A PRACTICAL COMMENTARY

ON THE

GOSPEL ACCORDING TO ST. MARK

A

PRACTICAL COMMENTARY

ON THE

GOSPEL ACCORDING TO ST. MARK

BY

JAMES MORISON, D.D

AUTHOR OF

" *Commentary on the Gospel according to St. Matthew* " *etc.*

EIGHTH EDITION

Wipf & Stock
PUBLISHERS
Eugene, Oregon

Wipf and Stock Publishers
199 West 8th Avenue, Suite 3
Eugene, Oregon 97401

Practical Commentary on the Gospel of St. Mark
By Morison, James
ISBN: 1-59244-500-4
Publication date 1/27/2004
Previously published by Hodder and Stoughton, 1896

CONTENTS.

	PAGE
PREFATORY NOTE	ix — xi

INTRODUCTION. (Pages xiii. to lxxx.)

§ 1. GOSPEL AND GOSPELS	xiii
§ 2. TITLE OF ST. MARK'S GOSPEL	xiii
§ 3. THE NAME 'MARK'	xv
§ 4. ST. MARK THE EVANGELIST THE 'JOHN MARK' OF THE Acts of the Apostles	xv
§ 5. COVERT REFERENCE TO THE EVANGELIST IN THE BODY OF THE GOSPEL	xvii
§ 6. THE RELATION OF THE APOSTLE PETER TO THE GOSPEL: PATRISTIC EVIDENCE. (Pages xix. to xxxiv.)	
(1.) Testimony of Jerome	xx
(2.) Testimony of Epiphanius	xx
(3.) Testimony of Eusebius	xxi
(4.) Testimony of Origen	xxi
(5.) Testimony of Tertullian	xxii
(6.) Testimony of Clemens of Alexandria	xxii
(7.) Testimony of Irenæus	xxiv
(8.) Testimony of Justin Martyr	xxvi
(9.) Testimony of Papias	xxviii
§ 7. RELATION OF THE GOSPEL TO THE APOSTLE PETER: IN- TERNAL EVIDENCE	xxxiv.—xxxviii

CONTENTS.

§ 8. THE INNER RELATION OF THE GOSPEL TO THE SYNOPTIC GOSPELS OF ST. MATTHEW AND ST. LUKE. (Pages xxxviii. to lxi.)

	PAGE
Augustine's theory	xxxviii
Griesbach's theory	xli
Dr. Henry Owen	xlv
The Tübingen School	xlv
Ewald's theory	xlvii
Gaussen's solution	xlviii
The Eichhorn theory	l
The 'Mark-hypothesis'	liv
General observations on the problem	lvii
Gieseler's hypothesis	lx

§ 9. DATE OF THE GOSPEL. (Pages lxi. to lxvi.)

Common view	lx
Patrizi, Storr, Berks	lxiii
Volkmar	lxiv
Tübingen School	lxiv
Data for approximative date	lxvi

§ 10. THE PLACE OF THE GOSPEL'S PUBLICATION AND THE LANGUAGE IN WHICH IT WAS ORIGINALLY WRITTEN . lxvii.—lxix

§ 11. THE PLAN, AIM, AND STYLE OF THE GOSPEL . lxix.—lxxii

§ 12. INTEGRITY OF THE GOSPEL lxxii

§ 13. THE TOPICAL POSITION OF ST. MARK'S GOSPEL IN THE GROUP OF GOSPELS lxxiii

§ 14. THE CONTENTS OF THE GOSPEL . . . lxxiv.—lxxx

EXPOSITION OF THE GOSPEL 1–470

INDEX TO THE EXPOSITION 471–481

PREFATORY NOTE.

THE following *Commentary on the Gospel according to St. Mark*, though latently complementive of the author's *Commentary on the Gospel according to St. Matthew*, is yet entirely 'self contained.' There are, indeed, occasional references to some fuller discussions or expositions in the *Commentary on St. Matthew*; but the thread of continuous exposition in St. Mark is never suspended or broken off. The author conceives that he was not entitled to postulate the reader's possession of the earlier volume; and he imagines that it would have been a blunder in the structure of his present work, had it imposed, even on those readers who possess the companion volume, the irksome task of turning to it, and turning it up, ere they could ascertain his opinion on any particular passage in St. Mark.

In thus endeavouring to avoid a 'rock' on which many had struck, the author was not unmindful that there was a little mälstrom-like 'Charybdis' on the other side of 'Scylla,' no less dangerous to navigators. Hence he has been on his guard not to allow any of the materials which have done duty in the *Commentary on St. Matthew* to float silently away into the whirlpool of circulatory repetition, in order to do double service in expounding the coincident representations in St. Mark. He hopes that whatever else his readers may miss in the present volume, they will find throughout fresh veins of representation and illustration, the result of fresh labour and research.

In *St. Mark's Gospel*, moreover, there is a pervading peculiarity of phraseology, (inartificial indeed, yet idiosyncratic,) which to the lover of delicate tints and flickers of presentation affords a continual incentive to fresh investigation. Hence, in truth, much of the charm, as also much of the difficulty, in expounding St. Mark. The charm is intensified if the conviction can be substantiated, (as it undoubtedly can, provided the sum of the existing evidence be impartially weighed,) that St. Peter's teaching within the circle of the early catechumens was the chief fountainhead from which St. Mark drew the substance and even the minutiæ of his Gospel. The flicker of St. Peter's subjective conceptions is thus passing before us as we read. It is a fact fitted to stimulate. We feel as if we should not like to let slip any of that subtle essence, or quintessence, of mind which made the primary observations of the chief of the Lord's personal attendants distinctive as well as distinct, and his subsequent reminiscences and representations invariably vivid and frequently picturesque.

Whether attributable to St. Peter's tenacity of memory, or to that unique element in his dialect which made his manner of speech, like that of every other original mind, peculiarly his own, or whether merely attributable to the reproductive idiosyncrasy of the writer, 'vexed expressions' abound in St. Mark, and give ample scope for patient, yet exciting, research.

There are 'vexed' questions in addition, belonging to the department of *Introduction*, as distinguished from *Exposition*. In particular, there is the question of *the genetic inter-relationship of the three Synoptic Gospels*, a subject around which a peculiarly thorny and 'vexatious' thicket, or rather forest, of literature has, during the past eighty or ninety years, been growing up. Into this forest the expositor is invited to enter, the moment he passes from one to another of the synoptic narratives.

In this new edition of his Commentary the author has, with as much care as was possible to him, revised the whole contents; and he hopes that it may prove a help to students, preachers, Sunday school teachers, and other lovers of Bible exegesis.

He may add that he has taken counsel throughout of the English *Revised version*; but he has been gratified to observe that a very large proportion of the Revisionists' emendations had been anticipated in the author's previous editions.

FLORENTINE BANK HOUSE,
GLASGOW.

INTRODUCTION

TO THE

GOSPEL ACCORDING TO ST. MARK.

§ 1. Gospel and Gospels.

It is a matter of interest and significance that, in the biblical records, we have not only *gospel* but *Gospels*.

We have *gospel*, running like a golden thread through the whole Bible, connecting history, precept, proverb, prophecy, and binding the entire constituents of 'the volume of the Book' into unity. We should certainly have had no Bible at all, had there been no *gospel*.

But in particular portions of the progressive revelation the golden gospel line becomes doubled as it were, or trebled, or multiplied in some still higher ratio. The whole texture of certain paragraphs or larger sections gleams and glows with *gospel*. Such are the Messianic Psalms. Such is the fifty-third chapter of Isaiah. And such, of course, are the four Gospels of the New Testament. The *gospel* is so efflorescent in these *Gospels* that the lovers of the Bible have, from a very early period of the Christian era, agreed to call them, 'par excellence,' *the Gospels*.

§ 2. Title of St. Mark's Gospel.

The Gospel ascribed to St. Mark was neither by himself, nor by the subsequent compilers of the New Testament canon, designated *the Gospel 'of' Mark*. The word *gospel* was not specifically employed, in the time of the evangelists, to denote *a particular kind of book* or *biography*. It had a more generic import. It meant *good news*; and just because it had that meaning, it was specially applied by Christians to *the best of all good news*, the news regarding Jesus Christ as the Divine Saviour of sinners.

Hence the united compositions of the four evangelists were often, in the post-apostolic ages, called collectively *the Gospel*.[1] And each evangelical record in particular was *the gospel 'according to' the particular evangelist who compiled it*. The gospel in each case was *one*, 'the gospel of Jesus Christ, the Son of God' (Mark i. 1); but it was that one gospel under the peculiar phase of a particular biographical presentation.

Hence the phrase '*according to.*' It is not, as some critics have contended, precisely equivalent to '*of*,' for the gospel was not regarded as an emanation from the mind of the writer.[2] It was not, in its essence, the product of any human compiler or composer; but, as delivered by the evangelists, it assumed in its form as distinguished from its essence, a peculiar phase in harmony with the size, shape, and symmetry of 'the earthen vessels' in which it was 'handed out,' that it might be 'handed on.'

In the great majority of manuscripts, inclusive of the Alexandrine, the title of the Gospel according to St. Mark is either substantially, or entirely, the same as in our common English version. In the Syriac Philoxenian version the word *holy* is introduced before the word *Gospel*, and the phrase *according to* is merged: *the Holy Gospel of Mark*. In the Syriac Peshito version there was an attempt, though not remarkably felicitous, to do more justice to the idea suggested by the preposition: *the Holy Gospel, the Announcement of Mark the Evangelist*.

It is noteworthy that in the two most venerable manuscripts extant, the Sinaitic and the Vatican, the title is fragmentary. It is simply *According to Mark*; it being assumed apparently that the entire fasciculus of the compilations of the four evangelists was but one manifold Gospel.

---

[1] See, for instance, Tertullian *De Baptismo*, c. 15; and compare Irenæus, *Adv. Hæreses*, iii. 11, and Origen's *Comment. in Joannem*, vol. iv., p. 98, ed. Delarue (καὶ τὸ ἀληθῶς διὰ τεσσάρων ἕν ἐστιν εὐαγγέλιον). See also Griesbach's *Commentarius Criticus*, Particula ii., p. 202.

[2] See *Introduction to the Gospel according to Matthew*, § 4.

§ 3. The Name 'Mark.'

Marcus or Mark was a Latin name, and became a common Latin *prænomen*, as, for instance, 'Marcus' Tullius Cicero. The diminutive Marcellus was a surname of the Claudian family. A distinguished member of that family, Marcus Claudius Marcellus, defeated Hannibal at Nola. Cicero has an oration '*Pro* Marco Marcello.'

The evangelist Mark however was, notwithstanding his Latin name, a Jew. His entire Gospel bewrays his nationality, and breathes the spirit of an Israelite who, though delivered from Jewish narrowness and bigotry, was still 'an Israelite indeed.' In the letter too, as well as the spirit of his composition, the *mark* of a Jewish mind is indelibly impressed.[1]

The reason why the evangelist either assumed, or got imposed on him, his Latin name is now unknown; probably he found it convenient, when out in the wide world, to wear a Gentile name. It might be even to himself, as well as to his friends, and to all with whom he had to do, a significant badge, indicating that he was now a Christian cosmopolite.

Perhaps it was for a similar reason that Saul of Tarsus, after he got rid of the spiritual fetters which the Palestinian Jews were perpetually imposing on him, and had got fairly under weigh in the career of his Gentile apostolate, called himself Paul, a word significant in Latin, and honourable in the estimation of all who could enumerate the most illustrious of the Roman families.

Marcus or Mark may have been at first a mere surname added to the original Jewish name of the evangelist; and then by and by it may, from casual or conventional circumstances, have acquired such a peculiar emphasis as at length to supersede and finally extinguish its Hebrew forerunner. (See next Section.)

§ 4. St. Mark, the *Evangelist*, the John Mark of the *Acts of the Apostles*.

Grotius[2] was of opinion that the evangelist was *not* 'John, whose surname was Mark,' the son of that Mary of Jerusalem to whose

---

[1] See, for instance, the construction in chap. i. 7, vii. 25.
[2] *Proœmium in Marcum.*

house Peter betook himself, on the night when he was so marvellously liberated from prison. (Acts xii. 12.) The distinguished critic was 'moved,' he says, to this opinion, partly by the fact that 'the ancients' never call our evangelist John, and partly by the fact that they never speak of him as the travelling companion of Barnabas and Paul, but invariably as the attendant and interpreter of Peter. Calov in Germany, though always differing, as much as he ever could, from the great Dutchman, agreed with him in this opinion;[1] as did Cave[2] in England, and Cotelier in France,[3] and some other able men, such as a-Lapide and Tillemont. Petter[4] hesitated a little, but on the whole swung in the opposite direction. In more modern times the same opinion has been occasionally revived, as by Schleusner, Kienlen, Da Costa, and Patrizi in his great work *De Evangeliis*.[5]

But there is no good reason for calling in question the unanimous tradition of 'the ancients,' that Mark the evangelist was 'John whose surname was Mark.'

De Wette unites the voices of all the Christian ages when he says, "The Mark to whom ecclesiastical tradition ascribes the "second Gospel is undoubtedly the John, or John Mark, of *the Acts* "*of the Apostles*."[6] Dr. Davidson, though not believing that the second Gospel was really the composition of Mark, says: "It is pro-"bable that the Mark, to whom the second Gospel is commonly "assigned, is the same who is called John (Acts xiii. 5, 13) and "John Mark (Acts xii. 12, 25; xv. 37)."[7]

True, 'the ancients,' of whom Grotius speaks, uniformly call him Mark, not John. But naturally so, for there were many conspicuous Johns in the early Christian circles. In the New Testament writings the tendency of the surname to displace the original Hebrew name is noteworthy. In Acts xii. 12, the first passage in which the bearer of the names is expressly referred to, he is called 'John, whose surname was Mark'; and in the 25th verse this double appellation is repeated. In the succeeding chapter, ver. 5 and

---

[1] *Biblia Illustrata*, in loc.
[2] *Scriptorum Ecc. Historia Literaria*, vol. i., 24.
[3] *Constitutiones Apostolorum*, ii. 57, note 36.
[4] The author of the *largest* Commentary on Mark, in two volumes folio, 1661.
[5] Lib. i., cap. ii., Quæstio 1. See also the first Appendix to his *Commentarium in Marcum*.
[6] *Lehrbuch des N. T.*, § 99.
[7] *Introduction to N. T.*, vol. ii., p. 76, ed. 1868.

13, he is referred to under his original Hebrew name exclusively, John. Then in chap. xv. 37 he is once more called 'John, whose surname was Mark.' But in the 39th verse of the same chapter he is called simply Mark. And this is the only name that is given him in the remaining passages of the New Testament: Col. iv. 10; 2 Tim. iv. 11; Philem. 24; and 1 Pet. v. 13. The remark of Jerome on the third of these passages is equally applicable to the rest, 'I think that the Mark here mentioned is the author of the Gospel.'[1]

As to the fact that 'the ancients,' when referring to St. Mark as the writer of the second Gospel, signalize exclusively his ministerial relation to the apostle Peter, as distinguished from his corresponding relation to Barnabas and Paul, nothing was more natural.

He was for a season, indeed, the companion of Barnabas and Paul. See Acts xii. 25, xiii. 5. But he got wearied of that relationship, or of the work which it entailed, and returned to his mother's house. (Acts xiii. 13.) Some of 'the ancients' use strong language in reference to this retreat, and ascribe to him a kind of spiritual 'poltroonery.'[2] Moreover, when Barnabas and Paul were subsequently arranging for another joint tour, Mark was ready to join them; but Paul objected, while Barnabas insisted, "and the contention was so sharp between them that they departed "asunder one from the other; and so Barnabas took Mark, and "sailed unto Cyprus, and Paul chose Silas and departed." (Acts xv. 36-40.) As was to be expected however of good men and true, this 'coolness,' as Grotius calls it, at once between Paul and Barnabas and between Paul and Mark, passed away, so that Mark was restored to intimate and confidential relations to the apostle. In the Epistle to Philemon (ver. 24) the apostle names Mark as one of his 'fellow-labourers.' In Col. iv. 10 he says, "Mark, sister's son "to Barnabas,—touching whom ye received commandments; if he "come unto you, receive him,—saluteth you." And then in 2 Tim. iv. 11 the apostle says again, when now near the very close of his

---

[1] "Marcum ponit, quem puto Evangelii conditorem."—*Comment. in Philemonem, in loc.* "Es ist höchst wahrscheinlich," says Michaelis, "dass Marcus "der Evangelist, der Sohn Petri, und der Geführte Pauli, eine Person gewesen "ist."—*Einleitung in N. B.*, p. 1051, 4th ed.

[2] Hence the remarkable expression of Hippolytus, in the recently recovered *Philosophumena*, vii. 18, Μάρκος ὁ κολοβοδάκτυλος. See also the Prologue in the Codex Amiatinus, '*amputasse* sibi post fidem *pollicem* dicitur.' Consult Tregelles' *Canon Muratorianus*, p. 75.

terrestrial career, "Take Mark, and bring him with thee, for he is "profitable to me for the ministry."

Still, as neither Paul nor Barnabas was able to supply, at first hand, the full historic details that were essential to a biographical Gospel, it is not to be wondered at that Mark, having either a purpose, or an instinct, leading him in the direction of an evangelist, should attach himself to Peter, and derive from him the information which he has embodied in his Gospel. And it is still less to be wondered at that 'the ancients,' who spoke of him, and felt interested in him, solely on account of his Gospel, should bring exclusively into view, so far as his authorship was concerned, his ministerial relation to Peter.

It is certain moreover that St. Peter was, from a very early period, on terms of the greatest intimacy with Mark and his mother. See Acts xii. 11–17. Not unlikely it might be by his preaching on the day of Pentecost, or subsequently, that both the lady and her son became acquainted with the true career and character of the Saviour. And it is probably for this reason that we are to account for the peculiarly endearing manner in which St. Peter refers to the evangelist, at the conclusion of his First Epistle, "The church "that is at Babylon, elected together with you, saluteth you; *and* "*so doth Mark my son.*" There is no reason for doubting that it is *our* Mark, and *Paul's* Mark, who is thus so affectionately mentioned. But there is less than none for imagining, with Heumann[1] and Credner,[2] or half imagining, with Pott,[3] that he was Peter's *literal son.*

§ 5. COVERT REFERENCE TO THE EVANGELIST IN THE BODY OF THE GOSPEL.

It is probable that the evangelist makes a covert reference to himself in the body of his Gospel.

His whole narrative indeed, like that of St. Matthew, is remarkably impersonal. Both the writers retire behind their themes, and shut themselves out of view. They are so absorbed 'objectively' in their narrations, that they become 'subjectively' oblivious of themselves.

---

[1] *Nöthiger Anhang zur Erklärung Marci*, pp. 736, 737. He rejoices over the imagination, as over a brilliant discovery.
[2] *Einleitung in das N. T.*, §§ 48, 237.
[3] *Annotationes* in 1 Pet. v. 13.

Nevertheless it is in the highest degree probable that St. Matthew refers to himself by name in the 9th verse of the 11th chapter of his Gospel, and to his home in the 10th verse. It is almost certain too that St. John refers to himself, as one of the two disciples spoken of in the 1st chapter of his Gospel, ver. 35–38. It is certain that it is of himself that he speaks in chap. xiii. 23, xix. 26, as 'the disciple whom Jesus loved.'

We believe that it is, in like manner, to himself that St. Mark refers when, in chap. xiv. 51, 52, he makes mention of 'a young man' who had been aroused out of bed by the uproar connected with the conveyance of Jesus from Gethsemane to the residence of the high priest. Full of youthful impetuosity, he had rushed, it seems, out of the house with only 'a linen sheet thrown around him,' to see what the disturbance was about. The incident was so trifling, intrinsically, that we can scarcely conceive of it being recorded by the evangelist unless he had some private reason for its insertion. But if it touched the vital turning point of his spiritual career we can at once understand why he should delight to link it on, and thus in a modest and covert way to attach his own personal and spiritual history to the great events he was recording. It is worthy of being noted, in addition, that it is not likely that he should have learned the unimportant incident from either Peter or any other of the apostles, for in the immediately preceding verse he states that 'they had all forsaken' the Lord 'and fled.'[1]

§ 6. THE RELATION OF THE APOSTLE PETER TO THE GOSPEL: PATRISTIC EVIDENCE.

It was the almost unanimous conviction of 'the fathers' that the apostle Peter's oral discourses were the special source, or well-

---

[1] See *Commentary*, in loc. "Why was a circumstance apparently so trifling," asks Greswell, "and certainly so irrelevant, inserted in the midst of so grave an "account? If the young man was the writer of the account, and an eye-witness "of the transaction at the time; partly implicated himself in the danger of our "Saviour; mistaken for a follower or disciple, when not really such; afterwards "converted to the faith; and finally St. Mark the evangelist; I think he might "naturally look upon this as the most interesting circumstance of his life; and "its introduction into the rest of the account, under such circumstances, be- "comes anything but foreign or irrelevant."—*Dissertations on the Harmony of the Gospels*, vol. i., p. 100, ed. 1837.

spring, from which St. Mark drew the information which is communicated in his Gospel.

Not that we need to suppose that he learned nothing from others. He would have ample opportunities in his mother's house and elsewhere for getting information from the other apostles and their coadjutors, companions, and acquaintances. The little paragraph too regarding himself (§ 5) would of course be contributed directly by himself to himself. But still it was the current report and belief of antiquity that he drew upon St. Peter in particular for the great body of the facts which he records.

(1) Jerome, who flourished toward the close of the fourth century and the beginning of the fifth, says in his *Catalogue of Illustrious Men*: "Mark, disciple and interpreter of Peter, wrote a "brief Gospel, at the request of the brethren in Rome, *in accord-* "*ance with what he had heard related by Peter*. This Gospel, when "read over to Peter, was approved of, and published by his "authority, to be read in the churches." [1] Putting no stress upon minutiæ of details in this statement, and bearing in mind that a fact when got hold of was liable, in the course of manipulation and transmission, to be unduly stretched and inconsiderately applied; still it is evident that Jerome had got handed down from the 'fathers' who preceded him, that Mark was indebted, for the contents of his Gospel, to the communications of Peter.

In his Letter to Hedibia he tersely represents St. Peter as the *narrator*, and St. Mark as the *writer*, of the Gospel.[2]

(2) Stepping back from Jerome, we come to Epiphanius, who flourished just a little earlier. He says: "But immediately after "Matthew, Mark, *having become an attendant of the holy Peter in* "*Rome, had committed to him the task of setting forth the Gospel*. "Having completed his work he was sent by the holy Peter into "the country of the Egyptians." [3] The dependence of the evan-

---

[1] "Marcus, discipulus et interpres Petri, juxta quod Petrum referentem "audierat, rogatus Romæ a fratribus, breve scripsit Evangelium. Quod cum "Petrus audisset, probavit, et ecclesiis legendum sua authoritate edidit."—*De Viris Illustribus*, cap. viii.

[2] "Marcum; cujus Evangelium, Petro narrante, et illo scribente, compositum est." (Cap. xi.)

[3] Εὐθὺς δὲ μετὰ τὸν Ματθαῖον ἀκόλουθος γενόμενος ὁ Μάρκος τῷ ἁγίῳ Πέτρῳ ἐν Ῥώμῃ, ἐπιτρέπεται τὸ εὐαγγέλιον ἐκθέσθαι. κ.τ.λ.—*Hæresis*, 41, p. 428.

gelist on the apostle is the substrate, and indeed the sum and substance, of this statement.

(3) Eusebius preceded Epiphanius, and flourished toward the close of the third century and the beginning of the fourth. He says, in his *Evangelical Demonstration*, that though the apostle Peter "did not undertake, in consequence of excess of diffidence,[1] "to write a Gospel, yet it had all along been currently reported "that Mark, who had become his familiar acquaintance and attend- "ant, made memoirs of his discourses concerning the doings of "Jesus."[2] The distinguished 'father' then proceeds, after some other details, to take notice of the fact that there is in Mark's Gospel a minute and particular account of St. Peter's lamentable denial of his Lord. After which account he adds: "It is Mark "indeed who writes these things. *But it is Peter who testifies them* "*concerning himself; for all the contents of Mark's Gospel are re-* "*garded as memoirs of Peter's discourses.*"[3] We need not press the remark regarding Peter's 'excess of modesty.' It was probably suggested to Eusebius by the representations of Clemens of Alexandria,[4] and may have been a subjective conjecture rather than a historical fact. But it is obvious that he got handed down to him as a fact that Mark, in the representations of his Gospel, is to a large extent but the echo of the narrations of Peter.

(4) Origen flourished before Eusebius, in the early part of the third century. In his *Commentary on the Gospel according to Matthew* he mentions that there were four unchallenged and unchallengeable Gospels received throughout the universal church. "The second of them," he says, "is that according to Mark, *who* "*composed it under the guidance of Peter*, who therefore, in his "Catholic Epistle, acknowledged the evangelist as his son, saying, "*The co-elect in Babylon saluteth you, and Mark my son.*"[5] We

---

[1] δι' εὐλαβείας ὑπερβολὴν.
[2] Τούτου Μάρκος γνώριμος καὶ φοιτητὴς γεγονὼς ἀπομνημονεῦσαι λέγεται τὰς τοῦ Πέτρου περὶ τῶν πράξεων τοῦ Ἰησοῦ διαλέξεις.—*Demonstratio Evangelica*, lib. iii., c. 5, p. 120.
[3] Μάρκος μὲν ταῦτα γράφει· Πέτρος δὲ ταῦτα περὶ ἑαυτοῦ μαρτυρεῖ· πάντα γὰρ τὰ παρὰ Μάρκῳ τῶν Πέτρου διαλέξεων εἶναι λέγεται ἀπομνημονεύματα.—*Id.*, p. 121.
[4] See Eusebius's *Ecclesiastical History*, lib. ii., c. 15, and lib. vi., c. 14.
[5] The original is preserved in Eusebius's *Ecclesiastical History*, lib. vi., cap. 25: δεύτερον δὲ τὸ κατὰ Μάρκον, ὡς Πέτρος ὑφηγήσατο αὐτῷ, ποιήσαντα, κ.τ.λ. It is thence transferred by Delarue into his edition of Origen's Works, vol. iii., p. 440.

must not press the sequence that is intimated here in the inferential *therefore*; but the special relationship of the evangelist to the apostle is unequivocally and unwaveringly asserted.

(5) Tertullian preceded Origen. He was born at Carthage about the year A.D. 160. Converted from heathenism when between thirty and forty years of age, his greatest literary activity was in the early part of the third century. In his book *Against Marcion*, which was published in the year 207 or 208, he enumerates the four authoritative Gospels,[1] noting that we have two of them, namely those of John and Matthew, 'from apostles,'[2] and other two, namely those of Luke and Mark, 'from apostolicals.'[3] He vindicates in particular the apostolical authority of the Gospel according to Luke, and then he adds, " the same authority of the apostolic (*or*, " *in other words*, the primitive) churches will likewise endorse the " other Gospels which have been handed down to us in their integrity " from these churches, I mean those of John and Matthew; not " excluding that also which was published by Mark, for *it may be* " *ascribed to Peter, whose interpreter Mark was.*"[4]

(6) Clemens of Alexandria, one of Tertullian's contemporaries, has also something to say of St. Mark, and his intimate connection as an evangelist with the apostle Peter. In a passage of his *Hypotyposes*, preserved in the *History* of Eusebius, he says:—" The " occasion for writing the Gospel according to Mark was as " follows: After Peter had publicly preached the word in Rome, " and declared the gospel by the Spirit, *many who were present* " *entreated Mark, as one who had for long attended the apostle, and* " *who knew by heart what he had said. to reduce to writing what had* " *been spoken to them.* Mark did so, and presented to his petitioners " his Gospel. When Peter became cognisant of this, he neither " laid an interdict on the undertaking nor urged its fulfilment."[5]

---

[1] Lib. iv., c. 2.
[2] "Ex apostolis."
[3] "Ex apostolicis."
[4] "Eadem auctoritas ecclesiarum apostolicarum cæteris quoque patrocinabitur " evangeliis, quæ proinde per illas, et secundum illas, habemus,—Joannis dico " et Matthæi; licet et Marcus quod edidit, Petri affirmetur cujus interpres " Marcus."—*Adversus Marcionem*, lib. iv., c. 5.
[5] τοῦ Πέτρου δημοσίᾳ ἐν Ῥώμῃ κηρύξαντος τὸν λόγον, καὶ Πνεύματι τὸ εὐαγγέ-λιον ἐξειπόντος, τοὺς παρόντας πολλοὺς ὄντας παρακαλέσαι τὸν Μάρκον, ὡς ἂν ἀκολουθήσαντα αὐτῷ πόρρωθεν καὶ μεμνημένον τῶν λεχθέντων, ἀναγράψαι τὰ

Eusebius makes, in an earlier part of his *History*, another reference to the representations of Clemens. "So charmed were the "Romans with the light that shone in upon their minds from the "discourses of Peter, that, not contented with a single hearing and "the viva-voce proclamation of the truth, *they urged with the* "*utmost solicitation on Mark, whose Gospel is in circulation, and who* "*was Peter's attendant, that he would leave them in writing a record* "*of the teaching which they had received by word of mouth.* They "did not give over till they had prevailed on him; and thus they "became the cause[1] of the composition of the so-called Gospel "according to Mark. It is said that when the apostle knew, by "revelation of the Spirit, what was done, he was pleased with the "eagerness of the men, and authorized the writing to be read in "the churches."[2] There has been considerable discussion on the relation of the last statement in this quotation to the remark at the close of the preceding quotation.[3] De Wette[4] and Fritzsche[5] are positive that there is absolute contradiction; Credner[6] concedes that there is, attributing it however to the reproductive representation of Eusebius. But de Valois thinks, apparently with reason, that the two statements are not irreconcilable;[7] although he fails to lay his hand precisely on the principle of conciliation, *the supposition of 'successive stages' in the case.* The apostle's diffidence, or repugnance, in relation to the writing of a Gospel is assumed. He is not therefore at the outset of the enterprise made acquainted with Mark's intention. By and by, nevertheless, he finds out what is going on; yet remains neutral, neither dissuading nor encouraging. At length, when the finished work is submitted to his inspection, it meets his approval, so that he sanctions it as a correct representation of the substance of his own statements. Such seems to be the view entertained by Clemens of the apostle's

---

εἰρημένα, ποιήσαντα δὲ τὸ εὐαγγέλιον, μεταδοῦναι τοῖς δεομένοις αὐτοῦ. Ὅπερ ἐπιγνόντα τὸν Πέτρον, προτρεπτικῶς μήτε κωλῦσαι μήτε προτρέψασθαι.—*Eccles. Hist.*, lib. vi., c. 14.

[1] αἰτίους.
[2] *Eccles. Hist.*, lib ii., c. 15.
[3] See Lardner's *Credibility of the Gospel History*, Part II., chap. xxii., pp. 212-218 of vol. ii., ed. 1788.
[4] *Lehrbuch*, § 98, p. 172.
[5] *Prolegomena in Ev. Marci*, § 2.
[6] *Einleitung*, § 51, p. 113.
[7] Annotatio in *Euseb. Hist.*, vi. 14.

relation to the Gospel. The dependence of the evangelist upon St. Peter for the substance of his narrations is the central idea, and the only one probably to which we should attach historic weight.

(7) We go back now to Irenæus, Bishop of Lyons in Gaul, but undoubtedly a native of the East. He flourished in the latter half of the second century; and was, as he tells us himself,[1] a young disciple of Polycarp, who was personally acquainted with the apostle John. We are therefore now treading on the border land of the apostolic age.

This celebrated father, like Origen and Tertullian, makes particular reference to the four accredited evangelists. For even in his day, it would appear, they stood apart from all competitors, on their own quadruple pedestal.

In the beginning of the third book of his *Treatise against Heresies*[2] he mentions that *after the apostles were clothed with the power of the Holy Spirit, and fully furnished for the work of universal evangelization, they 'went out'* (exierunt) *to the ends of the earth, preaching the gospel. Matthew went eastward to those of Hebrew descent, and preached to them in their own tongue, in which language he also published a writing of the Gospel;*[3] *while Peter and Paul went westward, and preached, and founded the church, in Rome.* "But," adds he, "after the departure of these, *Mark the disciple and interpreter of "Peter, even he, delivered to us in writing the things which were "preached by Peter.*[4] And Luke, the attendant of Paul, set down in "a book the gospel as preached by him."

It has been debated among critics, what can be meant by the expression, "*after the departure of these.*" Grabe would interpret it thus, *after the departure of Peter and Paul from Rome.*[5] Mill strongly advocated the same view.[6] C. Gottlob Hofmann contended for it too,[7] and Kuinöl.[8] Patrizi also leans toward it.[9] But such

---

[1] See quotation from his Letter to Florinus in Eusebius's *Eccles. Hist.*, v. 20.
[2] Chapter 1, preserved in Rufinus's Latin translation. The original Greek of the most important part of it is preserved in Eusebius's *Eccles. Hist.*, v. 8.
[3] καί γραφὴν ἐξήνεγκεν εὐαγγελίου.
[4] μετὰ δὲ τὴν τούτων ἔξοδον, Μάρκος ὁ μαθητὴς καὶ ἑρμηνευτὴς Πέτρου, καὶ αὐτὸς τὰ ὑπὸ Πέτρου κηρυσσόμενα ἐγγράφως ἡμῖν παραδέδωκε.
[5] See his note in his edition of Irenæus, p. 199.
[6] *Prolegomena in Nov. Test.*, § 101.
[7] *Introductio in Nov. Test.*, c. xiii., p. 170.
[8] *Prolegomena in Marcum*, § 2.
[9] *De Evangeliis*, vol. i., pp. 37, 38.

an interpretation seems to involve a somewhat aimless or insignificant specification.

If it had been possible to carry back the reference to the expression "*they 'went out' to the ends of the earth*," so as to suppose that Irenæus was informing us that it was after the 'exodus' or final dispersion of the apostles, and thus at a late stage of the apostolic epoch, that St. Mark wrote his Gospel, several difficulties affecting the harmony of the various representations of 'the fathers' would be met.

But it is probable, nevertheless, that we may be shut up to accept the view of de Valois,[1] endorsed as it is by the united judgments of Father Simon,[2] Michaelis,[3] Eichhorn,[4] Bertholdt,[5] Hug,[6] Credner,[7] Guericke,[8] Ebrard,[9] Klostermann,[10] Weiss,[11] that the expression means, *after the 'decease' of these apostles*. Eichhorn ingeniously suggests that the word 'departure' or 'exodus' is used in allusion to what is said in 2 Pet. i. 15, "I will endeavour that "you may be able, after my *decease* (literally *departure*) to have "these things always in remembrance."[12] If this interpretation be accepted, then we have, as regards the precise date of St. Mark's Gospel, and the consequent authentication of its contents by the apostle Peter, a representation which conflicts with that which we have found in Jerome, Epiphanius, Origen, and Clemens Alexandrinus. But it may be admitted, as we have already intimated, that in minute details of things 'the fathers' made free to vent their subjective subsumptions, assumptions, applications, and divinations, while yet the historic substance, or substrate, of the information handed down to them, and thence passed on, was a matter of indisputable validity.

We are not sure however that the real testimony of Irenæus has been conclusively ascertained. Christophorson, the author of an

---

[1] See his note in his *Eusebius*, p. 172, Migne's ed.
[2] *Historia Critica Textus N. T.*, i., c. 10.
[3] *Einleitung in den N. B.*, § 141, p. 1054, 4th ed.
[4] *Einleitung*, § 119, p. 607, 2nd ed.
[5] *Einleitung*, § 335, p. 1281, 3rd ed.
[6] *Einleitung*, Zweiter Theil, § 16, p. 61, 4th ed.
[7] *Einleitung*, § 54, p. 118.
[8] *Gesammtgeschichte*, § 15, p. 139, 1st ed.
[9] *Wissenschaftliche Kritik*, § 133, p. 795, 2nd ed.
[10] *Markusevangelium*, p. 336.
[11] *Marcusevangelium*, p. 4.
[12] *Einleitung*, vol. i., pp. 607, 608.

admirable Latin version of Eusebius's *Ecclesiastical History*, first published in 1570,[1] proposed to alter the text to the following effect, *after the publication of this*,[2] that is, *after the publication of Matthew's Hebrew Gospel*, as spoken of in the preceding sentence. Grotius accepted the alteration.[3] But de Valois expresses his astonishment at such an extraordinary emendation, 'not knowing,' as he says, on what ground Christophorson could venture to suggest it.[4] Yet it is a remarkable fact that in the 'Hypothesis,' or Prefatory Note to Victor of Antioch's *Commentary on the Gospel according to Mark* (sometimes ascribed to Cyril of Alexandria),[5] the same turn is given to Irenæus's observation. The entire quotation runs thus: "*After the publication of the Gospel according to* "*Matthew*,[6] Mark, the disciple and interpreter of Peter, even he, "delivered to us in writing the things that were preached by "Peter." If this reading is no survival or echo of the original statement of Irenæus, it is at all events evidence that at a very early period some difficulty was found with the text as it now stands.

Whatever, however, may have been the exact expression or idea of Irenæus, he is indisputably at one with the fathers who succeeded him, in ascribing to the apostle Peter the *matériel* out of which the Gospel according to St. Mark was compiled.

(8) Going back from Irenæus we come to Justin Martyr, who flourished in the first half of the second century. Though not making so frequent quotations from the Gospel of St. Mark as he undoubtedly does, recent objections notwithstanding, from the Gospels of St. Matthew and St. Luke, yet he does sometimes quote from our evangelist. And there is a remarkable passage in his *Dialogue with Trypho the Jew*, in which he uses an incidental expression, of some significance and importance for our present purpose. He is referring, in his own ingeniously theorizing way, to the fact that our Lord imposed the name *Peter* upon the chief of the apostles, and the name *Boanerges* upon James and John. The

---

[1] See Ittig's Preface to his *Historiæ Ecclesiasticæ Secundi Seculi Selecta Capita*.
[2] μετὰ δὲ τούτου τὴν ἔκδοσιν.
[3] *Proœmium in Marcum*.
[4] Note on Eusebius's *Eccles. Hist.*, v. 8.
[5] See first volume of Cramer's *Catena*, pp. 259-417
[6] μετὰ τὴν τοῦ κατὰ Ματθαίον Εὐαγγελίου ἔκδοσιν.

imposition of this latter name is recorded by Mark alone. But Justin speaks of the matter in the following terms: " And when it s said "that He imposed on one of the apostles the name Peter, *and when* "*this is recorded in* '*his Memoirs,*' *with this other fact that He named* "*the two sons of Zebedee Boanerges, which means Sons-of-Thunder*, "this is a sign that it was He by whom Jacob was called Israel, "and Auses, Jesus (*i.e. Oshea, Joshua*)."[1]

Justin thus speaks of the record of St. Peter's change of name as being in '*his* Memoirs.' In *whose* Memoirs? Lardner[2] and de Wette[3] say, *in Christ's*. Lang and Maranus, in their Latin versions, slur over a decision, translating 'in the *apostolical* Memoirs.' But Schwegler,[4] Norton,[5] and Smith of Jordanhill[6] legitimately contend that the reference of the pronoun must be to St. Peter himself, '*in Peter's* Memoirs.' In many other passages Justin speaks of *the Memoirs of the apostles*, meaning invariably *the Memoirs emanating from the apostles*, that is to say, *the Gospels*, which he thus recognised as all, directly or indirectly, of apostolic origin, and consequently of apostolic authority. With him the genitive connected with the word *Memoirs* is constantly the genitive of authorship, and not of the subject matter on which the authorship is exercised. In other words, he never speaks of *Christ's Memoirs*, but always of *the apostles' Memoirs* (concerning Christ).

Smith contends that the apostle Peter was literally the literary author of the Primitive Gospel, the New Testament 'Protevangel,' the *Urevangelium* as it is called by the Germans. It was composed, he assumes, in Aramaic. St. Matthew and St. Luke derived from it, he supposes, by simple translation, a large proportion of their materials; while St. Mark translated it entire, only adding to his version some minutiæ, such as the title in the first verse of the first chapter, and the epilogue of twelve verses which forms the conclusion of the last chapter. It is, as Smith conceives, because of this translation that Mark is so frequently called, as by Jerome,

---

[1] καὶ τὸ εἰπεῖν μετωνομακέναι αὐτὸν Πέτρον ἕνα τῶν ἀποστόλων, καὶ γεγράφθαι ἐν τοῖς ἀπομνημονεύμασιν αὐτοῦ γεγενημένον καὶ τοῦτο, μετὰ τοῦ. κ. τ. λ.— § 106, Migne's ed.

[2] *Credibility of the Gospel History*, v. ii., chap. x.: *Works*, vol. ii., p. 121, ed. 1788.

[3] *Lehrbuch des N. T.*, § 66.

[4] *Das nachapostolische Zeitalter*. vol. i., p. 221.

[5] *Genuineness of the Gospels*, vol. i., p. 131.

[6] *Dissertation on the Origin and Connection of the Gospels*, p. lxxii.

Tertullian, Irenæus, and Papias, *the interpreter*, that is, *the translator of Peter*.

It is an ingenious theory. But we cannot accept it, for this, were there no other reason, that the Gospel, if really Peter's, could never have got to be universally ascribed to Mark. The great name of Peter would never have been eclipsed, and indeed annihilated, behind the name of Mark, if Mark did nothing more than merely translate the apostle's Gospel into Greek.

The exceptional representation of Justin is no evidence to the contrary; neither is the somewhat analogous representation of Jerome, in the first chapter of his *Catalogue of Illustrious Men*, in which he says of Peter, "But the Gospel according to Mark, who "was his disciple and interpreter, is also spoken of as his."[1] These statements are obviously to be explained as free and easy applications of the principle, that *the cause of the cause is the cause of the caused*. St. Peter's relation to the Gospel was something like that of a literary grandfather.

Hilgenfeld's theory is, up to a certain point, in accordance with Smith's. He supposes that Justin had no knowledge of our canonical Mark, but quoted from a real *Gospel of Peter*, which was, says he, "if you will, the original Mark," only "richer." The canonical Mark, as he conceives, was but an epitome or abstract (*Auszug*).[2] But is it not 'passing strange' that the entire Christian community should so prefer the impoverished epitome, that they allowed it, without a single word of remonstrance or of murmur, or even of remark, on the part of any of the churches or any of the disputatious fathers, not merely to supersede the 'rich' apostolic original, but also to become its burial place and the everlasting Lethe of its existence? It looks like a 'miracle' in the history of the church.

(9) We go farther back still than to Justin Martyr. We go to Papias, who flourished in the earliest part of the second century. He was, says Irenæus,[3] the companion of Polycarp,[4] one of the disciples of John the Apostle. He was himself the disciple of

---

[1] "Sed et Evangelium juxta Marcum, qui auditor ejus et interpres fuit, "hujus dicitur."

[2] *Kritische Untersuchungen über die Evangelien Justin's*. pp. 278, 279. See also his *Markus-Evangelium*, pp. 93–117.

[3] See Eusebius's *Eccles. Hist.*, iii. 39.

[4] Πολυκάρπου ἑταῖρος.

another John,[1] John the Presbyter, who was 'a disciple of the Lord.'[2] From this veteran, and from such other seniors or patriarchs as he could meet with, he eagerly collected, (but not with much discrimination of judgment it would appear,[3]) all the apostolic fragments of things on which he could lay his hands, "all that "could be remembered, in particular, of the sayings of Andrew, or "Peter, or Philip, or Thomas, or James, or John, or Matthew, or "any other of the Lord's disciples." He thus raked together, amid some important items of information, many tittles and trifles of tradition, which he afterwards elaborated and published in his *Interpretation of the Lord's Oracles*, a work consisting of five books.[4] It has perished, whether happily or unhappily it might be difficult to determine, for its contents would no doubt be unequal. But Eusebius has preserved in his *Ecclesiastical History* what the worthy compiler recorded, from the lips of John the Presbyter, concerning the Evangelist Mark. It seems to have been one of the most important 'anecdotes' in the work.

"The Presbyter said this: Mark, *having become the interpreter of* "*Peter*, wrote accurately whatever he [5] recorded.[6] He did not "present however in regular order the things that were either "spoken or done by Christ; for he had not been a personal auditor "or follower of the Lord. But afterwards, as I said, he attached "himself to Peter, who gave instructions according to the necessi- "ties of his hearers, but not in the way of making an orderly "arrangement of the Lord's words. So that Mark committed no "error in thus writing such details of things as he recorded; for "he made conscience of one thing, not to omit on the one hand, and "not to misrepresent on the other, any of the details which he "heard."[7] These things, says Eusebius, are left on record by Papias concerning Mark.

---

[1] Ἰωάννου ἀκουστής.
[2] Klostermann, after Zahn and Riggenbach, supposes that John the Presbyter is just John the Apostle (*Markusevangelium*, p. 326). Unlikely.
[3] σφόδρα γάρ τοι σμικρὸς ὢν τὸν νοῦν. Eusebius, *loc. cit.*
[4] Eusebius, *loc. cit.*
[5] That is, Mark; not Peter, as Mr. Badinel contends (*English Review*, xiii., p. 276).
[6] So should ἐμνημόνευσε be rendered, according to the favourite usage of Eusebius. Cruse renders it thus; and Dunster, and Badinel. *Remembered* is the translation of de Valois, Lardner, Michaelis, Routh, Thiersch, Meyer, Klostermann, Weiss.
[7] καὶ τοῦτο ὁ πρεσβύτερος ἔλεγε· Μάρκος μὲν ἑρμηνευτὴς Πέτρου γενόμενος, ὅσα

They embody, notwithstanding the medium through which they were handed down to the historian and posterity, the most important ecclesiastical information in reference to the evangelist that has come to us from post-apostolic antiquity.[1] They embrace almost all that is reliable in the testimonies of the succeeding 'fathers'; and, as there is nothing intrinsically improbable in the record, there seems to be no valid reason why we should discard or ignore its testimony. Everything in it, on the contrary, is in harmony with the most trustworthy of the results that are attainable by inward examination of the texture of the Gospel, and its peculiar relation, as regards matter, method, and phraseology, to the two other Synoptics.

It will be noticed that Mark is called *the interpreter of Peter*. It is the first instance on record of the use of that expression; and it is to be attributed, we presume, not so much to Papias himself as to his informant, John, who, we may conclude, found it circulating among the compeers and immediate successors of the evangelist.

What is the meaning of the designation? A much debated point.

Eichhorn,[2] Bertholdt,[3] Kuinöl,[4] Nendecker,[5] and many others, assume that the apostle felt himself unequal to the effort of using the Greek language freely, while engaged in preaching the gospel. He would be accustomed therefore, they suppose, to preach in Aramaic; and St. Mark would be employed by him as his interpreter, or 'dragoman,'[6] to render his addresses into Greek. It is an unlikely supposition.

Bleek saw its unlikelihood; but, attaching the same radical meaning to the word, conjectured, as Wilhelm Wilcke had done

---

ἐμνημόνευσεν, ἀκριβῶς ἔγραψεν, οὐ μέντοι τάξει τὰ ὑπὸ τοῦ χριστοῦ ἢ λεχθέντα ἢ πραχθέντα· οὔτε γὰρ ἤκουσε τοῦ κυρίου, οὔτε παρηκολούθησεν αὐτῷ, ὕστερον δὲ, ὡς ἔφην, Πέτρῳ, ὃς πρὸς τὰς χρείας ἐποιεῖτο τὰς διδασκαλίας, ἀλλ' οὐχ ὥσπερ σύνταξιν τῶι κυριακῶν ποιούμενος λόγων· ὥστε οὐδὲν ἥμαρτε Μάρκος, οὕτως ἔνια γράψας ὡς ἀπεμνημόνευσεν. Ἑνὸς γὰρ ἐποιήσατο πρόνοιαν, τοῦ μηδὲν ὧν ἤκουσε παραλιπεῖν, ἢ ψεύσασθαί τι ἐν αὐτοῖς.—Eusebius, *Eccles. Hist.*, iii. 39.

[1] See Olshausen's *Echtheit der Evangelien*, p. 101.
[2] *Einleitung*, § 117, p. 597.
[3] *Einleitung*, § 334, p. 1277.
[4] *Prolegomena*, § 2.
[5] *Lehrbuch*, § 30, p. 226.
[6] Eichhorn's word.

before him,[1] that it would be when the apostle's hearers understood Latin alone that he would need a dragoman.[2] That dragoman he presumes to have been St. Mark. Also an unlikely supposition.

Schenkel, attaching the same radical import to the word, combines the two preceding conjectures. He supposes that the apostle, although having considerable experience in speaking to foreigners, could not use fluently either the Greek or the Latin tongue, at least for lengthened discourse, and that he hence employed St. Mark, for both languages, as the translator of his addresses.[3] Likewise unlikely, as gathering up into itself the separate unlikelinesses of the two preceding conjectures.

Smith of Jordanhill, still attaching the same radical idea to the word, and supposing therefore that Mark was so called simply because he was 'the *Translator* of Peter,' imagined, as we have remarked in a former page,[4] that he received the appellation because he translated into Greek the apostle's Aramaic Gospel.[5] An equally unlikely conjecture, built on the basis of a conjecture more unlikely still.

Jerome's idea was better, though not entirely satisfactory. He assumed that Peter, 'like Paul,' was not satisfied with his own proficiency in Greek, and hence took advantage, so far as his written communications were concerned, of the superior acquirements of a qualified *amanuensis*. "Paul therefore," he tells us, "employed Titus as an *interpreter*; just as the blessed Peter em-"ployed Mark, whose Gospel was composed by the latter out of the "narrations of the former. And the two epistles also," he continues, "which are ascribed to Peter, differ from one another in "style and character and verbal structure; from which fact it is "evident that he had been constrained to make use of different "*interpreters*."[6] Jerome thus understood by the word 'interpreter' *an amanuensis who expressed in his own improved phraseology the ideas that were dictated to him.*

---

[1] *Tradition und Mythe*, p. 50.
[2] *Einleitung*, pp. 112, 113, ed. 1862.
[3] *Das Charakterbild Jesu*, p. 332.
[4] See page xxvii.
[5] *Dissertation*, p. lxxiii.
[6] "Habebat ergo Titum interpretem: sicut et beatus Petrus Marcum, cujus "Evangelium, *Petro narrante, et illo scribente*, compositum est. Denique et "duae Epistolae quae feruntur Petri, stylo inter se et charactere discrepant, "structuraque verborum." Note *narrante*, not *dictante.—Epist.* cxx, c. x. (*ad Hedibiam.*)

Meyer approves of Jerome's views, and suggests the word *secretary* as an approximative synonym for the term employed by the 'fathers.'[1] Dean Alford adopts the suggestion.[2] Holtzmann too,[3] and Dr. Davidson.[4] But there is not a particle of evidence in all antiquity, that St. Mark was a greater master of Greek than the apostle St. Peter. If one might form an estimate from a comparative examination of the writings of the two authors, St. Mark was by no means more versant than St. Peter in 'the wisdom' of any kind of 'words.' St. Peter's connection moreover, at once by birth and by residence, with such a Gentilised region as Galilee, and his free intercourse with such Gentile individuals as Cornelius, constitute a sufficient guarantee that he would possess, for all practical purposes, a sufficient 'working' acquaintance with the Greek language.

Dunster thinks that the expression means *the editor in writing, or publisher to the world, of the oral discourses of Peter.*[5] But this conception of the case seems neither to be in harmony with the essential import of the term, nor with the ideas that were prevalent among the fathers' regarding the work of our evangelist.

Michaelis strikes the right vein: " When Mark is called Peter's "*Interpreter* or *Hermeneut*, we must not think of a translator. "Peter had no need of such a helper; and in truth he writes Greek "much better than Mark. But we should understand the word in "a sense analogous to what it bears when applied to Mercury, *the* "*interpreter of the gods*, the messenger, that is to say, who commu- ' nicated to mortals what the gods had commissioned him to com- "municate. So Mark was, as it were, the message bearer of Peter, "*an under teacher, who taught others what he had heard from Peter,* "*or what had been entrusted to him by Peter.*"[6]

This, we believe, comes very near the 'mark' regarding the rationale of the designation given to St. Mark. It was not so much

---

[1] *Einleitung*, § 1.

[2] *Prolegomena*, chap. iii., § 1.

[3] *Die Synoptischen Evangelien*, p. 367.

[4] *Introduction*, vol. ii , p. 79.

[5] He refers to Milton's use of the word in reference to Uriel, in *Par. Lost*, iii., 657. See his able *Discursory Considerations on the Supposed Evidence of the Early Fathers that Matthew's Gospel was first written*, pp. 77, 78.

[6] " Er ist Bote Petri, ein Unterlehrer, der andere das lehret, was er von Petro "gehört hat, oder ihm von Petro aufgetragen ist, und so werde ich es übersetzen, "nicht wie andere gethan haben, Dollmetscher."—*Einleitung*· § 141, p. 1052.

apparently because of any general assistance rendered to the apostle in the discharge of the ordinary duties of the apostolate, as because of the specific relation of the contents of his Gospel to the mind of St. Peter, as their literary source, that St. Mark was called the apostle's *Interpreter* or *Hermeneut*. Unlike St. Matthew and St. John, he wrote at second hand, and drew his secondary inspiration from 'the chief of the apostles.' The events which he narrated, and the discourses and Divine remarks which he recorded, were communicated to him by St. Peter. *And thus, in the matter of his biographical account of the Saviour, he was St. Peter's interpreter.* This, we may add, is the view that is taken of the expression by Fritzsche,[1] Thiersch,[2] and Klostermann.[3]

We may remark, ere we leave this testimony of Papias, that what the Presbyter says regarding the absence of a strict 'order' in the contents of St. Mark's Gospel must not be stretched so tightly, and therefore so unreasonably, as it was co-ordinately by Schleiermacher[4] and Credner.[5] They drew from the expression the inference that the writing referred to by Papias could not be our present canonical Gospel, which is at least as *well ordered* throughout as the other Gospels, but must have been some pre-existent compilation of a less developed and more miscellaneous character. 'Fragmentary' is Schleiermacher's word.[6] And changes have been eagerly rung on it, and, in particular, on the idea that underlies it, by a numerous array of critics, who have the misfortune to imagine that it is in the interest of truth that they should find some lever or other that might enable them to shake the reliability of the Gospel history. But John the Presbyter did not mean that there was no 'order' in the composition of St. Mark. Not even did he mean that there was no observance of chronological order. The Gospel *is orderly*; and the events recorded are grouped on a basis of true chronology. But it is nevertheless of the highest moment that the modern critic should bear in mind the truth of the Presbyter's observation. *There was no attempt, on the part of the evangelist,*

---

[1] "Res Petri, verba Marci."—*Prolegomena*, § i., p. 26.
[2] *Versuch zur Herstellung des historischen Standpuncts für die Kritik der N. T. Schriften*, p. 181.
[3] *Das Markusevangelium*, p. 329.
[4] *Studien und Kritiken*, 1832, pp. 735-768.
[5] *Einleitung*, § 57, pp. 123, 124.
[6] *Einleitung*, § 68, p. 250. See also § 67.

to introduce exact historic order into the details of his narrative. There was no attempt at a strictly scientific chronology. It would be doing the evangelist the greatest injustice to endeavour to impose it on his narrations. He allowed himself, like St. Peter in his discourses to the catechumens, scope and latitude in grouping. His work was not meant to be annalistic, or historically complete. But all that it aimed at was realized to perfection. It was meant to be *the gospel* in a biographical form; and it is therefore *a Gospel*. Like the other Gospels it is the announcement, and unpretending presentation, of some of the salient doings and sayings of Him who, in His own living presence in our nature, in our world, and in the world of glory, is Himself the Everlasting Gospel of the grace of God.

§ 7. Relation of the Gospel to the Apostle Peter: Internal Evidence.

There is certainly nothing in the contents or texture of St. Mark's Gospel which can decisively determine that it was drawn from the wellspring of St. Peter's discourses.

But, on the other hand, there is nothing that is, in the least degree, at variance with the patristic tradition.

Here and there, moreover, phenomena of representation occur, as also, in some cases, phenomena of omission, or things 'conspicuous by their absence,' which admit of felicitous explanation on the hypothesis of a peculiarly intimate relationship to Peter.

It is not to be doubted indeed that all the synoptic Gospels bear, to a considerable degree, the impress of this apostle's idiosyncrasy. He was the leader of the original twelve; he was their chosen spokesman; he would be their chief speaker. The forms consequently in which he put his descriptions of his ocular and auricular observations would naturally become models to the rest of the circle, or moulds in which their public representations of what they themselves, as well as he, had seen and heard, would take definitive shape. His image would be unconsciously stamped on the whole currency of their ministrations.

Nevertheless, each of his brethren would, in his individual exhibitions of the facts which constitute the biographical contents of the Gospel, contribute something out of his own individuality. Hence there would be differences in setting, differences in grouping, differences in modes of expression, differences in the admission or omission of scenes or minuter details. In such an original mind moreover as that of John there would be an amount of peculiarity that would entirely overlap, or perhaps completely supersede, the distinctive one-sidedness of Peter's presentations, or the parallel replacements, modifications, and additions of the rest of the apostles.

No wonder therefore that critics in general should have agreed to class the first three canonical Gospels as 'synoptic,'[1] setting St. John's apart on a pedestal by itself. No wonder moreover that a considerable school of investigators, of whom more hereafter, should have conceived that St. Mark must have borrowed from St. Matthew. No wonder that another considerable school should have imagined that he borrowed from both St. Matthew and St. Luke. And no wonder, in addition, that still another school should have contended, reversely, that it was on St. Mark that St. Matthew and St. Luke unitedly drew for the main body of their materials. Undoubtedly they did derive a large amount of the contents of their Gospels from the copious wellspring from which St. Mark still more directly drew.

When we assume, in accordance with the emphatic testimony of 'the fathers,' that St. Mark drew directly from the discoursings of St. Peter, then we understand how it comes to pass that it is in his pages that we have the most particular account of that lamentable denial of his Lord, of which the apostle was guilty (chap. xiv. 30, 31, 54, 66-72). On no other person's memory would the minute particulars of the prediction, and of its unanticipated fulfilment, be so indelibly engraven. It is also noteworthy that while the very severe rebuke which our Lord administered to St. Peter, in the neighbourhood of Cæsarea Philippi, is faithfully and circumstantially recorded in St. Mark's pages (chap. viii. 33), the splendid eulogium and distinguishing blessing, which had been previously pronounced, are as it were modestly passed by. (See Matt. xvi. 17-19.) Doubtless the great apostle would not be guilty of making frequent or egotistic references to such marks of distinction. *It is likely*, says Eusebius, *that Peter maintained silence on these points; hence the silence of Mark.*[2]

Then the very house which he occupied in Capernaum, though in the other synoptic Gospels simply called *Peter's* or *Simon's*, is in St.

---

[1] They can, to a large extent, be exhibited in a *synopsis* of parallel columns. See, for instance, Griesbach's *Synopsis*.

[2] *Demonstratio Evangelica*, iii. 5, p. 121.

Mark's called 'the house of Simon *and Andrew*' (i. 29). It is as if the evangelist were reproducing the statement that would naturally drop from the lips of the apostle, 'the house that was occupied *by my brother and me.*' Then again, when, in the account of the transfiguration, we read of St. Peter's proposal to erect three tabernacles, it is naively added, 'for he wist not what to say' (ix. 6). One almost hears the apostle rehearsing the whole matter; and, when coming to the project of erecting the tabernacles, he would pause and add something to the following effect: "*I thought I should say "something; but really I did not know what to say, I was so con- "founded and overwhelmed with awe. In the end I actually said "something foolish.*" This latter part of his account is reproduced in St. Luke's narrative (ix. 33). The way too in which the angel, who appeared to the women in the empty sepulchre, makes reference to the faithless apostle strikes us as peculiarly touching, if it be regarded as reproduced by the evangelist from the lips of the apostle himself, 'Tell his disciples *and Peter*, He goeth before you into Galilee' (xvi. 7). The apostle would delight to give emphasis to the semi-redundant clause, involving, as it did, the forgiving mercy of the Master he had so shamefully mistrusted and denied.

There are besides, throughout the entire Gospel, multitudes of minute graphic touches, which bewray the evangelist's connection with some peculiarly observant eye-and-ear-witness, such as the apostle no doubt would be. For instance, the personal looks and gestures of our Lord are more frequently specified than in either of the other synoptic Gospels. (See chap. i. 31; iii. 5, 34; v. 32; vii. 33, 34; viii. 12, 33; x. 27.) Then there are such vivid circumstantialities as the 'pillow' in the boat (iv. 38), the 'green grass' at passover time on the hill side (vi. 39), the 'roundabout road' from Bethany to Bethphage (xi. 4), the colt tied 'outside,' not *inside*, the quadrangle of the owner's house (xi. 4), and the 'one loaf' which the flustered disciples had with them on the sea (viii. 14). These are singularly luminous points.

The two other synoptic evangelists record, as well as St. Mark, *the little children scene*. But St. Mark alone makes mention of the interesting circumstance that our Lord, in blessing the little ones, 'folded them in His arms' (x. 16). He alone too mentions that, on another occasion, the same gentle 'embrace' was given to the little child, who was set in the midst of the disciples as the model of an unambitious spirit (ix. 36). Something of the same motherly tenderness of spirit was displayed in our Lord's treatment of the little girl of twelve years of age, whom He restored to life. Not only did He 'take her by the hand' in the act of reviving her, as both St. Matthew and St. Luke, as well as St. Mark, record; He spoke to her, as we learn from St. Mark alone, in her own familiar mother-tongue, *Talitha cumi* (v. 41). Peter was present (v. 37), and would hear.

The circumstantialities connected with the case of the woman who came behind and touched the hem of the Saviour's garment have all along, in Christian circles, excited the special interest of the pious. They are given by St. Mark more graphically, and in fuller detail, than by the other evangelists (v. 24-34). And so, to a noteworthy extent, is the history of the cure of the demoniac lad at the base of the mount of transfiguration. The whole scene is drawn to the life; but when we come to that notable home-thrust so felicitously dealt by our Lord, and with such readiness, by which He turned back on the stupefied father the '*If it be possible to Thee,*' we cannot doubt that we are listening to the report of one who had been just such a keen and tenacious observer as we picture the apostle Peter to have been. (See ix. 23, and *Commentary* in loc.)

There are other vivid circumstantialities, agreeing well with the idea that St. Peter was drawn upon: for instance, the taunt which the Nazarenes threw at our Lord, 'the carpenter' (vi. 3); the name of the blind beggar at Jericho, evidently ' a character,' 'Bartimæus (x. 46); the earnest bilingual address, 'Abba-Father,' in the Lord's agony prayer in Gethsemane (xiv. 36); and that little insignificant, yet most significant, particular in *the cornfield scene*, unhappily slurred over both by Luther and in King James's English version, but incontestably bewraying the autopticity of the narrator, 'they began to make a way' (ii. 23, and see *Commentary*). It is enough. We would only specify, in conclusion, one other incidental circumstantiality. When Peter got a place at the fire, in the court of the high priest's house, he had, we are told in St. Mark's narrative, his face, unfortunately or fortunately, '*to* the light,' so that his features stood out in full relief (xiv. 54). Who so likely to remember the fact, and to give it emphasis, as Peter himself?

In short, if we assume the patristic tradition regarding the apostle's relation to St. Mark, we find the contents and texture of the Gospel to be, without a jar at any point, in perfect accord with the idea.

§ 8. THE INNER RELATION OF THE GOSPEL TO THE SYNOPTIC GOSPELS OF ST. MATTHEW AND ST. LUKE.

The oldest ecclesiastical writers say nothing regarding the inner relation of our Gospel to the other two synoptic Gospels. But Augustine speculated on the subject. Assuming the chronological anteriority of St. Matthew's Gospel, he imagined that St. Mark followed his predecessor on foot as it were, only taking shorter cuts, or abbreviating the evangelical narrative as he went along.[1] "He "has," says Augustine, "nothing in his Gospel which he shares with "John alone. He has very little that is peculiar to himself. He has "still less in common with Luke alone. But he has very much in "common with Matthew, often expressed too in just so many, and "indeed the very same, words. In these instances he sometimes "accords with Matthew alone, and sometimes with the other "Gospels in addition, when they run parallel with Matthew."[2]

Augustine had somewhat minutely observed the remarkable correspondences and variations of the four Gospels, though he speculated no further regarding their inner inter-relationship. It is a fact that there are no correspondences that are peculiar to St Mark and St. John. It is also a fact that there are but few incidents in the life of our Lord, and but few of His discourses or remarks, that are recorded by St. Mark alone. It is likewise a fact that there is still less that is peculiar to St. Mark and St. Luke as a pair. Eichhorn,[3] followed by Bertholdt,[4] specifies only five paragraphs of this description, four of which are very brief. The five are these: (1) Mark i. 21-28, Luke iv. 31-37; (2) Mark i. 35-39, Luke iv. 42-44; (3) Mark iii. 7-19, Luke vi. 12-16; (4) Mark iv. 21-29, Luke viii. 16-18; (5) Mark xii. 41-44, Luke xxi. 1-4.

Eichhorn has made a mistake in specifying the third of these paragraphs, for it is almost as fully given in Matthew x. 1-4 as in Luke vi. 12-16. There is a mistake too in the fourth specification, for ver. 21-25 of chap. iv. have their homologues as really in

---

[1] "Marcus eum subsecutus, tanquam pedissequus et breviator ejus videtur." —*Consensus Evangelistarum*, i. 2.

[2] "Cum solo quippe Joanne, nihil dixit; solus ipse, perpauca; cum solo Luca, "pauciora; cum Matthæo vero, plurima, et multa pene totidem atque ipsis "verbis, sive cum solo, sive cum cæteris consonante."—*Consensus Evv.*, ut supra.

[3] *Einleitung*, vol. i., § 70, p. 348.

[4] *Einleitung*, vol. iii., § 301, p. 1103.

Matthew (v. 15, x. 26, vii. 2, xxv. 29), as in Luke; and ver. 26-29 have nothing in either Luke or Matthew that is analogous. So that only three peculiar paragraphs remain. Of these, it is merely the first, and longest, in which there is a verbal agreement. And that verbal agreement is complete only in two verses, namely the 24th and 25th of Mark, and the 34th and 35th of Luke. In these two verses, however, the phraseology is all but identical, absolutely so in the Received or Erasmian text.

Ferdinand C. Baur gives a list of the peculiar coincidences of St. Mark and St. Luke, somewhat different from Eichhorn's. He has Eichhorn's first, second, and fifth instances. But he has other three, viz.: (1) Mark iii. 7–12, Luke vi. 17–19; (2) Mark ix. 38–40, Luke ix. 49, 50; (3) Mark xii. 38–40, Luke xx. 45–47.[1] Let them be accepted. Augustine was right in saying that the precise correspondences that are found between St. Mark and St. Luke, without homologues in St. Matthew and St. John, are few, fewer indeed than the peculiarities in incident or discourse that are found in St. Mark alone.

He is also correct in saying that the correspondences between St. Mark and St. Matthew are very numerous. If we take, for instance, such a work as Griesbach's *Synopsis of the three Synoptic Gospels*, we find that in a sum total of a hundred and fifty sections into which he subdivides his *Synopsis*, there are between sixty and seventy in which there are marked correspondences between St. Matthew and St. Mark. If again we take, let us say, Robinson's *Harmony of the Four Gospels*, we find that in the hundred and seventy-three sections into which he distributes the harmonised narrative, there are above eighty in which the harmony of St. Mark and St. Matthew is regarded as evident.

Augustine therefore was correct in the general result of his collation.

But there are insuperable objections to his theory of the genetic relationship of St. Mark's Gospel to St. Matthew's. His great name indeed bore down, for many centuries, so far as the Western church was concerned, everything like opposition to his view; only there were now and again put forth, tentatively, small tinkering efforts to reconcile St. Mark's 'footman'-relationship to St. Matthew with the 'interpreter'-relationship to the apostle Peter ascribed to him by the other fathers. Even after the Revival of letters, and the sub-

---

[1] *Markusevangelium*, p. 114.

sequent genesis and development of a somewhat independent spirit of biblical criticism and theological inquiry, Augustine's opinion remained for long comparatively unchallenged. Le Fèvre d'Etaples however, with his characteristic independence, strongly opposed it.[1] But Erasmus acquiesced in it.[2] And so did even Wetstein, in his day, though he made some little allowance for the independent influence of Peter's instructions.[3]

It is however an utterly indefensible theory, and has been long abandoned by all critics, as a crudity of nascent speculation. It would account indeed for the minute verbal correspondences that sometimes occur in the two Gospels, as for instance in Matthew xxiv. 4-36 and Mark xiii. 5-32. But it can never account for the divergences of phraseology, which also frequently occur; and the divergences in order too. Still less can it afford a clue to a principle of omission, that would account for the absence of some of the most interesting contents of St. Matthew's narrative. And yet less still can it account for the multitudes of vivid touches in details, which are present in St. Mark but wanting in St. Matthew, and which have all the appearance of 'autopticity'; such for instance as the circumstantialities connected with the cure of the demoniac lad at the foot of the mount of transfiguration (chap. ix. 14-29). And then the theory not only fails, it entirely founders, when the fact is taken into account that there are incidents, discourses, and remarks, found in St. Mark, of which there are no traces whatsoever in St. Matthew. See, for instance, the remarkable parable contained in chap. iv. 26-29; and the remarkable miracles recorded in chaps. vii. 31-37 and viii. 22-26. See also the fact of the pairing of the apostles when sent out on their first apostolical tour (vi. 7). See likewise those great deep utterances in chaps. iv. 22, iv. 28, ix. 23, ix. 40, ix. 49; and those remarkable expressions in chap. vii. 3 and xiv. 41: all of which are peculiar to St. Mark.

When we take the sum total of these details of things into consideration, we cannot hesitate to come to the conclusion that Koppe was right in the title of his Dissertation, published in 1782, *Mark not the Abbreviator of Matthew*.[4]

---

[1] *Commentarius in Marcum;* Prooemium, fol. 216, ed. 1522.
[2] *Annotationes in Marcum;* Prooemium, in all the editions.
[3] *Novum Testamentum;* Prooemium in Marcum.
[4] *Marcus non Epitomator Matthæi:* published in Pott and Rupert's *Sylloge*, vol i., pp. 35-69.

Neither did the evangelist, as Griesbach imagined,[1] *cut and cull his narrative, in an alternating manner, out of the two Gospels of St. Matthew and St. Luke.* It is an extremely artificial and mechanical theory. And yet the distinguished critic actually supposed that he could reproduce the precise zig-zag process that was pursued by the evangelist, as he elaborated his Gospel out of the two anterior Gospels lying before him.

St. Mark had resolved, according to Griesbach, to compile out of the two a shorter account than either, and to make it suitable for Gentile readers. That was his general determination.

He then started with St. Matthew, to whose leadership he intended to adhere in the main. He omitted however, at the outset, the whole contents of the first and second chapters, as having no immediate reference to the public ministry of Christ. Coming down therefore to the third chapter, he passed carefully along its course, and thence down to the 22nd verse of the fourth chapter,— appropriating the facts recorded in that stretch, and condensing the substance of the narrative into the first twenty verses of his own first chapter.

Then, looking forward to the fifth, sixth, and seventh chapters of St. Matthew, and noticing that they contained a long and 'verbose' discourse[2]—the Sermon on the Mount—which he wished, as Ferdinand C. Baur expresses it, 'completely to ignore,'[3]—he turned to St. Luke. Following the thread of this evangelist's narrative, he comes to chap. iv. 31, which seems to refer to the same period that is spoken of toward the close of that paragraph of St. Matthew which he had already turned to account. He goes on therefore with St. Luke iv. 31-44, reproducing that paragraph into ver. 21-39 of his own first chapter. Then he looks forward to St. Luke v. 1-11, which seems to him to be not unlike what he had already recorded in ver. 16-20 out of St. Matthew iv. 18-22. He therefore pretermits that paragraph; but makes use of what follows from v. 12 to the end of the chapter, and thence on to vi. 11. All this he reproduces in his own Gospel, throughout chaps. i. 40-45; ii. 1-28; iii. 1-6.

Then he thinks it time to go back to St. Matthew, where he finds in chap. xii. 14 a parallel statement to his own in chap.

---

[1] *Commentatio qua Marci Evangelium totum e Matthæi et Lucæ commentariis decerptum esse monstratur.* See pp. 358-425 of his *Opuscula Academica*, vol. ii.
[2] "Nimis enim verbosa videbatur ei."—p. 371.
[3] "Er die Bergrede völlig ignorirte"—*Markusevangelium*, p. 143.

iii. 6. Hence, for some inexplicable reason, he spins out a paragraph consisting of ver. 7-12 in his own third chapter, to correspond with ver. 15 and 16 of Matthew xii. But noticing that what follows in St. Matthew is a quotation from the Old Testament, he feels as it were repelled,[1] and turns once more to St. Luke, taking up the narrative where he had formerly left it, and transferring, in his own way, ver. 12-16 of chap. vi. into ver. 13-19 of his own chap. iii. Then he seems to have got wearied of St. Luke, and turned to St. Matthew once more, and made use of xii. 22-32 in his own iii. 20-30.

He then passes over ver. 33-45 in St. Matthew, as containing matter that he did not wish; but instead of turning abruptly on that account to St. Luke, as might have been expected, he reproduces, in that portion of his own narrative which extends from chap. iii. 31-35 to chap. iv. 1-20, what he found in Matthew xii. 46-50 and xiii. 1-23. Then he turns once more to St. Luke, and makes use of viii. 16-18 in his own iv. 21-25. After which he reverts again to St. Matthew xiii. 24-30; but in place of reproducing the parable there contained he is reminded, by the expression '*while the men slept*,' of another parable in which not the '*men*,' but *the husband-'man*,' *slept*, and so he inserts it instead, in iv. 26-29. Then he copies from St. Matthew once more, reproducing St. Matthew's two verses, xiii. 31, 32, into his own three, iv. 30, 31, 32. After that, passing over the little parable in the 33rd ver. of St. Matthew, he condenses what he finds in the 34th and 35th verses into his own statement as contained in his ver. 33 and 34. And at length, 'fatigued' with the multitude of St. Matthew's parables, 'he bids good-bye for a little' to his chosen leader,[2] and, betaking himself again to St. Luke, resumes the thread of narrative which he had let go when he turned to St. Matthew xiii. 24. He finds, however, on resuming the thread, that he had already obtained out of St. Matthew what corresponds to St. Luke viii. 19-21, and hence he passes on to the following paragraphs, in ver. 22-25, and ver. 26-56. These he reproduces in his own chap. iv. 35-41, and chap. v. 1-43. Then he once more relents, though still only half recovered from the inundation of parables,[3] and turns to St. Matthew xiii. 53-58: etc., etc., etc.

---

[1] " Consulto omittit locum prophetæ comm. 17-21 laudatum."—p. 372.

[2] "Cum vero Matthæus porro parabolis adderet parabolas, Marcus velut " fatigatus hunc ducem aliquantisper valere jussit."—p. 374.

[3] " Marcum nimia parabolum Matthæi cap. 13 copia quasi obrutum, Lucæ

Enough! As a theory of genetic relationship, this *hypothesis* is, to the last degree, unlikely. Certainly, it entirely fails to give a sufficient reason for its hop-and-skip principle of transition from the one Gospel to the other. It also equally fails to account for those peculiarities of incident, discourse, and remark, which are found in St. Mark alone. Griesbach says that these occupy in all only about twenty-four verses.[1] But this is utterly unreal, when we add the copious circumstantialities, which besprinkle the Gospel throughout, to the sections which deal with scenes that have no parallels in either St. Matthew or St. Luke.[2] The theory likewise fails to account for those characteristic touches of description, which impart vividness, by single flashes, to the scenes depicted, and suggest that the evangelist must be drawing on the reports of some eye-witness, who had the tact of felicitously seizing, in what he saw and heard, points of irradiation and salient items of detail. Then too it entirely fails to account for the thorough homogeneousness, all through the Gospel, of the evangelist's style of composition,— simple, artless, and homely though that style confessedly is.[3] If he had been borrowing his *matériel*, alternately, from the writings of St. Matthew and St. Luke, one would have expected, as the unavoidable result of his double dependence, to find, in alternative sequence, a certain reflection, distinct or dim,— a '*nuancirung*' at least,—of the two different styles, to which the pendulum of his attention successively turned. But there is no such alternation of reflection or shade. And thus the theory again breaks down; as it also conspicuously does, when one attempts, in consistency with

---

"se adjunxisse comitem vidimus. Verumtamen cum Matthæum potissimum "sibi elegisset, ad cujus ductum memorabilia Christi scripto consignaret, jam "ad Matthæum suum redit."—p. 375.

[1] "Marcus totum libellum suum, *si viginti et quatuor circiter commata*, quæ "de sua penu addidit, excipias, e Matthæi et Lucæ commentariis compilavit."— p. 369, also p. 380.

[2] See the detailed evidence in Willes's *Specimen Hermeneuticum de iis, quæ ab uno Marco sunt narrata, aut copiosius et explicatius ab eo, quam a cæteris Evangelistis, exposita.* There is a summary in pp. 188-192. See also August Knobel *de Evangelii Marci Origine*, pp. 29-56.

[3] "Of all the New Testament writers," says Michaelis, "none appear to "have given themselves less concern, than Mark, concerning elegance of "diction and purity of Greek." (*Unter allen Schriftstellern des N. T. scheint keiner um die Zierde der Rede, und um die Reinigkeit des Griechischen weniger bekümmert gewesen zu sein, als Marcus.*)—*Einleitung*, § 147, p. 1076.

it, to account for the many minute diversities which, amid the multitudes of minute coincidences, mottle the representations of St. Mark, and stamp them with a phase that is entirely his own.

The theory is certainly untenable. But as it is positive on the one hand, and completely removed from the region of mystical haze on the other; as it happily stirred the stagnant waters of criticism, and disturbed the old, shallow, self-arrogating hypothesis of St. Mark's exclusive dependence on St. Matthew; as it was wrought out moreover, and propounded, by an author renowned for ability, learning, critical acumen, and independence of judgment; it was, although amid much contention and opposition, extensively espoused. Saunier, in particular, elaborately defended it in a special treatise on *The Sources of Mark's Gospel*.[1] Sieffert too defended it; though he tried to reconcile it with the testimony of Papias regarding the relationship of the Gospel to the teachings of the apostle Peter.[2] Fritzsche also espoused it zealously, and made it the basis of his *Commentary on Mark*,—a commentary remarkable alike for scholarly ability and for critical tyranny of tone. It was asserted moreover in the most positive manner imaginable by Evanson, in his *Dissonance of the Four generally received Evangelists*.[3] It is contended for by Dr. Davidson; only he postulates, in addition, that the unknown evangelist must have made use of "the primitive Mark, or Petrine Gospel, referred to by Papias."[4] Strauss too accepted it with eagerness as demonstrated.[5] He found it to be subservient to his own ulterior critical aim,—for it is obvious that there could be no place for the mythical theory of the *Gospel-History*, if St. Mark's *Gospel-Writing* rested directly on the authority of an actual eye-and-ear-witness, such as the apostle Peter. Strauss therefore, in his later work, persists in his adherence to the theory of Griesbach.[6] Gfrörer also, as might be expected from his kinship of spirit to that of Strauss, accepts it,

---

[1] *Ueber die Quellen des Evangeliums des Marcus.* (1825.)

[2] *Prolusio, qua diversæ recentiorum criticorum sententiæ de fontibus Evangelii St. Marci antiquissimæ traditionis ecclesiasticæ ope conciliantur* (1829). See also his subsequent *Abhandlung über den Ursprung des ersten kanonischen Evangeliums* (1832), p. 178. The former work is little known even in Germany.

[3] He represents Mark's narrative as "compiled entirely of passages copied, "often literally, either from the Gospel called Matthew's, or Luke's"—p. 212 of 1st ed. (1792), or p. 275 of 2nd ed. (1805).

[4] *Introduction*, vol. ii., pp. 90–103.

[5] "Ist zur Evidenz erhoben."—*Leben Jesu*, vol. i., § 12, p. 65, ed. 1835.

[6] *Leben Jesu für das deutsche Volk* (1864), p. 86.

and "holds it for *an established fact*, that St. Mark not only had "the two other synoptic Gospels lying open before him, *but trans-* "*cribed them.*"[1] The underlying principle of the theory, viz. that St. Mark made use of the Gospels of both St. Matthew and St. Luke, had been, at an earlier period, ably and reverently advocated by Dr. Henry Owen, in his *Observations on the Four Gospels* (1764).[2] It was accepted as a 'very probable' hypothesis by Harwood;[3] and it has been contended for, or maintained, by many critics since, inclusive of Neudecker,[4] de Wette,[5] and Bleek.[6] It is also maintained, under a certain developed phase, by Ferdinand C. Baur,[7] Schwegler,[8] Köstlin,[9] and the other adherents of the Tübingen school.

De Wette gives effect to his opinion on the subject, by arranging his *Handbook-Exposition of the Gospels* thus: (1) Matthew, (2) Luke, (3) Mark, (4) John. Köstlin, in like manner, in his treatise on the *Origin and Composition of the Synoptic Gospels*, divides his work into three books or sections, arranged thus: (1) *the Gospel according to Matthew*, (2) *the Gospel according to Luke*, (3) *the Gospel according to Mark*. Although he holds that there was an original Mark, anterior to both St. Matthew and St. Luke, yet he maintains that the canonical Mark was subsequent to these other synoptics, and dug out of their materials.

In addition to the general notion that St. Mark made use of the Gospels of both St. Matthew and St. Luke, the critics of the

---

[1] "Markus die beiden Anderen nicht nur vor sich gehabt, sondern ausge-"schrieben hat. Dass Lezteres wirklich der Fall sey, halte Ich wenigstens für "eine ausgemachte Thatsache."—*Geschichte des Urchristenthums, Band* iv., *Kap.* 9, p. 123.
[2] See, in particular, pp. 62-75.
[3] *Introduction to the Study and Knowledge of the New Testament*, vol. i., chap. iv., § 3, p. 135.
[4] *Lehrbuch der historisch-kritischen Einleitung*, § 32, p. 232.
[5] *Lehrbuch der historisch-kritischen Einleitung*, § 94.
[6] *Einleitung in das N. T*, p. 243. See also his *Beiträge zur Evangelien-Kritik*, pp. 72-75.
[7] *Das Markusevangelium*, and *Kritische Untersuchungen über die kanonischen Evangelien*, pp. 548-561.
[8] *Das Nachapostolische Zeitalter*, pp. 456-475.
[9] *Der Ursprung und die Komposition der Synoptischen Evangelien*, pp. 310-385.

Tübingen school,—such as F. C. Baur, Schwegler, Köstlin, already referred to,—attribute to the evangelist a particular doctrinal aim or 'tendency,' having a particular relation to the parties that were co-existing, at the time of the composition of the Gospel, within the circle of the churches. St. Matthew is regarded as having had an Old Testament 'tendency,' on the side of the Judaic party. St. Luke in his 'tendency' is regarded as having been anti-Judaic and Pauline. And St. Mark, coming after both as is assumed, and mediating as it were between them, is looked upon as meeting a more matured condition of the divergent parties,[1] when their wisest leaders were wishful to shake hands and agree. His Gospel is therefore 'neutral' and 'irenic.'[2] 'It is the product,' says Köstlin, 'of the idea of catholicity.'[3]

It may, on all hands, be admitted that there is a certain generic element of truth in the representations of the school that surrounded F. C. Baur. St. Mark's Gospel is undoubtedly 'neutral.' It is 'colourless,' in relation to all grave party questions within the circle of the early churches. It is eminently 'catholic.' It is 'irenic.' It is also, at the same time, as Hilgenfeld represents it, [4]'Petrinic,' though not in any one-sided, or obtrusive, or sectarian, or anti-Pauline sense. It is 'Pauline' too, as Michelsen contends,[5] but in no anti-Petrine spirit. It is thoroughly unsectarian.

All this *may* be admitted, and *should* be admitted. It is patent, lying on the surface of the Gospel. It wells up from its heart.

Nevertheless, there is not so much as one straw of evidence that the Gospel of Mark occupied a position of mediation, or iren c neutrality, *in relation to the other two synoptic Gospels*. It is in the mere wantonness of a creative imagination that its penman is depicted as warily steering his critical bark between some Scylla in St. Matthew's representations and some Charybdis in St Luke's. There is no Scylla in the representations of St. Matthew. It must be invented, if suspected. There is no Charybdis in the

---

[1] Schwegler, *Das Nachapostolische Zeitalter*, p. 456.
[2] Ibid., pp. 474–481. See a shadow of the Tübingen idea cast before, in Owen's *Observations*, pp. 50, 51.
[3] *Der Ursprung*, p. 373.
[4] *Die Evangelien*, pp. 125–144.
[5] *Het Evangelie van Markus, Inleiding*, p. 4. "Our Mark," was written, he says, "door een christen uit de joden, doch niettemin een hevig aanhanger van "Paulus."

representations of St. Luke. Neither is there any indication in St. Mark of wary steering, or of some latent aim of destination kept, like sealed orders, under lock and key. There is, in all the Gospels, perfect transparency and simplicity, 'the simplicity that is in Christ.' It is not needful to mine into profound depths, or to climb into giddy heights, in search of 'tendency.' No intricate involution, baffling to ordinary eyes, need be suspected. No divining power is required. There may have been, to a certain incidental degree, a desire, as Mill conjectured, to correct apocryphal or erroneous representations,[1] that were getting afloat over society. But doubtless the one dominant and overmastering aim would just be that of all the apostles of our Lord, and of all, in all ages, who have imbibed aught of the apostolic spirit; to tell, for the sake of sinful and suffering humanity, the unvarnished but vivifying story of the life-and-death-work of Christ the Saviour. In other words, and in popular phraseology, the aim would be *to unfurl the banner of 'the gospel.'*

The peculiar Tübingen theory has been repudiated and opposed by the illustrious Heinrich Ewald, in terms of the most stinging severity. The school from which it emanates is denounced by him as 'mischievous' and 'false.'[2] But in his own theory of the interrelationship of Mark to the other Gospels he formed, as is his wont, such peculiarly vivid conceptions that, to himself, they have started out from the canvas of his imagination, with all the self-evidencing or self-asserting authority of objective historical facts.

He postulates a considerable variety of documents or books, now lost, but more or less incorporated in our existing Gospels. The respective peculiarities of these books are, he conceives, clearly discernible, in the particoloured texture of the synoptic Gospels. And hence, in the first edition of his *Translation of the First Three Gospels*, the edition of 1850, the respective portions which, as he conceives, had been derived from these prior works, are actually represented to the eye by being printed in *nine varieties of type*.

He holds, moreover, that there have been three distinct editions of Mark,—Mark *a*, Mark *b*, Mark *c*,—the second much altered from the first, though appearing only about a year later, and the third (which appeared in the second century) still further altered and impoverished.[3] In the second edition, as he supposes, there were

---

[1] *Prolegomena*, § 111.
[2] *Die drei ersten Evangelien u. d. Apostelgeschichte* (1871-72), pp. 2, 3.
[3] *Die drei ersten Evv.*, pp. 77-174.

numerous interpolations introduced from two still earlier evangelical documents, *the oldest Gospel* (now lost,—the Gospel that was used, he is convinced, by the apostle Paul),[1] and *the Lord's Words* or the "*Spruchsammlung*" (also now lost).

In direct opposition, however, to the hypothesis of the Tübingen school and of Griesbach, Ewald maintains strongly that the Gospel of Mark was not only a thoroughly 'original' work, but antecedent in date to the Gospels of both Matthew and Luke, and was used by these evangelists in the composition of their respective books.

The entire theory of the distinguished author is emphatically his own. No other independent mind could be expected to accept it. Geniuses, who wander in orbits of infinite conjecture, differ from each other, like planet from planet, not only in bulk, substantiality, and the hue and intensity of their lustre, but also *in their paths*.

But how then are we to account for the remarkable coincidences that characterize the synoptic Gospels? Whence the whole paragraphs of coincident phraseology? Whence the coincidences in detached and minute phrases, as for instance in Matthew xii. 13, Mark iii. 5, Luke vi. 10? Whence the coincidences too in the order or arrangement of the evangelical materials?

Eichhorn, for instance, gives a tabulated list of 44 sections, which are parallel or coincident in the three synoptic Gospels. In all these sections, with the single exception of the 38th, the 'order' of Mark and Luke is identical; and, from the 20th onward, the order in the three evangelists, with the single exception already specified, is one and the same.

Whence such coincidences?

It is not enough to refer the whole matter, with Gaussen[2] and others of the same school, to the sovereignty of Divine inspiration and dictation. God indeed 'hath spoken once' and again and again. (Ps. lxii. 11; Heb. i. 1.) He still speaks. His very works are words. He spoke and speaks through the evangelists. Like the prophets of the older dispensation, 'they spake as they were moved by the Holy Ghost' (2 Pet. i. 21). Doubtless the omnipresent Spirit is brooding and breathing everywhere; and He 'blows where He listeth' (John iii. 8). This is not a worn-out antiquated idea. It is a perennial truth, just as really a dictate of

---

[1] *Die drei ersten Evv.*, p. 62
[2] *Théopneustie*, chap. i., § 4.

deep philosophy as it is a doctrine of simple and biblical theology. If so, we shall not be astray in our thoughts if we believe that the Living Spirit of Christianity was 'blowing' 1860 years ago, along the plains and around the hills of Galilee and Judæa. His influence, without stint, must undoubtedly have descended on the Christ (John iii. 34), and would be 'poured out' plenarily on His chosen representatives and commissioners. (Acts ii. 17, 18.) It *actuated* the apostles and evangelists, but always, let it be borne in mind, in perfect accordance with the divinely constituted laws that, in the sphere of free human agency, regulate idiosyncratic observation of phenomena, colligation of facts, collation of particulars, logical classification, rhetorical combination, and literary representation. (1 Cor. xiv. 32.)

We return then to our inquiry. There must be 'a sufficient reason' to account for the literary coincidences of the Gospels.

Le Clerc threw out the conjecture that the three synoptic evangelists may have derived their materials in common from the same sources, *the written Memoirs or Memorials of eye-and-ear-witnesses.*[1] Priestley reproduced the conjecture.[2] Koppe too reproduced it in part, contending in the Dissertation to which we have already referred[3] that St. Mark, so far from being a mere abbreviator of St. Matthew, never saw St. Matthew's Gospel. The coincidences between the two are, he conjectures, to be accounted for on the principle that they both drew from the same fountains, whether oral or written. Michaelis came to be of the same opinion substantially; only he gave emphasis to the conviction that it was '*written* Reports' (*schriftliche Nachrichten*) of which the three evangelists made use. "None of the three evangelists," he says, "seems to have read the Gospels of the other two."[4] Semler, though like 'a rolling stone' in his opinions, gave for a season more

---

[1] ". . . quidni enim credamus, tria hæc evangelia partim petita esse ex "similibus aut iisdem fontibus, hoc est, e commentariis eorum, qui varios "Christi sermones audiverant, aut actorum ejus testes fuerant, eaque, ne ob- "livioni traderentur, illico scriptis mandarant."—*Historia Ecclesiastica* (1716), p. 429.

[2] He speaks of the Gospels as "originally written *in detached parts.* Some of "these," he adds, "might have been committed to writing by the apostles "themselves, and some by their auditors, corrected by themselves."—*Observations on the Harmony of the Gospels* (1780), pp. 72, 73.

[3] Page xl.

[4] *Einleitung*, § 129, p. 929

definite shape to the conjecture, by saying that it was probable
that all the three synoptic evangelists used various original
Aramaic documents.¹ Lessing became more definite still, and
conjectured that the basis of the three synoptic Gospels was the
Aramaic Gospel spoken of by the fathers as *the Gospel according to
the Hebrews*, or, what was identical as he contends, *the Gospel of
the twelve apostles*.² Niemeyer took up the conjecture and elaborated it, maintaining that the divergences of the existing Gospels are
to be traced to different recensions of the primitive Aramaic Gospel.³
And then the hypothesis, thus amplified, got into the hands of
Eichhorn, who, with a consummate genius in the direction of ingenuity, elaborated it to its culminating point, during the process
of a long series of years. He was able, he conceived, to reproduce
the original document, or *Urevangelium*, so far at least as its essential contents are concerned. It consisted, he supposed, of the sum
of those forty-four⁴ sections of the history of our Lord, to which
we have already made reference,⁵ and which, in their substance, are
common to all the three synoptic Gospels. The additional sections
of the history, which are found coincidently, not in all, but only
in pairs of the Gospels, as (1) in St. Matthew and St. Mark, (2) in
St. Mark and St. Luke, and (3) in St. Matthew and St. Luke, were
documentary *Additions* or *Supplements*, incorporated in the particular copies or recensions which had come into the hands of the
respective pairs of evangelists. The sections again, which are
peculiar to each of the evangelists, were apparently either peculiarities in his particular recension, or contributions from private sources
of his own. Eichhorn is not quite positive about them.⁶ But he
is quite positive about the actual existence of the Aramaic *Urevan-*

---

¹ See his notes to his *Townson's Abhandlungen über die vier Evangelien*,
vol. i., pp. 146, 221, 290.

² "Matthæus, Marcus, Lucas sind nichts als verschiedene und nicht ver-
"schiedene Uebersetzungen der sogenannten hebräischen Urkunde des Mat-
"thæus, die jeder machte so gut er konnte."—*Neue Hypothese über die Evangel-
isten blos als menschliche Geschichtschreiber betrachtet* (1778), § 50.

³ *Conjecturæ ad illustrandum plurimorum N. T. Scriptorum silentium de
primordiis vitæ Jesu Christi* (1790), pp. 8–10.

⁴ *Forty-two* in his first draft.

⁵ Page xlviii.

⁶ As to Mark, he says: "*Diese Stücke verrathen vielmehr einen eigen gestimm-
"ten Concipienten, von dem wir sonst weiter nichts besitzen. Ob nun dieser Con-
"cipient Markus selbst sey, oder eine von ihm verschiedene Person, muss man unent-
"schieden lassen.*"—*Einleitung*, § 89, vol. i., p. 390.

gelium, with different sets of *additions* or *interpolations* in different copies : such as *Copy A*, containing additions ultimately incorporated in St. Matthew ; *Copy B*, containing additions ultimately incorporated in St. Luke ; *Copy C*, combining both *A* and *B* and translated by St. Mark ; *Copy D*, which, when combined with *B*, formed the basis of St. Luke's Gospel, while as combined with *A* it formed the basis of the text of St. Matthew.[1] He also became positive, in the ultimate form of his theory, that, in addition to the Aramaic additions in the various codices referred to, there had got into circulation early Greek translations of *Copies A* and *D*.

Hence, as he concludes, the coincidences on the one hand, and the variations on the other, of our canonical Gospels. All the coincidences are to be accounted for by the common possession of identical documents. The majority of the most important variations are to be attributed to the possession of one or more peculiar documents on the part of each particular evangelist.

We have referred to the ultimate form of Eichhorn's hypothesis. Intermediate between that form and its original draft, Dr. Marsh's *Dissertation on the Origin and Composition of our Three First Canonical Gospels* (1801) came in.

Equal to Eichhorn in zeal, and possessed of an ingenuity which, if not so inventive, was yet as keen in its edge and more critically consistent in its application, Dr. Marsh supplied several of the steps, by means of which Eichhorn at last mounted to the pinnacle and consummation of his theory.

The phase of the theory, as it left the hands of Dr. Marsh, may be learned from his own deliberate deliverance : " St. Matthew, St. " Mark, and St. Luke, all three, used copies of the common Hebrew " document ' א,' the materials of which St. Matthew, who wrote in " Hebrew, retained in the language in which he found them, but St. "Mark and St. Luke translated them into Greek. They had no " knowledge of each other's Gospels; but St. Mark and St. Luke, " besides their copies of the Hebrew document ' א,' used a Greek " translation of it, which had been made before any of the additions " ' α,' ' β,' ' γ,' ' A,' ' B,' ' Γ ' had been inserted. Lastly, as the " Gospels of St. Mark and St. Luke contain Greek translations of " Hebrew materials, which were incorporated into St. Matthew's " Hebrew Gospel, the person who translated St. Matthew's Hebrew " Gospel into Greek frequently derived assistance from the Gospel

---

[1] *Einleitung*, § 84, pp. 272–375.

"of St. Mark, where St. Mark had matter in common with St. "Matthew; and in those places, but in those places only, where " St. Mark had no matter in common with St. Matthew, he had " frequently recourse to St. Luke's Gospel."[1]

But the theory culminated, as we have intimated, in the hands of Eichhorn. It thenceforward became arrested. Though somewhat simplified by Gratz,[2] and defended, with reservations that turned longingly to the future for light, by Bertholdt,[3] it ceased to undergo development. It ceased by and by to live; and now, in Germany, it is nothing more than a memory.

No wonder. For it is, as a developed hypothesis of the genetic relationship of the Gospels, very far indeed from being satisfactory, and especially in its most developed or culminated form. It is, in the *first* place, too artificial by far. In the *second* place, it is a mere pile of conjectures, with no unchallengeable basis in historic fact. The postulated documents are never referred to by 'the ancients.' No trace of their existence is found, *except in the theory*. In the *third* place, it is unnaturally complicated, bristling cumbrously with its tabulated codices. And then, in the *fourth* place, it is essentially only a transition theory, that was destined in its very nature to be left behind, 'high and dry,' in the rapid succession of hypotheses. It proceeds on the assumption that the synoptic evangelists were dependent, for their materials, *on written documents*. And this assumption, by removing the canonical biographers of our Lord to a distance from the fountains of primary knowledge, leads, by a short route, to the surmise that the Gospels attributed to them were not their own compositions, but supposititious products of a later age. This surmise has been actually evolved, and is at present quite a postulate with a certain circle of theorists. It is claimed by F. C. Baur, and the adherents of his school, as the legitimate finding of distinctively *historical criticism*.

The claim, however, cannot be conceded. It is at variance with real history. It makes it impossible to find a sufficient reason, or an adequate cause, for the actual form which was assumed by post-apostolic Christian literature. That literature, amid many glaring excrescences and a strange combination of crudities and senilities,

---

[1] *Dissertation*, chap. xv., p. 195.

[2] *Neuer Versuch die Entstehung der drey ersten Evangelien zu erklären* (1812). See in particular §§ 26, 27.

[3] *Einleitung*, § 829. vol. iii., pp. 1249, 1250.

together with other imperfections, is pervaded by a spirit of reverence for our existing Gospels, and is frequently saturated with the expressed juices, not only of their general essence, but of their particular contents. It demands therefore, as the indispensable condition of its existence, the pre-existence of the Gospels as we have them.

In another respect, too, is the theory on which we are remarking unhistorical and unphilosophical. It leaves unaccounted for the unanimity of the Christian churches of the second century in regard to the great outstanding Christological phenomena which constitute the essence of the Gospels. For, while there were manifold diversities of speculation in reference to the interpretation of these phenomena, there was remarkable unity, attested even by the vagaries of heretics and the objections of heathens, in reference to the actual occurrence of the works and words ascribed to our Lord.

Indeed, the theory leaves unaccounted for the deeply imbedded unanimity in Christological essentials that underlies all the varied developments of Christian life, Christian speculation, and Christian organization, in all the succeeding centuries. The peculiarities of the present century demand, as part of their sufficient reason, the antecedent peculiarities of the century that preceded. The peculiarities of that preceding century demand for their adequate cause the presence of the antecedent peculiarities of the century that went before. And so the regress continues, until we arrive at the peculiarities of the second century, which demand a sufficient reason for themselves in something that is comprehensive of the antecedent peculiarities of the first. But that sufficient reason can never be found, if the facts that are embodied in the existing Gospels be ignored. And when we get into the sphere of these facts, it would be utterly unaccountable if the Matthew of the first century, who had the full use of his own eyes and ears, and the Mark of that same century, who had the privilege of being associated with probably all the apostles, and certainly with St. Peter, on terms of intimacy, were yet dependent for their narrations on some prior Gospel and connected Supplements, out of which they had painfully to weave the texture of their immortal compositions. The actual coincidences of the synoptics must be sought for in some other cause than in the common possession of an *Aramaic Urevangelium*, now lost.

What then is this cause? Many of late have looked, or are still looking for it, *in Mark's own Gospel*. They suppose that that Gospel has been, either in its present or in some prior form, the original, or archetype, out of which the Gospels of both Matthew and Luke were developed.

This Mark-hypothesis was Storr's theory. He handled it reverently, but immaturely.[1] It slumbered in its immaturity for long after the decease of Storr. But in the year 1838 it woke up in full maturity, and,—strange to say,—in two independent forms.

In that year Wilke published his *Urevangelist*,[2] and maintained, in an elaborate induction of particulars, and by most vigorous if not rigorous processes of argumentation, that our canonical Mark was *the original evangelist*, from the fountain of whose narrative both St. Matthew and St. Luke drew almost all their waters. He held however that St. Luke was anterior to St. Matthew, so that St. Matthew had not only the fountain of St. Mark from which to draw, but also the intermediate cistern of Luke.

Weisse again, in the same year, published his still more elaborate *Gospel History, critically and philosophically handled*,[3] in which, with still more comprehensive sweep of minutely detailed criticism, he contended, as zealously as Wilke, for the priority of St. Mark's Gospel, as we have it, to both St. Matthew's and St. Luke's, maintaining at the same time, just as Wilke does, that the compilers of these latter Gospels drew from the storehouse of the former. But, in contrariety to the simpler theory of Wilke, he maintained that both St. Matthew and St. Luke availed themselves, in addition, of the Aramaic *Oracles* ascribed by Papias to Matthew, the *Spruchsammlung* of which we have spoken in our notice of the hypothesis of Ewald. He contended, moreover, that St. Matthew and St. Luke wrote quite independently of one another, so that neither of the two made use of the other's cistern. In a subsequent publication, the author, influenced by the representations and reasonings of Ewald, so far modified his theory, retrogressively, as to hold that St. Mark's Gospel, as we now have it, is not so full or rich as it was at

---

[1] *Ueber den Zweck der evangelischen Geschichte und der Briefe Johannis* (1786), pp. 274 ff. See also his Prolusio *de fonte evangeliorum Matthæi et Lucæ* (1794) in Velthusen, Kuinöl, and Ruperti's Commentt. Theoll., vol. iii.; likewise his *Opuscula Academica*, vol. iii., p. 66.

[2] *Der Urevangelist, oder exegetisch kritische Untersuchung über das Verwandtschaftsverhältniss der drei ersten Evangelien.*

[3] *Die evangelische Geschichte kritisch und philosophisch bearbeitet.* (Zwei Bände.)

the time when St. Matthew and St. Luke unitedly drew from its wellspring.¹ Thiersch, in the main, has followed in the wake of Wilke and Weisse, of Wilke in particular.² So, in a sense, has Smith of Jordanhill; but independently, and by means of self originated research. He supposes, as we have already noted,³ that St. Mark's Gospel is merely *St. Mark's translation of St. Peter's original Aramaic Gospel.* He holds that it was the Aramaic original, which both St. Matthew and St. Luke made use of; St. Matthew first, and then St. Luke, who had in his hands not merely St. Peter's original document, but also our present canonical *Gospel according to St. Matthew,* or St. Matthew's Greek translation of his own prior Aramaic Gospel.

Holtzmann⁴ too supposes that all the three synoptics are compositions at second hand. At the basis of them all is an original Mark, or *Urmarcus,* of which however very special advantage was taken by the canonical Mark, and hence the transmission of the name; while the canonical Matthew and Luke had the advantage of using another important evangelical document, a Greek version of the *Oracles* which, in its original Aramaic form, was ascribed by Papias to the apostle Matthew. This *Collection of the Oracles of the Lord* constituted, says Holtzmann, the original Matthew, or *Urmatthäus,* and was freely used by both the canonical Matthew and the canonical Luke, but to a greater extent by the latter than by the former.⁵ The canonical Mark had not, it seems, the advantage of being acquainted with the work, and hence that comparative paucity of the words of the Saviour which is characteristic of his Gospel.

More recent investigators are still out at sea, and refuse to follow in the wake of either Wilke, Weisse, or Holtzmann.

Klostermann,⁶ for example, abjures the idea of an *original Mark* now lost. He believes that the canonical Mark is the Mark of

---

¹ *Die Evangelienfrage in ihrem gegenwärtigen Stadium* (1856), pp. 156 ff.
² *Die Kirche im apostolischen Zeitalter und die Entstehung der neutestamentlichen Schriften* (1858), p. 102.
³ Pages xxvii., xxxi.
⁴ *Die Synoptischen Evangelien, ihr Ursprung und geschichtlicher Charakter* (1863).
⁵ *Die Synoptischen Evangelien,* pp. 128, 162, etc.
⁶ *Das Markusevangelium nach seinem Quellenwerth für die evangelische Geschichte* (1867).

Papias. But he maintains its dependent or secondary relationship to St. Matthew.

In this last particular he treads in the footsteps of Augustine in ancient times, as also of Hilgenfeld in modern times, who, in a long series of consecutive treatises, maintains that St. Mark made use of St. Matthew, while he still more emphatically and persistently maintains, in opposition to Griesbach and F. C. Baur, that he did not make use of St. Luke.

Volkmar too, like Klostermann, though belonging to a totally different school, abandons the idea of an *original* or *chrysalis Mark*; though he holds that it is not unlikely that the canonical Mark made use of the canonical Luke, while it is certain, he supposes, that he made use of four of Paul's epistles, as also of 'the bitterly anti-Pauline Apocalypse.'[1]

Michelsen of Holland, on the other hand, contends confidently for a succession of Marks. He is certain indeed that both St. Matthew and St. Luke had before them the two editions. St. Matthew however, as he conceives, more frequently followed Mark the First, while St. Luke in general gave the preference to Mark the Second.[2]

Scholten followed Michelsen, and is equally positive that there was an original Mark, the precursor of the canonical. Indeed it must have been, as he represents it, of a very humble chrysalis character. It was, however, one of the chief sources of Matthew. But then, be it remembered, there were three successive Matthews: Matthew the First (*i.e.* the *Oracles*); Matthew the Second (drawn from Mark the First, and the Oracles, and another original Gospel now lost); and Matthew the Third, or our canonical *Gospel according to Matthew* (containing, in addition to the three constituent elements specified, some pieces or patches of anecdote unknown to Luke).[3]

A far more reverent spirit is that of Dr. Bernhard Weiss, who has devoted himself to the study of this question for a long series of years, and published in 1872 an elaborate work on Mark.[4]

---

[1] *Die Evangelien, oder Marcus und die Synopsis der kanonischen und ausserkanonischen Evangelien, nach dem ältesten Text, mit historisch-exegetischen Commentar* (1870), p. 646.

[2] *Het Evangelie van Markus.* (1867.)

[3] *Het Oudste Evangelie, critisch onderzoek naar de samenstelling, de onderlinge verhouding, de historische waarde en den oorsprong der evangeliën naar Mattheus en Marcus* (1868), pp. 70–72, etc.

[4] *Das Marcusevangelium und seine synoptischen Parallelen.* (1872.)

He has, however, a complicated theory of his own. He turns back to the testimony of 'the fathers,' and believes, in accordance with the general tradition, that St. Mark's Gospel was inspired by the direct teaching of the apostle Peter. So far good. But running, too artificially as we conceive, in the groove of the Mark-hypothesis, he also believes that the Gospel, as thus inspired by the chief of the original apostles, 'lies at the basis' of the other two synoptic Gospels, and gave rise to 'their entire inner economy.' But he believes, still further, that the problem of the inter-relationship of the three Gospels can never be solved, unless we postulate, with Holtzmann, that there was a still earlier apostolic document, which was made use of by all the three evangelists, viz. a Greek translation of that original Aramaic writing of Matthew which is spoken of by Papias, *the Oracles of the Lord*. It was because this was largely absorbed in the first canonical Gospel, that occasion was given to the name, *the Gospel according to* 'St. Matthew.' This earliest of all the evangelical documents is, as Weiss holds, 'the missing link,' after which the hands of Lessing, Eichhorn, Marsh, and their followers, were anxiously groping, but which, unhappily for the success of their critical researches, eluded their grasp.

We cannot say that we are satisfied with the 'Mark-hypothesis' in any of its forms, or with any of the other hypotheses which we have passed under review. They are all too artificial, and most of them too subtle.

The problem is in some respects insoluble.

A witness in a court of law, if he has a long story to tell twice, will produce a minglement of coincidences and variations, which postulate, as their factors, conditions which it might baffle the most judicial and judicious to unravel and enumerate.

Even the same author, if not trusting to a stereotypical memory, will be, perhaps unconsciously, the subject of different factors of representation, when, at different times and in different circumstances, he presents the story of his experience or information. Witness, for example, the apostle Paul's accounts of his 'apprehension' by the Saviour on the road to Damascus, as given, the one to the people of Jerusalem while he stood on the stair of the castle Antonia (recorded in Acts xxii.), and the other in the presence of King Agrippa at Cæsarea (recorded in Acts xxvi.). Compare, moreover, both of these accounts with that of Luke in the ninth chapter of the Acts, an account no doubt furnished to the faithful historian from the mouth of the apostle himself. The factors that influenced rhetorical or literary representation were, of necessity, peculiar in each case, and produced the noteworthy variations which occur in each of the accounts. But certain of the factors were uniform throughout, and hence are to be accounted for not only the essential harmony of the accounts, but also the coincidences in particular items of the phraseology. Yet who could now reproduce the sum total of the factors? And how exceedingly cumbrous, artificial, absurd, and comical, it would be to proceed on the assumption that, to explain the coincidences and variations, a complex series of prior documents or *Urdocumente* must be postulated, out of one or more of which something must have been derived to all the representations, while the variations are to be accounted for on the assumption that document A was not followed in the one case, while document B was substituted in its place, and document C was overlaid while document B was being used.

The factors of rhetorical or literary representation, that produce coincidences and sometimes even lengthened harmonies or identities, are not always or necessarily documentary. Especially was this the case in an age when the facilities for actual penmanship were comparatively few and rare, and among a people who did not enjoy the advantage of being trained to the use of 'letters.' Take the old English and Scottish ballads for example. It was long ere some of them, at least, were committed to writing. Bard handed them down to bard; and when the bards died out, amateurs of less practised memories kept hold of them, often with remarkable tenacity as regards essence and substance, though not with uniform identity as regards every word, line, rhyme, or verse.

It is suggestive to take note, moreover, of the peculiarities or idiosyncrasies of story tellers. Some cannot repeat the same story twice in identical terms. Others cannot repeat the same story at all except in identical terms; even when it is given by them at second hand, the identical terms of the first narrator are, in the salient points at least, faithfully reproduced. A third class of story tellers swing alternately toward either pole of peculiarity.

It is the same with preachers of the gospel. While some seldom, if ever, repeat themselves in phraseology, others, except when in special circumstances, slide insensibly, and as it were inevitably, into repetition.

In 'free' or 'extemporary' prayer too there is, with some, a continual up-welling of originality, while with others there is but little that is really 'extemporary' and ' free,' beyond a certain limited latitude in adjustment. There are in their memory actual forms or formularies of adoration and petitions, which are repeated and re-repeated with precision.

These phenomena of retentiveness or adhesiveness of memory are quite common, and would be far more so, when writing was cumbrous on the one hand and a rare accomplishment on the other; and when, besides, there was but a slender apprehension and appreciation of the charm of phraseological variety.

The phraseological coincidences therefore of the synoptic evangelists do not demand, for their explication, the hypothesis of some original document or documents possessed in common by them all.

It is admitted, indeed, on all hands that, at a very early period, there were other documents in existence besides our extant Gospels. St. Luke, in his Introduction, makes express mention of them. "*Many*," says he, "have taken in hand to set forth in order an "account of those things that have been accomplished among us" (i. 1). It is most reasonable to suppose that there might have been, and indeed must have been, soon after the Saviour's decease, if not in some instances even before it, various epistolary or anecdotical and semi-biographical accounts of His marvellous career, circulating in those spheres of society which had felt the thrill of His words and works. But we have no reason to suppose that St. Matthew, for instance, would be much dependent on such writings for the materials of his Gospel. He had been, himself, an eye-and-ear-witness of the works and words. And he was living in the closest intimacy with those who could assist his memory, or furnish him with information on facts beyond the sphere of his personal cognisance. St. Mark too, we have found reason to believe,[1] could not be, to a very large degree, dependent on such partial and casual memoirs, records, or reports. He drew fresh from the fountain of one who had enjoyed peculiarly favourable opportunities of acting as a privileged eye-and-ear-witness.

We may presume therefore that both St. Matthew and St. Mark trusted much to memory, the one to his own, the other to the memory of the apostle Peter.

But still we need not imagine that St. Matthew trusted exclusively to his own recollections, as distinguished from the recollections of his brethren in the apostleship; or that St. Mark

---

[1] See pages xix.—xxxvii.

trusted wholly to the memory of St. Peter. Such an idea of the state of the case would be an unnatural narrowing and limiting of the factors of literary reproduction and representation.

Doubtless, the first apostolic narrations of the gospel would be oral. Herder was right in giving emphasis to this idea.[1] The apostles and their helpers went about *preaching the gospel by word of mouth*. They proclaimed it as 'from the house-tops.' And when they passed beyond the little circles of those who had known by personal observation, or popular hearsay, the particulars of the Saviour's extraordinary career, they would be called upon, by such as became disciples or catechumens, to tell in detail the story of the unique and marvellous Life.

As happens however in all such cases, those who, like Peter, could report their observations and express their conceptions with facility and force, would give literary shape to the story. The others, who had in their nature more of the faculty of reproduction or representation, and less of the power of primary or original presentation, would follow in the footsteps of their leaders. Not slavishly however, we may suppose. All the eye-and-ear-witnesses would, we may presume, contribute somewhat to the grand result. But as apostle listened to apostle, narrating to the assembled disciples what their Lord had done and said and suffered, the specific forms of 'setting' the scenes, and even in many cases of 'putting' the minute details of the scenes, would, when vivid or striking, be appreciated, remembered, by and by reproduced, and at length regularly, and with only partial and occasional variations, repeated. The narratives would gradually run into moulds which would, in course of time, become stereotypical.

This is, in substance, Gieseler's hypothesis, to account at once for the coincidences and for the variations of the synoptic Gospels.[2] It no doubt contains in itself a large proportion of the realities of the case. But we see no good reason for isolating the indubitable factors it embraces from other possibilities and probabilities. Some of the 'numerous' memoirs, narratives, or reports, which were lying before St. Luke (i. 1), or which were circulating in other circles, may have been known to St. Matthew and St. Mark, and may have had an influence on their minds and pens. These very

---

[1] See especially his *Regel der Zusammenstimmung unsrer Evangelien, aus ihrer Entstehung und Ordnung* (1797), at the beginning.

[2] *Historisch-kritischer Versuch über die Entstehung und die frühesten Schicksale der schriftlichen Evangelien* (1818).

documents may indeed have been second-hand reflections, and thus more or less correctly taken literary photographs of the very rehearsals which the apostles, inclusive of St. Matthew himself and of St. Peter in particular, had been accustomed to make in the meetings of the catechumens. *Most probably all of them would be of this description.* And if so, it is no violent stretch of imagination to suppose that they might, in their distinctive individualities, have contributed their appreciable, though now indeterminable, quota of influence in giving shape and fixity to certain moulds of presentation and certain methods of arrangement.

A Higher Hand than that of man is always operative in human history, though it does not do everything, or supersede the unfettered activity of human hands, and heads, and hearts. Indeed, if there was a special Divine manifestation in Him who was Himself *the Living Word*, it is reasonable to suppose that there would be a correlative Divine manifestation in *the written word*. To fulfil the ends contemplated in the appearance of the *Impersonated Word*, the mirror of the *impersonal word* was required, in which, not His flitting shadow alone, but the fixed photograph of His glory, might from age to age be contemplated. We have the mirror. We have the fixed photograph. Indeed we have synoptic photographs; and others besides. Their variety is beautiful. Their unembarrassed harmony is perfect. The hands of the human artists had not a little to do in the matter of arrangement and adjustment. But for the 'speaking likenesses' or 'express images,' which come out in their pages, we are indebted to the irradiation of that very Light from heaven which is 'the true Light that lighted' the evangelists, and that still, though in a secondary way, 'lighteth every man that cometh into the world.'

§ 9. Date of the Gospel.

It is not possible, at present, to determine the particular year of the publication of the Gospel before us. Not even is it possible to determine the decade of years, within which the publication must have taken place. All is mere conjecture regarding years and decades.

Of conjecture, however, there has been no lack.

The majority of conjecturists have taken their cue from the statement of Irenæus, which has been already, in a former section of this *Introduction*,[1] passed under review. This early father says,

---

[1] Pages xxiv.—xxvi.

according to the currently received text of his *Work against Heresies*, that "*after the departure of Peter and Paul*, Mark, the dis-"ciple and interpreter of Peter, even he, delivered to us in writing "the things which were preached by Peter." On the assumption that the word '*departure*' refers to the *decease* of the apostles named, the publication of the Gospel has been connected with the date of Peter's martyrdom. The tragical event, (with which the martyrdom of Paul is, according to the current ecclesiastical tradition, supposed to have been either precisely[1] or very nearly coincident,) is generally or rather indeed unanimously assigned to the seventh decade of the first Christian century. The narrative concerning Paul in the *Acts of the Apostles* brings down the progress of events to the two years during which he dwelt, as a prisoner at large, 'in his own hired house' in Rome. These two years are supposed by Spanheim, Pearson, Tillemont, Bertholdt, Köhler, Feilmoser, Anger, Conybeare and Howson, to extend from A.D. 61 to A.D. 63. According to Hug, Schmidt, de Wette, Schrader, Schott, Ewald, Meyer, they extend from 62 to 64. According to Ussher, Michaelis, Heinrichs, Eichhorn, Olshausen, Sanclemente, Ideler, they extend from 63 to 65. Paul was martyred, according to Schrader, in the year 64;[2] according to Lardner, either in 64 or 65;[3] according to Hemsen, either toward the close of 65 or toward the beginning of 66;[4] according to Patrizi, in the summer of 67;[5] according to Conybeare and Howson, in the summer of 68.[6] Soon thereafter, and no doubt within the seventh decade of the century, if the chronology of Irenæus were correct, must *the Gospel according to Mark* have been published. Hug, in the earlier editions of his *Introduction*, fixed on the year 69. "The publication," he said, "took place in the sixty-ninth year after the birth, and in the "thirty-seventh year after the death of Jesus."[7] But he ultimately saw reason to conclude that there is no real historic ground on which to determine the precise year.[8]

---

[1] ἐμαρτύρησαν κατὰ τὸν αὐτὸν καιρόν, says Dionysius, bishop of Corinth in the second century. See Eusebius's *Hist. Eccles.*, ii. 25.

[2] *Der Apostel Paulus*, vol. i., p. 264.

[3] *History of the Apostles and Evangelists*, chap. xi. *Works*, vol. vi., pp. 300, 301, ed. 1788.

[4] *Der Apostel Paulus*, p. 742.

[5] *De Evangeliis*, vol. i., p. 42.

[6] *Life and Epistles of St. Paul*, vol. ii., pp. 502, 560, ed. 1855.

[7] *Einleitung*, vol. ii., § 31.

[8] *Einleitung*, 4th ed., vol. ii., § 32.

He was right. The coincidence of the martyrdoms of Paul and Peter in Rome is by no means a settled historical fact. And though it were, the chronological connection with it of the publication of Mark's Gospel rests only on the statement of Irenæus. And, in this statement, he is contradicted by counter statements on the part of Clemens Alexandrinus, Origen, Epiphanius, and Jerome, which have apparently as much title, as the asseveration to which they are opposed, to be regarded as authoritative and correct.

Irenæus's asseveration then must, in the present state of patristic criticism, be held in abeyance. Patrizi contends strenuously that it must be set aside; and reasoning on Christophorson's reading of the text, he fixes on the latter half of the year A.D. 42, or the former half of the year 43, as the date of the publication of Mark's Gospel.[1] This is, however, a mere conjecture of the distinguished Roman chronologist, a conjecture toppling on the point of a critical needle.

The conjecture, however, did not originate with Patrizi. The same date is found in the colophon of several respectable manuscripts of the Gospel, including the uncials G K S. In these manuscripts there is an express statement to the effect that the Gospel *was published ten years after the ascension of Christ*, that is, in the year 43.

Storr,[2] long ago, so far agreed with Patrizi and these manuscripts as to contend for a very early date. He supposed that the work was published in Antioch, soon after "the men of Cyprus and "Cyrene," who were scattered abroad upon the persecution that arose about Stephen, "came to Antioch and spake unto the Grecians, "preaching the Lord Jesus." (Acts xi. 19, 20.) He connected this occurrence regarding some *men of Cyrene* with the statement in Mark xv. 21, "And they impress one Simon *a Cyrenian*, who was passing "by, coming out of the country, *the father of Alexander and Rufus*, to "bear His cross." Storr thinks it probable that Alexander and Rufus were among *the men of Cyrene* who went to Antioch; and hence, as he supposes,—Mark's mention of them in connection with their father. This is, however, just another needle point of conjectural criticism.

T. R. Birks, also, pleads for an early date of publication. He

---

[1] See his Dissertation *Quando scripserit Marcus*, pp. 36–51 of the 1st volume of his *De Evangeliis*.

[2] *Ueber den Zweck der evangelischen Geschichte u. Briefe Johannis*, pp. 278 ff.

thinks that "the second Gospel was written by John Mark, about "the year A.D. 48, and probably at Cæsarea, with a reference, not "only to Jewish believers, but to Gentile Roman converts, who "would have multiplied there in seven or eight years from the con"version of Cornelius."[1] It is an ingenious conjecture, reverently wrought out, but resting, like Storr's, on not much broader evidence than can rest on the point of another needle.

Volkmar, fixing on a later date, is far more definite and positive on the 'point.' "The time of publication," he says, "is easily and "indubitably determined."[2] Easily! Indubitably! How? For the strangest of reasons, reader. Only turn to Mark i. 13, and you have it, half hidden in a mystery, but self revealing to the initiated. Do we not read there that Jesus was " in the wilderness, *forty days*, "tempted of Satan?" What of that? Why, it is obvious, contends Volkmar, that there must be a deep significance in that particular number of days. Moses too was *forty days* in the wilderness (Exod. xxxiv. 28). Elijah also was *forty days* in the wilderness (1 Kings xix. 8). And the people of Israel were *forty years* in the wilderness (Num. xiv. 33). What could be clearer and more indubitable to the initiated? The days of the Saviour's trial were *forty*, in order to cast shadows both behind and before. And they obviously therefore foreshadow *forty years* of trial to His people after His decease on the cross in the year 33, forty years to be succeeded by that glorious coming which was to take place before all the personal disciples of the Lord 'tasted of death' (Mark ix. 1). Add then 40 to 33, and 'the birth-year of the book'[3] is at once determined —73! This needle has a very sharp point indeed.

The critics of the Tübingen school project the date of composition and publication far beyond A.D. 73. They admit that the original Mark of Papias must have belonged to the first century; but they contend that the canonical Gospel, which superseded the original, cannot have been earlier than the second. Köstlin comes to the conclusion that it emerged in the first decade of the second century.[4] Dr. Davidson would date it 'about A.D. 120.'[5] Others of the school would carry the date still farther forward, say to some point or other between A.D. 130 and A.D. 150.

---

[1] *Horæ Evangelicæ*, p. 238.
[2] *Marcus und die Synopsis*, p. 646.
[3] " Geburtsjahr des Buches."—*Marcus, etc.*, pp. 49, 50.
[4] *Der Ursprung und die Komposition der Syn. Evv.*, pp. 384, 385.
[5] *Introduction*, vol. ii., p. 111.

But this entire theory of the supersession and absorption of the original Gospel of Mark by a fictitious Gospel of the second century rests on another needle point. It rests on the assumption of the soundness of Strauss's theory. It assumes that the mythical interpretation of the Gospel history is substantially correct, though incomplete as originally propounded by its author, and needing for its complement the establishment of the inauthenticity of the four canonical Gospels. Hence the literary task assigned to itself by the school: *Let the inauthenticity of the Gospels be made out! There cannot have been miracles. Paulus's method of reducing the supernatural to the natural is absurd and grotesque. Therefore the Gospels we possess cannot be of apostolic origin or authority. They must have originated in a time far removed from the days of the apostles!*

But the assumption of a fictitious Gospel according to Mark, composed by a well-meaning impostor of the second century, though essential, (along with corresponding assumptions in reference to Matthew, Luke, and John,) to the validity of Strauss's theory, is itself, so far as the scientific determination of the date of our canonical Gospel is concerned, nothing better than a mere unhistorical assumption. It is in fact a critical myth. As unlikely too as it is unhistorical. For where can be found even so much as a needle point's breadth of probability that a Gospel, originated in the apostolic circle, and bearing what was equivalent to the imprimatur of the chief of the original apostles, could, in the course of the second century, be not only unceremoniously, but also unanimously, laid aside, to make room for an upstart composition, written by nobody knows who, but filchingly bearing the honoured name of the genuine original document? How could it happen that all the copies of the original Gospel should have been not only superseded and shelved, but annihilated, so that, at the present day, not a single transcript, or fragment of one, can be found? How could it come to pass that, in the midst of the keen conflicts and mutual jealousies that abounded toward the conclusion of the second century, there should be a perfectly unanimous consent that never should one word be written about the substitution of the false for the true Gospel, so that all the records that would likely go down to posterity should be entirely destitute of any note or hint on the subject? How could all these improbabilities become actualities?

But are there then no data at all on which an approximate date may be assigned to the composition and publication of St. Mark's Gospel?

There are.

There is nothing indeed, as we have already intimated, that will afford a warrant to fix on any given year or decade of years. But the succession of patristic testimonies back to Papias, as exhibited in the sixth section of this *Introduction*, makes it certain that the Gospel was in existence, and well known, during the first century of the Christian era.

Since, moreover, it is all but certain that the John Mark of *the Acts of the Apostles* was the writer of the Gospel, and since it is probable that he was quite 'a young man' at the time of the crucifixion, and consequently still young when he was assumed by Paul and Barnabas as their ministerial attendant, we may reasonably suppose that he would not defer the composition of his Gospel till he was overtaken by extreme old age. If he did not, then we have something like a foothold on which to reach some data for an approximate date. It is not likely, at all events, that the composition of the Gospel would be deferred to a period later than the year 70, the date of the overthrow of Jerusalem. Indeed it is most unlikely that it would be deferred till that period. If St. Mark was about twenty years of age at the time of the crucifixion, he would be nearly sixty about the year 70.

Besides, there seems to be, in the peculiar inter-stratification of the contents of the 13th chapter of the Gospel, (the prophetical chapter,) taken in conjunction with the statement in chap. ix. 1, '*Verily I say unto you, that there be some that stand here, who shall not taste of death till they have seen the kingdom of God come with power,*' evidence on which we may, with probability, support the conclusion that Mark, at the time he composed his Gospel, connected in his mind, as a matter of 'private interpretation' and expectation, the glorious personal appearing of our Lord with the anticipated destruction of Jerusalem. The precise 'times and seasons' were not distinctly and minutely unrolled to the eyes of evangelists and apostles. The prophetical perspective did not show the length of the intervals that intervened along the path of the future; and the inspired writers were consequently left, like the prophets of old, to 'search what and what manner of times' were referred to. This being the case, there is, in the inter-stratification referred to, evidence that increases the probability that the Gospel must have been written before the year 70.

PLACE OF PUBLICATION. lxvii

There is another incidental item of evidence that leans and leads toward the same conclusion. It is found in the verse which occasioned Storr's theory, viz. chap. xv. 21, "and they impress one "Simon a Cyrenian, who was passing by, coming out of the country, "*the father of Alexander and Rufus*, to bear His cross." Why should the evangelist particularize the fact that Simon of Cyrene was *the father of Alexander and Rufus?* Obviously, as Grotius remarks, because *Alexander* and *Rufus* were living at the time when the Gospel was published. Simon himself seems to have been deceased. *His identity is remembered by means of his surviving sons.* He would probably be in middle life, or beyond it, when he undertook his journey to the city of his fathers to celebrate the passover. But it was 'the beginning of days' to him; and not to himself only, it would appear, but to all his household. His sons became men of mark in the Christian circle. It would however be quite improbable and unnatural to go forward to a period near the close of the century, for the time of their prominence. A period before the destruction of Jerusalem is far more likely to have been the season when they were conspicuous. At all events, we could not, with the least shadow of probability, pass the terminating decades of the first century, and go over into the second. The Tübingen date must of necessity be abandoned.

§ 10. The Place of the Gospel's Publication, and the Language in which it was Originally Written.

As to the *place* where the Gospel of St. Mark was originally circulated, nothing can be positively determined. We have seen, incidentally,[1] that Storr conjectured it to be Antioch, and that Birks conjectured it to be Cæsarea. The ancients in general assumed it to be Rome. Chrysostom, however, in the introduction to his *Homiletical Exposition of Matthew*, mentions another tradition, which seems, nevertheless, never to have obtained extensive currency:— "Mark is said (λέγεται) to have composed his Gospel *in Egypt* at "the solicitation of the disciples there." Modern critics in general acquiesce in the common opinion of the ancients. Some of them suppose that we have in the considerable list of Latinisms that is found in the Gospel,[2] internal evidence in favour of the tradition.

---

[1] Pages lxiii., lxiv.
[2] Such as κεντυρίων (*centurio*), ξέστης (*sextarius*), σπεκουλάτωρ (*speculator*), τὸ ἱκανὸν ποιεῖν (*satisfacere*).

Not much weight should be attached to the occurrence of the Latinisms, for they are found also in St. Matthew and St. Luke. There was naturally a considerable sifting in of Latin words and phrases over the whole extent of the Roman empire. They abound, as Volkmar remarks,[1] in the Talmud; and yet no one would conclude, from that fact, that it was written in Rome.

Another plea has been put in for Rome. St. Paul, in his Epistle to the Romans, chap. xvi. 13, says, 'Salute *Rufus,* chosen in the Lord, and his mother and mine.' This Rufus was evidently a somewhat conspicuous disciple, dwelling or sojourning in Rome. And it is quite natural to suppose that he may have been the brother of Alexander, and the son of Simon. If so, he would be well known in the Christian circles in Rome; and hence it might be natural for St. Mark, if writing there, to particularise his brother and him. But on the other hand it is reasonable to suppose that the Cyrenian family would be marked and well known over the whole extent of the Christian brotherhood, if, as is probable, the entire household traced their conversion to the father's intimate conjunction with the Saviour, when impressed to bear the cross. (See *Commentary* on chap. xv. 21.)

In the colophons of several of the cursive manuscripts it is said that the Gospel was written *at Rome.* In some it is said that it was written *in Latin* (ῥωμαϊστι) *at Rome.* The colophon of the Syriac Peshito version runs, correspondingly, thus: "Here ends the Holy "Gospel, the Announcement of Mark, which he spoke and "preached at Rome in the Roman language." In the Philoxenian version the postscript is to the same effect, only briefer: "Here ends the Holy Gospel of Mark, which he spoke in the "Roman language in Rome." These colophons, however, are of no authority. They merely mirror the opinion which was prevalent around the transcriber of the volume, or which was entertained by himself.

Yet Cardinal Baronius, assuming that the Gospel was published at Rome, and thinking it natural that a writing, which was intended for the use of the Romans, should be in their own language, strenuously contended, in his *Ecclesiastical Annals,*[2] that the colophons to which we have referred represent the true state of the case.[3] The

---

[1] *Marcus und die Synopsis,* p. 646.
[2] An. 45, n. 37 ff.
[3] "His igitur prope necessariis rationibus non solum suademur, sed obstricti.

idea was welcome to him as a controvertist, in the interest of the Vulgate version of the New Testament, as against the Greek original. It got connected too with a report that the Latin autograph of the evangelist was actually preserved in the library of St. Mark in Venice. This report however was a fabrication 'for the nonce.' And the whole of the ingenious reasoning of the cardinal dissolves, when it is remembered (1) that St. Paul's *Epistle to the Romans* is in Greek; (2) that the Jews everywhere, and consequently the Jewish Christians, were more familiar with Greek than with Latin; and (3) that St. Mark's Gospel, though doubtless intended for diffusion among the Gentiles, would be, in the first instance, handed over to the Christian Jews, and those Greek-speaking Gentiles who were associated with them in ecclesiastical communion. Father Simon did himself credit, as a critic, when he boldly assailed the cardinal's conceit, as utterly irreconcilable at once with the unanimous conviction of the fathers, and with the literary principles on which the apostles and their coadjutors conducted their New Testament enterprise.

It is needless to make specific reference to the crowd of critical 'repetents,' who, for a series of years, echoed the cardinal's conceit. Neither is it needful to discuss a corresponding conceit of Wahl's, that the Gospel was originally composed in Coptic, and then translated into Greek.[1] It is true, however, that the patriarch of the Coptic church regards himself as the true successor of St. Mark, and sitting in his cathedra.

§ 11. The Plan, Aim, and Style of the Gospel.

The 'Gospel according to St. Mark' does not claim to be a *Scientific History*. It does not aim at tracing the processes of social evolution around the Saviour of mankind, or at manipulating the fully linked concatenation of causes and effects, which permeated the specific moral condition of the Jews eighteen hundred and fifty years ago. To view the Gospel under this aspect, or to demand from it the conditions of such a species of literary composition, would be doing it very great injustice. It would, among other

---

" ferme devincimur atque plane cogimur affirmare, Evangelium Marci ab eo " Latine potius quam Græce esse conscriptum."—*n.* 41.

[1] Wahl's *Magazin für alte, besonders biblische und orientalische Literatur*, 3te Leiferung, pp. 8 ff.

fatal consequences, be exciting illegitimate expectations, which would necessarily issue in illegitimate disappointment.

Neither is the Gospel a little *Compilation of Christian Annals*, something like the embryo, or first instalment, of the *Ecclesiastical Annals* of Cardinal Baronius. It would be doing it, as we have already remarked,[1] a very great injustice to exact of it, or to expect from it, the strict chronological sequences of *Annals*. There is, to be sure, a certain obvious outline of genuine chronology forming the substantial framework of the narrative. That was indispensable. It was inevitable. Our Lord's public career, like every other career, lay along a given chronological path. It had a beginning, middle, and ending. It was a growth. But the interest and value that attach to it did not depend on any of the minute items of chronology. And thus there is no attempt, on the part of the evangelist, to work these items into a scientifically jointed adjustment.

His Gospel is not even *an elaborated or scientifically constructed Biography*. It is, of course, biographical. But there is no evidence of an intention to furnish 'a full and particular account' of the career and character of our Lord. There is no attempted analysis of the elements of His idiosyncrasy. It is entirely wilful on the part of any critic or reader to assume that St. Mark, or any other of the evangelists, should have given us such an analysis, and thence to conclude that it is an imperfection that he does not attempt it. It is wilful likewise to assume that he recorded all the incidents, discourses, and sayings of which he had reliable information. It is wilful to assume that the diversities in the respective Gospels are to be accounted for on the principle that the respective evangelists emptied out as it were, and exhausted, their respective measures of personal knowledge or secondary information. (Comp. John xxi. 25.) To follow out any of these lines of assumption leads far astray from the all-important practical standpoints of observation, which should be occupied by readers in general and by critics in particular.

The evangelist's literary task, though in one respect almost the sublimest imaginable, was, in another, nearly the simplest conceivable. It was to give, for practical and spiritual purposes, free and easy *Memoirs*, or *Memorabilia*, or *Memorials of our Lord*.

His Gospel, in truth, is *a Gospel*, just because it is *the gospel*, not *history proper*, or *annals proper*, or *a regular and exhaustive*

---

[1] Pages xxxiii., xxxiv.

biography. Dr. Bernhard Weiss lays down, as a principle, that 'the last motive of the evangelist's writing was not biographical but didactic.'[1] It is emphatically true. The evangelist meant his narrative to be *a simple biographical representation of the gospel.* It is, that is to say, and was meant to be, a simple mirroring or photographing of Him who is, in His own living personality, the sum, substance, and subject of the gospel. The mirroring or photographing is partial indeed. That was inevitable. But it is real. And it is sufficient: for the grand Object mirrored was and is, in all the phases of His peculiar character and career, the Living Gospel. He is, as it were, *the Gospel alive.* In His life, with all its effluents of work and word, and all its influents of opposition and suffering, the gospel lives, and moves, and has its being. It must be so. His life incarnated His love. And His love was really that Divine, world-infolding love, which, when manifested, *and as manifested,* is the very essence of *gospel* to the erring children of men (John iii. 16). This essence of gospel is the 'open secret' of all the Gospels. And just as the individuals, whether professional or lay, who in these modern times appreciate and promulgate the gospel, often vary from one another in their presentations, and frequently indeed from themselves when they have occasion to write more treatises than one or to deliver more addresses than one, (now omitting what they formerly admitted, and now admitting what they formerly omitted; now employing one 'form of sound words,' and now making use of another,) so the original evangelists differed from one another, more or less, in their respective presentations. And if each had written a second time, we need not doubt that he would have introduced still farther variations.

It is not in the least unnatural therefore that St. Mark, when intending to give a biographical presentation of the gospel, freely ran off its precious ore, so far as form was concerned, into his own peculiar cast of some of the moulds that were in common use among the apostles and their coadjutors. He might, no doubt, have used other casts, slightly different in details. But as there was a necessity for individualising, he made his selection, so far as the factor of his own agency was concerned, freely, easily, perhaps instinctively, and certainly without taking into account the elements which would have been of moment if there had been any definite

---

[1] *Das Marcusevangelium und seine synoptischen Parallelen,* Einleitung, § 5, p. 23.

aim in the direction of scientific adjustment, minute chronological sequence, or literary purity and elegance.

This brings us to the *style* of the evangelist. It is unclassical, provincial, and destitute of every species of 'the wisdom of words.' It is homely, humble, unadorned, and devoid of literary artifice or art. This artlessness is partly a charm, and partly a source of hermeneutical difficulty. See, as outstanding specimens of it, chaps. i. 2, 4, 9, 39; ii. 1, 15, 18, 21, 23; iii. 8, 16; iv. 25, 27, 31; v. 14, 19, 30, 35; vi. 8, 9, 11, 14, 16, 17, 43, 56; vii. 1, 2, 3; viii. 16, 19, 24; ix. 13; x. 10; xi. 1; xii. 11, 23, 34; xiii. 34, 35; xiv. 9, 49, 50; xv. 24; xvi. 4, etc. See moreover the 'vexed expressions' in chaps. vii. 3; viii. 26; ix. 13, 23; xiv. 41, 72; xvi. 13.

Like most other writers, whether inartificial or cultured, Mark has his favourite phrases, or mannerisms of expression. He deals very largely indeed, after the fashion of the true Hebrew, with the conjunction *and*, but is sparing in the use of *for*. (See Tischendorf on chap. xiii. 6.) When introducing a new topic of discourse, or something that was said *furthermore*, he frequently uses the expression *and He said to them*. (See chaps. iv. 9, 13, 24, 26, 30, 40; vi. 10; vii. 9, etc.) He has too a partiality for fixing attention on *beginnings*, employing, in a manneristic way, the phrase *began*. (See chaps. i. 45; iv. 1; v. 17, 20; vi. 2, 7, 34, 55; viii. 31, 32; x. 28, 32, 41, 47; xi. 15; xii. 1; xiii. 5; xiv. 19, 33, 65, 69, 71; xv. 8, 18.) But the most remarkable of all his favourite expressions is the word *immediately*, which however, as employed by him, means in general nothing more than *without loss of time*. It occurs with extreme frequency, nearly as often as in all the other writings of the New Testament put together.

§ 12. Integrity of St. Mark's Gospel.

It is, as we have elsewhere remarked,[1] one of Ewald's opinions that the canonical Gospel according to St. Mark has, relatively to his original Gospel, been impoverished by omissions, as well as enriched by interpolations. It has both lost and gained.

Such an opinion however is a mere conjecture, unnecessary, arbitrary, and improbable. It would be superfluous to enter into a detailed criticism of it, after the full discussions in § 8.

Along with many other critics, and notably with Eusebius in

---

[1] See pages xlvii., xlviii.

ancient times, and Griesbach, Fritzsche, Scholz, Credner, Tischendorf, Tregelles, Michelsen, Scholten, Volkmar, Weiss, in modern times, Ewald regards the last twelve verses of the last chapter of the Gospel as 'a later addition.' This notion has grown into a romance of criticism, which has thrown a spell of doubt over spirits that have not the least sympathy with biblical scepticism. But we have shown, in a full discussion of the subject, in the body of the *Commentary*, that the romance has culminated. There would appear to be no good reason for questioning the authenticity of the passage. See pages 446-449, 463-470.

§ 13. The Topical Position of St. Mark's Gospel in the group of Gospels.

Clemens of Alexandria mentions a tradition which he had received from certain 'elders,' regarding the chronological order of the Gospels. *Those were written first*, it was said, *which contain the genealogies.*[1]

According to this tradition St. Luke's Gospel should have stood before St. Mark's in 'the volume of the Book.' And so it actually does in the ancient manuscript that belonged to Beza (*codex Bezæ*), and which is now one of the 'lions' of the University Library of Cambridge. The order of the Gospels in the manuscript is 'Matthew, John, Luke, Mark.' And hence this is the order that is followed in *Whiston's Revision of the English New Testament*.

If the topical arranging of the Gospels had been committed to Macknight, Dunster, or Büsching, they would have put St. Luke first, and then, in succession, St. Matthew, St. Mark, and St. John. If Beza had got his will, he would, while keeping St. Matthew before St. John, have put St. Luke before St. Mark,[2] just as Owen and Griesbach, with all their followers, would have done.

The adherents again of the 'Mark-hypothesis,' such as Wilke, Weisse, Ewald, Holtzmann, Weiss, think that St. Mark should lead the chorus of evangelists, as being the earliest of them all, and the fontal source of the Gospels of both St. Matthew and St. Luke.

It would appear that the ancients in general regarded the present order as representing the chronological succession of the Gospels. It may be so in fact. But it is not proved. And it will be no

---

[1] Preserved in Eusebius's *Ecclesiastical History*, vi. 14.
[2] *Proœmium in Marcum.*

great calamity to the interests of Christianity in particular, or of 'pure and undefiled religion' in general, although the true chronological order of these primitive evangelical records should remain for ever undetermined and indeterminable.

§ 14. The Contents of the Gospel.

The contents of the Gospel may be tabulated as follows:—

Chap. and Ver.

I. The Preliminaries of the public career of Jesus.
   Chap. i. 1–13.
   1. The forerunnership of John the Baptist . . . . .   i. 1–8
   2. The baptism of Jesus . . . .   i. 8–11
   3. His temptation . . . .   i. 12, 13

II. The public career of Jesus in Galilee and its neighbourhood. Chap. i. 14—ix. 50.
   1. He begins to preach . . . .   i. 14, 15
   2. He calls four fishermen to become His disciples and attendants . . . .   i. 16–20
   3. He teaches, and delivers a demoniac, in the synagogue at Capernaum . . . .   i. 21–26
   4. The people were amazed at His words and works; and He becomes instantly famous . . . .   i. 27, 28
   5. He heals Peter's mother-in-law, who was sick of a fever . . . .   i. 29–31
   6. Many other sick persons, as also demoniacs, are brought to Him, and He heals them . . . .   i. 32–34
   7. In the morning He retires to a solitary place for prayer; but Peter and his friends go in quest of Him . . . .   i. 35, 36
   8. He visits with His disciples various towns, preaches, and casts out demons . . . .   i. 37–39
   9. He heals a leper, who blazes the matter abroad, so that crowds from all quarters flock to Him . . .   i. 40–45
   10. In Capernaum a paralytic is brought to Him, to whom He says, *Son, thy sins be forgiven thee* . . . . .   ii. 1–5
   11. The scribes that were present were scandalized, and thought that He was guilty of blasphemy . . .   ii. 6, 7
   12. Jesus proved His right to speak as He had done, by healing the paralytic . . . .   ii. 8–12
   13. He calls Levi to be one of His attendant disciples .   ii. 13, 14
   14. In Levi's house He sits at meat with 'publicans and sinners,' and defends His conduct against the carping of the scribes and Pharisees . . . .   ii. 15–17
   15. He answers complaints of the disciples of John and of the Pharisees in reference to fasting . . . .   ii. 18–22

	Chap. and Ver
16. His disciples are charged with desecration of the sabbath, and He defends them	ii. 23-28
17. He revitalizes a withered hand on the sabbath day and defends the act.	iii. 1-5
18. The Pharisees and Herodians have their malignity stirred, and plot His destruction.	iii. 6
19. Jesus withdrew to the shore of the sea of Galilee, but was followed by numerous crowds from far and near, many of whose sick He healed	iii. 7-12
20. He chooses twelve, whom He might send forth, as apostles, to assist Him in preaching and teaching .	iii. 13-19
21. He is still however tasked to the uttermost to minister to the crowds who press in upon Him	iii. 20
22. His relatives begin to think that He is 'beside Himself'	iii. 21
23. Scribes are sent down from Jerusalem to act as inquisitors, and they allege that He did His wonderful works by the aid of Beelzebul	iii. 22
24. Jesus refutes their cruel blasphemy of His character, and solemnly warns them	iii. 23-30
25. In reference to His relatives who were busying themselves intermeddlingly, He declares who are His truest relatives	iii. 31-35
26. He began to teach in vivid parables	iv. 1, 2
27. The parable of the sower	iv. 3-20
28. A cluster of other striking sayings	iv. 21-25
29. Other vivid parables	iv. 26-34
30. He passes over toward the eastern side of the lake; and, overcome with fatigue, sleeps during the passage. A storm arises, which, when He is waked up, He stills.	iv. 35-41
31. On the eastern side of the lake He relieves a demoniac who called himself Legion. The demons are allowed to enter a herd of swine, which go mad and are drowned in the lake	v. 1-13
32. The inhabitants get alarmed, and entreat Him to leave their district. But the cured demoniac goes forth and proclaims the miracle round and round .	v. 14-20
33. Jesus returns to the west coast of the lake, and restored to life the deceased daughter of Jairus. On the way a woman is healed of hæmorrhage by touching His garment	v. 21-43
34. He visits Nazareth, where He spent His youth, but is received coldly and incredulously	vi. 1-5
35. He marvelled at their unbelief, and went elsewhere teaching	vi. 6
36. He sent forth His twelve attendant disciples to preach and heal	vi. 7-13
37. The tetrarch Herod hears of Him, and thinks that He	

INTRODUCTION.

	Chap. and Ver
is John the Baptist returned from the world of the disembodied	vi. 14
38. Others had different opinions regarding Him, but Herod stood to his own notion, for he was ill at ease for having murdered John	vi. 15, 16
39. The story of the murder of John	vi. 17–29
40. The apostles return to Jesus, and report progress, and they all go to get retirement and rest for a season. They go by boat to the other side of the lake	vi. 30–32
41. They were watched however by multitudes, who hasted by land to get near the wonderful Rabbi. He had compassion on them, and taught them	vi. 33, 34
42. He fed about five thousand, in an uninhabited place, on five loaves and two fishes	vi. 35–44
43. Having spent a great part of the evening in prayer, He walked on the sea to His disciples, who were toiling at their oars in a storm	vi. 45–52
44. When they landed on the coast of Genuesaret, He was pressed by multitudes, who were eager to get their sick ones healed, and 'as many as touched Him were made whole'	vi. 53–56
45. The Pharisees and scribes find fault with Him for allowing His disciples to eat with unbaptized hands. He defends His disciples, and exposes the wretched outwardliness of the religious manners of their accusers	vii. 1–13
46. He teaches the people in general, and His disciples in particular, the inwardliness of true religion	vii. 14–23
47. He makes a detour into the neighbourhood of Tyre and Sidon, and heals, at a distance, the daughter of a Syrophœnician woman	vii. 24–30
48. He returns to Galilee by the way of Decapolis, on the north-east, and restores his hearing and speech to a deaf and dumb man	vii. 31–37
49. A second time He feeds miraculously in the desert a great multitude, about four thousand	viii. 1–9
50. He goes to Dalmanutha, and is asked by the Pharisees to prove what He was by some great 'sign from the sky.' He declines to pander to their frivolous, sceptical, and curiosity-hunting spirit	viii. 10–13
51. While crossing the lake with His disciples, He speaks to them of the leaven of the Pharisees and of Herod, but they have difficulty in understanding Him	viii. 14–21
52. At Bethsaida He gives sight to a blind man	viii. 22–26
53. In going toward Cæsarea Philippi, He interrogates His disciples regarding the conflicting opinions	

THE CONTENTS OF THE GOSPEL. lxxvii

	Chap. and Ver.
that were floating about in the public mind in reference to Him. When He asks them for their own judgment on the matter, Peter says 'Thou art the Christ'.	viii. 27–30
54. He begins to predict His rejection by men, His ignominious death, and His glorious resurrection	viii. 31
55. Peter, fixing his mind on the announcement of his Lord's ignominious death, 'began to rebuke Him,' and Jesus had to reprove him sharply	viii. 32, 33
56. He announces the necessity of cross-bearing as a condition of discipleship	viii. 34—ix. 1
57. Jesus is transfigured in presence of Peter, James, and John	ix. 2–8
58. He charged the three favoured disciples to tell no man what they had witnessed, till after His resurrection; and they wonder what He means by His resurrection	ix. 9, 10
59. They have a difficulty about Malachi's prophecy regarding Elijah; and Jesus explains what was meant	ix. 1–13
60. He heals, at the foot of the mount of transfiguration, a poor demoniac lad	ix. 14–29
61. He seeks to pass incognito through Galilee; and speaks to His disciples again regarding His coming death and consequent resurrection. But they did not understand Him	ix. 30–32
62. In Capernaum He rebuked His disciples for their self-seeking eagerness to get honours in the kingdom of which He was to be King, and He bids them be childlike	ix. 33–37
63. A cluster of remarkable instructions and sayings	ix. 38–50

III. THE CAREER OF JESUS ON HIS WAY FROM GALILEE TO JUDÆA, AND THENCEFORWARD TILL HIS DECEASE IN JERUSALEM. Chap. x.–xv.

1. Jesus goes toward Judæa by the eastern side of Jordan	x. 1
2. On the way, Pharisees propose to Him, temptingly, a question concerning divorce	x. 2–12
3. His heart yearns over certain little children who were brought to Him	x. 13–16
4. He deals faithfully with a rich young man, who asked, What shall I do that I may inherit eternal life?	x. 17–22
5. He speaks of the difficulty of being both rich and good	x 23–27
6. He speaks of the reward of those who make sacrifices for His sake and for the sake of the gospel	x. 28–31
7. He again makes known to His disciples His approaching sufferings and death, and His consequent resurrection	x. 33–34

lxxviii   INTRODUCTION.

                                                        Chap. and Ver.
8. James and John, the sons of Zebedee, prefer an un-
   wise and selfish request, and are faithfully dealt
   with . . . .   x. 35–40
9. When the rest of the disciples knew what James and
   John had been asking, they were incensed; but
   Jesus unfolded the true glory of man, the glory of
   ministering and giving . . . .   x. 41–45
10. The company reaches Jericho, where Jesus restores
    sight to Bartimæus, a blind beggar . . . . . .   x. 46–52
11. The company reached Bethany, and two disciples are
    despatched to Bethphage to obtain a colt. . . .   xi. 1–6
12. The colt is brought, and Jesus, riding on it, enters
    Jerusalem triumphally . . . .   xi. 7–11
13. He returns in the evening to Bethany . . . . .   xi. 11
14. Coming in next day to Jerusalem, He sought figs on
    a leafy fig tree. Finding none, He invokes a blight
    on the tree . . . .   xi. 12–14
15. He enters the temple and purifies it . . . . .   xi. 15–17
16. The scribes and chief priests were intensely offended,
    and plotted 'how they might destroy Him' . .   xi. 18
17. In the evening He left the city; and next morning
    the disciples saw that the fig-tree had withered.
    Jesus took occasion to impress them with the power
    of faith and prayer . . . .   xi. 19–24
18. A forgiving spirit must be joined with prayer . . . xi. 25, 26
19. When He was in the temple, the chief priests, scribes,
    and elders come and demand His authorization for
    acting as He did . . . .   xi. 27, 28
20. Jesus asked them a preliminary question, which they
    would not answer. He therefore declined to answer
    the question which they had put to Him . . .   xi. 29–33
21. He spoke to them, and the people, a parable, *the
    parable of the iniquitous vineyard tenants* . . .   xii. 1–11
22. The authorities were enraged, and sought to arrest
    Him, but feared the people . . . .   xii. 12
23. They then sent Pharisees and Herodians to get Him
    entrapped politically, if possible, in His words, but
    He saw through the manœuvre and confounded
    His interrogators . . . .   xii. 13–17
24. Some Sadducees then tried to overthrow Him in
    argument; but they too were utterly foiled and
    nonplussed . . . .   xii. 18–27
25. A scribe asked Him which is the first commandment
    of all; and was delighted with the answer . . .   xii. 28–34
26. None dared to interrogate Him any more . . . .   xii. 34
27. Jesus exposed the shallowness of the scribes' teach-
    ing regarding the Messiah . . . .   xii. 35–37
28. He denounced the scribes . . . .   xii. 38–40

THE CONTENTS OF THE GOSPEL. lxxix

	Chap. and Ver.
29. He noted the great liberality of a poor widow in giving two mites	xii. 41–44
30. Sitting on the mount of Olives with His disciples He revealed some of the great scenes of the future, both nearer and more remote	xiii. 1–37
31. The chief priests and scribes plotted to get Him arrested 'by craft'; but wished to postpone the execution of their plot till after the passover	xiv. 1, 2
32. Jesus, at an entertainment in Bethany, was anointed by a woman	xiv. 3
33. Some were offended at the 'waste of the ointment,' especially Judas	xiv. 4–10
34. When Jesus had vindicated the woman and rebuked the grumblers, Judas went to the chief priests to betray Him	xiv. 11, 12
35. Jesus observed the passover with His disciples; made touching reference to the treason of the traitor; and instituted the New Testament passover-supper	xiv. 12–25
36. He went with the eleven to the mount of Olives, and intimated to them that they would all that very night be stumbled in reference to Him	xiv. 26–28
37. Peter expressed his confidence that *he* at least would not be stumbled. Jesus tells him that before the cock crowed twice he would be guilty of a triple denial	xiv. 29, 30
38. The agony in Gethsemane	xiv. 31–42
39. The traitor comes with his company, and Jesus allowed Himself to be arrested	xiv. 43–49
40. His disciples all forsake Him and flee	xiv. 50
41. A young man is aroused out of bed as the noisy company pass along, and he follows Jesus	xiv. 51, 52
42. Jesus is taken to the high priest's house to be examined	xiv. 53
43. Peter follows afar off, and gets into the court of the house	xiv. 54
44. Jesus is accused, but could not be convicted. In answer to the high priest's adjuration, He confessed that He was 'the Christ, the Son of the Blessed'	xiv. 55–63
45. He is condemned to be worthy of death	xiv. 64
46. He is shamefully maltreated by the officials who were around	xiv. 65
47. Peter thrice denies his Lord	xiv. 66–72
48. In the morning the sanhedrim, after a hurried meeting, delivers Jesus over to Pilate, the Roman procurator, as one who was worthy of death	xv. 1
49. Pilate saw no evidence of criminality, and wished to release Him; but the chief priests moved the people	

	Chap. and Ver
to ask Barabbas instead, and to demand that Jesus should be crucified in place of Barabbas	xv. 2–14
50. Pilate yielded; and his soldiery cruelly mocked the innocent prisoner	xv. 15–19
51. He is led off to be crucified, and Simon of Cyrene is impressed to assist in carrying the cross	xv. 20, 21
52. He is crucified on Golgotha between two robbers . .	xv. 22–28
53. The passers by mocked Him as He hung on the cross, and even the chief priests came out to gloat over His agonies	xv. 29–32
54. It is darkness from the sixth to the ninth hour; and at the ninth hour Jesus, after uttering significant exclamations, expires	xv. 33–37
55. The veil of the temple was rent	xv. 38
56. The Roman centurion was awed, and felt convinced that the Crucified One was 'God's Son'	xv. 39
57. The holy women were looking on afar off	xv. 40, 41
58. Joseph of Arimathæa craves the body from Pilate, obtains it, and interred it in a sepulchre, to the door of which a stone was rolled	xv. 42–46
59. Two of the holy women beheld where He was laid .	xv. 47

IV. THE RESURRECTION OF JESUS ON THE THIRD DAY AFTER HIS DECEASE. Chap. xvi.

1. After the sabbath, some of the women come to the sepulchre very early in the morning	xvi. 1, 2
2. They are concerned about the great stone; but when they look, lo it is rolled away	xvi. 3, 4
3. As they enter the sepulchre, an angel informs them that Jesus is risen. He also tells them to say to 'the disciples *and Peter*' that their Lord would meet them in Galilee.	xvi. 5–7
4. The women run to fulfil their errand	xvi. 8
5. Jesus appeared first to Mary of Magdala	xvi. 9–11
6. He then appeared to two of the disciples going into the country	xvi. 12, 13
7. Afterward, He appeared to the eleven as they sat at meat	xvi. 14
8. He gives the eleven their evangelical commission . .	xvi. 15 18
9. He ascends to heaven	xvi. 19
10. His apostles were faithful to their commission, and were blessed in their work of faith and labour of love	xvi. 20

THE
GOSPEL ACCORDING TO ST. MARK.

CHAPTER I.

1 THE beginning of the gospel of Jesus Christ, the Son of

CHAPTER I.

VER. 1. **Beginning of the gospel of Jesus Christ.** The absence of the article shows that the expression is a kind of *Title*. Some have thought, indeed, that the evangelist intended it to be the title of his entire work. But on that hypothesis the word *Beginning* seems awkward. Alexander would interpret thus, *This is the beginning of the Gospel of Jesus Christ*, or, *Here begins the Gospel of Jesus Christ*. Klostermann thinks that all the events of the public life of Christ were but the *beginning of the Gospel*. The contents of the immediately succeeding verses, however, prove that the evangelist was thinking of events that were preliminary to the public life of Christ. He is going back, in retrospect, to the dispensation of the Saviour's forerunner; and, in the events of that dispensation, he finds the *Beginning of the Gospel of Jesus Christ*. Of course he might have gone further back still, and found other fountains, the feeders of the fountain at which he pauses. Or he might have continued to ascend till he reached the absolute Beginning, the Fountain of fountains. His purpose, however, was served by taking up his position beside the things that were the immediate antecedents of the public career of our Lord. When he calls these things the *Beginning of the Gospel of Jesus Christ*, he was not so much thinking, as Petter and Bengel properly remark, of a Title for his book, or even of a Heading for its initial section, as of the actual commencement in time of the things themselves, which he proceeds to specify. As his thoughts, however, and the words which were their vestures, were to him the mere subjective mirrorings of the objective historical realities on which his gaze was fixed, they became, as he detained them in the presence of his consciousness, *a kind of indistinct Title*,—the expression *the Gospel of Jesus Christ* referring to the events of the life of the Saviour, as these are about to be narrated in the body of the following Memoirs, and the word *Beginning* referring to the introductory events of the career of John the Baptist, as represented in the few initial sentences which commence with ver. 4, and merge and melt into the greater history at ver. 9-11. It would be assuming an unnatural involution were we, with Lachmann, to throw ver. 2 and 3 into a parenthesis, and to connect ver. 1 and 4 in such a manner that ver. 1 supplied the nominative

God; 2 as it is written in the prophets, Behold, I send my

---

to the verb in ver. 4,—(*The*) *beginning of the Gospel of Jesus Christ, God's Son, was John baptizing in the wilderness*, etc. The genitive expression *of Jesus Christ* is, as grammarians phrase it, *the genitive of the object*, not *the genitive of the subject;* thus making the meaning of the whole expression to be *the good news concerning Jesus Christ*, not *the good news proclaimed by Jesus Christ*. It is true that Jesus Christ did proclaim His own gospel ; but He is here represented as the Sum and Substance of the gospel which both He and His apostles proclaimed. See Rom. i. 1-3, 9, 16. *Jesus Christ :* the finely significant proper name of our Lord. He was called *Jesus*, because He was *a Saviour*. (See Matt. i. 21.) He was called *Christ* or *Messiah*, because He filled the office of Saviourhood by sovereign appointment. The Divine Father appointed Him, and hence as it were *anointed* Him. The word *Christ* is Greek; the word *Messiah* is Hebrew : and both the terms mean *Anointed*. There was poured out on our Lord, anointingly, by the hand of the Father, all that was needed to fit Him to be a Saviour. Great officers in church and state, among the Jews, and kings emphatically, were installed in their offices by anointing. Jesus, as the King of kings, had His anointing.

The Son of God. Or, more literally, and as Sir John Cheke gives it, *God's Son*. Our Lord, in His life on earth, had claimed to be at once *the Christ* and *God's Son*. He was condemned by the Jewish Sanhedrim for insisting on the claim. (See Mark xiv. 61-64; comp. Matt. xxvi. 63-66.) His resurrection sublimely verified the legitimacy of His claim, and instamped an imperishable significancy on the double designation. Hence it was exceedingly appropriate in Mark to prefix to his Memoirs the twofold appellation. It has been doubted, however, whether the words *God's Son* were in the autograph text of the evangelist. Tischendorf has omitted them in his eighth edition. Schenkel assumes that the omission is correct. They are not found in the original Sinaitic manuscript (א*); and they are wanting in an important quotation of the passage by Irenæus (iii. 11), as also in five distinct quotations of Origen. But, on the other hand, they are found in all the early versions, and, with the exception of the original Sinaitic, in all the best manuscripts. They are found, likewise, in two passages of Irenæus. And indeed it seems to us that, in the other passage where they are omitted, they should be found. *The preceding context seems to demand their presence.* On the whole it is probable that the words are genuine, and that their omission in the quotations of so many of the early Fathers is to be accounted for on the principle, that the Fathers, in their references, used the freedom, for brevity's sake, of dropping out of view unessential clauses. And hence, indeed, Epiphanius, in quoting the passage before us, omits even the preceding words *of Jesus Christ*, and connects at once the words of the second verse with the expression *Beginning of the Gospel*. (*Hæres.*, li. 6, p. 427, ed. 1682.) We do not pause to unfold here the theological significancy of the designation, *God's Son*. As applied to our Lord, it involves the great idea, that He had in Him a higher nature than man's. He was of one nature with God. Man needed a Divine Saviour.

VER. 2. As it is written, or, more literally, *As it has been written*. Some

messenger before thy face, which shall prepare thy way be-

editors and expositors, putting a full point at the close of ver. 1, regard this expression as bending anticipatively forward, and hooking itself on to ver. 4. Whedon, running on the same line, but running faster still, says, " the second "and third verses, by a strong inversion, should come after the fourth." This is unnatural, and assumes an artificial involution of structure which is quite unlikely in such a simple writer as Mark. It is better to put, with Tischendorf (in his eighth edition), a comma at the conclusion of the first verse, and thus to regard the contents of the second and third verses as appended to the first in a free and easy manner, with the intent of showing that the events about to be narrated had thrown their shadows before them in the Old Testament Scriptures; for it is really true that the *Beginning of the Gospel of Jesus Christ, God's Son*, was *in accordance with what had been written.*

In the Received Text there follows the expression in the prophets. King James's translators would find it in all the editions that were lying before them. It is, however, a tinkered reading, as both Erasmus and Beza were convinced, and Bengel too.

The reading of the autograph of Mark was, undoubtedly, in Isaiah the prophet. Such is the reading of the Sinaitic manuscript, and the Vatican, and the Cambridge, as also of 33, 'the queen of the cursives.' It is the reading too of the Vulgate version, and the Older Latin, the Peshito Syriac, the Harclean Syriac, the Coptic, and the Gothic. It is the reading of the principal Fathers too. It has been re-imported into the text by Griesbach, Scholz, Lachmann, Tischendorf, Tregelles. It would never have been disturbed had not some timorous students of the Gospel felt it difficult or impossible to account for the fact that, preceding the quotation from Isaiah, there is a quotation from Malachi (iii. 3). Eusebius says that the word *Isaiah* stands in the text as an erratum instead of *Malachi*. (See Cramer's *Catena*, in loc.) And Porphyry, the early enemy of Christianity, cast it in the teeth of the Christians that Mark had made a mistake. (See *Jerome on Matt.* iii. 3.) Griesbach too, alas! suspected that he had. (*Comm. Crit.* in loc.) Even Meyer thinks that there is a mistake, and that the evangelist's memory must have been at fault; surely a most unlikely occurrence on the part of one who, in that early age, and in the midst of the young fervour of admiration and love and zeal, was eager to persuade his fellow-men everywhere that Jesus was the Saviour who had been promised from of old in the writings of the prophets. Beza thinks that the evangelist had really quoted only the passage from Isaiah, and that the preliminary passage from Malachi had been subsequently intruded into the text from a marginal annotation suggested by Matt. xi. 10. The real solution of the case is to be found in the fact that *the passage from Malachi is strictly preliminary*. It is the mere porchway through which we are ushered into the quotation from Isaiah. The evangelist's mind went rapidly through it, and fixed its attention on the contents of the earlier and more remarkable oracle, lying beyond. (Comp. Matt. xxi. 5.)

Behold, I send My messenger. It is 'the Lord of hosts' who speaks. See the concluding clause of Mal. iii. 1. He is just on the eve of turning the future into the present. Hence the expression *I send*, instead of *I will send*. The imminency of the act is indicated. *My messenger:* My servant, to whom

fore thee. 3 The voice of one crying in the wilderness, Prepare ye the way of the Lord, make his paths straight.

I say 'Go,' and 'he goeth.' It is the word that is generally translated *angel*, which word *angel* just means *messenger*. Heumann, indeed, insists on translating it *angel* in the passage before us. It is John the Baptist who is referred to. See ver. 4.

Before Thy face. A full way of saying *Before Thee*. Attention is graphically fixed upon the *countenance* or *face*, which is the index to the whole man. *Before*: The Baptist was to be the forerunner of the Lord, or His harbinger. It is noteworthy that in Malachi the expression is not *before Thy face*, or *before Thee*, but *before Me*. The Lord of hosts speaks 'of' Himself. When Mark however quotes the passage, he so modifies the form of expression that *the Lord of hosts is represented as speaking 'to' the Lord of hosts*. It was a perfectly warrantable modification, for there is a sublime sphere of things in which all things are 'in common' between the Father and the Son. See Matt. xi. 10.

Who shall prepare Thy way. So that it shall be fit for Thee to travel upon. In the East few good roads are ever made; and such roads as have been made are generally kept in most wretched repair. Hence when a sovereign is about to visit any part of his dominions, it is requisite that a messenger, or quartermaster, as Hofmeister has it, be sent on before to get the way made ready. Such, in things spiritual, was John's mission. Men's ways were in a wretched state. Encumbrances and stumbling-blocks lay everywhere scattered about. Mud and mire were the order of the day. It seemed impossible for any one to get along through life with unpolluted garments, or without stumbling and falling, and getting bruised and broken. The real preparation that was needed was in *the hearts of the people*. See Mal. iv. 5, 6.

Ver. 3. Now comes the prophetic passage on which the evangelist's mind has been fixed. It is found in Isaiah xl. 3.

The voice of one crying in the wilderness. Or rather, *A voice of one crying in the wilderness!* That is, *I hear the voice of one calling aloud in the wilderness!* It is as if the prophet had been listening from afar. Bending forward, and hushing all noises within and around, he strains his ear to hear. At length, *Lo, a voice!* He fixes his attention. It is *a voice of one calling aloud in the wilderness, Prepare ye the way of the Lord! Make His paths straight!* It is not John himself who is called *a Voice*, as many—far too many—have imagined, inclusive even of Cajetan, Petter, de Veil, and Klostermann. Petter's remark is: "John is said to be a Voice, in respect of the "execution of his ministerial office, which was to speak and sound forth the "doctrine of the gospel touching Christ, and touching salvation by Him." *Of one crying: of one calling aloud* as with a herald-cry. *In the wilderness:* Not in the great city, nor in any city, but in the wilds and prairie pasture-grounds of the wilderness. John did not go to the people; he let the people come to him. It was different with Jesus.

Make ye ready the way of the Lord. John himself *made ready* the Lord's way (see ver. 2),—by calling upon the people to make it ready. Thus he did not do everything himself. He could not. He could not, by his single

4 John did baptize in the wilderness, and preach the baptism

agency, prepare the hearts of the people. Even God could not wisely do everything. The co-agency of the people was indispensable: and hence the herald of the Lord called upon them to act. Self-action, indeed, would not be enough. Something from above is needed. God must begin and God must end the preparation of the heart (Prov. xvi. 1). But between His beginning and His ending human spontaneity comes in; there must be response to the Lord's initiatory 'knock'; there must be preparation for His final enthronement in the soul. *Make YE ready the Lord's way!*

Make His paths straight. The word *straight* is the opposite of *crooked*. See Luke iii. 5; and comp. Acts ix. 11. Roads that have not been properly prepared at the beginning are generally more or less crooked. So are the ways of men, when no preparation has been made for the Great King. When John cried, *Make His paths straight!* he meant, *Have done with all your crooked ways of acting! Be straightforward with yourselves! Let there be no winding and doubling! Be honest!* The Lord will not enter into hypocritical souls.

VER. 4. **John came.** Viz., upon the scene. *It came to pass that John made his appearance on the scene.* At a certain unspecified time, John *made*, as it were, *his* 'début,' as a great public functionary, the harbinger and herald of the Messiah.

Who baptized in the wilderness and preached. The evangelist might have said, transpositively, *There appeared in the wilderness John, who baptized and preached.* But there is no occasion for disturbing the order of the evangelist's words; for it is true that John *baptized in the wilderness*. The wilderness referred to embraced a considerable tract of comparatively uninhabited land, stretching away eastward from Jerusalem and northward from the Dead Sea, but coming down, all along, to the banks of the river Jordan. It was chiefly in the Jordan, as it swept along *the wilderness of Judæa*, that John performed his baptisms. See Matt. iii. 1, 5, 6; Luke iii. 3. The *baptizing* is mentioned before the *preaching*, because it was the outstanding peculiarity of John's ministry. The participial form of the expression, *the baptizing* (ὁ βαπτίζων), denotes continuity, or characteristic habit. The word intimates that John engaged himself *in administering to the people a purificatory rite*. He *ritually purified* them, in order that they might be prepared to be admitted into the approaching 'kingdom of heaven.' (See John iii. 23-26; Mark vii. 4, 8; Heb. ix. 9-23.) In thus ritually purifying them, he would throw or pour water upon them,—'sprinkling them with clean water.' (See Joel ii. 28; Ezek. xxxvi. 25; Acts x. 44, 47, xi. 15, 16.) It was a beautiful symbolism, fitted to remind the people that the influence which truly purifies the heart is shed down from above (see *Comm.* on Matt. iii. 6). *In the wilderness:* By avoiding the frequented haunts of men, John indicated his profound sense of the corruption that was pervading the institutions of human society. Pollution was rampant everywhere. Had he been a man, however, of only ordinary calibre of mind and force of character, he would have been simply lost in the wilderness; only one here and there would have known

of repentance for the remission of sins. 5 And there went

anything about him. But he was Elijah-like,—a man overtopping all his fellows in grandeur of character; when common people came in contact with him, they felt at once his superiority; he was a lion among men. And then too he belonged to a conspicuous family, a family of priests. So soon, therefore, as it was known that he was asserting that he had a message for his countrymen, and that he had undertaken to help them in preparing for the approach of the kingdom of heaven, the population, as it were *en masse*, flocked out to him. *And preached:* or *proclaimed (in a heraldic way).* The word is participial in the original, and comes under the influence of the article which renders the preceding participle characteristically attributive. It thus conveys the idea of continuously repeated action or habit.

The baptism of repentance. Or, very literally, without the article, *baptism of repentance*, that is *repentance-baptism*, or *penitential-baptism*, that baptism of which repentance was a characteristic. It was thus not simply and abstractly the duty of baptism, that John proclaimed. It was the duty of that peculiar kind of baptism, which, when voluntarily and intelligently received, mirrors forth, in its outward act, the acceptance of that inward purification which is essential to the enjoyment of the privileges of the Messiah's kingdom. Hence John did not attribute any real purificatory virtue to his baptismal rite. (See Matt. iii. 2, 7–10.) He knew that it was but the shadow of the one really efficacious baptism. (See Matt. iii. 11, 12; 1 Pet. iii. 21.) No one would know better than he, that it is 'the water of life,' as Justin Martyr says, which is ' the only baptism that can purify the repentant.' (*Dialog. Trypho,* § 14.) John's baptism, nevertheless, was a beautiful figure of the true. And hence he unhesitatingly proclaimed, with heraldic cry, that it was the duty of the people to come to him, that they might receive it at his hands. *Repentance:* that is, *afterthought*, or *change of mind*, or *turning to a right state of mind,* namely, as regards things moral and spiritual. Such a turning begins in the intelligence (the νοῦς), but prolongs itself into the feelings, and runs out into the ultimate choices of the will, and then terminates in the fixed activities and habits of the whole complex man. Repentance may thus be incipient, or progressive, or complete. It was only incipient repentance that was enjoined by John *as the prerequisite of his baptism*, and hence the *first* word of his ministry was, 'Repent.' (Matt. iii. 2 ; and comp. ver. 5-8.) Hence, too, as he looked to the end, and realized profoundly the necessity of progression and completion, he ' baptized *unto* repentance.' (Matt. iii. 11.)

Unto remission of sins. The meaning is, *in order to*, or *with a view to*, *remission of sins.* But, of course, we are not to suppose that either the people's repentance on the one hand, or John's baptism on the other, or any combination of the two, could be either the efficient or the meritorious cause of forgiveness. God only is the Efficient Cause. The sacrificial Lamb, who bore the sin of the world (John i. 29), and He only, is the Meritorious Cause. Repentance-baptism could be nothing else than *a kind of instrumental cause,*—pædagogically leading the mind out and up at once to the Efficient and to the concurrent Meritorious Cause. It was really in the faith, which was underlying the

out unto him all the land of Judæa, and they of Jerusalem; and were all baptized of him in the river of Jordan, confessing their sins. 6 And John was clothed with camel's hair, and

---

repentance baptism, that the link was found which united the soul to the indispensable Causes. *Remission:* or *forgiveness.* It is realized in deliverance from the penal consequences of sins, and is to be carefully distinguished from moral cleansing of the soul, which, however, is a still greater and grander blessing. (See Matt. vi. 12, xviii. 21-35; Luke xvii. 3, 4.)

VER. 5. And there went out unto him all the country of Judæa. More literally still, *all the Judæan country.* The evangelist used that figure of speech called by grammarians *metonymy*,—naming the *country* while meaning its *inhabitants.* So we sometimes say, *London at this season is out of town.* It is the same licence that is employed, when, in the dispensation of the Lord's Supper, we speak of 'drinking this cup.' (1 Cor. xi. 27.)

And all they of Jerusalem. More literally still, *and all the Jerusalemites.* The adjective *all*, which in the Received Text occurs in the next clause, properly belongs to this, and is so placed in the texts of Griesbach, Lachmann, Tischendorf, Tregelles. *All:* The word is used in a free and easy, and popular, way. And yet, as Alexander remarks, " it must mean more than *many*, namely, "the great bulk and body of the population." *All the Jerusalemites:* not only all Judæa in general, but also all the Jerusalemites in particular. Even they

And they were baptized of him in the river Jordan. John would stand, perhaps, at some suitable point or angle within the margin of the river, and when the people came to him in file, he would lave them in succession. Or they might station themselves in rows along the margin, and, as he passed by inside he would sprinkle them in detail.

Confessing their sins. The word rendered *confessing* (ἐξομολογούμενοι) strictly means *confessing out*, that is, *confessing openly* or *aloud.* It is not implied, therefore, that the people made private confession, auricularly, one by one, of particular sins. But when charged by John, in general terms, with unfaithfulness to their own consciences, and to the claims of their neighbours, and to God, they admitted the justice of the charge, acknowledged that they were 'verily guilty,' and that they thus stood greatly in need of being cleansed or baptized from unrighteousness. Both the Latin word *confess*, and the corresponding Greek word, bring out the idea of *two parties speaking*; and when applied, as here, to sins, it is implied that some one—from without or within—charges the sinner with his sins, and that the sinner consents to the charge. Thus there is a *togetherhood of speaking* in the matter, that is to say, a *confession.*

VER. 6. The evangelist passes on to a description of some of the personal peculiarities of the Baptist. He was just a modern edition of the ancient Elijah.

And John was clothed with camel's hair. It is not said, as Hofmeister remarks, *with a camel's skin*, but *with camel's hairs.* (Vestimentum non *de pelle*, sed *de pilis* camelorum.) The old sacred artists misunderstood the ex-

with a girdle of a skin about his loins, and he did eat locusts and wild honey; 7 and preached, saying, There cometh one

---

pression, and painted the Baptist as arrayed in a camel's skin. The reference was no doubt to a coarse kind of sackcloth manufactured out of the strongest hairs of the camel. It made a rough hairy robe; and thus John would be, like Elijah, 'an hairy man.' (2 Kings i. 8.) He was entirely self denied to all luxury in dress.

And had a girdle of skin about his loins. Tyndale's first translation (1526) was, *and wyth a gerdyll off a beestes skyn about hys loynes*. In his second version (1534) he left out the word *beestes*, but unhappily left standing *the indefinite article*, and hence its presence in King James's version. Coverdale's version is *and with a lethron gerdell aboute his loynes*. "The *leathern girdle*," says Horatio B. Hackett, "may be seen around the body of the common "labourer in the East, when fully dressed, almost everywhere; whereas men of "wealth take special pride in displaying a rich sash of silk or some other costly "fabric." (*Illustrations of Scripture*, p. 61.) Chardin tells us that the dervishes in the East, in his time, wore great leathern girdles. (Harmer's *Observations*, vol. iv., p. 416.) They still wear them. And these dervishes, it may be noted,— at least the highest specimens of them,—most nearly resemble, in their character and in the functions of their ministry, such men as John and Elijah. "All the "great men in the East," says Dr. Wolff, "who have been celebrated either as "poets, or historians, or lawyers, have been dervishes. . . . If they did not "exist, no man would be safe in the deserts among the savages. They are the "chief people in the East who keep in the recollection of those savages that "there are ties between heaven and earth. They restrain the tyrant in his "oppression of his subjects; and are, in fact, the great benefactors of the human "race in the East. . . . All the prophets of old were dervishes, beyond all "doubt, in their actions, in their style of speaking, and in their dress." (*Travels and Adventures*, p. 297.)

And did eat locusts and wild honey. That is, *his customary food was locusts and wild honey*, the plainest of fare. He not only refrained from pampering 'the flesh,' he 'kept it under' (1 Cor. ix. 27), and made it 'endure hardness' (2 Tim. ii. 3) for great militant purposes. *Locusts:* "A kind of great "fly," says Petter, "which useth to eat and devour the tops of corn, herbs, "and trees." Jerome mentions that he had seen the whole land of Judæa covered with them. (*Comment.* on Joel ii. 20.) "It is well known," says Horatio B. Hackett, "that the poorer class of people eat them, cooked or raw, "in all the eastern countries where they are found." (*Illustrations*, p. 61.) *Wild honey:* Not *honey-dew*, as Robinson and Grimm suppose, a kind of gum that is found on the leaves of certain trees. The expression doubtless denotes real *wild honey*, the product of wild bees. Henry Maundrell mentions that when he was passing through the wilderness of Judæa, between the Dead Sea and Jericho, he "perceived a strong scent of honey and wax, the sun being hot; "and the bees," he adds, "were very industrious about the blossoms of that salt "weed which the plain produces." (*Journey*, p. 86, ed. 1749.) Dr. Tristram says: "The innumerable fissures and clefts of the limestone rocks, which every-

ST. MARK I.

mightier than I after me, the latchet of whose shoes I am not worthy to stoop down and unloose. 8 I indeed have baptized

---

"where flank the valleys, afford in their recesses secure shelter for any number of "swarms of wild bees; and many of the Bedouin, particularly about the wilder-"ness of Judæa, obtain their subsistence by bee-hunting, bringing into Jerusalem "jars of that wild honey on which John the Baptist fed in the wilderness." (*The Land of Israel*, p. 88.) The asceticism of John in food and raiment has its lessons. There are persons who ought always to be ascetics. It is their only chance for freedom from grossness and moral degradation. There are times, too, when all men should put both bit and bridle on the animal within them, keeping it on scanty diet and working it hard. And all moral reformers, who have it as their peculiar mission to expose the vices of a self-indulgent age, and to lead their fellow-men into cleaner ways and a nobler style of life, would require to be, in their own persons, unmistakable examples of the higher types of sobriety and self-denial.

VER. 7. **And he preached.** That is, *proclaimed* (*like a herald*).

Saying, There cometh after me He that is mightier than I. It is as if he had said, *My Suzerain, my Lord Paramount, is coming after me.* Instead, however, of employing a merely generic term to designate the Prince whose harbinger he was, he brings into view His superiority in might or strength. *He who is stronger than I is coming after me.* 'This is the gospel,' says Zuingli, ' though in epitome.' The people were prone to think that John himself had immense 'power' with God, and that all would be well with them if they should only get a baptism from his hands; they had an exaggerated idea of his power. He sought to undeceive them. He was but a humble servant, a herald, a forerunner. But his Master was 'mighty'; his Master had real power with God. He could wield all influences; touch all springs; ascend all heights; descend to all depths. He was '*able* to save to the uttermost,' to pardon the most criminal, and to purify the most unclean.

The latchet of whose shoes I am not worthy to stoop down and undo. *Undo* is Wycliffe's word, and better than the apparently contradictory *unloose* of our English versions. Purvey, in his revision of Wycliffe, has *unlace*. The word translated *latchet* means properly *thong*; but there is a connection between *latch*, *latchet*, and *lace*. John alleges that there was no standard of comparison, by means of which the relative superiority of the Messiah to himself could be measured. The Messiah was his master, and John was His herald and harbinger. Nevertheless, he did not deserve the honour of that post; he did not even deserve the honour of being permitted to stoop down and undo the latchets of his Master's sandals; that was a far higher honour than any man deserved. How exceedingly high, then, must the dignity of Jesus be!

VER. 8. **I baptized you with water.** A good translation, so far at least as the substance of the meaning is concerned. In the Received Text the original expression is *in water*. But Tischendorf and Alford have thrown out the preposition *in*, under the sanction of the manuscripts ℵ B H Δ 33 and others, and of the Vulgate version. If the omission be legitimate, then the evangelist's expression corresponds to Luke's (iii. 16), and is strictly translated *with water*,

you with water: but he shall baptize you with the Holy Ghost.

9 And it came to pass in those days, that Jesus came from

---

denoting the material employed. If, however, the reading of the Received Text should be retained, then the form of the expression corresponds to Matthew's (iii. 11), and could only be freely rendered *with water*. The preposition *in* would probably be accounted for by the original meaning of the verb *to baptize*; this original meaning leaving its impress on the form of expression, even when the purificatory act was effected by some other mode than *merging*. (See *Comm.* on Matt. iii. 6, 16.)

But He shall baptize you. There is here no emphasis on the *you*, and it would be wrong therefore to lay weight upon the word, in determining the question of the extent of the baptism which Christ administered, and still administers. Nevertheless it is worthy of note that the Baptist did not feel himself fettered in the pronominal phraseology which he employed.

With the Holy Spirit. There is a somewhat corresponding uncertainty in reference to the *with* in this clause, as there is in relation to the preceding clause. Tischendorf indeed, in his eighth edition, inserts in this clause the preposition *in*, though he omits it in the preceding clause. Lachmann, on the other hand, doubts its genuineness here, though he does not doubt it as regards the preceding clause. Alford omits it in both the clauses, supposing that the Received Text has been artificially assimilated to Matthew's form of phraseology. It is a matter of no practical moment whether it be admitted, as in Matthew, or omitted, as in Luke. If it be omitted, the expression is literally translated '*with* the Holy Spirit.' If it be retained, the expression is only freely thus rendered. *The Holy Spirit:* The article is wanting in the original. It was not needed, as the expression was, of itself, in Greek, sufficiently definite. Our usage however, in reference to the article, does not correspond absolutely to the usage of the Greeks; and hence it is according to the spirit, though not according to the letter, of the evangelist's phraseology that we say *the Holy Spirit*. When Wakefield rendered the expression *a holy spirit*, and Godwin, similarly, *a Divine Spirit*, they forgot that there is, in the letter of the original text, no more warrant for *a* than for *the*. The English language is richer than the Greek in the matter of articles, and if, in such a case as the one before us, the definite article be objected to, much more should the indefinite. The idea of the Baptist was not, that the Messiah would institute a more mystic style of water baptism, or a style of water baptism that would be instinct with a more efficacious spiritual energy, but it was that the Messiah would transcend altogether, in His purificatory operations, the sphere of the material and corporeal. He could act on spirit; He could act on spirit with Spirit; and He would thus act. He would furnish to men the influence from above that was needed in order to purity of heart and life; He would procure and pour out the influence of the Divine Spirit.

Ver. 9. **And it came to pass in those days.** *Those days*, namely, when John was engaged in preaching and baptizing in the wilderness that stretched along the banks of the Jordan.

Nazareth of Galilee, and was baptized of John in Jordan.
10 And straightway coming up out of the water, he saw the

That Jesus came from Nazareth of Galilee, and was baptized of John in the Jordan. In the Greek it is not *in*, but *to*, or *into*, *the Jordan*. It is as if the evangelist had been intending to say, *Jesus came from Nazareth of Galilee to the Jordan, and was there baptized by John*. But the evangelist, though having distinctly in view the Saviour's arrival at the Jordan, was yet in haste, as it were, to mention the fact of His baptism; and hence the peculiar collocation of the phraseology. It was quite in accordance with his ordinary inartificial style of composition, as exemplified for instance in ver. 1–4 and ver. 39. A similar transposition occurs in Matt. ii. 23, where we read, ' and He came and dwelt *in a city* called Nazareth.' In the original it is *to a city* or *into a city*, the idea being that Joseph *came to a city called Nazareth and then dwelt there*. Of course, we cannot suppose that Mark meant that Jesus *was baptized into the Jordan*. This interpretation is out of the question, when we take into account that in the verse immediately preceding we have Mark's way of construing the word *baptized*. Jesus came *to the Jordan*, and was baptized *in the Jordan*. His baptism was finely significant. It was a visible picture of the invisible descent into His humanity of the fulness of the Divine Spirit. He hence became full, officially, of the Holy Spirit. He received the Spirit 'without measure'; so that the Divine Spirit had His hand, not only in the preparation of the body of our Lord (Luke i. 35), but also, and gloriously, in the preparation of His spirit (Isa. xi. 2, 3; lxi. 1).

Nazareth of Galilee. There are still many traces of this despised little 'city,' and quite a thriving modern town is springing up on the steep slope of the hill. It is thriving, says Dr. Tristram, in part, because it is 'a Christian not a Moslem place,' and in part because it is ' the centre for the commerce of the districts east of Jordan.' (*The Land of Israel*, p. 122.) "Bare and featureless, singularly unattractive in its landscape, with scarcely a tree to relieve the "monotony of its brown and dreary hill, without ruins or remains, without one "precisely identified locality, there is yet a reality in the associations of Naz-"areth which stirs the soul of the Christian to its very depths. . . . It was "the nursery of One whose mission was to meet man, and man's deepest needs, "on the platform of common-place daily life. 'Can any good thing come out "of Nazareth?' might naturally be asked, not only by the proud Jew of the "south, but by the dweller among the hills of Galilee, or by the fair lake of "Gennesaret." (*The Land of Israel*, p. 123.)

VER. 10. *And straightway.* Or, *immediately.* Thiess supposes that the term was intended to indicate that there was, on the part of the Saviour, a certain hastiness of movement. " The baptism," says he, " was for Him no baptism ; " He needed it not. It was only the people and the Baptist who needed it. " The people needed the example ; John needed the honour." It was befitting, therefore, in the Saviour to be quick in leaving the scene of the ordinance. Thiess misunderstands the case, however. It is not hastiness that is indicated, but uninterrupted sequence.

Coming up out of the water. Or rather, *going up out of the water*, that is,

ST. MARK I.

heavens opened, and the Spirit like a dove descending upon him: 11 and there came a voice from heaven, *saying,* Thou art my beloved Son, in whom I am well pleased.

going up to the bank of the river. (Comp. Matt. iii. 16.) Our Saviour, with the Baptist, had been within the margin of the stream. For the meaning of the word which we render *going up,* see Matt. v. 1, xiv. 23, xv. 29; Mark iii. 13, vi. 51, x. 32; John i. 51, iii. 13, vi. 62, xx. 17.

He saw the heavens rent asunder. Or *cleft,* or *parted.* Our word *schism* comes from the term employed by the evangelist; and so does our geological word *schist* or *splitting rock.* When it is said '*He* saw the heavens parted,' the reference is not to John, but to Jesus, although it is also true that John saw the wonderful phenomenon as well as Jesus. (See John i. 33.) The revelation from above was primarily intended for our Lord Himself, in His humanity; for, of course, there must have been steps of gradation, and times and seasons of progression, in the development of His humanity.

And the Spirit, as a dove, descending upon Him. That was His true baptism, the thing signified. It was His formal inauguration, in the year of His perfect maturity, His thirtieth year (Luke iii. 23), to His great work, a work that gathered up into itself all the greatest offices of human society. Henceforth the Lord was replenished, not only in actual fact, but to His own subjective consciousness, with all the fulness of influences that were required in His complex personality, to constitute Him the official Head of the human race, the Prophet of prophets, the Priest of priests, the King of kings. It was *as a dove* that the Spirit descended on Him, a most captivating symbolism. The eagle too was in our Lord; everything about Him was mingled with the sublime; but the dove was predominant. Not only in His terrestrial career, but all along the ages, it is the power of His gentleness and tenderness and meekness, His love in short, that has been victorious. He has 'wooed' and 'won.'

VER. 11. And a voice came out of the heavens, Thou art My beloved Son, in Thee I am well-pleased. Very literally, *I was well-pleased,* viz. in Thy pre-existent state. The voice would thrill a variety of chords in our Lord's human heart, which would vibrate at once into the infinity of His higher being. The fulness of the Messianic self-consciousness would awake. Not the shadow of a film would obscure the glory of the fact that He was the Father's Son, and that He had been His darling from everlasting (*dilectus singularissima dilectione:* CAJETAN). His thoughts might shape themselves into some such forms as the following: *My Father has said it. I know My Father's voice. Everlasting memories come rushing in. He says that I am His Beloved! He used to say it before the foundation of the world. This mission which I have undertaken is dear, beyond expression, to His infinite heart. It is dear to Mine too. I rejoiced from of old, in the habitable part of the earth, while as yet there was none of it, 'nor the highest part of the dust of the world.' He says, 'In Thee I was well-pleased!'*—'*was*' from the first, and still '*am.*' *Oh how I delight, My Father, to do Thy will! 'Thy' will is 'My' will.* There has ever been, there will ever be, the inmost union of the two. Instead of *in Thee,* the Received Text reads *in whom,* a reading borrowed from Matt. iii. 17, which presents the whole utterance

13] ST. MARK I. 13

12 And immediately the spirit driveth him into the wilderness.
13 And he was there in the wilderness forty days, tempted of

from heaven, not as it was directly addressed to our Lord, but as it was indirectly apprehended by John who stood by. The two representations, we need
scarcely say, are in absolute harmony.

VER. 12. **And immediately.** Forthwith after His formal inauguration into
His great Messianic work.
The Spirit driveth Him forth. The Divine Spirit, to wit, whose influence He
had received in its fulness. *Driveth Him forth.* Very literally, *casteth Him out.*
It is the very verb that is employed to designate our Lord's *expulsion* of demons
(Mark i. 34, 39; iii. 15, 22; etc.). Wakefield renders it *leadeth out*, a translation that completely draws the teeth of the original emphasis. Vehemency of
impulse is represented; the Saviour felt an influence that must be yielded to
without delay. The translation of the English Geneva of 1557 is graphic,
driveth Him sodenly. Sir John Cheke has *threw Him*, which would suit Cartwright's idea that the reference is to a miraculous transport of our Saviour's
person through the air. The expression means, as Petter says, *thrusteth Him
forth*; and perhaps it may subindicate the existence of some innocent reluc-
tancy or shrinking of 'the flesh.'
Into the wilderness. We know not what wilderness, and we do not need to
know. Petter and others suppose that it was most likely the great wilderness
of Arabia, in which the children of Israel wandered for forty years, and where
Sinai is situated, the scene of the giving of the law and of the fasting of
Moses. The traditional locality, however, is near Jericho, a wild enough region,
where rises the Mons Quarantania, or Jebel Kuruntil, "with its precipitous
"face pierced in every direction by ancient cells and chapels, and a ruined church
" on its topmost peak." There are multitudes of antique frescoes still fresh on
the walls, "and generally," says Dr. Tristram, "every spring a few devout
" Abyssinian Christians are in the habit of coming and remaining here for forty
"days, to keep their Lent on the spot where they suppose our Lord to have
" fasted and been tempted." (*The Land of Israel*, pp. 207-217.)

VER. 13. **And He was in the wilderness forty days.** Our Lord thus linked
Himself on, in consciousness, to the marvellous and marvellously self-denying
experiences of Moses and Elijah, the greatest souls of the dispensation that
foreshadowed the more spiritual dispensation which He Himself was about to
introduce. (See Exod. xxxiv. 28; Deut. ix. 9; 1 Kings xix. 8.) The foundations of all true greatness in human institutions must be laid in self denial.
Tempted by Satan. That is, *undergoing temptation by Satan*. It was fit, and
perhaps inevitable, that our Lord should come into personal conflict with the
great adversary, whose works and usurped dominion He had come to destroy.
There needed to be a great moral struggle, for there was already great antagonism between the two. And unless our Lord should have been able, while having
all the secret springs of His aspirations and actions sifted to the uttermost, to
pass through the fiery test unscathed, coming off an untarnished conqueror and
indeed 'more than a conqueror,' He would not have been fit to take His place

Satan; and was with the wild beasts; and the angels ministered unto him.

at the head of the race, to recover for mankind the paradise that had been lost. None but the 'Stronger than the strong' could deliver 'the captives of the mighty.' "The Second Adam therefore," says Archbishop Trench, "taking up "the conflict exactly where the first had left it, and inheriting all the con- "sequences of his defeat, in the desert does battle with the foe; and, conquer- "ing him there, wins back the garden for that whole race, whose champion and "representative in this conflict He had been." (*Studies in the Gospel*, p. 8.) *Satan:* or, as it is very literally, *the Satan*; just as we say *the Devil*. The word is as significant in Hebrew as the word *Devil* or *Diabolos* in Greek. It means *adversary*, just as *Devil* means *accuser* or *slanderer*. The being so named is *the adversary both of God and of men*. He is no myth; his actual agency bewrays itself. The unity, which is characteristic of the varied wickednesses of men, suggests it. The suicidal infatuation, which is a curious and inseparable element in almost every species of crime, but which is obtrusively conspicuous in some of the most popular forms of iniquity, bespeaks the presence of some mighty malice behind the scenes, moving the springs of human action. We need not therefore discuss with C. Friedrich Gelbricht the question which he proposes, *whether we should require to 'think ill' of Jesus if He found His temptations simply springing up within Himself*; or, as Gelbricht more strongly expresses it, *if He Himself was His own tempter!* Gelbricht answers his question in the negative, while he concedes that the hypothesis on which it is erected is probably to be accepted as true. We object, however, to the hypothesis.

And He was with the wild beasts. This is added, not as Hilgenfeld supposes, to suggest an analogy between our Lord and Adam in paradise (*Die Evangelien*, p. 126), but, as Petter says, "to show the desolate and forlorn state in which "our Saviour now was in the wilderness; being destitute of all help and com- "fort from men, and having none to be His companions but wild beasts, which "were so far from helping or comforting Him that they were more likely to "annoy and hurt Him, yea, to devour Him." Of what kind the wild beasts were we do not know, and need not care to know. Even to the present day the desert places in and around the Holy Land swarm with such denizens, more especially wherever there are convenient *wadies* at hand, in which they may fix their homes or haunts. Dr. Tristram, in referring to Kuser Hajla, near Jericho, says: "In its gorge we found a fine clump of date palms,—one old tree, and "several younger ones clustered round it, apparently unknown to recent travel- "lers, who state that the last palm tree has lately perished from the plains of "Jericho. Near these palm trees, in the thick cover, we came upon the lair of "a leopard or cheetah, with a well beaten path, and the broad, round, unmis- "takable footmarks quite fresh, and evidently not more than a few hours old. "However, the beast was not at home for us. Doubtless it was one of these "which M. de Saulcy took for the footprints of the lion. But inasmuch as "there is no trace of the lion having occurred in modern times, while the others "are familiar and common, we must be quite content with the leopard. Every- "where around us were the fresh traces of beasts of every kind; for two days

14 Now after that John was put in prison, Jesus came into

"ago a great portion of the plain had been overflowed. The wild boar had
"been rooting and treading on all sides; the jackals had been hunting in packs
"over the soft oozy slime; the solitary wolf had been prowling about; and
"many foxes had singly been beating the district for game. The hyæna too
'had taken his nocturnal ramble in search of carcases. None of these, how-
"ever, could we see." (*The Land of Israel*, pp. 245, 246.) When in the Wady
Hamâm again, in the district of Gennesaret, he says : " We never met with so
"many wild animals as on one of these days. First of all, a wild boar got out
"of some scrub close to us, as we were ascending the valley. Then a deer was
"started below, ran up the cliff, and wound along the ledge, passing close to us.
"Then a large ichneumon almost crossed my feet, and ran into a cleft; and
"while endeavouring to trace him, I was amazed to see a brown Syrian bear
"clumsily but rapidly clamber down the rocks and cross the ravine. While
" working the ropes above, we could see the gazelles tripping lightly at the
"bottom of the valley, quite out of reach and sight of our companions at the
"foot of the cliff. Mr. Lowne, who was below, saw an otter, which came out of
"the water and stood and looked at him for a minute with surprise." (*The
Land of Israel*, p. 451.)

And the angels ministered to Him. In what way or ways we are not told, nor
how frequently, or at what conjuncture or conjunctures. See Matt. iii. 11.
Meyer infers from the extreme brevity of Mark's account of the temptation that
his report must be chronologically earlier, and less mythically developed, than
that of Matthew. Baur again infers, from the obscurity that is involved in its
brevity, and from the consequent need of Matthew's fuller narrative to make it
plain, that it must be of the nature not of a germ, but of a subsequent condensation or epitome. (*Kritische Untersuchungen*, p. 540.) It is thus that conjecture devours conjecture. We take neither of the alternatives. We do not think,
on the one hand, that we have in Mark, or ' the proto-Mark,' the germ of Matthew ; neither do we think on the other that the mystery of the relationship of
the two evangelists is solved when we try to school ourselves into Augustine's
conviction, that we are but hearing the echoes of Matthew when we listen to
the brief biographical sketches of Mark.

VER. 14. **Now after that John was delivered up.** See Matt. xiv. 3–5 ; Luke iii.
19, 20. The rendering of King James's translators, *was put in prison*, while
true to historic fact, is rather too free a translation. Perhaps the Baptist had
been *betrayed*, or *surrendered*, (as Dickinson renders the word,) into the hands of
Herod Antipas ; perhaps he was violently seized by the tyrant, and then
delivered over to the custody of a guard of soldiers, and thus imprisoned.
Taken is Wycliffe's version and Tyndale's and Coverdale's. *Delivered up* is
the version of the Rheims ; and Luther's corresponds (*überantwortet ward*).

Jesus came into Galilee. The district where He had spent His youth. Not
unlikely, in consequence of its distance from the capital and its proximity to
the Gentiles, it would not be so thoroughly priest-ridden, and Pharisee-ridden,
as the district of Judæa.

Galilee, preaching the gospel of the kingdom of God, 15 and saying, The time is fulfilled, and the kingdom of God is at hand : repent ye, and believe the gospel.

Preaching the gospel of God. Jesus *preached*, or, very literally, *heralded*; that is, as Petter popularly explains it, 'published openly, by lively voice and word of mouth.' He preached *the gospel*; He proclaimed that which is, by pre-eminence, *good news* or *glad tidings*. It was not His aim to accuse, or denounce, or condemn. It was in sadness of heart if He ever, as in parenthesis, spoke words of accusation, denunciation, or condemnation. The burden of His proclamation was altogether different. It was a message of mercy. He 'preached *the gospel of God*.' He preached the good news which He had received in commission *from God*. The genitive *of God* is what grammarians call *the genitive of the author* (genitivus auctoris).

VER. 15. **And saying, The time is fulfilled.** Or, more literally, *has been fulfilled*; that is, *the measure of time that required to be completed has been completed*. A certain amount of time required to come and go ere the world was ready for the establishment of the new order of things, or for the inauguration, in its more developed phase, of the kingdom of heaven. That amount of time had now *elapsed*. The appointed *measure* had been filled to the brim,—*fulfilled*, that is *filled-full*. The accumulation of days and weeks and months and years was complete. It was now 'the fulness of the time' (Gal. iv. 4).

And the kingdom of God is at hand. Or, *has come nigh*. What Matthew in general calls *the kingdom of heaven* (see Matt. iv. 17) is designated by Mark and Luke *the kingdom of God*. No other New Testament writer but Matthew employs the expression *the kingdom of heaven*, though Paul has *the Lord's heavenly kingdom* (2 Tim. iv. 18). The two expressions, *the kingdom of heaven* and *the kingdom of God*, are coincident in substrate; they vary only in phase. The kingdom is Divine, and hence heavenly. It is a thing of heaven ; it originated in heaven, tends to heaven, culminates in heaven. It is a heavenly community, with a heavenly Sovereign at its head. All its subjects are heavenly, whether they be on earth or in heaven. Our whole earth should have been a part of heaven ; but it is a runaway world, having gone off from heaven. It is not, however, finally lost to heaven. God, the Great Moral Governor, has not and will not let it go. He desires, not in the use of physical omnipotence, but by glorious moral means, to win it back. Long ago He took the initiative for the accomplishment of this end; He reclaimed a foothold for heavenly institutions. And now the time was come for establishing, in a somewhat developed and as it were completed form, the heavenly community, 'the kingdom of God.'

Repent. It was the burden of John's wilderness 'cry.' Our Saviour takes it up ; for it never can become obsolete until sin has ceased to be. *Repentance from dead works* (Heb. vi. 1), *repentance toward God* (Acts xx. 21), must ever be an integrant elementary theme of exhortation with all true preachers of righteousness. It implies, *firstly*, that men have been wrong in their conduct and character. It implies, *secondly*, that if they will but calmly and candidly *think back* over their ways, they will get to see that they have been wrong. Hence

ST. MARK I.

16 Now as he walked by the sea of Galilee, he saw

the solemn call *Repent!* as the antecedent of the joyful call *Believe!* Our English word is by no means a perfect or precise synonym of the original Greek term (μετανοεῖτε). The English *Repent* brings prominently into view the duty of *a penitent state of feeling* (note the French *repentir*). The Greek term brings prominently into view the duty of *a preliminary retrogressive acting of the intelligence* (or νοῦς). This retrogressive acting of the intelligence, or *afterthought*, is only intended indeed to be preliminary; and if it did not issue in the conviction of the conscience, the sorrow of the heart, and the reformation on the life, it would be of no moral moment. It would be a useless mental fragment, a beginning without its appropriate ending. Nevertheless it is the indispensable beginning of a right state of spirit and life on the part of all such moral creatures as have already been wrong in their character and conduct. (See on Matt. iii. 2.)

And believe in the gospel. It is men's duty both *to believe the gospel* and *to believe in it*. The one expression may replace the other; but they differ in aspect of import. When we are said *to believe in the gospel*, the attention, so far as the form of the expression is concerned, is not carried farther than the gospel; our faith is viewed as terminating *in* the gospel. When, again, we are said *to believe the gospel*, the attention is carried forward beyond the gospel to the object concerning which the gospel testifies. The gospel is regarded as the medium whereby we may reach the Glorious Object. Both representations are true to the actual philosophy of the case; but the latter goes deeper in its draught. There are always two objects of faith or belief,—a proximate and an ultimate. The proximate is the testimony (the *objectum quo*); the ultimate is the reality testified (the *objectum quod*). The *gospel* to which the Saviour referred is, of course, just the good news that the time had now been fulfilled, and that the kingdom of God had come near.

VER. 16. **And passing along by the sea of Galilee.** Or, *the sea of Tiberias*; or, *the lake of Gennesaret*. It was the centre of the circle of Galilee, and was called *the sea* by the surrounding inhabitants, for the same reason that Winder*mere*, Butter*mere*, Thirle*mere*, Gras*mere* were regarded of old as seas. It was *an expanse of water*. The Jews had also their *Dead Sea* or *Salt Sea*. But the Mediterranean was 'the *great* sea.' Dr. Tristram, describing his approach to the sea of Galilee from Nazareth, says:—" For nearly three hours we had ridden "on, with Hermon in front, sparkling through its light cloud-mantle, but still "no sight of the sea of Galilee. One ridge after another had been surmounted, 'when on a sudden the calm blue basin, slumbering in placid sweetness be- "neath its surrounding wall of hills, burst upon us, and we were looking down "on the hallowed scenes of our Lord's ministry. We were on the brow of a "very steep hill. Below us was a narrow plain, sloping to the sea, the beach of "which we could trace to its northern extremity. At our feet lay the city of "Tiberias, the only remaining town on its shores, enclosed by crumbling forti- "fications with shattered but once massive round bastions. Along that fringe, 'could we have known where to find them, lay the remains of Chorazin, Beth- "saida, and Capernaum. Opposite to us were the heights of the country of the

Simon and Andrew his brother casting a net into the sea: for they were fishers. 17 And Jesus said unto them, Come ye

"Gadarenes, and the scene of the feeding of the five thousand. On some one
"of the slopes beneath us the sermon on the mount was delivered. The first
"gaze on the sea of Galilee, lighted up with the bright sunshine of a spring
"afternoon, was one of the moments of life not soon or easily forgotten.
"It was different from my expectations; our view was so commanding. In
"some respect it recalled in miniature the first view of the Lake of Geneva,
"from the crest of the Jura, as it is approached by the old Besançon road;
"Hermon taking the place of Mont Blanc, the plain of Gennesaret recalling the
"Pays de Vaud, and the steep banks opposite the bold coast of Savoy. All
"looked small for the theatre of such great events, but all the incidents seemed
"brought together as in a diorama. There was a calm peacefulness in the look
"of these shores on the west, with the paths by the water's edge, which made
"them the fitting theatre for the delivery of the message of peace and recon-
"ciliation." (*The Land of Israel*, pp. 426, 427.)

He saw Simon. Or, Simeon. See Acts xv. 14; 2 Pet. i. 1 (Gr.). The pronunciation *Simeon* is nearest the Hebrew original. He was called Peter by our Lord.

And Andrew the brother of Simon. Andrew, unlike Simon or Simeon, is a Greek word, bearing the idea of *manliness*, whereas Simeon brings out the idea of *listening* or *hearing*.

Casting a net in the sea. ('Αμφιβάλλοντας ἐν τῇ θαλάσσῃ), *throwing about in the sea* (viz. a hand net). It is one of Mark's vivid touches. The thing that the men were throwing about is not named. (See Tischendorf and Tregelles.) It is supposed that it would be sufficiently understood; and no doubt the phrase *throwing about* would just be an idiom of the trade. It represents the fishermen throwing now on the one side of their boat, and now on the other (note the connection between ἀμφί and *ambo*). Hand-nets differed from drag-nets, which were trailed along the bottom of the fishing place. Hand-nets were let down and lifted up, and were more or less of a bag shape.

For they were fishermen. Of a humble calling indeed; but still, in the exercise of it, the men were trained to habits which were, in many respects, well fitted to prepare them for higher duties. The successful use of the hand-net requires in the fisherman, says Dr. W. M. Thomson, "a keen eye, an active "frame, and great skill in throwing. He must, too, be patient, watchful, wide "awake, and prompt to seize the exact moment to throw." (*The Land and the Book*, p. 402.)

VER. 17. **And Jesus said to them, Come ye after Me.** This, of course, was not the first time they had met. Simon and Andrew had been disciples of John the Baptist, and, while following him, had introduced themselves to the Saviour. (John i. 35-42.) They had evidently been earnest men, looking out wistfully for the good time of which the prophets had spoken, and longing to be engaged in any labour of love that might be helpful to the glorious cause of God. The expression *Come ye after Me*, while conventionally meaning *Become My pupils*, was moulded on the natural and seemly custom of allowing precedence to the rabbi, while walking along.

after me, and I will make you to become fishers of men.
18 And straightway they forsook their nets and followed him.
19 And when he had gone a little farther thence, he saw James
the *son* of Zebedee, and John his brother, who also were in the
ship mending their nets. 20 And straightway he called them:
and they left their father Zebedee in the ship with the hired
servants, and went after him.

And I will make you to become fishers of men. I will fit you for higher work, for a spiritual sphere, a sphere in which you will operate on men, and be successful in catching them. The figure must not be pressed or strained.

Ver. 18. And straightway. Without any hesitation.

They left the nets, and followed Him. They left *the nets* that were in their boat. Simon and Andrew, having drawn their boat ashore, left it in the hands of some assistants, and *followed* Jesus, or, as Wycliffe has it, picturesquely, *thei sueden Hym* (they pur*s*ued Him). It is interesting to note the brotherliness of the brothers; they had worked together in their secular calling, and they were not divided in their attachment to Jesus.

Ver. 19. And going on a little farther, He saw James the son of Zebedee and John his brother. Another pair of brotherly brothers. John, though afterwards the more conspicuous of the two, was evidently the younger, and hence is generally named after James and distinguished as ' the brother of James.' In Mark he always occupies this secondary position, as also in Matthew. In Luke however he is, on one occasion, mentioned before James, as if the knowledge of his ultimate eminence had, for the time, displaced the original association of sequence. (See Luke ix. 28.)

Who also were in the boat. The boat, namely, that belonged to them, and hence it might be legitimately rendered *in their boat*. The Unitarian 'Improved Version' has *in a ship*, which is certainly no improvement on the Authorized translation. Principal Campbell has *in a bark*, borrowing from, but deteriorating, the version of Mace, *in the bark*. It is noteworthy that Wycliffe and Sir John Cheke have *boat* instead of *ship*, which was Tyndale's word, and not equal to *boat*.

Mending the nets. Viz. that belonged to them, making them, as the word means, *complete*.

Ver. 20. And straightway He called them: and they left their father Zebedee in the boat with the hired servants, and went after Him. There would be something in the call, and in the mien and bearing of Him who gave it, that would entirely forestall any questioning or doubting. The behest was, as it were, from heaven; and it conferred at once the highest honour and the greatest privilege. They felt that they must not be disobedient to it. But, at the same time, they did not leave their father unprovided for; he had *hired servants*. " These " disciples," says Petter, " did not so wholly and utterly forsake their goods and " friends, as never afterward to use them any more upon occasion; but they " forsook them in regard of the ordinary use of them, and so far forth only as " they might hinder them in their ordinary conversing with Christ, and follow- " ing of Him."

21 And they went into Capernaum; and straightway on

Ver. 21. **And they enter into Capernaum.** Note the present tense, *they enter*. We are carried back in imagination to the time referred to, and see them walking along and entering the adjacent town. It was Capernaum, the home for the present of Simon and Andrew. (See ver. 29, and comp. John i. 44.) The precise spot on which the town lay is disputed. It has in modern times been generally supposed to be the place now called Tell Hûm, at the north-west angle of the lake, where three or four acres of ground are strewed with interesting architectural remains; "sarcophagi of white marble; fragments of marble "shafts, some of them double columns; friezes, pilasters, capitals, and portions "of elaborate carvings, most of them in a debased style, besides a few large fragments of walls, extending to some distance beyond; yet, excepting one large "piece of an entablature curiously carved, there is nothing to particularize, but "quite enough to prove ancient wealth and importance." (Tristram's *Land of Israel*, pp. 441, 442.) Dr. Robinson, however, argues strongly in favour of Khân Minyeh as the site, at Ain et-Tin, considerably south of Tell Hûm. (*Later Researches*, pp. 347-359.) Dr. Porter is disposed to agree with Dr. Robinson, more especially as Major Wilson has discovered there the remains of an ancient aqueduct, which conveyed the waters of Ain Tabighah "across "the low ground and round the cliff of Khân Minyeh by a striking piece of en-"gineering, at a sufficient altitude to irrigate the whole plain of Ghuweir," or Gennesaret, "from end to end." (*Syria and Palestine*, p. 407; *The Recovery of Jerusalem*, p. 377.) Dr. Tristram again contends that the situation of the city must have been more to the south and farther west, at the Round Fountain of Mudawarah. Josephus, in his description of the plain of Gennesaret, (or Gennesar as he calls it,) says that it is 'watered by a most prolific fountain, which the people of the place call Kapharnaum' (πηγῇ διάρδεται γονιμωτάτῃ, Καφαρναούμ αὐτὴν οἱ ἐπιχώριοι καλοῦσι). He proceeds to say that 'this fountain produces a fish like the *coracine* which is found in the marsh-pool at Alexandria.' (*War*, iii. 10 : 8.) This coracine or catfish is quite a remarkable siluroid, which delights to bury itself in sediment, leaving only its feelers exposed. Dr. Tristram *found it abounding in the Round Fountain of Mudawarah*, and carried off specimens a yard long, some of which he has deposited in the British Museum. In 'the fountain of the fig' (*Ain et-Tin*) at Khân Minyeh, there are no coracines. The fountain there, says Dr. Tristram, 'could neither supply it with cover nor food.' And as regards Tell Hûm there is, it seems, no fountain at all in the place. Neither is there any in its neighbourhood, nearer than Ain Tabighah, that could possibly correspond to the Kapharnaum of Josephus. But Ain Tabighah is two miles south of Tell Hûm; and Dr. Tristram could not discover in it any trace of the coracine. How marvellous that there should be such difficulty in identifying the Lord's 'own city' (Matt. ix. 1). How thoroughly has it been brought down to the dust! (See Matt. xi. 23.)

And straightway. Without 'losing any time,' as we say, or letting slip any opportunity. The word rendered *straightway, forthwith*, or *immediately*, is a favourite with Mark. He has already used it in ver. 10, 12, 18, 20. He uses it also, before the end of the present chapter, in ver. 28, 29, 30, 31, 42, 43.

On the sabbath day. A correct translation, though the expression is plural

the sabbath day he entered into the synagogue, and taught.
22 And they were astonished at his doctrine : for he taught them

in the original, and translated plurally in Luke iv. 31 by King James's translators. It is plural, because the Aramaic form of the word sounded, to the ears of Greeks, like a plural: *shabbata, sabbata*. Compare our English word *riches*, which, though plural in form, was, originally at least, a singular noun, *richesse*, and is so used by Chaucer for instance, who makes it rhyme with *princesse*. (l. 1831. See on Matt. xii. 1.) Euthymius Zigabenus was misled by the plural form of the evangelist's word, and interpreted the word as meaning *on the sabbath days*. The Vulgate translator made the same mistake; Luther too, and Tyndale and Coverdale, Matthew Henry likewise. Apparently Wakefield also, for he renders the whole clause thus: *and He constantly went on the sabbath day*. King James's translators in several places made the same mistake.

He entered into the synagogue. Tischendorf omits the word *entered*. But if it was not in the evangelist's autograph it requires to be mentally supplied. The Elzevir edition of 1624 has *into synagogue*, instead of *into the synagogue*. Wrongly, however. The good manuscripts have the article; and there would most probably be only one synagogue in so small a place as Capernaum. It had apparently been but recently erected. When the elders of the Jews, at a subsequent time, said to our Lord concerning the centurion 'and he hath built us *our synagogue*' (Luke vii. 5), it is *the synagogue* in the original. The word *synagogue* primarily meant a *meeting*, and thence came to denote *a meeting-place*, its meaning here. Luther renders it *school*. It denotes the edifice in which the Jews met together for the reading and explaining of their Scriptures, and the offering up of prayers.

And taught. Liberty of speech was allowed in the synagogues, though of course under certain conventional restrictions. (See Vitringa *de Synagoga vetere*, iii. 1: 7.) All therefore who had a word to say, and could say it with propriety, more especially if they were manifestly rabbis, or were apparently fit, either by man's teaching or by God's, to be rabbis, had an opportunity of addressing their fellow worshippers. It was a plan that would tend in some instances to confusion and irreverent disputing; but it was fitted, on the other hand, to foster a spirit of freedom and freshness. It was a counterpoise to the absolute officialism of the sacerdotal service.

VER. 22. **And they were astonished at His teaching.** Not so much because of its subject matter as because of its peculiar manner. Even Wycliffe employs here the term *techynge*, though translating from the Vulgate, which has *doctrina*. Tyndale has *learninge*, by which perhaps he may have meant *teaching*, as the word was for long 'ambidextrous,' and still is so in certain localities. In Anglo-Saxon the word *leorning-man* means indifferently either a schoolmaster or a scholar; and the verb *læran* means *to teach*.

For He taught them as having authority. He could not conceal from Himself that He was *a master* and *the master* in all things moral, spiritual, and scriptural, and entitled therefore to do something more than merely propose His opinion. He did not need to speak as one who was in doubt, or as one who

as one that had authority, and not as the scribes. 23 And there
was in their synagogue a man with an unclean spirit; and he

---

realized that he might be mistaken. He could not, in honesty, thus speak.
There would be meekness indeed, and the sweetest condescension; but there
could be no doctrinal diffidence. (See Matt. v. 20, 22, 28, 32, 34, 39, 44.) Not
only, however, would there be the absence of doctrinal diffidence, there would
at the same time be the presence in His teaching, to an unprecedented degree,
of the self-evidencing power of the truth. The light would shine, as in a
blaze, through all that He said; and it would be impossible for ingenuous men
to puzzle themselves into a debate whether it was really light or darkness.
Jesus, says Matthew Henry, was 'a *non-such* preacher.'

And not as the scribes. The *scribes* were the learned men of the Jewish
nation, the men who had to do with letters (γραμματεῖs). Almost all the writing
that was required in the nation would be done by them; most of the reading
too. The transcribing of the Scriptures would devolve on them; and as the
nation was emphatically ecclesiastical, the chief currents of their engagements
would flow in a biblical and religious direction. Hence the interpretation of
the law and the prophets, in the synagogues, would devolve chiefly on them;
and the people would, to a large degree, be dependent on their instructions.
They would vary greatly, like other men, in ability, character, and qualifications; but it would appear that in the time of our Lord the great bulk of
them were pedantic in things that were obvious enough, and frivolous and
jejune in all things that lay beyond. They would be admirable guessers, and
mighty in platitudes. They would be ingenious in raising microscopic doubts,
and perfect adepts in conjuring up conceit to do battle with conceit. They
would be skilful in splitting hairs to infinity, and they would be proud of their
ability to lead their hearers through the endless mazes of the imaginations of
preceding rabbis, imaginations that ended in nothing or in something that was
actually worse than nothing. But they would have no power, or almost none,
to move the conscience toward true goodness, or to stir the love of the heart
toward God and toward men. They might speak, indeed, with positiveness
enough; but it would not be with moral power. They might assert with dic-
tatorial self sufficiency; but it would not be with 'demonstration of the Spirit,'
demonstration flashing in conviction even upon reluctant and hard-winking
souls.

VER. 23. **And straightway.** No sooner had the Saviour concluded His address
than there arose a peculiar commotion.

There was in their synagogue a man with an unclean spirit. Or, more literally,
a man '*in*' *an unclean spirit*, that is, a man under the influence of an unclean
spirit; just as we say, *a man* '*in*' *drink*, or, more pleasantly, *a man* '*in*' *love*.
For the time being the man is absorbed, as it were, in love or in drink. So
the demoniac was absorbed as it were *into* the demon, and was completely
under its power, or, as we may say, *within* its power. There were such demoniacs of old; and there is little reason for doubting that there are such
demoniacs still, though demonism, like many other agencies, obvious and

cried out, 24 saying, Let us alone; what have we to do with

---

occult, has varied in its phases in the course of the ages. There is manifestly a spiritual side of things, the counterpart of that material side that is open to our apperception through our senses. It is entirely arbitrary to suppose that in this spiritual side of things there is no other spiritual element, no spiritism, except what is human. The universe is large ; worlds are linked to worlds ; evil and good are strangely commingled. God is everywhere; and He is a Spirit. There is therefore some other spiritism than what is human. And, as regards the sphere of creation, we may be sure that it is not a mere spiritual wilderness, or waste, or vacuum, round about man. There are hosts of spirits, at once hierarchically ascending, and contrariwise descending. Influences from both directions press in upon men ; and hence the demoniacal possessions of Scripture. It is in some respects a marvellous mode of influence, but yet by no means more marvellous than some other modes distinctively mental. If human spirits be wonderfully correlated to their bodies, as they are, it need not amaze us that demonic spirits, if having influence at all beyond the circle of their spiritual selves, should seek to enter and should be able on certain conditions to enter into some abnormal correlations, not to human spirits only, but to the bodies of these spirits. The man of whom the evangelist speaks was in the power of *an unclean spirit.* Possibly he was 'suffering,' as Schenkel will have it, 'from religious mania.' (*Character of Jesus*, v. 3.) But that explains nothing. Religious mania requires itself to be explained. The demon was *unclean, impure, unholy.* Holiness is cleanness. Wickedness or unholiness is foulness, or the defilement of the soul

And he cried out. Godwin translates, *and 'it' cried out.* But the nominative to the verb is the word *man,* whose mouth and voice were employed by the unclean spirit.

VER. 24. **Saying.** Immediately following this word we have in King James's version the exclamation *Let us alone!* But the interjection (ἔα) which is thus freely translated has most probably been imported into the text from Luke iv. 34, where it is no doubt genuine. It is omitted by Lachmann, Tischendorf, Tregelles, Alford. It is not found in the manuscripts ℵ B D, nor in the Italic, Vulgate, Syriac Peshito, Coptic, Æthiopic, Arabic, and Persic versions. It is an exclamation denoting displeasure. (See Fritzsche.)

What have we to do with Thee? Or rather, *What hast Thou to do with us?* Very literally, *What to us and to Thee ?* It is an idiomatic expression, meaning *What is there in common to us and to Thee ?* As here applied it is deprecatory, and means *Why dost Thou interfere with us?* (See Kypke ; and comp. John ii. 4 ; also Jud. xi. 12, 2 Sam. xvi. 10, 1 Kings xvii. 18, 2 Kings iii. 13, Matt. viii. 29.) The Saviour had not, so far as appears, been formally interfering by any specific action. But His very presence on the scene was felt to be interference. There emanated from Him, round about, an influence that went in upon men blissfully, counterworking all evil influences. The unclean spirit felt the power, and resented it as an interference, an interference not with itself in particular, but with the entire circle of kindred spirits. 'What hast Thou to do with *us ?* '

thee, thou Jesus of Nazareth? art thou come to destroy us? I know thee who thou art, the Holy One of God.

Thou Jesus of Nazareth ! There is no *thou* in the original; and it rather encumbers the address. It is properly omitted by Luther and the Rheims translator. It was inserted, however, both by Wycliffe and by Tyndale, and by King James's translators. Beza supposes that there was diabolic artifice in referring to Nazareth instead of Bethlehem. Trapp echoes the idea, and Matthew Henry. Petter says, ' but this I leave as uncertain, although it is not altogether unlikely.' It is however a manifest strain, and gives the evil one more than was his due: see Luke xxiv. 19; Acts ii. 22, iii. 6, iv. 10, x. 38, xxii. 8. Jesus belonged to Nazareth as truly as to Bethlehem; and His connection with Nazareth would be much better known, and would be therefore more discriminative as an appellation, than His connection with Bethlehem.

Art Thou come to destroy us? Or, more literally, *Camest Thou to destroy us?* It is not quite certain, however, whether we should read the words interrogatively, or affirmatively, *Thou camest to destroy us.* The majority of editors and expositors take them interrogatively. Luther however gives them affirmatively. Wetstein also. Bengel gave them interrogatively in his first and second editions, but in his third edition of 1753 he removed the interrogation point. In his German version also, of the same date, he gives the expression affirmatively. So Griesbach and Scholz; also Knapp, Tittmann, Vater, Näbe, Ornsby; Tischendorf too in his seventh and eighth editions, though not in his preceding edition of 1849. Fritzsche pleads for the affirmative reading. Ewald assumes it. It is not a matter of much moment which of the two views be embraced. In what goes before there is interrogation, and in what comes after there is affirmation. On the whole we prefer the interrogative view, though we would not have the interrogation strongly pronounced. It is much of the nature of exclamation, and expresses deprecation. The evil spirit knew, in general, what was the aim of the mission of Jesus, but we need not suppose that he knew with absolute precision and far-reaching range; and hence the interrogative element. Grotius votes for the interrogation, chiefly on the ground of correspondence with Matt. viii. 29. Note the *us: Camest Thou to destroy* ' *us* '*? Is it the intent of Thy mission to put down all demonic power?* Note the word *destroy.* It has no reference to the annihilation of being; usurpers are destroyed when their usurpation is destroyed.

I know Thee who Thou art. The Sinaitic manuscript and Tischendorf read *We know Thee,* instead of *I know Thee.* Were it the correct reading, it would represent the unclean spirit as speaking in the name of his fellows. They had inter-communication one with another about their affairs, and they all knew that Jesus had come and that He was from above. Doubtless, however, *I know Thee* is the correct reading. It is overwhelmingly supported by the real authorities; and it is the reading of Luke iv. 34.

The Holy One of God. That is, *the Holy One belonging to God,* viz. as God's great Agent in relation to the salvation of men. The demon gives emphasis to the moral transcendency and sinlessness of the Saviour. It was the phase of our Lord's being that was in the most absolute antagonism to the character and influence of ' the spirit that now worketh in the children of disobedience.' It

25 And Jesus rebuked him, saying, Hold thy peace, and come out of him. 26 And when the unclean spirit had torn him, and cried with a loud voice, he came out of him. 27 And they were all amazed, insomuch that they questioned among themselves, saying, What thing is this? What new doctrine *is* this? for with authority commandeth he even the unclean spirits, and they do obey him.

was the edge of the sword that was about to gain the victory. The confession, we may suppose, would be extorted under the pressure of the moment; or it may have been crookedly contrived to throw discredit on our Lord, as receiving commendation from a questionable quarter.

VER. 25. **And Jesus rebuked him.** Instead of *rebuked*, Coverdale has *reproved*, and Wycliffe *thretenyde*. The original word is very peculiar (ἐπετίμησεν), and strictly means *rated*. Our Saviour chid the evil spirit. He never on any occasion gave any quarter to anything demonic.

Saying, Hold thy peace, and come out of him. Whether the demon's confession were simply extorted, or diabolically contrived, our Lord laid His interdict upon it. He knew that it could not emanate from any good intent, or from any real appreciation. It was one of His aims in coming into the world to silence Satan. The word translated *Hold thy peace* (φιμώθητι) is exceedingly graphic, *Be muzzled*. It is a word for a beast: see 1 Cor. ix. 9, 1 Tim. v. 18.

VER. 26. **And the unclean spirit convulsing him, and crying with a loud voice, came out of him.** *Convulsing him,* no doubt epileptically, throwing him to the ground, and, as it were, *tearing at* him, though not actually, as Cardinal Cajetan remarks, *severing member from member*. *And crying with a loud voice.* "Not "that he uttered any words or speech," says Petter, "as he did before, but "only a confused hideous noise." It was with a grudge that he let go his prey.

VER. 27. **And all were amazed, so that they questioned among themselves.** Or rather, *so that they questioned together*. Such is the translation of Tischendorf's text (ὥστε συζητεῖν αὐτούς), as supported by the Sinaitic and Vatican manuscripts. Tyndale's version is, *in so moche that they demaunded one of another amonge themselves*. Each turned to his neighbour, in astonishment, to ask his opinion.

Saying, What is this? New teaching with authority! And He commandeth the unclean spirits, and they obey Him! Such is, apparently, the correct reading and rendering of the abrupt remarks which the astonished people made to one another (διδαχὴ καινὴ κατ' ἐξουσίαν· και τοῖς πνεύμασιν κ.τ.λ.). *New teaching with a witness! New certainly in relation to authority! We never heard anything like that before! And He lays His injunctions on the unclean spirits, and they obey Him!* The Revised version, following Lachmann and Tregelles, puts a stop after *New teaching!* and attaches the expression *with authority* to the following clause: *with authority He lays His injunctions even on the unclean spirits, and they obey Him!* The other method of construction, however, is simpler, and more in accordance with what is said in ver. 22, *He taught them as having authority.* The *authority* had impressed itself on the people's

28 And immediately his fame spread abroad throughout all the region round about Galilee.

29 And forthwith, when they were come out of the synagogue, they entered into the house of Simon and Andrew, with

---

hearts and consciences; *and, in addition to that,* they marvelled at the decisive and successful way in which He dealt with the unclean spirit. They say *the unclean spirits,* for by an easy process of generalization they referred the particular case in hand to the category to which it belonged.

VER. 28. **And the report of Him went out immediately in all directions into the whole surrounding region of Galilee.** It flew, as it were, on the wings of the wind. *The report of Him :* or, more literally still, *the hearing of Him,* that is, the hearing of which He was the object. *Immediately :* this word is omitted in the Sinaitic manuscript (א*), but not in the Vatican, as Tregelles had been led to suppose; it is omitted also in the important cursive manuscripts 1 and 33. But doubtless it is genuine; it was just like Mark to insert it (see on ver. 21 and 30). And it is peculiarly appropriate in such a case as the present, for no doubt the report concerning Jesus would spread like wildfire. *In all directions,* or *everywhere* (πανταχοῦ): a word not in the Received Text, nor admitted by Lachmann, but received by Tischendorf on the authority of X^c B C L, 69, etc. *Into the whole surrounding district of Galilee :* such is evidently the meaning of the evangelist's expression. King James's translators seem to have supposed that the reference was to *the district which surrounded Galilee.* So Tyndale, *all the region borderinge on Galilee.* The Geneva follows Tyndale. Cajetan takes the same view, and Erasmus, Beza, Petter, Elsner, Fritzsche, Meyer, Lange; some of them misled apparently by Matt. iv. 24. Grotius hesitates. But both the Peshito version and the Vulgate give the right view. Wycliffe's translation is, *in to al the cuntree of Galilee.* So le Fèvre, Diodati, de Dieu strongly, Beausobre, Wolf, Bengel, Principal Campbell, Burton Baumgarten-Crusius, Rilliet, Webster and Wilkinson, Klostermann.

VER. 29. **And forthwith.** The same word that is rendered *immediately* in the preceding verse. The two verses, however, run out with their respective '*immediately*' on different lines. The former takes note of the rapid general impression produced in the district at large; this takes note of what happened in Capernaum just after the dismission of the people from the synagogue.

When they were come out of the synagogue. *They,* that is, Jesus and His four disciples. The evangelist is not studying his phrases. He was thinking of our Saviour and His four disciples generally, and begins to speak of them collectively; but, as he proceeds, he descends to particulars, in a manner that might be regarded as confused by a fastidious composer, but that is in reality subservient to a distinct apprehension of the state of the case.

They came into the house of Simon and Andrew. See ver. 16.

With James and John. See ver. 19. Although the evangelist, when commencing this verse, had in his mind Jesus and His four disciples, inclusive of course of James and John; yet, when he proceeded to tell where the company

James and John. 30 But Simon's wife's mother lay sick of a fever, and anon they tell him of her. 31 And he came and took her by the hand, and lifted her up; and immediately the fever left her, and she ministered unto them. 32 And at even, when the sun did set, they brought unto

---

went, he deemed it a fitting particularization to add *with James and John*, lest they should be lost sight of in the generalization of the first part of the verse. It is not an utterly extravagant idea of Klostermann's that the evangelist's phraseology may probably be moulded on a report from Peter himself (see Papias in Eusebius's *Eccles. Hist.*, iii. 39), which might run in some such way as the following: "*And immediately on coming out of the synagogue we* "(that is, Jesus, James and John, and my brother Andrew and I) *went into* our "*house.*"

VER. 30. **But Simon's wife's mother.** Tyndale, in his 1526 edition, has *Symones motherelawe*. In his subsequent edition of 1534 he opens up the crushed expression, *Symons mother in lawe*. This is also Coverdale's translation, and that of the first Geneva in 1557. The subsequent Geneva, or the Geneva proper, and the Rheims, have the translation that is repeated in our translation.

Was lying in fever. She *lay prostrate* (κατέκειτο). *In fever:* as if she had been *on fire* (πυρέσσουσα). "Country fever is to this day," says Tristram, "very "prevalent in this seething plain and on its borders; and such a position as "Ain Mudawarah would be peculiarly subject to it." (*The Land of Israel*, p. 448.)

And straightway they speak to Him concerning her. No doubt with wistfulness in their hearts.

VER. 31. **And He came, and took her by the hand, and raised her up.** Or, as we should say, *assisted her up*. The perfect self possession and calm confidence of our Lord are beautifully indicated. There was no hesitancy on the one hand, and no bustle on the other. He simply put Himself *en rapport* with the patient, and the matter was done.

And the fever left her. The 'virtue' that went forth from the Lord restored instantaneously the physical equilibrium of the patient. He willed, 'and it was done.' He is thus the great healer and rectifier not only in the inner or moral sphere of the nature which He assumed; but also in the outer or material sphere. When once His will shall be absolutely dominant in the world, as one day it shall be, there will be no more disease.

And she ministered to them. She served them, or waited on them, when they sat down to partake of their humble repast. The fever had not burned up her strength before it was expelled, and left her prostrate. It was itself burned out and left her strength unimpaired.

VER. 32. **And at even, when the sun set.** *At even*, or, as Purvey has it, *whanne the eventid was come*; that is, when the sabbath was ended. It was a matter of religion with the Jews to do as little work as possible, even in the way of curing diseases, on the sabbath day; not a bad principle of action,

him all that were diseased, and them that were possessed with devils. 33 And all the city was gathered together at the door. 34 And he healed many that were sick of divers diseases,

when kept in the guidance of love and reason, instead of being committed to the leading strings of superstition. (See Danz's *Curatio Sabbathica*.)

They brought to Him all the diseased and the demoniac. The term *diseased*, in its current modern acceptation, is perhaps a trifle too strong to represent the import of the original expression (κακῶς ἔχοντας); but when looked at etymologically, *dis-eased*, that is, *sundered from ease* or *ill at ease*, and thus *unwell*, it is all that could be desired. The demoniacs referred to are described, in our English version, as *they that were possessed with devils*. It is no doubt a correct enough description; but the word *devil* or *devils* is never used in the original, when demoniacs are spoken of. It is always the word *demon* or *demons*, or the generic term *spirit* or *spirits*. In Greek mythology the word *demon* had a rather peculiar history or development of meaning. As Homer used the term, it was almost, if not altogether, equivalent to the word *god* or *deity*. Hesiod however distinguished between *gods* and *demons*; according to his representation in his *Works and Days*, " the latter are invisible tenants " of earth, remnants of the once happy ' golden race ' whom the Olympic gods " first made. . . . They are generically different from the gods, but essentially " good, and forming the intermediate agents and police between gods and men." (Grote's *History of Greece*, vol. i., part i., 2, pp. 58, 60.) By and by, however, Empedocles and Xenocrates represented the ghosts of the ' silver race ' as demons too; and, as the ' silver race ' were " reckless and mischievous toward " each other, and disdainful of the immortal gods," they made *bad demons*. This representation grew in the public mind, and at length overlapped the other, so that the word *demon* " came insensibly to convey with it a bad sense, " the idea of an evil being as contrasted with the goodness of a god." (Grote's *History*, vol. i. part i., 2, 16, pp. 61, 348, 349.) It was at this ultimate stage of the word's history that it got into use among the Greek-speaking Jews; and hence, in New Testament usage, it denotes *an evil spirit, of an order of beings superior in knowledge and power to men*. In short, it was regarded as a fitting Greek designation for *a fallen angel*. As to the possibility and probability of possession, see on ver. 23. When the evangelist says that the people brought ' all ' the *diseased and the demoniac*, the *all* is to be interpreted in accordance with the way in which it is often freely used in popular parlance. Comp. ver. 5, 33, 37.

VER. 33. **And the whole city was gathered together at the door.** They came to the door (πρὸς τὴν θύραν), and were thus *at the door*, crowding around it. *The whole city* thus came, that is, *the whole body of the citizens*. The evangelist is speaking popularly in his use of the word *whole*; and Capernaum, we must bear in mind, would be but a small city or town. (Compare the use of πόλις and κώμη in Luke ii. 4 and John vii. 42.) Dr. Samuel Clarke's paraphrase of the verse is, " *and such a vast multitude gathered together about the house*, " *to see what was done, that almost the whole city seemed to be there*."

VER. 34. **And He healed many that were sick with divers diseases; and many**

and cast out many devils; and suffered not the devils to speak,
because they knew him. 35 And in the morning, rising up a great while before day,
he went out, and departed into a solitary place, and there
prayed. 36 And Simon and they that were with him followed

---

demons He cast out. The evangelist distinguishes between natural diseases and
demoniacal possessions; though, not unlikely, the line that separated them
was not intended to be very rigidly drawn.

And He suffered not the demons to speak, for they knew Him. Beza, overlooking the proper import of the word rendered *speak* (λαλεῖν), renders the clause
thus, *and He suffered not the demons to say that they knew Him.* The demons
knew Him to be the Messiah, and were ready, in their anguish and anger, to
address Him as such. (See ver. 24; comp. Matt. viii. 29.) But Jesus did not
wish to be borne onward in His career by the aid of their testimony; see on
ver. 24, 25.

VER. 35. **And in the morning, while it was yet very dark, He rose up and went
out.** Namely, from the house where He was lodging. The expression in the
Authorized and Revised translations, *a great while before day*, brings into view
a length of time which is not indicated in the original phraseology (πρωῒ ἔννυχο
λίαν), and which might with difficulty be harmonized with the expression in
Luke iv. 42. Coverdale, following Luther, errs on the other hand in omitting
to translate the adverb which intensifies the idea of the *nocturnal darkness*. His
translation is, *in the mornynge before daye. Before daylight* would be better
(Luke iv. 42). The original expression is a plural adverb, in the accusative form,
meaning literally, when combined with the intensive adverb, *while the darkness
of the departing night was still very great*; that is, *while it was yet very dark*.
(See ἔννυχον in 3 Macc. v. 5, which Kypke translates *exeunte nocte*.) The morning is not a mere *point*, but a *line* of time, an elongated progress or procession.
At the one extremity it is *in the night*; at the other it is *in the day*. Wycliffe's
version is admirable, *in the morewynge ful erly*.

And departed into a desert place, and there prayed. Instead of '*desert* place,'
King James's version has '*solitary* place,' the only instance in which the
evangelist's adjective is so rendered. It means, however, more than *solitary*,
for a garden might be solitary, especially in the early morning. Indeed, Matthew Henry actually supposes that the reference here might be to 'some remote
garden or outbuilding.' It is a mistake however. Our Saviour went to one of
the bare and barren spots stretching away north or west from Capernaum. He
was there engaged *in praying, lifting up His spirit communingly to His Heavenly
Father*. The word rendered *prayed* (προσηύχετο) does not simply denote *asking*.
"Prayer," says Petter, "is a holy conference with God."

VER. 36. **And Simon and they that were with him went in pursuit of Him.**
When they awoke in the morning and found Him gone, they seem to have got
alarmed lest He should have left them, betaking Himself to some other sphere of
labour. So too the inhabitants of the little city in general seem to have felt.
Hence the haste and eagerness of Simon and his companions (Andrew, James
and John), as indicated by the strong verb employed (κατεδίωξεν); they *pursued*

after him. 37 And when they had found him, they said unto him, All *men* seek for thee. 38 And he said unto them, Let us go into the next towns, that I may preach there also: for

Him, as if *He were fleeing from them*. The Syriac Peshito version softens the evangelist's phrase, using a verb which simply means *sought*. They *went in quest of Him*. But the Philoxenian Syriac adheres to the literal idea, using a verb and preposition which mean *pursued after*. Peter was the leader of the pursuing party, thus giving early indication of the impulsive ardour of his nature.

VER. 37. **And they found Him, and say to Him, All are seeking Thee.** That is, though indefinitely, *all the people* (*in Capernaum*). The people in general had no sooner risen in the morning than they thought of the wonderful preacher and healer and demon expeller. They wanted still to hear more, and to see more; and hence they came, one after another, to the house where He had been lodging, in quest of Him; His popularity had leaped up instantaneously to the superlative degree

VER. 38. **And He says to them, Let us go elsewhere.** "Behold," says Sarcerius, "the philanthropy of Christ." The word *elsewhere* (ἀλλαχοῦ) is inserted by Tischendorf, Tregelles, Alford, Candy. It is found in the Sinaitic, Vatican, and Ephraemi manuscripts, and 33 (' the queen of the cursives '), and in the Coptic, Armenian, Æthiopic, and Arabic versions. It brings out generically what is specifically expressed in the following clause.

Into the next towns. The smaller places round about, *the adjoining towns and villages*. The compound word (κωμοπόλεις), translated in our English version *towns*, means *village-cities* as it were, or *village-towns* as Petter renders it, *country-towns* as Cajetan explains it. It is a word that occurs only here, in the New Testament. Strabo however uses it; and it is common in the Byzantine mediæval writers. It would include, as employed by the evangelist, imperfectly enclosed towns, and unenclosed *villages* or *hamlets* (Thucyd. i. 5), where however there would be some synagogue or place of social worship. (See next verse, and compare Lightfoot *in loc.*) There were many such towns and villages in Galilee. Josephus says, concerning the two Galilees upper and lower: "The cities (πόλεις) lie thick, and the multitudes of villages (κωμῶν) are "everywhere so full of people, in consequence of the richness of the soil, that the "very least of them contains above fifteen thousand inhabitants." (*War*, iii. 3 : 2.) But this surely is exaggeration.

That I may preach there also; for to this end came I forth. *To this end*, that is, that I may preach the good news, not in one place only, but far and wide amongst the lost sheep of the house of Israel. The Saviour came forth from His invisible condition into the world, *to this end*. Not indeed *to this end* only; He had other ends in view, higher still. But this was one of the aims which actuated Him. The expression *came I forth*, or *came I out*, was probably used by our Saviour with intentional indefiniteness. He does not specify whence or from whom He came. The truth was left to dawn gradually upon the disciples' minds. He *came into the world*; He *came out* into it, *out* from beyond or from above. *He came out from the Father.* (See John viii. 42; xiii. 3; xvi. 27, 28,

therefore came I forth. 39 And he preached in their synagogues throughout all Galilee, and cast out devils. 40 And there came a leper to him, beseeching him, and

---

30; and compare Hegendorphinus *in loc.*) Compare also Matt. xiii. 49, where we read that " the angels *shall come forth* (or *shall come out*), and sever the wicked "from among the just." (See Luke iv. 43.) De Wette thinks that the expression means *for to this end came I out (from Capernaum)*. Meyer insists on the same view, *for to this end came I out (of the house)*. So Fritzsche, *for to this end came I out (into this desert place)*. Godwin too. Such an interpretation however amazes us. It involves a sudden, arbitrary, and most unpleasant descent into bathos. It is to assume moreover that our Lord had resolved, as if in caprice, to go off elsewhere without His newly called disciples, and without so much as even informing them of His intended movement! It is to assume, besides, that it is not likely that our Saviour would wish to quicken thought by occasionally using two-edged expressions, which would lead His hearers to think at one and the same time of a lower and a higher relationship of things,—a most improbable assumption.

VER. 39. **And He went into their synagogues throughout all Galilee, preaching and casting out demons.** A simple and easily understood historical statement, but, in the original, thrown very inartificially together, as in a heap of phrases. If the correct reading were literally rendered, it would run thus: *And He came preaching into their synagogues, into the whole of Galilee, and casting out the demons* (καὶ ἦλθεν κηρύσσων εἰς τὰς συναγωγὰς αὐτῶν εἰς ὅλην τὴν Γαλιλαίαν καὶ τὰ δαιμόνια ἐκβάλλων). The reading '*into*' *their synagogues* is overwhelmingly supported by the manuscripts of importance. And the introductory expression *He came*, supported by the Sinaitic and Vatican manuscripts, as well as by the Coptic and Æthiopic versions, is received into the text by Tischendorf (in his eighth edition) and by Tregelles. The Received Text has apparently been touched into harmony with the text of Luke (iv. 44).

Throughout all Galilee. Josephus says, but surely with a touch of exaggeration, that in his day there were "two hundred and forty towns and villages in "Galilee." (*Life*, § 45.)

VER. 40. **And there cometh to Him a leper.** We know not in what place. Luke says it was 'in one of the cities' (see chap. v. 12-16). Matthew too records the miracle (viii. 1-4), but does not specify the place. To this day lepers' quarters are found outside the walls of many of the towns of Palestine. (Tristram's *Land of Israel*, p. 417.) *A leper*: one infected with what Mead calls 'the most dreadful of all the diseases to which the Jews were subject' (*atrocissimus erat, qui Judæorum corpora frequenter fædabat, morbus:* MEDICA SACRA, cap. 2). Many diseases have their peculiar haunts or habitats; and leprosy seems to have been emphatically, and as existing under some peculiarly aggravated type or phase, a Syrian, Arabian, and Egyptian disease. (See Smith's *Bible Dictionary*, sub voce.) Perhaps the Jews brought it from Egypt, which Lucretius (*Rerum Nat.*, vi. 1112-3) and other ancient writers (see *J. Mason Good's note on Lucretius*) assert to be the birthplace and the favourite abode of elephantiasis. It is disputed indeed among nosologists whether or not elephantiasis be

kneeling down to him, and saying unto him, If thou wilt, thou canst make me clean. 41 And Jesus, moved with compassion, put forth *his* hand, and touched him, and saith unto

---

really *leprosy*. The dispute is, to a great degree, a matter of terminology. (See J. Mason Good's *Study of Medicine*, vol. ii., pp. 851-862, and vol. iv., p. 578.) But it seems to be certain that what is, at the present day, regarded as *leprosy* in Jerusalem, and throughout Palestine and Syria, is not so much the disease which the old Greek and Latin physicians called *leprosy*, as the still more loathsome malady called *elephantiasis*. Diseases indeed sometimes vary in their development, in the course of ages; they culminate and wane; they run out their course, or pass into new varieties. (See Hecker's *Epidemics of the Middle Ages*.) Whether or not this may have been the case with the old Jewish leprosy we need not at present inquire. Dr. Robinson says: "Within the Zion gate of "Jerusalem, a little towards the right, are some miserable hovels, inhabited by "persons called leprous. Whether their disease is or is not the leprosy of "Scripture I am unable to affirm; the symptoms described to us were similar "to those of elephantiasis. At any rate they are pitiable objects, and miserable "outcasts from society. They all live here together, and intermarry only with 'each other." (*Biblical Researches*, vol. i., 359.) We ourselves saw the poor creatures, and noted the erosive and dismembering nature of their malady. The disease riots tubercularly and ulceratingly, attacking and destroying feature after feature of the face, and the fingers and the toes, and other parts, till ' the patient becomes a hideous spectacle, and falls in pieces.' (See Michaelis's *Mosaisches-Recht*, §§ 208, 209.)

Beseeching Him, and kneeling down to Him, and saying unto Him, If Thou willest, Thou art able to cleanse me. The disease was correctly regarded, not only as constituting a ceremonial uncleanness, but also as embodying a real physical impurity. Hence when the leper applied to the Saviour for cleansing, he did not refer to ceremonial purification, which a priest alone could confer. He made exclusive reference to physical purification, which would consist in restoration to such a normal state of health as, when acknowledged by the priest, would be his passport into the privilege of living in communion with the population at large, as an admitted member of society. When he said to our Lord, *Thou art able to cleanse me*, he manifested, as Alexander remarks, a very high degree of faith in our Lord's Divine or Messianic power. Leprosy stood apart by itself from all other diseases, as a malady that signally manifested the judicial displeasure of God (see 2 Kings v. 27; 2 Chron. xxvi. 19-21). It was admitted to be in general incurable. When the afflicted man said, *If Thou willest*, he admitted that he did not know whether it might be within the range of our Lord's mission, or within the scope of His aim and intent, to grant relief to such a humiliated and outcast class of sufferers as that to which he belonged. *We* know; but *he* did not.

Ver. 41. And being moved with compassion. An exceedingly fine translation (σπλαγχνισθείς), far exceeding the renderings of all the older English versions.

He put forth His hand, and touched him. The evangelist pictures the act, and you see it. The Saviour did not fear contamination from contact with the leper;

him, I will; be thou clean. 42 And as soon as he had spoken, immediately the leprosy departed from him, and he was cleansed. 43 And he straitly charged him, and forthwith sent him away; 44 and saith unto him, See thou say nothing

and surely, if it was competent to the priest, in administering ceremonial purification, to touch the healed patient (see Lev. xiv.), much more was it competent to our Lord, and a becoming thing, when imparting real purification, to touch lovingly and sympathetically the patient whom it was His pleasure to heal. He was, as Hegendorphinus says, *the Lord of the law (dominus legis)*. The touch would be moreover, at once to the patient himself and to the onlookers, an optical indication and demonstration of the actual transit of the healing virtue from the curer to the cured.

And saith unto him, I will, be thou cleansed. He spoke with sublime fiat, calmly and collectedly, and in the full consciousness of His perfect power.

Ver. 42. **And immediately the leprosy departed from him, and he was cleansed.** The cure was instantaneous and complete. It would be a grand spectacle, and fitted to arouse, to the highest pitch, enthusiasm and expectation in the onlookers. Wakefield, misapprehending the bearing of Matthew's expression (viii. 3) on the phraseology of Mark, translates the clause, absurdly enough, thus: *the leprosy went from the man and was cleansed.*

Ver. 43. **And He strictly charged him.** The evangelist's word is a very strong one (ἐμβριμησάμενος), and was originally employed to denote, onomatopoetically, the mutter or rumble-grumbling growl of chafed or fretted beasts or persons. (Compare the kindred Latin word *fremo*.) As here used it indicates that the Saviour spoke to the man peremptorily, and with a kind of unmistakeable sternness in His tone. The man would doubtless need to be thus addressed. Not unlikely he would be far too demonstrative in his gratitude, and going beyond bounds at once in his words and in his actions. Perhaps, forgetting himself, and losing sight of the fact that he was still ceremonially unclean, and must continue so until the priest should examine him and pronounce him to be clean, he may have prostrated himself and clasped the feet of our Lord, or he may have pushed himself too near the person of our Lord, or too near the persons of those who were surrounding our Lord. Hence he might require to be somewhat sternly repressed. Young renders the expression, *sternly charged him*. Mace, *severely charging him*. Coverdale, *forbad him strately*. Comp. Matt. ix. 30.

And straightway sent him out. Or, *and immediately dismissed him*. The original expression in this clause too is strong. It is literally, *and immediately threw him out* (ἐξέβαλεν αὐτόν). Our Saviour probably required to be exceedingly peremptory with the man, giving him to understand that it would be abusing the grace that had been showed him, were he to come, just as he was, in contact with the persons of others, or to persist in a premature and unauthorized attempt to attach himself to his Deliverer as one of His personal attendants.

Ver. 44. **And saith to him, See thou say nothing to any man.** Literally, *to no one*, an instance of the double negative. The Saviour's fame as an exorcist

to any man : but go thy way, shew thyself to the priest, and offer for thy cleansing those things which Moses commanded, for a testimony unto them. 45 But he went out, and began to

and healer had already got wind enough, and more than enough. It was in danger of blowing into a perfect hurricane of popularity. A check was therefore needed. There was a tendency to attach too much importance to the merely physical element of the work in which He was engaged ; the far more important moral and spiritual elements were scarcely at all apprehended. Hence confusion in the minds and hearts of the people. Speedily, very likely, would they begin to weary, waiting for the tide of events ; they would seek to precipitate results. *Was not this the long-looked-for Deliverer ? Is He not the true Messiah? Should we not have Him instantly enthroned ?* (John vi. 15.) *If we had Him but once crowned, He would put all things to rights in the nation, and in all other nations too ! The sooner, surely, the better !* It was thus no wonder that the Saviour said to the enthusiastic person before Him, *See thou say nothing to any one*. His injunction shows us that certain truths may be unseasonably and prematurely promulgated. "Gol," says Petter, "is sometimes glorified by "a discreet concealment of some truth for a time, as well as by the bold and "constant confession of it at other times." A moral preparation is not infrequently needed to pave the way for the enunciation or publication of certain deep-drawing truths, which, without that preparation, would be misunderstood and misapplied. The transit from the esoteric to the exoteric must be wisely timed and tended.

But go thy way. Or, *go away*. So the word is rendered in John vi. 67, xiv. 28. It is rendered *get thee hence* in Matt. iv. 10, the rendering of Tyndale and the Geneva in the passage before us.

Show thyself to the priest. Namely, in Jerusalem, that he may professionally examine thee and authoritatively pronounce thee clean. See Lev. xiii. and xiv.

And offer for thy cleansing what things Moses enjoined. These are specified in Lev. xiv. 1–32. *Offer*, or *present*. The things were to be presented through the priest unto God, as an acknowledgment of the grace of God. *For thy cleansing :* that is, *for the sake of thy (ceremonial) cleansing*. See Lev. xiv. 14. The expression is literally *concerning thy cleansing*, or still more literally, *about*, or *round about, thy cleansing* (περί). The ceremonial cleansing of the man is regarded as the *central* object contemplated in the entire circle of the ceremonies that required to be observed.

For a testimony to them. Act thus, in order that the officiating priest, and the other officials who are associated with him, may learn the facts that are transpiring in Galilee. These facts have an important bearing upon the fulness of the time and the fulfilment of the Scriptures.

Ver. 45. But he went out. From where ? Fritzsche and Meyer say from *the house* where the miracle had been wrought; so Patrizi. But it is not certain that the miracle had been wrought in a house. It might have been difficult for a leper, contact with whom occasioned uncleanness, to get into any house where our Saviour was likely to be. It is therefore enough for us to say, with Maldonato, that *the leper went out* from the place where the cure had been effected,

publish *it* much, and to blaze abroad the matter, insomuch that Jesus could no more openly enter into the city, but was without in desert places: and they came to him from every quarter.

---

and thus, as Volkmar puts it, from the circle of people who were round about the Saviour.

And began to publish (it) much. It is better to leave out the supplementary *it*, and to carry forward the reference of the verb to the noun that is specified in the immediately succeeding clause. So Grimm. The adverbial word translated *much* is plural in the original (πολλά). It is rendered *many things* by Tyndale and in the Geneva version; and it is strangely rendered *in many places* by Godwin. It just means *much*, however, the quantitative idea going naturally over into the qualitative or intensive. Comp. Mark iii. 12; v. 10, 23, 43; ix. 26; Rom. xvi. 6, 12; 1 Cor. xvi. 12. Elsner would translate the word *vehemently* (*vehementer*). When the evangelist says that the man '*began* to publish much,' he draws our attention, graphically, to the commencement of his career, and then leaves the continuation of it to go off, under our eyes as it were, into the unseen.

And to blaze abroad the matter. Or rather, *the account* (viz. of the matter). The expression *blaze abroad* is a happy and striking translation (διαφημίζειν). King James's English translators got it from the Rheims. Wycliffe gives a duplicate version, ' diffame (or *puplishe*).'

Insomuch that He—our Authorized and Revised versions, after Tyndale, replace the pronoun with the name *Jesus*, for the sake of perspicuity—**insomuch that Jesus could no more openly enter into a city.** *Into a city*, not *into the city*, as in the preceding English versions. The meaning is *into any city*, as Rilliet renders it (*dans aucune ville*). So too Patrizi. The literal translation would be *into town*; only this phrase had not quite the same idiomatic import among the Greeks that it has in English. *Into towns* would bring out the idea intended. Jesus, says the evangelist, *could not* enter openly into towns. The language is popular. The inability was, as metaphysicians would say, not physical but moral; not absolute, but upon a condition. Our Lord could not, in consistency with the high moral and spiritual aims which He had in view. He could not, because the moment that His presence was recognised in a town He was liable to be surrounded and hemmed in by a surging crowd of ignorant and ignorantly expectant gazers, wonderers, and volunteer followers. One sees now how wise it was to tell the leper to hold his tongue. The phrase *no more*, in the expression *He could no more openly enter into towns*, has reference to the particular period spoken of; it was a period that continued only for a limited season. See chap. ii. 1.

But was without in desert places. Now here and now there. He *was* in these places *continuously* (ἦν); He *continued* in them. *Without:* out of town, out of towns.

And they came to Him from all parts. The people *kept coming* to Him (ἤρχοντο), notwithstanding the difficulty of reaching Him, and the inconveniences connected with a sojourn, even for a very limited period, in an unpopulated district.

CHAPTER II.

1 AND again he entered into Capernaum after *some* days;

CHAPTER II.

So far as Chapter I. carries us into the career of our Lord, we find Him pursued by a most inconvenient amount of popular enthusiasm and curiosity. The whole district of Galilee was heaving and ringing with excitement concerning Him. *Is this 'He'? Who else can it be? Surely it must be 'He'! The day at length is dawning! Soon shall the Romans be put down! Soon shall God's people be exalted! The kingdom of heaven is at hand! Is not this the Son of David, and the King of the kingdom, though in disguise?* His fame thrilled almost instantaneously all over the region, and ran along vibrating chords into the surrounding localities.

These were the beginnings of things. But other elements soon sprang up. When once both high and low were fairly waked up into interest, and were straining their minds to comprehend ' who this should be,' the ecclesiastical formalists and critics found multitudes of things, both in our Lord's words and works, which did not fit into the angles of their preconceived notions. Hence came collision; and this collision grew, and grew, till Christ was crucified, and Judaism was shivered into pieces, and a new spiritual constitution of things was inaugurated. The first shocks of collision are exhibited in a variety of scenes, which are consecutively depicted from the beginning of this second chapter down to the sixth verse of the third. Had the chapters been more skilfully bounded off by Hugo de Sancto Caro, the second would have extended over the first six verses of the third.

The scene that is depicted in chap. ii. 1-12 is also depicted by Matthew, chap. ix. 1-8, and by Luke, v. 17-26. Michelsen contends that the paragraph bears marks of an overhauling by the Deutero-Markus. (*Het Evangelie van Markus*, pp. 88-90.) This is however an entirely arbitrary supposition. The paragraph only bears marks of a plurality of subjective factors in the mind and memory of the one Mark.

VER. 1. **And when He entered again into Capernaum after a lapse of days.** Or, *after a time*. Literally, *through days*. Tyndale's version is, *after a feawe dayes*; Coverdale's, *after certayne dayes*. (See L. Bos, *Exercitat. Phil.*, in loc.)

It was reported. Literally, *it was heard*. So Wycliffe; only he has it in the present tense, *it i*·*herd*. Every report is two-sided; it is something said and something *heard*. The English phrase exhibits the one side of the reality, the Greek the other.

That He was in the house. Such is the free translation of our Authorized and Revised versions. The demonstrative particle *that*, however, is 'recitative' in the original. It introduces the citation of the report heard, in the 'direct' orm of reporting; and hence the verb, in the original, is in the present tense, *Ie is*, not *He was*. Hence too the *that* is superfluous in English, as being in our idiom the introductory formula of an 'indirect' report. *It was reported,*

ST. MARK II.

and it was noised that he was in the house. 2 And straightway many were gathered together, insomuch that there was no room to receive *them*, no, not so much as about the door:

'*He is in the house*'; or more literally, '*He is into the house*'; or more literally still, '*He is into house*' (εἰς οἶκόν ἐστιν). Neither of the three translations, however, does full justice to the original idiom. So far as the preposition *into* is concerned, we may retain it, usage in some places at least allowing it. It indicates the *motion* that preceded the *rest*; *He has gone* '*into*' *the house, and is* '*in*' *it.* But we cannot say *into house*, as the Germans say *zu Hause* or *nach Hause*; and yet our phrase *into the house* points, as a phrase, determinately to some particular house, an idea that is not phraseologically involved in the Greek expression. Of course the Saviour was in some particular house, most probably Peter's; but the evangelist's phrase does not bring out this fact into prominence. It indicates more, however, than would be indicated by our expression, *He is into a house*. His meaning very much accords with our English idiomatic expression *in town*, or *into town*, only instead of the generic idea of *town* we have the specific idea of *house*. If our idiom would have allowed us to say *in house* or *into house*, as we say *in town* or *into town*, there would have been a perfect correspondence between the English and Greek expressions. *Into town* does not mean *into a town*, and hence Wycliffe's, Tyndale's, and Godwin's translation ('in a house'), and Euthymius Zigabenus's interpretation (εἰς οἶκόν τινα), are wrong. Lachmann, Tischendorf, Tregelles, suppose that the original expression was *in house* (ἐν οἴκῳ), instead of *into house* (εἰς οἶκον). They have the authority of the important manuscripts א B D L, 33; but, as the reading of the Received Text is obviously the more rugged, and in some respect the more difficult of the two, it is to be presumed that it would be the original. Hence Meyer, Lange, Alford retain it. A transcriber might readily turn the more rugged phrase into the smoother, thinking that he was doing no harm; but it is more difficult to imagine that he would wilfully transmute a smooth, correct, and easy-going reading into one that was rugged and peculiar. The Alexandrine manuscript (A), and the Ephraemi (C), and the rest of the uncials, with the exception of א B D L, read *into*, not *in*.

VER. 2. In the Received Text and the Authorized English version we read **And straightway.** But Lachmann and Tregelles query the genuineness of the *straightway* or *immediately*; and Tischendorf throws it out, in his eighth edition. Bengel too was in doubt about it; and Mill condemned it as "irreptitious" (p. clii.). It is omitted by the manuscripts א B L, 33, and by the Vulgate, Coptic, Syriac Peshito, Armenian, and Æthiopic versions. The word is a favourite with Mark (see chap. i. 21), and seems to drop down very naturally into the expression before us. But for this very reason it is more likely that it would be added, than that it would be subtracted, by transcribers.

Many were gathered together. Entering with oriental freedom into the house where the Saviour was. It would be a humble house; and the public apartment, or family room, in which our Saviour would be seated, was soon crowded to the door.

Insomuch that there was no longer room, not even about the door. So great

and he preached the word unto them. 3 And they come unto him, bringing one sick of the palsy, which was borne of four. 4 And when they could not come nigh unto him for the press,

and closely packed was the crowd, inside and outside. The evangelist makes us spectators of the scene, just *as if we were present, and looking on*. We see the public room rapidly filling up, till it is crowded to the door. The people, however, still come flocking toward the door (πρὸς τὴν θύραν) and choke up the whole space around, till there is no longer (μηκέτι) room. Those who are outside stretch their necks eagerly to get a glimpse of the Rabbi, or to catch something that He says.

And He spake the word to them. *The word*, in the collective import of the term, the import which it bears when the reference is to *vocables* '*laid*' *in order* (λόγος from λέγω. Compare the Latin *lego* and the Anglo-Saxon *lecgan*; compare also the Latin *sermo*). It is some particular *word* that is referred to, '*the* word.' It was what Luke and Paul so often call *the word of God*. It was no doubt *the word of truth, the word of the truth of the gospel* (Col. i. 5), *the word of the kingdom* (Matt. xiii. 19), *the 'good-spell' regarding the kingdom of heaven*. Our Saviour *spake the word*. Note the term *spake*, or *was speaking*. It is in the imperfect tense, and intimates that He was engaged in speaking when the occurrence just about to be narrated took place. The term *preached* employed in King James's version summons up before our imagination more of the nature of *a public proclamation* or *harangue* than is indicated by the evangelist's expression. The Saviour was in a private house, and sat *talking* to the people. Such is the import of the term (ἐλάλει).

VER. 3. And there come (persons) bringing to Him a paralytic (ἔρχονται φέροντες πρὸς αὐτὸν παραλυτικόν). The expression *to Him* does not necessarily mean *up to Him* or *into His immediate presence*. The preposition denotes, as Webster says (*Gram*., p. 183), 'the direction of motion.' Hence the saying of our Lord in John xii. 32, 'and I, if I be lifted up, will draw all men *unto Me*.' The direction of the drawing, rather than the accomplished result, is indicated. *Borne of four:* he would be suspended on his pallet between two pairs of bearers; a bearer would have hold of each corner.

VER. 4. And when they could not come nigh to Him for the crowd. The Vulgate version is, *et cum non possent offerre eum illi præ turba, and when they could not bring (him) to Him because of the crowd*. It represents a very ancient reading (προσενέγκαι instead of προσεγγίσαι), the reading of ℵ B L, 33, and also of the Philoxenian Syriac, and the Coptic, and Æthiopic versions. It has been taken into the text by Tischendorf in his eighth edition; Ewald accepts it. Certainly it seems to be the more difficult reading of the two, as there is no noun or pronoun to represent the person whom they wished to lay before the Lord. Volkmar however thinks that it has arisen from comparing the expression in Luke v. 18. Unlikely. But the reading itself is likely. That of the Received Text runs smoother, and would not be so likely to be voluntarily modified on the one hand, or unintentionally misread on the other, in a somewhat carelessly written manuscript.

they uncovered the roof where he was : and when they had

They uncovered the roof where He was. Very literally, *they unroofed the roof where He was*. They undid the roofing at the spot which was right in front of the place where He was sitting. Purvey has a picturesque translation, *thei unheeliden the roof*,—the verb *to heel* or *heal* meaning originally *to cover*. (The *heel* is a peculiarly *covered* part of the body; he who is *healed* is *recovered*.) The Gothic version is not unlike Purvey's, *andhulidedun hrot*. As to the *hrot* or *roof*, which was partially uncovered, Shaw the traveller supposed it to be the awning that is sometimes drawn over the quadrangular court, around which larger houses are built. He supposed that our Saviour would be sitting and teaching in the court below, and that the bearers of the paralytic, leaning over the terrace of the house, would fold back a portion of the awning, and then let down (by ropes), not 'through the tiles,' but '*by the side* of the tiles,' the couch of the patient. (*Travels in Barbary and the Levant*, vol. i., pp. 381–6, ed. 1808.) The supposition, when laid hold of by the imagination, forms itself readily into an interesting picture. But it is too romantic, and invested with too much 'pomp of circumstance.' It proceeds on the assumption that our Saviour *was in a great house*, where there was ample accommodation, with many of the appliances of luxury. Dr. Kitto modifies, and in some respects exaggerates, Dr. Shaw's conception. He supposes with Dr. Shaw that the people were gathered together in the quadrangular court of a great house; but he thinks it probable that Jesus, instead of sitting in the midst of the people in the court, was occupying a commanding position in the gallery or verandah that ran round the second storey of the house. "The roofing of this gallery "was distinct from that of the house," and "of very slight construction." "We think therefore that the men, having mounted to the terraced roof, pro- "ceeded to remove a part of this light roofing of the gallery, over the place "where Jesus sat below." (*Pictorial Bible*, on Luke v.) Webster and Wilkinson adopt what is substantially Dr. Kitto's view; Bishop Wordsworth too. But it is inconsistent with the humble position in society of the occupants of the house; and it does violence, moreover, to the phraseology of the representation. Even the supposition of Lightfoot, Bland, Meyer, Bisping, and many others, that our Saviour must have been in an 'upper room' is entirely arbitrary, and improbable too; more particularly improbable when we take the crowding around the door into account. The house would doubtless be a very humble one, a mere cottage. When Alexander says that 'eastern houses are always built around an open court,' he writes under an entire misapprehension. Such a mode of construction is indeed the prevailing style for the larger class of houses; *but for them only*. The cottages of the mass of the people, and especially in the villages and hamlets, are quite different, and are really very humble, low roofed, one-storeyed residences, opening directly, without any intervening porch or vestibule, into the one apartment of which they consist, though sometimes there is an inner apartment; and in other cases there is a confused aggregation of subordinate apartments, stretching backward, and sometimes under distinct roofs, like cot attached to cot. With a little agility, and, if need be, with some simple appliance far less elaborate than the application of a ladder, there would be no difficulty at all in getting on the flat roof of the fisher-

broken *it* up, they let down the bed wherein the sick of the

---

man's cottage. There would be just as little in undoing such a portion of the roofing as would be needed to admit of the descent of the paralytic on his couch. The flippant objections which have been persistently urged by Woolston (*Miracles*, iv. p. 57), Strauss, (*Leben*, § 92), Bruno Bauer (*Kritik*, § 35), and other scoffers, are founded on an entire misconception of oriental house construction, in the sphere of the humbler classes of society. See next clause.

And when they had broken it up. Or, more literally, *and when they broke it up*. The word thus translated (ἐξορύξαντες) explains, more particularizingly, what it was which they did to the portion of the roof which they removed. They *dug it out*, or *scooped it out*. (See Gal. iv. 15; Matt. xxi. 33, xxv. 18; Mark xii. 1.) A more appropriate term could not have been selected, even by Thucydides or Xenophon. The roofs of the humble class of oriental houses are such that *digging* or *scooping* is necessary whenever there is the intent to effect an entrance. And such *digging* or *scooping* does no injury whatever to the fabric. Dr. Robinson, speaking of the district about Lebanon, says: "The flat roofs of "the houses in this region are constructed by laying, first, large beams at in- "tervals of several feet; then rude joists; on which again are arranged small "poles close together, or brushwood; and upon this is spread earth or gravel "rolled hard. This rolling is often repeated, especially after rain; for these "roofs are apt to leak. For this purpose a roller of stone is kept ready for use "on the roof of every house. Grass is often seen growing on these roofs." (*Later Researches*, p. 39.) Referring to his lodging in Jerjû'a, on the way between Beirut and 'Akka, he says: "Like all the other houses of the village, it "had but one storey. . . . The roof was of the usual kind, supported by rude "props. It rained heavily during the night; and the water found its way "through upon us. Quite early in the morning we heard our host at work "rolling the roof; and saw the same process going on with other houses. "Goats also were cropping the grass growing on several roofs." (*Later Researches*, p. 44.) "We must banish from our minds," says Dr. W. M. Thomson, "every form of European or American houses. . . . All that it is necessary for "us to know is that the roof was flat, low, easily reached, and easily opened, so "as to let down the couch of the sick man; and all these points are rendered in- "telligible by an acquaintance with modern houses in the villages of Palestine." (*The Land and the Book*, pp. 358, 359.) In some cases, says Dr. Thomson (p. 359), stone slabs are laid across the joisting; and in the case before us there had been slabs of tile or dried clay underneath the thick compost of earth and gravel. (See Luke v. 19.) The roofs of the houses in Palestine required, and require, to be *thick* for the same reason that the people require to wear thick turbans on their heads,—to keep out, as far as possible, the heat.

They let down the bed whereon the paralytic was lying. "Examine," says Dr. W. M. Thomson, "one of the houses of the modern villages in this same "region, and you will see at once that the thing is natural and easy to be "accomplished. The roof is only a few feet high; and by stooping down, and "holding the corners of the couch (merely a thickly padded quilt, as at present "in this region) they would let down the sick man without any apparatus of "ropes or cords to assist them." (*The Land and the Book*, p. 358.) When

palsy lay. 5 When Jesus saw their faith, he said unto the sick of the palsy, Son, thy sins be forgiven thee. 6 But there were certain of the scribes sitting there, and reasoning in their

---

Woolston wildly depicts the danger of 'a broken pate,' incurred by our Lord and His disciples during the process, from 'the falling of the tiles,' he simply allows his flippancy to run riotous. The word translated *bed* (κράβαττος, such is its correct form) was an unclassical term for a narrow couch or litter, on which only one person could lie. (It corresponds to the Attic σκίμπους. See *Phrynichus* in voc., and *Lobeck* in loc., p. 62.)

VER. 5. **And Jesus seeing their faith.** The faith of the whole party, consisting of the paralytic himself and of his friends who had acted with him and for him. Jesus could look into their hearts and see; and no doubt He did thus look; but at the same time their inward faith was signally manifested by their outward acts.

Saith to the paralytic, Son, thy sins are forgiven. Or, *have been forgiven*. The verb is in the indicative mood of the perfect passive, Doric form (ἀφέωνται). If however we should adopt the reading of Tischendorf and Tregelles (ἀφίενται), the translation will be *thy sins are forgiven*. If this latter reading be accepted, the Lord is represented as referring to a present occurrence, *thy sins are forgiven* (viz. now). If the reading of the Received Text be retained, the Lord is represented as referring to a past occurrence, *thy sins have been forgiven* (viz. from the moment when thy faith began). The Received reading has the support of a great majority of the important manuscripts. The other has the support of the Vatican manuscript, and of 'the queen of the cursives' (33), and of the Syriac versions, and the Vulgate, and the Coptic. The Lord, looking into the heart of the afflicted man, saw that he was more distressed on account of his sins than of his sickness; and so He first of all spoke peace to his conscience. Not unlikely the young man had been foolish, possibly he had brought his disease upon himself by means of his sins; but he was now penitent, and a firm believer in the Messiah, superadding to his general faith the specific conviction that the Messiah was before him in the person of Jesus. Jesus calls him *son*, or more literally, *child*, partly no doubt because he was young, but principally, as we may believe, because there was a beautiful filial confidence in his heart.

VER. 6. **But there were certain of the scribes sitting there.** They had scented heresy from afar, and had come to pry censoriously and inquisitorially into the teaching of the wonderful upstart Rabbi. See Luke v. 17. They "carried," says Trapp, "gall in their ears." On the word *scribes*, see chap. i. 22.

And reasoning in their hearts. The reference of the expression *their hearts* is simply and generically to *the interior sphere* of their complex being, not specifically to the sphere of the affections. They *reasoned*: the term is graphic in the original. They *started a dialogue with themselves* within their own minds (διαλογιζόμενοι). *Themselves spoke to themselves*, as it were, but with bated breath.

hearts, 7 Why doth this *man* thus speak blasphemies? who can forgive sins but God only? 8 And immediately when Jesus perceived in his spirit that they so reasoned within

---

VER. 7. **Why doth this Man thus speak? He blasphemes.** He does an injury to the fame of God; He detracts from the true glory of God. "Blasphemy," says Sir George Mackenzie, in his *Laws and Customs of Scotland in matters Criminal* (Tit. iii. § 1), "is called in law, *Divine lese Majesty* or *Treason*; and "it is committed either (1) by denying that of God which belongs to Him as "one of His attributes, or (2) by attributing to Him that which is absurd, and "inconsistent with His Divine nature," or, as it may be added (3), by assuming to oneself, or ascribing to others, what is an incommunicable property or prerogative of God. It is with a reference to this third form of the crime that the word is used in the passage before us. See next clause.

Who can forgive sins except One, even God? It is God's incommunicable prerogative to forgive sins, to *dismiss* them from the sinner, as the original word signifies (ἀφιέναι). Men may forgive trespasses that have been committed against themselves in so far as they are injuries done to themselves. But these trespasses, besides being injuries to men, are sins against God. So far indeed as they are sins at all, they are *relative only to God*. (Ps. li. 4.) None but He, therefore, can forgive them. In this fundamental idea the censorious scribes were right; but then in all other respects they were wrong. They were censoriously presumptuous in rushing to the conclusion that the wonderful Personage before them had neither power nor authority to forgive sins. Why not justly judge of Him by His works, instead of censoriously criticising His mere words?

VER. 8. **And immediately Jesus, perceiving in His spirit that they so reasoned within themselves.** He had an intuitive perception of the contents of their hearts; and, by explicitly presenting these contents to their recognition, He implicitly rebuked them for their unwillingness to acknowledge the supernatural element that was characterizing Him. We may either say, on the one hand, "instantly perceiving '*in*' *His spirit*" (Jelf), or, on the other, "instantly perceiving '*by*' *His spirit*" (Le Clerc, Beausobre et L'Enfant), or '*with*' *His spirit* (Piscator, Heumann, Volkmar), or '*through*' *His spirit* (Bisping). The dative case employed may be either 'the *where* case' or 'the *how* case.' It is not likely that the locality idea is here intended; for, of course, perception or knowledge can never be localized anywhere but *in the spirit*, and there would therefore be no significancy in the specification. We should undoubtedly render the expression *by His spirit*, a rendering that brings into prominence *in what way* it was that our Lord read the hearts of His censors. It was not by what His ears heard or His eyes saw. It was not by means of any of those outward things that are objective to our percipient 'senses'; His knowledge did not reach Him in that circuitous way, by the route of any of 'the five gateways' in the periphery of the complex person. It was direct, the knowledge of spirit by spirit. Wells translates the expression *by His spirit*, and explains it as meaning *by His Divine spirit*. Potter gives the same explanation, *by His Divine nature*. Grotius contends at length, and learnedly, for the same explanation.

9] ST. MARK II. 43

themselves, he said unto them, Why reason ye these things in your hearts ? 9 Whether is it easier to say to the sick of the palsy, *Thy* sins be forgiven thee ; or to say, Arise, and take up

---

So Euthymius Zigabenus (πνεῦμα ἐνταῦθα τὴν θεότητα καλεῖ) ; and Erasmus (*Paraphrase*); and Calvin ; Bengel also, and Calmet, and many others. Elsner, on the other hand, thinks that there is a reference to *the Holy Spirit*, which was given to our Lord without measure. The same view was taken by Wycliffe, who hence translates the expression *by the Holy Goost*. Dionysius à Ryckel oscillates between the two interpretations, but tends toward the former. The reference to the Holy Spirit is altogether improbable. Neither is there any reason to believe that the evangelist was formally referring, in the spirit of a systematic theologian, to the Divine nature of our Lord, as distinguished from the spiritual element of His human nature. He was not formulating to himself the distinction of the two natures, although it no doubt lay embedded in his thoughts as the logical substrate of his representations. He simply makes reference, indefinitively and generically, to the inner and invisible or spiritual element of our Lord's complex being. In virtue of that element, and by means of it, our Lord saw at a glance through all interposing veils. He saw things as they really were. Materialisms were transparent to Him. So were the spiritual inwrappings of things, even in the hearts that were most coiled up and self involved. He ' needed not that any should testify of man ; for He knew what was in man.' (John ii. 25.)

Saith unto them, **Why reason ye these things in your hearts?** *Why reason ye* (διαλογίζεσθε)? Why put questions and give answers to yourselves, in the way that ye are doing? *In your hearts :* that is, *within yourselves.* See the preceding clause. It is as if He had said, *in your minds,* or, still more exactly, *in the heart of your being.*

VER. 9. **Which is easier? to say to the paralytic, ‘Thy sins have been forgiven,' or to say, ‘Arise, and take up thy bed and walk'?** The Saviour, in the most felicitous manner imaginable, brings the case to the simplest of issues. There was no need for any long discussion. The whole matter could be settled by a few words. The inward could be certified by the outward, without any circumlocution ; the upward could be reflected by the downward, immediately ; the invisible could be manifested in the visible, just at once. And if therefore it would be more satisfactory to them, or would carry more of the evidence of Divine authority, He could speak a few words of fiat in reference to the visible and downward and outward; and He would do that just as easily as He had authoritatively said *thy sins have been forgiven.* They might call in question His authority to say *thy sins have been forgiven,* inasmuch as they could not actually see the dismissal of the sins. But if when He said, *Arise, take up thy bed and walk,* they could see with their eyes that the fiat was fulfilled, then surely they would have no just reason for calling in question the fulness of the Divine authority that was behind all that He was saying and doing. When the resources of Divinity are available, it is just as easy to move a mountain as to remove a molehill, to cancel the liabilities of a soul as to strike off the fetters of a body. King James's translation, *whether is it easier,*

thy bed, and walk? 10 But that ye may know that the
Son of man hath power on earth to forgive sins, (he saith to
the sick of the palsy,) 11 I say unto thee, Arise, and take up

---

is not nearly so literal as Coverdale's, *whether is easier*, that is, *which of the
two is easier.* Coverdale reproduces Luther's translation (*welches ist leichter*).
Instead of the word *walk,* or *walk about* (περιπάτει) at the close of the verse,
Tischendorf reads *go thy way* (ὕπαγε), under the sanction of the Sinaitic manuscript and a few other authorities. The Cambridge manuscript and 'the queen
of the cursives' (33) read *go thy way to thy house.* Both the fuller reading,
however, and the briefer seem to have been borrowed from ver. 11. Not unlikely they had originally been jotted down as marginal explanations of the
word that is found in the Received Text.

VER. 10. **But that ye may know.** Godwin, overlooking or misapprehending
the nature of the word translated *ye may know*, renders it *ye may see.* The
word indeed has obviously enough a primary reference to *seeing*, but it does
not mean *I see.* It is in the perfect tense, and thus originally meant *I have
seen*, that is, *I know.* We have no alternative between the two translations *that
ye may have seen* and *that ye may know.*

That the Son of Man has power on earth—or, rather, *has authority upon the
earth*—to forgive sins. Mark the word *authority* (ἐξουσίαν). The Saviour is not
referring to a matter of mere *power.* Mere power might suffice for removing
paralysis from a paralytic; but the forgiveness of sins is a moral act, connecting
itself with a moral system, and having to do therefore with moral rights and
liabilities. Hence the idea of law comes in; and thus the power to forgive sins
must be more than mere power or omnipotence. It must be power *that is lawful* (ἔξεστι). Such power is *right*, and hence it is, in the highest sense of the
phrase, *a right.* It may however be either an original or a derived right. In the
Saviour's case it was both. Viewed as Divine, He had the right in Himself.
Viewed as Messiah, He had authority from the Father, His authority being
authorization. The Father was the *author* of the *authority* (Matt. xxviii. 18,
John xvii. 2; comp. Matt. viii. 9, Luke vii. 8). No doubt the Saviour refers
here to His mediatorial authorization, although, in the substrate of things, this
authorization reposed on His own intrinsic right.

He saith to the paralytic. This is a parenthetic note of the evangelist, turning our attention to the sublime transition in the Saviour's address.

VER. 11. **I say unto thee, Arise, take up thy bed, and go thy way to thy house.**
Or, as Tyndale picturesquely has it (1526), *Aryse, and take up thy beed, and get
the hens in to thyne awne housse.* How thoroughly conscious the Saviour must
have been of His Divine authority and power! His whole influence in the
country and the world at large, in the age and for all ages, lay trembling
as it were in the balance, and perilled so to speak on the result of His fiat. If
failure had been the result, His humiliation would have been overwhelming and
final. The supposed blasphemy of His assumption in reference to the forgiveness of sins would have been demonstrated. The triumph of His censors would
have been complete and legitimate. This being obviously the case, He must
have known, ere He spoke, that there was really no peril; otherwise, His fiat

13] ST. MARK II. 45

thy bed, and go thy way into thine house. 12 And immediately he arose, took up the bed, and went forth before them all; insomuch that they were all amazed, and glorified God, saying, We never saw it on this fashion. 13 And he went forth again by the sea side; and all the multitude resorted unto him, and he taught them.

---

would have faltered on His tongue, and would indeed have been utterly irreconcilable with the lowest degree of prudence, not to speak of the highest degrees of good sense and sincerity.

VER. 12. **And immediately he arose, and took up the bed, and went forth before all.** "Stoutly making his way," says Lightfoot, "with his bed upon his shoulders." There is some difference of opinion regarding the proper place for the adverb *immediately*. Tischendorf, Tregelles, and Alford insert it in the second clause, *and he arose, and immediately took up the bed*. They have the high authorization of the manuscripts ℵ B C* L, 33. But in a case like the present more evidence would be needed to warrant an alteration of the Received Text. It is not, however, a matter of any exegetical moment.

So that all are amazed, and glorify God, saying, The like of this we never saw! The Geneva version is, *We never saw such a thing!* The Rheims, *We never saw the like!* When it is said that they *glorify God*, the reference is to the exclamations which sprang up to their lips and flew out from their mouths, the moment they witnessed the marvellous transformation of the man's person,— *God be praised! Glory be to God!* At such moments, as on all occasions of very great intensity of feeling, the spirit of man instinctively opens into the presence of the Infinite Spirit. Even in the profane oaths of the wicked and the atheistic, when such persons are roused into intensity of passion, there is a strange, though strangely distorted, recognition of the presence of Divinity. In some wonderful way spirit touches Spirit, and in moments of intensity the touching thrills into consciousness.

VER. 13. For the paragraph that extends from this verse to the 17th, comp. Matt. ix. 9-13, and Luke v. 27-32.

And He went forth again. Namely, from the city of Capernaum. Comp. ver. 1. The *again* has reference to the previous exit that is mentioned in chap. i. 35. Michelsen admits that the entire verse is one of the true connecting links of the Proto-Markus (*een van die tusschenvoegsels van Markus:* p. 148). Doubtless.

By the sea side. Tischendorf, on the single authority of the Sinaitic manuscript, reads *to the sea*. But that, surely, is tilting on its apex the pyramid of textual criticism; more especially as the reading of the Received Text, and of all the other important manuscripts, is the more difficult. The evangelist's expression is condensed, but its meaning is evident,—*Jesus went again out of the city, and walked by the sea side*. Jesus was a lover of nature, at once in its open reaches and its elevated peaks. No wonder. It was His own workmanship.

And all the multitude resorted to Him, and He taught them. Or, more literally, *and all the multitude kept coming to Him, and He kept teaching them*. The

14 And as he passed by, he saw Levi the *son* of Alphæus

multitude of people, whose curiosity and wonder had been excited by the words which they had already heard from His lips, and the works which they had witnessed from His hands, kept crowding after Him and gathering around Him. *And He kept teaching them:* now talking to those of them that had pressed nearest Him, as He walked along, and now perhaps seating Himself on some simple 'coigne of vantage' or some boat drawn up upon the shore, and discoursing to the whole company. Our Lord, as Richard Baxter says, "taught the people and preached the gospel in field-meetings, house-" meetings, mountain-meetings, ship-meetings, synagogue-meetings, and " temple-meetings."

VER. 14. **And passing by.** The evangelist, after narrating in epitome the Lord's journey to the lake, and His walk by its shore, steps back to take up a certain thread of incident which happened on the way.

He saw Levi. The same individual, apparently, who was afterwards known by the name of Matthew; comp. Matt. ix. 9. It was quite customary among the Jews for persons who were entering upon an entirely new career to assume, or to get imposed upon them, a new name, or a surname that had hitherto been lying in comparative abeyance. Hence the names Paul and Peter. Hence too apparently the name Matthew. Some however have supposed that Levi and Matthew were different individuals. This opinion was entertained by Heracleon (Clem. Al., *Strom.*, iv. 9) and Origen (*Cont. Cels.* i., § 376) in ancient times; and by Grotius, Michaelis, and Ewald in modern times. Grotius conjectures that Levi might be a supervisor (ἀρχιτελώνης), like Zaccheus (Luke xix. 2), and that Matthew might be his subordinate officer. Unlikely.

The son of Alphæus. As Alphæus was a common Hebrew name, there is no good reason for assuming with Ewald that the father of Levi was the father of James ' the little,' the apostle (Matt. x. 3).

Sitting at the tax office. Or, as it stands in King James's version, *sitting at the receipt of custom.* The word employed by the evangelist means *customs, office,* or *custom-house* as it were. Principal Campbell renders it *toll-office.* Wycliffe, *tolbothe.* Levi is said to have been *sitting* '*at*' it, or, more literally, *sitting 'on'* it (ἐπὶ τὸ τελώνιον). The preposition 'originally expresses the position of one thing *on* another,' and sometimes, when governing the accusative, the idea of motion is merged. (See Jelf, § 633 and 635-6. Collate Rev. iv. 4, iii. 20.) Levi was *sitting* ' *on* ' *the elevated counter, or* ' *bank*,' *which constituted the central and essential part of the tax-office.* The common shops and banks in the eastern bazaars are somewhat like *box-beds,* ' in ' and ' on ' which, as we have ourselves often witnessed, the shopman or banker sits cross-legged, while either waiting for or actually transacting business. No doubt Levi's tax-office would be something of the same kind; and the elevated platform ' on ' which he would be sitting, being also the counter, bench, or ' bank ' on which the business was done, would be the real *tax-place.* The rest of the ' box-bed ' would be the mere surroundings and incidental conveniences of the ' office.'

And He saith to him, Follow Me. Or, as Wycliffe has it, *Sue Me.* Our Lord would wish Levi to follow Him literally, that is, to take his place behind in the

15] ST. MARK II. 47

sitting at the receipt of custom, and said unto him, Follow
me. And he arose and followed him.

15 And it came to pass, that, as Jesus sat at meat in his house,

---

company of His personal disciples or constant attendants; comp. chap. i. 17.
There is no reason, however, for supposing that our Lord and Levi had never
met before. The abruptness of the call, and the analogy of the case of Peter
and Andrew, would rather lead us to the conclusion that there had been some
previous intimacy. (See John i. 35-42, and Mark i. 16-18.)
And he arose and followed Him. *He suede Him*, says Wycliffe. There was
authority in the Lord's 'call.' Levi felt that it must be obeyed. Honour
moreover was conferred by it, as well as duty imposed; and hence it was gladly
obeyed. Levi however, we may be sure, would not leave the duties of the tax-
office neglected. If he was a subaltern, his place would be easily supplied. If,
as is most probable (see next verse), he was a superior officer, some one or other
of his subordinates would be ready to step into his place, until final arrangements should be made. (See Lightfoot's *Works*, vol. xii., p. 182.)

VER. 15. **And it came to pass.** Or, according to the more probable reading
of the manuscripts ℵ B L, 33, *it comes to pass* (γίνεται). The evangelist takes
us back with him in imagination, and makes us spectators of the scene, just as
it occurs. This present-tense reading is accepted by Tischendorf, Tregelles,
Alford.
That as Jesus sat at meat in his house. Such is the translation in King
James's version. It calls for various remarks. (1) The phrase rendered *as*
(ἐν τῷ) is wanting in the same manuscripts which give the present-tense reading
in the preceding clause; it is wanting in some other authorities besides, and
should be omitted, as it is in the Revised Version. (2) The word *Jesus* is in none
of the manuscripts at all; there is simply the pronoun *he*. It was Tyndale
who substituted the noun for the pronoun, for perspicuity's sake. The Geneva
version followed; and hence our King James's version. There is no doubt,
however, that Tyndale was right in assuming that it is Jesus, and not Levi, who
is referred to. (3) The expression *sat at meat* means literally *was reclining at
table*. The verb is the same as that which occurs in chap. i. 30, 'Simon's
wife's mother *lay* sick of a fever.' See also chap. ii. 4. The Greek and
Roman custom of taking a recumbent posture at table, at least on occasions of
formal entertainments, seems to have been common in Palestine in our Lord's
time; see John xiii. 23. (4) The reference of the pronoun *his*, in the expression *in his house*, has been of late much disputed. Meyer maintains that it
refers to Jesus. So do Holtzmann (*Die synoptischen Ev.*, p. 218), Schenkel
(*Charakterbild*, § 7, 1), Scholten (*Het oudste Evang.*, p. 95), and Volkmar (*Die
Evangelien*, pp. 150, 151). These critics indeed do not forget that Luke says
explicitly that the entertainment was *in the house of Levi* (v. 29); but they think
that Luke 'misunderstood' the Proto-Mark. 'Luke first of all,' says Volkmar, 'misunderstood the expression, and then all succeeding interpreters.'
Fritzsche again is certain that Luke and Mark entirely coincide in their repre
sentation. But, says he, Matthew (ix. 10) represents the entertainment as
being in Christ's own house. But, to one who does not eagerly wish to find

many publicans and sinners sat also together with Jesus and

war among the evangelists, there is not a shadow of evidence that there is the least conflict in the case before us. Fritzsche is obviously right when he asserts that Mark and Luke are at one, and Matthew is as obviously at one with them both. The house was evidently Levi's. It is utterly gratuitous to suppose that Jesus made an entertainment in His own house for 'many publicans and sinners.' (See next clause of the verse.) True, the pronouns of the narrative are not wielded by the evangelist with the highest classical skill. The 'wisdom of words' is absent; and hence, so far as the mere terminology of the first clause of the verse is concerned, there is scope for a fray over the reference of the pronouns. But though there had not been the explicit representation of Luke there would nevertheless be nothing whatever of the similitude of a reason for doubting the intentional reference of Mark, in the second at least of his pronouns. If it be the case that Luke borrowed from Mark, or the 'Proto-Mark,' or, as Michelsen will have it, the Deutero-Mark, then what Holtzmann, Scholten, and Volkmar call his *mistake* was simply his *correct interpretation*.

And many tax collectors and sinners were reclining (*at table*) along with Jesus and His disciples. It was just such a company as might be expected in the house of Levi. *Tax collectors* in particular, and *sinners* in general; all of them persons who made little or no pretension to religiousness. They were simply 'men of the world.' The word translated *publicans* in the Vulgate version, and hence in our English version, means simply *tax collectors* or *officers of revenue*. It occurs only, so far as the New Testament is concerned, in the three synoptic Gospels. The word was a Latin term (*publicani*), denoting the great officers, chiefly belonging to the equestrian order, who farmed the Roman revenue (*publicum habebant*), and paid into the public treasury (*in publicum*) a certain definite sum agreed upon by contract with the government. These *publicani*, who were all wealthy individuals, sublet the tax-gathering to agents (*magistri*), who also became bound by contract to return a given amount of money. These agents again engaged local officers, or *portitores*, to collect the dues. It was these local officers, or *portitores*, who are referred to in the New Testament under the name of τελῶναι. They needed to belong to the native population, that they might know the ways of the people and run little risk of being circumvented. And indeed they almost invariably succeeded in circumventing, oppressing, and fleecing the taxpaying population. They had a definite sum to return to their superiors, and it was needful of course to have a surplusage for their own remuneration. All over the Roman empire they were hated. They were looked upon as the 'bears and wolves' of society. (See Suiceri *Thesaurus*, and Smith's *Bible Dict.* in voc.) But a double and concentrated portion of hate attached to them in Palestine, for many of the people, more especially of the professedly religious sort, maintained that it was an indignity to God for the favourites of heaven to have to pay taxes to a foreign and heathen potentate. Hence none but such as were willing to set the popular patriotism and superstition at defiance could accept the office of tax-gatherers. And all who did accept it lost religious caste instantly and entirely, and were mercilessly driven into the outskirts of religious society, or farther out still. They were 'joined,' says Lightfoot, 'with cut-throats and robbers'

his disciples: for there were many, and they followed him.
16 And when the scribes and Pharisees saw him eat with
publicans and sinners, they said unto his disciples, How is
it that he eateth and drinketh with publicans and sinners?

(*Works*, vol. xi., p. 130). Hence the evangelist associates them with *sinners*, that is, with *such as were emphatically sinners*. The term is used in a plane of things that corresponds to what is related in Luke vii. 37, ' Behold a woman in the city, which was *a sinner*.' We still use the word in a partially corresponding way when we speak of 'saints and *sinners*.' It is too, apparently, on this principle of emphasis that we are to understand John when he says (1 John iii. 9) ' whosoever is born of God *cannot sin*.'

For there were many. The evangelist justifies his expression, '*many* tax-collectors and sinners.' It was, he intimates, literally true. There was a large company, and all of the tabooed class.

And they followed Him. This clause should have been transferred by Robert Stephens, the originator of the verse-divisions of our New Testament, to the commencement of the next verse, and connected with the first words thus, *And there followed Him also scribes of the Pharisees.*

VER. 16. **And there followed Him also scribes of the Pharisees**, or, *the scribes of the Pharisees*. Such is the connection of the clauses given in the text of Tregelles ; and it has been accepted by Tischendorf in his eighth edition. It is, we feel persuaded, the original reading; that of the Received Text being modified after Luke's phraseology. *Certain scribes, scribes belonging to the sect of the Pharisees*, had now got fairly on the inquisitorial scent. They followed our Lord to pry into His private ways. And on the present occasion they seem to have entered, with oriental freedom, into the hall or guestchamber where the company were seated at table. It was the apartment corresponding to the *k'hāwah* of modern Arabian houses, such we mean as belong to the higher and middle or moneyed class of society.

And when they saw that He was eating with the tax collectors and sinners. In the Vatican manuscript, and ' the queen of the cursives,' the indicative of the present tense is employed, *that He is eating* (ἐσθίει).

They said to His disciples, 'He eats with the tax collectors and the sinners!' Such is probably the evangelist's original text. There is however in the manuscripts and the ancient versions an almost bewildering variety of small and practically unimportant modifications and amplifications. Many of the manuscripts, for instance, add *and drinks* to the expression *He eats*. So A C E F H K L M S U, etc. The Vulgate version agrees with these manuscripts; and so do the Peshito Syriac and the Philoxenian Syriac, and the Coptic and Gothic versions. Augustine also notes that the words *and drinks* are found in Mark, though not in Matthew. (*Consensus Evv.*, ii. 27.) They were evidently in his day found in such copies of the Italic text as were in his hands. But on the whole we incline to the conclusion that they were added out of Luke. They are wanting not only in the Vatican manuscript, but also in the Sinaitic and the Cambridge. They are omitted too in those manuscripts of the Old Latin version which are noted *a b e ff*². It is more likely that they would

17 When Jesus heard *it*, he saith unto them, They that are whole have no need of the physician, but they that are sick : I came not to call the righteous, but sinners to repentance.

---

be deliberately added than either intentionally abstracted, or accidentally omitted. Again, some of the best old manuscripts (א C L Δ, 69), as well as the Coptic, Æthiopic, Arabic, and Persic versions read '*Your Master eats and drinks.*' It is an obvious addition from Matthew. Some again, instead of the simple exclamation, *He eats with the tax collectors and sinners !* have, in one form or another, the interrogation, *Does He eat,* or *Why does He eat with the tax collectors and sinners ?* (Tischendorf understands the initial ὅτι as having an interrogative import. But with Michelsen we regard it as simply 'recitative,' and therefore in English untranslatable.) *He eats with the tax collectors and the sinners !* As if that were one of the greatest and most unpardonable of misdemeanours ! As for themselves they had no scruple indeed in taking advantage of the customary oriental freedom that permitted the neighbours to enter the tax gatherer's comfortable *k'hāwah,* or reception-room. And when once inside the chamber they had no scruple in seating themselves on the comfortable matting that would be garnishing the sides of the walls all round. They could freely speak too with the tax gatherer and his company; there was no sin in such things ! But *to eat* with them ! (See Gal. ii. 11-14.) That was altogether a different affair ! It would indeed be one of the pinnacles of profanity, almost as wicked as to commit adultery or to worship idols ! So artificial and angular, and angularly arbitrary, had the notions of the Pharisees become in reference to moral demeanour.

Ver. 17. **And Jesus heard.** We need not say that He *overheard*, for doubtless the censorious scribes, though awed to such a degree by the moral majesty of His bearing that they did not dare to address Himself directly, yet intended for His ear what they said to His disciples.

And saith to them, They who are well have no need of a physician, but they who are unwell. A truism on the physical side of things ; but, for that very reason, of the greatest possible significance in its ethical application. It was the complete explanation, and the unanswerable vindication, of our Saviour's conduct in going into the society of the moral waifs of the population. The validity of the idea which the truism embodies *is* the foundation of all those philanthropic movements which enlist the upper classes of society in the blessed work of bending down to meet in love the lower classes, so that the snapped circle of humanity may be restored. It is the philosophy, in a nutshell, of all home and foreign missionary operations. Christ went among the moral waifs, be it observed, not as a boon companion, but as a physician. The word rendered *a physician* is peculiarly significant in the original, *a healer*. To whom should a healer go, as a healer, but to such as are needing to be healed ? But granted that the tax collectors and the sinners were ' unwell,' were the scribes and Pharisees ' well ' ? Were they ' whole,' or hale ? So thought not Jesus. But so thought many of themselves ; and hence they were not prepared to accept the attentions of the Physician, and take His Divine panacea.

I came not to call the righteous, but sinners. The superadded words, in King

18] ST. MARK II. 51

18 And the disciples of John and of the Pharisees used to

James's version and the Received Text, *to repentance*, were not in the evangelist's autograph. They were subsequently added, as Mill correctly judged (*Prolegom.*, p. cvi.), from Luke v. 32. Augustine, in his *Consensus* (ii., c. 27), notes that they were found only in Luke. They are omitted by Griesbach and Scholz, as well as by Tischendorf, Tregelles, Alford; they were suspected by Erasmus. The supplement brings out, however, into full development the Saviour's idea. It was His aim, in His manward mission, *to speak to men in an inviting way*, that is, *to call them*, in order to prevail with them *to stop in the career which they are pursuing, and to turn toward God and goodness*. When He here says that He 'came not to call the *righteous*,' the term is not used, as Grotius supposed, in its comparative but in its absolute import. They who are only comparatively righteous are also unrighteous. They are sinners; and therefore Jesus came to *call them to repentance*. In the absolutely righteous indeed, wherever they are to be found, the heart of God and of Jesus must have inexpressible interest and delight. But Jesus did not come to the earth to *call* such. They are not to be found on the earth. The Messianic aim of His Father, and of Himself, was to meet the wants of a different class of beings altogether, of *sinners*. The Saviour leaves His censors to consider with themselves whether they were *sinners* or *righteous*. Petter's notion of the word *righteous* is farther aside from the correct idea than that of Grotius; he supposes that it means 'such as think themselves righteous.' Theophylact gives the same interpretation. But it inverts the Saviour's idea. None had greater need than such self-deceivers to be called, and called to repentance. There is no article in the original before the word *righteous*, but we must either supply it in our English idiom, or use some other supplementary expression, such as *righteous persons*.

VER. 18–22. A new paragraph, corresponding to Matt. ix. 14–17 and Luke v. 33–39. It has relation to *fasting*, an important exercise of self-denial when wisely regulated as to time and other circumstances, but an odious bit of self-righteousness when simply regarded as a feat of religious superiority or meritoriousness.

VER. 18. **And John's disciples and the Pharisees were fasting.** Such is the proper translation of the correct text (καὶ ἦσαν οἱ μαθηταὶ Ἰωάννου καὶ οἱ φαρισαῖοι νηστεύοντες). The evangelist connects the Saviour's teaching regarding fasting with an actual fact that had occurred. The disciples of John on the one hand, and the Pharisees on the other, were coincidently fasting. Instead of *were fasting*, King James's translators have *used to fast*. They followed in the wake of the Rheims version. Luther unhappily took the same view of the expression; and Grotius too, and Fritzsche; and Michelsen also, who hence regards the whole first clause of the verse as 'an archæological elucidation' interpolated into the Proto-Markus's text by the Deutero-Markus (*vers* 18$_a$ *is een archeologische opheldering van II-Markus*). Hammond's paraphrase brings out the right idea, *John's disciples and the Pharisees*, '*according to their custom of frequent fasting, were now on a day of fast.*'

fast: and they come and say unto him, Why do the disciples of John and of the Pharisees fast, but thy disciples fast not? 19 And Jesus said unto them, Can the children of the bride-

And they come and say to Him. Some representatives, namely, of the two parties come, the Pharisees cunningly playing, no doubt, upon the simplicity of John's disciples.
Why do John's disciples and the disciples of the Pharisees fast? It will be noted that the question proper, which was proposed to our Lord, comes after this twofold clause, which is but the stepping-stone by which it is to be reached. It will also be noted that the evangelist, so far as this stepping-stone clause is concerned, gives his report not in the *ipsissima verba* of the questioners, but freely. If the *ipsissima verba* had been given, the report would no doubt have been somewhat as follows: *Why is it that while 'we,' the disciples of John, are fasting, and also the disciples of the Pharisees, Thy disciples fast not?* Comp. Matt. ix. 14. The expression *the disciples of the Pharisees* is noteworthy. For the time being the individuals of the Pharisaic community are regarded as the disciples of the body. As a matter of fact, all the individuals composing the community would one by one occupy, in relation to the whole, the position of pupils or disciples.
But Thy disciples fast not. *Why fast they not?* This was the real question. Surely you will not allege that 'we' and the Pharisees are too self denied. But if not, why is it that Thy disciples fast not?

VER. 19. And Jesus said to them, Can the sons of the bridechamber fast, while the bridegroom is with them? Would not fasting at such a time be most incongruous? The time referred to by our Lord, in His fine parabolic logic, is the period of festivity (often extending to a week, and sometimes even to a fortnight: see Tobit viii. 19), which was consequent on a happily consummated marriage. If there be a time at all when fasting would be inappropriate, it is such a time. A well-consorted 'wedding' should undoubtedly be a 'gala' occasion, though far removed from rioting and revelling and 'unhallowed mirth.' The expression *the sons of the bridechamber* is a Hebraistic phrase for *the groomsmen*, whose duty it was to convey the bridegroom to the bride's residence, and, when she was 'taken,' to accompany the couple back to the bridegroom's home, giving expression all along the way, and during the whole festivity, to their feelings of gaiety, congratulation, and gladness. They had, in accordance with the usage of Hebrew society, various little duties to perform in connection with the bridal chamber. This bridal chamber is, with admirable literality, designated, in our English version, *the bridechamber*. The most of the older translators were somewhat at sea regarding the precise import of the term. Wycliffe, Tyndale, Coverdale, rendered it *wedding*; Purvey *espousals (sposailis)*; the Rheims, *marriage*. But the Geneva version, though not the preliminary edition of 1557, made a great stride in the right direction when it rendered the term *marriage chamber*. The word however really means *bridechamber* (νυμφών from νύμφη, like γυναικών from γυνή, ἀνδρών from ἀνήρ, παρθενών from παρθένος). It was the particular chamber which was set apart for the bride. And as that chamber was the local centre of interest on a wedding occasion, the very groomsmen who officiated on behalf of the bridegroom were called

ST. MARK II.

chamber fast, while the bridegroom is with them? As long as they have the bridegroom with them, they cannot fast. 20 But the days will come when the bridegroom shall be taken away

its *sons*. They owed their official function, or, so to speak, their existence as groomsmen, to the existence of the chamber. *Can the sons of the bridechamber fast?* The word *can* is of course not used absolutely. It does not refer to what metaphysicians call *physical ability*, but to *moral ability*. The sons of the bridechamber *could not fast* consistently or congruously. *While the bridegroom is with them.* This is the correct translation of the expression. The phrase rendered *while* is literally *in which*; and Erasmus and Cajetan understood the reference to be to the bridechamber, *Can the sons of the bridechamber, in which the bridegroom is with them, fast?* But not only is there a parabolic incongruity in representing the groomsmen as being 'in' the bridechamber ' with ' the bridegroom, there is a further objection to the interpretation. The word *bridechamber*, though lexically a distinct and self contained word, is really, in the case before us, but a fractional part of a compound word, *sons-of-the-bridechamber* (= παρανύμφιοι), so that the relative *which* could not, without some degree of violence, look back to it as a detached antecedent. No doubt the expression refers, not to *place*, but to *time*: *in the time in which the bridegroom is with them*. *The bridegroom*: the Saviour beautifully subindicates that He is the Bridegroom of the church. (Comp. Ps. xlv; Song of Songs; 2 Cor. xi. 2; Eph. v. 24-32; Rev. xix. 7-9.) He is the Lover of the souls of men, and woos them. When He wins their hearts He becomes wedded to them, or most intimately and lovingly connected with them, and endows them, so far as the circumstances of the case will permit, with all the prerogatives and blessings of His own high estate. But there are tides of things in the 'times and seasons' of the Saviour's relationship to men which cannot be adequately set forth within the circle of the limitations of marriage. Hence we must not press the parable at all points.

As long as they have the bridegroom with them they cannot fast. We might have expected that the Saviour would have said, *As long as they are with the bridegroom*, viz. at his house. But He was looking through the transparency of His parable to a peculiar and exceptional case, His own. He had come from afar to the bride's house, to be there wedded to His bride; and by and by He must leave, and return for a season to His ' Father's house.' There is a good and peculiar reason for such leaving, though it could not with propriety be brought into view in connection with a marriage solemnity. No single human relationship can do justice to the unique reality of Christ's relationship to men. *They cannot fast.* Viz., unless they should act with the utmost incongruity.

VER. 20. **But days will come, when the bridegroom shall have been taken away from them.** There is a fine mystical meaning embedded in the word that is translated *shall-have-been-taken-away* (ἀπαρθῇ). The simple verb means *shall have been lifted up*, and the preposition in composition means *away*. The whole word covertly refers to what began with the crucifixion and ended with the ascension. (See John xii. 32.) It is noteworthy that it is this identical verb which is employed in the corresponding reports of Matthew (ix. 15) and

from them, and then shall they fast in those days. 21 No man also seweth a piece of new cloth on an old garment: else the new piece that filled it up taketh away from the old, and

Luke (v. 35), and that it is employed nowhere else in the New Testament. No doubt it would be the very word that our Lord Himself would use; for in the gentilized district of Galilee He would be almost always speaking in Greek. (See Diodati's *Christus Græce loquens*, and Roberts' *Discussions.*)

And then will they fast in that day. The Received Text reads here *in those days*, but by a manifest tinkering of the transcribers to make the phrase identical with the expression at the beginning of the verse and also with Luke's expression (v. 35). *In that day* was approved of by Mill (p. cxxii.); and though Bengel in his 1734 edition decided against it, yet in his 1753 edition, as also in his *German Version* and his *Gnomon*, he rev·rsed his decision. It is received into the text by Griesbach, Scholz, Lachmann, Tischendorf, and Tregelles. Fritzsche indeed could not make up his mind to receive it, he pronounced it 'intolerable.' Yet there really is not the shadow of a doubt that it stood in Mark's autograph. All the best manuscripts have it; and it is beautifully and touchingly significant, partly by rolling the days referred to at the commencement of the verse into the unity of one long dreary day, and partly by leading the mind back through the indefinite number of days to the first and darkest of them all, *the day of the lifting up on the cross*. That day would give colour and character to many succeeding days.

Ver. 21. **No one seweth a patch of unfulled cloth upon an old cloak.** Such patching would be most inappropriate and injudicious. The word *patch* is the proper term for the original ἐπίβλημα. It is Wycliffe's word, *pacche*. The patch supposed is an unfulled piece-of-cloth (the genitive of *the material*). It is the business of the *fuller* to make the cloth *full* and compact by precipitating the process of contraction. *Upon an old cloak:* the term which we have rendered *cloak* was the conventional term for the outer garment worn by the Jews, a loose cloak-like robe; it is rendered *cloke* in Matt. v. 40.

Else. Literally, *but if not*, that is, *but if it be 'not' the case that 'no one' sews a patch of unfulled cloth upon an old cloak*, which way of negativing a negative just amounts to the positive supposition, *but if it be the case that 'some one' sews a patch of unfulled cloth upon an old cloak.*

The piece-that-fills-up takes from it, the new from the old, and a worse rent is made. The patch sewed on is here called the *piece-that-fills-up* (the hole). It is the *complement* (πλήρωμα), the *insertion* as it were. Whenever it is damped it shrinks and draws to itself a margin of the old tender garment. There are several minute variations in the reading of the text, which have been somewhat perplexing to textual critics. In Michelsen's judgment (*Markus*, p. 150), the text is 'nearly unintelligible.' He can only resolve the difficulty by supposing that 'two glosses' from the hand of the Deutero-Markus have been bunglingly incorporated! But there is really no difficulty at all of the kind that Michelsen fancies, no difficulty of exegesis or construction, when we bear in mind that Mark makes not the slightest pretension to classical concinnity of phraseology or 'excellency of speech.' We approve of the reading given in the texts of

the rent is made worse. 22 And no man putteth new wine into old bottles : else the new wine doth burst the bottles, and the wine is spilled, and the bottles will be marred : but new wine must be put into new bottles.

Lachmann and Tischendorf (αἴρει τὸ πλήρωμα ἀπ' αὐτοῦ τὸ καινὸν τοῦ παλαιοῦ). It is the reading which the English Revisionists have followed in their translation of the clause ; and, when assumed, it makes it easy to account for all the little variations. It is approved of by Alford and Klostermann. Dr. Abraham Geiger, the Frankfort rabbi, has a different sort of difficulty with the passage. Or rather, he imagines a difficulty for the Christian, and imagines it to be insuperable, though he himself can easily overvault it, by landing on the other side of Christianity. He thinks that Christ's illustration is entirely erroneous ! (*So ist dies, so viel ich davon verstehe, geradezu unrichtig*.) He fancies that Christ is teaching that it is of no use patching up with new notions a religious system that has become, from age, much the worse of the wear (*Das Judenthum und seine Geschichte*, i. Abt, p. 173) ; and such teaching Geiger conceives to be wrong. He entirely misconceives, however, the mind of Christ, who is simply illustrating, by a striking little parable, the principle of incongruity, as it would have been exemplified had His disciples given themselves to fasting at a time of feasting. The illustration is perfect, and exceedingly graphic.

VER. 22. **And no one putteth new wine into old wine-skins.** Skins, such as of the goat, are still used all over Syria and Egypt for carrying water, and they were much used in former times for holding wine. At present these countries are under Mohammedan rule, and in the Koran wine is interdicted ; but in our Saviour's time it was a universal beverage, and, when not mixed with noxious ingredients or otherwise adulterated, or internally spoiled, it was a drink at once wholesome and delicious. *New wine :* That is, the new season's wine, 'young wine,' the wine which had just recently been drawn off from the wine vat, after the gathering and crushing of the grapes of the season. *Old wine-skins.* That is, old and frail. The reference is to skins of a relative age and frailty corresponding to the age and frailty of the old cloak referred to in the preceding parable.

Else. Literally, *but if not*, as in the preceding verse.

The wine will burst [*or rend*] **the skins.** This reading is supported by א B C D L, 33, very high and weighty authorities. The future tense of the verb is the more difficult reading, when we take the succeeding clause into account, in which there is a recurrence to the present tense. It is not so likely therefore that it would owe its place in the text to the modifying touch of a transcriber.

And the wine is destroyed, and the skins. Such is the reading of Tischendorf and Tregelles (καὶ ὁ οἶνος ἀπόλλυται καὶ οἱ ἀσκοί). It is preserved in the Vatican manuscript, and L, and the Coptic version, and is most likely the autographic reading of Mark. The variations in the manuscripts and versions are numerous, being traceable chiefly to an uncritical attempt in transcribers to conform the condensed, abrupt, and somewhat rugged phraseology of Mark to the more flowing phraseology of Matthew (ix. 17) and Luke (v. 37).

But new wine must be put into fresh wine-skins. An import of a clause

56   ST. MARK II.   [23

23 And it came to pass, that he went through the corn

dragged in by unskilful harmonists from Luke and Matthew. It is omitted by the Sinaitic manuscript and the Vatican, and by Tischendorf and Alford in their editions of the text. Tregelles encloses it, as doubtful, within brackets. Geiger, in this verse too, joins issue with our Saviour. He joins issue even in reference to the form of the parable. He doubts whether new skins were less liable to burst than old ones, and appeals to Job xxxii. 19, where we read of 'new bottles ready to burst.' He did not notice that *the great distention* of the 'new bottles ready to burst,' the idea that gets prominence in the poet's representation, is in consequence of an elasticity that is entirely wanting in old skins. He is sure, besides, that the inner meaning of the parable is far aside from the mark. It is "at variance with every historical development," for "the law of all development is the gradual metamorphosis of the old by the "influence of the new." (*Judenthum*, i., p. 174.) What paltering! and all so far away from the sphere of our Saviour's ideas! Our Saviour was not thinking of the development, or non-development, of old things into new. He was not making the least reference to 'the law of development.' Still less was He inculcating that His disciples should break with the past, and strike out into novelties of religious belief and practice. Does Geiger suppose that old wine-skins might, by the law of development, be transformed into new? Does he suppose that it would be an advantage to get old wine changed into new? If not, why refer to development and carp at the Saviour's parable? *Our Saviour simply meant to illustrate the incongruity that would be committed were His disciples to give themselves to fasting at a time of feasting.* They would be committing, in things spiritual, the very mistake that is committed in things natural, when new wine is put into old frail skins. At the least accession of 'after fermentation' the old frail skins will rend, and both wine and skins be destroyed. It is a mistake of incongruity which the Saviour exposes. (See Luke v. 39.)

VER. 23-28. A paragraph that has occasioned, in some of its details, a very great amount of perplexity to careful and reverent students of the word. Reckless and irreverent critics, on the other hand, have gloried over it, under the conviction that it affords them incontrovertible evidence that there has been blundering on the part of all the three synoptical evangelists. The corresponding paragraphs in the synoptical Gospels are Matthew xii. 1-8 and Luke vi. 1-5.

VER. 23. **And it came to pass.** Or, *And it happened:* at what particular time or in what particular circumstances we know not; and we need not be anxious to conjecture.

That on the sabbath He was going along through the cornfields. The expression rendered *on the sabbath* is the same that occurs in chap. i. 21. The word *was-going-along* is graphic (παραπορεύεσθαι), suggesting to us a picture. We see Jesus *walking along through extensive stretches of standing grain.* These stretches, spreading far and wide over the plain of Gennesaret, come down on either side close to the path on which our Lord and His disciples and a miscellaneous troop of others are leisurely and gravely walking along in the

fields on the sabbath day; and his disciples began, as they

stillness of the sabbath. It is an unenclosed path, a mere track, such as is common in the same district at the present day. It leads right *through* the standing grain. Several critics, including Köcher, Krebs, Palairet, Ernesti, object to the translation *through*, and laboriously try to prove that the preposition must here mean *alongside of*. They think that the Saviour must undoubtedly have kept on the public highway. It would have been wrong to have used the liberty of trampling through the standing corn of the farmers! The desire of these critics to shield the character of the Saviour is admirable; but their knowledge of oriental roads and cornfields is singularly deficient. The word translated *cornfields* means simply *sown places*; but we learn from what follows that the seed sown had sprung up, and eared, and was now nearly ready for the sickle.

And His disciples began, as they went, to pluck the ears of corn. An extremely free translation, and the clause so translated is the great difficulty of the paragraph. But yet such an expositor as Bloomfield quietly passes over the whole verse, without a single hint or remark of any description. The expression as it stands in the original, καὶ οἱ μαθηταὶ αὐτοῦ ἤρξαντο ὁδὸν ποιεῖν τίλλοντες τοὺς στάχυας, literally means *and His disciples began to make a way, plucking the ears*. The word *began* has, in the first place, been perplexing to many; more especially as it is not connected, in the original, with *plucking the ears*. It perplexed Beza among others. 'There seems,' said he, ' to be a displacement of the verbs.' Hence he arbitrarily connected it with *plucking the ears*, 'they began to pluck the ears.' It perplexed Hammond too. 'The phrase here in the Greek is,' says he, 'a little unusual.' He would regard the word *began* as an 'unsignificant expletive,' a mere pleonasm. So would Elsner and Wolf, who would consequently ignore the word in translation, *and His disciples walked on and plucked the ears*. Köcher however, and Raphel, Rosenmüller, Kuinöl, and others, would rather approve of Beza's 'hypallage.' Erasmus preceded Beza in his expedient, and Luther too. Tyndale used the same liberty, and the authors of the Geneva version, and hence the rendering in our present translation. It is, however, a licentious liberty. How then should we construe the expression? Coverdale comes nearer to the original than his great forerunner, Luther. He translates it thus: *and His disciples begane to make a waye thorow, and to plucke the eares of the corne*. Erasmus Schmid's translation is somewhat to the same effect, but very much more clumsy, *and His disciples began (so) to go, that (at the same time) they plucked the ears*. Both translations do justice to the '*began*.' But they differ as to the import of the expression that is directly governed by that verb. Coverdale says *to make a waye thorow*; Erasmus Schmid says *to go*. A rather hot controversy hooks itself on to the phrase thus rendered (ὁδὸν ποιεῖν, or ὁδοποιεῖν as Theophylact gives it, and Lachmann too under the sanction of the Vatican manuscript). The great majority of expositors, ancient and modern, translate it as E. Schmid does; but contrary, says Dresigius (*De Verbis Mediis*, § 29), to the idiom of the Greek language. When the verb is in the middle voice (ὁδὸν ποιεῖσθαι), the phrase means *to set out, to advance, to make way* (*iter facere*). But when the verb is in the active (ὁδὸν ποιεῖν), the phrase means, as Viger had remarked before

went, to pluck the ears of corn. 24 And the Pharisees said

Dresigius, not *to make way*, but *to make a way*, or, as Coverdale gives it, *to make a waye thorow* (*viam facere*). Fritzsche insists on the distinction being observed. Lange gives in to it. So did Bretschneider and Wahl and Winer. Meyer is most determined in adhering to it, and founds on it a theory of irreconcilable discordance between Mark's representation and that of Matthew and Luke. He is sure, that as Mark makes no explicit reference to the disciples' rubbing the spikes and eating the disintegrated grains, so he had no implicit reference to such acts. The Pharisees he holds, so far as Mark's representation is concerned, blamed the disciples, not for doing on the sabbath day what would have been quite lawful on any other day, but for doing on the sacred day what would have been unlawful on any day, viz. *making a road through other people's standing corn, by plucking the spikes*. Holtzmann takes the same view of the expression, and of the intent of the Pharisees in their censure (*Synopt. Evang.*, p. 73). And so does Michelsen (*Het Ev. van Markus*, p. 152), and Scholten likewise (*Het oudste Evan.*, p. 26). These three critics insist on it, moreover, that Mark's account is the original story, and that both Matthew and Luke have ' misunderstood ' it. Grimm, on the other hand, supposes that if we must interpret the expression as Meyer does, then there is no avoiding the conclusion ' that Mark did not report the truth, but miserably corrupted (*misere corrupisse*) the report which he had received from others.' (*Clavis*, sub voce ποιέω.) Krebs, again, has no doubt that Mark's expression properly means *to make a road*, but he thinks that, in using it, he was *Latinizing*, or rendering into Greek a common Latin phrase (*iter facere*, *proficisci*), and that therefore, as Mark intended it, the meaning is that the disciples *advanced*. (*Observationes*, in loc.) Others, inclusive of Kypke, Lösner, Rosenmüller, Kuinöl, Bisping, Alford, assume or maintain that in the later and provincial Greek the distinction between the active and the middle voices of the verb, in the expression under question, got to be to a great degree confused or effaced. Jud. xvii. 8 is appealed to, as an instance in point ; but the expression there is rather peculiar, and does not simply mean, as we presume, *to journey* or *advance*. Yet, whatever it means, we see no reason for abandoning the simple and natural interpretation of the expression in Mark ; more particularly when we bear in mind the word *began*. We must picture to ourselves, as Klostermann remarks, the ' scene.' No doubt Mark is retailing the abrupt and graphic phrases of Peter or of some other reporter, who is speaking from a vivid recollection of what he had witnessed with his eyes and heard with his ears. We must picture then to ourselves the Saviour going along through the cornfields. His disciples are with Him, and a group of others, inclusive of a band of disputatious and censorious Pharisees. They are on their way to or from some adjoining synagogue. Conversation and lively disputation go on, all along the way. At a certain point where there is a crossing, or nearer cut, or a smaller diverging footpath, there is a pause on the part of our Saviour and of some of the Pharisees with whom He was discoursing. Perhaps they paused, merely that they might stand and talk for a little, the earnestness of their spirits putting an unconscious arrest upon their physical progress. Or perhaps they were about at that point to separate into different routes. While they stand and talk. the

unto him, Behold, why do they on the sabbath day that which

Lord's disciples move on; they 'began' to advance. Here is the explanation of the 'began.' Cajetan rightly supposes that they *began to go ahead of our Lord*. But the very narrow path along which they had to advance, being comparatively unused, was overgrown apparently at that particular spot with the crop. When the soil had been prepared, and the seed sown, no care was taken to keep off that narrow strip, along which the people had right of way; the farmer knew that it was easy for the public to renew the path, just by walking upon it. The disciples then began to walk in upon this line of transit, '*making a way.*' They were hungry too; they had been long fasting. And hence, instead of simply trampling down the intervening stalks, they stooped, as they 'began' to walk, and plucked some handfuls of the spikes. They plucked them not from the fields by the side (although that would not have been seriously objected to), but considerately and economizingly from the stalks that were obstructing the road, and thus *they began to make a way, plucking the spikes, or by plucking the spikes.* There is thus not the slightest necessity for having recourse to any rack or strain or out-of-the-way peculiarity, to get the evangelist's expressions bent from their natural import.

VER. 24. **And the Pharisees said to Him, Behold!** Or, *See!* The word was used as an exclamation, *Lo!* But in such a case as the one before us its primary meaning is not to be lost sight of. The Pharisees turned their attention to what the disciples were engaged in doing, the moment that they 'began' to press in among the standing corn. *What are they about? They are actually plucking the spikes as if they were reapers! and they are rubbing them too in the palms of their hands, and eating the threshed out grains! Who could have thought it? What daring wickedness!* Immediately they turn round, as with surprise, to the Lord, and say, *See!*

Why do they on the sabbath what is not lawful? It is an inartificial way of saying, *Why do they what is not lawful on the sabbath?* Meyer however, along with Holtzmann, Michelsen, and Scholten, will have it that the meaning is, *Why do they, and that too on the sabbath, a thing that is (at all times and under all circumstances) unlawful?* Scholten is positive that the mere plucking and eating of the spikes 'could hardly have afforded an occasion of offence and complaint,' (*wat kwalijk eene oorzaak van ergernis kon hebben opgeleverd*). He seems to know little of the censorious spirit of ancient phariseeism, or of its modern oriental analogue, 'wahhabeeism.' He seems likewise, along with Michelsen, Meyer, and Holtzmann, to be strangely unwilling to look at what is obviously implied in the reply which the Saviour made to the censorious Pharisees. What can be clearer than that it is implied that His disciples were hungry, and that what they did to the standing corn *they did because they had need?* This was so obvious to the mind of the inartificial narrator, who was bending his thoughts forward toward the words of the Saviour's reply, that he does not make formal mention of the fact. The proprietor of the crop had no right (Deut. xxiii. 25), and would not be disposed, to find fault with the disciples for assuaging their hunger as they passed along. But the sanctimonious Pharisees thought it a dreadful desecration of the sabbath to do things so like to week-day

is not lawful? 25 And he said unto them, Have ye never read what David did, when he had need, and was an hungred, he, and they that were with him? 26 How he went into the

reaping and threshing as plucking the ears of the corn and rubbing them in the palm of the hand. (See *Comm.* on Matt. xii. 2.)

VER. 25. **And He saith to them, Did ye never read what David did, when he had need and was hungry, he and they that were with him?** See 1 Sam. xxi. 1–6. Note the generic *had need* and the specific *was hungry*. Note also the inartificial and conversational way in which the expression, *he and they that were with him*, is appended to the affirmation *he had need and was hungry*. His followers had need too, and were hungry; but it is on the acting of David, as one of the most eminent of the Jews, that our Lord concentrates attention. Note likewise the archaic expression *an-hungred* in King James's version and the Revised. It came down from Tyndale, who gives it thus—*anhongred*. The prefixed *an*, like the *a* in *athirst*, is a preposition, equivalent to *on* or *in*, so that the whole expression means *in (the state of being) hungered* or *hungry*. See *Comm.* on Matt. xii. 1.)

VER. 26. **How he entered into the house of God.** The tabernacle, to wit, while it was located in Nob, an ancient sacerdotal town (1 Sam. xxii. 19) near Jerusalem (Isa. x. 32). See 1 Sam. xxi. 1–6.
In the days of Abiathar (the) high-priest. This is the other expression in the paragraph which has occasioned difficulty to many, and over which irreverent critics have rejoiced, under the idea that it furnishes them with evidence that the evangelist has committed an historical blunder. They allege that a blunder there must be, inasmuch as we learn explicitly from 1 Sam. xxi. that it was not Abiathar but his father Ahimelech, who was high-priest, when David entered into the house of God and ate the shewbread, giving part of it to them that were with him. How then are we to account for the expression? *That may be somewhat uncertain; but it is absolutely certain that it is absolutely impossible to prove that there is anything of the nature of a blunder.* 'There is no need,' as Dr. Wall says, 'of that supposal' (*Notes*, in loc.). (1) Some have drawn attention to the fact that it is not said in 1 Sam. xxi., or in any other passage in the Bible, that Ahimelech the father of Abiathar was *high-priest*; he is only called *the priest*, and never *the high-priest*. Theophylact threw out the conjecture that this might probably have to do with the solution of the difficulty. Patrizi is of opinion that Abiathar was actually high-priest at the time that David came to Ahimelech (*Comm.* in loc., and *De Evangel.*, xxviii. n. 38). Wall and Whiston held the same opinion. *It is probable however that Ahimelech was high-priest*, for he 'inquired of the Lord' and had '*the* ephod' (see *Whitby*). Josephus, himself of the priestly order, again and again speaks of him as *high-priest* (*Ant.* vi., xii., 4, 5, 6). (2) Some have supposed that a solution of the difficulty is to be found in 2 Sam. viii. 17, and 1 Chron. xxiv. 6, in which passages there is a transposition of the names *Abiathar* and *Ahimelech*, the latter being spoken of as the son of the former. Comp. 1 Chron. xviii. 16. It is probable however that this transposition is merely transcriptional; and, if so, it would be in vain to look to it for an explanation

house of God in the days of Abiathar the high priest,

of the expression before us. (3) Lightfoot imagined that the phrase *Abiathar the high-priest* had already in our Saviour's day acquired its curious cabbalistical import of *Urim and Thummim*, so that the whole expression *in the days of Abiathar the high-priest* meant *in the days of the Urim and Thummim*, in the days, that is to say, when the mind of the Lord was ascertainable and ascertained by means of *the Urim and the Thummim*. But this is quite an oddity of interpretation. (4) Jansen, Petter, a-Lapide, and others, suppose that both Abiathar and his father may have had each other's names for surnames, so that Ahimelech would be surnamed Abiathar, while Abiathar would be surnamed Ahimelech. Beza, in his day, had caught hold of this idea as an alternative explanation, founding on the passages already referred to (2 Sam. viii. 17 and 1 Chron. xxiv. 6). It has, however, all the appearance of an exceedingly artificial device. (5) Beza threw out another conjecture, in the editions of his *Annotations* which succeeded that of 1565. The entire phrase *in the days of Abiathar the high-priest* is wanting in the very ancient manuscript (D) which belonged to him, and which he subsequently presented to the University of Cambridge; and hence he wondered whether the phrase might not have crept into the text from an early marginal note. The phrase is wanting not only in D, but also in some important manuscripts of the old Latin version. Archbishop Newcome would have liked to let it go; and, walking in his leading-strings, the authors of the *Improved Version* (Unitarian) actually omit it; Bloomfield too is disposed to part with it. *But without good reason;* the evidence in support of the clause is overwhelming. And if it should be supposed that the words involve a historical difficulty, it would be unaccountable, on the supposition of their spuriousness, that they should have been almost universally received into the text. But what then? Do they really involve a historical difficulty? (6) Michaelis thought that the historical difficulty was very great, and, in a kind of despair, suggested that the phrase, instead of being rendered *in the days of Abiathar the high-priest*, might have a topical reference, *in the section* or *paragraph of Abiathar the high-priest*. Comp. Luke xx. 37. Saunier accepts this solution of the imagined difficulty as the best upon the whole. (*Quellen des Ev. des Marcus*, pp. 57, 58.) But there is really no evidence that the word *Abiathar* was appropriate from its conspicuousness to give a title to a Scripture section or paragraph, at least in or about 1 Sam. xxi. And then, besides, the phrase would have required to have stood nearer to the expression *did ye never read?* in the 25th verse. (7) Le Clerc tries another shift. He supposes that the preposition ($\dot{\epsilon}\pi\dot{\iota}$) employed by the evangelist, instead of being rendered temporally *in the time of*, should be rendered locally, *in* or *into the presence of* (*chez, apud, ad*). Wetstein gives the same translation, and Godwin. The passages appealed to in support of it (1 Tim. vi. 13; Acts xxiv. 19, xxv. 10; 1 Cor. vi. 1; add Matt. xxviii. 14, Mark xiii. 9, Acts xxvi. 2) are all idiomatic, having a reference to the elevated position of a judge. And no difficulty is escaped, if difficulty there be, by means of such a translation; new difficulties, on the contrary, are incurred. (8) Bishop Hammond saw clearly that the preposition must have a reference to time, but he conjectured that it might mean *a little before the time of*. He says, apolo-

and did eat the shewbread, which is not lawful to eat but

gizingly: "The notation of the preposition for the time not then present, but "soon after succeeding, is remarkable." He ingeniously appeals, however, to Matt. i. 11 in support of his 'remarkable' interpretation; and Richard Baxter, Samuel Clarke, and Owen agree with him. The passage in Matthew however has this peculiarity, that it refers to a definite occurrence, and thus to a point of time, whereas this expression in Mark refers either to the period of a lifetime or to the period of a pontificate. In the case therefore of such an expression as Matthew's the preposition is naturally employed to denote *close upon the time of*; but in the case of Mark's expression it as naturally means *on* or *in the time of*. (See Raphel's *Annotations*, in loc.) Wells's translation therefore, *about the time of*, is inexact. But what then? (9) Brameld translates the phrase *during the high-priesthood of Abiathar*. Schleusner gives the same translation; it corresponds with the Syriac Peshito, *when Abiathar was chief of the priests*. The English Revisionists agree, *when Abiathar was high-priest*. But this is certainly a most unnecessary leap into the heart of a historical difficulty; there is assuredly no propriety in giving such a free and *interpretative translation*, when the interpretation of the phrase is the very matter in dispute. Bisping's interpretation coincides with Brameld's, but his translation is correct, *in the time of Abiathar the high-priest*. What is the difference between the two translations? and how does it affect the true interpretation? (10) Bishop Middleton supposed that the presence of the article before the word *high priest* is the key that unlocks the whole supposed difficulty. If the article had been wanting, the phrase he thinks must have been interpreted as meaning *in the time of the high-priesthood of Abiathar*; but the presence of the article makes that meaning, Bishop Middleton contends, 'a sense which the words will not bear.' The phrase then means, according to him, *in the time of Abiathar, the (celebrated) high-priest*, it not being implied that he was high-priest at the time referred to. We think that Middleton and Wetstein are both right and wrong. They are right, we conceive, in the meaning which they attached to the evangelist's phrase; and thus the difficulty of the phrase, if difficulty there be, is really solved. Their exegetical instinct led them, as it did Grotius before them, to the true mark. *The phrase refers to the lifetime of the high-priest, not to the time of his pontificate.* But the reason on which Middleton grounds his interpretation is as unsound, in its onesidedness, as the interpretation itself is sound. The word '*high-priest*' *without the article* has not necessarily, by any means, the force of a participle (like Herodotus's ἐπὶ Λέοντος Βασιλεύοντος, i. 65). It may simply be added appositively, in order to discriminate, embellish, or characterize the name that is specified; somewhat like the word *Christ* put anarthrously after Jesus (Matt. i. 1, etc.), or the anarthrous word *apostle* after Paul (Gal. i. 1, etc.), or the anarthrous expression *Doctor of Divinity*, or *Doctor of Laws*, or *Knight*, or *Baronet*, after any proper name in our own times. It is undoubtedly thus added in the case before us. There is a decided preponderance of authorities against the genuineness of the article. It is found indeed in the manuscripts A C Δ Π, 1, 33, 69. But it is wanting in ℵ B L E G H K M S U V Γ. Lachmann, Tischendorf, Tregelles, and Alford omit it. Bishop Wordsworth both accepts the reading of the text

for the priests, and gave also to them which were with him?

which omits the article, and gives the correct interpretation of the phrase. "The reference is made to Abiathar as one well known to the readers of the "Old Testament *as a celebrated high-priest.*" When however the bishop says that the expression, in itself, 'rather suggests that he was *not* the high-priest' at the time referred to by our Lord, he greatly overstrains the case, and overlooks at once the usage and the regulative principles of Greek phraseology. In that he is decidedly wrong; but it is to the point that he adds: "If our Lord "had mentioned *Ahimelech*, the Pharisees' answer might have been that Ahi-"melech was punished by God for this profanation of sacred things; he and his "were soon overtaken by Divine vengeance and slain. But by specifying Abia-"thar, who was then with his father (1 Sam. xxii. 20), and who (we may "reasonably *infer* from our Lord's words, which are the words of Him who "knows all history) was a party to his father's act, and was afterwards blessed "by God in his escape and in a long and glorious priesthood, our Lord "obviates the objection of the worldly-minded Pharisees, and strengthens His "own argument, by reminding them that this action took place in the time "and under the sanction of one whom they held in reverence as a venerable "ornament of the pontifical family and dignity." De Lyra brings out a "similar idea.

And ate the shewbread Or, as the Rheims, translating from the Vulgate, renders the expression, *and did eate the loaves of proposition.* The word *proposition* is here used in its primary acceptation, *position before*, the loaves referred to being *the cakes which were put in position before the Lord.* The reference is to the twelve loaves or cakes, which were regularly kept on the golden table in the holy place. (Lev. xxiv. 5–9.) They were *the loaves of the Face*, as the Jews called them, that is, *the loaves of the Divine Presence*, the loaves which were kept in the presence-chamber of Jehovah, one for each of the twelve tribes of Israel. It was a sublime symbolism, being intended to remind the children of Israel that it was the Lord, their Father, who was their bountiful Provider. It was thus *the bread of God* (see John vi. 33) which David ate. (See *Comm.* on Matt. xii. 4.)

Which it is not lawful for any but the priests to eat. The reading of Tischendorf, in his eighth edition, is οὓς οὐκ ἔξεστιν φαγεῖν εἰ μὴ τοὺς ἱερεῖς. It is the reading of the Sinaitic and Vatican manuscripts. It was needful, in the spiritual tuition of the children of Israel, that the whole symbolism of the temple should be treated with the utmost reverence. To *stand in awe before God* is one of the first and most important lessons which men who are but emerging into spiritual culture can learn. It was fit, therefore, that the very bread which symbolised the Provision that was divinely made for the whole of the people should be eaten only by the representative priests. (See Lev. xxiv. 9.)

And gave also to them who were with him. So that the rule of the sanctuary was relaxed to meet an emergency, not only in the case of David, a man of exceptional eminence, but also, and for his sake, in the case of those who were associated with him. Rules that had to do with the circumstantials of things, as distinguished from the essentials, were stretched for their benefit. All such rules are elastic still, whether they have reference to the sanctuary, or to the

27 And he said unto them, The sabbath was made for man,

sabbath, or to any other 'positive' institution. They are meant to bend to a certain extent, when exposed to stress of weather.

VER. 27. **And He said unto them.** He added this other weighty observation. **The sabbath was made for man, and not man for the sabbath.** One of the simplest and most obvious, but yet one of the deepest and most important, of the apophthegms of our Lord. Thiess is in raptures with it, and exclaims: "What else is intolerance, that most inhuman and unchristian of dispositions, "than a perpetual forgetting or reversing of this grand principle of Christ?" (*Intoleranz, diese allermenschenfeindlichste und allerunchristlichste Gesinnung, was ist sie anders, als ein beständiges Vergessen und Misbrauchen des Grundsazes Christi?*) The verb rendered *was made* (ἐγένετο) means *was brought into existence*. The Syriac version is, *was created*. The preposition somewhat barely rendered *for* (διά with the accusative) means *because of*, or *on account of*. Coverdale's translation of the apophthegm, in all but epigrammatic terseness, is fully better than that of our Authorized version, *The sabbath was made for man's sake, and not man for the sabbathes sake*. The idea is, that the reason of the existence of the sabbath is to be found in man, not *vice versa*. Man needs a sabbath, man universal. He needs it in order to the highest development of his idiosyncrasy. It would be a total inversion of relationship to suppose that the reason or cause of the existence or idiosyncrasy of man is to be found in the sabbath. The sabbath is therefore subordinate to man, not man to the sabbath. The sabbath is *a means* in order to some *end* or *ends* terminating in man. And thus, as final ends are 'first in intention,' so that we have to come back through them in order to understand the rationale of the means by which they may be reached, we get to the reason of the sabbath by going, as it were, '*through*' man. (The fundamental idea of the preposition διά is *through*.)

VER. 28. **So that the Son of Man is Lord also of the sabbath.** This is an inference, though a-Lapide had difficulty in seeing it, from the incontrovertible axiom enunciated in the preceding verse. Since it is the case that the sabbath is an institution that finds the reason of its existence in man, the law that enjoins the details of its observance is something altogether different from those eternal and immutable principles which are identical with the moral perfections of the Divine Being. It is elastic in its application to the circumstances of men. It is susceptible of modification by the superinduction of higher laws into the sphere of its operation. And hence He who is emphatically 'the Son of Man,' and who has in charge all the higher interests of man, has full authority to regulate, as He may see cause, the amount and modes of that rest from worldly work which is needful for the highest weal of men. The regulation is safe *in His hands*, though it would not be safe in the hands of every man. Grotius thinks indeed that the phrase *the son of man* does not refer exclusively or particularly to Christ, but generically to *man*. Fritzsche takes the same view. So does Principal Campbell, who says, "one would con- "clude that *the son of man* in this verse must be equivalent to *man* in the "preceding; otherwise a term is introduced into the conclusion which was not

and not man for the sabbath: 28 therefore the Son of man is Lord also of the sabbath.

"in the premises." But nothing is more manifest than that our Saviour was not constructing, in the unity of these two verses, a single formal syllogism. His reasoning is an exemplification of that '*polysyllogism*' *condensed*, which is the characteristic of all untechnical processes of argumentation. Some of the involved syllogisms might be easily disintegrated. *If man was not made for the sabbath, and if Christ was a man, it follows that He was not made for the sabbath.* This simple hypothetical syllogism is undoubtedly involved in our Saviour's reasoning. Again, *If He who is emphatically and pre-eminently man and the Son of Man be greater than all other men, and if Christ be, as He is, emphatically and pre-eminently man and the Son of Man, it follows that He is greater than all other men.* This is another simple hypothetical syllogism involved in our Saviour's reasoning; and no term is introduced into its conclusion which is not in its premises. Again, *If He who is emphatically and pre-eminently man and the Son of Man of God and the Lord of glory, and if Christ be, as He is, emphatically and pre-eminently man and the Son of Man, it follows that He is also the Son of God and the Lord of glory.* This syllogism too is involved in our Saviour's reasoning. And again, *If He who is the Lord of glory be the Lord also of the sabbath, and if Christ be, as He is, the Lord of glory, it follows that He is the Lord also of the sabbath.* This other hypothetical syllogism is also involved in the Saviour's reasoning ; and so good a logician as Principal Campbell might easily have found, if he had looked a little more inquisitively, that there is really no term in the conclusion of the polysyllogism which is not found in its premises, *when those premises are explicitly unfolded*. The expression *the Son of Man is*, in Christ's own usage, most definitely appropriated to Himself, although the same expression, without the article, is applicable to others as well as to Him. Ezekiel is constantly called, in his prophecies, *son of man*; and in Syriac the corresponding phrase is the common designation of *man*, and is employed for instance in the preceding verse, in both the Peshito and Philoxenian versions. When it is said that *the Son of Man is Lord ' also ' of the sabbath,* the *also* proceeds on the assumption that the lordship of the Son of Man has a wide domain. He is the Lord of heaven, the Lord of earth, the Lord of men, the Lord of the sanctuary, and the Lord 'also' of the sabbath. He hence 'doeth with it according to His pleasure,' and has a right thus to act. And if so, He had a perfect right on the part of His disciples, and taking their peculiar circumstances into account, to waive compliance with those rigid and petty prescriptive usages of the Pharisees, which embodied, not the Divine ideas of things, but only their own narrow and narrowly misshapen and superstitious conceptions of the rest of the sabbath.

CHAPTER III.

1 AND he entered again into the synagogue; and there was a man there which had a withered hand. 2 And they watched him, whether he would heal him on the sabbath day ; that they might accuse him. 3 And he saith unto the man which had

CHAPTER III.

IT would have been a happier arrangement of the chapters if Hugo de Sancto Caro had included within the second chapter the first six verses of this. (*See the Remarks on Chap.* ii.)
Corresponding paragraphs to ver. 1–6 are found in Matt. xii. 9–14 and Luke vi. 6–11.

VER. 1. **And He entered again into the synagogue.** Apparently in Capernaum; compare chap. ii. 1. *Again.* He had been there before, though we know not how often; see chap. i. 21 ; comp. Luke vi. 6. *Into the synagogue.* In the Sinaitic and Vatican manuscripts the expression is anarthrous, *into synagogue*, just as we say *into church.*

And there was there a man having the hand withered. It was his right hand, and hence the article '*the*' *hand.* (Comp. Luke vi. 6.) It had met with some accident, or otherwise suffered some injury, and had in consequence stiffened and shrunk up. The participial expression rendered *withered* indicates, says Bengel, that it was not a congenital defect.

VER. 2. **And they kept watching Him.** *They*, the scribes and Pharisees. See chap. ii. 24, and Luke vi. 7. They *kept watching. Thei aspieden Hym*, says Wycliffe, keeping eagerly on the outlook, like watchmen.

Whether He would heal him on the sabbath. Very literally, *if on the sabbath He 'will' heal him.* The reader is taken back by the evangelist to the time when the spying and watching were going on, and looks forward from that standpoint to the uncertain future. Instead of *if He will heal*, Tischendorf, in his eighth edition, reads *if He heals*; a future precipitated backward into the present. It is the reading of the Sinaitic manuscript, but most likely an accidental variation.

That they might accuse Him. Namely, to the ecclesiastical authorities in Jerusalem. They were eager to get some ground on which they might denounce Him as a person who should not be allowed to go at large. (See ver. 6.) The true spirit of ecclesiastical bloodhounds was roused within them, and they were resolved to do their utmost to hunt Him to death.

VER. 3. **And He saith to the man who had the withered hand, Stand forth.** *Stand forth* is a free but admirable translation, a fragment of the Old Geneva rendering, *Arise, stand forth in the middes.* Wycliffe's version is literal, *Rise into the mydil*, that is, *Rise, come into the midst, and stand there.* Our Saviour saw that it was a time of crisis, and so He chose to make the man conspicuous, the 'cynosure of eyes.'

the withered hand, Stand forth. 4 And he saith unto them, Is it lawful to do good on the sabbath days, or to do evil? to save life, or to kill? But they held their peace. 5 And when he had looked round about on them with anger, being grieved

VER. 4. **And He saith to them, Is it lawful on the sabbath to do good or to do evil?** He assumes that if a man does not do good when he can, he does evil. To refuse to do good is to choose to do evil. There is *doing* in both cases; there is the outgoing of energy in volition; and thus, radically, it is a question of doing right or wrong, and not merely of doing or not-doing.

To save life, or to kill? Our Lord puts the case strongly, carrying out the alternatives of activity into their most momentous issues. The principle of action, which He wishes to vindicate, is thus seen in its strongest light. All good-doing to men's bodies lies on the line of life; all withholding of good-doing lies on the line of killing or of death. If it would be wrong, in the absence of higher claims, to withhold the good-doing that would save life, it must also be wrong, when the higher claims are still absent, to withhold the good-doing that may be needed to develop life into its fulness of vigour and beauty. What is true of bodies is equally true, on a loftier plane of things, of souls.

But they held their peace. They *kept silent* (ἐσιώπων). They did not wish to discuss principles of action; they did not even wish to look into them, that they might understand them. They were simply resolved to hold on by the notions with which they were pre-occupied, and to put down all that might be contrary to these notions.

VER. 5. **And having looked round about on them with indignation.** Viz., because of the bigotry and tyranny of their spirit. Our Saviour's anger would be no outburst of ill-natured passion. There was no ill-natured passion in Him to burst out. And yet in all anger there is intense feeling; only in the Saviour's anger the intense feeling would not be that of chafed and irritated selfishness. There was no selfishness in His heart to get chafed and irritated. His indignation, like the indignation of God, would be pure and holy (*ira per zelum*, not *ira per vitium*). It would be the recoil and regurgitation of benevolence. His benevolence was wilfully resisted by the scribes and Pharisees, and thus thrown back into an attitude of antagonism.

Being grieved. The expression in the original is significantly full, bringing into view a certain peculiar element of *togetherhood* (συνλυπούμενος). There is a difference of opinion among critics as to *the precise phase of togetherhood* that is referred to. Some think that it is the union of *the Saviour's grief with His anger*. Hence the translation of the word in the Geneva version, *mourning also*. Beza had the same view, *simul dolens*; and Calvin, *pareillement marri*. Calvin's translation of the phrase was received into the French Geneva version, supplanting the older translation, *contristé*. Martin retained the same view of the togetherhood in his French version; Ostervald too. So also Sebastian Schmidt and Erasmus Schmid, in their respective Latin translations; and Elsner likewise, and Petter, and Dr. Robinson. But it is more likely that it is the idea of *sympathy* which is indicated, so that the Saviour's feeling was a

for the hardness of their hearts, he saith unto the man, Stretch forth thine hand. And he stretched *it* out: and his hand was restored whole as the other. 6 And the Pharisees went forth, and straightway took counsel with the Herodians against him, how they might destroy him.

---

kind of *condolence*. Such is the classical import of the word (see *Herodot*. vi. 39, ix. 94). Only in the case before us there was a wonderful peculiarity in the condolence. The scribes and Pharisees were not themselves grieved. But they should have been. Not thus does malevolence mourn over the woes of its object; it is utterly destitute of any wellspring of tears. It is only benevolence that weeps.

At the hardening of their heart. The Saviour was grieved *at* this, or, more literally, *over* this. Bending *over* it, He inwardly wept. Instead of *hardening* or *hardness*, it is *blindness* in the Vulgate; and so J. D. Michaelis translates. Wrongly however; the word means *callousness*. As here applied to the *heart* or *mind*, it denotes that *moral insensibility* which is the prominent characteristic of religious formalists and bigots. Formalism is like a coating of callosity over the soul. Bigotry is another brawny coat. When it is in its superlative degree there is an assumption of practical infallibility, which is an exceedingly insensible coat. This assumption is naturally followed by another assumption that all others *should be compelled* to think 'as *we* think,' and to act 'as *we* act'; the hardest and toughest coat of all. He who is incased in these coatings is proof against almost all appeals that would go to the conscience or the heart.

He saith to the man, Stretch forth thy hand. Or, as Wycliffe gives it, *Holde forth thin honde*. The Saviour wished the whole assembly to see the hand, and to take note of its shrunk and shrivelled condition.

And he held it out. The arm was not impotent.

And his hand was restored. Viz. into its former condition of soundness. It would be a sublime spectacle. When the tide of returning health rushed expandingly through the shrivelled member, the presence and operation of some supernatural power could not be gainsaid. And, so far as history informs us, *there was no attempt to gainsay the intromission of such a power, all through the period of our Saviour's career*. Some said indeed that the power was from beneath, but none denied that a might higher than human was in operation.

The appended words *whole as the other* seem, as Tischendorf remarks, to have been imported from Matt. xii. 13. They are wanting in all the most important manuscripts. They are wanting too in the most important ancient versions: the Vulgate, the Peshito Syriac, the Philoxenian Syriac, the Gothic, Coptic, Armenian, and Æthiopic; the Arabic too, and Persic.

VER. 6. **And when the Pharisees went out.** From the synagogue where the miracle had been performed.

They straightway, with the Herodians, took counsel against Him. *Straightway*, or *immediately*; Mark's favourite adverb. All things in connection with Jesus were now moving on in hot haste. The whole district was in a whirl of commotion. Hence the Pharisees, being, with the rest of the population, under the

ST. MARK III.

7 But Jesus withdrew himself with his disciples to the sea:

spell of the movement, resolved to lose no time in getting some scheme concocted for laying violent hands on the Disturber. They took the Herodians into their counsels. It is not quite certain who the Herodians were. They were probably a court party among the Jews, who were politically attached to the rule of the Herods, and who either thought, or affected to think, that the glowing predictions of the Old Testament in reference to the Messiah were sufficiently fulfilled in the jurisdiction, military power, and social magnificence of Herod the Great and his family. (See *Comm.* on Matt. xxii. 16.) They would not be *a religious party*, or much influenced by religious principles. And hence the Pharisees, in seeking their co-operation to put down the great Opponent of the irreligiousness of mere religious formality, bewrayed the depth of their own irreligious hate. *Took counsel:* Such is our English phrase. The Greek expression means *made counsel*, or *made consultation* (συμβούλιον ἐποίησαν; see Tischendorf, eighth edition). Wycliffe renders it, *maden a counseil*. The Rheims has it, *made a consultation*.

How they might destroy Him. The conjunction (ὅπως) has, in its make, a reference to *mode* or *manner*. But here the reference is not to the mode or manner of the destruction as already contemplated, but to the mode or manner in which they might be able to reach such a desired result as that of destruction. The Vulgate version renders the conjunction *how* (*quomodo*), but Beza substituted *that* instead (*ut*), and Tyndale translates the clause *that they might destroye Him*. The word *destroy* has reference to a *violent death*. See Matt. ii. 13, xxi. 41, xxvii. 20. Comp. Luke vi. 9 with Mark iii. 4.

De Wette says that Mark's mention of the combination of the Pharisees with the Herodians is an erroneous anticipation of the subsequent coalition which is recorded in Matt. xxii. 16. Ferdinand C. Baur gives expression to the same idea (*Markus.*, p. 179). But wantonly. Why should it be supposed unlikely that there should be co-operation between groups of the two parties more than once? If the co-operation took place once, why should it be supposed incredible that it took place more than once? And why, again, should it be supposed strange that Mark alone takes notice of this early coalition? Why, when events are in themselves many-sided, should it be deemed improbable or unaccountable that different writers should give different details?

VER. 7–12. In the brief paragraph extending from ver. 7 to ver. 12 there is a condensation of many details of our Lord's Galilean ministry. He spoke again and again words of grace; He performed again and again works of mercy. But the generic sameness of men's wants occasioned a somewhat corresponding sameness in the manifold ministrations of our Saviour's benevolence. Hence one of the reasons that account for the condensation of all the evangelistic narratives.

VER. 7. **And Jesus with His disciples withdrew.** Such is the collocation of the words in most of the best manuscripts.

To the sea. Viz. of Galilee. Our Saviour, in retiring thither from Capernaum, would move from place to place on either side of the lake, seeking opportunities, as they were required, for seclusion with His disciples (comp.

and a great multitude from Galilee followed him, and from
Judæa, 8 and from Jerusalem, and from beyond Idumæa, and
from beyond Jordan; and they about Tyre and Sidon, a great

Mark vi. 31), and halting for little seasons at the various villages and hamlets, such as Chorazin and Bethsaida.
And a great multitude from Galilee followed. The Saviour could not get seclusion. His fame was ringing all round about in the neighbourhood, and crowds sought to see and hear Him.
And from Judæa. A semicolon should precede these words, and thus they should be classed with the clauses of the next verse. It would have been well indeed if Robert Stephens had transferred them altogether to ver. 8. Not only was our Saviour's fame ringing throughout Galilee, it was sending its peals and echoes far and wide beyond; many, for instance, in Judæa were stirred.

VER. 8. **And from Jerusalem.** Even in the capital city people's wonder and curiosity were excited.
And from Idumæa. Or Edom, the territory that lay across the south of Palestine, stretching toward the south-east. The fame of Jesus had penetrated even thither. Numbers of Jews would be resident in Idumæa; for, though crushed as a people, they were a prolific race, and were widely distributed over the western parts of Asia, the eastern of Europe, and the northern of Africa. The Herod family came from Idumæa.
And beyond-the-Jordan. This expression *beyond-the-Jordan* is a kind of indefinite name for the territory that lay east of the Jordan, stretching southward to the Dead Sea, from the sea of Galilee or the river Hieromax. The district was called in Greek *Peræa*, which just means *the country on the other side*. It is classed by the evangelist with *Idumæa*, as forming part of one circuit of country, and hence the preposition *from* is not repeated, *and from Idumæa and Peræa*.
After the last clause Beza, Wetstein, Fritzsche, and many others, place a colon, and Principal Campbell and Volkmar a full point, looking upon the clauses *and from Judæa, and from Jerusalem, and from Idumæa and Peræa*, as constituting the train of the preceding clause, *from Galilee*. It is much better, however, with Heumann, Lachmann, and Meyer, to detach the train, and to connect it with what comes after. See the last clause of the verse.
And about Tyre and Sidon. That is, *and from the territory about Tyre and Sidon*. This territory is added to Idumæa and Peræa as completing the circuit of country round the Holy Land; and hence all the three localities are classed together under the one preposition *from,—and from Idumæa, and (the territory) beyond Jordan, and (the territory) about Tyre and Sidon*. The evangelist's language is to a large extent aggregative, and the jointing of the aggregated parts is left a little loose. But there is no difficulty in determining where the train begins and ends. See next clause.
A great multitude, hearing what things He was doing, came to Him. This 'great multitude' was *from* Judæa, Idumæa, Peræa, and the vicinity of Tyre and Sidon. They 'came' to Jesus. Note the verb. It is said of the 'great multitude' from Galilee that they 'followed' Him,—a word that was appropriate for the inhabitants of the Galilean towns, out from which Jesus 'withdrew to the sea,' but inappropriate to express the primary movement of the

multitude, when they had heard what great things he did, came unto him. 9 And he spake to his disciples, that a small ship should wait on him because of the multitude, lest they should throng him. 10 For he had healed many; insomuch that they pressed upon him for to touch him, as many as had plagues.

---

inhabitants of the remote places specified. These, *hearing what wonderful things He was doing* (ἀκούοντες ὅσα ἐποίει), '*came'* to *Him* to see and to hear.

VER. 9. **And He spake to His disciples.** No doubt after He had already been long engaged in ministering to the growing and exacting multitude.

That a small boat should wait on Him. Or, should keep in constant attendance on Him (προσκαρτερῇ). The conjunction translated *that* is literally *in order that* (ἵνα), so that the clause explains for what purpose it was that the Saviour had turned aside and spoken to His disciples.

Because of the crowd, in order that they might not press upon Him. The Geneva version of 1557 gives a very exaggerated translation to the verb, *lest they should thronge Hym to death*. The word however does denote *squeezing* or *jamming* (Felbinger, *drükketen*). It is not expressly said, as Meyer remarks, that our Lord taught the people out of the boat; but we like to imagine that He did. (Comp. chap. iv. 1, 2.)

VER. 10. **For He healed many.** The evangelist thus explains how it came to pass that the people pressed in upon the person of our Lord. Had He merely taught, like a great rabbi, they would probably have kept at a respectful distance. But He healed as well as taught; healing 'virtue' seemed to stream out from Him at all points.

So that as many as had plagues were pressing upon Him. Or, literally, *were falling upon Him* (ὥστε ἐπιπίπτειν αὐτῷ). The verb employed almost invariably receives the same translation in the other passages where it occurs. (See Luke xv. 20; Acts x. 44, xi. 15, xiii. 11, xix. 17, xx. 10; etc.) In English, however, the phrase, with subject and object such as it has before us, has got stiffened into an idiom that expresses hostile attack or assault. In the case before us it appropriately represents the eager and impetuous pressing, and bending forward almost to the angle of falling, that would be characteristic of the crowd of patients who gathered around our Lord and sought to come in contact with His person. Hammond thinks that interpreters have 'mistaken' the import of the phrase, and that it means 'so that they *fell down before* Him.' But he has entirely failed to realize to himself the peculiarity of the represented scene. *Plagues*: or *scourgings*, as the word literally signifies, and as it is translated in Acts xxii. 24, Heb. xi. 36. The phrase here denotes *diseases*, or *syknessis* as Purvey has it: only it graphically represents, on the one hand, the torture which they frequently inflict, while it suggests on the other that they are themselves *inflictions*. There is something '*penal*' in their '*pain*' (see *pœna*). The idea is true, though it leads the thought into an exceedingly complicated subject, which, if one's clue be insufficient, would speedily issue in an inextricable tanglement. The word *plague* has now a more restricted signification than it once had. It originally just meant *a stroke*. In its more modern acceptation, it is, says Archbishop Trench, "a title given to great pestilences, because

11 And unclean spirits, when they saw him, fell down before him, and cried, saying, Thou art the Son of God. 12 And he straitly charged them that they should not make him known.

"the universal conscience of men, which is never at fault, believed and confessed "that there were *strokes* or *blows* inflicted by God on a guilty and rebellious "world." (*Study of Words*, p. 40.)

In order that they might touch Him. For it was the Saviour's pleasure that there should in general be some perceptible connection between Himself and the objects of His healing ministrations.

Ver. 11. And the impure spirits. Note the article, pointing to those particular impure spirits who acted their part in the wonderful scene.

Whensoever they beheld Him (ὅταν αὐτὸν ἐθεώρουν), fell down before Him. Or, as the Rheims renders it, *fell down unto Him*. They fell down at His feet, doing homage as it were. *The impure spirits* thus acted in the way of actuating the bodies of the possessed. It was a cunning demonic 'dodge.' (See on chap. i. 23.)

And exclaimed, saying, Thou art the Son of God. That is, *Thou art no mere man! no mere son of man, like other men! Thou art come direct from God, in fulfilment of ancient prophecies, to put an end to our dominion over men!* We need not suppose, with Cajetan, that they uttered this confessional exclamation only tentatively, to find out whether or not our Saviour was the Son of God. It is unwaveringly affirmative; but it would no doubt be wrung from them under the influence of disappointment and hate. (Chap. i. 26.) They felt that they could not retain their hold on their prey, in the presence of the Great Deliverer. The 'virtue' which went out from Him constrained them to let go. But they hoped, we may imagine, that the audible utterance of their acknowledgment might suggest a suspicion of collusion with themselves. "It is certain," says Petter, "that in making their confession they aimed at evil and "sinister ends."

Ver. 12. And He charged them much. So the term is rendered in chap. i. 45, v. 10; John xiv. 30; Rom. xvi. 12; Rev. v. 4; etc. Wycliffe renders the adverb *gretely*; the Geneva, *sharply*; the Vulgate, Erasmus, and the Rheims, *vehemently*; Whiston and Bisping, *earnestly*; Mace, Wakefield, Principal Campbell, Thomson, Young, *strictly*. *Charged*: the original term means *rated* (ἐπετίμα). It indicates that our Saviour spoke sharply and peremptorily. *Them*: it is too generally assumed that the reference of this pronoun is exclusively to *the impure spirits*. The evangelist however had already, in the language of the preceding verse, intertwined a double reference to the spirits and their victims. He speaks of *their prostration at the feet of our Lord*. His thoughts thus oscillated for a little from the one party to the other. But as he mentally traced the actual progress of the events to which he refers, he sees the demoniacs delivered; he takes note of their noisy demonstrations of ecstasy and zeal, when once they felt themselves free; he then naturally classes them with the others who had been healed (see ver. 10); and then, while thinking of the whole number of the cured, he says, *and He spake very peremptorily to them.* Such was Matthew's

14]   ST. MARK III.   73

13 And he goeth up into a mountain, and calleth *unto him*
whom he would : and they came unto him.   14 And he or-

---

understanding of the case; chap. xii. 16-20. And, even although we had not
Matthew's testimony, a careful and unbiassed effort to disintegrate the elements
of Mark's artlessly condensed representation should lead us to the same result.
Surely it is a much more natural conclusion than to suppose, with Volkmar
(p. 239), that Matthew, in condensing Mark's narrative, imprudently copied
ver. 12, while leaving out ver. 11 !

In order that they might not make Him known, or *manifest* (φανερόν). These
words represent, not exactly what our Lord said to the healed persons, but what
was the end He had in view in saying what He said (ἵνα). He wished to prevent
them, as far as possible, from spreading themselves abroad over society, and
zealously proclaiming that He was the great Deliverer. His popularity with
the common people was already inconveniently great. There was besides too
much tendency to make use of Him for merely physical relief. A time too of
quiet was needed for the progressive instruction of His disciples in things
moral, spiritual, and Messianic. And He shrank, with true delicacy of spirit,
from the din and dust and 'muscular' rush and roar and rant of those excited
mobs of admirers, in the tides of whose applause moral and political mounte-
banks think themselves glorified.

VER. 13-19 constitute another snatch of narrative, exceedingly condensed.
Comp. Matt. x. 1-4 and Luke vi. 12-16.

VER. 13. **And He goeth up into the mountain.** We know not exactly when;
we know not exactly where. Neither the precise chronology, nor the precise
topography, of the event was interesting to the evangelist. He had heard,
however, from the lips of his informant, that it was '*the* mountain' into which
the Lord ascended, that is, *the particular 'highland' of the locality that was
present to the thoughts of the narrator.* Comp. Matt. v. 1. Of course it was
some one or other of the numerous upland spots in the vicinity of the sea of
Galilee, at its northern extremity. Our Lord 'ascended *into* the mountain,'
that is, *into* some of the scoops or gorges that intersect the face of the
eminence.

And calleth to Him whom He Himself pleased. We need not fancy anything
like vociferation in the call; for we need not suppose, on the one hand, that our
Saviour had ascended to any very great height, and we must bear in mind, on
the other, that in those still regions of comparatively bare rock, and thus of
universal 'sounding-board,' the voice is easily carried. Our Lord called to Him
'whom *He Himself* pleased' (οὓς ἤθελεν αὐτός). He did not allow any of His
general followers to offer themselves, ultroneously, for special work and special
privilege.

And they departed to Him (ἀπῆλθον πρὸς αὐτόν). Namely, from the rest of the
people who remained below.

VER. 14. **And He appointed twelve.** Literally, *And He made twelve*, an exceedingly artless expression; and, in conjunction with the following clause, just
as artlessly though not literally rendered by the Vulgate, *And He made that
twelve should be with Him* (Rheims translation). Tyndale and Coverdale,

dained twelve, that they should be with him, and that he
might send them forth to preach, 15 and to have power to
heal sicknesses, and to cast out devils. 16 And Simon he

instead of the generic *made*, have the specific *ordained*; the Geneva, Norton,
Sharpe, Rotherham, the English Revisionists, *appointed*; Principal Campbell,
selected. The term may be freely so rendered; but still it just means *made*.
It would appear that our Lord had called up to Him a select number of His
most attached followers; and then *from these* He selected twelve. See Luke vi.
13. Standing somewhat apart from the company, He would tell Peter to
advance nearer to Him: that was one. Then He would call perhaps on
Andrew, the brother of Peter: that would make two. Then He would call on
the other pair of brothers, James and John: that would make four. And
thus He would proceed, till *He made twelve*, the full number of the children of
Israel. The Lord, it would appear, delighted to realize, in His institution of
the apostolate, His relation to the whole of the Israelites, as representative of
the whole of mankind.

In order that they might be with Him. He had a particular aim in '*making
twelve*.' It was, first of all, in order that they might be His constant attendants. He wished to have them beside Him, that He might pour His spirit into
them, and train them, at once by light and by love, to be His fellow-labourers
and His successors in teaching the people.

And in order that He might send them forth to preach. Namely, by and by,
when they were inwardly equipped. *That He might send them forth* (ἀποστέλλῃ),
that is, that He might make *apostles* of them (ἀπόστολοι). This was His
ulterior aim. Our Lord could not Himself reach very many with His own
individual voice; and hence He multiplied it as it were. He knew that it was
all-important for the Israelites in particular, and thence for all men, that they
should be earnestly *spoken to* in reference to the kingdom of God. Hence
'preachers,' or *heralds of good news*, were needed.

VER. 15. **And to have authority to cast out the demons.** '*The* demons,' to
wit, which were so rampant in human society, annoying, oppressing, defiling,
and abusing men. (See chap. i. 23, 32.) Note the expression *to have authority*.
We might have expected the evangelist to have said simply, *and to cast out the
demons*. But the power of exorcising was so different from the power of
preaching, that the evangelist makes special mention of the Divine authorization
with which they would require to be endued.

VER. 16. **And He made the twelve.** This artless repetitive clause, with the
addition of the retrospective article, is inserted by Tischendorf in his eighth
edition of the text; apparently on good authority, the authority of the
Sinaitic, Vatican, Ephraemi, and San Gallensis manuscripts (א B C* Δ), and the
Æthiopic manuscript m. The clause had got to be early dropped, as bearing
the aspect of a useless repetition.

And He imposed on Simon the name Peter. Another exceedingly artless expression. The evangelist intends to enumerate the apostles, and begins with
Peter. But instead of introducing the surname in a subordinate clause, *Simon,
on whom He imposed the name Peter*, he narrates the imposition of the name in

ST. MARK III.

surnamed Peter; 17 and James the *son* of Zebedee, and John the brother of James; and he surnamed them Boanerges,

a capital clause, and then leaves the narration as sufficing for the enumerative object that he had in view. The word *Simon* or *Simeon* is Hebrew, meaning *hearing*; the word *Peter* is Greek, meaning *stone*. As imposed, however, upon the chief of the apostles, it is not to be regarded as referring to any little pebble in the brook, or any accidental chip of rock lying on the road or in the field. Galilee and the surrounding lands were remarkable for massive stone structures. The most conspicuous of these were sacred edifices, temples; and the foundation stones of these temples were invariably large and imposing. It would be with a view to these large and conspicuous foundation stones that our Lord would call Simon a Stone. He was spiritually large and strong, massive and shapely, fit to constitute an important part of the substructure of the great spiritual temple of God. (See Matt. xvi. 18.) There is no reason for supposing, with Cajetan and Meyer, that the name *Peter* was imposed on Simon just at the particular time referred to. (See John i. 42.) The evangelist simply takes the opportunity, in his own artless way, of recording the new name and of mentioning that it was given to Simon by our Lord.

VER. 17. Mark does not classify the apostles in pairs, as Matthew does (x. 2-4), although it is he who mentions that by and by they were sent out in pairs (chap. vi. 7). He heaps their names together in an artless manner, but is particular, like the other evangelists, about the first and the last. He is also particular, unlike Matthew, and Luke in his Gospel (vi. 14), to introduce James and John between Peter and his brother Andrew, thus recognising the pre-eminence of the triumvirate who were admitted by our Lord into His most intimate fellowship. (See Mark ix. 2, xiv. 33.) The same intersection occurs in the Acts of the Apostles (i. 13).

And James the son of Zebedee. James is thus patronymically marked out, to distinguish him from the other apostolical James, the son of Alphæus. See next verse.

And John the brother of James. John had no doubt been the younger brother, and hence his position in the list, though he ultimately became much more distinguished than his brother. See chap. i. 19; and comp. Luke ix. 28.

And them He surnamed Boanerges, which is, Sons of thunder. The expression rendered *surnamed* means literally *imposed on them* '*names*.' Note the plural 'names.' It seems to justify us in concluding that each of the brothers would bear the 'name' *Son-of-thunder* or *Bar-r^eges*. The two names combined make *Sons of thunder*, or *Boanerges*, that is *Boanè-r^eges*. The word *Boanè*, meaning *Sons of*, must have been a provincial or otherwise peculiar way of pronouncing *Benê* or *Benai*. (*Benê* is Hebrew and Chaldee; *Benai* is Syriac.) Drusius indeed was perplexed with the broadness of the pronunciation, and supposed that the word, as found in the evangelist's text, must have been accidentally mis-spelled, and that it should be written *Banê*. (*Præterita*, in loc.) Beza was nearly of the same opinion. 'It is obvious,' says he, 'that the *o* should be expunged.' But this is going much too far in an assumption of purism of pronunciation among the Galileans. There are often the strangest freaks of

which is, The sons of thunder : 18 and Andrew, and Philip,

variation in pronunciation. There would be in Galilee, especially in the 'broad' direction. (See Matt. xxvi. 73.) The manuscripts are unanimous in reading *oa* ; and Hugh Broughton says, " At this day scheva is sounded by the " Jews themselves as *oa*, as for example *Noaby-im*," (for *Neby-im*). (*Works*, p. 706.) The other moiety of the surname, viz. *r*ges* or *r*gesh* (רֶגֶשׁ or רִגְשׁ-ַ י), has also occasioned to critics unnecessary difficulty. It is true that in the classic passages in which the term occurs, it means, not *thunder*, but an *assembly* or *crowd*. (See Ps. lv. 14.) In no passage of the Targums, it would appear, or of the Talmud, does it indisputably mean *thunder*. (See *Patrizi*, in loc.) It is, however, very evidently onomatopoetic, having primarily a reference to *noise*. (See Buxtorf's *Lexicon Talmud.*, sub voce.) Hence the translation which the cognate verb receives in the Septuagint version of Ps. ii. 1 ($\dot{\epsilon}\phi\rho\dot{\nu}\alpha\xi\alpha\nu$), a translation to some extent reproduced in our English version, ' why do the heathen *rage* ?' in the margin it is *tumultuously assemble*. Castell conjectured that there was a connection between the word and our Saxon *rush*, which is undoubtedly onomatopoetic. (*Lexicon*, sub voce.) We may be sure, at all events, that in the Galilean dialect the word did mean *thunder*. The whole compound word was perplexing to Jerome. He looked at it apparently from too classic a standpoint, both as regards the pronunciation of the first part, and as regards the conventional acceptation of the second. He hence proposed to amend it into *Bene-re'em* (that is, בְּנֵי רַעַם). " The name," says he, " is not, " as most suppose, *Boanerges*, but is more correctly read *Bene-reem*." (*Comm.* on Dan. i. 7 ; see also his *Comm.* on Isa. lii. 4. and his *Lexicon of Hebrew Names*.) Luther was so far swayed by Jerome's authority as to introduce his word into the text; he gives it thus, *Bnehargem*. Stunica too accepted it, and Maldonato, and le Clerc. Grotius, again, supposed that the second moiety of the word was neither *r*ges* nor *re'em*, but *re'es* or *ra'ash* (רַעַשׁ), which is sometimes translated *rushing*, sometimes *earthquake*, and in Isa. ix. 5 *confused noise*. Hammond followed Grotius, but unwisely ; for *re'es* or *ra'ash* is expressly distinguished in its meaning from *thunder* in Isa. xxix. 6. There is really no occasion for racking ingenuity to account for the evangelist's term. There is no difficulty in accepting it just as we have it, when we take the power of pronunciation into account, and the obvious onomatopoetic force of the term. The rationale of its application to James and John has, like everything else about the term, been keenly disputed. *It is unknown*, as le Clerc observes ; it can therefore be only conjectured. The Fathers in general conjectured in a spiritual direction. They supposed that the term glances at the general power of the gospel as preached by the two apostles. (See *Suiceri Thesaurus*, sub voce $\beta\rho o \nu \tau \dot{\eta}$.) Heumann conjectured in another direction, that the name was intended to be a term of reprimand or reproach (*ein Schelt-Nahme*), because James and John had said, in reference to certain Samaritan villagers, " Lord, " wilt Thou that we command fire to come down from heaven, and consume them, " even as Elias did ? " (Luke ix. 54.) It is a most unlikely interpretation, though approved of by Whitby. Our Lord would not deal in nicknames ; and if He had ever allowed Himself in such a licence, He would have called His inconsiderately ardent disciples *Sons of fire* rather than *Sons of thunder*. A-Lapide

and Bartholomew, and Matthew, and Thomas, and James

supposed that the name was imposed because the Lord designed that the brothers should excel the other apostles in their power of preaching and propagating the gospel; he thinks in particular that the commencement of John's Gospel evinces all the peculiar majesty of thunder and lightning. Luther took a corresponding view (*Glos.*, in loc.). It is however far more likely that there is a simple reference, in the surname, to some deep-toned peculiarity of voice which was characteristic of the brothers, and which would eminently fit them, when engaged in addressing their fellow men, for rolling in on the mind and heart, with awe inspiring effect, the solemnities of religion. This view of the import of the surname was taken by Beza, and Pfeiffer (*Ebraic. et Exotic.*, xviii. 4). It is not quite the same idea as was suggested by the peculiar style of Pericles' oratory, the 'thunder and lightning' style (*ut non loqui et orare, sed quod Pericli contigit, fulgurare ac tonare videaris*: QUINCTILIAN, *Inst.* ii. 16), but it does lie to a certain extent on the same line of thought. The filial element of the phrase, namely *Sons of*, is an exemplification of a favourite idiom among the Hebrews. (Comp. chap. ii. 19.) The entire compound surname was on the whole equivalent to *Thunderers* (οἱ βροντῶνες: Euthymius Zigabenus); but it suggested this idea over and above, that the brothers *derived* no little portion of their differentiating peculiarity as preachers from the solemn thunder-tone that was inherent in their voices.

VER. 18. The remaining names are heaped together.

And Andrew. A Greek name, meaning *Manly*. It is an incidental proof of the prevalence of the Greek language in Galilee. He was the brother of Peter (chap. i. 16), and has left behind him in history but few traces of his career. He is reported, says Eusebius, on the authority of Origen (*Hist.*, iii. 1), to have gone to Scythia to preach the gospel; and he is said to have suffered martyrdom on a decussated cross (or X), which is hence called the *St. Andrew cross*.

And Philip. Another Greek name, meaning *Fond of horses*. It was this Philip who said to Nathanael *Come and see*. (John i. 43-51.) Little is known of his career. He is said to have died at Hierapolis (Eusebius, *Hist.* v. 24).

And Bartholomew. A Hebrew patronymical name, signifying *Son of Tholomew* or *Talmai*. It is not unlikely that he was Nathanael (John i. 43-51); and he might be generally called *Bartholomew*, to distinguish him from some other Nathanael in the same circle. (Comp. John xxi. 1, 2.) He is said to have gone to India to preach the gospel. (See Eusebius, *Hist.* v. 10; and Jerome, *de Viris Illustribus*, xxxvi.)

And Matthew. The tax collector, or officer of revenue (Matt. x. 3),—no doubt also the evangelist. (See *Introd. to Comm. on Matt.*) His name is Hebrew, and means *Gift-of-God* or *Theodore*.

And Thomas. Another Hebrew name, meaning *Twin*. Its Greek synonym is *Didymus*. (See John xi. 16, xx. 24, xxi. 2.) There are many traditions regarding his ultimate career. Origen reports that he preached the gospel in Parthia (Eusebius, *Hist.* iii. 1). There is extant a *Gospel according to Thomas* among the New Testament Apocrypha.

And James the (son) of Alphæus. Wycliffe's translation is, *and James Alfey*.

the *son* of Alphæus, and Thaddæus, and Simon the Cu-

Jerome, in his treatise *On the Perpetual Virginity of Mary*, written against Helvidius, maintains that Alphæus was the husband of Mary the sister of the Virgin Mary ; and he hence supposes that the James here specified was one of our Lord's ' brethren,' being elsewhere called ' James the little ' (Mark xv. 40). By ' brethren ' he understands *cousins-german.* W. H. Mill maintains the same view. (*The Descent and Parentage of the Saviour*, sect. 3.) There seem however to be almost insuperable difficulties in the way of accepting such a genealogical theory. It is not likely that Mary our Lord's mother would have a sister also called **Mary.** The statement in John xix. 25, on which the whole theory is based, may be legitimately interpreted on the principle that four women are referred to, not three. It is on this principle that the Peshito translation of the passage is constructed : " Now there stood by the cross of Jesus His mother, "and the sister of His mother, *and* Mary (the wife) of Cleophas, and Mary Mag-"dalene." The older theory regarding the ' brethren ' of our Lord (that they were the children of Joseph by a previous marriage), the theory that preceded both that of Helvidius (that they were Mary's children) and that of Jerome (that they were the children of Mary's sister Mary), is the most probable of all. It has the advantage, in addition to other recommendations in its favour, of accounting for the air of superiority and precedence assumed by the ' brethren ' in relation to our Lord. (John vii. 3–10 ; Mark iii. 21.) It is certainly not at all probable that any of the apostles would be of the number of the ' brethren.' (See John vii. 5.) *Alphæus :* There is no reason for supposing that this is the same *Alphæus* who has been already referred to as the father of Levi, or Matthew. (Mark ii. 14.) The name was common among the Hebrews ; whether it be but another form of *Clopas* (not *Cleophas*), referred to in John xix. 25, is uncertain. The archetypical Hebrew word *Chalphai* might readily mould itself in the direction of both poles of pronunciation ; but we need not seek to determine. If, however, the *Clopas* of John xix. 25 be Alphæus, then the *Cleopas* of Luke xxiv. 18 must be a different person from *Clopas*, for Luke, as well as Matthew and Mark, uses the form *Alphæus* (vi. 15 ; Acts i. 13).

And Thaddæus. Or *Lebbæus*, as he is called by Matthew (x. 3). He is otherwise called *Judas* or *Jude* ' (the son) of James.' (See Luke's Gospel, vi. 15, Acts i. 13 ; see also John xiv. 22.) He is, as Luther remarks, ' the good Judas,' (*der fromme Judas*). It is most probable that *Judas* or *Jude* would be his ' proper name.' *Lebbæus* or *Thaddæus*, sometimes the one and sometimes the other, would be a kind of characteristic designation or surname. The two words are affiliated as designations, *Lebbæus* coming from *leb* (לֵב) the Hebrew and Aramaic for *heart*, and *Thaddæus* from *thad* the Aramaic for *breast* or *bosom* (תַּד, Hebrew שַׁד). In the *breast* or *bosom* we have, to a certain extent, the outer development of the *heart* ; the *full-breasted* is as it were the *large-hearted.* We know nothing of the ultimate career of this Judas or Jude. He is doubtless to be distinguished from the Judas or Jude, the ' servant of Jesus Christ ' and ' brother of James,' who wrote the little epistle that comes after the Epistles of John.

And Simon the Cananæan. There is no reference at all to the people called *Canaanites.* Neither is there any reference, as Luther seemed to think, to the

naanite, 19 and Judas Iscariot, which also betrayed him. And they went into an house. 20 And the multitude

---

town *Cana*. He translates the expression 'Simon of Cana'; so do Coverdale, Piscator, Bengel, Zinzendorf. Tyndale has *Symon of Cane*. The evangelist's term however is not *Canaite*, but *Cananite*, or better still, and as Edgar Taylor gives it, *Kananite*, or *Canancean* as it is in the original and as Alford gives it in his translation. The word is an Aramaic word, signifying *zealot*. And hence it is translated into Greek by Luke, *Zelotes* (Gosp. vi. 15 ; Acts i. 13). Norton renders the phrase here *Simon the Zealot*. The zealots were an extreme political party among the Jews, somewhat corresponding to the Irreconcilables of our own day, who were determined on no account to acquiesce in the Roman rule. They were persuaded that any public or private measures or acts, however bloody or revolutionary, which were intended and fitted either to break down or to embarrass the dominion of the Romans, or of any other heathens, within the Holy Land, were not only legitimate but meritorious. They played in subsequent times a terrible part in connection with the 'reign of terror' that preceded the destruction of Jerusalem. (See Josephus' *Wars of the Jews*, from the 4th Book onward.) At the outset of the movement there would most probably be a purer zeal than was afterwards developed ; it would be pious as well as patriotic. And no doubt it would be at this comparatively pure stage of things that Simon would get connected with the movement. The diviner zeal, emanating from Jesus, and flowing in the direction of the kingdom of the true Jews, ' the kingdom of heaven,' would change the current of his life.

VER. 19. **And Judas Iscariot.** The last and lowest in the list. He would receive the designation *Iscariot* to distinguish him from other Judases in general, and from Judas Thaddæus or Lebbæus in particular. It is generally supposed that the designation is just *ish-Kerioth*, meaning literally *man of Kerioth*, or *Keriothite*. Kerioth was an obscure town of Judah (see Josh. xv. 25), and it is not unlikely that Judas's father Simon had removed from it to Galilee. Hence he too, when once he became a 'residenter' in Galilee, would be called *Simon Iscariot*, or *Simon the Keriothite*. And so indeed he is called in the text of John vi. 71 and xiii. 26 which is given in the editions of Tischendorf and Tregelles.

Who also betrayed Him. Or, *who also delivered Him up*, namely, to those who were thirsting for His blood. It is the black mark on Judas that differentiates him from the other apostles, and from all other men. It may be asked, *Why did our Lord choose such a man to be an apostle ?* It is enough, meanwhile, to answer (1) that as our Lord, for the grandest of purposes, had appeared among men in a peculiar sphere of human society and at a particular time, so the men whom He chose to be disciples and apostles *might not be the best that were absolutely imaginable* ; they might merely be the best that, in the circumstances, were actually attainable. And then again (2) there is no good reason for supposing that Judas would be an unprincipled man at the time he was chosen.

And He cometh into a house. With these words a new brief paragraph commences. *They should have formed part of the 20th verse*. Robert Stephens, the verse-maker, included them in the 20th verse ; but unhappily Beza differed in his judgment, and in his editions tacked them on to ver. 19 ; so did Henry

cometh together again, so that they could not so much as eat

Stephens in his editions. Our translators, no doubt influenced by their authority, walked in their footsteps. Inconsiderately however. And yet Mill and Wetstein followed. The Elzevirs before them had wavered; in their earlier editions (1624, 1633, and 1641) following Beza and Henry Stephens, but returning in their later editions (1658, 1662, 1670, 1678) to Robert Stephens. Bengel saw that the words belonged to a new paragraph, and he hence commenced a new paragraph with them, but he marked them in his 1734 edition as belonging to ver. 19. Afterwards he discovered that they properly belonged to ver. 20, and hence in his 1753 edition and his German version he not only kept them at the commencement of the new paragraph, but restored them to the 20th verse. Both Zinzendorf and Griesbach commence with them a new paragraph; so did Luther and Tyndale. Lachmann and Tischendorf both commence a new paragraph with the words; but they both mark them as belonging to the 19th verse. Ewald however and Tregelles restore them to the 20th verse. It is not easy to give the words a correct idiomatic translation. The literal translation would be *and He cometh into house*. The narrator's standpoint is *at the house*; hence the verb *cometh* instead of *goeth*. But the phrase *into house*, or *to house* as Coverdale has it, or *unto housse* as Tyndale has it, is not an English idiom. Yet the original expression does not mean *into a house*, as Wycliffe has it. Neither does it exactly mean *home*, as in the margin and the Geneva version. It corresponds to our idiomatic expression *into town*, only it narrows the reference to a particular house. (See on chap. ii. 1.) The meaning is that *in process of time Jesus returns to Capernaum with His disciples, and they go into the house where He was accustomed to live when in that town*. Tischendorf's reading, in his eighth edition, '*He cometh*' instead of *they come*, is supported by the Sinaitic and Vatican manuscripts and some other considerable authorities. Not unlikely it is the correct reading; but it is implied, of course, that the apostles were with our Lord. See next verse.

Ewald thinks that in Mark's original Gospel, an abstract of *the Sermon on the Mount* would intervene between the words of this clause and the words of the preceding clause, but that somehow it had got dropped out. Hence he interposes between the clauses the signs of a hiatus or gap (a *Lücke*). It is an arbitrary conjecture, founded on an arbitrary theory as to what Mark might be expected to record and what he might be expected to leave unrecorded. We must take Mark's *Memoirs of our Lord* just as we have them, and be contented with them. They are indeed in many respects, semi-detached snatches of biography, artlessly pieced together. But how charming!

VER. 20. **And a crowd cometh together again.** The excitement, curiosity and eagerness of the people were still flowing as in spring-tide. Note the *again*. It glances back, not exclusively to what is recorded in chap. ii. 2, but to the many notices of crowds that are contained in the entire preceding narrative. **So that they could not so much as eat bread.** The expression is peculiarly emphatic (ὥστε μὴ δύνασθαι αὐτοὺς μήτε ἄρτον φαγεῖν). *Among many other things, less indispensable, which they were not able to do,* our Lord and His disciples *could not even secure for themselves such a modicum of seclusion and leisure as was needful for their meals.* The people kept thronging in irrepressibly, eager to

bread. 21 And when his friends heard *of it*, they went out to lay hold on him: for they said, He is beside himself.

---

see, eager to hear, eager to experience or to witness, the wonderful effects of the outgoing 'virtue.'

Ver. 21. And when His friends heard. Viz. about what was going on. When reports reached them regarding their Kinsman's persisted-in preachings, and His fearless disputings with the ablest and most learned of the scribes and Pharisees, and His actual selection of a band of twelve coadjutors and apostles, not to mention other rumours of most daring exorcisms and cures. The expression rendered *His friends* has caused perplexity to many critics. Unnecessarily however. It literally means *they who were from beside Him* (οἱ παρ' αὐτοῦ), that is, in this connection, *they who were by origin or birth from beside Him*, *they who were 'closely connected' with Him by birth*. It is quite an appropriate phrase to denote one's *kinsmen*. So the term is translated by Wycliffe. The Geneva has the corresponding word *kinsfolkes*. Tyndale meant to bring out the same idea when he rendered the expression, *they that longed unto Him*, that is, *they that belonged unto Him*. Luther missed the mark, and misled Coverdale, when he rendered the phrase *they that were about Him (die um ihn waren)*. Wolle however contended for the same translation (*De Parenthesi Sacra*, p. 33). And Krebs's rendering is kindred, *they who were with Him*. Schöttgen gives the same rendering with Krebs, both in his *Lexicon* and in his *Horæ Hebraicæ*; it is approved of too by Köcher. All these critics suppose that the phrase refers to our Saviour's *disciples*. Wolf took the same view of the reference (see his note on ver. 31), and Griesbach and Vater. And so too Sir Norton Knatchbull (*Annotations*, in loc.) and Hombergk (*Parerga*, in loc.); only they interpreted the phrase as meaning *some from Him*, that is, *His messengers*, or *they who were sent by Him*.

They went out. Or, better still, *they came out*. The evangelist's mental standpoint was not at Nazareth, *whence the Saviour's kinsfolk went*, but at Capernaum *whither they came*. If we were to drop his mental standpoint out of view altogether, we might render the verb freely *they set out*.

To lay hold on Him. Namely with their hands, that they might take Him home and keep Him under family restraint.

For they said, He is beside Himself. Literally, *He is standing out of Himself*; He is *out of His senses* (ἐξέστη). With their small ideas of things, they could not otherwise account for His conduct. The verb translated *they said* is in the imperfect tense (ἔλεγον); *they kept harping on the matter*. Many expositors have felt scandalized at the application of such language to our Saviour on the part of His kinsfolk; and, in particular, they have been unable to reconcile themselves to the idea that His mother could allow herself to speak thus of her Son. Hence they have tortured their ingenuity to excogitate some other interpretation. The writer of the very ancient Cambridge manuscript (D) represents the verse thus: *And when the scribes and the rest heard concerning Him, they went out to lay hold of Him, for they said, He is driving them mad* (ἐξέσταται αὐτούς, *exentiat eos!*). The Gothic version represents the sense thus: *And scribes and others hearing of Him went out to lay hold of Him; they also said that He is out of His senses* (*usgaisiths*). The Old Latin version presents a

G

82   ST. MARK III.   [22

22 And the scribes which came down from Jerusalem said,

---

corresponding transformation, swinging in some of its manuscripts to the representation preserved in the Cambridge codex, and in others to the milder misrepresentation preserved in the Gothic translation. It is evident that some of the old transcribers and translators had been sorely perplexed. So in more modern times. Schöttgen, for instance, though reverently retaining the unexceptionally supported reading of the Received Text, puts it on the rack, and extorts from it the following interpretation: *And when the disciples heard (the crowd tumultuating outside the door), they went out to restrain it, for they said, It is furious!* Sir Norton Knatchbull, with his characteristic love of the peculiar, gives a corresponding explanation, and speaks of *the multitude being mad.* Coverdale, again, contented himself with toning down the force of the verb, *He taketh too much upon Him.* Grotius, on the other hand, found relief in the other verb, *they said,* or *they were saying.* He thinks that it is used impersonally, *it was said, it was rumoured.* Euthymius Zigabenus had a similar idea, interpreting the phrase thus, *for certain envious persons said, He is beside Himself.* Griesbach, again, thinks that Christ had gone out to the crowd, though this is not expressly stated by the evangelist; and he would explain the verse as follows: *And when they who were with Him* (His disciples and other friends) *heard (how He was over exerting Himself among the crowd), they went out to bring Him in, for they* (i.e. *some of the crowd) were saying, He is carried beyond Himself, so as to be no longer master of Himself.* Vater takes the same view. And still other and equally violent modifications of interpretation have been proposed by other interpreters, more influenced perhaps, as Maldonato observes, by piety than by prudence. Unhappily however. It is by no means needful to suppose that our Lord's kinsfolk understood Him, or were careful to avoid all strong expressions in reference to Him. (See John vii. 3-10.) Neither is it on the other hand needful to suppose that every one of them, inclusive even of Mary herself, used the very strong phraseology recorded. Nothing is more reasonable, as Maldonato remarks, than to assume a free and easy *syllepsis* or *synecdoche* of representation on the part of the evangelist. And it is, at the same time, quite reasonable to assume that, even to Mary, our Saviour was in many respects an Inexplicable Mystery. So doubtless would He have been to *us*, had we had no other light, by means of which to see, than the twilight in which Mary and the 'brethren' were walking.

Ver. 22. **And.** The evangelist, having in the preceding verse led us in thought from Capernaum to Nazareth, and shown us the departure of the Saviour's kinsfolk on their officious mission, leaves that thread of things, to be afterwards resumed: see ver. 31-35. Meantime, and while the kinsfolk are as it were on the road, he introduces us abruptly and artlessly to another scene.

The scribes who came down from Jerusalem. For it would appear that the great ecclesiastics in the capital were feeling uneasy in reference to the Galilean Reformer. He had not got His training at the feet of any of the accredited rabbis, and yet He was already quite a power in the country. They deemed it prudent therefore to depute some of the ablest of the scribes to go down and make inquisition. *Down:* Jerusalem was perched on the summit of a broad

He hath Beelzebub, and by the prince of the devils casteth he out

mountain ridge; the highest point of the city was more than 2,300 feet above the level of the Mediterranean. Hence people in all parts of the Holy Land spoke of *going up to* Jerusalem and *coming down from* it.

Said, He hath Beelzebub. Or rather *Beelzebul*. Such is the form of the word in Greek, although unhappily it is *Beelzebub* in the Syriac Peshito and the Latin Vulgate. It was from the latter version that the corrupted form passed into the Anglo-Saxon and the old English versions, inclusive of Wycliffe's; and thence it descended into our Authorized version and the Revised. It passed likewise, from the same source, into Luther's German version, and Emser's, Piscator's, and Zinzendorf's; also into the older French versions; and into the old Dutch version, though it was rectified in the revised version of the Synod of Dort. It passed likewise into Diodati's Italian version, and Martini's. But in Brucioli's Tuscan version a compromise is made between the two forms; or rather, the peculiarity of both the forms is dropped. His word is *Belzebu*. The evangelist's word was no doubt *Beelzebul*, which however was an intentional travesty of *Beelzebub* or *Baal-zebub*. This latter word was the real name of the tutelary deity of the Ekronites (2 Kings i. 2, 3, 16), and meant *Fly-Lord*. But the Jews, by the change of a single letter, turned it quaintly into *Filth-Lord* (see *Comm.* on Matt. x. 25); and then, pleased with their own theological pleasantry, they proceeded farther in their grim humour, and applied the name in its parodied form to Satan. Hence when the scribes said of our Lord, *He has Beelzebul*, they meant to destroy His influence with the people by throwing into their minds the terrible idea that *the devil was in league with Him*. (See ver. 23.) There is far greater malice in the imputation than Rosenmüller and Kuinöl imagined; they thought that it simply meant *He is mad*.

And, By the prince of the demons He casts out the demons. Note the connective particle *and*; it is not part of the report; and hence it does not introduce a second clause in the terrible accusation, or lead us to understand that they who said *He has Beelzebul* immediately added *and by the prince of the demons He casts out the demons*. The repetition of the quotation particle in the original (the recitative ὅτι after the καί) shows us that the evangelist is recording *two distinct reports*,—although, it is true, they were but different forms or phases of one diabolical accusation. If we were, according to a suggestion of Philippi, to represent ocularly, by means of inverted commas, the power of the quotation particle, the verse would stand thus: *And the scribes, who came down from Jerusalem, said, " He has Beelzebul," and, " By the prince of the demons He casts out the demons."* It is Satan of course, or Beelzebul, who is called *the prince* or *ruler of the demons*. (See next verse.) The expression *by the ruler of the demons* is rendered freely by Tyndale, *by the power of the chefe devyll*. It is literally '*in*' *the ruler of the demons*, and represents our Saviour's personality as *merged in* the personality of Satan. The imputation was that Satan had taken Jesus *into himself*; or, to exhibit the case under a slightly different phase, that he had, as principal, entered into a compact with Jesus as subordinate. He had entered into this compact, it was insinuated, *for the purpose of putting down the inestimably beneficent influence of the Pharisees!* Hence, it was alleged, all the strictures and criticisms of Jesus on the godly ways of the godly people! Power

devils. 23 And he called them *unto him,* and said unto them in parables, How can Satan cast out Satan? 24 And if a kingdom be divided against itself, that kingdom cannot

---

was given from beneath, power even to cast out demons, so that the people might be thoroughly deceived ! (As to demons, see on chap. i. 34.)

VER. 23. **And He called them unto Him.** The horrible imputation was not directly addressed to Himself, but to some of the surrounding people. Perhaps it would be elicited in the course of some keen debate which was going on aside. Not unlikely it would at first be only broached in some half smothered insinuation, gnashed between the teeth. But the Saviour was cognisant of it, and it brought collision to a crisis. Hence He called His accusers to Him.

And said unto them in parables. Such as are recorded in ver. 24, 25, 27. The argumentative *parables* there recorded are short indeed; still they are *parables,* for it is not essential to a *parable* that it be a fully developed narration or story. The word means etymologically a *side-throw.* The thing signified by the word is therefore *something thrown by the side of another thing,* it may be *to hide it,* or it may be *to show it off.* The parable is in general some kind of similitude, illustrating by something common, well known, or easily understood, some other thing lying more remote from popular apprehension. It is based on a profound law of correspondences, pervading and binding into harmony the whole universe. Instead of the Greek word *parables,* Tyndale, Coverdale and the original Geneva version of 1557 have the Latin word *similitudes,* which however is not quite broad enough to cover the whole expanse of *parables.* (See Luke iv. 23, in the Greek.)

How can Satan cast out Satan? This does not mean, as Fritzsche supposed, and Luther and Coverdale before him, *How can one Satan cast out another Satan?* but *How can Satan cast out himself?* (See ver. 24, 25.) When the Saviour says *can,* He does not refer to *physical ability* as it is called, for it is conceivable that Satan could, as a mere feat of ability, make a feint of casting out himself. He could cast himself out (as regards some forms of his indwelling presence or energy) from some individuals, in order that he might throw a 'glamour' of misconception over the minds of others. Our Saviour is referring however to a certain kind of *moral ability,* so called, to ability inter-related to consistency of demeanour. *How could it be consistent in Satan to cast out Satan?*

VER. 24. **And.** The *parables,* referred to in the preceding verse, now come in. But as the argumentative query which has already been proposed has really settled the whole question, they are not introduced as demonstrations by means of the ratiocinative particle *for,* but are just artlessly linked on as appended illustrations. Hence the *and.*

If a kingdom be divided against itself. That is, *If perchance it should happen that a kingdom has been divided* (μερισθῇ) *against itself.* The expression *against itself* is literally *upon itself* (ἐφ' ἑαυτήν); if part has turned *upon* part with hostile intent. The preposition denotes *motion with a view to superposition;* if each party has sought to come *down upon* the other, so as to *overthrow* it and keep it *under.*

stand. 25 And if a house be divided against itself, that house cannot stand. 26 And if Satan rise up against himself, and be divided, he cannot stand, but hath an end. 27

That kingdom is not able to stand. Note the present tense of the verb, *is not able*, coming after the præterite tense of the preceding clause. If the division in the state is already an accomplished fact, the consequence is not merely *a prospective* but *a present weakness*, and hence *imminent prostration*. If the parties are well balanced, and the feud be incurable, (two elements in the case that are parabolically assumed,) the kingdom must collapse. For the meaning of the passive verb rendered *to stand* (σταθῆναι), and correctly so rendered, see Luke xviii. 40, xix. 8, xxi. 36; Acts ii. 14, v. 20, xvii. 22, xxv. 18, xxvii. 21; Rev. vi. 17, viii. 3.

VER. 25. The Saviour gives another and analogous parable, only shifting His scene to a smaller community.

And if a house be divided against itself, that house will not be able to stand. The word *house* has, of course, its rarer meaning of *household*, the meaning which it has in John iv. 53 and 1 Cor. xvi. 15. It is translated *household* in Phil. iv. 22. If thorough intestine antagonism be once an accomplished fact in a family, *that* family must be *broken up* and thus *broken down*.

VER. 26. **And if** (εἰ) **Satan has risen up against himself** (ἀνέστη ἐφ' ἑαυτόν). As is actually the case, *provided the malicious imputation of the scribes be well founded*. It is a most graphic picture. Satan, ' himself a host,' *rises up* in all the panoply of his might to *put himself down!*

And has been divided. Such is probably the correct reading (καὶ μεμέρισται). It is the reading of the Received Text, and of Lachmann, Tregelles, Alford. It is supported by the great body of the uncial manuscripts, inclusive of the Alexandrine (A), and by the Peshito Syriac, the Philoxenian Syriac, the Coptic and Gothic versions. In the Vatican manuscript there is a slight variation of reading; the verb is in the aorist instead of the perfect (ἐμερίσθη), but the conjunction *and* is retained in front, thus postponing the predicate of the sentence to the next clause. In the Sinaitic manuscript (ℵ*) and the Ephraemi (C*) the verb is in the same tense as in the Vatican, but the conjunction follows the verb, as it also does in the Vulgate version, and in certain important manuscripts of the older Latin. Tischendorf has accepted, in his eighth edition, the reading of the Sinaitic and Ephraemi manuscripts, thus finishing the subject of the sentence with the words, *if Satan has risen up against himself.* It is more likely, however, that the subject includes the second clause; and it is also more likely that the verb in this second clause is in the perfect tense, *and has been divided*, that is, *and has thus been divided against himself*, like an embattled host splitting up into two that it might rush into deadly conflict with itself.

He is not able to stand, but has an end. The Saviour's conception of Satan does not confine itself to that of a personality. He pictures him as a power, a principality, a royalty, a kingdom. If, as such, he has been divided against himself, and is thus counterworking himself, and turning all his artillery against himself, *he cannot stand*; his adversative relationship to others is anni-

No man can enter into a strong man's house, and spoil his goods,

hilated. *He has an end*; there is an end of his Satanic influence among men. The Saviour, in His reasoning on the imputation of the scribes, assumes, and was entitled to assume, that He Himself was intensely earnest in the part which He was acting against Satan and sin. He allows this moral earnestness to assert its own reality. It was shining by its own light. The unsophisticated *people* did not doubt it, and could not. No one who came near Him, and conscientiously watched Him, could doubt it in his heart. You might as soon doubt whether God were good. If Jesus be not Nobody or Nothing, He is the Impersonation of anti-Satanic earnestness. " For this purpose the Son of God " was manifested, *that He might destroy the works of the devil*." (1 John iii. 8.) If therefore Satan were making a tool of Him, as the scribes maliciously insinuated, he was making a tool of the most intense anti-Satanic earnestness in the universe. Was it likely? To suppose it is to suppose that the adversary of God and of men wilfully chose, and with his eyes wide open, to become his own adversary, his own Satan and Apollyon.

VER. 27. But ('Αλλ'). This adversative conjunction is omitted in the Received Text, and hence in our King James's version. It is also omitted in the Vulgate version, and in most of the manuscripts of the older Latin, and in the Syriac Peshito version, and the text of the Philoxenian Peshito, and the Gothic version. It is wanting too in the Alexandrine manuscript (A), and the Cambridge (D), and a majority of the other uncials; Lachmann omits it. But Tischendorf, Tregelles, Alford have rightly inserted it, on the authority of the Sinaitic and Vatican manuscripts and C* L Δ, 1, 33, 69, etc. It is likewise represented in the Coptic and Armenian versions. It is the more difficult reading, and not likely therefore to have been intruded. The Saviour, instead of further pursuing the same line of argumentation along which He was moving in the preceding verses, turns in a *different direction.*

No one, after entering into the house of the strong one, is able to plunder his vessels. There is much difference of opinion among textual critics regarding the precise order of the phrases and clauses of this part of the parable; but there is none regarding their interpretation. The difference of reading would no doubt arise from the evangelist setting down his expressions inartificially, more so than they stand in the text which Tischendorf has exhibited in his eighth edition of the New Testament. The picture represents the house of the strong one *as already entered* (εἰσελθών). The difficulty comes after that. The person whose house has been entered is emphatically *strong* ; the Saviour thinks of him very individualizingly as '*the*' *strong one.* It would be impossible to plunder such an individual's vessels if he were standing by unmastered. Note the expression *his* '*vessels*,' rendered freely in King James's version and the Revised *his goods.* This free rendering was Tyndale's ; Wycliffe gave the more exact and significant rendering, *vessels.* It is supposed that the individual who goes into the strong one's house desires to get hold of certain specific things, *the precious vessels of silver and gold.* His eye is upon these particular 'goods'; and he thus leaves unregarded the other goods or effects that may be within the house. The word used for the act of *plundering* is graphic (διαρπάσαι). It represents a man *snatching on the right hand and the left.*

28] ST. MARK III. 87

except he will first bind the strong man ; and then he will spoil his house. 28 Verily I say unto you, All sins shall be forgiven unto the sons of men, and blasphemies wherewith soever they

Unless he first bind the strong one. *Bind*, or otherwise get rid of. The Saviour however is contemplating a particular case in which riddance by transportation or death must not be thought of. He allows the reality which He is parabolically representing to mould and modify the form of His parable. He was thinking of Satan, who had his home in this world before man appeared, and who besides was constituted immortal because constituted moral. His transportation therefore, or annihilation, was not to be thought of. But as he had surrounded himself unlawfully with certain precious vessels, which were fitted to be of ' honourable ' use in a much greater ' house ' than his, it was meet that he should be *bound*, and then deprived of his ill-gotten ' goods.' Jesus had come to bind him ; and He had succeeded, even already, in His enterprise. Satan was restrained, and men were being delivered. That was the true significancy of those wonderful miracles which gave relief to demoniacs.

And then shall he plunder his house. *Then*, viz. after he shall have bound the strong one. The evangelist mingles his lines of thought inartificially but clearly. Note the two expressions *plunder his house* and *plunder his vessels*. Both representations are true to nature. The plundering takes effect both upon the house—*the object containing*, and upon the vessels in the house—*the objects contained*.

VER. 28. Our Saviour follows up His reasonings with a solemn warning.

Verily I say unto you. This is the first time that the adverb *amen* or *verily* occurs in Mark. It seems to have been, in its original Hebrew form, a favourite phrase with our Lord, when He wished to give emphasis to an idea. It is rendered *trewly* by Wycliffe. In the Rheims version, as in the Gothic and Vulgate, the original term is left untranslated, just as it is in the text of the evangelist himself. It corresponds to the expression *Of a truth*: see John vi. 14, Acts iv. 27, x. 34. *I say to you*, that is, *to you scribes, who have been so wantonly maligning Me, by alleging that I am acting in league with Beelzebul.*

All shall be forgiven to the sons of men. The expression *all* is looking forward to the classified things which are immediately specified. It has reference therefore to a limited universality, the universality of a certain class of things. They are such things as need forgiveness, sins. All these, with one exception, *shall be forgiven to the sons of men*. Note the *shall*. It expresses more than *may*, though *may* might have been employed. It suggests that there is but one phase of sin that is an absolute bar to forgiveness; it is at one point of things alone that the principle of unpardonableness comes in. The multiplicity of sins becomes merged as it were in the unity of sinfulness; and when this unity of sinfulness is free from a certain peculiar element, about to be specified, *it* '*shall*' *be forgiven.* (See *Comm.* on Matt. xii. 31.) Note the expression *sons of men*; it is a mere variation in form of the simpler expression *men.* (See Matt. xii. 31, and compare the Syriac idiom.)

The sins and the blasphemies, wherewith they may blaspheme (τὰ ἁμαρτήματα καὶ αἱ βλασφημίαι, ὅσα ἂν βλασφημήσωσιν, the correct reading). The preceding

shall blaspheme: 29 but he that shall blaspheme against the Holy Ghost hath never forgiveness, but is in danger of eternal

all has reference both to the generic *sins* and the specific *blasphemies* ; and when it is added '*wherewith*' *they may blaspheme*, the *wherewith* (ὅσα with ℵ B D E G H Δ II, Lachmann, Tischendorf, Tregelles; not ὅσας as in the Received Text) has condensed reference to the generic *sins* as well as to the specific *blasphemies*. If the reference had been unfolded, the expression would have run thus, *the sins wherein they may sin, and the blasphemies wherewith they may blaspheme*. The phraseology is inartificial ; but a deep theological meaning is embedded. It is implied that all sins, when analysed into their substrate, have an element of *blasphemy* in them. They cast dishonour on God ; they cast it wilfully. Blasphemy, considered in its form, is *injurious speaking* ; but considered in its essence it is *despite* or *scorn*. In all sin there is such essential blasphemy ; God's wish and will are proudly set aside and resisted. All such proud resistances of the wish and will of God will be forgiven, if they do not culminate in a particular phase of blasphemy. See next verse.

Ver. 29. **But whosoever shall blaspheme against the Holy Spirit.** Whosoever shall be guilty of blasphemy that goes out *to* (εἰς) the Holy Spirit. What of him? See next clause. But meanwhile note that the peculiarity of his crime arises from its relation to the dispensation of mercy. It is the only crime which, in its own nature, closes the door of the soul and keeps it closed, against the ingress of Divine mercy. The Holy Spirit is the revealer of the propitiousness of God ; and when, as such, He is blasphemed, or scorned, or slighted, the only possible means of the soul's acquaintance with the mercy of God is set aside or resisted ; the only avenue to salvation and sanctification is thus closed. Augustine was right, the blasphemy against the Holy Spirit is wilfully-persisted-in impenitence or disbelief. (See *Comm.* on Matt. xii. 31, 32.)

Hath never forgiveness. A free but fine translation ; it was Coverdale's. It is more literal than Tyndale's, *shall never have forgevenes*. The Rheims version is more literal still, *he hath not forgiveness for ever*. The expression *for ever* is literally *to the age* (εἰς τὸν αἰῶνα). It is an idiom, and substantially means, as Alexander renders it, *to eternity*. And hence a peculiar symphony between this clause and the next.

But is in danger of eternal damnation. So is the expression rendered in King James's version. It is a strong translation of an incorrect text. The text was that of Erasmus ; the translation was Tyndale's. It is to be borne in mind however that the word *damnation* meant originally nothing but *condemnation* ; and such undoubtedly was the import of the term in Tyndale's version. The Greek word indeed, in the text that was lying before him, strictly meant *judgment* (κρίσεως), and so Coverdale here renders it. But as *judgment* is in itself ambidextrous, left-hand judgment is *condemnation*. The word however which Tyndale found in his Erasmian text was really a marginal correction of the word that was in the evangelist's autograph, and which Lachmann, Tischendorf, Tregelles, Alford, have wisely restored, the word *sin* (ἁμαρτήματος). Griesbach, in his day, saw clearly that the reading of the Erasmian text was a critical correction (*Comm. Crit.*, in loc.) ; Mill too (*Prolegomena*, p. xliii.). The case is

damnation: 30 because they said, He hath an unclean spirit.

obvious. No one would have substituted, for perspicuity's sake, the expression *eternal sin* for the expression *eternal judgment* or *condemnation*. But many a critic might think that he was only innocently smoothing a rugged phrase when he quietly introduced *judgment* or *condemnation*, for *sin*. Both the Vatican and the Sinaitic manuscripts, as well as ' the queen of the cursives,' read *sin*; so do the Italic, Vulgate, Coptic, Armenian, and Gothic versions. Instead then of the expression *is in danger of eternal damnation*, we should read *is guilty of an eternal sin*. As to the word translated *guilty* (ἔνοχος), see its use in 1 Cor. xi. 27 and Jas. ii. 10. It denotes that the person spoken of is *in the grip of his sin*. It has *hold* of him, and *holds* him *in*, so that he cannot escape from the punishment that is his due. As to the expression *eternal sin*, it is peculiar and in some respects unique, but thoroughly intelligible. It denotes a sin that cannot be *taken away*, *blotted out*, or *cleansed*. Griesbach compares John ix. 41, '*your sin remaineth*.' An *eternal sin is a sin that remaineth for ever*. Forgiven sins are sins that are taken up by God from the burdened conscience of the sinner and cast as it were ' behind His back' or 'into the depths of the sea '; but unforgiven sins abide for ever on the souls that committed them. The language is of course strongly pictorial, but most solemnly significant.

VER. 30. **Because they said.** They *persisted in saying* (ἔλεγον). Our Saviour addressed to the scribes His solemn warning, *because* they were persisting in their malign and wanton allegation.

He hath an unclean spirit. That is, *a demon*. They could not deny that His works were supernatural. But instead of admitting that they were from above, and full of Divine mercy to men, they wilfully, casuistically, and malignantly accused Him of being voluntarily assisted from beneath. He does not intimate to them, as Petter and many others suppose, that they had thereby blasphemed the Holy Spirit and committed the unpardonable sin. Neither does Mark, as Köstlin imagines, confound the two blasphemies (*die βλασφημία τοῦ πνεύματος τοῦ ἁγίου, ausdrücklich in die Lästerung der Person Jesu selbst gesezt*: URSPRUNG DER SYN. Evv. iii., § 1). But our Lord intimates to His slanderers that they were treading close on the borders of the sin that hath never forgiveness. They were on its brink; another step, and they might topple irretrievably into the abyss. They were malevolently rejecting and thus blaspheming the Son of Man as an impostor. If they should proceed the least degree farther, and malevolently reject and blaspheme the Holy Spirit also as an impostor, and His testimony as an imposition, their salvation would become an impossibility. It was within the limits of possibility to reject Jesus of Nazareth and yet believe in a Propitiator to come, as revealed by the Holy Spirit of God. But if they proceeded to reject the Holy Spirit Himself and all His revelations of the Divine propitiousness, they would thereby reject every possible element of Divine evangelism, and hence there would no avenue remain by which saving and sanctifying influences could enter their souls. (See *Comm*. on Matt. xii. 31, 32.)

VER. 31. The evangelist, having left as it were the Saviour's kinsfolk on the road between Nazareth and Capernaum (see ver. 21), rejoins them on their arrival. Hence the paragraph ver. 31-35. Comp. Matt. xii. 46-50 and Luke viii. 19-21.

ST. MARK III.

31 There came then his brethren and his mother, and, standing without, sent unto him, calling him. 32 And the multitude sat about him, and they said unto him, Behold, thy mother and thy brethren without seek for thee. 33 And he answered them, saying, Who is my mother, or my brethren? 34 And he

And there come His mother and His brethren. The *mother* is put last in the Erasmian text, that she might be shaded off behind the *brethren*. Tischendorf however goes too far when he reads, chiefly on the authority of the Sinaitic manuscript, '*comes*' (ἔρχεται) instead of '*come*.' The singular verb had doubtless got into some manuscripts by mistake, on account of the proximity of the singular nominative, *His mother.* There is a subjacent reference to what is mentioned in ver. 21. The *brothers of our Lord* were probably, as we have remarked on ver. 18, the sons of Joseph by a previous marriage. Thus would they be only our Lord's half-brothers. They would hence be considerably older than our Lord, and would thus very likely think themselves both qualified and entitled to exercise some peculiar guardianship and authority over their youthful and unintelligible Kinsman. Their names are given in chap. vi. 3.

And, standing without, they sent to Him, calling Him. At the time when they arrived our Lord was in some house, surrounded by a crowd of people. The very doorway was packed full. There was no way of access for His solicitous kinsfolk (Luke viii. 19). Hence they sent in a message by word of mouth, conveying their desire that He should then and there come out to them, as they wished to speak with Him (Matt. xii. 47).

VER. 32. **And a crowd was sitting round about Him.** In a 'squat' position, after the usual oriental fashion, though not unlikely the outer margin of the throng might consist of persons who would be standing on their feet, and leaning forward to hear and to see.

And they say to Him. Such is the best reading, instead of *and they 'said' to Him.* We are led in spirit into the assembly, and see and hear as if we had been really present. One would whisper the message to another, and it would be transmitted round and round even while our Saviour was speaking. At length at some pause or break in the discourse some one would muster courage to repeat it aloud. (See Matt. xii. 47.)

Lo, Thy mother and Thy brothers outside are seeking Thee. They are outside, and have come hither in quest of Thee. After the clause *and Thy brothers* Tischendorf adds *and Thy sisters*, under the authorization of the Alexandrine and Cambridge manuscripts (A D), as also of E F H M S U V Γ. But it is omitted in ℵ B C G K L A II, 1, 33, 69, and by the Vulgate, Syriac Peshito, Coptic, Æthiopic, and Armenian versions. It is not unlikely that the clause had been originally inserted in the margin by some annotator who drew with too great confidence a historical inference from the doctrinal statement of ver. 35.

VER. 33. **And answering them, He saith, Who is My mother and My brethren?** A question intended to lead His auditory to a very lofty standpoint of thought Perhaps they had been already ascending with Him, and were more or less prepared to step still farther aloft. Most likely He had been discoursing on some

1] ST. MARK IV. 91

looked round about on them which sat about him, and said, Behold my mother and my brethren! 35 For whosoever shall do the will of God, the same is my brother, and my sister, and mother.

CHAPTER IV.

1 AND he began again to teach by the sea side: and there was gathered unto him a great multitude, so that he entered

---

high topic. Possibly at the very time the message was delivered He may have been reaching the climax of some grand exhibition of the spiritual relationships of men, and of the superiority of these relationships to mere outward ties of consanguinity. Hence He would not allow the exhibition of His great theme to be materially interrupted by the officiousness of His kinsfolk. On the contrary He seizes hold of their meddling message to illustrate the great principle He had in hand and at heart.

VER. 34. **And looking round about upon those who were sitting around Him** in a circle. Such is the literal translation of the text as given by Lachmann, Tischendorf, Tregelles (περιβλεψάμενος τοὺς περὶ αὐτὸν κύκλῳ καθημένους). It is supported by the uncial manuscripts ℵ B C L Δ.
He says, Lo My mother and My brethren! My nearest of kin! See next verse.

VER 35. **For whosoever shall do the will of God, he is My brother and sister and mother.** A great preponderance of the best manuscripts omit the *my* before the word *sister*. If any one do the will of God, and be thus Godlike and good in character, holy and whole in spirit, in him does the Saviour recognise, in relation to Himself, true kinship. He is at once His 'brother and sister and mother.' The deepest affinity is that of the spirit. Hence the supremacy, even in the present provisional state of things, of the wedlock relationship. Hence too the still higher supremacy of the relationship that will rule in the world of glory (Matt. xxii. 30). It is noteworthy that Jesus does not add 'father' to His 'brother and sister and mother.' A high and hallowed consciousness kept back that august term; He realized that His relation to His real and only *Father* towered far aloft above all other relations.

CHAPTER IV.

HERE follows one of the most graphic of illustrative stories, *the parable of the sower*, ver. 1–20. Comp. Matt. xiii. 1–23 and Luke viii. 4–15.

VER. 1. **And again He began to teach by the sea side.** By the side of the lovely 'sea of Galilee.' It was *again* that He *began*; He had taught by the same place before. See chap. iii. 7–9.
And there is gathered unto Him a very great crowd. No sooner had He gone to the shore and begun His teaching, than the people came pouring toward Him from all directions. There was *a very great crowd* (ὄχλος πλεῖστος). Such is

into a ship, and sat in the sea; and the whole multitude was by the sea on the land. 2 And he taught them many things by parables, and said unto them in his doctrine, 3 Hearken; Behold, there went out a sower to sow : 4 and it came to pass, as he sowed, some fell by the way side, and the fowls of the air came and devoured it up. 5 And some fell on stony

the reading of Tischendorf, Tregelles. Alford, instead of the reading of the Received or Erasmian text, *a great crowd* (ὄχλος πολύς). The same important manuscripts (א B C L Δ) which support the *superlative* reading have the verb in the present tense, *is gathered* (συνάγεται). We are taken back in imagination to the time referred to, and see the people in the very act of congregating.

So that **He entered into a boat**. Such is Wycliffe's translation, *in to a boot*.

And sat in the sea, and all the crowd were (ἦσαν) **by the sea on the land**. Some might be sitting on the beautiful 'white beach,' some standing. The Great Rabbi however, according to the universal custom of the rabbis, *sat* as He taught. He *sat* '*in the sea*.' The boat in which He sat was *afloat in the sea*. If the place referred to was near Bethsaida, there "the beach rises rapidly," says Mr. Macgregor, "and there is deep water within a few yards of the shore, "while at the same time a multitude of hearers could place themselves so as "to see the Saviour in the boat; and there is no such *natural church* along the "other coast by Gennesareth." (*The Rob Roy on the Jordan*, p. 350.)

VER. 2. **And He taught them many things in parables.** The *things* were conveyed to them 'in' parables (ἐν παραβολαῖς', and thus they were partly revealed and partly concealed. (See ver. 10–12.) Parables are not direct representations of realities, but indirect. What they directly represent is *thrown* in the direction of something that lies beyond. (See on chap. iii. 23.)

And said to them in His teaching. The word employed is just the noun-form of the verb that is rendered *taught* in the preceding clause (διδαχή—ἐδίδασκεν).

VER. 3. **Hearken; Behold, the sower went out to sow.** It is '*the*' *sower* in the original. The Saviour casts upon the canvas of the imagination a particular individual. This individual *went out* to sow. He went out from the village or hamlet, where the farmers in the East are accustomed to reside, duly furnished for his work.

VER. 4. **And it came to pass, as he sowed.** Or, still more literally, *and it happened in the sowing*. *It happened* is Coverdale's translation. Tyndale's version is, *it fortuned*.

Some fell by the wayside. That is, *some seed*. It fell on the margin of the hard trodden pathway that ran along, or, as the case might be, right through the unenclosed field.

And the birds came. Or, the *briddes*, as Wycliffe gives it.

And devoured it. The word (κατέφαγεν) is just '*de*'-*voured* or *ate down*. "Our "horses," says Dr. W. M. Thomson on a certain occasion, in his eastern travels, "are actually trampling down some seeds which have fallen by this "wayside, and larks and sparrows are busy picking them up." (*The Land and the Book*, p. 82.)

ground, where it had not much earth; and immediately it sprang up, because it had no depth of earth. 6 But when the sun was up, it was scorched; and because it had no root, it withered away. 7 And some fell among thorns, and the thorns grew up, and choked it, and it yielded no fruit. 8 And other fell on good ground, and did yield fruit that sprang up and

Ver. 5. **And other fell on rocky ground** (ἐπὶ τὸ πετρῶδες). Our Saviour imagines a field with a particular rocky part protruding slightly here and there above the general level of the ground, or else revealing itself to the tread as lying immediately below the surface. This is '*the*' *rocky ground*. It is not expected by the farmer that anything sown upon it will come to full maturity; but the place comes within his sweep as he sows the grain, and so some seeds fall upon it.

Where it had not much earth. For it is not of a *stony* place, properly so called, but of a place that is *rocky*, that the Saviour speaks.

And immediately it sprang up because it had no depth of earth. Or, *because of not having depth of earth.* There was no scope for development downward, and hence the forces of the plant rushed prematurely upward.

Ver. 6. **And when the sun arose, it was scorched.** *Scorched*, a fine translation, originated by the editors of King James's version.

And, on account of not having root, it withered away. It *had not sufficient root*. Its supplies beneath were not sufficient to sustain it in the process of a complete upward development.

Ver. 7. **And other fell among thorns.** Or, more literally, *into the thorns*, such namely as our Saviour was *realizing in His picture of the field*. He was thinking of some clump of thorny plants which had been burnt down according to oriental custom, but not eradicated, before seed-sowing time. In among these roots some seeds fell.

And the thorns grew up, and choked it. Or, as Wycliffe renders it, *strangled it*. The thorns suffocated the growing plant, compressing it together συνέπνιξαν, and thus preventing it from getting the free air of heaven and a sufficiency of the nourishment of the soil.

And it yielded no fruit. It rose high enough in its stem, perhaps too high; but it was by the help of artificial props. The tide of vital energy was so impoverished by the surroundings that the real final end of the plant's existence was never reached. There was no 'fruit.'

Ver. 8. **And others fell into the good ground** (εἰς τὴν γῆν τὴν καλήν). In some important manuscripts (ℵ B C L, 33), there is in this clause the plural word *others* (ἄλλα), instead of the singular *other* (ἄλλο), which is found in ver. 5 and 7. Tischendorf has introduced it into his eighth edition of the text.

And yielded fruit growing up and increasing. Meyer thinks that the word *fruit* denotes here, not *the grains*, but *the stalks* of the corn, which conspicuously *ascend* and *increase*. He was misled by thinking of *the disintegrated grains* (Körner), instead of the entire *spikes*, the *ascent* and *increase* of which are obvious and beautiful phenomena. That the reference is to *the grains in the*

increased; and brought forth, some thirty, and some sixty, and some an hundred. 9 And he said unto them, He that hath ears to hear, let him hear.

10 And when he was alone, they that were about him with the twelve asked of him the parable. 11 And he said unto

---

integer of the spike is demonstrated by ver. 20. Comp. Matt. xiii. 8, and Luke viii. 8.

And bore to thirty and to sixty and to a hundredfold. Such is the literal translation of the true text (καὶ ἔφερεν εἰς τριάκοντα καὶ εἰς ἑξήκοντα καὶ εἰς ἑκατόν). It is the text that is given by Tischendorf, Tregelles, and Alford, supported by the manuscripts ℵ B C L Δ. It could not well be accounted for unless it had been in the original autograph. The reading of the Received Text (ἐν for εἰς) seems to have been artificially accommodated, as Tischendorf remarks, to the mode of expression in Matt. xiii. 8. The various degrees of fertility specified by our Lord were nothing extraordinary in such a paradise of a place as the plain of Gennesaret. 'Its fertility,' says Dr. Robinson, 'can hardly be exceeded.' (*Biblical Researches*, vol. iii., p. 285.)

VER. 9. **And He said, He who has ears to hear, let him hear.** Calvin, Petter, a-Lapide, and others, think that our Saviour assumes a distinction among men, between *those who have ears*, that is, ears fit to listen to Divine communications, and *those who have none*. It is much more probable, however, that He assumes that all without exception have been divinely provided with fitting organs of hearing, and that He draws attention to the fact of the provision in a way that is calculated to lead each individual to reflect on his individual responsibility. It is quite a common phenomenon among men to misuse the ears, so as not to hear the still small voices that speak the most important truths. In a world like ours, in which there is such a din of noises and voices, there must be eclecticism in hearing.

VER. 10. **And when He came to be alone.** Not indeed absolutely *alone*, but relatively to the public crowd who had pressed down to the shore to see and hear; *when He got into comparative seclusion*.

They who were about Him with the twelve. No doubt there would be frequently in the presence of our Lord other attached disciples besides the apostles; the pious women for instance, and occasionally the relatives and acquaintances both of them and of the apostles; and others besides. It is only Mark who here takes notice of these other adherents. (Comp. Matt. xiii. 10, Luke viii. 9.) It is one of the minute touches which show that he was not writing a compendium of any of the other synoptic Gospels.

Asked Him the parable. That is, *interrogated Him concerning the import of the parable*, or, as Wycliffe gives it, *axiden Hym for to expowne the parable*. Such is the import of the Received Text. It is the reading of Lachmann; and it is found in the Alexandrine manuscript and a majority of the other uncials, as also in the Clementine Vulgate, the Peshito Syriac, and the Gothic, Armenian, and Coptic versions. It is certainly the easiest reading; and in this instance it is, most probably, the correct reading. A preponderance indeed of the more important manuscripts (ℵ B C L Δ), supported by some important

them, Unto you it is given to know the mystery of the kingdom of God : but unto them that are without, all *these* things are done in parables : 12 that seeing they may see, and not perceive ;

manuscripts of the Vulgate, inclusive of the Codex Amiatinus, read, in the plural, *parables* (τὰς παραβολάς), instead of *parable*. Tischendorf in consequence, and Tregelles and Alford, have introduced the plural word into their texts. But it is probable that it owes its place, in the codices from which they copy, to the use of the plural word in the 11th verse.

VER. 11. **And He said to them, Unto you the mystery of the kingdom of God has been given.** *Unto you as the 'subjects' of knowledge.* The *mystery* of the kingdom of God is its *secret*, or *the sum of its secrets.* It is that inner reality of spiritual things which the masses of the Jews did not like to think of, and which had therefore to be veiled when it was spoken of in their presence. The same inner reality of things, though under other phases, is still an object of aversion to the masses of men, rich and poor, high and low, learned and illiterate. When an approach is made to an esoteric exhibition of it, symptoms of impatience and dislike are speedily encountered, so that the object must be shaded off exoterically as *a secret* or *mystery*. It is not in any peculiar respect *an incomprehensibility*, although no doubt in its heights it ascends, and in its depths it descends, into incomprehensibilities enough.

But to them who are without. Who are outside the circle of disciplehood. The phrase was frequently used by the Jews to denote *the Gentiles* ; but it was also applicable, according to the specific standpoint occupied, to all who did not gravitate toward any given centre of attraction.

All the things take place in parables. The phrase *all the things* (τὰ πάντα), or indefinitely, *all things* (πάντα), as Tischendorf, under the authority of the Sinaitic and a few other manuscripts, has it, refers to the universality that is found within the circle of the Saviour's teachings at that particular period. His teachings to the masses of the people took the shape of parables. Why ? See next verse.

VER. 12. **That seeing they may see and not perceive.** Or, *In order that looking they may look and not see.* The verb in the Hebraistic expression, *looking they may look*, is translated *look* in Matt. v. 28, John xiii. 22, Acts iii. 4, 2 John 8. It is here used to denote that exercise of *the beholding faculty* which stops short of perfected perception. The Hebraistic expression draws attention to a process, involving a progress which should culminate in a completed result. The result however is not reached ; *they do not see.* And Jesus did not wish them, at that particular stage of things, to *see.* The parables were spoken in order that (ἵνα) they should not 'see.' Why? Was it because He did not wish them *to know* and *to enjoy* ? Everything the reverse. But He was aware that, in consequence of the inveteracy of their prepossessions, they could not, in the first instance, *see* ' the secret of the kingdom ' without being repelled in spirit, and confirmed in their dissent and dislike. He wished therefore that they should not ' see.' But at the same time He graciously wished that they should ' look,' and keep ' looking,' so that they might, if possible, get such a glimpse of the inner glory as might fascinate their interest and attention, and

and hearing they may hear, and not understand; lest at any time they should be converted, and *their* sins should be forgiven them.

13 And he said unto them, Know ye not this parable? and how then will ye know all parables? 14 The sower soweth

---

by and by disarm their prejudices, so that they might with safety be permitted to 'see.'

And hearing they may hear and not understand. A parallel representation, drawn from another of the outward senses. The Saviour wished that the deeply prejudiced multitude should not 'understand,' in the first instance, the fulness of His ideas, but that yet they should 'hear' and continue to 'hear.' If what they 'heard' were in itself fitted to stimulate interest and inquiry, and also adapted, when once inquiry was excited, to guide the mind toward the right goal, it might ultimately lead on to the mo.t important secrets of the kingdom of heaven.

Lest they should ever turn. The verb is in the active voice ($\dot{\epsilon}\pi\iota\sigma\tau\rho\dot{\epsilon}\psi\omega\sigma\iota\nu$), and thus brings into view the important truth that the sinner's own agency is an indispensable element in his conversion. When it is said '*lest*' they should *turn*, the 'lest' expresses the idea of aversion; and the question naturally arises, *in whose mind is the aversion to the turning?* Is it in the Saviour's (and God's), or in that of the sinner himself? The sentence is so inartificially constructed that, unless common sense step in as interpreter, one might suppose that it was the Saviour who was opposed to the sinner's conversion. It is manifestly, however, the sinner himself. It is implied in the preceding clauses that it is the sinner's *deeply rooted wish* that he should not 'see' and 'understand.' And in this expression the reason of his wish is given. *He is afraid lest he should be prevailed on to turn.* Comp. Matt. xiii. 15, and also John xii. 40, and Acts xxviii. 27.

And it should be forgiven to them ($\kappa\alpha\grave{\iota}$ $\dot{\alpha}\phi\epsilon\vartheta\hat{\eta}$ $\alpha\dot{\upsilon}\tau o\hat{\iota}s$). In the Received Text the expression *the sins*, that is, *their sins*, is incorporated, *and their sins should be forgiven to them*. The supplement brings out exactly the idea of the original phrase; but it is not unlikely that it was exegetically added. The people spoken of would not be averse to *forgiveness*, abstractly considered, though there are some that profess to wish simple justice and no favour. But, in the case of most, it is the moral antecedents, and in particular the moral consequences, of forgiveness that are disliked. In explicitly shrinking from these they implicitly shrink from the involved forgiveness itself.

VER. 13. **And He says to them.** This expression indicates that another thread of thought is taken up in what immediately follows. Note the present *says*; we are carried back in imagination, and can ourselves listen.

Know ye not this parable? *Is that the case? Are ye so slow in learning? Have ye such difficulty in getting to the standpoint from which the whole expanse of these spiritual truths is seen?*

And how shall ye know all the parables? The language at the beginning of the clause is abrupt, *and how?* that is, *and how, if that be the case?* Note the future expression, *shall ye know?* It implies an intended order in the parables

the word. 15 And these are they by the way side, where the word is sown; but when they have heard Satan cometh immediately, and taketh away the word that was sown in their hearts. 16 And these are they likewise which are sown on stony

referred to. The order is such that the mind should commence with the consideration of the first, and thence proceed, *in the future*, to the remainder. The Saviour does not refer to *all possible parables*. His expression is not *all parables*, but *all the parables* (πάσας τὰς παραβολάς). Very probably however He may refer, not only to those which He delivered before He retired from the multitude to whom He spoke the parable of the sower, but also to such as He might deem it proper to deliver on future occasions in reference to the kingdom of heaven.

VER. 14. The Saviour explains the parable of the sower.

The sower sows the word. The sower in the parable represents *the preacher of the word*. The Holy Spirit is the Great Preacher, the Holy Spirit in Jesus or in those who are filled out of the fulness of Jesus. All ordinary preachers have but to echo the preaching of the Holy Spirit. It is to them however, in particular, that the Saviour refers. The *word* which they preach, if they preach as they ought to preach, is just *the manifested thought* of the Holy Spirit, His thought concerning God, and goodness, and the way back for sinners at once to goodness and to God. This *manifested thought* is *the gospel*.

VER. 15 **And these are they by the wayside, where the word is sown.** The demonstrative *these* points forward to those who are about to be described in the remainder of the verse. But as the Saviour has them already in His eye while He is speaking, He introduces the next clause by means of the conjunction *and*. There is *a wayside* in the place 'where the word is sown.' There is, that is to say, a class of people *who correspond to the wayside* in the parabolic field. Who are they? See what follows.

And whenever they have heard, immediately Satan cometh, and taketh away the word which has been sown in their hearts. Instead of the expression *in their hearts*, Tischendorf (eighth edition) reads *in them*, and Tregelles *into them*. The former has the support of the Sinaitic, the latter that of the Vatican manuscript. It is probable that one or other of the readings, as developing a less developed mode of phraseology than the expression of the Received Text, is authentic; most likely the former, which is sustained by the manuscripts C L Δ, as well as by the Coptic (*edd*) and Armenian versions, and the marginal reading of the Philoxenian Syriac. The wayside hearers are those who never allow the word to get under the surface of their thoughts; and hence any little superficial influence which it may exert is easily and speedily removed by any of the winged and watchful agencies of Satan, the great adversary of souls. It is well to retain the Hebrew word *Satan*. The evangelist himself retained it, though writing in Greek. It would however be unidiomatic, so far as English is concerned, were we to follow him in the use of the article, *the Satan* (that is, *the Adversary*).

VER. 16. **And these in like manner are they who are sown upon the rocky places.** *In like manner*, for the second part of the parable admirably *corresponds*

H

ground; who, when they have heard the word, immediately receive it with gladness; 17 and have no root in themselves, and so endure but for a time. Afterward, when affliction or persecution ariseth for the word's sake, immediately

---

to the first in its susceptibility of application. Note the inartificial nature of the representation. The significates of the parable are, for the moment, shifted, the hearers of the word being represented *by the seeds sown* instead of *the ground on which they were sown*. But the idea remains unembarrassed for all practical purposes.

Who, whenever they have heard the word, immediately receive it with gladness. The word does get under the surface in their case, and immediately produces some effect. It touches the superficial feelings, and is hastily welcomed. Perhaps because it is a new thing; perhaps because it is evidently a good thing, good in particular for objects that terminate on self, good for getting safety and everlasting glory.

VER. 17. **And have not root in themselves.** They *have not root*, that is, they are deficient in root. The word of God, though under the surface, does not get far down in its influence; and hence it does not get free scope and fair play. Its influence is speedily arrested by an impenetrable hardness underneath. Religion does not get rooting; there is no receptivity for it in the hidden depths of the being, almost all that is of it has rushed up to the outside. *They have no root 'in themselves.'* The expression finely suggests that religion must be a personal matter; it is either *something in one's self*, or else nothing at all.

And so endure but for a time. King James's version, and a fine free translation; but certainly free. It is literally *but are temporary*. There is in the expression a kind of hasty anticipation of the hasty termination of the hasty religious profession. The measure of the comparative temporariness is to be found in the time that would have been required for the full development of the grain. A full moral spring-time and a full moral summer-time would have been required.

Then when tribulation or persecution for the word's sake has come to pass (γενομένης). It is assumed that such tribulation or persecution may be expected. The prevailing hatred of 'the word,' on the part of 'the world,' will, in one way or another, bring it to pass. The words *tribulation* and *persecution* are just two specific modes of representing suffering for the gospel's sake. The one word (*tribulation* = Ϟλίψις) denotes *oppression*; the other (persecution = διωγμός) denotes *pursuit*.

Immediately they are offended. Literally, and as the Rheims has it, *they are scandalized*. The word *scandalized* is just the Anglicised form of the Greek word; and the Greek word was provincial. It does not occur in the classics. It is a term moreover which it is impossible to translate literally, into Latin or English or French or German or Dutch. It paints a complex picture. The original *scandal*, or *scandalon*, was a part of a trap for catching noxious animals. It was that part on which the animal was expected to strike unawares; when once this *scandal* was struck, the animal was ensnared. A

ST. MARK IV.

they are offended. 18 And these are they which are sown among thorns; such as hear the word, 19 and the cares of this world, and the deceitfulness of riches, and the lusts of

scandalized person, therefore, is a person who has unawares struck, or stumbled on, what entraps and ruins him. The persons referred to by our Lord are in this respect *scandalized*. Their religion becomes a thing on which they stumble and stagger, and are held fast, or fall. Tyndale's translation is, *they fall immediately*, or, as it is in his 1526 edition, *anon they fall*. It is all over with their profession.

VER. 18. **And others are they who are sown into the thorns. These are they that have heard the word.** The demonstrative *these*, which had erroneously extruded in the Received Text the word *others* in the preceding clause, comes in here.

VER. 19. **And the cares of this world.** Or rather *of this age*, or better still, *of the age*. The *this* is omitted in the manuscripts ℵ B C D L Δ, 1, and in the Vulgate and Armenian versions. Griesbach, Lachmann, Tischendorf, Tregelles leave it out. *The cares of the age* are the *distractions* ($\mu\acute{\epsilon}\rho\iota\mu\nu\alpha\iota$) *that are incident to this preliminary period of the world's history*, a period when things are exceedingly out of order. They are men's '*secular*' *cares* (*ærumnæ seculi*). They come more or less upon all men; but some men lay themselves peculiarly open to their influence, and allow them to twine and twist themselves, like the serpents of Laocoon, around every energy and susceptibility of their being.

And the deceitfulness (or *deceit*) **of riches.** Tyndale has *disseytfulness*, Wycliffe *disseit*. The word for *riches* ($\pi\lambda o\widehat{v}\tau o s$) etymologically connects itself with the idea of *much* ($\pi o\lambda\acute{v}s$). A rich man is a man who has *much*, and who, just because he has *much of what* '*answereth*' almost '*a'l things*,' is exposed to peculiar temptations, which but few can altogether withstand. "If a man "suffer the habit of acquisition," says one who was eminently entitled to speak on such a subject, Joshua Wilson, Esq., " to predominate and prevail over him, " (as it must predominate and prevail unless carefully held in check and reso- " lutely counteracted), he may become, before he is aware, a miserable victim of " 'the pitiful passion for accumulation.' Hence the immense importance of " early forming and diligently cultivating the habit of liberality, of beginning to " give as soon as a man begins to get, and increasing the amount of his givings " in proportion to the increase of his gains. One of the greatest deceptions, " that men are too apt to practise upon themselves, is to defer being bountiful " till their means have greatly increased. This is indeed a striking proof of " what our Lord calls *the deceitfulness of riches*." (*Memoir of the Life and Character of Thomas Wilson, Esq.*, p. 69.)

And the lusts of other things. Namely, besides money. The expression is literally *and the lusts concerning the other things*. Note the definitive articles, '*the*' lusts (*so common in society*) *concerning* '*the*' *other things* (*so commonly longed for*). The word *lust* has now for long got narrowed in its reference to sensual desire of a hateful description, as being either improper in kind or improper in degree. But originally it had a much wider reference, and just meant, generically, *desire, longing, inclination* or *liking*. The Greek term

other things entering in, choke the word, and it becometh unfruitful. 20 And these are they which are sown on good ground; such as hear the word, and receive *it*, and bring forth fruit, some thirtyfold, some sixty, and some an hundred.

(ἐπιθυμία) is occasionally used in the New Testament when some *good and holy longing* is referred to: see Luke xxii. 15, Phil. i. 23, 1 Thess. ii. 17. But though occasionally thus used, it is nevertheless, in its general New Testament usage, *like a ball loaded on the left side*. It thus reflects the sad fact that somehow or other the affections are the favourite seat of human depravity. The Rheims translation of the clause, copied from the Vulgate and therefore omitting the articles, is, *and concupiscences about other things*. The Saviour might be referring to 'concupiscences' concerning such things as houses, lands, works of art and vertu, posts of honour, gaiety of garments, grandeur of entertainments, and in general the myriad appliances of luxury.

Entering in. If a very precise adherence to the parabolic imagery had been aimed at, some such phrase as *growing up* would have been employed instead of *entering in*.

Choke the word. They *crowd in stiflingly upon the word* (συνπνίγουσιν). Comp. Luke viii. 14. They *strangle* it, as Wycliffe has it; his word is *strangulen*.

And it becomes unfruitful. It gets no farther than the leaf of profession, struggling feebly toward the light amid the thicket of thorns. It has not strength to seed. It does nothing for the *propagation* of the word in the world. See on ver. 7.

VER. 20. **And those are they that were sown on the good ground.** *Those*, instead of *these*, is the correct reading given by Tischendorf, Tregelles, Alford (ἐκεῖνοι).

Such as hear the word, and accept it. They accept it *to themselves*, and *for themselves* (παραδέχονται).

And bring forth fruit, one thirty, one sixty, and one a hundredfold. Such is the reading (ἕν) of the Received Text; and it is retained by Lachmann and Alford. It was the reading that was before our translators. It is the reading too that had been accepted by the authors of the Italic, Vulgate, Coptic, Armenian, and Gothic versions. It is in some respects the easiest reading. (Comp. Matt. xiii. 8, 23.) But the word which with a certain 'breathing' is a numeral meaning *one* (ἕν) is, when pronounced with another 'breathing,' a preposition meaning *in* (ἐν). It is with this latter breathing that the word is given by Tischendorf and Tregelles, on the authority of the important cursive manuscripts 1, 33, 69, and also of the uncials E F G H K M U V II (in which uncials the 'breathings' are indicated; see Tischendorf). No doubt these cursives and uncials are right, for the phraseology is thus brought into harmony with the representation employed in ver. 8. The clause then, when literally translated, runs thus, *And they bring forth fruit in thirty, and in sixty, and in a hundred*, that is, in the proportional ratios of thirty, sixty, and a hundredfold of increase. These threefold ratios however are specified only representatively. All who hear and heartily receive the word are more or less fruitful; but some, according to a peculiar innate energy or peculiarly favourable surroundings, are

21] ST. MARK IV. 101

21 And he said unto them, Is a candle brought to be put under a bushel, or under a bed ? and not to be set on a candle-

---

fruitful to an eminent or even to a pre-eminent degree. All propagate what is good, but some more largely than others.

VER. 21. **And He said to them.** We know not, and we do not need to know, who are definitely referred to under the pronoun *them*, whether it be the disciples alone or the people at large. Neither do we know *when* and *where* it was that our Saviour said what He said, whether it was on the day when He delivered *the parable of the sower* to the people, or at the time when He explained it to His disciples, or at some other time. The evangelist's memoirs are remarkably *anecdotical*, but not remarkably *chronological*. The sayings recorded in ver. 21-23 were probably some of our Saviour's favourite seed thoughts. The likelihood is that He would often drop them by the way. Perhaps He would even drop them repeatedly, and need thus to drop them, into the very same soil. The seed thought contained in this 21st verse is found in Luke viii. 16, xi. 33; Matt. v. 15.

Is a candle brought [so we read in King James's English version] *to be put under a bushel, or under a bed? and not to be set on a candlestick?* We have here a remarkable instance of the definite article being overlooked. It occurs four times in the original: Is 'the' lamp brought, that it might be set under 'the' bushel, or under 'the' couch, not that it might be set on 'the' lamp stand? A still more literal translation of the first clause would be, *Does the lamp come?* There is motion observed in the lamp; but for the time being it is left undecided whether it be self-motion or motion by another. Even in the classics (see Kypke and Raphel), as also in our modern idioms, it is common in many cases to represent inanimate objects as *coming*, when they are only *brought*. Tyndale's translation is freer still than the Authorized version, *Is the candle lighted? Lamp* is better than *candle*, for the lamp was the common household nightlight among the Jews. '*The*' *lamp*: it is implied that in general only one was used in the family apartment. *Under the bushel*, literally *under the modius.* The word is Roman, so that it is probable that the vessel referred to had got into use among the Jews in consequence of their subjection to the Romans. It is not unlikely that it would be found to be more exact, and therefore more to be depended on, than the native-made measures. Hence householders might wish to have it beside them as security against imposition, both in buying and selling. The Roman *modius* however was, as to capacity, nearer a *peck* than a *bushel. Under the couch*: the reference here too bespeaks the influence of Roman customs. Our Saviour must have had in view, not the native *mat, matting*, or *mattress*, which when simply spread on the floor served for bed or couch, but the Roman *triclinium* or raised couch that was used at formal meals, when the guests reclined at three sides of a table. *Not that it might be set upon the lamp stand?* The lamp stand was not set upon the table, but stood on the floor, rising aloft. Our Saviour's fine parabolic seed-thought might have many applications. He wished His disciples and all people to make a generous use of all the light, whatever it might be, that had been vouchsafed to them. It was a trust committed to them. No man is illumi-

stick? 22 For there is nothing hid, which shall not be manifested; neither was any thing kept secret, but that it should come abroad. 23 If any man have ears to hear, let him hear.

nated from above for his own sake alone. No man should try to hoard his light, or to consume it in secret. At the same time he need not force it upon the unwilling. The saintly Cæsar Malan of Geneva said about fifty years ago to the author, then a young student of theology : *Hold up your lamp before men ; hold it up fearlessly, and let it shine ; but do not dash it into anybody's face !*

VER. 22. **For.** In what follows a reason is given for letting the light shine. But the immediately succeeding clause is very perplexed as regards some minute details of expression, in consequence partly of the inherent peculiarity of the original reading, and partly of the varied forms in which the seed-thought occurs in Matt. x. 26, Luke viii. 17, xii. 2. We doubt not, however, that Tischendorf, following up the labours of Griesbach and Lachmann, has succeeded in presenting the text in its original form : **There is not anything hidden unless that it might be manifested** (οὐ γὰρ ἔστιν τι κρυπτόν, ἐὰν μὴ ἵνα φανερωθῇ). It is one of the longest plumblines of thought that our Saviour ever let out in conversation. God hides some things ; it is His glory to hide them (Prov. xxv. 2). He hid several very important things under the shadows of the Jewish dispensation. He has hidden millions of other things ; in the crust of the earth for instance, perhaps in its flora, perhaps in its fauna, perhaps in invisible telluric influences. He has hidden innumerable things in the sun and moon and stars. Christ Himself hid many things under the parables which He spake (ver. 11, 12). He hid in His own heart many other things which even His nearest disciples could not have 'stood' (John xvi. 12) or 'understood' (John xiii. 7). But this hiding on the part of Christ and of God is, in every case, not final but provisional. *The truth is hidden, that it may be found out and manifested* ; and *no one thing is hidden, unless that it may be by and by manifested.* Nothing is to be hidden for ever. There is always a final end in hiding ; and the end is *that it may be manifested.* Hence human progression in science and in all the applications of science. Even when men try to hide things, it is divinely permitted for a season, only that after a season all may be revealed. The whole universe by and by, with all its contents, will be as it were absolutely transparent to every illumined eye. To the eye of God there is already everywhere complete transparency.

Neither was anything kept secret, or rather *made secret,* **but that it should come to light** (Alford), or, *but that it should come into sight,* (Sharpe) εἰς φανερόν. It is an emphatic repetition of the idea of the preceding clause, but simply bringing into view the intentional *making of a thing secret.* Whoever has the intention, it either is, or is divinely permitted to be, just that in due time the wrapping may be taken away and the thing exposed to universal view.

VER. 23. **If any man has ears to hear, let him hear.** It is subsumed that *every one actually has ears to hear.* Then let every one hear ; let him voluntarily listen till he understand. It was one of the Saviour's fine didactic seed-thoughts, which He seems to have very frequently dropped by the way (ver. 9). It needs still to be dropped, and dropped time after time into the same ears.

24] ST. MARK IV. 103

24 And he said unto them, Take heed what ye hear. With what measure ye mete, it shall be measured to you: and unto you

There are, comparatively speaking, but few patient and impartial hearers, but few patient and impartial thinkers, in the world.

VER. 24, 25. Another little cluster of anecdotical sayings.

VER. 24. **And He said to them.** To whom? We know not, and do not need to know. The value of the apophthegms does not depend on the incidents of their utterance. They are of universal application.

Take heed ' what' ye hear. It is a slightly different idea from that which is brought out in Luke viii. 18, *Take heed ' how' ye hear*. Both injunctions are needed; and indeed they wonderfully intertwine, so that he who takes heed *how he hears* will likely be careful as to *what he hears*, and *vice versa*. There is no scope, it is true, for the exercise of will in reference to many of the things which we hear; and hence every man often hears things which it would be better for him, in his present circumstances, not to hear. But there are on the other hand many other things, which we may either hear or not, as we choose. We are responsible therefore for much that we hear, as well as for all that we speak. And if, for instance, we be eager to hear words of detraction or censorious tittle-tattle and scandal-talk, in reference to our neighbours, we must take the retributive consequences. Most likely there will be 'counterpart' retribution. See next clause.

With what measure ye mete, it shall be measured to you. Literally '*in*' *what measure*. The reference is to *a measure of capacity*. The same measure 'in' which we mete out our treatment of others will be retributively employed for measuring out to ourselves the treatment which we shall receive. Comp. Matt. vii. 2, Luke vi. 38. It is a law of retribution in morals, somewhat analogous to the law of reaction in physics. It will sooner or later, except in certain peculiar cases modified by repentance, be fulfilled in the experience of all. It will be fulfilled either in kind or in equivalent; either imminently or ultimately; either from without or from within; and if from without, either from around or from Above. *As we treat, so shall we be treated*. *What we sow, that we shall reap.*

And more shall be added to you. A clause that has been tampered with, and badly tinkered, by unperspicacious critics. It was supposed that there is a close connection between the injunction *Take heed what ye hear* and the words of the preceding verse, *If any man have ears to hear, let him hear*. It was hence supposed that in the words *what ye hear* there is a reference only to what is good, a reference to Christ's own explication of the mysteries of the kingdom of heaven. And then it was supposed that when He adds, *in what measure ye mete it shall be measured to you*, He means, *in what measure ye mete out your hearing and attention, in that same measure shall the subject matter of hearing and attention be meted out to you*. And then and thence it was inferred that our Saviour meant to add, *and unto you ' that hear*,' or as the Gothic version gives it, *unto you ' that believe ' shall more be given*. That is, *the more you hear of Divine truth, the more shall you get to hear*. The idea is admirable in itself, but it is foisted in upon the phraseology of the evangelist. The injunction *Take*

104   ST. MARK IV.   [24

that hear shall more be given. 25 For he that hath, to him shall be given : and he that hath not, from him shall be taken even that which he hath.

26 And he said, So is the kingdom of God, as if a man

---

heed what you hear implies the duty of discrimination in reference to the objects on which hearing may terminate; and in what follows there is a warning against hearing what should not be heard. *If we hear concerning others what we should not hear, others will in all likelihood hear concerning us what we would not like them to hear;* there will be retribution. In the clause that is added the idea is, *There will be more than merely equal retribution, there will be retribution with a surplus.* We shall be *paid back with interest.* Griesbach suspected that the entire clause was spurious, a ' gloss.' Hence he omits it entirely from the text; it is omitted in the Cambridge manuscript (D). But this is going too far. There is no doubt however that the words *that hear* (τοῖς ἀκούουσιν), found in the Received Text, were originally a marginal gloss added by some one who, forgetting or not knowing the anecdotical character of the passage, misapprehended the meaning of the Divine counsel. They are wanting in א B C L Δ, and in the Italic, Vulgate, Coptic, Armenian, and Æthiopic versions. They are omitted by Lachmann, Tischendorf, Tregelles, Alford. The clause as it originally stood was simply, as the Rheims has it, *and more shall be given unto you.*

VER. 25. **For he who hath, to him shall be given.** A principle of very wide applicability. Whosoever has something good, having acquired it by the right use of his powers, to him shall more be given. If, for instance, by not hearing what should not be heard, time and opportunity are left for hearing what should be heard, and if consequently something is learned which it is a privilege to learn, then the learning faculty is enlarged, and more and still more will be progressively acquired.

And he who hath not, even what he hath shall be taken from him. The other side of the principle, though put so far as the grammatical phraseology is concerned in an exceedingly inartificial manner. Whosoever *has not the good which he ought to have acquired,* and has it not in consequence of the misapplication of *the good power of acquisition which he has,* will suffer loss in his good power. The power is abused, and will be weakened. If the weakening goes on, the power will by and by become a wreck.

VER. 26. **And He said.** The time and connection are not absolutely certain. **So is the kingdom of God.** This is the beginning of a little parable that is preserved by Mark alone. Strauss indeed (*Leben,* ii., vi. § 74) threw out the suggestion that it might be but ' another recension ' of *the parable of the tares* or *darnel* (Matt. xiii. 24–30), but without the reference to the darnel, somewhat apparently on the principle of *the Play of Hamlet with the part of Hamlet left out!* Hilgenfeld (*Evang.,* p. 133) takes the same view ; and, sad to say, Ewald (*Evang.,* p. 234). Michelsen too ; only he holds that the form of the parable in Mark is the original form, out of which the fuller form in Matthew was ultimately elaborated. (*Het Evan.,* p. 56.) Wantonly all through. Such conceptions can

should cast seed into the ground; 27 and should sleep, and rise night and day, and the seed should spring and grow up,

---

only be reached by an indiscriminate application of a thumbscrew species of exposition. Scholten admits the originality and self contained distinctness of the parable (*Het Oudste Ev.*, p. 197). *So is the kingdom of God*, viz. in a certain aspect of its multiform spiritual phenomena. The particle *So* looks forward to the similitude that is about to be expressed.

As if a man should have cast the seed upon the earth (βάλῃ τὸν σπόρον ἐπὶ τῆς γῆς). We are not to suppose, with Theophylact and many other expositors, that the *man* here parabolically pictured forth is the Saviour Himself. The ignorance that is ascribed to him at the end of the 27th verse, not to speak of other items of the representation, lays an interdict on this idea. It is evidently the ordinary preacher of the gospel who is referred to. The *seed* represents the *word* of God, or the *word* of the kingdom of God, that is, the *word* of the truth of the gospel. Note the article, '*the*' *seed*, that is, *the particular seed* which the man had got to sow. He sowed it *upon* the prepared soil; and he would finish up the process by using what simple means were available to him, to get the grain duly bedded and protected.

VER. 27. **And should sleep and rise night and day.** Note the present tenses of the verbs *sleep*, and *rise*, after the past in the preceding verse, *have cast*. When once the casting of the seed upon the ground is *past*, the husbandman *goes to rest*, and thenceforward continues, day by day, to prosecute his varied avocations. In the alternations of *sleeping* and *rising* a precedence is given, in the parable, to the former, because the speaker's mind begins to consider the alternating series from the point of time when the seed was sown. On the night following that day the husbandman *sleeps*; in the morning he wakes and *rises*. And thenceforward the same alternations are repeated for an undefined length of time. In King James's version there is a comma strangely inserted after *and should sleep*. and then another comma after *and rise night and day*. It is almost as if the translators had thought, with Theophylact, that the husbandman is represented as anxiously rising both by night and by day to see that all was going on well; or as if they had been influenced by Erasmus, who, in the fourth edition of his New Testament, proposed to arrest the parabolic reference to the husbandman at the conclusion of the words *and should sleep*, ascribing the succeeding words *and rise day and night* to the *seed*. Purvey, in his revision of Wycliffe's version, gives the same interpretation, *and he slepte, and it rise up nighte and dai*. It is an impossible construction, as is evident from the fact that reference to the seed is expressly introduced in the following clause. *The husbandman sleeps and rises night and day*. It is an inartificial expression; the word *night* is to be connected with *sleeps*, the word *day* with *rises*. The husbandman is not blamed for his *sleeping*, no more than for his *rising*. He needs both to *sleep*, and when he wakes, to *rise*. And if he has done his daily duty, as he is presumed to have done, he may lay himself down to sleep and rise again without any carking care.

And the seed should sprout and grow up. Literally, *and should lengthen*. The living thing in the seed, which constitutes its vital germ or inner essence, does sprout and lengthen into the stalk and its culminating spike. It will be

he knoweth not how. 28 For the earth bringeth forth fruit of

noticed that the clauses of the parable are artlessly aggregated, but yet quite clearly.
He knows not how. Or, according to the collocation in the original, *how he know not*. Erasmus would strangely interpret thus, *in such a way as it (the seed) knows not*. The seed sprouts and shoots up in a way unknown to the husbandman. The Saviour does not say that no husbandman, or philosopher, or investigator, will ever know how a seed sprouts and shoots up. He is simply supposing a case which would in His day be common enough, and which is common still, the case of a man casting seed into the ground, and then sleeping and rising for days in succession without ever touching again the seed which he sowed. Not only does the man not touch the seed, or seek by his own skill and energy to operate *in* it, he does not even know its inner essence or the nature of its inner energy. It sprouts and shoots up in a way he knows not. The Saviour's meaning is that, *in the case supposed*, the man knows not how the seed germinates and grows up to maturity.

VER. 28. **For.** This ratiocinative particle is dropped out of the text by Lachmann, Tischendorf, Tregelles, Alford. It is not found in the very important manuscripts ℵ A B C L ; and it is omitted in the Coptic version (both Wilkins's and Schwartze's editions), and in the Philoxenian Syriac, and the Æthiopic. It is evidently not needed.
Of itself the earth beareth fruit. The adjective that is very imperfectly rendered *of itself* means *self-moving* or *self-acting* (αὐτομάτη). The earth is represented as *automatic*; there is a kind of *unconscious spontaneity* in it. There is indeed no real spontaneity attributable to the earth : real spontaneity is a property of consciousness and mind ; and the earth is impersonal. But there is a Spontaneity, altogether distinct from the consciousness and mind of men, pervading the earth. And hence, relatively to man, the earth is automatic. It is not, relatively to God, an automaton. It 'has its being, and moves, in God.' In all its motions He is moving. But it is the aim of the Saviour, in the expression before us, to represent not what the earth is in its relation to God, but what it is in its relation to man. Multitudinous motions go on in the earth in absolute independence of man's volitions and efforts. In this respect *the earth beareth fruit 'automatously.'* The word was a favourite with the classical writers. They frequently speak of automatous or spontaneous plants or fruits, meaning such as grow without the help of man. Herodotus represents the Nile as irrigating the fields of Egypt *automatously* (ii. 14). The hand of man is not needed to spread out the water ; in like manner the hand of man is not needed to push up the sprouting of the grains of corn, or to give shaping to the stalks or to the ears.
First the blade. Out of the compound verb which is rendered in the preceding clause *beareth fruit* (καρποφορεῖ) we must mentally detach the element that simply means *bringeth forth* or *beareth*, and carry it forward to this and the succeeding clause : *the earth bringeth forth, first, the blade*. The word *blade* denotes *the grassy part* of the plant, or simply *the grass*, as Purvey here renders it in his revision of Wycliffe. It is the word that is commonly used to

herself; first the blade, then the ear, after that the full corn

denote *grass*. (See Matt. vi. 30, xiv. 19; Mark vi. 39; John vi. 10 ; 1 Pet. i. 24 ; Rev. viii. 7.) It here denotes *the leaf-equipped stalk* of the corn-plant.
Then the ear. Or *spike*. See Luke vi. 1.
Then the full corn in the ear. The reading of Lachmann, Tischendorf, and Tregelles is, *then (there comes) the full corn in the ear*. *The full corn*, or *the full grain*, or *the full wheat*. The word is generally rendered *wheat*, which was the grain in common use for human food. See Matt. iii. 12, xiii. 25, 29, 30 ; Luke xvi. 7, xxii. 31 ; John xii. 24 ; Acts xxvii. 38 ; 1 Cor. xv. 37 ; Rev. vi. 6. The '*full*' *grain* means the '*filled up*' *grain*. The grain is at first small, flaccid, pulpy. But by and by, under ordinarily propitious circumstances, it swells out to its full size, and then gets compact and hard. *And all this without any manipulation on the part of man*. It is not meant indeed that man is utterly unable to do anything either to help or to hinder the growth. Man can do much. It is evident that he can do much *in the way of hindering* ; he might trample the growing stalks, or let them be choked by weeds and thorns. He can also do not a little *to help* ; and hence the vast advances that may be made, and that have been made, in the science of agriculture. He can carefully prepare the soil ; he can drain his field, when that would be beneficial ; he can manure it properly ; he can pluck up certain weeds and noxious shrubs ; he can here and there let in additional sunlight by removing overshadowing trees ; he can see to his fences, so that the grain may not be trampled and injured by the foot of man or of beast ; he can scare away the birds that flock around ; and he can entrap such other animals as might wish to prey on his crop. The husbandman has much that he can do to help forward the crop. *But still there are limits to his power*. When the Saviour speaks of the man casting the seed on the ground, and then sleeping and rising for a series of days and weeks, He does not intend, by specifying *the casting of the seed*, to exclude all other operations. *On the contrary the operation of* '*casting the seed*' *is mentioned by Him as representative of a certain limited number of agricultural operations*. And the idea that He would impress is this, that there is a limit beyond which the agriculturist cannot go, and at which consequently he must abandon all efforts of his own and trust to a greater power. He cannot go to each grain, and elaborate it into the stalk and the spike and the fulness of the spike. *In like manner there is a limit to ministerial labour in reference to the growth of true religion in the soul*. Ministers of the gospel may do much, either to help or to hinder the growth of true religion, in the souls of those to whom they minister. They may mismanage the preparation of the soil ; they may neglect the fences of the field ; they may fail to watch as they ought to watch. Or on the other hand they may use all diligence to plough, and harrow, and pluck up briers and thorns and weeds, and to ward off the birds and beasts of prey. But they soon reach the limits of their power. Man, as Theophylact here says, is a free agent, he continues to be free while he is being operated on by his fellow men, his heart is automatous. And then too a higher Spontaneity than his own is at work within him, and is needed to be at work. 'My Father worketh hitherto,' says Jesus, ' and I work ' (John v. 17). It is God who 'gives the increase' (1 Cor. iii. 7). The word of the truth of the gospel is a wonderful kind of grain :

in the ear. 29 But when the fruit is brought forth, imme-

there is *life* in it (1 Pet. i. 23); there is automatism (αὐτοματισμ/ς) in it, as well as in the heart in which it is sown. There is *automatic thought* in the *word*. And automatic thought, every real thought, is just a germ in a living mind. The thought that is in the word of the truth of the gospel is *the thought of the Holy Spirit of God*. The moment that we get beyond the mere husk or symbolism of the ' word,' the moment that we get into the ' thought,' we are in the spontaneities of the Divine Mind. Hence the power of the Holy Spirit. It is no mere mechanical operation. Hence the power of the word of the truth of the gospel. It is the power of the living mind and heart of the Living God.

VER. 29. Ὅταν δὲ παραδοῖ ὁ καρπός. An exceedingly difficult expression. Tyndale's translation, *But when the fruit is brought forth*, must have been originally given, and subsequently reproduced, under a kind of critical despair. The same despair seems to have seized upon the old Syriac translator, who renders the expression *when the fruit has been fattened* (that is, no doubt, *when it has been matured*). The Philoxenian has it correspondingly and as freely, *when the fruit has been filled*. The Arabic, Æthiopic, and Persic translations are equally free. So is the Gothic, *when the fruit is given out (atgibada)*. The translation in the margin of King James's version, and adopted in the Revised version, is similarly free, *when the fruit is ripe*, a rendering adopted into their texts by Mace and Wakefield. Rodolphus Dickinson has *when the grain is matured*. The verb however is active, not passive (παραδοῖ or παραδῷ). It means literally *has delivered up*. Klostermann supposes that it must have been a technical agricultural phrase, denoting the ripened condition of the grains. The majority of critics, inclusive of Henry Stephens, Beza, Felbinger, Wolf, Bengel, Fritzsche, suppose that it must be used reflexively, or intransitively, *whenever the fruit has delivered ' itself,'* or *shall have delivered ' itself,' up*. The verb is used in this reflexive or intransitive acceptation in the Alexandrine text of the Septuagint version of Josh. xi. 19, *and there was no city which did not ' surrender '* (ἥτις οὐ παρέδωκεν) *to the children of Israel*. Meyer, Lange, Bisping, Grimm, and not a few others, suppose that the verb has here its occasional meaning of *permit* (a mode of *delivering up*), *when the fruit shall permit* or *shall have permitted*. This meaning is found again and again in Herodotus (v. 67, vi. 103, vii. 18, ix. 78) and other classics. But it is unbiblical, and yields a rather awkward and constrained sense, when applied, not to persons as in Herodotus, nor to *circumstances* as in our corresponding modern idiom, but to *fruit*. We wait for fuller light. But meantime we would either accept the reflexive import of the verb, or suppose that the language abruptly and inartificially leaves the reader to supply, out of his own consideration of the case in hand, *what it is that is delivered up by the fruit*. In the parable as a whole we have *successive working* exhibited. The *working* passes along, in trust as it were, now *through* man, now *from* man, now *to* man. We have first the *working* of the sower; he casts the seed into the soil. Then the working passes from him; and the seed itself automatously works; it sprouts and grows up, and 'brings forth the blade and the ear and the full corn in the ear.' There is similar synchronous working, unspecified in the parable but implied, on the part

diately he putteth in the sickle, because the harvest is come.
30 And he said, Whereunto shall we liken the kingdom
of God? or with what comparison shall we compare it?

---

of the rain from heaven and the sun. By and by the working of the soil and its cosmical accompaniments is finished; so is the working of the plant itself, and of the maturing fruit. But still the full complement of working is not finished; something remains to be done; and the fruit, when by its own automatous operation it has become fully matured, ' *delivers up* ' (the working power which had been divinely committed to it, or transmitted through it). The working must now be *taken up again* by man. See next clause.

Straightway he putteth forth the sickle. *He*, that is the *man* (ver. 26), the *husbandman*. He '*putteth forth*'; literally, *he sendeth out*, ' apostolically ' as it were (ἀποστέλλει). He sendeth out *the sickle* in the hands of the reaper. The 'lord of the harvest' is supposed to hire reapers, and to ' send them forth into his harvest.'

Because the harvest is come. The time for gathering in and enjoying the fruits is come. The time thus parabolically referred to is assumed by Theophylact, Dr. Samuel Clarke, Meyer, and many others, to be the consummation of all things. But this assumption is based on the prior assumption that it is the Saviour Himself who is represented by the husbandman. It is however as we have seen, not the Divine, but the human workman, who is meant by the *man*. The parable teaches the limitations, not of *Divine*, but of *ministerial agency*, in the moral effects of the gospel. It is very limited; but if it be faithfully exerted at the time when it is really required, there will, in due season, be the enjoyment of a 'harvest home' of blessed results. We do not need to assume, with Archbishop Trench, that the reaping of the grain refers to the gathering of believers, ' when they are ripe for glory,' ' into everlasting habitations.' (*The Parables*, p. 283.) ' Certainly,' says Dr. Adam Clarke, ' the parable does not say so.' What is to hinder us from supposing that the reaping meant corresponds to that which is spoken of in John iv. 35, 36: " Lift up " your eyes, and look on the fields; for they are white already to harvest. *And* " *he that reapeth receiveth wages, and gathereth fruit unto life eternal* "? Comp. Ps. cxxvi. 6; Matt. ix. 37, 38. "The reapers," says Arnot, "are the human " ministers of the word, and the reaping is the successful ingathering in conver-" sion here, not the admission of the redeemed into glory at the end of the " world." (*The Parables*, p. 316.)

VER. 30. **And He said.** Here follows another of the Saviour's parables.

Whereunto might we liken (ὁμοιώσωμεν) **the kingdom of God?** The Saviour, sympathetically and with fine oratorical tact, stimulates His hearers to thoughtfulness by associating them with Himself in His search for appropriate similitudes. Hence the *we*. Instead of *whereunto* (τίνι) Tischendorf, Tregelles, Alford have the corresponding word *how* (πῶς). It is the reading of ℵ B C L Δ.

Or in what parable might we put it, or *set it forth ?* Such is the reading of ℵ B C* L Δ, 63. The Saviour continues to speak as if He were searching about for a parable that would serve as an appropriate setting for the truth which He wished to enforce, in reference to a certain phase of the kingdom of God.

31 *It is* like a grain of mustard seed, which, when it is sown in the earth, is less than all the seeds that be in the earth: 32 but when it is sown, it groweth up, and becometh greater than all herbs, and shooteth out great branches; so that the fowls of the air may lodge under the shadow of it.

33 And with many such parables spake he the word unto

VER. 31. **We might liken it** (such is the unfolded import of the initial ὡς) **to a grain of mustard seed, which when it is sown upon the earth is a less thing than all the seeds that are upon the earth.** The language is broken, but the sense is obvious. The mustard seed is an exceedingly small seed, not indeed absolutely smaller than all other seeds known to modern botanists, but smaller than all the seeds that the Jews were accustomed to sow in their fields and gardens.

VER. 32. **Yet when it is sown.** It is an artless repetition, but with a peculiar emphasis. It breaks the participial construction that was in progress at the conclusion of the preceding verse, and brings back attention to the time, whensoever that might be, when the seed may have been committed to the soil.

Groweth up. Or, as the Rheims has it, *riseth up*. It *ascends*.

And becometh greater than all the herbs. Namely, that people in Palestine were accustomed to rear in their gardens. The word rendered *herbs* (λάχανα) denotes a peculiar species of herbs, viz. *potherbs* or *garden herbs*.

And throweth out great branches. Literally, *maketh great branches*, great relatively to the branches of other garden herbs. Bishop Ryle says: "The "enormous size to which the rhododendron, the heath, and the fern will grow, "in some climates which suit them better than ours, should be remembered by "an English reader of this parable." (*Expository Thoughts on Mark*, p. 79.)

So that the birds of the heaven are able to lodge under its shade. *To lodge*, or as Wycliffe has it, *to dwell*. So Purvey, Tyndale, Coverdale, and the Rheims. The Geneva has *to build*, and in Cranmer's Bible it is *to make their nestes*. The original term properly means *to pitch their tents* (κατασκηνόω). Here it would appear to mean *to roost*.

The parable seems intended to teach the vast resources of extension that were summed up in the minute germ of the kingdom of heaven. The community, in the day of our Saviour's humiliation, was indeed exceedingly small. But it was destined to have a great and glorious development, transcending that of all the other kingdoms and communities of the world. The same principle is exemplified in miniature in the experience of every individual subject of the kingdom. The heavenly principle within is small at the outset, but it gradually expands and grows and ramifies into the whole amplitude of the heart and intellect and life.

VER. 33. **And with many such parables.** *Such* as are recorded in what goes before, *such* in form and *such* in doctrinal aim. The evangelist has only preserved a selection of specimens.

Spake He the word to them. That circle of truth or truths whose centre is 'the gospel.'

them, as they were able to hear *it*. 34 But without a parable spake he not unto them. And when they were alone, he expounded all things to his disciples.

35 And the same day, when the even was come, he saith unto them, Let us pass over unto the other side. 36 And when they had sent away the multitude, they took him even as he was in the ship. And there were also with him other

---

As they were able to hear. Or as the same idea is represented in John xvi. 12, *as they were able to bear* or *carry*. The people, though not understanding much, were yet profoundly interested and charmed. There are limits however to the power of attention and the susceptibility of interest; when the vessel becomes full and is running over, it is needless to pour in more.

VER. 34. **And without a parable spake He not unto them.** Although He spoke much, as much as they could hear when straining their attention to its utmost limit of tension, yet He did not deviate from the parabolic form of instruction. The auditory that was before Him was not in a condition to endure other than parabolic truth.

But privately to His disciples He expounded all things. *Explicated* is the corresponding word in the Rheims version. The cognate noun is rendered *interpretation* in 2 Pet. i. 20. Instead of *to His disciples* the manuscripts ℵ B C L Δ, read *to His own disciples* (ἰδίοις), and Tischendorf has introduced this reading into his text.

VER. 35. **And He saith to them on that day when evening was come, Let us cross over to the other side.** Namely of the sea of Galilee. He refers to its eastern side, where, in consequence of the comparatively barren and rocky character of much of the coast and of the adjacent country, there was not nearly so dense a population as on the western side. "There is no recess," says Dean Stanley, "in the eastern hills; no towns along its banks corresponding to those "in the plain of Gennesareth. Thus this wilder region became a natural refuge "from the active life of the western shores." (*Sinai and Palestine*, p. 379.) As to the chronology of the occurrence that is about to be related, Mark seems to be precise. See on Matt. viii. 23.

VER. 36. **And having dismissed the crowd.** No doubt, by telling them firmly that the Master would give no more instructions on that occasion.

They take Him with them, as He was, in the boat. Just as He was, in that particular boat in which He had been sitting while addressing the people (ver. 1). They did not, on the one hand, go in quest of a more convenient or comfortable boat; neither did they, on the other, go ashore to get any special baggage or provisions. Time was pressing; and there might have been only additional pressure from the lingering remnants of the crowd if the boat had been brought to land.

And there were also with Him other boats. It would appear that while our Lord was engaged in teaching the people, who stood crowding far and wide on the shore, there had been individuals who availed themselves of the opportunity of the adjoining boats for getting nearer His person, and into a more

little ships. 37 And there arose a great storm of wind, and the waves beat into the ship, so that it was now full.

---

favourable position for listening to His discourse. Hence a little fleet had gathered round the boat in which our Saviour sat. Doubtless at that period of comparative national prosperity there would be many boats available. Josephus describes (*Wars*, Book iii., 10) a naval engagement that took place on the lake, when both the natives on the one hand and the Romans under Titus on the other had *many vessels*. The 'other boats' which had gathered round our Saviour's boat are said to have been *with* '*Him*,' for 'He,' as distinguished from the boat which bore Him and the 'apostolic' crew who manned it, was the great object of interest. It is, we presume, in an artlessly incidental manner that mention is here made of these 'other boats,' filling out however the picture which Peter autoptically drew when he narrated the facts of his Lord's life. It is probable that the occupants of the boats would, like the people on the shore, be assured by the disciples that the Master had concluded for that occasion, and that He now desired seclusion and rest.

VER. 37. And—by and by, as they are rowing across—there **ariseth a great storm of wind.** *A hurricane of wind*, such as the sea of Galilee is notoriously exposed to. Mr. Macgregor speaks of 'a headlong flood of wind like a waterfall' which he witnessed pouring down into the lake. He says: "The peculiar "effects of squalls among mountains are well known to all who have boated "much on lakes; but on the sea of Galilee the wind has a singular force and "suddenness; and this is no doubt because that sea is so deep in the world that "the sun rarifies the air in it enormously, and the wind, speeding swift above "a long and level plateau, athers much force as it sweeps through flat deserts, "until suddenly it meets this huge gap in the way, *and it tumbles down here* "*irresistible*." (*The Rob Roy on the Jordan*, p. 421.) On two distinct occasions Mr. Macgregor encountered this 'great storm of wind.' With reference to the first of the two he says: "A brisk breeze from Bashan had freshened "while we paddled along these bays, and the short 'choppy' waves at Jordan's "mouth were angry enough to require attention while crossing them. I "ascended Jordan to wait for the wind's pleasure if it might calm down; but "instead of that the sea rose more and more, and at last heavy clouds in the "east burst into a regular gale. . . . The wind whistled, and sea gulls "screamed as they were borne on the scud. Thick and ragged clouds drifted "fast over the water, which became almost green in colour, as if it were on the "salt sea, and the illusion was heightened by the complete obscurity of the "distance, for the other side of the lake was quite invisible. . . . The "waves burst in upon the oleanders, and broke high and noisy upon the rugged "rocks. . . . The storm lasted next day." (*The Rob Roy*, pp. 336, 339.)

And the waves were lashing into the boat, so that the boat was now filling. Notwithstanding no doubt the utmost efforts of the crew at 'baling.' Luther and Coverdale regard the word *lashing* as transitive, and construe the word *waves* as supplying the objective to the action of the verb. Coverdale's version is, *There arose a great storme of wynde, and daszhed the wawes in to the shippe.* The construction of our King James's translators however is evidently correct.

38 And he was in the hinder part of the ship, asleep on a pillow : and they awake him, and say unto him, Master, carest thou not that we perish ? 39 And he arose, and rebuked the wind, and said unto the sea, Peace, be still. And the wind ceased, and there was a great calm. 40 And he said unto them, Why are ye so fearful ? How is it that ye have no faith ?

VER. 38. **And He Himself was in the stern.** Where there would be some little cabin.

Sleeping on the pillow. That is, *sleeping with His head reposing on 'the' pillow*, the one pillow which belonged, as part of the boat's furniture, to the small cabin at the stern. How touching that our Saviour should have been so speedily asleep ! How suggestive of His great exhaustion that He should have been so sound asleep ! Those delicate energies of His humanity, that needed to be statedly replenished, had been subjected to an excessive drain in consequence of the urgent demands of the people for teaching and healing. See chap. iii. 20, and comp. vi. 31.

And they awake Him. Literally, *they arouse Him.*

And say unto Him, Master, is it no concern to Thee that we perish? They were evidently much alarmed ; but their alarm, however great, was no excuse for such a petulant expostulation. The word which our translators render *Master* properly means *teacher* or *rabbi* (διδάσκαλε).

VER. 39. **And He awoke and rebuked the wind.** *Rebuked*, though perhaps as good a term as can be got, is an exceedingly imperfect translation (ἐπετίμησεν). The term is sometimes rendered *charged.* (See Matt. xii. 16 ; Mark iii. 12, viii. 30; Luke ix. 21.) It primarily means *rated.* Wycliffe renders it here *manasside*, i.e. *menaced.* It means that our Lord as it were laid His commands on the wind, peremptorily and authoritatively, and as if it had been transgressing bounds. Such was the outer form with which, for gracious exoteric purposes, He clothed the forth going of His inner volition. And what, too, if it should have been the case that He saw that there was some malignant personality astir in the midst of the storm ?

And said to the sea, Peace, be still. Very literally, *Be silent! Be muzzled!* The personification adapted itself to the *roar* of the storm.

And the wind ceased. It *fell* as if it had been utterly *exhausted by the exertion of its own beating* (ἐκόπασεν).

And there was—*there came on* (ἐγένετο)—**a great calm.** *Greet pesiblenesse*, as Wycliffe has it, that is, *great peacefulness.* The lake would then be, as it appeared to the eye of Dr. Tristram when he got his first glimpse of its beauty, "a calm blue basin, slumbering in placid sweetness beneath its surrounding wall "of hills." (*The Land of Israel*, p. 426.)

VER. 40. **And He said to them, Why are ye fearful thus?** *Why are ye fearful 'on this fashion,' 'after this manner'*? The adverb is rendered in these different ways in Matt. xxvi. 54, Mark ii. 12, Matt. vi. 9, etc. The expression draws attention to the degree and manner of their frightenedness.

How have ye not faith? It was wonderful that with the Lord in the vessel

41 And they feared exceedingly, and said one to another, What manner of man is this, that even the wind and the sea obey him?

they should have allowed themselves to be so entirely flurried and unmanned. Had they not already witnessed enough to assure them that He held at His girdle the keys of the kingdom of nature? Had they not noticed that He had some secret access to all the resources of the universe? Must not all seas be His highways? Must not all winds be His messengers?

Ver. 41. And they feared exceedingly. Literally, *they feared a great fear*. They had already been conscious of far too great fear in the presence of the sudden hurricane. But their fear was now greater still, though calm and more noble, in the presence of Him who had willed the hurricane into repose. They were filled with *awe*. They felt that they were in the presence of a far greater Power than what had pressed upon their senses in the storm. They seem to have got a glimpse into the interior of something that stretched away into infinity.

And said to one another, Who then is this? The *then* has a touch of argumentativeness in its import, *since it is the case that He can do such wonders*. They were but beginning to see. There were heights and depths in the Saviour which they had not hitherto realized.

That both the wind and the sea are obedient to Him! The *then* of the preceding clause looked back argumentatively to the occurrences that had taken place. The *that* of this clause looks forward reduplicatively to a fresh statement of the case. Schenkel thinks that there was no other miracle than merely a wonderful self-collected calmness on the part of our Lord amid the tempest! "If Jesus," says he, "ruled nature with Divine omnipotence, His sway was without any "moral significance. How much more exalted and exalting is Jesus standing "there amidst the increasing danger, surrounded by the trembling, experienced "seafarers, in spite of the despair of the steersman, standing there in holy self "possession, rebuking, tranquillizing, and encouraging them, an image of perfect "faith in God and of the clearest insight into His own destiny." "He had," says Schenkel, "immovable faith in His destiny, unwavering conviction that His "hour had not yet come, that He had yet to do the great work of His life; and "hence the accident of a storm could not disturb the Divine plan for the salva "tion of mankind." (*Characterbild Jesu*, x. 1.) He does not notice that if he ascribes to Jesus a really 'Divine plan for the salvation of mankind,' which required to be wrought out to completion in His individual personality, he introduces at another point the very element of the supernatural which he seeks to withdraw from the Saviour's relationship to the winds and the waves. It need not be added besides that if Schenkel's theory be right, Mark's narrative is wrong.

CHAPTER V.

1 AND they came over unto the other side of the sea, into

CHAPTER V.

FROM the 1st to the 20th verse we have a minute narrative of the deliverance of the Gerasene demoniac. See the corresponding paragraphs in Matt. viii. 28-34, and Luke viii. 26-39.

VER. 1. **And they came to the other side of the sea, to the country of the Gadarenes.** Or rather *of the Gerasenes*, or *of the Gergesenes*. There can be no doubt that *Gadarenes* is an erroneous reading, although it is found in the Alexandrine manuscript and the Ephraemi (A C), as well as in E F G H K M Ss Vs, and in the Peshito Syriac version, and the text of the Philoxenian Syriac, and the Gothic. It had evidently become an extensively diffused reading when once it did get into the manuscripts. Gadara was a well-known Jewish town, celebrated for its warm springs, and not very far from the sea of Galilee. It was a good many miles distant however, and lay to the south-east of the lake. Unhappily Erasmus inserted *Gadarenes* in his editions, and Robert Stephens followed him, and then Beza; and thence it got into King James's English version, although it is the word *Gergesenes* that is found in the parallel passage of Matt. viii. 28. *Gadarenes* was not the word in the oldest manuscripts. It is *Gerasenes* that is found in the Sinaitic and Vatican and Cambridge manuscripts (א B D), as also in the Italic and Vulgate versions. Origen too expressly mentions (i. 239, ed. *Lommat.*) that *Gerasenes* was the general reading of the manuscripts, though in some ʻ few ʼ copies *Gadarenes* was found. He dismisses the reading *Gadarenes* as out of the question; but, in consequence of an orthographical misconception, he supposes that the prevalent reading *Gerasenes* was also corrupt, and he conjectured that *Gergesenes* should be substituted in its place. He was thinking of *the famous Gerasa*, an Arabian city a long way to the south-east of Gadara, one of the chief places in Decapolis, and exhibiting to this day ʻ beautiful and extensive ruins.ʼ (See Porter's *Syria*, pp. 294-298.) This Gerasa is far removed, as he justly remarks, from ʻ both sea and lake ʼ; it cannot be the place referred to. Hence he concluded that the reference is to *Gergesa*, an ancient city on the eastern shore of the lake of Gennesaret. Thenceforward *Gergesenes*, instead of *Gerasenes*, became a favourite reading in the manuscripts. It established itself in Matthew, and was given there by Erasmus. Epiphanius says expressly that *Gergesenes* is the reading of Mark (*Hæres.*, lxvi. 33, p. 650). And so the word appears in L U Δ, 1, 33, and in the margin of the Philoxenian Syriac version, and in the Coptic, Armenian, Æthiopic, and Arabic versions. Origen was no doubt right geographically, the reference is to Geresa or Gersa or Kersa on the eastern margin of the sea of Galilee; but he was wrong in assuming that the old reading *Gerasenes* could not and did not refer to that very town. The two words *Gerasenes* and *Gergesenes* are just two different ways of pronouncing one name. Origen's *Gergesa* is just the evangelist's *Gerasa* and the modern *Kersa*. The ruins of the town

the country of the Gadarenes. 2 And when he was come out of the ship, immediately there met him out of the tombs a man with an unclean spirit, 3 who had *his* dwelling among the tombs; and no man could bind him, no, not with chains:

---

lie to this day a little south of the Wady Semakh, which debouches into the lake nearly opposite Magdala. " It was walled," says Dr. Porter, " and the " remains of the wall can be traced. The houses are all prostrate, and heaps " of rubbish and hewn stones encumber the site. . . . The physical con " formation of the country south of Kersa appears to suit the incidents of the " narrative better than any other spot along the eastern shore of the lake." (*Syria and Palestine*, p. 401.)

VER. 2. **And when He was come out of the boat, immediately there met Him out of the tombs a man with an impure spirit.** *Met*, or, more literally, *encountered* (ὑπήντησεν), only the word conveys no hostile intent. *Out of the tombs:* The direction in which the man who is about to be specified came was *from the tombs*, not *from the town*; he did not live in the town; see next verse. *A man:* Matthew, in his account, makes mention of two. Nothing is more likely than that there should be more than one. There were no asylums for the insane in those days; the unhappy sufferers were scattered about; and sometimes individuals, when possessed of peculiar inter-relations of susceptibility, would draw together. There had been two thus associated in the neighbourhood of Kersa; but the personality of one of the two had been so strikingly outstanding and remarkable that the other individual had been apparently a mere semi-servile appendage. Hence Mark and Luke take notice only of the one. It is evident from this that Mark was no mere copyist and epitomizer of Matthew. *With an impure spirit.* The expression in the original is somewhat stronger, '*in*' *an impure spirit.* It is the same idiom that we employ when we speak of a man being '*in*' *a passion* or '*in*' *drink.* The demonic in the man was more conspicuous and obtrusive than the man's own manhood. Wycliffe and the Rheims version retain the primitive ' *in.*' Tyndale paraphrases the expression *possessyd of an uncleᴋe sprete* As to the existence of *demon spirits* and their *uncleanness*, see on chap. . 23 32.

VER. 3. **Who had his habitation among the tombs.** Or, more literally, *in the tombs.* Like many other maniacs he had a melancholy craze for frequenting the places of the dead; he felt no interest, or almost none, in the society of the living. In the whole of Syria the mountains are pierced with old excavated tombs, fit haunts for demoniacs. Dr. W. M. Thomson says expressly that ' an immense mountain rises directly above Chersa, in which are ancient tombs.' (*The Land and the Book*, p. 376.) Many of the existing Palestinian tombs belong to a period long anterior to the time of our Lord's ministry, and some of them perhaps to a period anterior to the occupancy of Palestine by the Hebrews.

And no man could bind him any longer, no, not with a chain. The plural *chains*, found in the Received Text, had been suggested apparently by the phraseology of the succeeding verse. It was common in Palestine, and till lately it was not uncommon in Great Britain, to chain with iron chains such of

ST. MARK V.

4 because that he had been often bound with fetters and chains, and the chains had been plucked asunder by him, and the fetters broken in pieces: neither could any *man* tame him. 5 And always, night and day, he was in the mountains, and in the tombs, crying, and cutting himself with stones.

---

the insane as were unfortunately furious or violent. No doubt it would be often a necessity; but it was sad, and sadly humiliating.

VER. 4. **Because that.** The evangelist explains why he said that no one could any longer bind him with a chain.

He had been often bound with fetters and chains. The experiment had been often tried, with *fetters* specifically and *chains* generically. The word *fetters*, like the corresponding word in Greek, properly means *shackles for the feet.* Compare the word '*fet*lock,' the lock of hair at the *feet* of horses. *Fet* is the Anglo-Saxon for *feet.* There is no reason for supposing with Fritzsche, Bloomfield, Bland, and others, that the generic word *chains* refers specifically and antithetically merely to *manacles* or *handcuffs.*

And the chains had been pulled asunder by him. By no means an unexampled degree of strength on the part of the maniacally violent, but yet incontestable evidence of a high type of frenzy or full-fed 'furor.'

And the fetters broken in pieces. Or *crushed together* (συντετρίφθαι), namely by the trampling of the feet, till at length they gave way. Wycliffe's version is picturesque, *and hadde broken the stockis to smale gobetis,* that is, *and had broken the stocks to small pieces.*

And no one was able to master him. No one could awe him into subjection. It is often the case that very violent maniacs are quite calm and submissive under the authoritative eye and bearing of instinctively commanding natures. But the Gerasene demoniac had not met any one who had power to soothe or to subdue him.

VER. 5. **And constantly, night and day, in the tombs and in the mountains.** Such is the order of the words *tombs* and *mountains* in the best manuscripts. At one time he would be sitting moodily in an empty tomb; at another he would be roaming about excitedly over the mountains, 'in' the gorges and wild nooks, and wherever any sequestered haunts could be reached in the thickets or by the most precipitous crags.

He was crying—no doubt with unearthly yells,—**and cutting himself with stones.** Instead of *cutting* Wycliffe and Coverdale have *beating.* Luther's word corresponds (*schlug*); so Tyndale (*and bet him silfe with stones*); the Geneva version is equivalent, *and strooke himself with stones.* But the translation of our English version is correct. The demoniac would use sharp-edged stones to cut and gash his person. There is sometimes a strong propensity in maniacs to wound and even to maim themselves. V. Swieten says that he himself "saw a maniac who "lacerated all the integuments of his body, and who during the inclemency of "a severe winter lay naked on straw for weeks, in a place rough with stones." (*Comment.*, iii., p. 521.) When poor human nature is raving, the judgment is inverted and the sensibility is benumbed. "Mania," says Feuchtersleben, "always proceeds from deceptive ideas and sensations." (*Medical Psychology*

6 But when he saw Jesus afar off, he ran and worshipped him,
7 and cried with a loud voice, and said, What have I to do with
thee, Jesus, *thou* Son of the most high God? I adjure thee by

---

p. 289.) "In insanity," says Dr. Mason Good, "the corporeal sensibility is "greatly diminished; but not more so than the moral sensibility." (*Study of Medicine*, vol. iii., p. 88.)

VER. 6. **And when he saw Jesus afar off.** Or, more literally, *from afar*. It is not the distance of Jesus from the demoniac that is noted; it is the distance of the demoniac from Jesus. The Vulgate version (*a longe*), and Luther's, and Bengel's (*von ferne*), are literal.

He ran and did obeisance to Him. There might be a combination of influences at work within the poor demoniac's spirit. His own oppressed soul, on the one hand, might be sensitive to the 'virtue' that was streaming out, we know not how far, from the Divine personality of the Saviour; the oppressive demonic spirits, on the other, might likewise be conscious of a power far higher than their own, restraining them in part and constraining them in part.

VER. 7. **And crying with a loud voice, he saith, What have I to do with Thee?** Or rather, *What hast Thou to do with me?* The idiomatic phrase is literally, *What to me and to thee?* It depends on the nature of the case which of the two poles of interposition should be emphasized, and whether consequently we should say, *What have I to do with Thee?* or reversely, *What hast Thou to do with me?* See chap. i. 24.

Jesus, Son of the most high God. The spirits who had possession of the poor man's body wielded his organism of speech as if it were their own. It is a marvel; but nevertheless it is at bottom no greater a mystery than the wielding of the same organism by the human spirit itself. The demonic spirits seem everywhere to have known the Saviour. They would no doubt have means of telegraphy, as well as media of perception, far more delicate than our coarse corporeal organisms. When they called out confessionally, *Jesus, Son of the most high God!* they might be conscious that there was a power above them, laying its hand upon them, and thus extorting from them involuntarily a confession of the truth. In other circumstances, and more especially when promiscuous crowds were around, they might malignantly hope that the confession might be construed as a proof of collusion.

I adjure Thee by God. Strauss carps at this, and thinks it an incredible adjuration on the part of 'one who believed himself to be possessed by a demon hostile to God' (*Leben*, ii. 9, § 89), or rather, as he should have said, on the part of a demon itself who knew that it was the enemy of God. But the objection is frivolous. Nothing is more common than swearing by God on the part of the ungodly, the infidel, and even the atheistic.

That Thou torment me not. That is, that Thou dismiss me not into the endurance of the torments reserved for spiritual rebels. Meyer supposes that this representation brings out a different idea from that which is expressed in Matt. viii. 29, *Art Thou come hither to torment us 'before the time'?* But in both representations the reference is alike to the final sufferings of those who will not be submissive to the moral will of God. "Farther curiosity as to the

God, that thou torment me not. 8 For he said unto him, Come out of the man, *thou* unclean spirit. 9 And he asked him, What *is* thy name? And he answered, saying, My name *is* Legion:

"*when* and *where* and *how* does not become" beings "whose main business and "greatest wisdom is to fly from, not to pry too close into, these terrible secrets "of the dark kingdom." (Bragge's *Observations on the Miracles*, vol. i., p. 74.)

VER. 8. **For He said to him.** Namely *before* the adjuration mentioned in the preceding verse. Hence the free translation of Tyndale brings out interpretatively the correct idea, *For He had said unto him.* Strauss (*Leben*, ii. 9, § 89) and Bruno Bauer (*Kritik*, v., § 33) insist that the representation is self-inconsistent. The inconsistency arises, says Bruno Bauer, from 'pure inconsideration'! It is most inconsiderately said; for there is neither self inconsistency, nor inconsistency with the accounts of the other synoptic evangelists. There is only simplicity of representation. The salient points and pinnacles of things are recorded. There is no attempt, and no profession of attempt, at a systematic and chronological unfolding. Note the expression *to* '*him.*' There is all through the narrative, to a greater or less degree, an interblending of reference to the man and to the spirit or spirits who were in possession of him. No wonder that there should be such *verbal* interblending in the representation; there was *real* confusion in the composite phenomenon.

Come out, thou unclean spirit, from the man. There were in reality, as we learn from the next verse, many spirits; but one had spoken representatively, *What hast Thou to do with* '*me*'? and therefore the Saviour addresses it in the same representative capacity. We need not picture to ourselves a mere chaotic mob of spirits. There was a 'legion'; and we may appropriately think therefore of some general of the corps.

VER. 9. **And He asked him, What is thy name?** We have no reason to suppose that the question was proposed for the Saviour's own information. But, *seeing as He did into the spirit world*, He saw that this was a peculiar case, and hence He took appropriate means to unfold to the view of His disciples and of the other spectators the fulness of the reality.

And he says to Him. We are taken into the presence of the demoniac, and listen with our ears.

Legion is my name, for we are many. It was the man, not the spirit, who was asked to tell his name. The man *seemed to answer*; it was his lips that moved, it was his voice that articulated; but it was really the representative spirit who spoke. He spoke however as if he were the man, *Legion is* '*my*' *name*. "He "answered," says Farmer, in the treatise in which he endeavours to prove that there were no real possessions, "like a madman *who thought himself pos-* "*sessed with a multitude of demons, or that he was one of the number*. . . . He "confounded himself with those spirits under whose influence he supposed him- "self to speak and act." (*Essay on the Demoniacs*, p. 273.) True, there was confusion. The man was insane, and misunderstood his own case; but his peculiar type of insanity is the very problem to be solved, and there seems to be no solution of it more reasonable than the evangelist's; he was 'possessed.' *Legion:* a

for we are many. 10 And he besought him much that he

Roman word, denoting a corps of foot soldiers to the number of between six and seven thousand, at least in the evangelist's time. Each legion consisted of ten cohorts; each cohort of three maniples; each maniple of two centuries. It is most likely that it was the man himself who imposed on himself, for the moment, the name. But we need not, from the fact that it was a Latin name, infer with Semler (*De Demoniacis*, p. 82) that the man was probably a Hellenist or a proselyte who could not speak Hebrew. Lightfoot however had the same idea. The word 'legion' was likely enough to fasten itself upon the popular Jewish mind as a term vividly representing the idea of overwhelming numbers. The poor man no doubt *felt overwhelmed*, and hence in his hallucination transferred his consciousness, as it would appear, to the overwhelming force. Such a transference of consciousness, or what appears to be such, is quite common in certain cases of insanity. Many of the inmates of our asylums imagine themselves to be kings, or queens, or angels, or Christ, or God, or (descendingly) beasts, birds, or inanimate things. For we are many: At this point in the interview the transference of the poor man's consciousness from the singular to the plural seems to have taken place. Or, to represent the case otherwise, the man's personality got merged at this point out of view, and the host of spirits that had possession of him came into the foreground of observation. Strauss maintains that such possession of an individual man by a multiplicity of spirits is 'unthinkable' (*undenkbar*); he reasons the matter (*Leben*, ii. 9, § 89). He says that to possess is by hypothesis "nothing else than to make oneself the "subject of consciousness in an individual." A possessed person therefore is one who has ceased to be the subject of his own consciousness. But, adds he, as consciousness can actually have only one culminating or central point (*nur eine Spitze, einen Mittelpunckt haben kann*), it is impossible to think that a plurality of demons would at the same time have possession of the man; the utmost that can be thought is that there may have been a succession in possession. Strauss forgot, in his zeal, that insanity is by hypothesis *a state of inconsistency*. He confounds, too, the subject and the objects of consciousness. The man in the unity of his own subjective consciousness seemed to himself to be objectively conscious of a plurality of demons usurping his powers and being. There was of course a hallucination of consciousness; but in no instance is possession so complete by hypothesis as to obliterate entirely every vestige of the original self-consciousness.

VER. 10. **And he besought Him much.** The consciousness of the man swung partially back to himself. Hence the *he* after the *we* of the preceding clause. *Much:* the word is plural in the original (πολλά), and suggests repeated entreaties.

That He would not send them. The *that* of the original (ἵνα) does not so much point out the subject-matter of the entreaty as its final end. The idea is, *in order that He might not send them*. The demons, in pleading through the man, had a particular end in view. Let no one marvel at the fact of their pleading or the fact of their aim. They had desires; they could not but have them; and, having them, what wonder that they should express them?

11] ST. MARK V. 121

would not send them away out of the country. 11 Now there was there nigh unto the mountains a great herd of swine

Out of the country. They had become localized in their associations. And why not? All *human spirits* are. All spirits, but the infinite, must be to a greater or less degree. The local reference however is not, as Hilgenfeld supposes (*Evangel.*, p. 134), a reference to heathendom as the appropriate sphere of demoniacal possessions (*der eigentliche Wirkungskreis der Dämonen*). There is no evidence that Gerasa was regarded as strictly belonging to heathendom or Gentiledom. And still less is there evidence that demoniacal possession was regarded as a strictly heathenish or Gentile experience. Neither is the representation in Luke, *and they besought Him that He would not command them to depart into 'the abyss'* (viii. 31), at variance, as Bruno Bauer alleges (*Kritik*, v., § 33), with the representation in Mark. Expatriation would have been to the Gerasene demons tantamount to banishment into the abyss of woe (see ver. 7). In petitioning therefore *not to be sent out of the country* they would really mean *not to be sent into the abyss*. It is assumed in the twofold representation that there would, for them, be no intermediate sphere available. Another country on earth was not to be thought of, and was not thought of, as an alternative localization.

VER. 11. **Now there was there.** *Now* or *but* (δέ). The attention is suddenly turned for the moment in a new direction.

On the mountain side. A little to the south of the Wady Semakh there is a considerable uneven plateau of fine fertile soil stretching westward from the roots of the mountain slopes. "A verdant sward is here," says Mr. Macgregor, "with many bulbous roots which swine might feed upon. And on this I "observed—what is an unusual sight—a very large herd of oxen, horses, camels, "sheep, asses and goats all feeding together. It was evident that the pasturage "was various, and enough for all, a likely place for *a herd of swine feeding on* "*the mountain.*" (*The Rob Roy on the Jordan*, p. 423.)

A great herd of swine feeding. Not a right kind of herd for a Jew, or for Jews, to possess. The animal was 'unclean' to the Jews (Lev. xi. 7, Deut. xiv. 8) as it was also to the Egyptians. (*Herod.*, ii. 47.) It was prohibited as one of a class of animals; but possibly the limits of the class were determined, to some extent, by reasons that had special reference to it as an individual species. (See Isa. lxv. 4.) There can be no doubt that there was something exceedingly disgusting and morally contaminating, connected with the use that was made of the animal in Egypt. (See Herodotus, ii. 37.) Similar customs, less modified and moderated by restrictions, may have been common in adjacent countries. (See Pausanias, vii. 15 : 7.) And hence it might be wise, in the peculiar ethical circumstances of the Jews, that the use of the animal should be prohibited altogether for the whole course of a Dispensation. If in addition to this it should be the case, as many have contended, that the flesh of the animal must have been dietetically injurious among a people in whom there was a sort of national tendency to leprosy and corresponding erosive affections, as well as other eruptive and contagious cutaneous diseases, then there would be reason upon reason for the prohibition. If the Canaanites moreover were eaters of

feeding. 12 And all the devils besought him, saying, Send us into the swine, that we may enter into them. 13 And forthwith Jesus gave them leave. And the unclean spirits went out, and entered into the swine: and the herd ran violently down a steep place into the sea, (they were about

---

swine's flesh and fond of it, that may have been another good reason for the prohibition, for as Michaelis remarks, " the most intimate friendships are "formed at table. Men," he adds, "whatever business relations they may have " with one another, seldom become familiar if they do not become each other's "guests." (*Mosaisches Recht*, § 203.) The Gerasenes must have got Gentilized in their ideas and customs, and languid in their attachment to the institutions of Judaism.

VER. 12. **And they besought Him saying, Send us into the swine**—or rather *Send us 'to' the swine*,—that we may enter into them. How could there, it is asked, be such a desire on the part of the demons? Why should there not? we would answer. We do not feel called upon to enter into the rationale of demonic desires, and to find them in harmony with our notions of what is reasonable or proper. The wish might, on their part, be a mere outburst of wantonness. Or there might be eagerness for *anything* on which to wreak their evil energy; they might be wishing, as Richard Baxter has it, 'to play a small game rather than none.' Or there might be cunning malice in their intent, malice toward Christ and toward all the other parties concerned. "They aimed," as Petter thinks, " at this, that they might move the owners of " the herd, and the rest of the people of the country, to be discontented at our " Saviour." It may be so, or it may not.

VER. 13. **And He gave them leave.** 'It was an injury done to the proprietors,' says the scoffing Woolston, 'and unbecoming of the goodness of the holy Jesus.' (*Discourses on the Miracles*, i. 38.) But it was not, if the proprietors had no right to have such property, and if they were moreover the subjects or the stewards of Him who was the true King of the Jews.

And the unclean spirits came out, and entered into the swine. ' When it is averred,' says Strauss, ' that the demons actually entered the swine, do not the evangelists narrate a manifest impossibility?' (*Leben*, ii. 9, § 89.) No. The demonic power that was adequate to take possession of the intricate organism of man's nature would be more than adequate to take possession of the simpler organism of beasts; if the castle of the human spirit could be surreptitiously entered and occupied, there could be little difficulty with the fortalices of irrational natures.

And the herd rushed. As the word is admirably rendered in Acts xix. 29. The movement was ' with a greet birre,' as Purvey has it.

Down the steep into the sea. The particular steep in which the plateau referred to terminated, close on the waters of the lake. "There are several "steeps near the sea here," says Mr. Macgregor, " but only one so close to the "water as to make it sure that if a herd *ran violently* down, they would go *into* "*the sea*." There "the gravel beach is inclined so steep that when my boat was "at the shore I could not see over the top even by standing up; while the water

15] ST. MARK V. 123

two thousand,) and were choked in the sea. 14 And they that fed the swine fled, and told *it* in the city, and in the country. And they went out to see what it was that was done. 15 And they come to Jesus, and see him that was possessed

---

"alongside is so deep that it covered my paddle (seven feet long) when dipped "in vertically a few feet from the shore." (*The Rob Roy on the Jordan*, pp. 423-4.)

To about the number of two thousand. Such is the import of the simple unparenthetical expression exhibited in the texts of Tischendorf, Tregelles, Alford (ὡς δισχίλιοι). It is supported too by the Vulgate version.

And were choked in the sea. A vivid mirroring, in a particular outward sphere, of the lamentable wrecking of things that would speedily be realized, if the demonic powers that are in the world had full and unfettered scope.

VER. 14. **And they who were feeding them fled and reported in the city and in the country.** Our word *reported* corresponds as nearly as may be to the radical import of the evangelist's term (ἀπήγγειλαν, not ἀνήγγειλαν). We can use too the word *reported* 'absolutely,' just as the evangelist has used his term. The double-folding expression *in the city and in the country* is a free but admirable translation. It is literally *into the city and into the fields*, and would be connected, in the evangelist's mind, not with the verb *reported*, as Lightfoot imagined, but with the preceding verb *fled*. The scene pictures itself readily and vividly upon the canvas of the imagination. There were several individuals tending the herd. The moment that they recover from the first stun which they would experience when they witnessed the consummated catastrophe of the herd, they flee, under the influence of intense excitement, first *into the city*, and then *into the surrounding fields*, where numbers of the inhabitants would be at work. They shout aloud, wherever they meet with individuals, that *the whole herd has rushed into the sea and is drowned, and that the wild man of the tombs is in his senses!*

And they came to see what it is that has happened. *They*, the people of the city and the workers in the fields. They were filled with blank amazement at the report which was shouted into their ears, and could not at first comprehend the state of the case. They must come and 'see' with their own eyes.

VER. 15. **And they come to Jesus.** Note the present *come*, as distinguished from the historic *came* of the preceding verse. The evangelist begins to depict the scene as if he and we were present in the midst of it and looking on.

And behold the demoniac sitting clothed and in sound mind. Note the word *behold* (θεωροῦσιν); it is more than *see*. They gaze upon the man. There is a fine harmony between the statement that the demoniac was now *clothed* and the statement in Luke that formerly he 'had worn no clothes' (viii. 27). The two statements mutually confirm each other's historic verity. The coincidence is so striking that Ewald (*Evan.*, p. 241) had to imagine that the expression 'he wore no clothes' must have originally stood in the third verse of Mark's narrative! And Holtzmann (*Synop. Ev.*, p. 222) supposes that Luke took the hint, from the Proto-Markus's remark, to insert the statement 'anticipatively.' Fancies!

with the devil, and had the legion, sitting, and clothed, and in his right mind: and they were afraid. 16 And they that saw *it* told them how it befell to him that was possessed with the devil, and *also* concerning the swine. 17 And they began to pray him to depart out of their coasts. 18 And when he was come into the ship, he that had been possessed with the devil prayed him that he might be with him.

Him who had the legion. Such is the proper position of this clause. The contrast of the man's former condition sets off to advantage the marvel of his present state. *Yes, the very individual who was now ‘sitting clothed and sound in mind’ was ‘he who had the legion’!*

And they were afraid. They felt in the presence of a power which inspired them with awe and alarm. It might, for aught that they could comprehend, be something weird and ‘uncanny.’

VER. 16. **And they who saw narrated to them how it happened to the demoniac.** How the things which had taken place did take place, in reference to the demoniac; or, as the Rheims version has it, *in what manner he had been dealt withal that had the divel.*

And concerning the swine. The spectators, (who would no doubt be principally, if not exclusively, the same persons who had carried the news excitedly into the city and into the fields, and who would return to the scene of the miracle with the body of the people,) recounted and explained in detail all that had happened ‘concerning the swine.’ The two clauses which specify the things recounted are inartificially connected.

VER. 17. **And they began to entreat Him to depart from their borders.** Namely, after they got to understand somewhat clearly how the events had come to pass. They were afraid that they might suffer other losses. They were afraid, at all events, of the consequences of having such a wonderful Being as Jesus in the midst of them. "With unparalleled—what shall I call it? 'tis a crime that "wants a name, and such as one would think people that were not themselves "possessed could never be capable of committing,—they were urgent with Him "to be gone and leave them. . . . And yet, if we consider it, is not the case "just thus with too many amongst ourselves? . . . Are we not afraid of "anything that would oblige us to a reformation? shy of a faithful friend who "would advise us better? and that because our swine would be in danger!" (Bragge's *Observations on the Miracles*, vol. i., pp. 79–82.)

VER. 18. **And as He was entering into the boat the delivered demoniac entreated Him that he might be with Him.** The clause, *that he might be with Him*, brings out rather the aim than the subject matter of the entreaty (ἵνα). It is probable that the man's heart was swelling with gratitude and love; he would feel ashamed too of the conduct of his countrymen. Euthymius Zigabenus and Theophylact suppose that, in addition, he would probably be afraid that, if his Deliverer should be at a distance from him, he would again be subject to assault from his old spiritual enemies. Maldonato and Dr. Samuel Clarke bring out the same idea.

19 Howbeit Jesus suffered him not, but saith unto him, Go home to thy friends, and tell them how great things the Lord hath done for thee and hath had compassion on thee. 20 And he departed, and began to publish in Decapolis how

Ver. 19. **And He suffered him not.** Such is the simple form of the expression as it is given, correctly, in the texts of Griesbach, Tischendorf, Tregelles, Alford. Hilgenfeld (*Evan.*, p. 148) supposes that the refusal to allow the delivered man to go along with our Lord bewrays, *on the part of Mark*, an anti-Gentile tendency. The whole Gospel is thus assumed to be a myth that was contrived in the interests of a small theological dogma and narrow ecclesiastical movement!

But says to him, Go home to thy own folk. Literally, *to those who are thine*, or as Wycliffe has it, *to thine*. Very literally it is, *to the thine*, which however, though idiomatic Greek, is not idiomatic English.

And tell them. Literally, *report to them* (ἀπάγγειλον αὐτοῖς, the reading of ℵ B C Δ, and of Lachmann, Tischendorf, Tregelles), or *announce to them* (ἀνάγγειλον αὐτοῖς, the reading of the Textus Receptus and the Alexandrine manuscript (A), and the great body of the secondary uncial manuscripts).

How great things the Lord hath done for thee. Or rather, *for thee*. What the Lord had done terminated *on* and *in* the person of the delivered man, and thus reached *to* him. It is only however from the history of the case, and from the peculiarity of the expression in the next clause, that we know that the things done *on*, *in*, and *to* him were *for* him and not *against* him. The Saviour, in saying *the Lord*, does not point to his own particular personality; He simply leads the man's mind upward, in a general way, to *the Divine Source* of the great things which had been done to him.

And compassionated thee. Or, *and had mercy on thee*. Here it is distinctly stated that the great things done were *for* the man. The expression, however, is very artlessly attached to the preceding clause. The mind of the reader is left to disintegrate, from the compositely qualitative expression *how great things* or *what great things* (ὅσα), the simplest qualitative element of 'conjunctive' thought—*how* (quasi ὡς, see Luke viii. 47, xxiv. 35), or *how that*, or *that* (ὅτι), and to carry it forward to be combined with the attached verb. Hence Tyndale's translation, *and 'how' He had compassion on thee*.

The Saviour, instead of imposing silence on this delivered demoniac, as He did on so many others, encourages and enjoins him to make proclamation of his miraculous deliverance. No doubt He saw, on the one hand, that the man was fit for the evangelistic work committed to him, and that he needed it besides; while He knew, on the other, that there would not be reason for apprehending, as the result of his labours, any formidable addition to the inconvenient crowding to which He Himself was subjected.

Ver. 20. **And he departed.** He acted in the promptest manner on his Deliverer's injunction.

And began to publish. To proclaim like a herald, *to preach* as Wycliffe has it.

In Decapolis. Literally, *in the Decapolis*, that is, *in the district of the Ten Cities*. It was a district that would seem to have varied in its boundaries from

great things Jesus had done for him: and all *men* did marvel.
21 And when Jesus was passed over again by ship unto the other side, much people gathered unto him: and he was nigh unto the sea. 22 And, behold, there cometh one of the rulers

---

time to time; and hence there is not perfect unanimity in the ancient writers in reference to all the cities which originally gave it its name. It lay for the most part east of the Jordan, and east and south-east of the sea of Tiberias. Bethshean however, or Scythopolis, on the west side of the river, was according to Josephus 'the largest city of Decapolis' (*War*, iii. 9: 7). Among its other cities were Pella, Gadara, Gerasa, Hippos (see *Relandi Palæstina*, pp. 203-4). Pliny says (v., 18) that Damascus too belonged to the 'Decapolitan region'; but this could not be the case in the time of Josephus, since he says that Scythopolis, which was of course far inferior in size to Damascus, was the largest city of the district. The word *Decapolis* occurs three times in the New Testament (see Matt. iv. 25, Mark vii. 31), and, as Reland says, twice in the writings of Josephus.

How great things. Or, *what great things*, or simply, as Alford gives it, *what things*. It is the same word that occurs in the 19th verse. In both passages it is rendered by Purvey, and in the Rheims, *how great things*. Tyndale again, in his 1534 edition, renders it *what great things*, while in his preceding edition of 1526 he renders it, as Alford has done, *what things*.

Jesus did to him. The delivered man identified in his mind what God the Lord had done with what Jesus did. *Christ*, says Euthymius Zigabenus, *had modestly ascribed the work to the Father; but the healed man gratefully ascribes it to Christ*. He would not however be thinking of any fine theological distinctions.

And all marvelled. They could not help marvelling, though in too many cases the appropriate moral result would probably be hindered by 'the idols of the cave,' and 'the idols of the theatre,' and 'the idols of the market place.'

VER. 21. **And when Jesus had crossed over again in the boat to the other side.** The western side of the lake of Gennesaret, and no doubt to that part of it where Capernaum was situated. See Matt. ix. 1.

A great crowd was gathered about Him. Or literally, *upon Him*. The expression ἐπ' αὐτὸν graphically indicates that the people came pressing *close upon His person*.

And He was by the sea: while the events about to be recorded began to transpire.

VER. 22. **And behold.** This *behold* has not unlikely been carried into the text from the margin. It is found in Matt. ix. 18, and Luke viii. 41; but it is wanting here in the Sinaitic, Vatican, and Cambridge manuscripts (אBD) and LΔ, as also in the Vulgate, Syriac Peshito, Coptic, Æthiopic, and Arabic versions. It is omitted by Tischendorf and Alford.

There cometh one of the rulers of the synagogue. For, in general at least, there was a plurality of rulers or elders in every synagogue (see Acts xiii. 15, and comp. Vitringa *De Synagoga*, p. 582ff.). It was their duty to conduct or superintend the services of the congregation. The word that is here employed

ST. MARK V.

of the synagogue, Jairus by name; and when he saw him, he fell at his feet, 23 and besought him greatly, saying, My little daughter lieth at the point of death: *I pray thee*, come and lay thy hands on her, that she may be healed; and she shall live. 24 And *Jesus* went with him; and much people followed him, and thronged him. 25 And a certain woman,

---

by the evangelist, and correctly rendered in King James's version *rulers of the synagogue*, is in the singular incorrectly rendered '*chief*' *ruler of the synagogue* in Acts xviii. 8, 17.

By name Jairus. Or *Ja-irus*, or very literally *Ya-eiros*, the Grecised form of the Jewish name *Jair* or *Ya-ir*. It is a significant Hebrew name, meaning *He will illuminate*. Josephus Grecises it into *Ya-eires* (*Antiq.*, v. 7: 6).

And when he saw Him,—after penetrating perhaps through the surrounding crowd,—**he falleth at His feet.** *Falleth*: we are taken back in imagination, and see him in the act of prostration. *At His feet*: literally, *toward His feet* (πρὸς τοὺς πόδας αὐτοῦ). With beautiful oriental facility he would drop upon his knees *before* the Saviour, and bring his forehead to the ground, *in the direction of the Saviour's feet*.

VER. 23. **And beseeches Him much** (παρακαλεῖ instead of παρεκάλει). His heart was full, and he urged his plea.

Saying, My little daughter is at the point of death. She was, Luke tells us, *about twelve years of age* (viii. 42). He tells us too that she was an only child. Perhaps she was lovely and engaging; at all events the father's heart was bound up in her. She was now, from some illness or other, 'in extremity' (ἐσχάτως ἔχει, an idiom of the later Greek. See Lobeck's Phrynichus, p. 389).

(*I make my request*) **in order that Thou mightest come and lay Thy hands upon her.** The father's address, as he spoke with choking voice, is abrupt and fragmentary, or else only fragments of it are recorded. When he prostrated himself and spoke of the condition of his little daughter, it was *in order that the Saviour might come and lay His hands upon her.* He seems to have known that it was the Saviour's practice *to lay His hands* on such as He cured; it established and exhibited a human connection between His Divine power and the patient.

That she might be saved and live. Such is the literal translation. *That she might be saved*, viz. from her malady. *And live* (καὶ ζήσῃ). Such is the reading of אBCDLΔ, and Lachmann, Tischendorf, Tregelles, Alford.

VER. 24. **And He went off with him.** Namely, in the direction of the ruler's house. He had no misgivings about His own power, and He was satisfied with the ruler's faith.

And a great crowd was following Him, and thronging Him. They were pressing together upon His person (συνέθλιβον αὐτόν). *Thronged* is Tyndale's fine word; and it was accepted by Coverdale, the Geneva, and the Rheims. Wycliffe had *oppresside*, Purvey *thruste*.

VER. 25. **And a woman.** Eusebius (*Hist.*, vii. 18) records a tradition that she was a Gentile, a resident of Cæsarea Philippi or Paneas. It was likewise reported that she caused to be erected in front of her residence a bronze (or

which had an issue of blood twelve years, 26 and had
suffered many things of many physicians, and had spent all
that she had, and was nothing bettered, but rather grew worse,
27 when she had heard of Jesus, came in the press behind,

---

copper) monument in commemoration of her cure. It consisted of two statues:
one representing herself in the attitude of supplication, another representing
her Deliverer, our Lord. Eusebius adds that he himself had seen the monument, though we should rather suppose that popular tradition had only capriciously associated an old work of art with the miracle of the passage before us.

Who had been afflicted with an issue of blood for twelve years. Such is Edgar
Taylor's translation. In speaking of the case the technical term *hæmorrhage*
may be fitly employed.

VER. 26. **And had suffered much of many physicians.** Or, as Wycliffe gives
it, *of ful many lechis*. The preposition rendered *of* (ὑπό) properly means *from
under*. She had been *under* many physicians, and had suffered much, not only
from her malady, but also from their methods of cure. They had attempted
strong or severe remedies. Lightfoot gives a graphic account of some of the
prescriptions that were used by the rabbinical doctors (*Heb. and Talmud. Exer.,
in loc.*). They were certainly severe enough. Webster and Wilkinson suppose
that the evangelist's expression only means that the woman had been 'subject
to much treatment.' But the verb translated *suffered* has, in New Testament
Greek, invariable reference to *a passive experience of pain*. See Matt. xvi. 21,
xvii. 12; Luke xxii. 15; Acts i. 3, xvii. 3; Heb. xiii. 12; 1 Pet. iv. 15, v. 10; etc.
Gal. iii. 4 is no exception.

And had expended all her resources (τὰ παρ' ἑαυτῆς πάντα). She had spared no
expense, within the reach of her circumstances, to get the best medical advice
and treatment.

And was nothing benefited, but had rather grown worse. Or, as Tyndale gives
the last clause, *but wexed worsse and worsse*; or, as Petter has it, 'was the
worser.' It was in short a very bad case, inaccessible to all ordinary methods
of cure.

VER. 27. **Having heard concerning Jesus.** What a wonderful Being, and in
particular what a wonderful Healer, He was. She had, it would appear, made
herself acquainted with His character and conduct. In some very important
manuscripts (א B C Δ, 33) the expression runs thus, *Having heard 'the things'
concerning Jesus* (τά). She made herself acquainted with *the facts* of His career,
and had thence come to believe that He was full of a Divine and gracious
energy. He was; and it only needed that men should willingly receive it, in its
fulness, in order to have realized within them the rectification of all their disorders, physical as well as moral.

Came in the crowd behind, and touched His garment. His outer garment, the
garment that was worn above the tunic. It is rendered *cloke* in Matt. v. 40,
Luke vi. 29; and in the passage before us Principal Campbell renders it *mantle*.
It was the peculiarity of this woman's touch that it was intentional or voluntary. It was the touch of faith, a touch consequently that indicated and con-

and touched his garment. 28 For she said, If I may touch but his clothes, I shall be whole. 29 And straightway the fountain of her blood was dried up; and she felt in *her* body that she was healed of that plague. 30 And Jesus,

summated the unreserved opening up of her entire being to the influx of the Saviour's influence.

VER. 28. **For she said.** Viz., to herself within herself. See Matt. ix. 21.

If I should touch though it were but His garments. Such is the real idea embodied in the original expression (κἂν τῶν ἱματίων αὐτοῦ). It has been partially missed by many translators. It was seized however by the Rheims translators, who were followed by the editors of King James's version; and hence they put their *but* after *touch*, not before it as Tyndale had done, *yf I maye butt tewche His clothinge*. The *but*, thus correctly collocated, as it was also by Luther, is transposed back to the wrong place by Mace, Principal Campbell, Rodolphus Dickinson, Sharpe, Brameld. The same mistake is committed by Edgar Taylor and Godwin, although they employ the word *only* instead of *but*; *if I can only touch His garments*. The woman's attention was fixed, not on her act of *touching* as contra-distinguished from some other mode of contact, but on the *garments* of our Lord as contra-distinguished from His person. It is an interesting fact that in the reading that is found in אBCLΔ, and admitted into the editions of Tischendorf and Alford, the verb *touch* comes before the expression which we have rendered *though it were but His garments*: in the Received Text it comes after. *Garments*: the plural is used indefinitely, *any part of His garments*. It would matter nothing at all, so far as efficacy was concerned, what portion should be touched.

I shall be whole. Rather, *I shall be made whole.* Comp. Matt. ix. 22. The idea is, *I shall be delivered from my malady.* Literally, *I shall be saved.*

VER. 29. **And immediately the fountain of her blood was dried up.** The cure was supernaturally instantaneous.

And she felt in her body. Or rather, *and she knew in her body*, that is, *she knew by her bodily sensations*. Her *body*, that is, the state of her bodily sensations, was the means of her knowledge. Hence Euthymius Zigabenus explains the evangelist's dative (τῷ σώματι) by the prepositional expression *through the body* (διὰ τοῦ σώματος).

That she had been healed of 'the' plague. We do not require a stronger demonstrative than our definite article, which very precisely corresponds to the article employed in the original. Erasmus introduced into the third edition of his Latin version the demonstrative *that* ('ab eo flagello'). Beza approved of this translation and adopted it; and hence the Geneva translation and King James's coincident version, *of that plague*. There was some excuse for Erasmus and Beza in their Latin versions, as there is no article in the Latin language. But there is no reason why in English we should deviate from an exact reproduction of the original; and yet Principal Campbell, following Mace, as so frequently on other occasions, has *that*, as have also Wynne, Wakefield, Edgar Taylor, Thomson, Sharpe, Anderson. Luther's version, though free, is much better, 'of *her* plague.' The word *plague* is to be understood in its archaic and

K

immediately knowing in himself that virtue had gone out of him, turned him about in the press, and said, Who touched my clothes? 31 And his disciples said unto him, Thou seest the multitude thronging thee, and sayest thou, Who touched me? 32 And he looked round about to see her that

---

original meaning, *scourge*; see chap. iii. 10. The Rheims gives a more generic but very admirable rendering, *malady*. '*Of*' *the plague*: literally, '*off*' *the plague*, or '*from*' *the plague*. The verb *healed* is, as Fritzsche remarks, used pregnantly, so that the full idea is, *that she had been healed and thus delivered from the plague*.

VER. 30. **And immediately, Jesus knowing.** The participle *knowing* is not present but præterite in the original (ἐπιγνούς). We might hence render the phrase freely, *and immediately, as Jesus knew*. The compound verb employed by the evangelist has a stronger import than the simple verb used in the preceding verse, and there translated *felt* in our Authorized and Revised versions. Our Lord *knew well*; He was *fully aware*.

In Himself. That is, *in His own self consciousness*. He did not need to reason inferentially on the matter. Neither did He need the testimony of His outer senses. Still less was it the case that "being secretly apprised of the woman's "faith, and touch of Him, He took the hint," as Woolston wantonly suggests (*Discourse on Miracles*, ii., p. 16).

The power—or *virtue*—that had gone forth from Him. The object of the Saviour's knowledge, in the sphere of His self consciousness, was thus complex. It was, in the first place, His *virtue* or *power*, and in the second place the fact that this virtue or power had been *in the act of transit from Himself*. All the old translators, with the exception of Coverdale, use the word *virtue*, following in the wake of the Vulgate version (*virtutem*). They mean by it, however, just *power*, Coverdale's word. Wycliffe often uses the term in this acceptation. He speaks of Christ being 'the Son of God *in vertu*' (i.e. *in power*: Rom. i. 4). He speaks of the gospel being 'the *vertu of God* in to helthe,' that is, 'the *power of God* unto salvation' (Rom. i. 16). He translates 1 Cor. xv. 56 thus : 'Forsoth the prick of deeth is synne; forsoth *the vertu of synne* is lawe.' Instead of the expression 'most of His *mighty works*' in Matt. xi. 20, he has 'ful manye *vertues*.'

Turned about in the crowd, and said, Who touched My garments? This He said only after He had *turned about*, and thus to those who had been behind Him, for He knew well in what direction His healing power had gone forth. Meyer thinks however that He did not know *upon whom* the power had taken effect. It is an entirely arbitrary idea, as well as *exegetically unlikely*, when the 32nd verse is taken into account.

VER. 31. **And His disciples said to Him, Thou seest the crowd thronging Thee! and sayest Thou, Who touched Me?** The word rendered *thronging* is the term that is employed in ver. 24. It admirably denotes the *united pressure*, on a person, of a crowd in contact.

VER. 32. **And He looked round about to see her who did this thing.** We are to suppose that, after she had touched His garment, she had shrunk back into the

had done this thing. 33 But the woman fearing and trembling, knowing what was done in her, came and fell down before him, and told him all the truth. 34 And he said unto her, Daughter, thy faith hath made thee whole ; go in peace,

crowd. Perhaps she had never got perfectly close to His person. Most likely she would be able to accomplish her object only by stretching out her hand, as it were stealthily, between others. Hence our Saviour naturally *looked round about upon the crowd* to see her. He was in no haste to dart a direct glance upon her. The verb is in the imperfect tense, *He continued looking round*. But of course His eye soon reached her ; and no doubt it would rest benignantly upon her. So strange however is the power of prepossession to blind its victims, Strauss cannot see that Mark meant that our Lord knew the individual who had believingly touched Him. He argues keenly on the subject in both his works (*Leben Jesu*, ii., § 93 ; *Leben Jesu für das deutsche Volk*, ii., 2, § 75). He holds the whole story to be a myth, and contends that it was in accordance with the natural growth of the myth out of its original form as it occurs in Matthew, that Mark should represent our Lord's person as so wonderfully charged with a divinely curative power, that mere believing contact with it should suffice for a cure, *even while the Lord remained ' ignorant,'* as Hilgenfeld too assumes, *of the individual who was drawing upon His resources !*

VER. 33. **But the woman, fearing and trembling.** Or, still more literally and graphically, *afraid and trembling* (φοβηθεῖσα καὶ τρέμουσα). She would be feeling that she had perhaps acted in too stealthy a way in reference to her wonderful Benefactor. Should she not have approached Him openly ? should she not have formally petitioned for His blessing ?

Knowing what was done in her—or rather, according to the reading of the Received Text, *knowing what had happened to her* (αὐτῇ)—**came and fell down before Him, and told Him all the truth.** Having had experience of her Benefactor's power, she added ' confession with her mouth ' to ' faith in her heart ' (Rom. x. 9, 10). In making this confession, she threw herself, with rapid oriental ease and grace, into a beautiful attitude of obeisance ; she *fell down before Him*.

VER. 34. **But He said to her, Daughter, thy faith hath made thee whole.** Literally, *hath saved thee*. Comp. ver. 28. Her faith of course had not been the efficient cause of her cure ; Christ's power had been that. And behind His power was His Person, the real Healer. But her faith was that *ethical condition of things* on her part, that rendered it fitting on His part to put forth His curative efficiency in her experience. It was the opening of the sluices of her being to the ingress of His overflowing energy as the great Rectifier of human disorders. Hence it might be represented as having, in a certain subordinate respect, ' made her whole.' *Daughter :* A term of affection, but perhaps, as employed by our Saviour, implying that all that was spiritually distinctive in her character had been *derived from Himself*.

Go thy way in peace. Literally, though scarcely in harmony with English idiom, *go thy way into peace*. The Saviour looks at her *peace* prospectively. He sees that the woman would enjoy much of it in time to come. And hence,

and be whole of thy plague. 35 While he yet spake, there came, from the ruler of the synagogue's *house, certain* which said, Thy daughter is dead: why troublest thou the Master any further? 36 As soon as Jesus heard the word that was spoken, he saith unto the ruler of the synagogue,

---

instead of giving emphasis to what of it she was already experiencing, He turns attention to the future that was stretching out before her. *Peace* is only a partial aspect, but it is certainly an indispensable element, of comfort and bliss. It stood prominently out to view before the Hebrew mind. The other elements were silently subtended. A state of constant battle with trouble or troublers makes a sad defalcation in the amount of *happiness* realized.

And be whole of thy plague. Literally, '*from*' *thy plague*. The expression *be whole* '*from*' is pregnant; *be whole (and thus delivered) from thy malady*. Comp. ver. 29. There is a connection between *whole* and *heal*, as well as between *heal* and *hail*, and *whole* and *holy*. The Greek word (ὑγιής) rendered *whole* means *sound* or *healthy*. When the Saviour says *Be whole*, He, for the moment, ignores as it were the chronological fact that she was already whole, that He might bring logically into view the dependence of her past, present, and prospective *health* on the autonomy of His will.

VER. 35. While He is yet speaking, there come from the ruler of the synagogue's house some who say. The phraseology is exceedingly inartificial. It is in the original *there come from the ruler of the synagogue*, and yet the ruler of the synagogue is the person *to whom* the message is delivered.

Thy daughter is dead. The verb is in the aorist tense. Her death is now a *past* event.

Why troublest thou the Master any further? The Master, that is, *the Teacher, the Rabbi*. The whole expression is a phrase of politeness. It assumes that the visit of the Great Teacher would most likely be a somewhat irksome addition to His already too numerous and overwhelming engagements. Hence the word rendered *troublest* is very strong in the original, *excoriatest* (σκύλλεις). Tyndale and the Geneva render it *diseasest*, that is, *dis-easest*. It was Coverdale who gave the admirable translation *troublest*. *Any further:* Yet or *still*, now that there is no prospect of any benefit being derived from His visit. It did not occur to them that restoration to life could be a possibility.

VER. 36. But Jesus immediately, having overheard the word that was spoken, says to the ruler of the synagogue. Such we conceive to be the correct and literal reproduction in English of the authentic text of the evangelist. (1) Note the *immediately*, Mark's favourite adverb (chap. i. 21). Lachmann and Alford put it within brackets, as of doubtful genuineness. Tregelles and Tischendorf (in his eighth edition) omit it altogether on the authority of ℵ B D L Δ, and of the Vulgate version (and a majority of Italic manuscripts), as also of the Syriac Peshito, Coptic, Armenian, and Æthiopic versions, etc. Mill condemned it. Its somewhat awkward position however makes it more likely, in accordance with Bengel's critical canon (*scriptioni proclivi præstat ardua*), that it would be omitted than that it would be intruded by transcribers. It is found in A C H and other nine uncial manuscripts, and in the Gothic and

Be not afraid, only believe. 37 And he suffered no man to follow him, save Peter, and James, and John the brother of James.

Philoxenian Syriac versions, as also in the 'a' copy of the Italic version (*statim*). (2) We might connect the *immediately* with the participle *overheard*: *But Jesus, having* '*immediately*' *overheard the word that was spoken, says*. It is more probable however that the evangelist made, in an inartificial manner, a pause after writing *immediately*, and mentally suspended the continuity of his expression till he reached the word *says*. He meanwhile interposed the statement *having overheard the word that was spoken*. Hence Schöttgen puts commas after *immediately* and the expression *the word spoken*. It is more likely in short that the evangelist desired to draw attention to the fact that Jesus *spoke immediately*, than to the fact that He *overheard immediately*. (3) Note the word *overheard* (παρακούσας). It has been introduced into the text by Tischendorf, Tregelles, Alford, on the authority of ℵ*B L Δ and the Italic 'e' (*neglexit*). It is undoubtedly the genuine autographic reading, the simple *heard* of the Received Text having been borrowed out of Luke's narrative (viii. 50). This simple *heard* was all the more likely to be substituted for *overheard*, as the term rendered *overheard* means, in the only other passage in which it occurs in the New Testament, not *overheard* but *disregarded*; see Matt. xviii. 17. This meaning of *disregarded* indeed was here given to the term by the author of the Italic manuscript 'e,' and it is contended for by Meyer. Klostermann too gives it, and the English Revisers. But unnaturally. If the message had been addressed to Jesus Himself, the term might have borne the meaning of *disregarded*, for then we might think of our Lord as *listening aside*, or as *listening to what was said to Him, carelessly* as it were, or *inattentively*. But the case is quite different when the message was not at all addressed to Him, or meant for His ears. He *heard it aside* however, that is, *overheard* it, for doubtless it would not be merely whispered. Such is the interpretation that is given to the term by Ewald, Alford, Lange, Bisping.

Fear not, only believe. Fear not for the result. Have faith in Me that I shall meet the desire of your heart. *If this be the state of your mind, it is all that is needed*. '*Only believe*,' I ask no more. How sublime the self possession of our Lord! How complete the self-consciousness that He held in His hand the key of all the resources of infinite power! Relatively to that power, it was of no moment whether the child was dead or alive. Could our Lord, or could any honest and worthy individual, have thus spoken to the agitated father, if his power had been limited?

VER. 37. **And He suffered no one to follow in His company** (μετ' αὐτοῦ συνακολουθῆσαι) except Peter, and James, and John the brother of James. The specially favoured triumvirate, specially favoured no doubt because of some special ethical susceptibility in relation to the ethical influence of the Saviour. The nearer they came to their Lord, and the longer they abode with Him, the more did they open up to the inflow of His spirit. Meyer thinks that there is a small contradiction between the representations of Mark and Luke. Mark, he says, represents the other followers of our Lord as kept back by Him *before* He had entered into the house, while Luke (viii. 51) represents them as kept back *after*. There is however nothing of the nature of contradiction. There is merely, on

38 And he cometh to the house of the ruler of the synagogue, and seeth the tumult, and them that wept and wailed greatly.

the part of Mark, an artless proleptic statement of the fact that only the three favoured disciples were allowed to accompany Him (viz. into the chamber of the maiden). And then he resumes, but still in an artless manner, the narrative of the events in their order. Some considerable portion of the general crowd might enter into the open court of the house. (See Luke viii. 51.) But only the triumvirate would be allowed to enter *the family apartment of the house*.

VER. 38. **And He cometh.** Or rather, *And they come.* Such is the reading of ℵ A B C D F Δ, 1, 33, and of the Vulgate, Peshito Syriac, and Coptic versions. It is approved of by Mill (*Prol.*, p. cxxix.), and received into the text by Lachmann, Tischendorf, Tregelles, Alford. *They*, that is, Christ and the company in general.

To—or rather *into*—**the house of the ruler of the synagogue.** That is, they enter through the gateway into the open court of the house.

And He beholds an uproar (θεωρεῖ θόρυβον) **and people weeping and wailing greatly.** The scene represented struck upon two of the outer senses, that of hearing and that of seeing. But the evangelist gives prominence to that particular sense which is our chief medium of observation, seeing. Our Saviour *beholds an excited company of people making 'an uproar,' and, prominent in that company, persons busily engaged in 'weeping aloud,' or 'crying,' and 'wailing.'* The word rendered *tumult* in our English version, after the example of the Vulgate, is translated by Wycliffe *noyse*. It usually denoted *the confused noise of an excited public assembly.* The noise on the present occasion was chiefly that of wailing, and would be raised by females. "There are," says Dr. W. M. Thomson, "in every city and community, women exceedingly cunning in this "business. They are always sent for, and kept in readiness. When a fresh "company of sympathisers comes in, these women 'make haste' to take up a "wailing, that the newly come may the more easily unite their tears with the "mourners." (*The Land and the Book*, p. 103.) The same artificiality and business-like way of mourning and crying was, and still is, common in Greece. Tournefort says in reference to the island of Candia, "the wife of one of the "principal men in the city, over against whose house we lodged, expired two "days after our arrival. Scarce had she given up the ghost before we heard "extraordinary cries, which made us inquire what was the matter. They told "us that, according to the ancient Greek custom, the public weepers were doing "their duty over the body of the deceased. These women," he adds, "really "earn their money hard, and Horace (*De Arte Poet.*) had good reason to say that "they give themselves more plague and uneasiness than those who mourn "naturally." (*Voyage into the Levant*, vol. i., p. 99.) This mourning *to order*, and *according to an approved pattern*, prevails still in many other places, even among those who do not literally '*sell* their sorrow.' Dr. Clarke found it in Russia. In describing a funeral at Nikitskoy he employs a word which admirably corresponds to the term employed by the evangelist (ἀλαλάζοντας, using the ἀλαλή): "The women kept up a kind of musical *ululation*, howling their "loud lamentations in strains truly dolorous." (*Travels*, vol. i., p. 251.)

39 And when he was come in, he saith unto them, Why make ye this ado, and weep? The damsel is not dead, but sleepeth. 40 And they laughed him to scorn. But when he had put them all out, he taketh the father and the mother of the damsel, and them that were with him, and entereth in where

VER. 39. **And when He was come in, He says to them, Why make ye this uproar? The child is not dead, but sleepeth.** Our Saviour occupied a peculiar, and peculiarly elevated, standpoint when He said *The child is not dead*. He had not yet seen the child with His human eyes, and He could not therefore speak from human observation. He knew that the mourners were aware that this was the case. Neither did He mean to depreciate the gracious miracle which He was about to work, by alleging that the case was by no means so desperate as they imagined. He was looking at the case from a lofty point of view. His idea is this: *The child's terrestrial course is not terminated. She has subsided indeed into unconsciousness toward things outward and terrene ; but, in virtue of My will, it is only for a little. The child is therefore, so to speak, but asleep.*

VER. 40. **And they laughed Him to scorn.** They *derided Him* (the Rheims). They did not understand what He meant when He said *The child is not dead*. They thought that He was meaning to deny the actual fact of her manifest decease. They would not, and did not, take time to ascend to that higher standpoint of observation, to which they had been invited by the lofty bearing of the Saviour. They hurriedly pre-judged and mis-judged His representation.

But He, when He had thrust them all out. Most probably by His mere word of command. There would be an authority displayed which would make them cower and crowd out ; for no doubt, when our Saviour chose, there would be a majesty of manner in His bearing which would be ineffable and irresistible. Comp. John xviii. 5, 6. But why did He *thrust them out?* He was not needing, on the one hand, to choose a very public theatre of representation. He was already inconvenienced by excess of publicity (see chap. iii. 20, iv. 1, 35). He might have been, and most probably would have been, annoyed on the spot, and harassed, and oppressed, by a sudden and yet only superficial revulsion of feeling on the part of the excited crowd. And then, on the other hand, there are some solemnities to which privacy and domestic quiet are peculiarly appropriate, and which would be spoiled by din and tumult and uproar, even when springing from a spirit of admiration and joy.

Taketh with Himself the father of the child, and the mother, and those who were with Him. That is, the three disciples formerly specified. The others might probably be left in the street amid the crowd, while the Saviour was working His way into the court, and thence into the apartment where the mother with her companions would be found. Ferdinand C. Baur, by a strange oblivion of memory, says that 'the three disciples also' are here represented as thrust out (*Er trieb sie alle hinaus, also auch jene drei Jünger : Markus.*, p. 38). They are however expressly excepted in the words before us.

And entereth in where the child was. In some inner apartment.

the damsel was lying. 41 And he took the damsel by the hand, and saith unto her, Talitha cumi, which is, being interpreted, Damsel, I say unto thee, arise. 42 And straightway the damsel arose, and walked; for she was *of the age* of twelve years. And they were astonished with a great astonishment.

VER. 41. **And having taken hold of the hand of the child.** Thus visibly connecting Himself with her, for the sake, as we may suppose, of the witnesses; at least for their sake principally.

He says to her, 'Talitha cumi,' which is, being interpreted, Damsel, I say unto thee, Arise. There is nothing that precisely and literally corresponds, in the Aramaic expression *Talitha cumi*, to the words *I say unto thee*. But every imperative is *the saying of some one*; and hence, when the Saviour said '*cumi*,' His idea, when fully unfolded, was exactly *I say unto thee, Arise.* The full unfolding might, with indifference, be either given as in Mark, or withheld as in Luke (viii. 54). It is Mark alone who preserves the native Aramaic form of the Saviour's command. The words would likely be just such as the little girl had been accustomed to hear and to employ; and there was a beautiful propriety in our Lord addressing her returning and re-animating spirit in her natural mother-tongue. '*Tali*' was a *boy*, '*Talitha*' a *girl*. (See Buxtorf's *Lex. Talm.*, p. 875, and *Lightfoot* in loc.) '*Cumi*,' or '*Cum*' as it is in some of the oldest manuscripts (ℵ B C L M, 1, 33), is the common Hebrew word for *arise*. Here the idea is, as it were, *arise out of sleep, wake up, rouse thyself up internally and thence arise externally.* The word is translated *awake* in Matt. viii. 25; Rom. xiii. 11; Eph. v. 14. Comp. Matt. ii. 13, viii. 26, xxvii. 52; Mark iv. 27.

VER. 42. **And immediately the damsel arose.** It is a different word that is rendered *damsel* here, and in the last clause of the preceding verse, from that which is employed in ver. 39, 40, and the first clause of the 41st verse. It properly means *damosel* or *damsel*, while the other means *child* or *little child*. The word *arose* too has no connection with the verb which is rendered *arise* in the preceding verse. It *strictly* means *arose* (ἀνέστη).

And walked about; for she was twelve years old. This last clause is added, as Euthymius Zigabenus properly remarks, because in the preceding part of the narrative the damsel is called *a little child* (παιδίον). The evangelist as it were says: *In one respect indeed she was but a little child, the little darling of her father.* (See ver. 23.) *But at the same time she was not so little as to be incapable of walking about.*

And they were astonished with a great astonishment. The important manuscripts ℵ B C L Δ, and 33 'the queen of the cursives,' add Mark's favourite *immediately* to the verb *were astonished*: '*and they were immediately astonished.*' Tischendorf and Alford have introduced it into the text. It is found too in the Coptic and Æthiopic versions, and it is scarcely likely that it would be intruded by transcribers; it seems rather to stand awkwardly in the way as a superfluity. It is probably therefore genuine. Instead of the repetitious expression *they were astonished with a great astonishment,* Tyndale, followed by Coverdale, has the more idiomatic phrase, *they were astonished out of measure.* **They**: the outstanding reference is doubtless to the father and mother of the child (see

ST. MARK VI.

43 And he charged them straitly that no man should know it; and commanded that something should be given her to eat.

CHAPTER VI.

1 AND he went out from thence, and came into his own

---

next verse), though of course there is no need for shutting out of view the other witnesses of the miracle.

Ver. 43. And He charged them much. Or, *He enjoined them much*. *Them:* the parents of the child.

That no man should know this. Literally, *in order that no one should know this*. His multiplied injunctions were laid upon them with the aim in view that *no one should know what had been done*. The expression *no one* is of course to be understood according to the nature of the case. The Saviour knew that there was outside a surging crowd of followers, loosely or more closely attached to His person, from whom the fact of the miracle could not be long concealed. He knew too that when once they got hold of the fact they would be sure to blaze it abroad. (See Matt. ix. 26.) But He wished that the parents of the child should not lay themselves out to trumpet abroad what had been done. *He desired that as far as possible no one should know*. Popular enthusiasm was already rushing on at tornado speed, and with tornado pressure. It was at the same time but superficially intelligent; and it had therefore but little need, at that stage of its development, to be fed and fanned and still farther inflamed.

And He said that something should be given her to eat. The expression *commanded* is too strong. It is an artless and beautifully homely incident. We need not suppose that the Saviour had exclusively in view the confirmation of the fact of the little maiden's resuscitation, as an actual fact, to be distinguished from a mere illusory appearance. This is the idea that Euthymius Zigabenus, Petter, and many others take. Neither need we suppose that He simply meant to prove to the parents her complete convalescence. There is no need for regarding our Saviour as acting for ever in the rigid character of a doctrinaire. He was not always bent on giving proofs and demonstrations. He was a loving man, genial in His feelings, full of human sympathies, fond of young folks. He would enter at once into the circle of the little damsel's self consciousness, and understand how sweet to her young fresh appetite, after the long abstinence to which she had been subjected in her illness, would be 'something to eat.' Even the child's mother was not so motherly as Jesus.

CHAPTER VI.

Ver. 1–6. This paragraph has its parallel in Matt. xiii. 53–58. There are also interesting points of correspondence in Luke iv. 16–30, which it may be instructive to note. We do not need however to come to a very positive conclusion regarding the relationship of the two paragraphs.

Ver. 1. And He went forth. Or *departed*, as the word is rendered in Matt. xxviii. 8 and Luke ix. 6. Tyndale, Coverdale and the Geneva have *departed*.

Thence. Saunier (*Quellen*, p. 85), Fritzsche, and Meyer insist on it that the

country; and his disciples follow him. 2 And when the sabbath day was come, he began to teach in the synagogue: and many hearing *him* were astonished, saying, From whence

---

reference is to *the house of Jairus*. But arbitrarily; the house of Jairus was not a prominent object in the mind of the evangelist while penning the immediately preceding narratives. The Saviour had taken refuge on the eastern side of the sea of Tiberias; but He could not find rest there. He had to return to the western side, where Capernaum was situated; and there He was pressed, hemmed in, and harassed, by accumulating crowds. This being the case, the evangelist says, *He departed thence*, that is, *He departed out of that district of country*. See next clause.

And comes. The Received Text has the past tense *came*, and Lachmann abides by it; but Tischendorf, Tregelles, Alford have the present, *comes*. The reader is thus taken back into the *presence* of our Lord, and sees Him on His journey.

Into His own country. Literally, *into His 'fatherland.'* The reference of the word however is not to the large district of country occupied by the nation, but to the small locality where the paternal home was situated. It is the district of Nazareth that is referred to, a district of quiet and seclusion as compared with the densely crowded district of Capernaum. The town would be easily reached by our Lord in the course of a day's journey.

And His disciples follow Him. The reference is doubtless to *the twelve. They accompany Him in the capacity of followers.* When the group was in motion, the Lord as a general rule would take a slight precedence and lead the way.

VER. 2. And when sabbath was come, He began to teach in the synagogue. '*The* synagogue,' for most probably there would be only one in so small a place. In all the Jewish synagogues there was a fine freedom of speech allowed; and there would be no objection therefore to one like Jesus, who had already achieved for Himself a name as a popular and somewhat remarkable rabbi, addressing the assembled congregation. The evangelist says '*He began* to teach.' We are thus taken back in imagination to the commencement of the address, and thence allowed or left to go forward with it, and take note of interruptions, if there should be any.

And many, hearing, were struck with amazement. Such was the effect, even before the conclusion of the address. Note the participle *hearing*. The idea is not, as Principal Campbell and Edgar Taylor, as well as Piscator and Felbinger and many others, give it in their respective versions, *and many who heard Him*. There was not on the evangelist's part any intention of discriminating two classes of auditors, one of which at least was numerous. Rodolphus Dickinson hits the idea in his free translation, *the numerous hearers*. The congregation was numerous, and *while hearing* they were struck with amazement. Norton in his translation brings out the idea exactly, *and many heard Him and were struck with astonishment*. In the Vatican manuscript (B) the article is inserted before the adjective, *the many, the multitude*. Tischendorf has received this peculiar reading into the text, but on too slender authority. Michelsen however approves

hath this *man* these things? and what wisdom *is* this which is given unto him, that even such mighty works are wrought by his

of the reading, but supposes that it was foisted into the text by the Deutero-Mark (*Het Ev. van Markus*, p. 102).

Saying. In the course, namely, of our Saviour's address; see ver. 4. Hence the propriety of the preceding expression, '*began* to teach.' He had not proceeded far ere He was interrupted; there was less of decorous repression of remark and criticism in a Jewish auditory than in a British congregation.

Whence hath this Man these things? Very literally, *Whence to this Man these things?* The *things*, namely, that He was *saying*. As the 'winged words' left in uninterrupted succession the Saviour's lips, and alighted on their ears, the simple people marvelled at His facility and power of utterance, and at the weighty character of the thoughts that were conveyed by the utterances. Such phenomena of oratory are always captivating to the masses; and when the orator is known to have had none of the advantages of school learning, the captivation gets transformed into amazement. But amazement may either be questioning or unquestioning; in the case of the Nazarenes it was questioning, and superstition brought the questions to the birth. *Whence hath this Man these things? Has He got them in a lawful way? Is there not something suspicious, something that looks suspiciously supernatural, in His acquisition of such a remarkable accomplishment?*

And, What is the wisdom that has been given to Him? It is probable that the introductory *and* is not part of the reported criticisms, but the evangelist's own link of connection, by means of which he adds one reported criticism to another, *Whence has this Man these things? and, What is the wisdom that has been given to Him?* This interpretation of the *and* as introducing a second and separate criticism is confirmed by the reading of Tregelles, Tischendorf (eighth edition), Alford, ' What is the wisdom that has been given *to this Man?* ' This repeated demonstrative, *to this Man*, is in the texts of ℵBCLΔ. It is the more difficult reading, and ought to be accepted; but if so, it proves that the query is detached and separate from the query of the preceding clause. When the people asked, *What is the wisdom that has been given to this Man?* they were looking at *wisdom* rather on its merely intellectual than on its more important moral side; they admitted the existence of great intellectual and rhetorical superiority, but they stood in doubt in reference to the origin of such superiority. Was it from above or from beneath?

And such mighty works are brought to pass through His hands. Such is the right reading (καὶ δυνάμεις τοιαῦται κ.τ.λ.). The observation is thus an appendage to the two preceding questions. The people refer, not to the wonders of works which they had seen, but to the wondrous works of which they had heard. Such wonderful works seemed to them to be unaccountable on any hypothesis that would leave the reputation of the Worker intact. *What are we to make of Him? Whence His wonderful words? What is this wisdom, which somehow or other He has got hold of? Is it right? And then too such wonderful works are brought to pass! They are not easily accounted for. But they do come to pass 'through' His hands! Aye, 'through.' But who is it that is behind?* Luther makes them say, Surely He will have to *do with the devil* (*Er*

hands? 3 Is not this the carpenter, the son of Mary, the

wird gewiss mit dem Teufel zu thun haben). The whole expression is rather an exclamation than an interrogation, and so Meyer has given it in his translation of 1829, though he afterwards changed his view. In the Received Text there is a *that* (ὅτι) before the expression, *that even such wonders are brought to pass through His hands*. It is manifestly spurious, and is omitted even by Bengel, Griesbach, Matthaei, Scholz. It was condemned of old by Mill; it is wanting even in the editions of Erasmus; as also in the first and second editions, the *O mirificams*, of Robert Stephens. It was however introduced into his folio of 1550, retained in the 1551 edition, and thence copied into all Beza's editions, and thus carried down into our Authorized version and the Elzevirs. Candy in his edition has given a reading for which there is *no* authority at all (αἱ καὶ δυνάμεις).

VER. 3. **Is not this the carpenter?** The word *carpenter* was given as an alternative translation by Wycliffe, and has descended into all the succeeding English versions; Wycliffe's primary translation was *smith*, the word that was used in the Anglo-Saxon version. It had in Anglo-Saxon a generic meaning, equivalent to *artificer*. A worker in iron was called in Anglo-Saxon *iren-smith*. A *smith* is one who *smites*; a *carpenter* is one who makes *cars*. The word *carpenter* therefore must be a much later coinage than the word *smith*. The original Greek term (τέκτων) means primarily a *producer*; the word *wright* very nearly corresponds to it, as being closely connected with *wrought* or *worked*. It just means *worker*, and occurs in Anglo-Saxon in the two forms *wryhta* and *wyrhta*. This is the only passage in which it is stated that our Lord worked at a handicraft. It is a different expression that is found in Matt. xiii. 53, *Is not this the carpenter's son?* There is no contradiction however between the two representations; both might be coincidently employed, and no doubt were, when the Nazarenes were freely and frettingly canvassing the merits of their wonderful townsman. Our Lord would not be trained to idleness; it was contrary to Jewish habits, and to the teaching of the best Jewish rabbis. (See *Lightfoot*, in loc.) It would have been inconsistent moreover with the principles of true civilization, and with the ideal of normal human development. It is no evidence of high civilization, either to lay an arrest on full physical development on the one hand, or on the other to encourage only those modes of muscular and nervous activity which are dissociated from useful working and manufacturing skill. While overmuch manual labour depresses both body and mind, handiwork in moderation is an inestimable blessing to men, physically, morally, intellectually, socially. Society will never be right until all classes be industrious and industrial: the higher orders must return to take part in the employments of the lower; the lower must rise up to take part in the enjoyments of the higher. Justin Martyr mentions, in his *Dialogue with Trypho the Jew* (§ 88), that the Saviour manufactured 'ploughs and yokes,' thus 'teaching the symbols of righteousness and the duty of an active life' (ἄροτρα καὶ ζυγά· διὰ τούτων καὶ τὰ τῆς δικαιοσύνης σύμβολα διδάσκων, καὶ ἀεργῆ (? ἐνεργῆ) βίον). We know not whether Justin preserves in this 'specific' remark a separate tradition, or merely gives an illustrative and imaginative explanation of the 'generic'

brother of James, and Joses, and of Juda, and Simon? and are not his sisters here with us? And they were offended at him.

expression before us. In the apocryphal *Gospel of the Infancy* (chap. xxxviii.) Jesus is represented as assisting His reputed father Joseph while working at his trade; but the assistance is always given in a miraculous manner. 'Neither was there ever any need,' it is added, 'for Him to do anything with His own hand.' It is evident that the author of this Apocryphal Gospel did not understand the true dignity of manual work; neither did Celsus, who insolently and ignorantly cast it in the teeth of Christians that Christ worked with His own hands. (Origen, *Cont. Cels.*, vi. 4: 3.)

The son of Mary. We would not infer from the specification of *Mary*, as F. C. Baur (*Markus Evang.*, p. 138) and Hilgenfeld (*Evangelien*, p. 135) do, that the evangelist was taking care to use no expression that might suggest that our Lord was the real or natural son of Joseph. We are as little to infer, with Köstlin (*Ursprung*, p. 323), that while Mark assumed that our Lord was really the natural son of Joseph, he yet wished, for 'irenic' purposes within the divided church, to give no certain sound on the subject. We would simply infer that Joseph was deceased, and had been so for such a considerable length of time that our Lord's filial relationship to the widowed Mary stood out overshadowingly, and almost exclusively, to public view. It is true that in the parallel passage of Matt. xiii. 55 Joseph is referred to; but it is in the way of bringing into view the humble nature of the trade on which the family had depended, *Is not this the carpenter's son?* The youngest of the criticizing Nazarenes knew that the trade had been hereditary in the family, and that therefore our Lord had never been in circumstances to obtain any high rabbinical training. It is entirely arbitrary in Holtzmann (*Synopt. Evang.*, p. 82) and Michelsen (*Het Evang. van Markus*, p. 102) to conjecture that in the text of the Proto-Mark the query ran thus, *Is not this the carpenter, the son of Joseph?* and that from this text of the Proto-Mark Matthew formed on his part his condensation, while the Deutero-Mark on his part, and for his own peculiar purposes, formed his dogmatic variation. Such licentiousness of conjecture is wild on the one hand, and mere 'rubbish' on the other.

And brother of James, and Joses, and Judas, and Simon. In what sense *brother*, see on chap. iii. 18, 31; half-brother, but not uterine. James in short, and the three brothers, would be the sons of Joseph by a previous marriage. In the correct text there is an *and* but no *article* before the word *brother*. Such is the reading of Lachmann, Tischendorf, Tregelles, Alford. Instead of *Joses* the Sinaitic manuscript (א) reads *Joseph*, as so many manuscripts do in Matt. xiii. 55. It was the comparative uncommonness of the name *Joses* that gave occasion to the variation. (See *Comm.* on Matt., in loc.)

And are not His sisters here with us? Their names are not specified, in accordance with the secondary place which was assigned to females in Semitic society.

And they were offended at Him. Or rather *in Him*. The word rendered *offended* is *scandalized* in the original. It is a very graphic word, but incapable of adequate translation. It presents to view a complex picture. Christ was to His kinsmen and townsmen like a *scandal*, or catch-stick, in a trap. (See on

4 But Jesus said unto them, A prophet is not without honour, but in his own country, and among his own kin, and in his own

chap. iv. 17.) They did not see what He was. They hence heedlessly ran up against Him and struck on Him, to their own utter ensnarement; they were spiritually caught; they became fixed in a position in which it was most undesirable to be fixed; they were spiritually hurt, and in great danger of being spiritually destroyed. Such are the chief elements of the picture. The actual outcome of the whole complex representation may be given thus: *They spiritually stumbled on Jesus. To their loss they did not accept Him for what He really was. They rejected Him as the Lord High Commissioner of Heaven. They came into collision with Him, and were ensnared, by suspecting that His indisputable superiority to ordinary men in word and work was owing to some other kind of influence than what was right and from above.*

VER. 4. **And Jesus said to them, A prophet is not without honour, but in his own country, and among his own kin, and in his own house.** He specifies three concentric circles of persons to whom every prophet is nearly related. There is (1) the circle of his *little fatherland*, or *district of country*, or township; there is no wider reference in the Saviour's expression. Within this outer circle there is (2) the circle of his *relatives* or '*kin*.' Then there is (3) the circle of his *nearest relatives*, the *family to which he belongs*. In each of these circles there is in general but little readiness to recognise native or nascent superiority. The principles of self-satisfaction, self-confidence, self-complacency, come in to lay a presumptive interdict upon any *adjoining self* rising up in eminence above the *my-self*. The temporary advantage of age, and thus of more protracted experience, asserts to itself for a season a sort of counter-superiority; and the mere fact of proximity makes it easy to open the door for the influence of envy, an ignoble vice that takes effect chiefly in reference to those on whom one can actually look (*invidia, in-video*). In the long run indeed real superiority, if time be granted it, will vindicate for itself its own proper place in the midst of all its concentric circles. But in general this will be only after victories achieved abroad have made it impossible for the people at home to remain in doubt. (Hofmeister quotes the proverb, '*quod rarum, carum*'). Our Saviour in uttering His apophthegm uses representatively the word *prophet*; He might have employed a more generic term, that would have embraced other examples of superiority; but the specification served His purpose, and it was at the same time broad enough to bring into view one of the great outstanding features of His own unique relationship to men. He had a commission, amid other behests, to *speak to them for God*. He was emphatically 'the *Word of* God,' and thus the Prophet of prophets. The term *prophet* has no particular reference to *prediction*; the true prophet was one who spoke *fore* God, and therefore *from* God, and thus *for* God. It is arbitrary in Schenkel to say that our Lord "still called Himself "*a prophet*, because He had not yet attained the conviction that He was, in a "new and higher meaning of the word, the fulfiller of the yet incomplete "Messianic promise of the Old Testament." (*Charakterbild*, x. 4.) Our Saviour was only laying down a generic principle for a specific purpose; and He left His auditors, as it is often wise to do, to make the specific application.

house. 5 And he could there do no mighty work, save that he laid his hands upon a few sick folk, and healed *them*. 6 And he marvelled because of their unbelief.

VER. 5. **And He was not able to do there any mighty work.** Instead of *He was not able*, Rodolphus Dickinson has *He was unwilling* : an unhappy freedom. It occurs however in some of the old Latin versions that existed before Jerome's Vulgate (*noluit*). Kuinöl merges altogether the idea both of ability and of will, and explains the phrase thus, ' *He was not able to do, that is, He did not do*,' an intolerable strain upon the evangelist's phraseology. The Saviour was really *shut up* to act as He did, and thus to withhold almost altogether from the Nazarenes miraculous manifestations, not because of any weakness on His part, but because of utter moral insusceptibility on theirs. His *power* never acted absolutely, or simply by itself, like mere blind force. It was invariably linked right and left with the highest wisdom, which, when regarded in its highest acceptation, is always coincident with the clearest intelligence on the one hand and the purest love on the other. The Saviour's power, as thus conditioned and regulated, *could not* go forth in the performance of mighty works among a people who would only have abused the gracious miracles to rivet their conviction that it was by some unlawful and demonic influence that He was actuated. Euthymius Zigabenus explains the inability thus, *He did not deem it admissible* (ἐνδεχόμενον). 'The door,' says Calvin, 'was so to speak shut upon the Saviour by the people's impiety.'
Save that He laid His hands on a few sick folk, and healed them. Wakefield's version is free but admirable, *beyond healing a few sick people by laying His hands upon them*. Such works, performed in all likelihood upon 'hidden ones,' would be inconspicuous, and therefore 'admissible' in the circumstances. They would be, however, intensely gratifying to the Saviour's benevolence.

VER. 6. **And He marvelled because of their unbelief.** It is not said, as several critics have remarked, that *He marvelled* ' *at*' *their unbelief*. The preposition *because of* (διά) brings into view, not the *object* of the astonishment, but the *cause* or *occasion* of it. Logically however, though not phraseologically, the *object* of the astonishment and the *cause* or *occasion* of it were identical. The unbelief of the Nazarenes *was* a wonder to our Lord. The wonder was 'real,' says Cardinal Cajetan, being 'caused' by the Saviour's 'experimental inacquaintance' with such an unreasonable state of mind. It was 'real' on another account. Unbelief in such circumstances as those of the Nazarenes was actually a most remarkable thing. It had a *cause* indeed ; it had *occasions* : but it had *no reason* for its existence. Far less had it a *sufficient reason* ; it was, that is to say, utterly *unreasonable*. It should not have been ; it was an utter anomaly. So is all sin (see Jer. ii. 12). It is an exceedingly strange phenomenon in the universe of God, and may well be wondered at. If wonder indeed were always *the daughter of ignorance*, one might wonder at Christ's wonder. Schleusner and Kuinöl wondered, and rendered the word, not *wondered*, but *was angry*. Fritzsche too wondered, and while too precise a scholar to admit that the word could mean *was angry*, he proposed that we should correct the text and read it thus, *and, because of their unbelief, they wondered*

And he went round about the villages, teaching. 7 And he called *unto him* the twelve, and began to send them forth by two and two; and gave them power over unclean

(viz. at Jesus). But one may most reasonably wonder at such feats and freaks of exegesis. *There is nothing really wonderful in Christ's wonder.* While it is the case that there is a vulgar wonder, which is the daughter of ignorance and dies when knowledge is attained, it is also the case that there is another wonder, of noble origin, the daughter of knowledge. This wonder dwells in the loftiest minds, and is immortal.

And He went round about the villages teaching. That is, *He visited the villages in circuit, teaching.* This does not mean that He visited the circle of villages *round about Nazareth.* The evangelist was taking topographically a much wider view. He means that Jesus, instead of tarrying at Nazareth, and thus confining His bootless labours to an unreceptive people, left that place, and extended His personal ministrations to the entire circle of the Galilean villages, retaining no doubt His headquarters in the central parts about Capernaum. This being the obvious meaning of the evangelist, it is to be regretted that Robert Stephens, the verse-maker, did not add the preceding clause of the verse to the fifth, and leave this clause to form by itself the sixth verse. Theophylact saw better into the connection, and commenced a new paragraph with this clause; so did Luther, and also Tyndale and Coverdale. So too, notwithstanding the awkwardness of rupturing a verse, do Lachmann, Tischendorf, Tregelles, Alford. These editors commence a new line with this second clause of the verse. So do Mace, Principal Campbell, Rodolphus Dickinson, Rilliet, Young. From this clause to ver. 13 inclusive is a distinct paragraph. Compare, for parallel paragraphs, Luke ix. 1-6 in particular, and also Matt. x. 1-15.

VER. 7. **And He calls to Him the twelve.** Note the present tense, *calls.* The evangelist transports himself and his readers to the scene.

And began to send them forth two by two. He *began.* It is a favourite way of speaking with Mark (see Scholten, *Het Oudste Evang.*, p. 149), founded on a favourite way of conceiving. He liked to look at the beginnings of things. When a process or progression was implied, he felt inclined to set down his thoughts at the starting places, and thence to look forward indefinitely and perhaps dimly toward the termini. (See chap. i. 45; v. 17, 20; vi. 2, 34, 55; viii. 32; x. 28, 41, 47; xi. 15; xiii. 5; xiv. 65, 69; xv. 18.) In the case before us there is no latent reference to the future mission of the apostles ' to all the world'; there is merely a certain graphic way of viewing the process of despatching the apostles. *Two by two :* that they might help and encourage one another, and take counsel together. Union is strength. It is remarkable that Mark alone mentions this pairing of the apostles on their first evangelistic tour; and yet, when enumerating the apostles in chap. iii. 16-19, he gives no indication of any order of pairing; whereas both Matthew and Luke, who do not mention that they were sent out in couples, actually introduce the coupling into their respective lists of the apostolate. (Matt. x. 2-4, Luke vi. 14-16.) It is one of those minute undesigned coincidences that establish the actual historical validity of the respective narratives.

spirits; 8 and commanded them that they should take nothing for *their* journey, save a staff only; no scrip, no bread, no money in *their* purse: 9 but *be* shod with

And He gave them authority over the unclean spirits. ' *The* unclean spirits ' that were then rampant in society, and that have ever been such formidable and cruel enemies to men. *Unclean:* characterized by and revelling in moral impurity. Witness the disgusting obscenities, and other abominations, in the talk of some of those who are *beside themselves*, and therefore *not themselves*, but *more than themselves*, and hence mercifully shut up in asylums. Our Saviour gave His apostles *authority*. If it had failed them in the time of trial, and turned out to be a mere myth of their Master's imagination, how could they have retained their allegiance to Him as the Lord? The fact that they retained it, and consecrated their lives to His service, amid obloquy, persecution, and ' deaths,' is surely proof sufficient that they were not befooled.

VER. 8. And He charged them that they should take nothing for their journey. Literally, *for the road*. They would not require to carry with them any *viaticum*. Not requiring to carry it with them, they would not require to *take it as they started*, literally *to take it up*, viz. that it might be carried. Their wants would be sufficiently supplied as they went along.

Except a staff only. Wetstein, by a temporary but singular lapse of thought, imagined that this expression means *except a single staff, one only for each pair of apostles*. But the word *only* is not an adjective here (note the gender), but an adverb. The Coptic and Anglo-Saxon translators however had committed the same oversight as Wetstein. In Matt. x. 10 the apostles were told *not to provide a staff*. (See *Comm.*, in loc.) The emphasis there is on the *provide*: *Do not acquire for yourselves what at present you are not possessed of*. Here the idea is substantially the same, though taken from another side of the reality. *Go as you are, without making any provision whatsoever. If you have a staff in your possession, and are accustomed to use it, you need not throw it away; but do not add to it; do not use it to suspend over your shoulders, for your future convenience, any bag or baggage. Take it by itself, and set out immediately. I shall be the Lord your Provider.*

No bread, no wallet. Such is the order of the words in the manuscripts א B C L Δ, 33, and in the Coptic and Æthiopic versions, as also in the texts of Tischendorf, Tregelles, Alford. The reverse order of the Received Text is the order of Luke ix. 3. In King James's English version, and all its precursors, Wycliffe, Purvey, Tyndale, Coverdale, the Geneva, the Rheims, *scrip* is used. That word however has now become quite obsolete as meaning *wallet*, and, as derived from another root, has a totally different meaning on the Stock Exchange. The Gothic translation of the word is *matibalg*, or *meat bag*.

No money in their girdle. Literally, *no copper*, for that is the metal that is got from the bowels of the earth. *Brass* is an artificial alloy, having in it a mixture of tin with the copper, and was unknown, as is supposed, to the Hebrews. The word is not used by the evangelist to denote any particular copper coin, but simply, though representatively, *copper money* in general. The underlying idea is *money in general*. Not even *coppers* would be needed,

L

sandals; and not put on two coats. 10 And he said unto them, In what place soever ye enter into an house, there abide till ye depart from that place. 11 And whosoever

not to speak of *silver* and *gold*. (Comp. Matt. x. 9, Luke ix. 3.) The original *purse* consisted of the folds of the girdle, sash, or zone ('*argentum in zonis habentes*': Liv. xxxiii. 29). The evangelist's expression, very literally, is *into the girdle*. He was artlessly thinking of *putting* money '*into*' that natural repository. The same artlessness comes out strikingly in the two succeeding clauses.

VER. 9. **But be shod with sandals.** *Have your sandals tied on.* The construction is broken. They were not indeed to have a change of shoes. (See Matt. x. 10.) That would not be needed for the limited time they would require to spend on their tour; but as they were to have a good deal of walking hither and thither, and often over rough places, *they must have on sandals*. The original expression has reference to the strings by which the sandals, as covering, for the most part, only the soles of the feet, were tied on (ὑποδεδεμένους σανδάλια). I have often looked with interest, while in Syria, on the primitive contrivance. A piece of thick tough skin, shaped somewhat like the foot, but every way larger, so that an edging may be turned up, constitutes a common specimen of the sandal of the poor. The edging is perforated at a considerable number of points to admit of elaborate lacing by means of thongs. The word employed in Matt. x. 10, and there translated *shoes* (ὑποδήματα), does not refer, as Picinellus, Salmasius, Heumann, and others, have supposed, to a more artistic cover for the feet. It is a word cognate to the verb that is here employed, and simply denotes *the undertied thing*, that is, *the thing underneath the sole of the foot that is elaborately tied on*.

And do not put on two coats. Or, *two tunics*, as Rilliet appropriately renders it. They were not to take any superfluity of dress, as if provision had to be made for a very lengthened tour. The *tunic* was the somewhat close-fitting garment that was worn next the skin; children and very poor persons frequently wore nothing else.

VER. 10. **And He said to them.** In addition to His other injunctions. It is a favourite phrase with Mark, when he introduces something *furthermore*.

Wheresoever ye may enter into a house, there remain until ye depart from that place. They were not to cater, self indulgently and restlessly, for the most agreeable quarters. When welcomed by any 'worthy' individual to his home, they were to be contented with it, however humble it might be, while they continued in the locality. (Comp. Luke x. 7.) All along their tour they were to maintain a spirit of restraint and self denial as regarded themselves, and, as regarded others, a tender regard to the benevolent feelings of the good.

VER. 11. **And whatsoever place shall not receive you.** Such, instead of *whosoever*, was no doubt the reading in the autograph of Mark (καὶ ὃς ἂν τόπος μὴ δέξηται ὑμᾶς). It is preserved in the manuscripts ℵ B L Δ, 69, as well as in the Coptic and Æthiopic versions, and in the margin of the Philoxenian Syriac. It is replaced in the text by Tischendorf, Tregelles, Alford, and approved of by

12] ST. MARK VI. 147

shall not receive you, nor hear you, when ye depart thence, shake off the dust under your feet for a testimony against them. Verily I say unto you, It shall be more tolerable for Sodom and Gomorrha in the day of judgement, than for that city.

12 And they went out, and preached that men should repent.

Meyer. It would never have been disturbed had it not been for the artless *anacoluth* of the succeeding clause.

Nor shall listen to you. In this clause the evangelist passes altogether, in thought, from the *place*, as a *place*, to its *living inhabitants*. And hence his verb *shall listen*, unlike the preceding verb *shall receive*, is in the plural number (ἀκούσωσιν). We cannot reproduce in English, without a circumlocution, the abrupt transition.

When ye depart thence, shake off the soil that is under your feet. The soil, that is to say, which is adhering to the soles of your sandals. What Mark, in his simple generic manner, calls *soil* or *earth* (χοῦς, not χνοῦς as in the editions of Erasmus), Matthew and Luke, more specifically and elegantly, call *dust* (κονιορτός). Wycliffe translates it freely, *powdre*.

For a testimony to them. A *testimony* that ye are constrained to regard them as unclean, somewhat as the heathen are. (See *Comm.* on Matt., x. 14.) Let them know that ye could not wish to take the least particle of their spirit along with you ; it would be defiling.

In the Received Text there follow the words, *verily I say unto you, It shall be more tolerable for Sodom and Gomorrha, in the day of judgment, than for that city*. But the critical editors have, almost unanimously, thrown them out, as an import from Matt. x. 15. Lachmann puts them within brackets. They are not found in the manuscripts ℵ B C D L Δ, nor in the Vulgate and Armenian versions, and many copies of the Italic. Against such authority, says Griesbach, *the weight of six hundred, or of six thousand, Constantinopolitan manuscripts is nothing at all (is 'nil': Comm. Crit.,* in loc.) Erasmus and Beza suspected the genuineness of the clause; and Mill condemned it, following Zacharias Chrysopolitanus. It is omitted in the editions of Tischendorf, Tregelles, Alford, and the Revised version; rightly. But Matthæi and Fritzsche nevertheless, in consequence of their peculiar and erroneous standpoint in textual criticism, contend for it.

VER. 12. **And they went out, and preached that men should repent.** This is one half of the brief unambitious narrative of the first apostolic tour of the apostles. The expression *that men should repent* does not so much exhibit the subject matter of the apostles' preaching as the aim that actuated them ; but that aim nevertheless would determine the subject matter ; and hence the subject matter of the speaking, and the aim of the speakers, would be coincident. The expression in the original is literally, *in order that* (ἵνα) *men might repent,* or, as Lachmann, Tischendorf, and Tregelles read it, *in order that men 'may' repent* (μετανοῶσιν). It was thus the apostles' great aim to induce men to turn, inwardly and then outwardly, from the error of their ways. That they might succeed in this their aim, they addressed themselves to the *intelligence* (the

13 And they cast out many devils, and anointed with oil many that were sick, and healed *them*.

14 And king Herod heard *of him*; (for his name was spread

νοῦς) of men, and thus sought to bring them to *a reconsideration of their ways*. (See chap. i. 4.) The term, says Petter, "which is translated *repent* is such "a word as doth properly signify *to change one's mind*, or to become more wise "than before."

VER. 13. In this verse we have the other half of the evangelist's report of the first apostolic tour.

And they cast out many demons, and anointed with oil many invalids, and healed them. There is no reference here to what Roman Catholics call *the sacrament of extreme unction*. So even a-Lapide admits and contends. The reference is to *medicinal anointing*, a favourite method of cure among the ancient Jews and many other peoples. (See Isa. i. 6 and Luke x. 34.) Josephus mentions that Herod the Great, in one of his illnesses, was 'immersed in a bath full of oil,' and obtained a surprising recovery for a season. (*Antiq.*, xvii. 6: 5.) Celsus, the famous Latin physician, in his great work *de Medicina*, makes frequent reference to the medicinal use of oil in connection with medical friction, etc. (Lib. i., cap. 3, etc.) Such a simple hygienic application has perhaps been too much neglected amid the multitudinous recipes of the modern pharmacopœia. The apostles made use of it, we should suppose, representatively, as being the sheet anchor of the ancient pharmacopœia; but assuredly they did not employ it in the way dreamed of by Paulus and Kuinöl, the way of simply applying by natural medical skill a natural medicinal remedy. Neither, on the other hand, would it be merely in a symbolical way that they would apply it, as Beza and Petter contend. They would employ it, on a principle of intercorrespondency or harmony, as a fitting material and visible medium, through which the invisible and Divine influence, which it was their prerogative to communicate, took effect. Not that we are to suppose that it was the only fitting medium. It was employed *representatively* only. There is no evidence that our Saviour ever Himself used the same medium. He used *words* at times and *touching* at other times. "He healed," as Michaelis remarks, " by a word, a command, a "simple touch; His apostles by ointment and medicines" (*Anmerkungen*, in loc.) But they healed miraculously nevertheless. As Lightfoot expresses it, "they used an ordinary medicine, and obtained an extraordinary and infallible "effect." (*Heb. and Talm. Exer.*, on Matt. vi. 17.)

VER. 14–16. A little paragraph, giving occasion for the insertion of the larger one that immediately follows. It corresponds to Luke ix. 7-9, and Matt. xiv. 1, 2.

VER. 14. **And the king Herod heard.** The Cambridge manuscript (D) and some few other authorities read reversely *Herod the king*. The evangelist does not tell what it was that he *heard*. His own mind was full of his great subject, of Christ, and of His sayings and doings; he hence artlessly writes as if his readers could not but understand what he was referring to. The Syriac Peshito version adds the words *concerning Jesus*. It is far too narrow a view to suppose,

abroad:) and he said, That John the Baptist was risen from the dead, and therefore mighty works do shew forth themselves in him. 15 Others said, That it is Elias. And others

with Meyer, that the intended reference is to the contents of ver. 12 and 13. The Herod spoken of, Herod Antipas, one of the sons of Herod the Great by Malthace the Samaritan, was not strictly and technically *king*, like his father. He was only *tetrarch*; and so he is designated by both Matthew (xiv. 1), and Luke (ix. 7). But as he was really sovereign in his own fraction of the old kingdom, the tetrarchy of Galilee and Peræa, he was popularly and by courtesy called *king*.

For His name was spread abroad. Or, as Coverdale gives it, *for His name was now known*; literally, *for His name was become manifest*, or as it were conspicuous; a parenthetical remark, accounting for the fact that even the tetrarch, though far removed from the circle of society in which Jesus was working, had heard of Him.

And he said, John the Baptist has been raised from the dead. That is, *from among the dead*. The report of Herod's remark is given, not in the indirect, but in the direct, form; and hence the introductory demonstrative *that*, found in King James's version, should be omitted in harmony with our English idiom. It is omitted both by Tyndale and Coverdale, and in the Geneva, but was introduced by the Rheims. The guilty monarch's conscience was haunted by ghastly reminiscences and weird forebodings; these, working in conjunction with a superstition which he found it impossible, notwithstanding his Epicureanism, to shake off, projected their own ghost-like shadows of things upon the wonderful personality of our Lord.

And therefore the powers are operative in him (ἐνεργοῦσιν αἱ δυνάμεις ἐν αὐτῷ). This is a snatch of Herod's theology and philosophy. He knew that the Baptist had in his natural lifetime wrought no miracles; but he thought that, in consequence of his connection with the unseen world, he had now become a prominent subject and agent of the occult forces of the universe. He knew not *what these forces were*; but he was sure *that they were*. He had too a wholesome dread of them, and was uneasy when the idea took possession of him that one of their terrestrial centres of operation was in the resuscitated person of his old faithful adviser, whom he had so unrighteously put out of the way. '*The* powers,' generically considered; *the existing* powers. Wycliffe's translation of the clause is, *and therfore vertues worchen in hym*, that is, as the Rheims gives it, *worke in him*.

VER. 15. Round about the peculiar opinion of Herod regarding the wonderful Galilean Rabbi other opinions were in circulation, and more or less ventilated. **Others said**; or rather, *But others said*. Almost all the good manuscripts insert the conjunction.

It is Elias. Or *Elijah*. For he was expected to reappear on the earth, to prepare the way for the establishment of the kingdom of heaven (see Mal. iv. 5). It was assumed by those who mooted this opinion regarding the Galilean Rabbi, that He could not be the Messiah himself. The Messiah was to be a great and glorious King, and would be found in some palace, surrounded with courtiers and generals and armies.

said, That it is a prophet, or as one of the prophets. 16 But when Herod heard *thereof*, he said, It is John, whom I beheaded: he is risen from the dead.

But others said, A prophet! Like one of the prophets! Such is the translation of the correct reading. A twofold form of the report is recorded: one was, *A prophet!* another was, *Like one of the prophets!* Elias too was a prophet; but he stood apart on a peculiar pedestal as 'the forerunner,' and as thus pre-eminently '*the* prophet.' Some, who could not imagine that Jesus was so great a personage, yet supposed that He might very likely be *a prophet*, say perhaps Jeremiah (Matt. xvi. 14); others, who could not go quite so far, yet admitted that He was *like one of the prophets*, one of them come to life again. In the Received Text there is an *or* inserted between the two forms of the report; it is wanting however in almost all the important manuscripts, inclusive of ℵ A B C and 33 'the queen of the cursives,' and in almost all the old versions, inclusive of the Vulgate and Syriac Peshito. It is thrown out of the text by Bengel, Griesbach, Matthæi, Scholz, Lachmann, Tischendorf, Tregelles, Alford. Besides this spurious *or* there is also in the Received Text the substantive verb, '*it is* a prophet'; but this too, though better supported than the disjunctive particle, was a transcriber's addition to Mark's own abrupt phraseology.

VER. 16. **But when Herod heard.** It is not said what. Meyer thinks that the reference is to the different opinions entertained regarding our Lord. Unlikely. It is more probable that the evangelist is simply reverting resumptively to what he had said in ver. 14. He repeats the abrupt phrase which he there employed, and which would be still standing out to view in his memory.

He said, It is he whom I beheaded, John ; he is risen from the dead. The construction is rugged in the original, but graphically exhibits such jerking and broken modes of phraseology as might be expected from one in Herod's position, speaking under the impulse of superstition and the sting of conscience. He turns the first part of his observation right round as it were, *whom I beheaded, John, he is risen from the dead.* It is somewhat doubtful whether the words *from the dead* may not be a marginal addition. They are omitted by Tischendorf and Alford on the authority of ℵ B L Δ and 'the queen of the cursives.' They are also omitted in the Coptic version and the Harclean Syriac ; Tregelles encloses them within brackets. It is of no moment whether they be retained or left out.

VER. 17-29 constitute a long and intensely 'sensational' paragraph. Its 'sensationalism,' however, is the quiet efflorescence of truth, not the noisy effervescence of fiction. It is 'truth stranger than fiction': deeply instructive truth moreover, giving glimpses into scenes behind the curtain of court life, and revealing the hollowness of the pleasures that are founded on immorality. At the bottom of these pleasures there is an opening into an abyss of disappointment and woe. The paragraph is introduced into the narrative to account for Herod's notion regarding Jesus. It would however be gladly introduced by the evangelist, partly because of the intensely striking character of the facts narrated, and partly because of the opportunity which it afforded for giving information regarding John the Baptist, who stood in so intimate a relationship to

19]   ST. MARK VI.   151

17 For Herod himself had sent forth and laid hold upon John, and bound him in prison for Herodias' sake, his brother Philip's wife: for he had married her. 18 For John had said unto Herod, It is not lawful for thee to have thy brother's wife. 19 Therefore Herodias had a quarrel against him, and

---

our Lord. A corresponding paragraph is found in Matt. xiv. 3–12, but not in Luke. Compare, however, Luke iii. 19, 20.

VER. 17. **For Herod himself.** This very Herod, whose opinion of Jesus has just been recorded.

Had sent forth. The verb is not in the pluperfect tense in the original, but in the aorist. He *sent out*, viz. at a former stage of things, when he had been irritated by the faithful remonstrances of the incorruptible preacher.

And arrested John, and bound him in prison. The idea is not that John was bound when once he was got into prison, but that *he was bound when arrested, and then shut up in prison.* Manacles would no doubt be put upon him, ere he was led off to prison. The language is constructed in a free and inartificial way.

Because of Herodias, the wife of Philip his brother. Philip was the brother of Antipas by the same father, Herod the Great, but not by the same mother. The mother of Antipas was Malthace the Samaritan; the mother of Philip was Mariamne, the daughter of Simon the high priest (Josephus, *Ant.*, xviii. 5: 1, 4). This Philip, to be distinguished, notwithstanding all the efforts of Volkmar (*Die Evang.*, p. 367–8), from Philip the tetrarch of Trachonitis (see Patrizi, *De Evangeliis*, vol. ii., p. 424–5), lived privately at Rome, and had a daughter Salome by his wife Herodias. Herodias was herself a granddaughter of Herod the Great, being the daughter of Aristobulus, who was Herod's son by Mariamne, the granddaughter of Hyrcanus. Philip her husband, and Antipas her subsequent paramour, were thus her uncles! So incestuously tangled was the family web! Agrippa the Great was one of her three brothers.

For he had married her. Or, more literally, *for he married her.* It was a sadly scandalous affair all through. He was not only Philip's brother; he was also his guest in Rome at the time that he stole Herodias's heart (*Joseph. Ant.*, xviii. 5: 1). He had moreover a wife of his own, to whom he had long ago been married, and who had been entirely faithful to him. She was the daughter of Aretas, king of Arabia. She fled to her father on discovering that it was the intention of her unfaithful lord to get her divorced, that room might be made for her sister in law. A bloody war, offspring of 'the lusts that war in the members' (Jas. iv. 1), was the result, and a total and humiliating defeat was inflicted on Herod. Thus 'hard,' in the long run, 'is the way of transgressors.'

VER. 18. **For John said to Herod, It is not lawful for thee to have the wife of thy brother.** The noble man had been faithful to the tetrarch. Instead of flattering him as the cringing creatures of the court would be doing, by some subtle Machiavellian reasoning to the effect that *might was right*, such reasoning as that of Callicles in Plato's Gorgias, he boldly asserted the supremacy of right and condemned the infamous marriage.

VER. 19. **And Herodias was urgent against him.** Literally, and idiomatically,

would have killed him; but she could not: 20 for Herod feared John, knowing that he was a just man and an holy, and

---

held in to him, instead of simply *holding off from him* (ἀπεῖχεν ἀπ' αὐτοῦ). Comp. Luke xi. 53, Gen. xlix. 23. She nursed her animosity and resentment in her heart.

And wished to kill him. It is a plain and unvarnished way of speaking on the part of the evangelist. He calls a spade a spade. The unprincipled woman could not brook the outspoken integrity of the man of God, and schemed to get quit of his living voice and influence. She had inherited, in a marked degree, the haughty, domineering, and unscrupulous spirit of her grandfather. George Buchanan, the prince of modern Latin poets, sketches her character and principles of action with a masterly hand in his drama entitled *The Baptist*. He makes her say to the vacillating Herod, just as Callicles would have taught her to speak:

> "Father in law, friends, kinsmen, son in law,
> Brother and sister, citizen and foe,
> Are chains for poor men; empty words for kings.
> Whoe'er puts on his head a diadem
> Should fling aside all kinds of common duty,
> Think nothing base that's useful to a king."—*Scene Twelfth*.

And was not able. She could not compass her end, for the reason stated in the next verse.

VER. 20. **For Herod feared John.** Kingliness changed places: the subject did not fear the sovereign; the sovereign feared the subject. He did not know what occult influences might be at the good man's disposal; but he felt that some influences or other, of a powerful and penetrating description, *did* vibrate into his heart and conscience, at the touch of the incorruptible preacher.

Knowing him to be a righteous and holy man. *Righteous* toward man, *holy* toward God. There was thus a part of Herod's soul that was, to some extent, responsive to the imperatives of righteousness and holiness. He bowed, though only alas at a distance, before the sceptres of these sovereign principles. But he was not prepared to be obedient to their behests.

And observed him. A wrong translation, and yet, strange to say, given by both Erasmus and Beza, and thence received into King James's version. Tyndale, too, had taken the same view; his translation is, *and gave him reverence*. So too Vatable, Calvin (see his *French version*), Grotius, le Clerc, Beausobre, Wakefield, Fritzsche, Wahl, Bloomfield, Patrizi. The translation of Webster and Wilkinson is also objectionable, *observed him strictly*, 'as if he would see whether Herodias had any good grounds for her enmity.' The word does not mean *observed*, but *conserved* (συνετήρει), and so it is used in the other New Testament passages where it occurs. See Matt. ix. 17; Luke ii. 19, v. 38. Rilliet's translation is, *and protected him*. Principal Campbell's is identical. And so the Vulgate, Coverdale, Henry Stephens, Jansen, Petter, Hammond, Elsner, Bengel, Bretschneider, Meyer, Alford, Lange, Grimm. Herod protected John against the machinations of Herodias, and hence *conserved* him, or, in accordance with our idiom, *preserved* him, *kept him safe*.

observed him; and when he heard him, he did many things, and heard him gladly. 21 And when a convenient day was

And when he heard him, he did many things. Such is the reading of the Received Text. Herod's conscience being touched, he tried to make a compromise with it by doing a variety of good things from which he would otherwise have abstained. It is likely, however, that the expression *he did many things* (πολλὰ ἐποίει) is a tinkered reading, occasioned chiefly by the word *gladly* in the following clause. The original expression seems to have been, *he was much perplexed* (πολλὰ ἠπόρει). Such was, for long, known to be the reading of the Vatican manuscript (B). It was also the reading of the Parisian manuscript L, and of the Coptic version. And now it turns out that the Sinaitic manuscript has the same reading. Ewald approves of it, and so does Meyer. Tischendorf has, in his eighth edition, received it into the text. We cannot but accept it. See next clause.

And he heard him gladly. Or with pleasure (ἡδέως). A statement not at all inconsistent with the preceding; for there was inconsistency in the heart of Herod. He was not bad throughout; and he was far from being good throughout. There was still a tender spot in his conscience. The genius of John, his ready oratory, the unsophisticated grandeur of his character, his manifest and incorruptible integrity, his loyalty to God, his manly and undeviating devotion to a life of self denial and godliness,—all these uncommon elements of idiosyncrasy would lend a nameless charm to his discoursings. The monarch would feel that he was in the presence of 'an honest man,' who was as great as he was good. But then the very charm of which he was conscious, by insinuating itself into his still susceptible conscience, and rousing the dormant forces that were there, would give occasion to a perplexing collision between a sense of duty and a desire to enjoy the revelry that had established for itself a kind of prescriptive right, and a home, in his court. We need not doubt the reality of the collision. We need not, with Cardinal Cajetan, suppose that there was the mere simulation of respect for John, for fear of the people (*ficte Herodes exercebat hos virtutum actus*). Yet de Lyra took the same view. Strauss gives emphasis to another supposed inconsistency, the inconsistency of Herod's interest in John, as here recorded, with what is said in Matt. xiv. 5, "*And when " he would have put him to death, he feared the multitude, because they counted " him as a prophet*" (*Leben*, ii. 1 : 44). Meyer echoes this assertion of inconsistency. But inconsistently. It is not to be wondered at that the first promptings of Herod's haughty heart should have been to put to death the man who had dared to criticise the legitimacy of his marriage. But when a regard to public opinion had held back for a season his uplifted hand, time was given for resentment to cool and conscience to utter its 'still small voice.' And perhaps too his infatuated attachment to his queen might have gradually become conscious of some thorns piercing into its quick. What wonder then that there should be some change in his feelings? Where is the inconsistency of the two accounts? There is not even what Ebrard would admit (*Wissenschaftliche Kritik*, p. 384), the 'appearance of contradiction' (*Schein eines Widerspruches*).

VER. 21. And an opportune day having come. *Opportune*, to wit, for Herodias

come, that Herod on his birthday made a supper to his lords, high captains, and chief *estates* of Galilee; 22 and when the daughter of the said Herodias came in, and danced, and

---

carrying out a machination which she had been concocting in her heart. Principal Campbell's translation, modelled upon Mace's, and improved, is free but admirable, *At length a favourable opportunity offered.*

When Herod (ὅτε, not δ τε as in Lachmann, p. xliii.).

On his birthday festivities (τοῖς γενεσίοις αὐτοῦ). The evangelist's phrase is not used in its current classical acceptation. Among the Attics it was generally employed, by a remarkable inversion of reference, to denote *the solemnities that were commemorative of decease* (see Hesychius and Phavorinus *in voc.*, and Lobeck, pp. 103, 184). *Death* was treated as *a birth* (compare the ecclesiastical '*Genethlia*'; Suiceri *Thes.*, i., p. 747). The evangelist, however, uses the phrase in its primary and natural acceptation. It is said that the Jews in general disapproved of observing birthday festivities. They esteemed "the "keeping of birthdays," says Lightfoot, "a part of idolatrous worship." He adds, however, "perhaps they would pronounce more favourably and flatter-"ingly of thine, O Tetrarch, because thine" (*Exercit. on Matt.*, xiv. 6). It is certain at all events that the Herods, after the manner of the great among the Egyptians, Persians, Greeks, and Romans, observed their birthdays with the utmost pomp and luxury (see *Joseph. Ant.*, xix. 71; *Persius Sat.*, v. 180).

Made a supper to his lords. *Lords,* an excellent idiomatic translation of the original word (μεγιστᾶσιν). It was a word which came into use *after* the Macedonian era (Lobeck *ad Phryn.*, p. 196-9), and literally means *chief ones* or *chiefs*. Salmasius says that it was probably introduced *by* the Macedonians (*De Hellenistica*, p. 110). Some of the Roman writers, such as Tacitus (*An.*, xv. 27) and Suetonius (*Calig.*, 5), adopted the term into the Latin language, *megistanes.*

And high captains. Or *high military officers, chiliarchs* as it is in the original, that is, *commanders of a thousand men*. These military dignitaries are specified, apparently, in contradistinction to the *lords* or civil dignitaries.

And the grandees of Galilee. Mace's translation of the clause is, *and persons of the first distinction in Galilee.* Old Purvey's translation is good, *the grettest of Galilee.* The *lords* and *high officers* would be the regular 'habitués' of the court, *the grettest of Galilee* might comprehend all the other distinguished men of the district.

VER. 22. **And the daughter of Herodias herself having come in and danced.** This clause is in consecutive apposition with the initial clause of the preceding verse, *an opportune day having come.* The idea is that it was *Herodias's own daughter* who danced. The aim is not so much *to particularize the Herodias already referred to*, after the manner of Tyndale's translation, *the daughter of the sayde Herodias,* **as to** emphasize the fact that *instead of a professional dancing girl or almeh being employed, it was Herodias's own daughter* who was cunningly put forward *to act as a decoy to the heart of the susceptible monarch.* "I should conclude," says Dr. Lardner, " that this dance was a very unusual if "not a very singular piece of complaisance" (*Credibility*, vol. i., p. 17). It was not customary for ladies of high rank to dance beyond the limits of the harem.

pleased Herod and them that sat with him, the king said unto the damsel, Ask of me whatsoever thou wilt, and I will give *it* thee. 23 And he sware unto her, Whatsoever thou shalt ask of me, I will give *it* thee, unto the half of my kingdom.

The oriental dance, still more than the occidental ballet that was in use among the voluptuaries of Greece and Rome, was of a libertine character; it was seldom appreciated unless it made irruptions across the borders of decency (see Sir Fred. Henniker's *Notes of Egypt*, etc., pp. 72-74). Indeed Dr. E. D. Clarke imagines that "if the history of this exercise be traced to its origin, it will be "found to have nearly the same character all the world over" (*Travels*, vol. v., p. 167). Cicero, from his standpoint, said, "Scarcely any sober man dances, "unless indeed he be mad" (*Nemo enim fere saltat sobrius, nisi forte insanit : Pro Murœna*, 6).

She pleased Herod and his guests. Literally *those who reclined with him,* viz. around the suite of *triclinia* (see Ciacconius, *De Triclinio*, p. 85; Ursinus's *Appendix*, p. 374; and Becker's excursus on the triclinium in his *Gallus*). The dancing women of the East used tambours of various kinds, and sometimes had little bells attached to their fingers to make musical jingling. They sang too. The Princess Salome's dancing and singing would, we may suppose, be more elegant, and more captivating, than any exhibition of mere professional almehs. Herodias, a very 'serpent under femininitee' (*Chaucer*, 4 : 780) would artfully introduce, moreover, such a piquant portion of the entertainment, just at the right time, and by way of conferring upon her lord, as from herself and her daughter, a very special honour.

And the king said to the damsel, Ask of me whatsoever thou desirest, and I shall give it thee. Flushed with flattery, inflamed with wine, and touched to the heart by the gratification which had been contrived for him by the mother of Salome, he felt in his most magnificent and generous mood, and wished to make the elegant *danseuse* the very best present she could desire. Hence the *carte blanche* of promise, which, not without a liberal infusion of ostentation, he put into her hand in the presence of his applauding guests.

VER. 23. Salome, abashed by the magnificence of the promise, and wincing too, let us hope, under the reproaches of her maidenly modesty, on which she had been so wantonly trampling as she danced, may have hung her head for a little, in mingled diffidence, perplexity, and shame. The spectacle moved still more the excited and gratified voluptuary. He 'came out stronger' still, and made efforts to assure her.

And he swore to her, Whatsoever thou mayest ask of me, I will give to thee, even to half of my kingdom. A most extravagant promise, in which one can easily trace the infatuating effect of voluptuous indulgence, and vanity, and ostentation. Perhaps the inflated potentate imagined that he was rivalling the magnificence of 'the great king Ahasuerus' in the promise which he made to Esther (Esth. v. 3, 6). *Even to half:* Our English idiom, like the Greek, admits of the suppression of the article. Purvey's translation of the clause is *though it be half my kyngdom.*

24 And she went forth, and said unto her mother, What shall
I ask? And she said, The head of John the Baptist. 25 And
she came in straightway with haste unto the king, and asked,
saying, I will that thou give me by and by in a charger the head

VER. 24. **And she went out and said to her mother, What shall I ask?** Or
rather, according to the reading of the best manuscripts and all the modern
critical editors, *What should I ask?* (αἰτήσωμαι, instead of the αἰτήσομαι of the
Received Text.)
And she said, The head of John the Baptist. Nothing would be so sweet apparently, or so dear to her, as the gratification, however coarsely, of her vindictive
feelings. And hence too the laconic form of her answer to her child. Somewhat of the ferocity may doubtless be legitimately attributed to the spirit of the
age; but still a large residuum remains of what was savage and unfeminine in
the character of Herodias.

VER. 25. **And she came in immediately with haste to the king.** *Immediately*,
without loss of time; *with haste*, with alacrity in her steps, and unhesitating
determination in her bearing. '*Avec empressement*' is the felicitous translation
of the modern editions of the French Geneva, as also of Beausobre and L'Enfant,
and Rilliet. She had been reinspired by contact with her mother, and was
herself no doubt a thorough Herodine.
**And made her request, saying, I wish that thou shouldest give me instantly,
on a platter, the head of John the Baptist.** Note the peremptoriness of the *instantly* (ἐξαυτῆς). The word is rendered *even now* in the Geneva, *straightwaye*
by Coverdale, *anoon* (i.e. *in oôn, in ône instant*) by Wycliffe, *immediately* by Mace
and Wakefield, *at once* by Sharpe, *forthwith* by Edgar Taylor, *now* by Norton,
presently by Young; all of them correct translations. So is King James's
version, got from Tyndale, *by and by*, only the expression has in modern parlance
drifted from its former moorings. When that version was published, the phrase
just meant *immediately*, as is evident from the other three passages in which it
occurs: Matt. xiii. 21; Luke xvii. 7, xxi. 9. In all these cases it is the rendering of the adverb which is generally translated *immediately* or *straightway*. By
the time of Dr. Samuel Johnson however the phrase had got to mean, as he
defines it, 'in a short time,' although in the examples which he adduces it
really means *instantly*. **On a platter:** Or *salver*, as Brameld renders it. Wycliffe,
Wynne, Wakefield, Norton, Edgar Taylor, Sharpe, Alford, Godwin, use the more
generic *dish*; Newcome, Principal Campbell, Rodolphus Dickinson, have *basin*;
the Rheims has *platter*; King James's translation and the Revised version have
charger, a word now antiquated, but formerly meaning a large 'assiette,' which
was *charged* with or on which was carried a *charge* or *cargo* of meat. (See
Comm. on Matt., xiv. 8.) The maiden indicated that it would be, as it were, the
consummation of the feast to her and her mother, if the Baptist's head were
presented to her. It was needful, in her opinion, that it should be actually presented *to herself*, no doubt that she might satisfy herself that no inferior head
had been surreptitiously substituted in its place. "Agrippina, wife of Claudius,
"and mother of Nero, who was afterwards emperor, sent an officer to put to
"death Lollia Paulina, who had been her rival for the imperial dignity. And

ST. MARK VI.

of John the Baptist. 26 And the king was exceeding sorry; *yet* for his oaths' sake, and for their sakes which sat with him, he would not reject her. 27 And immediately the king sent an

---

" Dio Cassius says that when Lollia's head was brought to her, not knowing it "at first, she examined it with her own hands, till she perceived some particular "feature by which that lady was distinguished. I have put down this instance, "because it seems to give us the reason of this practice among great people, "namely, that they might be certain their orders had been executed." (Lardner's *Credibility*, vol. i., p. 17.)

VER. 26. **And the king was made exceedingly sorry, but, on account of his oaths and his guests, did not choose to reject her.** The reason of his exceeding sorrow was to be found in his inward respect for John, and his desire to 'have his own way' in reference to him, notwithstanding the wishes and schemes of his consort. *On account of his oaths.* Note the plural number. He had repeated, and perhaps re-repeated, his *oath.* *He did not choose:* he did not wish (and will). *To reject her:* a free phrase, meaning *to repudiate her demand*, or *to deny her request.* Literally, *to displace her*; namely, from that standing-room which she got by his promise, and of which she had taken unhandsome advantage in preferring such an unwelcome request.

Was it right in Herod, it has often been asked, to choose not to displease Salome, and consequently to murder John? It is sufficient to answer that it can never be right to do wrong. But what then of the obligation of his oaths? He was conscious of their force; but still they could not bind him to do wrong. No power in the universe can ever make it right to do wrong. But is it not doing wrong to violate an oath? No, if the oath were itself entirely wrong (*rei illicitæ nulla obligatio:* Sanderson, *De Juramenti obligatione,* ii. 13). The making of such an oath is the first wrong doing; the keeping of it is the second. When one has begun wrong, repentance, as even Seneca teaches, is more honourable than pertinacity. (It is one of the bad effects of *ira*, he says, that *in male cæptis honestior pertinacia videtur quam pœnitentia:* De Ira, i. 16.) When it is said that Herod had regard *to his guests,* as well as *to his oaths,* the meaning probably is, not that ' these persons joined in with the request' of Salome, out of dislike to John, as Dr. A. Clarke supposes, but that the tetrarch could not brook the idea of doing in their presence what would lower him in their estimation, seeing they were themselves witnesses of the fact of the unconditional promise.

VER. 27. **And immediately the king sent off a soldier of his body-guard.** The evangelist, instead of employing a Greek term (δορυφόρος), uses a Latin technical word, which was at that time in fashion, *speculator* (not *spiculator*, as Erasmus and Beza give it; see, especially, Golling's exhaustive Monograph on the term). This Latin word originally meant *a scout*, but came by and by to denote, more generically, a military attendant on high officers in the army. At length it was used to denote one of the armed body-guard of the Roman emperor. (See Suetonius, *Calig.* 44, *Claud.* 35; Tacit. *Hist.*, ii. 33, etc.) Herod Antipas imitated the manners of the Roman court, and hence, like Claudius (Sueton. 35), had in

executioner, and commanded his head to be brought: and
he went and beheaded him in the prison, 28 and brought
his head in a charger, and gave it to the damsel: and the
damsel gave it to her mother. 29 And when his disciples
heard *of it*, they came and took up his corpse, and laid it in
a tomb.

---

attendance a company, or little 'cohort,' of *speculatores*. These *speculatores*
were employed, when occasion required, as *executioners*. (See Seneca, *De Ira*,
i. 16, and Golling, *ut supra*.) But it was by no means their distinctive characteristic to act in this capacity; and hence the translation in King James's version
is apt to suggest too narrow an idea. This idea was revoltingly exaggerated by
Tyndale, who rendered the expression '*the hangman*.' Yet Coverdale, the
Geneva, and the Rheims, followed in his wake. Wycliffe's version was not so
offensive, but it was wrong nevertheless, *a manqueller*, i.e. *a mankiller*.

And commanded to bring his head. Or, as it is freely rendered by Mace, *with
orders to bring the head of John the Baptist*.

And he went off and beheaded him in the prison. According to Josephus, it
was in the strongly fortified fortress of Machærus, east of the Dead Sea, that
John was beheaded. (*Antiq.* xviii. 5 : 2.) If this be the case, then Herod must
have kept the anniversary of his birthday in the magnificent palace which his
father had built within that fortress. (See Josephus, *War*, vii. 6 : 2.) Renan
assumes that the feast must have been celebrated there (*Vie de Jesus*, chap.
xii., p. 197). So does Hepworth Dixon (*The Holy Land*, p. 288); and many
others. And yet it is possible that Josephus may just have taken for granted
that John was put to death in the castle where he was originally confined; and
it may have been the case that he had been removed to Tiberias, the favourite
residence of Herod. The fact that *the grandees of Galilee* only, and *not those
also of Peræa*, are specified as having been present at the festival, rather favours
this supposition.

VER. 28. There is a small difference about the commencement of this verse.
Our translators have followed the division of Robert Stephens the verse-maker;
but Beza and Henry Stephens made a modification of the division. They
began the 28th verse with the preceding clause, *And he went off and beheaded
him in the prison*. The Elzevirs followed them, and thence too all the great
continental editors, earlier and later; Bengel, Wetstein, Griesbach, Matthæi,
Scholz, Lachmann, Buttmann, Tischendorf.

And brought his head on a platter, and gave it to the damsel, and the damsel gave
it to her mother. A fit presentation for cannibals, or other savages, whether
living in a palace or a wigwam.

VER. 29. And when his disciples heard of it, they came and took up his corpse,
and laid it in a tomb. Or, as Wycliffe has it, *in a buriel*. They *took up*, viz.
from the ground, *the fallen thing* (τὸ πτῶμα). It was not the noble man himself
whom they took up and buried. He was 'away' (2 Cor. v. 8). It was but his
prostrate 'remains.'

VER. 30–33 constitute a little paragraph, introductory to the paragraph con-

30 And the apostles gathered themselves together unto Jesus, and told him all things, both what they had done, and what they had taught. 31 And he said unto them, Come ye yourselves apart into a desert place, and rest a while: for there were many coming and going, and they had no leisure so much as to eat. 32 And they departed into a desert place by ship privately.

---

tained in ver. 33–44. It is of great intrinsic interest. It contains, says Dean Alford, 'one of the most affecting descriptions in the Gospels.' Corresponding statements are found in Matt. xiv. 13; Luke ix. 10, 11; and John vi. 1–3.

VER. 30. **And the apostles.** The only instance in Mark, in which the word *apostles* is found. But, as Bengel remarks, it is with peculiar fitness that it is introduced (*apta huic loco appellatio*). The disciples had just completed their first apostolic tour.

Gather themselves together. Or passively, as Erasmus, Beza, Bretschneider, Grimm, give it, *are gathered together*. Luther however, and Tyndale, and Bengel, give the middle acceptation, as in our English version. The two meanings are coincident.

Unto Jesus. Whose movements in the interval are not indicated by Mark. But see John v. 1–47.

And they reported to Him all whatsoever they did and whatsoever they taught. In the Received Text there is a conjunction after *all: and they reported to Him all,* '*both*' *whatsoever* (καὶ ὅσα) *they did, and whatsoever* (καὶ ὅσα) *they taught.* But it is not found in the best manuscripts, or in the best old versions. The returned apostles went into full details of their whole procedure.

VER. 31. **And He says to them**—in a spirit of fine human sympathy—**Come ye yourselves apart into a desert place, and rest yourselves a little.** *Ye yourselves*, that is, *ye by yourselves*. Erasmus renders the phrase *ye alone* ('vos soli'). *Apart:* or *privately*, as the expression is rendered in Matt. xxiv. 3; Mark ix. 28, xiii. 3; Luke ix. 10, x. 23; Acts xxiii. 19; Gal. ii. 2. It is Beza's rendering (*privatim*). *Into a desert place:* there were many such places in the neighbourhood of the lake of Gennesaret, more especially on its eastern side, places not only uninhabited but uncultivated, in consequence of the predominance of bare rock. *And rest yourselves a little:* that is, *a little while*.

For they who were coming and going were many. There was a constant stream of visitors arriving and departing.

And they had not sufficient leisure even to eat. The very times for their meals were constantly intruded on by the never-ceasing influx of individuals and groups, who were eager to hear the great Rabbi, or to witness His wonder-working. The proximity of the greatest of the festivals that were celebrated at Jerusalem would give occasion for a large increase of visitors. See John vi. 4..

VER. 32. **And they departed to a desert place by the boat privately.** 'By *the* boat,' which was at our Saviour's disposal, and which He generally employed. (See chap. iv. 36.) The desert place for which they set out was, as we learn

33 And the people saw them departing, and many knew him, and ran afoot thither out of all cities, and outwent them,

from Luke ix. 10, near 'a city called Bethsaida.' Reland conjectured that there must have been two towns of this name (*Fish-town*), one in Galilee proper, in the tetrarchy of Herod Antipas, and the other in Gaulonitis, in the tetrarchy of Philip. (*Palæstina*, pp. 654-5.) One of the towns would be *Bethsa da of Galilee* (John xii. 21), the city of Peter and Andrew and Philip (John i. 44); the other was on the east side of the Jordan above its embouchure into the lake (Josephus, *War*, iii. 10 : 7). It was increased and adorned by the tetrarch Philip, and called Julias in honour of the emperor's daughter (Josephus, *Ant.*, xviii. 2 : 1). It would no doubt be to some secluded spot in the vicinity of this eastern Bethsaida, in the tetrarchy of Philip, that our Lord retired with His disciples. There is reference to the other Bethsaida in ver. 45. Baur (p. 51) and Ewald however suppose that the place referred to must have been the Galilean Bethsaida on the western side of the lake, or near to Capernaum. Unlikely.

VER. 33. **And many saw them departing and knew them.** Notwithstanding the Saviour's desire to get off *privately*, by night perchance, many had been hovering about, and noticed their departure, and, though it was dusk, identified them. Instead of *knew them* (αὐτούς) it is *knew Him* (αὐτόν) in the Received Text, and in E F G H S V Γ. But it is *them* in ℵ A K L M U Δ II, and 33 ' the queen of the cursives,' as also in the Syriac versions, and the Coptic, and Æthiopic. This *them* is received into the text by Tischendorf in his eighth edition. Rightly, Griesbach, Lachmann, Tregelles, Alford, omit both *them* and *him* on the authority of the Vatican and Cambridge manuscripts (B D), and the fine cursive manuscript of Basle (1). If it should be the case that the *them* was really omitted in the original text, it is needful, at all events, to supply it mentally.

And on foot from all the cities they ran together thither (καὶ πεζῇ ἀπὸ πασῶν τῶν πόλεων συνέδραμον ἐκεῖ), that is, *and 'people' on foot from all the cities ran together in the direction that was taken by the boat* in which our Saviour and His disciples were. The reference is not exclusively to those who saw the disciples setting off. (Comp. Matt. xiv. 13.) They are artlessly merged, so far as the evangelist's narrative is concerned, in the greater multitudes who were influenced by their report. The body of the people would probably set out early in the morning, before sunrise, according to the oriental custom. They were *on foot*, or *afote* as Tyndale has it, not *in boats*. They ran *together*, or as the Rheims has it felicitously, *they ranne flocking.*

And outwent them. Or, as Wycliffe has it, *and came bifore hem* (i.e. *before them*), viz. to the place of destination. The Rheims version has the fine old word *prevented*, in its primitive old fashioned acceptation, *and prevented them.*

VER. 34-44, the paragraph to which ver. 30-33 are introductory. It contains a simple but graphic account of the miraculous feeding of five thousand persons in a desert place. Comp. Matt. xiv. 14-21 ; Luke ix. 11-17 ; John vi. 5-13.

ST. MARK VI.

and came together unto him. 34 And Jesus, when he came out, saw much people, and was moved with compassion toward them, because they were as sheep not having a shepherd: and he began to teach them many things. 35 And when the day was now far spent, his disciples came unto him, and said, This is a desert place, and now the time *is* far passed: 36 send them

VER. 34. **And when He came forth, He saw a great crowd.** Such is the reading in Griesbach, Tischendorf, Tregelles, Alford, without the word *Jesus*. *When He came forth:* even before He disembarked, the moment that He emerged from the little cabin, in which, as we may presume, He had been snatching some repose (comp. chap. iv. 38), He would witness the collected crowd. Most probably the vessel would lie at rest a considerable time on the still waters, to allow of repose.

And was moved with compassion toward them. A fine translation of the original expression (ἐσπλαγχνίσθη ἐπ' αὐτούς), as is also Purvey's, though archaic, *and hadde reuth on hem.* All that was 'within' our Lord was tenderly agitated 'over' the people. (See Buttig's admirable monograph on the word, *De Emphasi σπλαγχνίζομαι.*)

Because they were as sheep not having a shepherd. A very sad case in a land of only partial pasturage, and utterly unenclosed, running off too at many a point into defiles and gorges, which are the natural haunts and dens of wild beasts.

And He began to teach them many things. Instead of taking the rest for which He had longed, and which was so desirable at once for Himself and His disciples, He *began* to teach the people; and having begun, He was drawn on, and still on, until the day was far advanced.

VER. 35. **And when the day was now far spent.** A fine free idiomatic translation, obtained from Tyndale. Wycliffe's version is very literal, *and whanne moche our* (i.e. *much hour*) *was maad now,* that is, *and now when it was become late.* It becomes late in the day, when *much hour,* or *much time,* has come to pass. In the reading of the Sinaitic and Cambridge manuscripts (א D), a reading adopted by Tischendorf in his eighth edition, the verb is in the present participle instead of the past (γινομένης, not γενομένης), *and now when it is becoming late.*

His disciples approached Him, and said, **The place is desert.** And hence there would be no hamlets dotting it, in which the multitudes could get provisions for themselves. The farmers and workers did not, as a rule, live in detached houses, but clustered together in larger or smaller villages.

And now the time is far spent. Or literally, '*and now much hour,*' that is, *and now it is much hour, it is late.* The Romans had an idiom corresponding to that of the Greeks; they spoke of *much day* (*multo die*), when they meant to intimate that it was late. The disciples very properly and correctly took note of the facts of the place and of the time. But what then?

VER. 36. **Dismiss them.** But why obtrude ultroneously such a counsel? It was officiousness, well meant indeed, but not well weighed.

M

away, that they may go into the country round about, and into the villages, and buy themselves bread: for they have nothing to eat. 37 He answered and said unto them, Give ye them to eat. And they say unto him, Shall we go and buy two hundred pennyworth of bread, and give them to eat?

In order that they may go into the surrounding fields and villages. Wherever they might come upon *fields*, or *cultivated spots*, they would be sure to find a hamlet or hamlets hard by.

And buy for themselves bread, for they have nothing to eat. Or, according to the greatly abbreviated reading that is given by Tregelles, Alford, and Tischendorf in his eighth edition, *And buy for themselves somewhat to eat* (ἀγοράσωσιν ἑαυτοῖς τί φάγωσιν). This short reading approved itself to Mill (*Proleg.*, p. xliii.). It is more likely that the longer reading grew out of the shorter than that the shorter was crumbled down from the longer.

VER. 37. But He answered, and said to them, Give ye them to eat. An injunction that was eminently fitted to allay their officiousness on the one hand, and to quicken their consideration on the other, into an attitude and intensity of thoughtfulness that would fit them for a due appreciation of His intended miracle.

And they say to Him. Perhaps one after another, each echoing his companion's remark. But it was Philip who was the original spokesman. (John vi. 7.)

Should we go and buy two hundred pennyworth of loaves, and give them to eat? (δώσωμεν, the right reading.) Should we hasten to the nearest villages, and get, let us say, two hundred pennyworth of loaves? That quantity, at the very least, would be needed, to admit of every individual receiving a little (John vi. 7). It is *loaves*, or *cakes*, not generically *bread*, that is the evangelist's word. See next verse. The penny that is spoken of was a silver penny, the common Roman silver money, the *denarius*; somewhat equivalent to a shilling in our English money, but not so large. Though not so large, however, it would buy far more among the Jews than we can at present buy with a shilling in Great Britain. The relation between money and commodity continually varies. There was a time when bullion was so scarce, comparatively, in our land that a sheep could be bought for two shillings and sixpence. (See Jacob's *Precious Metals*, chap. xii.) It is needless then to try to estimate the number of loaves that would be obtained for two hundred denarii. Lightfoot mentions that this amount of money, corresponding to two hundred *zuzim* in Hebrew money, or fifty shekels, was a kind of standard sum in relation to large liabilities. And hence he imagines it was not unlikely that it was mentioned indefinitely by the disciples, 'because it was a most celebrated sum, and of very frequent mention in the mouths of all.' (*Exercitations*, in loc.) Grotius, on the other hand, and Hofmeister, and Dr. S. Clarke, and others, assume, with greater verisimilitude, (comp. John vi. 7) that *two hundred denarii or thereby* would be the amount that happened to be on hand in the common purse, 'bourse,' *byrsa*, or 'bag' of the disciples. (See John xii. 6, xiii. 29.) The phrase *two hundred pennyworth of loaves* does not originally and literally mean, as Alexander supposed, *loaves*

38 He saith unto them, How many loaves have ye? go and see. And when they knew, they say, Five, and two fishes. 39 And he commanded them to make all sit down by companies upon the green grass. 40 And they sat down in ranks, by hundreds, and by fifties. 41 And when he had taken the

---

of two hundred denarii. But the whole expression means *should we buy*, '*with*' *two hundred denarii, loaves?* See 1 Cor. vi. 20.

VER. 38. **But He says to them, How many loaves have ye? Go and see.** Or, as Tyndale has it, *Goo and loke.* "Questions," as de Veil remarks, "are not "always signs of ignorance, but are sometimes employed for the benefit and "instruction of those who are interrogated."
And when they knew, they say, Five, and two fishes. They had made no provision for luxurious entertainment in their retirement. *Fishes:* Dried, of course, according to a common custom of the country, and intended to be eaten as *opsonium*, or, as the Scots would express it, as 'kitchen.'

VER. 39. **And He ordered them**—the disciples to wit—**to cause all to recline by companies on the green grass.** Mark alone mentions that the *grass was green.* It is an interesting *autoptic* observation which had been communicated to him by his informant. During a great part of the year there is not such a thing as a blade of *green grass* to be seen on the slopes that ascend from the eastern shores of the sea of Tiberias ; all the grass that remains is browned and scorched. But, as we learn from John, though John alone, it was now spring time, just before the passover festival. (John vi. 4.) The whole district therefore would be richly carpeted with beautifully green grass, except at those spots where the bare rocks protruded. *By companies:* Our word *parties*, in its convivial acceptation, is, as nearly as possible, a reproduction of the original term (συμπόσια συμπόσια). The multitude was to be arranged *in a suite of parties*, no doubt *semicircularly* adjusted, after the form of Roman *triclinia* or Grecian *symposia.* Such a semicircular or 'horseshoe' style of parties had become common among the Jews, being adopted from the Greeks and Romans ; and hence the frequent reference, in the New Testament, to *reclining at meals.*

VER. 40. **And they sat down.** Or rather, *and they reclined.* The verb represents *the act of falling backward* (ἀνέπεσαν). It is translated *leaned back* in John xxi. 20.
In ranks. Like *leek-beds* in a garden (πρασιαὶ πρασιαί). They were symmetrically arranged.
By hundreds and by fifties. This does not mean, as Fritzsche and Meyer suppose, *in companies which were in some cases a hundred in number, and in some cases fifty.* It represents such a symmetrical arrangement of the whole suite of parties, that, viewed in one direction, *in rank*, from end to end of the respective triclinia, there was a succession of semicircular hundreds, in tier beyond tier ; whereas, when viewed laterally, or *in file*, counting off one at a time from each of the semicircles or triclinia, there was a succession of fifties. Viewed from front to back, there were fifty hundreds ; viewed from side to side there

ST. MARK VI.

five loaves and the two fishes, he looked up to heaven, and
blessed, and brake the loaves, and gave *them* to his disciples

---

were a hundred fifties; that is, there were *five thousand guests*. (See ver. 44.)
Wetstein and Wesley understood the arrangement, though probably erring in
reversing the proportions of *rank* and *file*. They counted *fifty by a hundred*,
instead of, as the evangelist, *a hundred by fifty*. Fritzsche and Meyer have
both misunderstood Wetstein, strangely supposing that he made out each company to consist of *a hundred and fifty*. Erasmus Schmid interested himself in
the arithmetical phase of the matter, and has inserted in his New Testament
two large plans of the parties. But he missed the idea of *triclinia*, and accordingly did not bend his hundreds into continuous semicircles, or what was
equivalent, to three sides of a parallelogram or square. Dr. Adam Clarke too
got perplexed in his conception; for, on referring to Mr. Wesley's perspicuous
representation, he says, ' but if they sat fifty *deep*, how could the disciples
conveniently serve them with the bread and fish?' The answer is obvious,
Just because the fifties (or rather the hundreds, for Mr. Wesley reverses the
ratios) were not packed closely together. Each hundred constituted a distinct
party or *triclinium*, and would be separated by a convenient interval from
all the other hundreds. The whole suite of hundreds, however, though thus
conveniently separated from each other, would bend up on the slope semicircularly and overlappingly, one beyond another.

VER. 41. **And having taken the five loaves and the two fishes, He looked up to
heaven and blessed.** *Blessed*, or *gave thanks*. See John vi. 11. He *gave thanks
for the food*, and in that sense *blessed it*. See Luke ix. 16. The English word
bless, like the corresponding Anglo-Saxon word, has got various remarkable
applications. When man *blesses* man, he gives him *bliss* (Ang. Sax. *blis*), or
makes him ' blithe.' In this way too, but reverently understood, does God *bless*
man. But we also speak of *blessing God*, as likewise of *blessing those blessings*
with which *we are blessed by God*. The Greek word is radically different both
from the Hebrew term and the English. It means *to speak well of* (εὐλογέω),
and can thus, wheel-like, be turned round toward any being or thing that has
any point in it of either actual or possible good. Our Saviour, on the present
occasion, would doubtless *speak well of His Father*; and, coincidently, He
would *speak well of the provision*, His Father's device and gift, which He was
about to distribute and increase. He might *speak well* too *in reference to the
people*, petitioning for their weal. He would thus coincidently *bless* the Father,
bless the food, and invoke *blessing* on the people. As He *blessed* He *looked up
to the heaven*; thus, in the outer sphere of things, instinctively representing
the elevation of His thoughts, in their own inner sphere, above the mere
materialisms that were around Him and beneath Him. " In prayer," says
Petter, " we should use such outward gestures as may most fitly serve to express
" the inward disposition and holy affections of our heart and soul."

And brake the loaves. Literally, *and broke down the loaves*, viz. into several
pieces. The Jewish loaves, it should be remembered, were of the form of
cakes.

And gave to the disciples. Viz. the broken pieces.

ST. MARK VI.

to set before them; and the two fishes divided he among them all. 42 And they did all eat, and were filled. 43 And they took up twelve baskets full of the fragments, and of the fishes. 44 And they that did eat of the loaves were about five thousand men.

To set before them. The verb that is here employed by the evangelist was the accredited term used by the Greeks to denote the action of servants in *placing the meat on the table beside the guests* ($\pi\alpha\rho\alpha\tau\iota\theta\eta\mu\iota$).

And the two fishes He portioned out to all. Viz. through the hands of the disciples, as the bread had been. The disciples would in all likelihood pass, in the first instance at least, along the respective termini of the semicircular rows, and hand a portion of food to each individual at the extremities. As the portion was diminished, lo it increased! It would be easy to speculate on the *how*, but difficult to determine it. It would be easy to speculate along different lines of possibility; but it is unnecessary, and would be unprofitable. Let what is divinely veiled in this matter continue veiled; but nothing except what involves a contradiction is 'too hard for the Lord' (Jer. xxxii. 17). He who can produce a forest of oaks from a single acorn, and in one spawn of a codfish can give existence, at one point of time, to a brood of not less than three millions six hundred and eighty-six thousand, seven hundred and sixty units of life, could be at no loss to condense, indefinitely, molecular action in time, and coincidently expand it in space.

VER. 42. **And all ate and were satisfied.** The word properly means *foddered* ($\dot{\epsilon}\chi o\rho\tau\acute{a}\sigma\theta\eta\sigma\alpha\nu$). Purvey has it here *and weren fulfillid*, showing finely the primitive meaning of *fulfilled.* (Comp. Chaucer, 5,079.)

VER. 43. **And they took up of fragments twelve basketfuls.** Very literally, *fillings of twelve baskets.* Wycliffe uses the word *coffins* instead of *baskets.* It is the original term, and is connected with *coffers.* It denoted, as used by the Greeks and Romans, (for they both employed it,) a sort of basket that was commonly used by the Jews. (Comp. Juvenal, iii. 14, vi. 542.)

And of the fishes. This clause is inartificially added to the preceding one; but its meaning is quite obvious. The fragments collected were not only *from the loaves*, but also *from the fishes.*

VER. 44. **And they who ate the loaves.** Such is the simple form of the expression in the original text. In Tyndale's version the expression is simply *they that ate*, for in Erasmus' editions the words *the loaves* were wanting. They were inserted however in the Complutensian New Testament, and thence copied into Stephens's editions, and Beza's, and the Elzevirs. They are wanting however in the Vulgate version, and in ℵ D, and in most copies of the Italic version. Yet they were no doubt in Mark's autograph. Under the outstanding word *loaves* there is of course a silently subtended reference to the *fishes*.

Were five thousand men. Note the word *men.* It is not the generic term, but the specific ($\check{a}\nu\delta\rho\epsilon s$). There were also *women and children* (Matt. xiv. 21); but these, according to oriental custom, would eat *by themselves.* They would be *sitting* apart, not *reclining* like the men. How beneficent, humanizing, civiliz-

45 And straightway he constrained his disciples to get into the ship, and to go to the other side before unto Bethsaida, while he sent away the people. **46** And when he had sent

ing, and literally '*familia*rising,' is that spirit of Christianity, the embodied spirit of the Saviour, which breaks down the middle wall of partition between the sexes by asserting that, in respect of privilege, 'there is neither male nor female.' (**Gal. iii. 28.**)

VER. 45-52. Compare for corresponding paragraphs Matt. xiv. 22-33 and John vi. 15-21.

VER. 45. **And straightway He constrained His disciples to enter into the boat.** They appear to have been loath to go without their Master. A gentle but decisive *constraint* was required, ere they would consent.

And to be going on before to the other side toward Bethsaida. That is, toward the Galilean Bethsaida. (See on ver. 32.) Lange and Klostermann strangely suppose the reference to be to the eastern Bethsaida. John says that they went 'toward Capernaum' (vi. 17), so that we should infer that the Galilean Bethsaida and Capernaum lay in one direction, as viewed from the point of departure at the north-east of the lake. The site of Bethsaida is not yet absolutely determined; but Dr. Robinson, after long uncertainty, fixed on *et-Tabighah* as the probable spot. (*Later Researches*, pp. 358-9.) Dr. Porter acquiesces in this decision. "No site," he says, "along the shore is so well adapted for a "fishing town. Here is a bay sheltered by hills behind, and projecting bluffs "on each side; and here is a smooth sandy beach, such as fishermen delight "in. The strand forms a pleasant promenade, and so far answers to the de- "scription in Matt. iv. 18-22." (*Syria*, p. 405.) "The beautiful white beach "of Bethsaida," says Mr. Macgregor, "is gracefully bent round its pretty little "cove in a gentle slope of gravel, shells, and purest sand. . . . The bay is "admirably suited for boats; it shelves gradually. The anchorage is good, "and boats can be safely beached. Rocks project at the south-west end about "fifty yards beyond those seen above water. These would form a good protec- "tion to the harbour. There appears to be no jetty. The water is deep, and "nearly free from boulders until near the south-west end." (*Rob Roy*, p. 351.) St. Willibald, who visited the Holy Land about the middle of the eighth century, found Bethsaida still in existence, just a little north of Capernaum. There was a church in it. A little farther north he found Chorazin. (*Vita*, §§ 16, 17.)

While He Himself dismisses the crowd. He simply assured His disciples that He would meet them on their way to Capernaum. They might imagine that He might either walk round by the shore, and hail them as they coasted along westward; or that He might join them, more rapidly and directly, by means of a '*little*' boat. (See John vi. 22, Gr., and also *Rob Roy on the Jordan*, p. 255.)

VER. 46. **And when He had sent them away.** The translation in King James's version, but rather too free, though exactly reproducing the Vulgate version. The original expression bore upon it a stamp of politeness, and had got, by the evangelist's time, to be technical and idiomatic. It means not so much *when He had dismissed them*, or *given them their leave*, as *when He had*

ST. MARK VI.

them away, he departed into a mountain to pray.
47 And when even was come, the ship was in the midst
of the sea, and he alone on the land. 48 And he saw
them toiling in rowing; for the wind was contrary unto them:
and about the fourth watch of the night he cometh unto

taken leave of them. Such is the translation that it receives in Acts xviii. 18 and 2 Cor. ii. 13. It is translated *to bid farewell* in Luke ix. 61. Phrynichus pronounces the phrase unclassical. Be it so; yet it got to be quite common in the Alexandrian style of writing, and is used by both Philo and Josephus. (See Krebs and Kypke on Luke ix. 60.) The reference of the pronoun *them* is evidently to *the people*, not to *the disciples*, as Beza supposed.

He departed into the mountain. The adjoining high land, at the sloping base of which the multitude had been fed. The whole district is mountainous. "On the east of the lake of Tiberias," says Dr. Porter, "the banks are nearly "two thousand feet high, destitute of verdure and of foliage, furrowed by "ravines, but flat along the summit, from which the plain of Bashan extends "eastward." (*Syria*, p. 394.)

To pray. It is the fine generic term that is employed ($\pi\rho o\sigma\epsilon\acute{u}\xi a\sigma\theta a\iota$), not the specific term that is used in John xvii. 9, 15, 20, and which properly means *to ask* ($\dot{\epsilon}\rho\omega\tau\acute{a}\omega$). The Saviour would no doubt *ask* as He *prayed*; but He did more; *He addressed Himself in a generic way to His Father.* He opened up heavenward His spirit, and let all that was within Him ascend, in a stream of inwardly articulated aspiration, to His Father.

VER. 47. **And when evening was come.** The *late evening*, that extended from sundown onward.

The boat was in the midst of the sea, and He alone upon the land. A wind had sprung up that was blowing them from the coast. This continued for hours, the wind increasing. See next verse.

VER. 48. **And as He saw** ($i\delta\acute{\omega}\nu$) **them toiling in rowing.** *Toiling* is a feeble word to express the force of the original term ($\beta a\sigma a\nu\iota\zeta o\mu\acute{\epsilon}\nu o\nu s$). Archbishop Newcome hit on a better term, *distressed.* Alford has adopted it, and the Revisers. The Greek word properly means *tormented.* The expression, freely rendered *in rowing*, literally means *in the driving*, that is, *in the propelling*, viz. of the boat by rowing. The disciples had to make violent and distressing efforts to keep the boat from drifting before the hurricane, and being dashed to pieces on the opposite shore.

For the wind was contrary to them. Blowing therefore from the north-west.

About the fourth watch of the night. That is, as Lightfoot remarks, 'after cock crowing.' The Jews, like many other peoples, divided the night into *watches*, or those portions of time that were occupied by relays of sentinels. These *watches*, according to the native Jewish division, were three. But the Roman custom was to have four; and to this custom, which would naturally attach itself to the military establishment of the Herods (Acts xii. 4), the later Jews conformed themselves. Hence the reference here to *the fourth watch*. It is quite arbitrary in Ewald, and quite uncalled for, to render the expression here 'about the *third* night-watch' (*um die dritte nachtwache*). The fourth watch

them, walking upon the sea, and would have passed by them.

extended from 'cock crowing' till sunrise, that is, from about three a.m. to about six a.m , just as the third watch extended from midnight half-way to sunrise, that is, to about three a.m. The first and second watches divided the time from sunset to midnight.

He cometh to them, walking upon the sea. Which would be just as easy to Him as to walk anywhere else, if indeed *He and the Father* were *One.* The 'progress' of Divinity, within His own dominions, cannot be confined to humanly constructed roads or solid ground. *Upon the sea :* Koppe, while lecturing on one occasion extemporaneously, as Lavater records, threw out the wild idea that this expression might mean *on the shore !* The shore forsooth being higher than the sea, our Saviour, when walking on it, might be truthfully represented as walking *above the sea !* (Compare the French expression *Boulogne sur mer.*) Next morning Koppe wisely withdrew his grotesque conjecture. But the great apostle of 'rationalism,' H. E. Gottlob Paulus, reinvented the interpretation in 1794, and thenceforward earnestly and learnedly contended for it, as one of his happiest achievements in the way of eliminating everything supernatural from the Gospels! The daringness of the exegesis, as well as the ridiculousness of the little-mouse-of-idea that came forth from it, roused into activity several able pens, but none so effective and trenchant as that of the celebrated J. K. Lavater, who at once denounced the interpretation as silly (*dumm*) and shameless (*frech*). How is it possible, he asks, that three evangelists should record the Lord's walking and its accompaniments as something marvellous, at which the disciples were 'sore amazed in themselves beyond measure,' if the whole matter just amounted to this, *that the Saviour actually went, and was actually able to go, on the solid ground !* The exposition proposed he designated 'philological legerdemain' (*philologische Taschenspielerei*). It is, he says, 'a laughable insult on logic, hermeneutics, good sense, and honesty.' (*H. E. Gottlob Paulus und seine Zeit*, Band i., pp. 268-308.) J. A. Bolten's notion is nearly as ridiculous as that of Paulus, and in some respects still more revolting. He translates the expression thus, *He came to them* '*swimming*' *!* Such feats of exegesis almost amount to a transference of miracles; the wonders are eliminated indeed from the Saviour's life; but they are thrust into the phraseology of His biography, under the transformed shape of prodigies of philological manœuvre.

And would have passed by them. Literally, *and wished to go past them.* Fritzsche thinks that the idea is that *He wished to finish the feat of crossing the entire sea on foot,* and was only drawn aside from His purpose by the agitation of His disciples. Surely too theatrical a notion. Ewald contends that the phrase must mean, *and wished to go over* '*to*' *them*, *to go over the water in order to reach them.* Norton had had the same idea. His translation is, *and wished to join them.* It is a violent philological strain ; and brings out moreover, when the preceding clause is considered, a redundancy of idea. Lange's notion is that the disciples were rowing in the wrong direction, easterly, and that the Saviour *wished to go on before them to show them the right way*, westerly. But the evangelist gives no hint to the effect that the disciples were on a wrong tack. Bishop Wordsworth thinks that 'here is a silent note of *inspiration*'; 'for who

49 But when they saw him walking upon the sea, they supposed it had been a spirit, and cried out: 50 for they all saw him, and were troubled. And immediately he talked with them, and saith unto them, Be of good cheer: it is I; be not afraid.

---

knoweth the *mind* of Christ but the Spirit of God?' But what if the evangelist is just describing *the appearance of things*? Jesus, instead of coming all at once directly to the disciples, comes near them indeed, but holds on His way as if He wished to go past them. 'He made as though He would have gone further' (Luke xxiv. 28; comp. Gen. xviii. 3). Did He really then wish to leave them behind, struggling in the storm? We need not suppose it; we cannot for a moment suppose it. But His real wish, nevertheless, would be a complex thing. He would wish His disciples to recognise Him. He would wish them to understand distinctly what He was doing, and what He had done, and what it was in His power to do. He would wish to pass onward by their side, and in their view, till it should be the very best moment to turn and give them relief. (Comp. Gen. xxxii. 26.) If that moment should not occur till He had Himself reached the shore, He would have held on His way. There was no duplicity. There was merely, as infinitely became Him, a complexity of desires, founded on a complexity of contingencies. 'In the nature of the thing,' as Jeremy Taylor remarks, 'it is proper and natural, by an offer, to give an occasion to another to do a good action.' (*Christian Simplicity:* Works, vi., 156.)

VER. 49. **But they, when they saw Him walking on the sea, thought, It is a spectre.** Such is the literal version of the original reading, as preserved in the manuscripts אּ B L Δ, and 'the queen of the cursives' (ὅτι φάντασμά ἐστιν). The object of the thought of the disciples is presented in the direct form of speech, just as it would start up in their minds and leap out from their lips. *A spectre:* the proper meaning of the word; or *apparition*, the word of Mace, Principal Campbell, and the Revisers. Wycliffe's version is, *a fantum*; the Rheims, *a ghost*.
And they cried out. In fright. They shrieked.

VER. 50. **For all saw Him, and were troubled.** They were *agitated* and *confused*. But *troubled* is the best translation.
But He immediately talked with them. When He saw them so agitated, and perceived that they misunderstood the case, He at once *entered into communication 'with them'* by word of mouth.
And says to them, Have courage! It is I; fear not. It was thus that He began to *talk*, soothingly and inspiritingly.

VER. 51. Mark passes over in silence the incident of Peter's petition, and the consequences that ensued. (See Matt. xiv. 28-31.) Why this silence? We cannot tell; we can only guess; and guessing in such a case is of little avail. Hilgenfeld sees in the *suppression* of the incident an incident not entirely creditable in some respects to Peter, a proof of the *Petrinism* of Mark's Gospel. (*Die Evangelien*, pp. 136, 137.) D'Eichthal sees no evidence of *suppression* at all, but supposes, on the other h nd, t at in Matthew we have a new sprouting and later growth of the older myth as given in Mark. The same is the opinion of

51 And he went up unto them into the ship; and the wind
ceased: and they were sore amazed in themselves beyond

Scholten (*Het oudste Ev.*, p. 297) and Meyer. But it is of course a mere opinion.
There may be a thread of truth in Hilgenfeld's notion. It is quite possible that
something of the nature of reverence for the chief of the original apostolate
may have inclined the evangelist, since he was condensing at any rate, to stride
rapidly onward to the conclusion of this section of his narrative. The private
peculiarities, in thought and feeling, of the respective writers of the Gospels were
not ignored, and still less obliterated, by the inspiring Spirit, but respected and
wielded, when not inconsistent with the great end divinely contemplated, *the
faithful exhibition of the wonderful personality of our Saviour in His manifold
relationships to the manifold wants of men.*

And He went up unto them into the boat. The expression implies that the
boat was of some magnitude, comparatively speaking, and standing considerably
out of the water. At the stern especially it would be elevated, according to the
ancient style of naval architecture. The little cabin would be there. The term
employed in John vi. 21 is the same; whereas the term that is employed in the
two following verses of John's narrative is different, meaning *a little boat*, or
yawl. Possibly the disciples used a little boat by which to get into their larger
boat. (See on ver. 45.)

And the wind ceased. It *fell*, as if thoroughly *exhausted*. Such is the
graphic idea suggested by the evangelist's expression ($\dot{\epsilon}\kappa\acute{o}\pi\alpha\sigma\epsilon\nu$). It was just,
it would appear, as the Lord stepped on board (Matt. xiv. 32), that the blast sub-
sided. He who is the Lord of all the elements willed it. When the wind blows,
or ceases to blow, it is, when we go to the ultimates of things, at His behest.
When any movement great or small in things material takes place, we must, if
we would understand the case, go 'back of' what is visible and tangible. We
could not otherwise get to the Cause of causes. Mind is behind matter; if it
were not, matter could not be, for *scientific principles are wrought out* in all its
elements and interrelations. ' *Thou* didst blow with *Thy* wind,' says Moses, on
the one hand, *to* God (Exod. xv. 10). ' *He* maketh the storm a calm,' sang the
psalmist, on the other, *of* God (Ps. cvii. 29).

And they were exceedingly beyond measure amazed in themselves. Note the
cumulative expression, *exceedingly beyond measure*. Not only was the amazement *beyond measure*, it went *exceedingly* beyond it. Our English word *sore*,
used in our English version (Scottice *sair*), is just the German *sehr*, = *very* or
much. The word rendered *amazed* ($\dot{\epsilon}\xi\acute{\iota}\sigma\tau\alpha\nu\tau o$) is in itself exceedingly strong.
Its cognate noun is ' *ecstasy*.' The disciples started out of themselves as it were,
and then *stood out of themselves!* That is the graphic idea. We sometimes
speak in English of a person being *out of himself* for joy. The disciples were
out of themselves with wonder. And yet it is added by the evangelist, *in themselves*. The expression seems to indicate that the amazement was inwardly felt
still more than outwardly expressed. It did not get vent, to any remarkable
degree, in outward exclamations.

And wondered. This expression is still further cumulative, though, when
viewed rhetorically, it does not exalt or crown the representation. It seems, on
the contrary, to be somewhat tame. It is omitted altogether in the Sinaitic and

ST. MARK VI.

measure, and wondered. 52 For they considered not the *miracle* of the loaves : for their heart was hardened.

Vatican manuscripts (א B), as also in L Δ and 1, and in the Vulgate version and the Coptic. It has been left out of the text by Tregelles, Alford, and Tischendorf (in his eighth edition). It was suspected by Griesbach. It was condemned by Mill (*Prol.*, § 403). It is omitted by the English Revisionists. Even Beza suspected it; and Erasmus before him. We have no doubt however that it is genuine. The very fact that it appears to be, when rhetorically considered, a somewhat ' lame and impotent conclusion,' militates strongly against the likelihood of its insertion by a transcriber. And the same fact accounts for its silent omission in the case of that small number of transcribers who have left it out. It would seem to them, not unnaturally, to be a redundancy, and a redundancy in which the representation dropped off flat. There is however no real redundancy, or tameness, or lameness. Not only were the disciples suddenly struck with amazement. After that sudden 'ecstasy' was past (ἐξίσταντο), they *continued more collectedly and thoughtfully in a wondering mood* (ἐθαύμαζον, imp.).

VER. 52. **For.** The evangelist explains why it was that the disciples were confounded and astonished.

They understood not by means of the loaves. The primary import of the Greek word *understand is to send together*. He who sends out his mind to an object, so as to bring together both the subject and the object of thought, *understands*. He who does not thus send out his mind, that a union of subject and object may be effected, *does not understand*. The disciples *did not understand*. The whole expression, if very literally rendered, would be, *for they did not understand* ' upon ' *the loaves*. It is *condensed* phraseology. The meaning is, *they did not take their stand* ' upon ' *the miracle of the loaves, so as to see things in their true light, as they might have done and should have done*. They did not reason, as they should have done, *by means of the loaves*, or *on the ground of the loaves*. If they had taken their standpoint of survey ' upon ' the miracle of the loaves, they would have *understood*, and not merely have *wondered* that the Saviour should have walked on the waters, and tamed the storm by a simple act of quiet volition. They would have seen that nothing was more natural than that He, who rules absolutely within the spheres of the earth's flora and fauna, and their products (such as *loaves* and *dried fish*), should also rule absolutely within the spheres of the inorganic elements of wind and water.

But their heart was hardened. In the Received Text, and hence in King James's version, the conjunction is *for* (γάρ) and not *but* (ἀλλ'). It is *but* however in both the Sinaitic and the Vatican manuscripts (א B), as also in 'the queen of the cursives ' (33), and L S Δ. This reading is supported by the Coptic version, and the margin of the Philoxenian Syriac. It has been received into the text by Tregelles and Tischendorf. Rightly. It is the more difficult reading, and yet opens up a deeper vein of thought. The evangelist is not giving a reason why the disciples did not understand. He had already subindicated the reason, *they did not take their stand* ' upon ' *the miracle of the loaves*. He is giving, *on the positive side,* a description of that state of mind which, in the preceding

53 And when they had passed over, they came into the land
of Gennesaret, and drew to the shore. 54 And when they

clause, he had characterized *on its negative side*. *Their heart:* that is, *their
mind*, viewed in its intellectual constituents. There is no reference here to the
emotional element of our nature. The reference, as Alexander remarks, is to
'sluggishness and obtuseness of intellect,' not to 'callous feeling or insensible
affection.' (See chap. viii. 17.) The word is used in its accredited biblical
sense, as denoting *the interior and central part of our being*, that is, *the spiritual
or mental part*, that part which is, as Carus expresses it, *the seat of consciousness
(Psychologie der Hebräer*, p. 283). *Was hardened :* was in a *callous* condition,
intellectually insusceptive, and thus intellectually irresponsive to the appeals
which were addressed to it by the wonder working of the Lord.

VER. 53. **And when they had crossed over they came into the land of Gennesaret.** Or, according to the reading of the Sinaitic and Vatican manuscripts
(א B), and 'the queen of the cursives' (33), a reading accepted by Tischendorf
and supported by L Δ, *and when they crossed over to the land, they came to Gennesaret* (διαπεράσαντες ἐπὶ τὴν γῆν ἦλθον εἰς Γεννησαρέτ). The expression *when
they crossed over to the land* is another instance of condensed phraseology, a
specimen of 'much in little.' The meaning is, *when they came 'upon' the land,
having finished their 'passage across the lake.'* When this took place they
found themselves at some point or other of Gennesaret, that fine rich level tract
of country which was the principal theatre of our Lord's public career on earth,
and in which Capernaum and Bethsaida were situated. Josephus calls it
Gennesar, and so does the Syriac Peshito version in the passage before us, as
also the fine old Cambridge manuscript (D). It is, says Josephus, about thirty
furlongs in length, and twenty in breadth (*War*, iii. 10: 8). " Its nature is
" wonderful," he says, " as well as its beauty. It soil is so fruitful that all sorts
" of trees can grow upon it; and the inhabitants accordingly plant on it all
" kinds. The temperature of the air is so well mixed, that it agrees with the
" different kinds. Walnuts, which require cold air, flourish there in the greatest
" abundance ; palm trees also, which grow best in heat ; fig trees likewise, and
" olives, which require an air that is more temperate. One may call this place
" the Ambition of nature, where it constrains those plants which are naturally
" enemies to one another to agree together. It is a happy strife of the seasons,
" as if every one of them laid claim to this country, for it not only nourishes
" different sorts of autumnal fruit beyond men's expectation, it preserves them
" a great while. It supplies men with the principal fruits, with grapes and figs,
" continually during ten months of the year, and the rest of the fruits, as they
" become ripe together, through the whole year." Such is Josephus's description of Gennesar, to which our Lord and His disciples returned from the east.

And moored their vessel (προσωρμίσθησαν). It is left uncertain, so far as the
word is concerned, whether the mooring was effected by dropping the anchor
in the roadstead, or by being chained to the landing place. The noun from
which the word is derived (ὅρμος) denotes primarily *a chain*, and then an
anchorage.

VER. 54. **And when they were come out of the boat, straightway they knew**

were come out of the ship, straightway they knew him, 55 and ran through that whole region round about, and began to carry about in beds those that were sick, where they heard he was. 56 And whithersoever he entered, into villages, or cities, or country, they laid the sick in the streets, and

Him. The people of the locality immediately identified Him. This might be the case even though they had never seen Him before. The Rheims version is, 'incontinent they knew Him.' He was now the Cynosure of all eyes.

VER. 55. **And ran about the whole of that region.** Informing the people at large of the arrival of the wonderful Healer.

And they began to carry about on their beds those who were unwell, wherever they heard that He was. The people of the district, when informed of the arrival of the great Healer, began immediately to trace His steps, carrying with them from place to place, in their pursuit, the invalids whom they wished Him to benefit. As to the kind of *beds* referred to, see on chap. ii. 4. Fritzsche is scandalized by the expression *carry about*, and is sure that the evangelist must have used a different term ($\pi\rho\sigma\phi\epsilon\rho\epsilon\iota\nu$). He simply failed to realize the scene depicted. There was nothing 'spectacular' intended. The expression *wherever they heard that He was* is simple, graphic, and quaint in the original; *wherever they heard, He is there.* The report heard is given in the direct form, and the local *there* may have been determined by pointing with the finger, or by previous naming. In the texts however of both Lachmann and Tischendorf, the *there* is omitted, on the authority of ℵ B L Δ, and the Syriac Peshito, Gothic, and Æthiopic versions. The phrase thus reads *wherever they heard (that) He is*. The *there* must be mentally supplied; and hence apparently its early insertion in the margin, and thence in the text.

VER. 56. **And wheresoever He entered, into villages, or into towns, or into fields.** The preposition is repeated in the Sinaitic, Vatican, and Cambridge manuscripts, and is inserted by Tischendorf in his eighth edition. Rightly. *Wheresoever:* in and around Gennesaret. The evangelist is now widening his reference. *Into fields:* where agriculture was going on, and where consequently people were to be found in numbers.

They laid the sick in the market-places ($\dot{a}\gamma o\rho a\hat{i}s$). *Market-places* is the only right rendering. Coverdale gave it, led by the hand of Luther (*auf den Markt*). The *market-places* of the East were sometimes inside the towns, and sometimes outside; but they were always the chief places of resort. They 'were equivalent,' says Webster-and-Wilkinson, 'to our village greens.' St. Mark speaks as if there were market-places in *fields*, as well as in the *towns* and *villages*. But no doubt he intended his expression to be applied only to the *towns* and *villages* of which he had spoken. And as regards the *fields*, the sick would be laid there in places corresponding to the market-places in towns and villages. They would be laid, that is to say, in *the most convenient places*, the places perhaps where the workers assembled under some friendly shade at the time of the midday siesta. The evangelist's form of speech is a kind of *zeugma*.

besought him that they might touch if it were but the border of his garment: and as many as touched him were made whole.

CHAPTER VII.

1 THEN came together unto him the Pharisees, and certain

And entreated Him that they might touch, if it were but the border of His robe. The *that* refers to the aim of the entreaties presented (ἵνα). They *entreated Him* '*in order that*' *the sick people might touch*. The word which we have translated *robe* denotes the outer garment, that was worn over the tunic. The term rendered *border* (κράσπεδον) is supposed by some to mean *tassel*; but it is likely that it just means *edge, border, fringe* or *hem*. (See on Matt. ix. 20 and xxiii. 5.)

And as many as touched Him were made whole. They were *physically saved* (ἐσώζοντο); they became *sound in health*. In the margin the pronoun *him* is rendered *it*, as if the reference might be to the *garment* or its *border*. So it might, so far as the pronoun is concerned. Our translators gave the alternative, following in the wake of Beza; le Clerc, in his French version, accepts the alternative (*qui la touchoient*). But almost all other translators and expositors suppose that the evangelist's mind was looking to the Saviour Himself, although he required to look *through the drapery* of the representation of the preceding clause. Correctly, no doubt. In whatever way the sick people got touching our Lord, there was virtue for all of them who were recipient.

CHAPTER VII.

IN ver. 1–16 we have an account (1) of the way in which our Lord was malevolently assailed by the Pharisees and scribes, on account of His disciples' neglect of a customary ceremonial usage; and (2) of the remarkably firm, faithful, and home-thrusting manner in which He met and repelled the assault. A parallel paragraph is found in Matt. xv. 1–11.

VER. 1. **And.** *And:* in using so very frequently the simplest of all conjunctions, St. Mark shows how thoroughly the constructive part of his phraseology was moulded on primitive Hebraistic simplicity.

There are gathered together to Him. But certainly it is not meant that it was by any external compulsion that they were collected. They were self moved. Neither is Lange's idea to be entertained, that they came together 'in synagogue form,' as a formal court of inquisition (*in Synagogenform zur Rüge*). Still less is there any likelihood in the very different idea of Michaelis that the persons referred to *put up at the residence of Jesus as His guests* (kehreten bey ihm ein).

The Pharisees. The evangelist uses the article artlessly; he does not mean of course that *the Pharisees in a body* came. He really means that *certain Pharisees* came (see Matt. xv. 1), though he did not intend his article to convey the idea expressed by our word *certain* or *some*; neither did he intend it to be used *indefinitely*. He was simply thinking of '*the*' *Pharisees* as distinguished from

ST. MARK VII.

of the scribes, which came from Jerusalem. 2 And when they saw some of his disciples eat bread with defiled, that is to say,

other classes of society. It was some of '*the*' *remarkably self assuming, self, righteous class of people* who gathered together ' to ' our Lord.

And some of the scribes. There had been a smaller proportion of these, and hence the selective expression *some of*. It is not meant that the *scribes* were not Pharisees; but they were a specific and limited fraternity or guild, and hence they are distinguished from the generic class to which they belonged. (See chap. i. 22.)

Who came from Jerusalem. The authorities in the capital city had got concerned about the influence of the remarkable Galilean Rabbi, and seem to have thought it high time to take some cognisance of His proceedings and doctrines. And hence some commissioners were delegated, either formally by the sanhedrim, or at the instance of some of the high officials, or it might be only of some of the officious, to go down to Galilee and make inquisition. They would have no doubt in their nature the true scent of inquisitors. They would be chosen because of their adaptation for the ignoble employment. They would be sleek, sanctimonious, sly, secretive, and splendid splitters of hairs. Cunning men and able, we may presume, but remorseless withal, and unprincipled. They knew not, however, with whom they had to do.

VER. 2. **And saw.** In King James's version we read, *and when they saw*. It is better however to regard the clause as a simple continuative addition to the last clause of the preceding verse; thus, *who came from Jerusalem, and saw*. It is in vain to seek in Mark, or to force upon his artless composition, precise rhetorical construction. Mill puts a full point at the close of ver. 1. So did Beza; so do Wetstein, Matthæi, Griesbach, Scholz, Fritzsche, Lachmann, Tischendorf. Meyer did so too in his 1829 edition of the text, but he threw it out in the second edition of his Commentary (in 1846), and adhered thenceforward to the simple continuative construction; Bengel too has merely a comma at the close of ver. 1; so has Erasmus in his various editions of the text (though not of his translation).

Some of His disciples eat. The expression in the original is, *that they eat* (ὅτι ἐσθίουσιν). It is not, as the Greek scholar will notice, *that they ate*. The verb *they eat* is given, as it were, in the direct form of report, as presenting immediately the object seen. *They saw some of His disciples.* Well, what is it that they saw about them? This to wit : *they eat*. (Comp. chap. vi. 55, last clause.)

Bread. The expression in the original is very primitive, *the loaves*, that is, *the cakes*, those namely that were lying before them.

With defiled hands. Perhaps a strong enough translation. The word is *common* in the margin, and that is the proper and distinctive meaning of the evangelist's term (κοιναῖς). Comp. Acts ii. 44, iv. 32; Tit. i. 4; Jude 3. In the Geneva version the word in the text is *common*, but the alternative word in the margin is *filthie*, a far more objectionable term than that implied in the text of our Authorized version. Our translators would be influenced by Beza, who has *polluted* in his translation, and vindicates it in his *Annotations*. Erasmus

with unwashen, hands, they found fault. 3 For the Pharisees,

---

has *common*; so had the Vulgate; so have Wycliffe, Tyndale, Coverdale, and the Rheims. The Gothic version has *c mmon* (*namainjaim*), but the Anglo-Saxon *defiled* (*besmitenum*). The disciples' hands were as men's hands *commonly* were. The hands of all heathens, however cleansed, were in the condition objected to on the part of the Pharisees. They could never be anything else than *common*, unless the persons who owned them became proselytes to Judaism. Michaelis's translation conveys admirably the idea of the original, *with unholy hands*. Wakefield gives the same translation; Mace's version corresponds, *with profane hands*. Kypke pleads for the word *profane*; it is admirable when taken in its original import. The expression does not in the least degree intimate that there was any *physical impurity* attaching to the disciples' hands.

That is to say, unwashed. The evangelist explains what the Pharisees meant (see ver. 5) by the expression *common* or *unholy*, as applied to the hands. *Unwashed*, that is, *ceremonially unwashed*; for, according to the Pharisees' doctrine, it was necessary to perform, before eating, the ceremonial lustration, although the hands should be perfectly clean in a physical point of view. It was not physical cleanliness which they esteemed; it was not physical uncleanliness which they reprehended and denounced.

VER. 3. The evangelist interrupts the continuity of his narrative by introducing a historical note in reference to the ceremonial customs of the Pharisees and the Jews in general. The note is really parenthetical, though not formally so; and hence it is unnecessary to throw ver. 3 and 4, as Lachmann and Tregelles have done, within the forms of a parenthesis. The introductory phrase of ver. 5 is *not* intended to dovetail into the construction of ver. 2; it starts a new detail; the language is aggregative; thing is added with simplicity to thing.

For the Pharisees, and all the Jews. The Pharisees in particular, and all the Jews in general. In the matter about to be specified all classes of Jewish society were in accord, Sadducees included. But the Pharisees, with characteristic obtrusiveness, made most of the matter, and acted as if they were the divinely appointed conservators and guardians of the public consistency and orthodoxy.

Except they have washed the hands diligently, eat not. The word translated *diligently* ($\pi\nu\gamma\mu\tilde{\eta}$) is one of *the crosses of the critics*, and has occasioned a very extraordinary amount of research and discussion. The ancients themselves, who lived comparatively near to the evangelist's time, and were familiar with Greek as a spoken language, regarded the word as peculiar and debatable. Hence in the old Latin versions (the 'Italic') which preceded Jerome's Vulgate it receives quite a variety of translations (*pugillo, prius crebro, primo, momento, subinde*). The word literally means *with closed hand*, or *with the fist* (comp. $\pi\acute{v}\xi$). But what the evangelist could mean when he says *except they have washed the hands 'with closed hand'* looks perplexing enough. Had it been the case that there was satisfactory evidence, derivable from the rabbinical writers, that the Jews were accustomed to close the operating hand when washing the other, so that the hand operated on was rubbed, not with the palm but with the knuckled part, that part which washerwomen use when washing clothes, then

and all the Jews, except they wash *their* hands oft, eat not,

there would never have been any dispute concerning the evangelist's meaning. But there is no such evidence, although the whole extent of rabbinical literature has been carefully ransacked. Some eminent critics, nevertheless, such as Beza, Fritzsche, Meyer, Grimm, adhere to the idea that Mark must have meant that the washing was performed *with the fist*. The same opinion seems to have been entertained by Michaelis, who in his translation inserts a long paraphrase of the word (*wobey aber das Waschen für genug gehalten wird, wenn auch die Faust geballet ist*). Grotius had somewhat of the same notion, only he supposed that the meaning is that the fist was washed by the other hand (*manum in pugnum compositam manu altera lavabant*). This seems almost to reverse the picture of the process that is naturally suggested by the evangelist's expression. Yet Calov approves of it. Lightfoot took an entirely different view of the phrase; he thought that the debatable word meant *to the wrist*; Hammond, Whitby, Wells, Bengel, took the same view. But (1) the word in itself does not mean *the wrist*, and (2) even though it did, the form in which it is employed could not mean *as far as the wrist*, or *up to the wrist*. Le Clerc saw this, and hence, in his Latin translation of Hammond, as well as in his French translation of the Gospel, he interpreted the word as meaning *by putting the fist into water* (en mettant le poing dans l'eau), an interpretation however that involves almost as large an amount of arbitrariness as is characteristic of the explication which he rejects. Theophylact exaggerates Lightfoot's notion, and interprets the word as meaning *up to the elbow* (ἄχρι τοῦ ἀγκῶνος), because, says he, the term does mean *the length from the elbow to the tips of the fingers*. Certainly the term is a measure of length *from the elbow to the fingers* (strictly, it would appear, *to the closed fingers*; see Stephens's *Thesaurus*, sub voc.); but it is difficult to see how it could ever be the case that the evangelist's expression could mean *up to the elbow*. Louis Cappel however took the same view (*Spicileg.* in loc.); and le Cene, Elsner, Beausobre-et-L'Enfant. So did Mace; he translates *up to the elbows*. So does Godwin; he translates the whole phrase thus, *unless for a pigmy's length they wash the hands and arms*. But (1) the Greek word *pygme* does not mean *a pigmy*, and (2) there is nothing in the original text that corresponds to the appended expression *and arms*. Scaliger, Drusius, Cameron, and many others take substantially the view of Theophylact, though under a peculiar phase derived from one of the petty precepts of the rabbis regarding ceremonial purification. The rabbis enjoined that a double washing of the hands should be attended to before eating. In the first of the two *the hands were to be held upward that the polluted water might run off at the elbow*. In the second, which 'purified the water of the first washing,' the hands were to be held downward! (See Buxtorf's *Lexicon Talm.*, p. 1,335.) The critics named suppose that the evangelist has reference to the elevation of the hands The evangelist's expression, however, remains as puzzling as ever, both (1) as regards the fact that it is *the fist* or *closed hand* that is spoken of, and (2) as regards the form of the phrase '*with*' *closed hand*. Wetstein, followed by Wakefield and Principal Campbell, takes an entirely different view. He supposes that the debatable word means *a handful (of water)*. Hence Wakefield translates, *for the Pharisees and all the Jews never eat 'without throwing a handful of water over their*

N

holding the tradition of the elders. 4 And when they come

hands.' Principal Campbell translates correspondingly, *For the Pharisees, and indeed all the Jews, eat not until they have washed their hands ' by pouring a little water upon them.*' It is an ingenious cutting of the knot; but it is entirely unwarrantable. The debatable word does not mean *a handful*; the debatable expression, standing absolutely as it does, cannot mean *a handful of water!* What then are we to make of the phrase? King James's translators have rendered the disputed word *oft*. It was Wycliffe's rendering, and Tyndale's, and Coverdale's. It was the rendering of the Anglo-Saxon version (*gelomlice*), and of the Gothic (*ufta*). It was adopted too into the Geneva, and reproduced in the Rheims. It was Erasmus s rendering. More than all, it was the rendering of the Vulgate (*crebro*), the fountain head of the whole series of repetitions. Erasmus conjectured that the debatable word was a corruption, and that Mark must have used another word that signifies *frequently* (' πυκνῶς aut πυκνα aut πυκνῇ'). The translation therefore, so far as Erasmus is concerned, is founded on a conjectural reading. And it is not unlikely that Jerome himself was just as completely puzzled as Erasmus; and hence the Vulgate version. It is a remarkable fact, however, that one of Erasmus's conjectural readings (the middle one) is actually found in the Sinaitic manuscript (א), and thence it has actually been introduced into the evangelist's text by Tischendorf, in the eighth edition of his New Testament. It is a marvellous deference to pay to the fine old manuscript. It is far too much, however. The writer of the manuscript had manifestly been puzzled by the term which he found in the text from which he copied, and, being unable to understand it, he assumed that it was a mistake and corrected it accordingly. *If the debatable word was not in the evangelist's autograph, it is inconceivable that any transcriber would ever have inserted it.* And when we dip into the matter a little farther, we may easily see that the reading of the Sinaitic manuscript, if interpreted according to the rendering of the Vulgate (*oft*, not *much*), could never have been the original reading. There is not an atom of evidence that either the Jews in general, or the Pharisees in particular, or any peoples or persons or person, ever made it a matter of conscience, or a matter of practice, *to wash the hands 'frequently' before partaking of food.* What then? There remains the interpretation of the Syriac Peshito version. It renders the debatable word adverbially by a term which means *carefully* or *diligently*. It is the same term which is employed in its translation of Luke xv. 8. And assuredly, if the debatable word can bear such an interpretation, all the exegetical exigencies of the case would seem to be met to a nicety. One should suppose that a perfunctory washing of the hands would not have satisfied the Pharisaic sticklers for fulness and thoroughness in all that was merely outward in religion. On the principle which led them 'to make broad their phylacteries, and to enlarge the borders of their garments' (Matt, xxiii. 5), they would be careful to give in all ordinary circumstances an ample lustration to their hands, however neglectful they might be of their hearts. But it is scarcely likely, notwithstanding their devotion to pettinesses, that they would insist on the cleansing being uniformly performed in one invariable way. It is not likely at all events that the whole people would be particular in insisting, or admitting, that, from among the many possible modes of cleansing the

from the market, except they wash, they eat not. And many hands with water, only one single and singular way should be legitimate. And hence the generic idea of *diligently* or *carefully* seems to meet all the requirements of the case. It is true that the debatable word does not occur elsewhere with this adverbial acceptation. Hence the difficulty. But it is nevertheless, when intrinsically considered, quite a natural acceptation, which may readily enough have obtained a local or provincial currency, although it never found its way up into classical usage or polite literary phraseology. Just as some people speak of doing a thing *with tooth and nail*, when they refer to an effort in which the eagerness of a vicious temper plays an important part; so people in other circles might be accustomed to speak of doing a thing *with the fist*, when the thing had to be done *energetically, vigorously,* and *effectively*, almost *pugilistically* as it were; that is Arius Montanus's word (*pugilatim*). The washing was to be done as if hand were to contend with hand which should be cleanest. (Comp. Suidas, *sub voce* πύξ.) Calvin gives, as one of his alternate translations, *à force.* Sharpe, in his translation, uses the admirable word *thorougly.* Piscator, in his, has *diligently* (*fleissig*); Count Zinzendorf, *very carefully* (*sehr sorgfältig*). The great Isaac Casaubon contended for this interpretation of the debatable word. (*Notæ,* in loc.) It had evidently been accepted too by Epiphanius in the fourth century. (See his *Hæreses,* xv.) It has also been accepted by many others, as by Petter for instance, and a-Lapide, among the older expositors, and by Kuinöl, Wordsworth, Alford, Rowlandson, and the authors of the Revised English version, among the more modern.

Holding the tradition of the elders. *Holding*, that is *holding firmly*, or *holding fast*, as the term is rendered in Heb. iv. 14, Rev. ii. 13, 25. The ceremonial washing of hands before eating was not an injunction, bearing upon it a written superscription of 'Thus saith the Lord.' It was a mere *tradition*, orally handed down, as was alleged by its patrons, from *the elders. These elders* or *ancients* were often represented as the contemporaries or immediate successors of Moses, and as persons therefore who might be expected to know the Divine will in reference to duties not formally enjoined in the Scriptures.

VER. 4. **And** (*when they come*). This supplement, substantially, is found in the fine old Cambridge manuscript (ὅταν ἔλθωσιν). In many copies of the 'old Latin' there is another form of supplement, equally excellent, 'when they return' (*redeuntes*).

From the market. Or, more literally, *from market*, where, in consequence of the crowding of the people, there would be the possibility and the risk of contracting ceremonial contamination. The *market* or *market place* in the ancient Jewish towns and villages would correspond to the modern *bazaar* of the East; it was *the place of concourse*, and hence *the place of merchandise.* The idea of *concourse* is that which is suggested by the Greek term (ἀγορά); and certainly, if crowding is anywhere in the East, it is in the *mart* or *bazaar*. Man rubs on man, and has often to squeeze his way through. "The great bazaars, where "the necessaries of life are sold, are also thoroughfares," says Miss Whately, speaking of Cairo, " and in the middle of the day so noisy and crowded that " it requires much skill on the part of the boy who guides one's donkey, as well

other things there be, which they have received to hold, *as*

"as considerable vigilance in oneself. . . . A sea of white and red turbans "is in front, here and there interrupted by a huge camel, towering above every "body, and apparently going to trample down some half dozen in his progress, "or by a long line of donkeys laden with dripping skins of water or great "stones for building, loosely fastened with cord netting, and threatening to fall "on the feet of the passengers; though indeed, from the density of the crowd, "they do not seem to have any feet, only heads. To penetrate the mass is a "puzzling affair; but the young guide calls out, *To the right! To the left!* "incessantly adding plenty of hints to individuals, *O boy! O man! O lady!* "*O camel-driver!* . . . If wishing to be more particular, he alludes to the "article the person is carrying, thus, *O chickens, O oranges, get out of the way!* "and so by degrees one gets along." (*Ragged Life in Egypt,* pp. 19, 20.) In Cairo there are numerous bazaars; but in small places, where there is only one, *it naturally becomes the favourite resort and lounge of the entire male population.* Hence a large amount of personal contact with individuals, whose secret physical or ceremonial condition cannot be known, is unavoidable. It was possible therefore, as the Pharisees argued, that ceremonial defilement might have been unwittingly contracted in the market. They exaggerated the divinely prescribed precautionary measures, referred to in Lev. xv. and other parts of 'the law,' and fancied that they were giving the highest possible evidence of extraordinarily meritorious holiness when they bound themselves to use more frequent ablutions than Moses had enjoined.

Except they have baptized themselves (ἐὰν μὴ βαπτίσωνται) they eat not. The reference of the baptism is to *themselves*, not to *the articles purchased in the market*, as Krebs, Matthæi, Kuinöl, Lange, and others suppose. But the real action denoted by the verb *baptized* has been much debated in 'the baptismal controversy.' There can be no doubt that the term, in its primary acceptation, denoted *dipping, merging, mersing, whelming*; this should never be disputed. But there should be as little doubt that the primary modal acceptation got merged out of consideration, when the term was *ritually employed among the Jews.* The idea of *purification* became then outstanding and overshadowing (John iii. 22, 25, 26), whatever the specific mode in which the purificatory act was effected. *In the case before us the immersion of the whole body in water was really an absolute impossibility.* We wonder that even Meyer contends for it. It would have involved a bath-room, or at least a sufficiently ample plunge-bath, in every house and cot in the land. It would have involved too a supply of water such as has never yet been in Palestine during the present geological epoch. For the water that was once used for purifying would be ceremonially 'unclean,' and therefore unfit for further use by a second member of the household; and what then would become of the household when three or four or more required to baptize themselves? For the same reason a common public bath in every village would have been an impossibility among the Jews; the use of it by a single individual would have rendered it 'unclean' for all the rest of the population, until it was replenished afresh for each. And even then the vessel itself would, until purified, be ceremonially defiled in consequence of contact with the unclean person (Num. xix. 22). *There is no evidence of any kind that*

the washing of cups, and pots, brasen vessels, and of tables.

the Jews ever had any public baths, or could indeed have ever allowed them, for the removal of ceremonial uncleanness. The baptism which 'the Pharisees and all the Jews' performed, on every occasion of coming home from the market-place, or from any crowded place whatsoever in which they might have got entangled among a mass of miscellaneous individuals, must have been something else than 'immersion.' It would no doubt, in all ordinary cases, be effected by 'sprinkling,' the common mode of purification. See Num. viii. 7, xix. 13, 18, 19, 20; Ezek. xxxvi. 25; Heb. ix. 13, x. 22. Add to these passages Ps. li. 7, 'purge me with hyssop,' the common instrument apparently of ceremonial 'sprinkling.' It is a remarkable fact that in the two oldest and most important of all the existing manuscripts of the New Testament, the Sinaitic and the Vatican (א B), the expression before us is not *except they have baptized themselves*, but *except they have sprinkled themselves* (ῥαντίσωνται). Volkmar accepts the word. It is not likely, however, that it exhibits the original reading; otherwise it would never have got superseded. But it shows us decisively what was the opinion entertained by the writers of these manuscripts in reference to the mode of the ceremonial custom which is referred to by the evangelist. And it need not be a surprise to any that a word, originally denoting a specific mode or form, should in the course of time merge its reference to its own primary import. Nothing is more common in living language. To *manufacture*, for instance, originally meant *to make 'by the hand'*; but now a very large proportion of *manufactured articles* are no longer '*hand made*,' but, on the contrary and in contradistinction, are *made by machinery*. Originally it was *vessels only with 'sails' that 'sailed'*; but now we constantly read and speak of the *sailing* of steamboats, although, in many cases, they have actually no *sails* at all, and thus cannot 'sail' in the primary acceptation of the term. Originally it was at the sound or '*blast*' of the trumpet that heralds described the armorial ensigns of those who entered the tournament lists; it was thus (compare the German *blasen*) that they *blazoned*; their description was '*blazed*' abroad over the whole assembled multitude. But now nothing in the world is done more quietly than the *blazoning* of coats of arms; and yet they continue to be *blazoned*. In fact '*coats* of arms,' so called, are no longer *coats* at all, just as the great majority of *spinsters* no longer *spin*. There are too other *hypocrites* besides those who are found on the boards of a theatre, though a *hypocrite* originally was *a stage-player who answered from under a mask*. So a *villain* was originally just a *villager*; a *pagan* was simply a *countryman*; a *scandal* was *a stick in a trap*. And to come back to the very word in dispute, the root verb from which it springs, though primarily meaning *to dip*, came also to mean *to dye*, in whatsoever way the *dyeing* was effected. And, as a matter of philological fact, the word *baptize* itself is now by the great majority of the people who use it all the world over employed to denote the performance of a purificatory rite, without the least atom of reference, in '*their*' *use of it*, to its primary import of *immersion*. If the term is *now* employed in this way, is it inconceivable that it should have been *formerly* thus employed? If not, is it inconceivable that we should have to push back the reference of the '*formerly*' to the very time of Mark himself? There is no good reason for doubting that

5 Then the Pharisees and scribes asked him, Why walk not thy

the 'six waterpots of stone, containing two or three firkins apiece,' which were 'set' in the house in Cana, 'after the manner of the *purifying* of the Jews' (John ii. 6), furnish us with a fair representation of the kind of vessels that were generally employed among the Jews to contain the water of baptism. The members of the family and their guests would, in passing into the house, *lift* the bunch of hyssop that would be lying conveniently, fixed on the extremity of a distinct and appropriate handle, and would dip it in the cleansing element and *sprinkle* their persons. The water and the hyssop, *being untouched by the unclean*, continued clean, and would be available for all. Lightfoot and Wetstein err in supposing that the purification referred to by our Lord passed *on the hands* alone.

And many other things there are which they received to hold fast. *Which they received*, as authoritative ordinances traditionally handed down. They *received* them, *that they might hold them fast*. When the ordinances were enjoined on them by their rabbis, the design was *that they might hold them fast*. (See Fritzsche.) But their reception of them was *a past thing* (hence the aorist tense of the verb), and *they were now holding them fast*. The language is equivalent to this, *there are many other things which they hold fast, having received them that they might hold them fast*. The evangelist mentions, as representative purifications, *baptisms of cups*, that is, '*ceremonial*' *purifications of cups*; and such purifications being *ceremonial*, and for another purpose altogether than the removal of physical impurity, would be performed in such a way as not t endanger the ceremonial purity of the aggregate of purifying water. *It would, in other words, be performed by sprinkling.* See the remainder of the verse. The Greek word *baptisms* is preserved in the Vulgate version, and it is much better than the partially synonymous term *washings*, which Erasmus, Luther, and Beza introduced into their respective versions. Erasmus says that he 'wondered' at the Vulgate version, 'inasmuch as the reference is just to common washing' (*vulgaris lotio*). He entirely misapprehended, however, the nature of the case; the Saviour does not refer to *common washing*. He would never have objected to the literal cleansing of cups. Such cleansing *must be regarded* as in accordance with the will of God. It has too a moral significance and effect, as well as a physical propriety.

Cups. That is, as the word means, *drinking vessels*.

And pots. These would be larger vessels than the ordinary *cups*, vessels out of which the cups would be filled. *Potts* is the Geneva translation; Tyndale and Coverdale have *cruses*; Wycliffe, *cruetis*. The word employed ($\xi\acute{\epsilon}\sigma\tau\eta\varsigma$) is properly a Latin word (*sextarius*), though it was adopted both into the Greek and Hebrew languages (Buxtorf, *Lex. Tal.*, p. 2,076). It etymologically signifies *a sixth*, and would denote *a jug* or *jar that held a sixth part of a congius*. A *congius* somewhat corresponded to the English gallon.

And coppers. See chap. vi. 8. These copper vessels would probably correspond to the large copper caldrons that are still used in Syria for cooking food, often being of a size that is apparently very disproportioned to the other articles that constitute the essential outfit of a domestic establishment.

In King James's version it is added *and tables*. But that is a mere guess of

disciples according to the tradition of the elders, but eat bread

a translation, arising apparently out of the difficulty of conceiving that *couches* or *beds* would be ceremonially purified either *by washing* in general, or by *immersion* in particular. The difficulty of the supposition is obvious enough; for if couches or *beds* required to be immersed, when they were about to be used afresh, not only would a very large supply of water have been required, they themselves would, by being soaked with water, have been rendered unfit for use. Yet *couches* or *beds*, and not *tables*, is the only possible interpretation of the evangelist's word (κλινῶν). The word never has, in any Greek writer of any age, the meaning of *table*, or any other meaning than that of *couch* or *bed*. It must have been in despair that both Luther and Tyndale rendered it *tables*; they were followed by Coverdale and the Geneva version. Wycliffe and the Rheims however, following the faithful Vulgate, have *beds*. Felbinger has *bedsteads*; Bengel and Heumann, *table-couches*. Such couches would of course be ceremonially purified only by sprinkling, for it is in vain for Dr. Carson to affirm that ' there is no furniture in a house that could not be immersed,' or to suppose ' that the couches might be made to be taken to pieces, in order to their more convenient immersion ' (*Baptism*, p. 451). It is noteworthy that in both the Sinaitic and Vatican manuscripts (א B), as well as in L Δ and the Coptic version, this phrase *and couches* is omitted altogether ; and, in his eighth edition of the New Testament, Tischendorf has actually dropped it out of the text. Unwarrantably, however; if the words had been wanting in the autograph of the evangelist, they would never have been arbitrarily added. The writers of the manuscripts mentioned, and of the Coptic version, or the writers from whom they copied, had evidently felt the very difficulty that led Luther, Tyndale, Coverdale, and our Authorized translators to hazard, by guess, the word *tables*.

VER. 5. **And the Pharisees and the scribes question Him.** *And* instead of *then* is no doubt the correct reading. The *then* had been intruded by transcribers who did not understand the relation of the second verse to the first, and its consequent relation to the fifth. It had been intruded to give the construction the appearance of greater concinnity. (See on ver. 2.) The *and*, Mark's favourite conjunction, is restored by Lachmann, Tischendorf, Tregelles, Alford ; it was advocated by Griesbach (*Comm. Crit.*, in ver. 2).

Why walk not Thy disciples according to the tradition of the elders? *Walk not* (οὐ περιπατοῦσιν). Life is thought of as a kind of perpetual motion ; it is a constant *peripateticism*. *The tradition of the elders :* The word rendered *tradition* properly means *the act of handing from one* (παράδοσις) or *of handing down* as it were. Here it refers to the object of the act, that is, *to the thing handed down*, the *ordinance* or *injunction* which is subindicated in the next clause. This injunction came, it was alleged, from *the elders* or *ancients*. It was not written indeed in the book of the law. (See Josephus, *Ant.*, xiii. 10 : 6.) But it was handed on from generation to generation by word of mouth, and had emanated, it was contended, from those fathers of the constitution who had been the assessors and friends of Moses, and thus, as was to be presumed, had been so near the fountain of inspiration as to know the mind of God.

But eat with common hands the bread. With hands such as heathens have;

with unwashen hands? 6 He answered and said unto them, Well hath Esaias prophesied of you hypocrites, as it is written, This people honoureth me with *their* lips, but their heart is far from me. 7 Howbeit in vain do they worship me,

---

with unsanctified hands. (See ver. 2.) *The bread:* note the article, and the consequent simplicity of the representation, ' *the* ' *bread which is before them.*

VER. 6. **And He said to them, Well did Isaiah prophesy concerning you the hypocrites.** Note the *well*. The same word is ironically repeated in ver. 9, and is rendered *full well*, the rendering which it receives here in the version of Coverdale. If very literally translated, it would be *beautifully* (καλῶς). Luther admirably reproduced its import, *finely (wohl fein).* The Saviour means that the words of Isaiah could not have been more apt and felicitous if he had had really present before him, for the purpose of taking their portrait, those very Pharisees and scribes who were finding fault with the disciples. Isaiah *prophesied.* The reference is not simply, or distinctively, or principally, to *prediction.* When the prophets *prophesied,* they spoke *fore* God, and *from* God, and thus *for* God, whether it was to things past, present, or to come, that they referred. (See chap. vi. 4.) The waters that welled up within them came from depths that were deeper than their own thoughts. (See Patrizi, in loc.) The Saviour then, as Calvin has judiciously remarked, does not mean that Isaiah was looking forward to the scribes and Pharisees of the New Testament age. He means that the prophet's utterances depicted these scribes and Pharisees to perfection. *Concerning you ' the ' hypocrites:* the article indicates that their hypocrisy, in the judgment of the Lord, was something conspicuous.

As it stands written. Such is Luther's habitual translation of the expression which, with somewhat less exactitude perhaps, is rendered in our English version *it is written.* In the first two issues of Luther's New Testament, the issues of 1522, the expression is frequently given as in our English version, *it is written.* In the 1524 edition however, and its successors, the less exact rendering is superseded by the more exact. The phrase is literally *it has been written.* (See Isa. xxix. 13.)

This people honoureth Me with the lips. Making, as Pet'er says, ' outward show and profession of holiness and religion.' When the prophet refers to *the lips* he specifies a part for the whole. Jesus had in His eye the baptism of cups and the washing of hands, as well as the saying of prayers and the utterance of solemn tones. ' The reason is,' says Petter, ' because the principal parts of outward worship are performed with mouth and lips.'

But their heart is far from Me. ' By *heart* understand,' says Petter, ' the inner man, comprehending all the faculties and powers thereof.' (See chap. ii. 6 and vi. 52.) The expression rendered *is far* is idiomatic and emphatic in the original (πόρρω ἀπέχει). It primarily means *holdeth off afar.* The heart of the scribes and Pharisees *held itself far off* from God ; it kept itself to itself, instead of taking itself to God. Nothing indeed is farther away from God than selfishness, under whatever phase or guise it may appear.

VER. 7. **But in vain do they worship Me.** (See Patrizi, in loc.) The *but* has retrospective reference to the more outstanding or obtrusive of the two pre-

teaching *for* doctrines the commandments of men. 8 For laying aside the commandment of God, ye hold the tradition of men, *as* the washing of pots and cups: and many other such like things ye do.

9 And he said unto them, Full well ye reject the commandment of God, that ye may keep your own tradition.

---

ceding clauses, that namely in which it is said, '*this people honoureth Me with the lips.*' Notwithstanding all this honour, *in vain do they worship Me.* Why? See next clause.

Teaching as doctrines the commandments of men. Very literally, *teaching teachings, men's commandments.* It is, as Calvin remarks, a case of *apposition.* Tyndale's version brings out clearly the prophet's idea, though somewhat paraphrastically, *teaching doctrynes which are nothing but the commandements of men.* The *for* of King James's version, borrowed from the Geneva, and found too in Calvin's French version (*pour*), is not altogether a happy supplement. It is liable to be misunderstood, and has been mistaken by many, as by Petter for instance, who explains the expression thus, *instead of true and sound doctrines.*

VER. 8. The quotation is ended, and the Saviour now speaks out of His own fulness. **Having left the commandment of God, ye hold fast the tradition of men.** The words *commandment* and *tradition* are used in the singular number, because the mind of the Saviour was concentrated anticipatively upon single illustrative cases.

Baptisms of pots and cups; and many other such like things ye do. These clauses are omitted altogether by Tischendorf in his eighth edition. They are enclosed within brackets by Tregelles and Lachmann (in his small edition). Alford brackets them too, but pronounces on the whole in their favour. The Revisers omit them. They are wanting in ℵ B L Δ, 1, and the Coptic version, and in all the manuscripts of the Armenian version, though not in Uscan's edition. We wait for further light.

VER. 9. **And He said to them.** This is one of Mark's favourite ways of introducing a new topic of discourse or some salient detail. Comp. chap. iv. 9, 13, 24, 26, 30, 40.

Full well. Or *finely*, as Luther has it (see on ver. 6). Coverdale has *how goodly*; the first Geneva, *verie wel.* It is *beautifully* in the original. Though there is no need of making much of it, yet there is undoubtedly, as Euthymius Zigabenus remarked of old, a dash of irony in the employment of the word. Castellio, Beza, Petter, Baxter, Alexander, all allow the ironical import. Willes too contends for it. 'By *full well*,' says Richard Baxter, 'is meant *full ill.*' 'He speaketh one thing in words,' says Petter, 'and intendeth the contrary.' Wakefield evaporates the life from the phraseology when he tries to merge the irony, and renders the clause thus, 'Ye *entirely* set aside the commandment of God.'

Ye reject the commandment of God, that ye may keep your tradition. Instead of *reject*, the Geneva word, it is *frustrate* in the Rheims. Neither rendering is

10 For Moses said, Honour thy father and thy mother; and, Whoso curseth father or mother, let him die the death. 11 But ye say, If a man shall say to his father or mother, *It is* Corban, that is to say, a gift, by whatsoever thou mightest be profited by

---

perfect. Tyndale's first rendering (in 1526) was, *ye putt awaye:* his last (in 1534) was a little stronger, *ye cast aside;* neither of them perfect either. The word (ἀθετεῖτε) has no absolute synonym in English; it lies somewhere between *nullify* and *abrogate.* Petter explains it: 'Ye abrogate or make of no force or authority.' The word in the next clause, excellently translated *keep* in our English version, is also excellently translated *maintain* by Tyndale and Coverdale.

VER. 10. **For Moses said, Honour thy father and thy mother, and, Whoso revileth father or mother, let him die for it** (θανάτῳ τελευτάτω). The Rheims rendering is Hebraistic, *dying let him die.* The original idea is, *let him finish (his career) by death (judicially inflicted).* It was Coverdale who introduced the translation which is given in our King James's version, the Geneva, 'the Great Bible,' and the Revised version. It is awkward however, and has not the merit of being literal. Our version is Tyndale's. The Old Testament passages quoted are found in Exod. xx. 12, Deut. v. 16, and Exod. xxi. 17, Lev. xx. 9.

VER. 11. **But ye say, If a man should say to his father or his mother, Corban!** (that is to say, 'A gi't.') It is the evangelist who parenthetically interjects the interpretation of the Hebrew word *Corban.* Josephus employs interpretatively the same Greek term (*Ant.,* iv. 4: 4; *C. Apion,* i. 22). The Hebrew word means *a gift (to God), a sacrificial gift* (δῶρον θεοῦ, *Joseph. c. Ap.,* i. 22). It occurs frequently in the Old Testament, and is translated in our Authorized version either *offering* or *oblation.* It etymologically means *what is brought near* (viz. *to God*). When an unnatural son wished, either in a temporary fit of passion or under the goad of an abiding selfishness, to get quit of the importunity of a destitute father or mother, he had just to say, in reference to whatever was craved, *Corban!* or, as it was sometimes veilingly corrupted, *Conam!* and then not only was he released from obligation to assist his needy parent, he was actually bound, as by the highest solemnity, to withhold the desired relief. So tortuously and tamperingly did the rabbis deal with the word of God and with the consciences of men.

Whatsoever it is by which thou mightest be benefited out of me. This was the most sweeping and thoroughly generic way of expressing the cruelty of selfish rage, or of putting an end inhumanly to importunity. It continued among the Jews for centuries after our Saviour's death. It crops out again and again in the tract *Nedarim,* in the Mishna, as a form of 'cursing' that was actually in use. Josephus speaks of the single word *Corban* being used as an 'oath' or 'curse' (ὅρκος, *C. Apion,* i. 22); but when to that single word was appended, as the area of the radiation of its influence, the generic statement, *whatsoever it is by which thou mightest be benefited out of me,* the 'curse' was embittered and intensified to the utmost degree. Often, we may suppose, would there be something less in actual life than the fulness of this sweep. The wide extent of the ban would be disintegrated or minced down, to meet particular details of

me; *he shall be free.* 12 And ye suffer him no more to do ought for his father or his mother; 13 making the word of God of

application. If a needy father should ask a sheep out of the son's flock, he might be answered *Corban!* that is, *Corban the sheep!* or *Let be Corban the sheep!* If he asked a measure of corn he might receive for answer, *Corban! that is, Let the corn be Corban!* (see L. Cappel's *Diatriba,* § 9); but if reproach ensued, and passion got towering, then the ban of Corban would be laid on everything that might be available, *Corban! whatever it is by which thou mightest be benefited out of me!* And the rabbis ruled that if an inhuman son thus swore or 'cursed,' he was bound to stand to his 'curse,' because of the holy word *Corban* which he had uttered. 'O most abominable and detestable imposture!' exclaims Faber Stapulensis. And the climax of the satanic quirk was this: the heartless wretch, though vocally vowing by the word *Corban* all his sheep and corn and other possessions to the temple, *was not bound after all to give them to the temple; he was only bound, until such time as by some other quirk he could get absolution, to give nothing to the person to whom he had uttered the sacred word!* (see Comm. on Matt., xv. 5). This was a refinement of rabbinical jesuitism in 'cursing' that has never been exceeded in the annals of the sleekest of human snakes. No wonder that it excited the indignation of our holy and loving Lord.

He shall be free. A supplement thrown in by King James's translators, following in the wake of the Geneva and of Beza. It was devised in despair, because of the barrier that was found in the first word of the following verse. The natural apodosis however of the sentence is found in that verse.

VER. 12. **And.** This conjunction must to all appearance be omitted. It is left out by Lachmann, Tischendorf, Tregelles. It is wanting in the manuscripts א B D Δ, 1, 69, and in the Coptic and Æthiopic versions. Its insertion in the other ancient authorities seems to have been occasioned by the difficulty of understanding the Hebraizing expression employed, and the rabbinical jesuitism involved in the phraseology of the preceding verse. "The words of that verse," says Petter, "are in themselves somewhat dark and difficult in the original "Greek text, and learned men do not at all interpret them alike." (See even Castellio and Dionysius à Ryckel.) With the omission of *and,* however, and the above interpretation of *Corban* and its adjunct, the connection of the two verses becomes simple and lucid. The *and* perplexed Principal Campbell; but he sagaciously concluded, though he did not know that there was critical warrant for his idea, that somehow or other it must be ignored.

Ye suffer him no more to do ought for his father or his mother. *No more* or *no longer,* viz. after he has said *Corban! 'Ought,'* or by a still better spelling, *aught,* that is *a whit.* (Compare the Anglo-Saxon *aht, awiht, awyht*). *Anything* is the translation of the Geneva version. The first Geneva (1557) had *oght.* Wycliffe has *ony thing;* the Anglo-Saxon, *ænig thing.*

VER. 13. **Making the word of God of none effect.** Depriving it of its authoritative force (ἀκυροῦντες), annulling it as it were. The word is rendered *disannul* in Gal. iii. 17. It occurs nowhere else in the New Testament, except in the passage of Matthew parallel to this (xv. 6).

none effect through your tradition, which ye have delivered: and many such like things do ye.

14 And when he had called all the people *unto him*, he said unto them, Hearken unto me every one *of you*, and understand: 15 there is nothing from without a man, that entering into him can defile him: but the things which come out of him, those are

---

By your tradition which ye handed down. The Saviour identifies them for the moment with their forefathers, *which 'ye' handed down.* (Comp. Matt. xxiii. 35.) They and their forefathers were *one* in spirit.

And many such like things ye do. The one instance of the Corban matter was but a specimen of many cases in which 'the word of God' was racked, wrenched, tortured, and reversed by the paltering conceits of the rabbis.

VER. 14. **And having called to Him all the crowd.** Viz., which was hanging about, but which it would appear had either spontaneously and respectfully retired to a little distance, or had been waved off by our Lord, while He had His interview, apparently at the dinner table (see ver. 2), with the strangers from Jerusalem. But instead of the adjective *all* ($\pi\acute{a}\nu\tau a$), there occurs in some of the highest authorities the adverb *again* ($\pi\acute{a}\lambda\iota\nu$), which in Greek bears some little analogy in appearance to the adjective: *and having called to Him 'again' the crowd.* This reading was defended by Mill (*Prol.*, § 403), and, on the whole, approved of by Griesbach (see *Comm. Crit.*). It is introduced into the text by Lachmann, Tischendorf, and Tregelles. It is supported by the manuscripts ℵ B D L Δ. and the Vulgate, Coptic, and Æthiopic versions, and the margin of the Philoxenian Syriac.

He said to them, Hear Me, all, and understand. This formality of introduction indicates that some principle of far-reaching importance was about to be enunciated.

VER. 15. **There is nothing from without the man.** The Saviour is mentally individualizing a representative case: *There is nothing outside 'the' man.*

Entering into him—or, as Tyndale has it, *when hitt entereth in to him,*—**which is able to defile him.** Literally, *to make him common*, like the unsanctified mass of mankind, *to make him profane* (in the original meaning of that term), *to make him unholy.* Had our Saviour been speaking as a physiologist, He would have admitted and contended that *many things from without*, if allowed to enter within, will corrupt the functions of physical life, and carry disorder and detriment into the whole fabric of the frame. But He was speaking as a moralist, and hence the antithetic statement of the next clause.

But the things—or, as Tyndale has it, *thoo thynges*—**which come out from him;** or, as it is in the texts of Lachmann, Tischendorf, Tregelles, Alford, *which come out from the man.* This repetition is the reading of the manuscripts ℵ B D L Δ, 33, and the Vulgate, Gothic, Coptic, Æthiopic, and Persic versions.

Those are they that defile the man. *That render the man common.* The Saviour, speaking as a moralist, lays His hand on the fundamental spring of all that moral impurity which is so *common* in the world. It originates *in the heart* of man's being, and thence wells out. It is not an import, but an export. Its origin is in self. Its genesis is in self-will. Nothing but what is the product

they that defile the man. 16 If any man have ears to hear,
let him hear.

17 And when he was entered into the house from the
people, his disciples asked him concerning the parable.

---

of free will can be sinful, or have moral guilt attaching to it. Nothing else is culpably excessive on the one hand, or culpably deficient on the other. Nothing else is culpably present, or culpably absent and wanting. Free will is ever the *causing cause*, and never the merely *caused cause*, of all the human or diabolic effluences that corrupt the sum total of moral being.

VER. 16. **If any one have ears to hear, let him hear.** This verse is bracketed by Fritzsche, Tregelles, and Alford, as of doubtful authenticity. It was 'vehemently (*vehementer*) suspected' by Mill (*Prol.*, § 1475). It was received by Lachmann, but it is omitted altogether by Tischendorf in his eighth edition. It is wanting in the manuscripts ℵ B L Δ, and the Coptic version. It is rather more likely however that it would be accidentally omitted by certain transcribers than intentionally intruded. Comp. chap. iv. 9, 23.

VER. 17. **And when He entered into the house.** In the texts which were lying before King James's translators the expression was not '*the* house,' but simply and anarthrously, *house*. Hence the Geneva translation, *into an house*, and the first version of Tyndale (1526), *into a housse*. Tyndale, in his second version (1534), has Germanizingly *to housse*; but Coverdale, the Great Bible, and the Rheims, as well as Luther, have *into* '*the*' *house*. Strange to say, Tischendorf in his eighth edition, under the authority of the Sinaitic and San Gallensis manuscripts (ℵ Δ), inserts the article. The authorization for the insertion is altogether insufficient; but we are not to suppose on the other hand that the phrase exactly means *into* '*a*' *house*. It is idiomatic (comp. chap. ii. 1; iii. 1, 19); and if an article must in English be inserted, *the* is to be preferred: *into the house*, that is, *into the house where He was lodging*.

From the crowd. Or, *away from the crowd*. Perhaps it was sunsetting time, and our Saviour would enjoin on the people to retire to their homes. Having thus spoken to them He would, as Petter expresses it, 'leave the multitude that He might be private for a time to refresh Himself with His disciples.'

His disciples asked Him concerning the parable. Or more literally and correctly, according to the reading of the modern critical editors, approved of too by Griesbach and Fritzsche, *His disciples asked Him the parable*, that is, they asked its meaning. The word *parable*, as here used, goes back to its primary import. There was no *story* in the case; *story* is not essential to the idea of a parable. It is an accident. The *parable* was a *side-throw* in contradistinction to *a direct utterance*; hence something was revealed, and something was at the same time concealed (chap. iii. 23). The reference here is to the apophthegm contained in ver. 15, which did not directly utter and unfold the whole truth of the case. It was, as the Germans would say, a *Denkspruch*, and needed to be unfolded; there was a husk around the kernel of its meaning. 'His *disciples* asked Him': we learn from Matt. xv. 15 that it was Peter who was the spokesman; and Hilgenfeld imagines that, as the question led to a reproof, we have in

18 And he saith unto them, Are ye so without understanding also? Do ye not perceive, that whatsoever thing from without entereth into the man, *it* cannot defile him; 19 because it entereth not into his heart, but into the belly, and goeth out into the draught, purging all meats?

Mark's suppression of his name an evidence of the Petrinism of the Gospel (*Evangel.*, p. 137). It may be so; but it may also simply be that the evangelist, without any peculiar reference to Peter, just avails himself of the eclecticism which is at once the privilege and the necessity of all historians and biographers. It was a fact that the whole company of the disciples were in a state of mental perplexity (see Matt. xv. 16).

VER. 18. **And He says to them, Are ye so without understanding also?** Or, *Is it the case that even you are so dull in apprehension?* Even *you*, who have so long been with Me, and have hence had such opportunities of understanding the principles of right and wrong, of true and false : *are ye in this matter so unintelligent?* Note the *so;* to *such an extent as not to understand the apophthegm which I uttered to the collective crowd, and which I put into the form which it received, because I wished them to turn it over and over in their thoughts, till they should see through it.*

Do ye not perceive that everything that entereth from without into the man is unable to defile him? Or literally, *to make him common*, that is, *to make him, as regards moral condition, to be in the state which is 'common' all over the world.* The Saviour refers to the material things, that enter into a man through his mouth. His principle however is applicable, on a higher plane of reference, to spiritual things too which come in from without. These, however noxious, cannot of themselves defile a man. 'The man within the breast' must act in reference to them, before guilt can be contracted.

VER. 19. **Because it entereth not into the heart.** The spiritual region of the being, the region in which alone can be found the entities and essences of moral purity and impurity. 'By *heart*,' says Petter, 'understand *the whole inner man*, comprehending in a large sense the principal faculties of the soul.'

But into the belly. The merely corporeal region, the region of the stomach and those other wonderful intestinal structures which have to do with the chymification, chylification, and sanguification of the food, and thus with the utilization of its nourishing ingredients.

And goeth out into the draught. The place whence refuse is with*drawn*.

Purifying all the meats. That is, *all the 'comestibles' that have been eaten.* The word *purifying* has been puzzling from time immemorial; and hence multitudes of the manuscripts turned its gender from a masculine ($\kappa\alpha\theta\alpha\rho i\zeta\omega\nu$) into a neuter ($\kappa\alpha\theta\alpha\rho i\zeta o\nu$). This neuter gender thus became the reading of the Received Text, and is defended by Griesbach. (*Comm. Crit.*) But the word is masculine in almost all the most important authorities, such as ℵABEF GHLSXΔ, 1, 69, and is so given in the texts of Lachmann, Tischendorf, Tregelles, Alford. The construction is extremely inartificial. There is indeed, take the words as we may, a grammatical *anacoluth*. But the expression must, apparently, refer to the *draught*, which, by receiving the refuse, draws off as it

ST. MARK VII.

20 And he said, That which cometh out of the man, that defileth the man. 21 For from within, out of the heart of men, proceed evil thoughts, adulteries, fornications, murders,

were the impurities of the food, or those elements that remain after the nutritive ingredients have been eliminated and assimilated. To suppose with Field, Farrar (*Expositor*, 1876), and the Revisers that the words are a parenthetically interjected doctrinal inference of the evangelist, and not an observation on the part of our Lord, involves a violent strain of exegesis.

VER. 20. **But He said.** Turning to the other, the spiritual, side of this case. **That which cometh forth from the man**—and has been originated within him—**that defileth the man.** Namely, when he is defiled at all or *made common*, as the phrase literally means, and as it is given in the Rheims version. The Saviour refers of course to a moral condition, for the scribes and Pharisees in His day had confounded what was ceremonial with what was moral. They were contending, blindly, pertinaciously, and pettifoggingly, for the variable letter, as if it were the immutable spirit. And not only did they insist on the everlasting permanence of the letter, they equally insisted on the rigid observance of all the little teasing tittles and jots of ritualistic righteousness, which had been gratuitously added to the Mosaic letter by the fertile ingenuity of small rabbinical interpreters.

VER. 21. **For from within, out of the heart of men, proceed forth evil thoughts.** Or rather *evil communications*, or *evil conversations*, or *evil disputings*. Still more literally *the evil disputings*, those namely that were so common in Jewish society, and so infectious. The Saviour may have been referring to such rancorous disputes as had just been exhibited by the inquisitorial scribes and Pharisees in the uproar which they sought to raise in reference to the conduct of His disciples. The word is rendered *disputings* in Phil. ii. 14, and *reasoning* in Luke ix. 46. The cognate verb (διαλογίζομαι) is almost always rendered *to reason*. It refers to some kind of *dialectical* exercise, inward or outward, the bandying of a matter backward and forward with oneself or another. The reference here is not to what is inward, but to what is outward, as having welled up from what is inward. *Out of the heart:* That is, generically, *out of the inward or spiritual element of our nature*, the inward or spiritual, as distinguished from the outward or corporeal. See ver. 6, 19; chap. ii. 6, 8.

Adulteries, fornications, murders. There is considerable difference in the manuscripts, and old versions, regarding the order of some of the words in this clause and in the succeeding verse. Hence Tischendorf and Tregelles put *fornications* first, then *thefts*, then *murders*, then *adulteries*. But manifestly there was no special principle of order intended; the terms were simply *showered down*. Fritzsche says that the vices which are miscellaneously specified are considered 'not in so far as they are *perpetrated*, but in so far as they are *meditated*.' It is an infelicitous distinction; for the specified vices are expressly referred to as coming out from within, and efflorescing into overt acts. They pass beyond intentions into accomplishments. There is indeed, in the interior region of our being, sphere within sphere; and intentions may be distinguished, not only from their consequents *ad extra*, but also from their

22 thefts, covetousness, wickedness, deceit, lasciviousness,

antecedents *ab intra*. When thus distinguished, we find, in their antecedents, vices of choice that spring directly out of the innermost fountain of personality, the heart of the heart. But it is not to these inter-relationships, *in the interior of the being*, that the Saviour here refers. He is drawing a broad distinction between what belongs to the inner or spiritual sphere (the *heart*) on the one hand, and what belongs to the outer or corporeal on the other.

VER. 22. **Thefts, covetings.** The original word (πλεονεξίαι), refers, like the preceding expressions, to overt conduct rather than to inward disposition. King James's translators rendered it *covetous practices* in 2 Pet. ii. 14. That is, as nearly as may be, its meaning here; and hence the 'plural number. The cognate verb originally denoted *to have more* (viz. *than one's proper share*). It thence naturally came to denote *the voluntary possession of an illegitimate overplus*, the *holding* of it. A kindred idea was, the *grasping at* it, and the *claiming* of it. It is something like *overreachings* that is meant here; yet not exclusively *overreachings*, but also *overgraspings* and *overholdings*,—all *acts*, in short, *that manifest a determination or a desire to have more than one's legitimate share*. Wycliffe gives, as an alternative translation or gloss, an admirable description of the vice, *overhard kepynge of goodis* (overhard keeping of goods). It is one of the subtlest of vices, and the wellspring of innumerable social and political corruptions and collisions. It has been the real cause of almost all the wars that have been waged between nations, as well as the prolific fount of the most irremediable of family feuds.

Wickednesses. The word means *knaveries* or *villanies* objectively considered, that is, *acts of knavery or villany* (πονηρίαι). *Knavery* originally denoted the rude and trickish conduct of a *servant lad*. The word *knave* meant *lad*; it is merely our English form of the German *Knabe*, 'a boy.' *Villany*, again, just means the gross, coarse, unprincipled conduct that was characteristic of the serfs or servile labourers who were attached to the *villas* or country houses of landed proprietors. These poor neglected *villagers*, living in clumps of wretched booths, 'bothies,' cots, or hovels, were in general extremely uncultured, not only æsthetically but morally. No one cared for their souls; no one cared for their minds. No wonder that they were often guilty of *villanies*, and that their wayward acts got enstamped upon them the name of *villanies*. The Greek word leads us back to the characteristic conduct of the same unfortunate toiling-and-moiling class. The root of the word (πόνος) means *labour, hard labour, drudgery, toil*. The word itself denotes, in the singular, *the action of a servile labourer*. When morally used it denotes *the moral action of a servile labourer*. Hence, as used here in the plural, it denotes *villanies, rascalities, knaveries*.

Deceit. This and the remaining items of the miscellaneous catalogue, or *Sündenregister* as Mehring would call it, are in the singular number. Petter spells the word *deceipt*, and explains it as meaning 'fraud and guile.' The English word literally means *the act of taking from*, stealthily no doubt (Lat. *decipio = de capio*). The primary idea of the Greek word (δόλος) is not so certain. It is supposed to have meant *bait* (for fish); Homer thus uses it (*Od.*

an evil eye, blasphemy, pride, foolishness: 23 all these

xii. 252). But whatever its primary reference, it came to denote *any cunning contrivance for catching or entrapping persons*, or *for getting an advantage over them*. "Deceipt is practised," as in other ways, so in this, says Petter, " by " using any kind of craft or cunning to cozen others of any part of the goods or " substance which belongs to them."

Lasciviousness. An excellent translation, superior to that of Tyndale, Coverdale, and the Geneva version, *uncleanness*. Wycliffe has *unchastitie*, and Wakefield contends for that term. The Rheims has *impudicities*; Principal Campbell, *immodesty*. Wolf, Rosenmüller, Kuinöl, Rowlandson, think that the reference is not to the wantonness of *lasciviousness*, but to the wantonness of *injuriousness*, '*masterfulness*,' *insolence*, or *outrageousness*; Mace renders it *impudence*. But the immodest companionships of the term in such passages as Rom. xiii. 13, 2 Cor. xii. 21, Gal. v. 19, make it evident that our translators have struck on the true idea.

An evil eye. That is apparently, and as Suicer concludes (*Thesaurus Ecc.*, vol. ii., p. 534), and also Patrizi, *an envious eye*; *an eye*, that is to say, *which manifests a spirit of envy*. Comp. Matt. xx. 15. It is the opposite of *a good eye*, or as it is rendered in our Authorized version, *a bountiful eye*: Prov. xxii. 9 ('a man *good as regards eye* will be blessed'). The mind looks through the eye; so does the heart. Lactantius beautifully compares the eyes to glazed windows (*fenestras lucente vitro aut speculari lapide obductas*), through which the mind beholds. 'And therefore,' adds he, ' the mind and will are often discerned from the eyes' (*De Opificio*, § 5). Salvianus of Marseilles uses the same comparison of *windows*, but adds that hence ' all wicked desires enter into the heart through the eyes, as through their natural avenues ' (*De Gubernatione Dei*, lib. iii., § 8). Certainly the *occasions* of the desires often thus enter into the heart, as the mind looks out. But the Saviour unfolds in the passage before us a far profounder moral philosophy, when He says that the evil desires *arise in the heart*, and come looking out wistfully at the eyes.

Blasphemy. The word apparently is not here used, as Luther supposed, in its highest reference, its reference to God. Its companionship is with vices that have reference to men. The term and its cognates are frequently employed in this lower plane, and then it means *railing, reviling, calumny, slander, evil speaking*. (See Matt. xxvii. 39; Mark xv. 29; Luke xxii. 65, xxiii. 39; Rom. iii. 8, xiv. 16; 1 Cor. iv. 13, x. 30; Eph. iv. 31; Col. iii. 8; 1 Tim. vi. 4; Tit. iii. 2; 1 Pet. iv. 4; 2 Pet. ii. 2; Jude 9) It is rendered *railing* in 1 Tim. vi. 4, and Eph. iv. 31; the Geneva renders it here *backbiting*.

Pride. Or *haughtiness of demeanour*, reflecting itself downwardly in *lofty and disdainful bearing*, such bearing as assumes a right to appear *conspicuous above others* (ὑπερηφανία). It is the vice of those who, owing it to accident that they are high in the social pyramid, take it for granted that others should be their humble servants, or if possible their serfs. It is the vice unhappily of some others too.

Foolishness. Or *senselessness* of demeanour. Some translators err in fixing on certain specific phases of senselessness. Mace fixes on *vanity*, Wakefield on *arrogancy*, far off from the mark; le Clerc has *intemperance!* Principal Camp-

evil things come from within, and defile the man.
24 And from thence he arose, and went into the borders
of Tyre and Sidon, and entered into an house, and

bell has *levity*. Patrizi wisely adheres to the generic notion of *foolishness*, but he unnecessarily narrows the word's scope when, like Fritzsche and Hammond, he confines the reference to *foolishness of speech*. Heumann, beyond all others, made the investigation of the word a kind of 'hobby' for years. He took his stand on Luther's translation, *unreasonableness* or *irrationality* (*Unvernunft*), and thence working inwardly, he saw in the term not only 'the greatest of the vices, the mother of them all,' but also the reason why all Roman Catholics and Jews and Mohammedans had not been converted from the error of their ways. *The church had not made use of 'reason' as it should.* This however, though by no means too wide or too deep a speculation in itself, is certainly going entirely out of the way of the simple moral philosophy of our Saviour, in the passage before us.

VER. 23. **All these evil things come forth from within.** They have an inward origin, and are vomited forth from the crater of the heart or soul. But whence then their origin? From 'self' no doubt. They are created, if one may so speak, within the selfhood. By what? A wrong question. 'Things' are created, but never create. By whom then? By God? It cannot be, for *moral evil* (as distinguished from *penal evil*, which is *moral good* : Amos iii. 6) is opposition to the will of God. By whom then? By the evil doer himself. In a little sphere of things, and as regards *acts*, though not as regards *substances* or *essences*, men may be spoken of as creators. Men, that is to say, are the efficient causes of their own choices. If they were not, will would not be really free. If it was not, there would be no real responsibility.

And defile the man. They make him *common*, *profane*, *unclean*, or *foul*. They 'defoulen' him, as Wycliffe has it. See on ver. 2, 15, 18, 20.

VER. 24–30 constitute a paragraph which gives us a glimpse into what was a kind of parenthesis in the life of our Saviour. See the corresponding paragraph in Matt. xv. 21-28.

VER. 24. **And from thence He arose, and went.** Or rather, (to avoid the awkward position of the *thence* or *from thence*,) *And He arose, and departed thence*. Such is Edgar Taylor's translation. Our English version however is a perfect parallel to the Syriac Peshito version. *Arose :* an artless statement of the natural antecedent of departure. Comp. Gen. xxxi. 13; 1 Sam. xxiii. 16, xxv. 1; Jon. i. 3, iii. 3. *Thence :* namely from the district that was contiguous to the sea of Tiberias. It is too stringent in Petter, Fritzsche, and Meyer, to insist that the reference must be to the specific locality of Genuesaret, at which the Saviour and His disciples had landed on the subsidence of the storm that is referred to in chap. vi. 47-53.

Into the borders of Tyre and Sidon. Great Phœnician cities, that had been conspicuous for centuries as centres of commerce and opulence. Tischendorf and Alford however omit from their texts the words *and Sidon*; so does Fritzsche. Meyer and Ewald approve of the omission; Griesbach too inclined

would have no man know *it*: but he could not be hid.

---

in the same direction, pronouncing the reading that is characterized by the omission as 'not improbable' (*Comm. Cr.* in loc.). And yet there is comparatively very little ancient authority for that reading. The words are found in the Sinaitic, Alexandrine, and Vatican manuscripts (א A B), and in all the rest of the uncials with the exception of D L Δ. They are also found in almost all the cursive manuscripts, including 1 and 33 'the queen.' They are found too in all the ancient versions, with the exception of some copies of the Old Latin. They are twice omitted however by Origen in quotations, in his Commentary on Matthew. There is then but little ancient authority for the omission of the words; and assuredly they would not have been repudiated by any modern critics, had it not been for a probable reading in the 31st verse, " and again, "departing *from the coasts of Tyre* He came *through Sidon* to the sea of Galilee." That this other reading is correct we cannot doubt; and were the Received or Erasmian reading of ver. 24 inconsistent with it, we should be obliged to accept the amputative reading of Fritzsche, Tischendorf, Ewald, Meyer, Alford. But there is no inconsistency between the two passages, the one as given in the Received Text, and the other as given in the critical texts. There is simply an inartificial freedom of composition in the direction of *generic* representation in ver. 24, and an equally inartificial *specific* representation in ver. 31. Such was the judicious view taken of the subject by Mill (*Prol.*, § 404); and both Lachmann and Tregelles have done wisely in retaining the words *and Sidon* in ver. 24, and giving the reading *through Sidon* in ver. 31. Alford says indeed that "there can be no possible reason given why *and Sidon* should have been "omitted, had it formed part of the original text." But the desire to produce literal uniformity with the correct reading of ver. 31 was certainly a 'sufficient reason.' The hand of some 'studious' person, as Mill remarks, is apparent in the tinkering. The expression, the *borders* or *confines* of Tyre and Sidon, leaves it indeterminate whether our Lord was actually beyond the Galilean territory and within the landmarks of Phœnicia, or only on the marginal ground of Galilee that marched with the lands of Tyre and Sidon. It is likely that He would still be on Galilean soil. Comp. Matt. xv. 22. It is likely that His temporary home would be the abode of some trusty Galilean friend.

And having entered into an house. It was not of moment to the narrator to give particulars regarding the householder; his mind was hastening on to another set of particulars. In the Received Text the expression is *into 'the' house*; but with the exception of the Cambridge (D), all the best manuscripts omit the article; so did Erasmus, Beza, and Bengel in their editions. The Peshito Syriac has what is equivalent to 'into "*ane*" hoose,' that is, *into a certain house, into 'an' house*.

He wished no one to know. Or, as Tyndale gives it very literally, *and wolde .hat no man shuld have knowen*. He wished seclusion with His disciples. See chap. iii. 20; iv. 35; vi. 1, 31. Note the word *wished*, translated *would* in Tyndale and our English version. It is not so much *volition* or *purpose* as *desire* that is expressed.

And He could not be hid. He could not remain *incognito*. His fame preceded Him; and His bearing and behaviour marked Him off as a remarkable

25 For a *certain* woman, whose young daughter had an
unclean spirit, heard of him, and came and fell at his feet.
26 The woman was a Greek, a Syrophenician by nation;

Personage. His 'following' of disciples moreover would make concealment
extremely difficult.

VER. 25. For a woman. Or, as Tischendorf, Tregelles, and Alford read it,
But forthwith a woman (ἀλλὰ εὐθύς). The reading is supported by the manuscripts ℵ B L Δ, 33, and other ancient authorities, and is likely, as the more
difficult, to be correct. The Saviour "was not able to escape observation, *but*
" *on the contrary, and immediately,* a woman came to Him as a suppliant."

Whose little daughter had an impure spirit. The word for *little daughter* is a
beautiful diminutive in the original (θυγάτριον), which the Germans can finely reproduce, as Luther has done (*Töchterlein*). Count Zinzendorf has a corresponding diminutive (*Töchtergen*). As to *impure spirits*, see on chap. i. 23, 32.

Having heard concerning Him. That is, having heard that the great Israelitish
Deliverer, whose fame had been ringing so loud and so long far and near, had
come to her own neighbourhood.

Came and fell down at His feet. Instead of *came*, Tischendorf in his eighth
edition reads *entered*. The reading is supported by the manuscripts ℵ L Δ and
the Vulgate and Coptic versions. And one could suppose that it had been modified into the Received reading by a desire to bring the narrative into minute
harmony with the narrative of Matt. xv. 22, 23. In reading Matthew's
narrative, we naturally think of our Saviour as walking in the open air at the
time when He was addressed by the woman; but, on the other hand, it is
possible that the reading of Tischendorf (εἰσελθοῦσα for ἐλθοῦσα) may have been
simply moulded by some semi 'studious' transcriber, on the expression of the
preceding verse, *entered into a house* (εἰσελθών). Whichsoever be the correct
reading, there is ample scope left for filling up the minute and unessential
details of the scene. The interview for instance *may have been lengthened;*
and our Saviour, during it, may have been both within and without the house.
Fell down at His feet: the preposition (πρὸς) indicates that she threw herself
toward His feet, imploringly, and no doubt with beautiful oriental facility and
gracefulness.

VER. 26. And the woman was a Greek. That is, *a Gentile,* an instance of the
specific being put for the generic; comp. Rom. i. 16. It was on a corresponding principle that, in former times, Europeans in general were designated
Franks by the Turks, Arabs, and other inhabitants of the south-western
portion of Asia. The designation continues even yet to a partial extent. The
Vulgate renders the term *Gentile,* and hence Wycliffe has *heathen, Sothli the
womman was hethene*. Fritzsche translates the word *pagan,* and supposes that
the reference is to the woman's religion. But the expression is only the first
indefinite step toward a more precise specification of her ethnological position.

A Syrophœnician by race. Or *by descent*. This was her precise ethnological
position. She belonged to the *race,* or ethnological *family* (the γένος), of the
Syrophœnicians. She was, as the Rheims version renders it, *a Syrophœnician
born*. The *Syropbœnicians* were distinguished from the *Libo-* or *Libyo-*

and she besought him that he would cast forth the devil out of her daughter. 27 But Jesus said unto her, Let the children first be filled: for it is not meet to take the children's bread, and to cast *it* unto the dogs. 28

---

phœnicians in the north of Africa, the *Carthaginians*. The Syrophœnicians were *Phœnicians* who dwelt *in Syria*. (See *Relandi Palest.*, pp. 50, 607). They were called in their own tongue *Canaanites*. (See Matt. xv. 22.)

And she besought Him that He would cast out the demon from her daughter. *Besought*, or *entreated*, or *supplicated*; literally, *asked*. The *thing* that she asked was coincident with the *aim* that she had in view in asking, and hence the expression, if very literally rendered, would run as follows, *and she asked Him* '*in order that*' *He might cast out* (ἐκβάλῃ the right reading) *the demon*.

VER. 27. **And He said to her.** Such is the simple reading of Lachmann, Tischendorf, Tregelles, Alford.

Let the children first be filled. Or, *Permit that the children first be satisfied*. Let them first get enough. Purvey's revision of Wycliffe's version is graphic, *Suffre thou that the children be 'fulfilled' first*. The Lord would no doubt have previously told the suppliant that His mission was *a mission to the children of Israel*. (See Matt. xv. 24.) He could not diffuse Himself universally. He must select His sphere and draw a circle. If all within that circle should welcome His ministry, they would soon be able to radiate out the influence to the ends of the earth. There was hope in the word '*first*.'

For it is not meet. Or *good*, as the Vulgate and Wycliffe render it. Literally, *beautiful*; that is, here, *becoming*.

To take the children's bread and cast it to the dogs. In Palestine and the surrounding districts dogs abound, but they are not favourites with the people. "As the traveller," says J. G. Wood, "traverses the streets, he finds that all "the dogs are alike, and that all are gaunt, hungry, half starved, savage, and "cowardly; more like wolves than dogs, and quite as ready as wolves to attack "when they fancy that they can do so with safety. They prowl about the "streets in great numbers, living as they best can on any scraps of food that "they may happen to find. They have no particular masters, and no particular "homes. Charitable persons will sometimes feed them, but will never make "companions of them, feeling that the very contact of a dog would be a pollu- "tion. They are certainly useful animals, for they act as scavengers, and will "eat almost any animal substance that comes in their way." (*Bible Animals*, p. 40.) There is however in the dog a deep instinct of yearning for human society; and the dogs of the East, though in general sadly neglected and degenerate, have a chord in their nature that becomes readily responsive to human kindness. This has often been exemplified in the experience of European travellers; and there can be no doubt that in ancient times *children* and *little dogs* would get into terms of good fellowship. Not unlikely, some specimen of such fellowship had been before the eyes of both our Saviour and the Syrophœnician woman just before the remark we are considering was made. The word rendered *dogs* is a diminutive, *little dogs*, probably *little* because *young*. Tyndale renders it *whelppes*. So the Geneva.

And she answered and said unto him, Yes, Lord: yet the dogs under the table eat of the children's crumbs. 29 And he said unto her, For this saying go thy way; the devil is gone out

VER. 28. **But she answered and says to Him, Yes, Lord.** She acknowledges the justice of our Saviour's observation. She concedes the principle of action that was implied. She would not regard it as a fitting thing that the ministry which was so wisely intended for the Jews should be transferred to the Gentiles. **Yet.** An imperfect rendering of the expression that was before our translators (καὶ γάρ). It is the same expression that occurs in Matt. xv. 27. But there is reason to believe that Mark's real phrase was only the conjunction καί, as meaning *even*. Such is the reading of both Tregelles and Tischendorf (in his eighth edition). It is the reading of the manuscripts ℵ B H Δ, 33, and 69, and is supported by the Syriac Peshito, Coptic, Armenian, and Æthiopic versions. The woman, as Trapp remarks, was ' of an heroicall faith.' **Even the little dogs under the table eat of the children's crumbs.** The word for *crumbs* (ψιχία) is a diminutive, and means *little crumbs*. The reference is not to considerable pieces intentionally thrown to the little dogs, but to small inconsiderable crumbs which children are so apt to let fall undesignedly on the ground. The children, she as it were reasons, cannot as a general rule use up absolutely all the bread that is given to them. As they break and crumble their portions, there is some superfluity, however little, that falls; and the little dogs get the benefit of it. The woman means that, in her view of the case, it would not be inconsistent with the prerogatives of the Jews that a poor Gentile in her position should get the advantage of the little superfluity of ministerial or mediatorial energy that was ready to drop, as it were, from the table, in the very fact of the Saviour's presence in that Gentilised district. Such was the admirable reasoning, or, as Luther expresses it, the ' comfortable dialectic ' (*tröstliche Dialektik*) of the Syrophœnician woman.

VER. 29. **And He said to her, For this saying.** Or, *because of this saying*. It is διά with the accusative. The Saviour discovered in it the evidence of a faith that was at once peculiarly enlightened and peculiarly strong. It was therefore ' rewardable.' In scholas ic language, it was a *cause* of reward or blessing; something good could be conferred ' *because* of it.' It was not, of course, the *efficient cause* of the blessing. Jesus was that. It was only of a *motive* nature (*causa motiva* aut *impulsiva*); it was something that *moved* into action the Efficient Cause. And yet it was not the principal motive. The inward love or grace of the Efficient Cause was that. The woman's faith was the secondary and external motive of the Saviour's act (*causa motiva externa*). Dr. Samuel Clarke's standpoint was not sufficiently elevated when he represented our Saviour as ' *vanquished*, as it were, by the woman's modest importunity.'

Go thy way, the demon has gone out of thy daughter. The woman's faith was munificently ' rewarded.' Volkmar thinks that the whole narrative is a cunningly devised New Testament counterpart to the Old Testament narrative concerning the widow of Sarepta (1 Kings xvii.) ! Hilgenfeld thinks that Mark, by the word ' first ' (ver. 27), intentionally ' softens the strong, hard, judaizing view ' that is given in Matt. xv. 24, 26, of the relation of Christ to the Jews !

of thy daughter. 30 And when she was come to her house, she found the devil gone out, and her daughter laid upon the bed.

31 And again, departing from the coasts of Tyre and Sidon,

Ewald, Holtzmann, Michelsen follow another line of conjecture, and think that in the fuller account of Matthew, in which the conversation out of doors is narrated, we have the true remains of a passage in the Gospel of the Proto-Mark, which has been for some reason or other cut down and abbreviated by the Deutero-Mark! What next?

VER. 30. **And when she was come to her house.** Or more literally, *and when she 'went' to her house.* Very literally, *and when she 'departed' to her house* (ἀπελθοῦσα). The completion of her journey homeward is assumed.

She found the demon gone out, and her daughter laid (or *thrown*) upon the bed. Such is the order of the clauses in the Received Text. The order is reversed in the texts of Lachmann, Tischendorf, Tregelles, Alford: *she found her daughter laid, or thrown, on the bed, and the demon gone out.* For this latter arrangement there is the authority of the manuscripts ℵ B D L Δ, 33, and of the Vulgate, Peshito Syriac, Jerusalem Syriac, Coptic, Æthiopic, and Persic versions, also of most of the Old Latin codices. *She found her daughter :* or rather, *she found the 'child'* (τὸ παιδίον). Such is the reading of the chief manuscriptural authorities, ℵ B L Δ, 33, as also of the Vulgate and most of the Old Latin codices (*puellam*). When the evangelist says *she 'found,'* he intended the mind to go forward from the mere personality of the 'child' to her condition as described in the words that follow. *Laid on the bed :* exhausted no doubt and prostrate (chap. i. 26), but nevertheless enjoying delightful repose. She had probably been subjected to some severe convulsions. *And the demon departed :* the child was herself again.

VER. 31-37 form a paragraph for which there is no parallel in the other Gospels. As it is wanting in Matthew, Hilgenfeld looks upon it as invented by Mark, or expanded, as it were, into specific form and details, out of the germinal generality of Matt. xv. 30!

VER. 31. **And again.** We must go forward with this *again* to the verb *He came* ; *He came again,* that is, *He returned.*

Departing. The participle is in the aorist, and thus points to what was past in relation to our Lord's action in returning to the sea of Galilee, '*after departing.*' (See Krüger's *Sprachlehre*, § 53, 6 : 6.)

From the coasts of Tyre. In the Received Text it is added, *and Sidon* ; but these words, as already intimated (ver. 24), are omitted by the best textual critics, Lachmann, Tischendorf, Tregelles, Alford. They were suspected by Griesbach, and condemned by Mill. Fritzsche too omits them from his text, and Meyer approves. They are wanting in the Sinaitic, Vatican and Cambridge manuscripts (ℵ B D), as also in L Δ and 33 'the queen of the cursives.' They are wanting too in the Old Latin version, and the Vulgate, Coptic, Jerusalem Syriac, and Æthiopic versions. They are manifestly an import from ver. 24. Our Lord had gone indeed to 'the coasts of Tyre *and Sidon,*' that is, to the

he came unto the sea of Galilee, through the midst of the coasts of Decapolis. 32 And they bring unto him one that was deaf, and had an impediment in his speech; and they

boundary lands of Galilee that marched with the maritime strip of land that belonged to Tyre and Sidon, or that constituted the territory of Tyre and Sidon. But nevertheless, in going northward to these boundary lands, He naturally came first of all to the neighbourhood of Tyre, which lay considerably south of Sidon. And it was there, as it would appear, that He met with the Syrophœnician woman.

He returned 'through Sidon' to the sea of Galilee. This phrase *through Sidon* is the reading of those manuscripts and versions which omit the words *and Sidon* in the preceding expression. There can be no doubt of the genuineness of the phrase. It would never have been invented by a transcriber, whether 'studious' or careless, for as Sidon lies north of Tyre it would never have occurred to any one that it was likely that *our Saviour would return from Tyre to the sea of Galilee by way of Sidon*. He did so, however; for He was still wishful to be as much as possible secluded He needed rest; and so did His disciples. And they also needed to get education and private preparation for the scenes of suffering that were so soon to throw into shadow, as far as *their* vision was concerned, the glorious personality and prospects of their Master. When it is said that He passed *through Sidon* we need not be positive with Meyer that He actually traversed the streets of the city. He may or He may not. Both Tyre and Sidon had boundary lands; they were the centres of territorial semicircles, which belonged to them, and thence took their denomination. These great cities, though peculiarly and emphatically cities, were also States, though very small ones.

Through the midst of the borders of Decapolis. Our Lord, while having the sea of Galilee as His goal, did not take the shortest route to it from Sidon. He made a still farther detour eastward, into the grand highland scenery of Palestine, and came down, somewhere on the east side of the Jordan, to the special scene of His ministerial activity. As to *Decapolis*, see on chap. v. 20.

VER. 32. **And they bring to Him.** We know not at what part of His journey.

One who was deaf (κωφόν). The word is two-sided in import. It often means *dumb*, just as it often means *deaf*. It is translated *dumb* in Matt. ix. 32, 33, xii. 22, xv. 30, 31; Luke i. 22, xi. 14. In Mark however it only means *deaf* as distinguished from *dumb*. See chap. ix. 25.

And had-an-impediment-in-his-speech (καὶ μογιλάλον). He spoke *with difficulty*; and what he said would no doubt be awkwardly spoken. He was almost speechless, or, as it were, dumb. See ver. 37. In the Vulgate the word is rendered *dumb* (*mutum*), which astonished Principal Campbell. He says 'this deviation from the meaning is not authorized by a single manuscript.' The Principal was under a kind of mistake. *The Vulgate word was intended to be a translation of the term in the text.* Luther gives it the same translation (*stumm*); so does de Dieu, Ernesti, Ewald; Meyer too, who *contends* for the meaning; and Bisping, who simply *concedes* it. The term is certainly used in the Septuagint

beseech him to put his hand upon him. 33 And he took him
aside from the multitude, and put his fingers into his ears, and

version of Isa. xxxv. 6, to render a Hebrew word which is always translated
dumb in our version. And in the Greek versions of Aquila, Symmachus, and
Theodotion, the same term is employed in Exod. iv. 11, to render the same
Hebrew word. One might say indeed of this Septuagint rendering, as Bloomfield says, that it is 'erroneous,' and thus object to the Vulgate version of the
expression before us; or we may, more respectfully and legitimately, presume
that the Greek translators assumed that in the passages referred to the dumbness spoken of included, not only those cases in which it was absolute, but also
those in which it was partial. There is certainly no good reason for supposing
that in the case before us there was absolute dumbness. But Tyndale's version,
on the other hand, understates the case, 'they brought unto Him won that was
deffe, *and stambred in his speche.*'
And they beseech Him to put His hand upon him. So as to heal him. They
would seem to have understood that it was the ordinary practice of our Lord to
make a visible connection of Himself with the recipient of His 'virtue.' The
phrase rendered, *they beseech Him* '*to put*' is literally *they beseech Him* '*in
order that He might put.*'

Ver. 33. And He took him away from the crowd, apart. To a private place;
most likely into a private house. Privacy is certainly suggested (see ver. 36).
The expression indeed which we render *aside* is not infrequently rendered
privately (Matt. xxiv. 3; Mark ix. 28, xiii. 3; Acts xxiii. 19, etc.). But why did
the Saviour take the man (and his friends) *aside*? Michaelis suggests that the
action might be a kind of parable to the eye. He supposes that the Saviour was in
some heathen place, amid a heathen multitude. Might not His action therefore,
he concludes, be regarded as vocal with this idea, *Ye must come out, and be separate, from your own people, from heathenism*? This however is too fanciful; and
there is really no reason for assuming that the crowd was composed of heathens.
Meyer is of opinion indeed that the aim of the Saviour was to secure an isolated or
undisturbed 'rapport' between Himself and the patient. It is likely however
that our Saviour was just shunning, under the influence of His personal feelings
on the one hand and His more impersonal judgment on the other, everything
that might appear to be *display*; and more especially when He took into account
the peculiar mental condition of the crowd of Jews that was surging around
Him. That crowd was intensely excited indeed in His favour. But its excitement was not taking the direction of things spiritual and heavenly; it was rolling strong and fast in the direction of things corporeal and terrestrial, things
that would be grateful to mere selfism and selfishness. The people were hoping
most likely that they would be able to get, by means of the mystic power of such
a Wonder-worker, social and political advantages that would free them from the
necessity of toil, and exalt them above those Gentiles who had so long been
domineering over them. (See John vi. 26-63, and comp. Mark v. 37-43.)

And put His fingers into his ears, and He spat, and touched his tongue (ver. 34);
and looking up to the heaven He sighed. Clauses these which have occasioned
to many, though unnecessarily, very great perplexity. Dr. Adam Clarke, for

he spit, and touched his tongue; 34 and looking up to heaven,

instance, says : " This place is exceedingly difficult. There is scarcely an action "of our Lord's life but one can see an *evident reason* for, except this." He would get quit of the difficulty by interpreting as follows: " *and (the deaf man)* "*put his fingers into his ears*, intimating thereby to Christ that they were so "*stopped that* he could not hear; *and having spat out*, that there might be "nothing remaining in his mouth to offend the sight when Christ should look "at his tongue, *he touched his tongue*, showing to Christ that it was so bound "that he could not speak ; *and he looked up to heaven*, as if to implore assist-"ance from above; *and he groaned*, being distressed because of his present "affliction, and thus implored relief, for, not being able to speak, he could only "*groan* and *look up*, expressing by these signs, as well as he could, his afflicted "state and the desire he had to be relieved." Rodolphus Dickinson introduces Dr. Adam Clarke's interpretation into his version. It is inadmissible however; because it is strained and romantic on the one hand, and ungrammatical on the other. The construction is such that *the person who took* the man aside must be *the person who put his fingers* into his ears (ἀπολαβόμενος . . . ἔβαλεν). There is moreover no real difficulty. See what follows. *And put His fingers :* very literally *and ' threw ' His fingers* : thrust them as it were, as if He would perforate or clear a passage for the sound to enter (*quasi clausas et obturatas aures terebraturus*: MALDONATO). The action was of course symbolic or parabolic, but very significant. It would be, in default of words, which would have been unsuitable because inaudible, of especial significance to the deaf man himself. *And He spat and touched his tongue :* or, as we might now express it, *and He touched his tongue with saliva :* symbolically of course, or parabolically, but yet most significantly, more particularly in relation to the times and the manners of the people ; for, as W. Gilpin remarks, ' we must not criticise the manners that prevailed two thousand years ago, by those of our own age.' (*New Test.*, in loc.) The man's tongue, we may suppose, would be hot, and stiff, and parched, and needing nature's lubrication. How was it to obtain its normal flexibility ? By nothing in the man's own nature ; by nothing that would be naturally medicinal ; but by a higher power. It was to be by the fiat of Jesus. But Jesus could not tell the man this in words ; the man was deaf. And hence our Saviour benevolently *acted* for his behoof, intimating on the one hand, and no doubt with the utmost delicacy, that nature's own delightful lubrication would be immediately experienced in the affected part, and announcing, on the other, with the utmost significancy, that the blessed change would be the result of a fiat to which there was nothing analogous in any ordinary medical treatment. As Maldonato expresses it, Christ's action was ' a *metaphor*, not in word, but in fact.' It is on this action of our Saviour that Roman Catholics found their custom of touching with 'spittle' the ears and nostrils of the person to be baptized, whether adult or infant. Thus, as Calvin says, "among other fool-"eries with which baptism has been debased by foolish men, the ceremony used "by the Lord is turned into a piece of buffoonery." "Avaunt therefore," exclaims Cartwright, "with this profane spittle, as that which is fitter for the "spital than for the church." (*Confutation of the Rhemists*, in loc.)

VER. 34. *And looking up to the heaven He sighed.* Or *groaned*, as the word

ST. MARK VII.

he sighed, and saith unto him, Ephphatha, that is, Be opened. 35 And straightway his ears were opened, and the string of his tongue was loosed, and he spake plain. 36 And he

is rendered in the Rheims, and in Rom. viii. 23 ; 2 Cor. v. 2, 4; comp. Acts vii. 34, and Rom. viii. 26. **Wycliffe has it,** *He sorwide withynne.* Heinsius and le Cene misunderstood the term when they rendered it *He cried aloud.* Our Saviour was touched with a feeling of the man's infirmities ; and perhaps, at the same moment, His spirit might take in, at a glance, the innumerable woes, both spiritual and physical, which have been rained down with just retribution upon men in consequence of their sins. It was *after looking up to heaven* that He groaned (ἀναβλέψας . . . ἐστέναξεν, see Krüger's *Sprachlehre*, § 52, 6: 6) ; for the deepest sympathy with man *springs out of* the loftiest communion with God. The lifting up of the desires, indicated by the lifting up of the eyes, is prayer.

And saith to him, Ephphatha (that is, Be opened). Or, *Be thou opened*, as both Wycliffe and the Rheims correctly give it. It is the man who is addressed. It was he who needed to be corporeally opened to the ingress of sounds and to the ready egress of words. The Aramaic imperative *Ethpathach*, or, in its abbreviated form, *Ethpach*, and the corresponding expressions in Greek and English, are applicable both to the organs of hearing and to the organ of speech, not strictly indeed to the tongue, but strictly to the mouth as a whole. Hence we read of Zacharias in Luke i. 64, 'and *his mouth was opened* immediately, and *his tongue (loosed*), and he spake, and praised God.' There is no word for *loosed* in the original. The word *opened* stretches, as it were overshadowingly, beyond its appropriate object, *mouth*, and is freely applied to the *tongue*, in the manner called zeugma by grammarians. In the passage before us there is somewhat of the same figure of speech, connecting the *mouth* with the *ears*; for in ver. 35 there is no *explicit* reference to the *opening of the mouth.*

VER. 35. **And straightway his ears were opened.** Very literally, *his hearings* (ἀκοαί). No doubt, originally, the *ear* was just the *hear*.

And the bond of his tongue was loosed. *Bond*, or *fetter*. *String* was Tyndale's word. Wycliffe and Coverdale have *bond* ; and in all the other passages in which it occurs in the New Testament it is rendered *bond* or *band* in our English version. The representation of the cure is of course popular, not scientific.

And he spake plain. Or rather, *right.* The former is Coverdale's word, and the Rheims' too ; the latter is Wycliffe's (*rightly*). The fact that the man now spoke *right* seems to make it certain that he had not been, as Petter expresses it, ' stark dumb before,' or absolutely *a deaf-mute*, and that hence his infirmity had not been congenital. He had once heard well enough, and could speak well enough ; but, either by some external accident or by an internal disease, he had lost his hearing entirely, and could only utter, with awkwardness, a limited number of articulated sounds.

The word *straightway* or *immediately* in the first clause of the verse is omitted by Tischendorf, Tregelles, Alford. It is wanting in ℵ B D L Δ, 33, the Coptic version, and several copies of the Old Latin. Tischendorf however restores it to the second clause of the verse, and '*immediately*' *the bond of his tongue was loosed*, under the authority of ℵ L Δ and the Æthiopic version.

charged them that they should tell no man: but the more he charged them, so much the more a great deal they published *it;* 37 and were beyond measure astonished, saying, He hath done all things well: he maketh both the deaf to hear, and the dumb to speak.

CHAPTER VIII.

1 IN those days the multitude being very great, and having

VER. 36. **And He charged them that they should tell no one.** He gave them *distinct* and positive orders (διεστείλατο). *Them :* the man who had been cured, and his friends. The fact of the cure could not indeed be concealed from the outside crowd; but our Saviour wished that it should not be blazoned abroad. The rush of sight-seers, and of others who were either morbidly or superficially excited, was still most inconveniencing. It was with difficulty that the Saviour obtained that statedly recurring seclusion, of which His own human weakness stood in need, and which was urgently required by His disciples in order to their spiritual development and evangelistic education and preparation.

But the more He charged them, so much the more exceedingly they published (it). They probably did not understand the reason why He sought to restrain them, imagining perhaps that He was only giving expression to His modesty; and they felt so amazed and captivated that they could not hold their tongues. Popularity has thus its drawbacks, as well as unpopularity.

VER. 37. **And they were beyond measure astonished, saying, He hath done all things well.** *All things* namely that He has done. Principal Campbell errs in rendering the clause, *He doth everything well.* The generalized asseveration comes in the next clause.

And (καί). So apparently the conjunction should be rendered, rather than either *both* or *even.* It seems to be no part of the reported exclamations, but the evangelist's own link of connection between the two exclamations which he records. (Comp. chap. vi. 2.) Both Wycliffe and Tyndale render it *and.* Luther, Coverdale, Zinzendorf, Heumann, Bengel, and many others, omit it altogether; as does the Peshito Syriac version, though not the Philoxenian.

He maketh the deaf to hear, and the dumb to speak. In the preceding exclamation the people had explicit reference to the particular actions which they had witnessed, and which were past and completed. In this they generalize their conception, and hence use the present verb representatively, instead of the perfect historically. Hence also, instead of using phrases that would have described to a nicety the special condition of the individual who had been so marvellously cured, they enlarge their reference to 'the dumb,' in all stages of 'dumbness,' as well as to 'the deaf.'

CHAPTER VIII.

VER. 1-10 constitute a paragraph, which finds its exact parallel in Matt. xv. 32-39. The variations in the two accounts are minute. The exact verbal coincidences are many.

VER. 1. **In those days.** The evangelist makes no attempt at very precise

ST. MARK VIII.

nothing to eat, Jesus called his disciples *unto him*, and saith unto them, 2 I have compassion on the multitude, because

---

chronological representation. It would therefore be unfair to endeavour to work out of his narrative a rigidly consecutive concatenation of events. Such a rigid chronology was not needed; and Holtzmann proceeds on an entirely fallacious principle when he seeks to make out a close historical connection between what is narrated at the close of chap. vii. and what is recorded in ver. 11–13 of this chap. viii., *and when*, consequently, *he fancies that he finds, in the interposition of ver.* 1–10, *a disturbance* (a Störung) *of the real connection of occurrences.* (*Die Synopt. Evangelien*, p. 85.) He seeks what he had no right to seek, and what consequently he cannot find. Wilke before him made the same mistake. (*Der Urevangelist*, p. 567.)

The crowd being very great. Or, still more literally, *there being a very great crowd*, a crowd namely that had gathered round the Saviour while He was seeking seclusion in rural and comparatively unfrequented parts. Instead of *very great* (παμπόλλου, *a word which occurs nowhere else in the New Testament, and not at all in the Septuagint*), there is, in a large preponderance of the oldest and best manuscripts, a different reading (πάλιν πόλλου), *there being again a great crowd.* This is the reading of ℵ B D G L M N Δ, 1, 33, 69, as well as of the Vulgate, Coptic, Gothic, Armenian, and Æthiopic versions, and of almost all the copies of the Old Latin. The Alexandrine manuscript (A), on the other hand, along with E F H K S U V Wᵈ X Γ Π, and the Syriac versions, supports the Received reading. There had evidently been an early divergence in the manuscripts, and it is somewhat difficult to decide between the readings. Matthæi, Fritzsche, Meyer, plead for the Received Text; Mill, Griesbach, Lachmann, Tregelles, Alford, decide for the other. This other was given by Tischendorf in his first critical edition, that of 1849; but he reverted to the Received reading in his second critical edition, that of 1859; and now in his third critical edition, the eighth edition in all, he has gone back to his first preference. His latest decision is probably right, for although it would seem to be unlikely that a word, nowhere else found in the New Testament, would be intruded into the text, to the displacement of a natural and eminently appropriate phrase, (and this is what has to be said in favour of the judgment of Matthæi, Fritzsche, Meyer,) yet, on the other hand, as an old ecclesiastical *Lection* began with this chapter, it may have appeared to some ecclesiastical readers that the omission of the retrospective expression made the lesson more self contained. Hence they might, with innocent intention, have substituted for the *again* the somewhat alliterative syllable by which they intensified the idea of *great*.

And having nothing to eat. In the original there is a disintegration of the *singular* word '*crowd*' into its *plural* constituents, the many individuals who composed it. *They* had nothing to eat.

He called His disciples unto Him, and saith to them. In the Received Text it is '*Jesus called.*' It was convenient, when commencing the public *Lection* in the church, to supply *Jesus*. Hence its occurrence in the Received Text.

Ver. 2. **I have compassion on the multitude.** Or, as Wycliffe finely renders it, *I have 'rewthe' on the companye of peple.* The word denotes such feelings, says Petter, ' as are in natural fathers and mothers toward their children.'

they have now been with me three days, and have nothing to eat : 3 and if I send them away fasting to their own houses, they will faint by the way : for divers of them came from far.

Because they have now been with Me three days. The expression (προσμένουσίν μοι) properly means, *they persist in remaining with Me*. They persist in this although it was *now the third day*, that is, the third day of their 'camp meeting' as it were. The word rendered *now* (ἤδη) means *by this time ; by this time it is three days*, that is, *by this time it is the third day*. The expression *three days* is exceedingly inartificial in the correct reading of the original (ἡμέραι τρεῖς, not ἡμέρας as in the Received Text). It has occasioned much perplexity to those who look for classic purity of diction in the evangelist. Rowlandson proposes to construe the clause thus, *there are already three days to them remaining with Me*. Alexander, more violently still, *three days now continue*. But there is no real difficulty ; the entire phrase is an artlessly condensed conglomerate, and means, *because by this time it is the third day, and yet they persist in abiding with Me*.

And they have nothing to eat. Literally, *and they have not what they might eat* ; their stock of provisions was completely exhausted.

VER. 3. **And if I should dismiss them fasting to their homes.** Literally, and as Wycliffe renders it, *to their house*. The multitude is mentally disintegrated into the individuals composing it, *each to his house*.

They will faint in the way. Or, *on the road*. Note the expression *they will faint*, instead of *they would faint*. The reader is led, as it were, to look upon the hypothetical standpoint of the preceding clause, *if I should dismiss*, as converted into a real standpoint. The people 'are' dismissed, let us say. What follows ? *They 'will' faint in the way*.

And some of them have come from far. It is Jesus who is reported by the evangelist as speaking these words ; some translators however have regarded them as a parenthetical observation of the evangelist himself. Luther for instance, and Heumann, and Zinzendorf; apparently too Tyndale, and the editors of the Geneva version, as also King James's translators. Webster and Wilkinson indeed refer to the primary edition of the Authorized version, that of 1611, as reading *for divers of them 'come' from far*, instead of *for divers of them 'came' from far* ; and this reading is actually found in the reprint contained in Bagsters' *Hexapla*, from which, as we presume, Webster and Wilkinson must have quoted. But the *come* is a typographical error in the *Hexapla* for *came* ; it is *came* in the primary edition. The exact translation however is neither *came* nor *come*, but *have come*. But if *come* be used, as it is by Wakefield, Newcome, Brameld, Godwin, it is evidence that the observation is ascribed not to the evangelist but to the Saviour. That it should be ascribed to the Saviour is still further evidenced by the fact that instead of the initial conjunction *for*, it is *and* that is found in the very important manuscripts ℵ B L Δ, 1, 33, and which has been introduced into the text by Lachmann, Tischendorf, Tregelles, Alford; no doubt rightly. Instead of *have come* (ἥκασι), the Vatican manuscript (B) and L Δ read *are* (εἰσίν), which Alford accepts. Tischendorf accepted the same reading in his 1849 and 1859 editions, but in his final edition wisely returned to the reading of Lachmann.

ST. MARK VIII.

4 And his disciples answered him, From whence can a man satisfy these *men* with bread here in the wilderness? 5 And he asked them, How many loaves have ye? And they said, Seven. 6 And he commanded the people to sit down on the ground: and he took the seven loaves, and gave thanks, and brake, and gave to his disciples to set before *them*; and they did set *them* before the people. 7 And they had a few small fishes: and he blessed, and commanded to set them also before

---

VER. 4. **And His disciples answered Him, Whence shall any one be able to satisfy these with loaves in the desert?** This last expression, *in the desert*, is literally *on (the) desert*. The people were *on the superficies*, as well as *within the circumference*, of the desert. The article is omitted idiomatically, just as we can say in English, *on sea*, or *a-field*, that is *on field*. Some have wondered that the disciples should have brought forward a second time their former difficulty (see chap. vi. 37). The wonder is unnecessary. The disciples' remark was just their respectfully semi-circuitous way of indicating how utterly impossible it would be to provide for the multitude by any ordinary means of purveyance. And it did not belong to them to lay down to their Master the law of a miraculous commissariat.

VER. 5. **And He asked them, How many loaves have you? And they said, Seven.** In Tyndale's spelling *loaves* is *loves*. Wycliffe has *looves*.

VER. 6. **And He issued orders to the crowd.** Or rather, *He issues orders*. Such is the reading of Lachmann, Tischendorf, Tregelles, Alford. It is supported by the manuscripts ℵ B D L Δ and Origen. The reader is transported back to the scene as it occurred, and looks on.

To recline on the ground. The verb employed very literally means not *to fall down* but *to fall up*; for, in assuming a recumbent posture, the body comes gradually in contact with the ground from below upwardly, the upper part is the last that comes to rest.

And He took the seven loaves, and, after having given thanks, He brake and gave to His disciples. The word *brake* is in the aorist tense (ἔκλασεν), whereas the word *gave* is in the imperfect (ἐδίδου). The evangelist might have put both in the aorist, but he chooses to bring into view *the continuity of giving after the act of breaking was past*.

To set before them. Or, more literally, *that they might serve out*; or, still more literally, according to the evangelist's autographic reading as preserved in the manuscripts ℵ B C L M Δ, 33, 69, *that they might be serving out* (παρατιθῶσιν, imperfect, instead of παραθῶσι, aorist). The disciples were to act as *serving men*. The word employed was the proper technical vocable, and meant primarily *to place beside*. In the particular case referred to however the food would not be *placed beside*, but *handed from the hand of the waiter to the hand of the receiver*.

And they did serve out to the crowd. Wycliffe's version is excellent, *and thei setten forth to the cumpany*.

VER. 7. **And they had a few small fishes.** Dried, of course. See chap. vi. 33. **And after blessing them He commanded to serve them out also.** The precise

them. 8 So they did eat, and were filled: and they took up of the broken *meat* that was left seven baskets. 9 And they that had eaten were about four thousand: and he sent them away. 10 And straightway he entered into a ship with his disciples, and came into the parts of Dalmanutha.

---

reading of the original is not easily ascertained; but the variations are not of the least exegetical moment. It would appear that our Saviour offered up to His Father separate acts of thanksgiving for the bread and the fishes. Matthew represents them in the gross (xv. 36). But there is nothing inconsistent in the two representations; the one is *involved*, the other is *explicit*. As to the meaning of the expression *blessing* when applied to food, see on chap. vi. 41. Zuingli correctly interprets it as here meaning *giving thanks* (id est, *gratias egit*).

VER. 8. And—(καὶ *the right reading*)—they ate and were satisfied. Literally, *were foddered*. Wycliffe's version is graphic, *fulfild* (that is, *filled full*). Tyndale has, *suffysed*; Coverdale, *satisfied*.

And they took up, of broken pieces that remained over, seven baskets. The word used for *baskets* (σπυρίς) is different from the term employed in the narrative of the corresponding miracle (chap. vi. 47, κόφινος). Matthew preserves the same distinction. The article here designated is supposed to have been of larger capacity than the other. It was the kind of vessel in which Paul was let down over the wall of Damascus (Acts ix. 25). Principal Campbell renders it *maunds*, too archaically.

VER. 9. And they were about four thousand; and He sent them away. Or, as the Rheims version has it, *and He dismissed them*.

The sceptical critics in general regard this whole narrative of the miraculous feeding of the four thousand as but the mythical echo of the corresponding narrative of the miraculous feeding of the five thousand (chap. vi. 35–45). The event is narrated, says Volkmar, 'as if it were distinct from the other; but it is not' (*Die Evangelien*, p. 396). Such is his, such is their, conjecture; but it is of course a mere conjecture and fancy. As a matter of fact, the emergencies of human life often repeat themselves under only minute variations of circumstance; and it is nothing wonderful therefore that many of the miracles of our Lord should have had, in their relation to one another, some striking points of correspondence or similitude.

VER. 10. And straightway He entered into the boat with His disciples and came into the parts of Dalmanutha. The expression *parts* is, in English and Latin, as well as Greek, used with a geographical acceptation. Territory everywhere is either naturally or artificially *parcelled* into *parts*. Dalmanutha is nowhere else referred to, so far as investigation has yet extended, either in Hebrew, Chaldee, Greek, or Roman writings. It must undoubtedly have been some obscure place, closely connected with another obscure place, *Magadan*, referred to by Matthew in the parallel passage (xv. 39). Augustine supposed that the one place must have borne the two names (*De Consensu Evangelist.*, ii., § 106). It is more likely however that Lightfoot is right when he supposes

ST. MARK VIII.

11 And the Pharisees came forth, and began to question with

Dalmanutha to be 'some particular place within the bounds' of the other. (*Chorographical Decad*, chap. v.) We know not in what part of the coast line of the lake the two places were situated; Lightfoot thought that they were situated at the south-east extremity; Volkmar is of the same opinion, in reference to Dalmanutha at least. (*Die Evangelien*, p. 399.) It seems probable however that the places were on the west side of the lake (see ver. 13). Baur has a singularly irreverent and wanton idea in reference to St. Mark's specification of Dalmanutha; he imagines that he designedly stuck in that name, to the exclusion of the place named by Matthew, 'in order to give his narrative the *appearance* of independent origin' (*einen Schein von Selbstständigkeit zu geben*: Marcusevangelium, p. 61). Holtzmann, on the other hand, reversing Baur's chronology of the inter-relationship of the Gospels, thinks that Matthew saw that Mark had made a geographical blunder in sending the Saviour and His disciples to the west of the lake (*Dalmanutha = Damon*), and therefore changed his Dalmanutha into Magadan! (*Die Synopt. Ev.*, p. 86.) Thus fancy fights with fancy; each annihilates the other. Dr. Tristram, assuming that Matthew's word was *Magdala* instead of *Magadan*, supposed that Dalmanutha may have been a little to the south of Mejdel, where there are "the ruins of a village, and some large and more ancient foundations of several "copious fountains." (*The Land of Israel*, p. 429.)

VER. 11-13 contain a little paragraph parallel to the paragraph in Matt. xvi. 1-4. The chronology and topography of the scene are left indeterminate in both Gospels; but there are more folds in the drapery of the representation as it occurs in Matthew than are found in Mark's narration.

VER. 11. **And the Pharisees came forth.** Whence we cannot tell, and need not conjecture. 'From their dwellings,' say Fritzsche and Meyer. It may be so. 'They came forth from their concealment, like persons who had been lying in wait,' says Lange. It may be so, though there is nothing to justify the specific supposition. Lange gives, as an alternative view, 'they came forth in solemn procession.' Even this is a gratuitous intensification of the import of the phrase. The evangelist's expression, however, does seem to indicate that the meeting was not casual on the part of the Pharisees. They 'came forth *of set purpose*,' as Petter explains it. Our evangelist makes mention only of the Pharisees. Matthew records that Sadducees were associated with them, (xvi. 1). The scene is thus described by the two evangelists from two standpoints of observation. In the one description there is a combination of more details than in the other. No doubt the Pharisees would be the predominant party, bustling about as usual with much self consequence, and making themselves obtrusively conspicuous.

And began to question with Him. Mark notices the commencement of their onset, *began*. The beginnings of things had a peculiar charm for him; and to note them, leaving the progress of events to the imagination, became *an idiom* in his mode of thought and speech. See chap. i. 45, iv. 17, 20, vi. 2, 7, 34, 55. *To question with Him*: or, as Purvey, Tyndale, Coverdale, the Great Bible,

him, seeking of him a sign from heaven, tempting him. 12
And he sighed deeply in his spirit, and saith, Why doth

---

and the Geneva render it, *to dispute with Him*. Our translators would seem to
have parted with this old translation under the idea that it implicated our
Saviour in something undignified. Principal Campbell's version is *to argue
with Him*. The majority of modern English translators however, such as Mace,
Worsley, Wakefield, Newcome, Norton, Edgar Taylor, Young, Brameld, recur
to the rendering of the old translators. Wynne mistakes the meaning. He
renders the phrase, *to examine Him*; it literally means *to inquire together with
Him* (συνζητεῖν αὐτῷ). As originally employed, it denoted the co-operation of
investigators. But as such co-operation became often replaced, in consequence
of human infirmity and the influence of partisanship, by embittered disputation, the phrase unhappily shifted its applicability, and was used when there
was nothing cordial or co-operative at all. Hence it came to mean *to dispute
with*. (See Acts vi. 9; 1 Cor. i. 20.) In the case before us the disputatious
spirit would be all on one side. See next verse.

Seeking from Him a sign from the heaven. That is, *a token, from the sky, of
His Divine mission*. They intimated to Him that they were not sure about the
'ways and means' of the miracles He was working. There was scope, they
insinuated, for illusion and delusion. Indeed, for aught that they could tell,
Satan might have his hand in all these wonders! Let Him therefore give
them something more decisive. *Let us see something striking coming from
a region where Satan can have no authority or power!* (Chap. iii. 22.) *Let us
see something coming straight down from the clear blue sky, say a shower of
manna, which we could all handle deliberately, and eat* (John vi. 30, 31); *or something else as unmistakeable*. It was a miracle of the nature of a phenomenal
curiosity that they pleaded for, not considering that if such a 'spectacular'
exhibition had been made, they would have been the very first, and the loudest,
to exclaim that it must be legerdemain, *for who could imagine that God was
going to entertain them, like children in a theatre, with mere displays of the
marvellous?* They were, in short, in a mood to find fault with everything that
our Saviour should do, so long as He did not become like one of themselves.

Tempting Him. That is, *trying Him*. It will be impossible to understand
temptation correctly, in the various branches of its signification, if this, the
radical meaning, be let go. God is said *to tempt* (Gen. xxii. 1; Ps. cxxxix. 23).
Christ is said *to tempt* (John vi. 6). Men are said *to tempt* (Mark xii. 15).
Satan is said *to tempt* (Mark i. 13). The point of coincidence in all these
applications of the term is *trial*. All the agents specified *made trial*. It is
the motive that determines whether the trial be good or bad. In the case
before us, the motive was base, and therefore the trial was bad. But it was
not specifically, like Satan's temptations, *a trial to get our Lord to commit a sin*.
It was a trial to get Him to attempt something in which He might signally fail,
something 'spectacular,' sensational, astounding, and coming from the sky.
They hoped, by skilful playing on His weakness, to excite His vanity or His
pride into rashness!

VER. 12. **And He sighed deeply in His spirit.** *He 'emitted' a groan from the*

this generation seek after a sign? Verily I say unto you,

---

depths of His spirit. The word employed (ἀναστενάξας) properly means *groaned upwardly.* It is a graphic touch from the hand of an eye-and-ear witness. And saith, Why does this generation seek a sign? (ζητεῖ not ἐπιζητεῖ.) He speaks to Himself as it were, reflectively, bewailingly. In the next clause He speaks directly to His critics. *This generation:* He does not refer exclusively to the critics who were standing in His presence. His view had expanded, till it embraced the great body of the people. 'The Jews require *a sign*' (1 Cor. i. 22). They demanded *a sign pure and simple,* a sign that would be nothing but a mere abstracted prodigy, or feat of Divine power. But they had no right to insist on such a mode of evidence. It was a style of demonstration which was suitable in only very peculiar circumstances (see Jud. vi. 37–40; etc.), and which would have been quite unsuitable in the case of the contemporaries of our Lord. If it had been resorted to, theories of illusion would have been instantly propounded, or Satan would have been introduced to cut the knot. The testimony of the eye-witnesses would have been challenged. Demands would have been made for illimitable repetitions of the marvel, and for a thousand-and-one securities that no 'glamour' was thrown over the eyes. Before any signs of the kind could have been advantageously given, a thorough moral preparation of the heart would have been requisite, a spirit of honest recipiency would have been indispensable. And then, why should there be abstracted, from the outgoings of the Divine energy, every element of mercy, humanity, and instruction? The works which our Lord actually performed bore ample and unmistakeable testimony concerning Him (John v. 36, x. 25, 38, xiv. 11); and their testimony was far from being marred or diminished by the fact that, instead of being wrought as on the stage of a theatre, and in the manner of a master of legerdemain, they were performed just as the natural emergencies of men's moral and physical condition cried aloud for merciful intervention. When God reveals Himself in nature and providence, He utilizes the forces and resources of His being, making them subservient to other purposes than those of mere self manifestation. And our Divine Saviour, in like manner, went about 'doing good,' filling most divinely the recipient vessels of men whenever they were longingly held up, and rectifying in the morally self-conscious, as far as was practicable amid the necessary limitations of time, space, and circumstances, the disorders inward and outward that are the woeful results of sin. Such works as these were the proper outgoings, manifestations, and signatures of Divinity, in its moral relations to moral creatures in a condition of sin. They were really the very best conceivable of all possible 'signs' (John ii. 11; Acts ii. 22). But as the elements of adaptation and moral utilization were inseparably inherent in them, they were rejected by the censorious and self-sufficient critics as being really irrelevant, and thus no signs at all, that is, no sufficient signs. Our Saviour, for the moment, catches up the word *sign,* in the arbitrarily abstracted sense abusively attached to it by His critics, and, in a kind of agony of spirit, because of the hopelessness of the moral condition indicated, says: 'Why, oh why, does this generation persist in seeking *a sign?*'

Verily, I say unto you. Both in the word *verily* and in the expression *I say*

There shall no sign be given unto this generation. 13 And he left them, and entering into the ship again departed to the other side.

14 Now *the disciples* had forgotten to take bread, neither had they in the ship with them more than one loaf. 15 And he charged them, saying, Take heed, beware of the

---

unto you, there is emphasis given to the declaration that follows. (See on chap. iii. 28.)

There shall no sign be given to this generation. No '*sign*' in the extremely partial, narrow, and unwarrantable sense attached to the term by His critics. The phrase that is rendered, and correctly rendered, *there shall no sign be given*, is a peculiar elliptical expression in the original. It is literally *if there shall be given a sign*, and is, as Euthymius Zigabenus remarks, ' an idiom of the Hebrew language.' It is based on a certain form of *swearing* that prevailed among the Jews. They were accustomed to imprecate some judgment of God on themselves, *if so and so were done by them*. Such imprecations were, of course, very strong denials or refusals. And hence there grew up, as a certain idiom of speech, the use of the hypothetical clause, *in a truncated form*, as a full and forcible denial or refusal. Comp. Heb. iii. 11.

VER. 13. **And He left them.** For there are limits to forbearance in dealing with creatures who abuse indefinitely the freedom of their will.

And having again embarked (πάλιν ἐμβάς). In the Received Text the phrase is *and having entered into the boat again*; but the expression *into the boat* is rightly omitted in the texts of Tischendorf and Alford. It is wanting in ℵ B C L Δ. Meyer approves of the omission.

He departed to the other side. The eastern side, apparently, of the lake of Gennesaret.

VER. 14-21 constitute a parallel paragraph, in the main, to Matt. xvi. 5-12. The representation is not so fully developed as in Matthew; but it has a touch or two that are peculiar to itself. Both the representations are but partial touchings of incidents and conversations, in which there would be manysided-ness of details.

VER. 14. **And they forgot to take bread.** *They*, that is the disciples, exclusive of the Master, for it would naturally devolve on them to make provision for the common physical wants of the company. *They forgot:* It escaped them (ἐπελάθοντο). *To take bread:* Literally, *loaves*.

And they had but one loaf with them in the boat. This little fact, like the *groaning* mentioned in the 12th verse, is one of those minute incidents that are recorded by Mark alone. It had stuck in the memory of Mark's informant. And no wonder. The very existence of the single cake would help to throw into bolder relief the awkwardness of the disciples' neglect.

VER. 15. **And**—in the course of His communications with them—**He charged them, saying, Take heed.** Literally, *See*, and so Wycliffe renders it *Se yc*. The Rheims has *Looke well*.

Beware of. The Saviour thus gives, says Petter, ' a double caveat or caution.'

leaven of the Pharisees, and *of* the leaven of Herod. 16

The expression literally means *Look from*, but yet does not mean, as some have supposed, *avert the eyes from*. It is borrowed from scenes of danger. In the event of a formidable wild beast threatening an onset, it might be of moment for the imperilled individual, not indeed *to avert his eyes*, but yet *to look from*, to look, that is to say, to the direction which it might be wise to take, in order to baulk or escape the infuriated beast.

The leaven of the Pharisees. That is the doctrine or teaching of the Pharisees. See Matt. xvi. 12. Wycliffe's version is very picturesque, *the sourdowgh of Pharisees*. We are not indeed to assume that the name, thus metaphorically given to the Pharisaic teaching, was intended of itself to suggest depreciation. The word is not explained in Matt. xvi. 12 as meaning *corrupt teaching*, but simply as meaning *teaching*. Neither is it clear that the leaven, yeast, or 'sour dough,' in use among the Jews, was regarded as a corrupting thing. But it was insinuative, penetrative, permeative. (Comp. Matt. xiii. 33.) The teaching of the Pharisees, in reference to the expected Messiah, in particular, was to be suspected and avoided. They were altogether wrong in their general ideas regarding moral goodness and moral evil, and hence they were altogether astray in their specific ideas regarding the mission, character, and work of the Messiah.

And the leaven of Herod. A clause that has occasioned to expositors unnecessary difficulty in relation to Matt. xvi. 6, in which there is reference to *the leaven of the Sadducees*, but none to *the leaven of Herod*. The two expressions are but two ways of putting one truth. The Saviour was not referring to the respective heads and particulars of the dogmatic creed of the Sadducees, any more than He was referring to the minute dogmatic items or details of the creed of the Pharisees. He was looking broadly at certain distinctive and outstanding principles of the sect. And in these principles, just as in the distinctive principles of the Pharisees, there was something far and fundamentally wrong. They misapprehended that which was the discriminative essence of moral goodness, and consequently that which was the discriminative essence of moral evil. Hence also they were in error in reference to the character and work of the Messiah, who is promised in the Old Testament prophecies. They looked for a sovereign who would be magnificent in his habits, powerful in his political influence, and either feared or respected by all surrounding potentates. It would appear that Herod had given himself out for such a sovereign, sufficiently satisfying the prophetic descriptions of the Old Testament, when these descriptions were 'liberally' interpreted. Herod developed into the Herod family. The Herod family were fulfilling, it would be argued by the 'Herodians,' the Messianic predictions. *They are fulfilling them in so far as it is reasonable that we should expect them to be fulfilled. Let us acknowledge it. Let us be content. Let us thus have 'peace,' the burden of the songs of our Scriptures. In no other way shall we get prosperity. This no doubt is the real prose of all the Old Testament poetry.* The Sadducees, as a whole, fell in with this Herodian policy. They temporised (ἔλεγον ὅτι ὁ Ἡρώδης ἐστὶν ὁ Χριστός: THEOPHYLACT). They eliminated from the mission, character and work of the Messiah everything spiritual and sublime, and of course everything

And they reasoned among themselves, saying, *It is* because we have no bread. 17 And when Jesus knew *it*, he saith unto

---

that had relation to propitiation for sin, and that was really needed as a *causa meritoria* for admission into the kingdom of heaven and for the enjoyment of life everlasting. Thus there was a point of coincidence in the notions of the Pharisees, Sadducees, Herodians, and Herod himself. And no wonder therefore that our Lord was careful to say to His disciples, *Take heed, beware of the leaven of these people!* No wonder too that one evangelist makes mention of *the leaven of the Sadducees*, and another of *the leaven of Herod*.

VER. 16. **And they reasoned among themselves.** The expression means that they *conferred and disputed with one another*, viz. in reference to their Lord's injunction. (See Mark ix. 33.) *Disputed* is Cardinal Cajetan's word. They tossed the matter among themselves, *dialogue-wise* (chap. vii. 21), whisperingly perhaps and with bated breath, yet eagerly and earnestly.

Saying, (*It is*) **Because we have not bread.** Or, *because we have not loaves*. The interlinking word *saying* is wanting in the three important ancient manuscripts, the Sinaitic (ℵ), the Vatican (B), and Cambridge (D). It is omitted from the text by Lachmann, Tischendorf, Tregelles, Alford. *But it must, at all events, be mentally supplied.* As the disciples talked and disputed with one another the assertion came up again and again, '*because we have not loaves*'; and they surmised that the Master was indirectly reprehending them *because they had not loaves.* What else can He mean? How else should He speak of '*leaven*'? And yet, can it be that He is *wishful* that we should have nothing to do with any article that emanates from the hands of Pharisees and Herodians? *Must we not, unless in the greatest emergency, make use of their bread or their leaven?* It does not seem likely that this should be the Master's meaning. But if not, why should He choose this time, when we have neglected to take loaves with us, to warn us of the '*leaven*' of the Pharisees and Herod? In the texts of Lachmann, Tregelles, Alford, we read *because* '*they*' *have not loaves* (ἔχουσιν), instead of *because* '*we*' *have not loaves* (ἔχομεν). This reading is grounded on the authority of the Vatican manuscript, and a few cursives, and some copies of the Old Latin version. A corresponding reading (εἶχαν) is found in the Cambridge manuscript; but the difficult reading of the Received Text, '*we*' *have not*, is overwhelmingly supported at once by the ancient manuscripts and by the ancient versions. *It must be the autographic reading*, the others being mere conjectural efforts to bridge the break in the construction. What Prebendary Gilpin says of the evangelists in general is particularly true of Mark : " Their narratives are all artless in the greatest degree." They write, he adds, " with that simplicity with which men, big with their subject, but unversed " in letters, might be expected to write." (*General Preface to Exposition of N. T.*) "Rhetoric *is artifice*, the work of man " (Cowper).

VER. 17. **And Jesus perceiving it saith unto them.** King James's version, *when Jesus knew it*, is a poor translation of the original expression (γνούς), and is fitted to convey the idea that some time elapsed ere our Lord became cognisant of the perplexity of His disciples. No such idea, however, is conveyed by the evangelist's own expression ; and hence Coverdale, true to the spirit of the

ST. MARK VIII.

them, Why reason ye, because ye have no bread? Perceive ye not yet, neither understand? Have ye your heart yet hardened? 18 Having eyes, see ye not? and having ears, hear ye not? and do ye not remember? 19 When I brake the five loaves among five thousand, how many baskets full of fragments took

original, translates the phrase *and Jesus understode that*. The Rheims version keeps nearer to the original idiom, *which Jesus knowing*. If our English idiom had permitted a preterite participle, then a perfect translation would have been, *and Jesus 'knewing.'* The *knowing* is represented as *past* before the following *saying* begins; but no hint is thrown out to the effect that some time elapsed *before the knowing began*.

Why do ye dispute because ye have not loaves? Do ye not yet perceive, nor understand? How could you suppose that I was aiming, by a side stroke, at your very pardonable oversight? I know well the many distractions to which you were exposed. It does not surprise Me in the least, far less does it offend Me, that it escaped you, on this particular occasion, to take with you a sufficient supply of loaves. But I am grieved to think that you should get perplexed on these matters, and that you should allow your minds to lie grovelling among them, while they should be soaring to the heights of great first truths and eternal realities.

Have ye your heart hardened? The word *heart* is used in its common biblical acceptation, as denoting, not specifically *the seat of the affections*, but generically *the seat of the self conscious principle*, or rather, *the self conscious principle itself*. It thus simply means *the inner element of the complex nature*, or *the mind*. And the reference here is specially to the *intelligence: Is it the case that spiritual ideas have still such a difficulty in penetrating into your thoughts?* See chap. vi. 52.

VER. 18, 19. **Having eyes, do ye not see? And having ears, do ye not hear?** Although duly furnished with the appropriate organs of apprehension, is it the case that still you do not apprehend? Petter says that the Saviour "amplifieth "their ignorance in *spiritual matters* by their contrary ability to conceive *earthly* "*things.*" He mistakes, however; the disciples are not blamed for failing to apprehend higher things, on the ground that they were qualified to apprehend lower and earthly things. The point of the reprehension is more reasonable. They had, by the gift of God, the powers that fitted them for apprehending the higher things; and yet they failed to exercise these powers as they should have done. (See Willes, *Specimen Hermeneut.*, p. 104.)

And do ye not remember when I broke the five loaves to the five thousand, and how many baskets full of fragments ye took up? Such seems to be the artless connection of the clauses; and there is no need for trying to effect a very precise disentanglement of the construction. The *and*, before *how many baskets*, is found not only in the Sinaitic manuscript (א), but also in C D M Δ, 1, 33 'the queen of the cursives.' It is introduced into the text by Tischendorf. The Saviour asks, firstly, if they remembered *the time when He divided the five loaves to the five thousand*, and secondly, if they remembered how many baskets of fragments they then took up.

ye up? They say unto him, Twelve. 20 And when the seven among four thousand, how many baskets full of fragments took ye up? And they said, Seven. 21 And he said unto them, How is it that ye do not understand? 22 And he cometh to Bethsaida; and they bring a blind

They say to Him, Twelve. See chap. vi. 43. Instead of simply affirming that they remembered the whole wonderful reality, they state the number of the basketfuls which they took up; and thus they do more than acknowledge the fact of their remembrance.

VER. 20. **And when the seven to the four thousand.** Tyndale repeats the verb in this clause, '*when* '*I brake* '*vii amonge iiii M.*" Instead of *among* it is *to* (εἰς), or *for*, in the original, both in this clause and in the corresponding clause of the preceding verse. Norton has *for*. Young has *to*.
How many basketfuls of fragments took ye up? And they say (λέγουσιν the right reading), **Seven.** Their memory was clear as to the facts, though their intelligence was confused as to the appropriate moral and Messianic principles which they should deduce from the facts.

VER. 21. **And He said to them, Do ye not yet understand?** How could you think that I was afraid that we should be shut up to make use of the loaves, or literal leaven, of the Pharisees and Herodians? *But surely the light is, now at length, breaking through into your minds !*

VER. 22-26 contain an incident which is recorded by Mark alone. Wilke contends however, though in quite an arbitrary manner, that Matthew must have been acquainted with Mark's narration. (*Urevangelist.*, pp. 680-685.)

VER. 22. **And they come to Bethsaida.** '*They* ' *come*, instead of *He cometh*, is not only found in a majority of the best old manuscripts, it is reproduced in a great majority of the old versions, the Italic, Vulgate, Coptic, Armenian, Gothic, Æthiopic. It is approved of by Mill, Bengel, Griesbach, Scholz, and adopted into the text by Lachmann, Tischendorf, Tregelles, Alford. *Bethsaida* = *Fish-town*. See Matt. xi. 21. Expositors are divided in opinion in reference to the particular *Bethsaida* referred to; some, such as Potter, supposing it to be the Galilean *Bethsaida* that was *near Capernaum* on the western side of the lake; others supposing that it was the Gaulonitish Bethsaida on the eastern side of the Jordan, a little to the north of the lake. This eastern Bethsaida was in the tetrarchy of Philip. He took a fancy to the place; and, with the architectural genius that was inherent in the Herod family, greatly improved it, and called it *Julias* in honour of the emperor's daughter. (See on chap. vi. 32.) Köstlin supposes that it must be the Galilean Bethsaida that is meant (*Ursprung*, p. 348). Griesbach, on the other hand, and Fritzsche, and Meyer, justly contend that the reference is to the Bethsaida that lay in the natural route to the district of Cæsarea Philippi. (See ver. 27.) Jesus was finding it needful to shun publicity and keep at a distance from Galilee. Both for His own sake, and for the spiritual and educational benefit of His disciples, He sought seclusion.
And they bring to Him a blind man. His blindness had been superinduced as

man unto him, and besought him to touch him. 23 And he took the blind man by the hand, and led him out of the town. And when he had spit on his eyes, and put

---

a disease ; he had not been born blind. (See ver. 24.) Note the present tense, *they bring*, lying in continuity with the preceding expression, *they come*. We are taken back by the narrator to the time when the events occurred, and see them *eventuating*,

And beseech Him to touch him. Literally, *in order that He might touch him*. They specify *touching*, under the impression, most probably, that contact was indispensable for the transition of the healing ' virtue.'

VER. 23. **And He took hold of the hand of the blind man, and led him outside the village.** The word κώμη naturally means village ; but it is applied by John to Bethlehem (vii. 42). Josephus mentions that the tetrarch Philip raised Bethsaida from the condition of a *village* (κώμη) to the status and dignity of a *city* or *town* (πόλεως παρασχὼν ἀξίωμα : *Ant.* xviii. 2, 1). Mark however would make no pretension to nice distinctions in the matter of municipal prerogatives, and would probably use, uncritically, the old appropriate term because of the relative smallness of the place. Jesus, still shunning publicity, *led the blind man outside the village*. Instead of *led* (ἐξήγαγεν), Tischendorf, Tregelles, and Alford insert in their texts, on some very high manuscriptural authority, a verb that suggests *bringing* or *conveying* (ἐξήνεγκεν), rather than *leading*. It is the reading of ℵ B C L, 33. It is just another way of expressing the idea that is embodied in the Received Text, only it throws into shade, comparatively, the agency of the blind man himself, and thus gives greater prominence to the agency of our Lord. The man, it would appear, did not belong to Bethsaida (see ver. 26) ; he had probably been brought from one of the adjoining hamlets. And hence our Lord took the precautionary plan of conveying him to some distance from the town before He operated on him. Had He cured him in the town, the man would have become a public spectacle, and the rush and crush of the excited multitude would still more have interfered with the spiritual and physical requirements of the disciples, and with the limitations of our Lord's own humanity. (See chap. ii. 2, iii. 7–10, 20 ; iv. 1 ; v. 24 ; vi. 31–33, 56.)

And when He had spit on his eyes. Literally, *into his eyes*. Petter, Heumann, and Dr. Samuel Clarke, interlace this expression with the clause immediately following, so as to bring out the idea that our Lord touched the man's eyes *with saliva on His finger*. It is enough however that we do not import into the statement our own British manners, customs, prejudices, and feelings. Deficiency in dignity on the one hand, and contempt on the other, have been often manifested by certain modes and circumstances of making use of what Tacitus calls ' the excrement of the mouth ' (*oris excrementum : Hist.* iv. 81). But saliva, when natural, is not excrementitious ; and a certain simple, semimedicinal, use of it, in certain exceptional conditions, is in no respect unnatural or unbecoming ; it is beneficial. And yet as it is only, to a very limited degree, and in the case of exceedingly slight disorders, that its beneficial influence is appreciable, its employment in the instance before us would all the more strikingly serve as a foil to display the presence and operation of a higher power.

his hands upon him, he asked him if he saw ought. 24 And he looked up, and said, I see men as trees, walking.

Its application indicated the *source* of the curative virtue, at the very time that it suggested the utter inadequacy of all ordinary remedial measures.

He put His hands upon him. The *and* which introduces this clause in our Authorized version is an import into the evangelist's text. It is not in *any* of the first-class manuscripts. The only uncial in which it is found is G. It is not in any of the critical editions, older or more recent. It is not even in the Textus Receptus. It is introduced however, interpretatively, into the Syriac version, and the versions of Erasmus, Luther, Beza. In these versions the construction of the passage is assumed to be as follows: *and He spit into his eyes, put His hands on him, and then asked him if he saw ought.* But it would be more precisely represented thus, *and when He had spit into his eyes He laid His hands on him and asked him if he saw ought.* (See Fritzsche.) The application of the saliva is represented as precursive in relation to the conjoint acts that followed consecutively, the acts of manual imposition and oral interrogation. The way in which our Lord imposed His hands, or the local direction which He gave to the act of manual imposition, is ascertained from the 25th verse; He laid His hands over the eyes of the patient.

And asked him if he saw ought. He desired to draw, and draw out, the attention of the man to the process of restoration. The phrase in the original finely '*presenti*ates' the scene, *He questioned him if he 'sees' ought.* **Ought,** or better still, *aught*: that is, *anything*, literally *a whit*. See chap. vii. 12.

VER. 24. **And he looked up.** Namely, toward the source of light, as was natural. That was the first visual movement which the man made. But he speedily looked *round* as well as *up*. See next clause.

And said, I behold the men, for I see them as trees, walking about. Note the *for*. Probably after he had looked up and looked round he would be asked whether he saw the men who were before him. They moved about, that he might the more readily notice and distinguish them. He saw them! but dimly, and indistinctly, and as persons magnified in a mist. *I behold them!* he exclaims. And he was sure that they were men; '*for*,' *though they seemed rather like trees than men, yet they were walking about!* This, no doubt the true reading of the text, is found in the Sinaitic, Alexandrine, and Vatican manuscripts, as well as in almost all the rest of the uncials. It was not approved of by Griesbach; but it is received into the text by Lachmann, Tischendorf, Tregelles, Alford. It is moreover the reading in all Stephens's editions and Erasmus's, and in the Elzevir of 1624 too. But it was changed by the Elzevirs in their edition of 1633 into the more easy-going reading from which King James's translation was made. They had been swayed apparently by the judgment of Beza, who in all his editions, after that of 1565, inserted and defended the easy-going reading. This easy-going reading was found in his ancient manuscript (D), and in the Complutensian edition. It is supported apparently by the Old Latin version, and the Vulgate, Coptic, Peshito Syriac, Philoxenian Syriac, Armenian, and Æthiopic versions. The Gothic however corresponds with the reading of the great body of the uncial manuscripts; and some of the other versions may be accounted for on the principle of free translation.

25 After that he put *his* hands again upon his eyes, and made him look up: and he was restored, and saw every man clearly.

VER. 25. **Then He put His hands again upon his eyes; and he looked steadfastly.** Literally, *he looked through* (διέβλεψεν), that is, *he looked so as to discriminate objects*. This is the reading of the manuscripts ℵ B C L Δ, 1, and of the Coptic and Æthiopic versions. The phrase seems to have been annotated at an early period, and hence the reading of the Received Text and some other rival readings. Griesbach felt so perplexed by their variety that he came to the conclusion that *all of them* were marginal, so that nothing should intervene between the clause *He put His hands again upon his eyes*, and the resultant clause *and he was restored*. (See his *Comm. Crit.*, in loc.) It is likely however that the reading of ℵ B is genuine. The same verb occurs in Matt. vii. 5, and Luke vi. 42, and is translated *see clearly*. When it is used *absolutely*, as in the case before us, it denotes *discriminative looking*, and thus brings into view the *energy of volition* in distinct seeing.

And was restored, and beheld all men clearly. But instead of *all men* a preponderance of the highest authorities reads *all things*. In the original there is only the difference of a single letter between the two readings (ἅπαντα for ἅπαντας). *All things* is the reading of ℵ B C D L Δ, 1, 69, and is supported by the great majority of the Old Latin codices, as also by the Vulgate version, the Syriac versions, and the Coptic, Armenian, and Æthiopic. The word rendered *clearly* (τηλαυγῶς or δηλαυγῶς) is properly objective in its import, *conspicuously*. But here it is used subjectively, *distinctly*.

It is somewhat remarkable that it is recorded by both Tacitus (*Hist.* iv. 81) and Suetonius (*Vesp.* c. 7) that when Vespasian was in Alexandria he was besought both by a blind man, and by a lame man, to cure them of their respective ailments. They had been directed, they alleged, by the god Serapis to apply to him. The blind man besought him *to spit into his eyes*; the lame man besought him to touch with his foot the disabled member. He treated the applications at first with disdain, says Tacitus, as something ridiculous. But as the poor men persisted in their suits, acting toward him as if he were a god, he ordered his physicians to examine the cases and report to him whether or not they were curable. *The physicians alleged that they were not incurable.* And at length therefore, yielding, or affecting to yield, to the entreaties of the poor men and the urgency of his flatterers, he did as he was desired. He dispensed his royal ' virtue,' as if he were divine; and immediately, it is alleged, *the blind man saw*, and *the lame man's lameness disappeared*. We need not say perhaps, with Casaubon, that 'the devil' was seeking to throw discredit on the miracles of our Lord by a piece of pantomimic ' buffoonery.' But we are justified in feeling suspicious in reference to the trustworthiness of the narrations. There are indeed cases in which the royal touch of right royal natures has been efficacious in rectifying certain nervous disorders. The imagination is potent in its influence; so is hope; so is faith. And *there are* subtle physical magnetisms too. But it is likely that there was *claptrap* in the cases that are signalized by Tacitus and Suetonius. The physicians saw through the real state of the case, and helped to work the wires behind the curtains. The whole affair seems to have been got up for the occasion, to yield Vespasian

26 And he sent him away to his house, saying, Neither go into the town, nor tell *it* to any in the town.

---

the incense of adulation on the one hand, and to sway the minds of the superstitious Egyptian multitude on the other into the full conviction of his divine right to the purple. (See Heumann's *Dissertation on the Miracles of Vesparian*, 1707.) The circumstances of 'the humble Nazarene' were altogether different.

VER. 26. **And He sent him away to his home, saying, Neither go into the village.** In telling him to go home, our Saviour insisted on his going directly. Hence the injunction, *Do not enter into the village*. Our Lord did not wish to make a spectacle of the man, and stir up the superficial curiosity and enthusiasm of the population in reference to Himself as a Thaumaturge or Wonderworker.

Nor tell it to any one in the village. A clause that has occasioned a great deal of perplexity from the remotest times. How was it possible, it was and is asked, for the man to tell the fact and mode of his cure *to any one in the village*, if *he did not enter the village*? How then could the Saviour give such a superfluous injunction? Was it not enough to have given either one or other of the two commands? In the Sinaitic and Vatican manuscripts, as well as in L and 1, the second clause is actually omitted; and Tischendorf, in his eighth edition of the text, follows in their wake and suppresses the last clause. Wrongly however For we may rest assured that no transcriber would ever have dreamed of adding such a clause as a mere invention or improvement of his own. The Vulgate version of the verse runs thus, *And He sent him to his home, saying, Go to thy home, and if thou shouldest enter into the village tell it to no one*. A similar reading is found in manuscript 69, and in the margin of the Philoxenian Syriac version. But it is an obvious tinkering to smooth away the apparent incongruity of the two injunctions. The incongruity is only apparent. The two injunctions might after all be only parts of what our Lord found it needful to say in the circumstances. Most likely the man would be in ecstasies, and anxious to rush right off into the village that he might herald the wonderful Deliverer, by proclaiming his own wonderful deliverance. Our Lord might need to add 'precept to precept,' and to emphasise and vary His expressions, in order to succeed in impressing the excited man with His real desire. *You must leave Me indeed;* '*but do not enter into the village.*' *Go home directly. Tell all that has happened, if you choose, to your own friends at your own home;* '*but do not tell it to any one in the village.*' *If you have acquaintances in the village who will be hovering about in the outskirts, on the outlook for you, and with whom therefore you would meet were you to go close by the quarter where they are, keep out of their way. Go in another direction. I wish at present to have seclusion with My disciples.* Grotius hit, *substantially*, on the right idea. The phrase is elliptical, he said, and means, *nor tell it even to any one (of those who are) in the village*, that is, *to any one of the inhabitants of the village*. Dr. Samuel Clarke, Rosenmüller, Bland, adopt his explication; Lange contends for it. It is too stiff and artificial as a precise interpretation; but it is in substance correct.

27 And Jesus went out, and his disciples, into the towns of Cæ-

VER. 27-30 form a condensed paragraph corresponding to the more detailed narrative in Matt. xvi. 13-20. See also Luke ix. 18-21.

VER. 27. **And Jesus went forth, and His disciples.** Namely, *from Bethsaida.* (See ver. 22.)

They went northward **into the villages of Cæsarea Philippi.** *The hamlets,* or *villages* (see ver. 23), *that dotted the district of country of which Cæsarea Philippi was the centre.* This *Cæsarea Philippi,* or *Philip's Cæsarea,* belonged to Philip 'the tetrarch of Gaulonitis, Trachonitis, and Paneas' (Josephus, *Ant.* xvii. 8:1). It not only belonged to him, it had in a great measure been built by him. (See Josephus, *Ant.* xviii. 2:1; *War* ii. 9:1.) It stood on the site of an old heathen city called *Paneas* (see Josephus, *ut supra*), and, strange to say, this its ancient name has survived its fashionable Cæsarean designation. The place is called *Banias* at the present day. It was in honour of the Roman Cæsar, the emperor Tiberius, that Philip called it *Cæsarea.* And it was necessary to call it *Philip's Cæsarea,* or *Cæsarea Philippi,* to distinguish it from the still more important *Cæsarea* in which the Roman procurator generally resided, and which was situated southward on the shore of the Mediterranean. (See Acts viii. 40, ix. 30, etc.) The northern Cæsarea, to which Jesus and His disciples now betook themselves, lay in the centre of some of the grandest scenery in Syria. "The situa-
"tion," says Dr. Tristram, "is indeed magnificent." He adds: "With tall
"limestone cliffs to the north and east, a rugged torrent of basalt to the south,
"and a gentle wooded slope for its western front, Banias is almost hidden till
"the traveller is among the ruins. These are not remarkable, the best preserved
"being the old Roman bridge over the impetuous stream which has hewn out
"its channel in the black basalt to the south. Everywhere there is a wild med-
"ley of cascades, mulberry trees, fig trees, dashing torrents, festoons of vines,
"bubbling fountains, reeds, and ruins, and the mingled music of birds and
"waters." (*The Land of Israel,* p. 586.) Such is Banias, or Cæsarea Philippi, as it now appears. The royal residence of Philip, when visiting in the district, would be the adjoining castle of Subeibeh, one of the marvels of the East. It "stands proudly," says Mr. Macgregor, "on a height guarded by sheer cliff
"all round, except at the entrance gate. . . . Heidelberg is not so large,
"nor has it anything like the view we have before us here. Towers and bas-
"tions are round about, and huge walls and courtyards fill the ample space
"within. A thousand men here, more or less, would not crowd the visitors'
"rooms, or weigh upon the grand old masonry. Built by the Herods first
"perhaps, or by Phœnician masons, it was an outwork afterwards of the Holy
"War, when nations were fired with frenzy for the land of the cross." (*Rob Roy on the Jordan,* p. 233.) The other object of transcendent interest at Cæsarea Philippi is the fountain, *that forms one of the sources of the Jordan.* It is, says Dr. Tristram, "a wonderful fountain, like a large bubbling basin, the
"largest spring in Syria, and said to be the largest single fountain in the
"world, where the drainage of the southern side of Hermon, pent up between a
"soft and a hard stratum, seems to have found a collective exit. Full grown at
"birth, at once larger than the Hasbany which it joins, the river dashes through

sarea Philippi: and by the way he asked his disciples, saying unto them, Whom do men say that I am? 28 And they answered, John the Baptist: but some say, Elias; and others, One of the prophets. 29 And he saith unto them, But whom say ye that

"an oleander thicket." (*The Land of Israel*,' p. 585.) Such was the central scene of the picturesque region in which our Lord sought and found seclusion with His disciples.

And by the way. Or, *in the way*, while journeying northward on the eastern side of the Jordan in the direction of Cæsarea Philippi.

He questioned His disciples, saying to them, Who do men say that I am? Very literally, *the men*. The meaning is, *who do ' the people ' say that I am?* The question would be asked, we may presume, not so much for the Saviour's personal information (John ii. 25) as to be a leader into the personal opinions or convictions of His disciples. (See ver. 29.) Instead of the nominative *who*, the older English versions, from Wycliffe downwards, have the objective *whom*. But see Bishop Lowth's *English Grammar*, p. 133.

VER. 28. **And they told Him, saying** (εἶπαν αὐτῷ λέγοντες), **John the Baptist.** That was one popular notion regarding Jesus, circulating no doubt chiefly among those who had never seen Him. Herod Antipas entertained it (chap. vi. 16). His imprimatur would give it currency in certain circles, and the Saviour's conspicuous purity and incorruptibility would lend it support. His miracles would be accounted for on the principle that he had brought back with him, as was to be expected, from the world of spirits, some distinctive additions to the powers which he had formerly possessed. (Matt. xiv. 2.)

And others, Elias. Or, Hebraistically, *Elijah*, the great ideal of a prophet and spiritual reformer. It was very generally expected that he was to return to the earth in connection with the Messiah's advent. (Mal. iv. 5.) And some, who could not entertain the idea that the humble Nazarene was the Messiah Himself, conjectured that He was nevertheless the veritable Old Testament Elias, the great precursor of the Messiah.

But others, One of the prophets. They could not go so far as to identify Him with Elias; neither could they be positive that He had any very special relation to the long expected Messiah; His rank was perhaps too humble for that. But they were quite sure that He was altogether different from all the modern men whom they had seen, or of whom they had heard; and hence they concluded that He must belong to a bygone heroic age. *Must He not be*, they would reason, *a re-incarnation of one or other of the old prophets?* A wild conjecture; but easy perhaps to the untutored imaginations of many Galileans in the days of our Lord.

VER. 29. **And He questioned them** (ἐπηρώτα), **But who say ye that I am?** Or, according to the emphasis of the original, *But ye, who say ye that I am?* The time was come when it was of the greatest moment that they should have a settled conception of His real character and mission. No doubt the true light on the subject had often gleamed through the darkness of their minds. (See John i. 29, 33, 34, 41, 45, 49, etc). But, though gleam succeeded gleam, in

I am? And Peter answereth and saith unto him, Thou art the

flashes that revealed the Illimitable, the darkness would ever, more or less, close in again. They could not altogether help it. They were witnesses of a ' humiliation' of state, which they could not reconcile with the notions they had inherited in reference to the power and pomp of the Messiah. And yet it was evident that He was entirely unlike all other rabbis. He was the Master of masters, and a Mystery over and above. An inner lustre was continually breaking through ; it was glorious ; it was unique. His character was transcendently noble and pure. He had not, moreover, obtruded self-assertions on them. He had left them, in a great measure, to observe for themselves ; and they *had been* observing. But they needed time to steep their minds in what they observed ; they needed time to combine and compare their observations, one with another, and then to work out the inferences that were involved. But now they had got sufficient time, and the end of the Master's terrestrial career was looming, big with both human and Divine interests, into view. He saw that it would be of the utmost moment that the faith of His nearest adherents should, from henceforth, faithfully and fixedly reflect the actual realities of His high condition and commission. Hence the decisive question here recorded.

Peter answered. With that honest readiness and impulsiveness which were so characteristic of his nature, and which fitted him for being a leader of the little circle.

And says to Him. Note the conjunction of tenses ; he *answered* and *says*. We are led, firstly, to look back and notice the historical fact that Peter *answered*. Then, secondly, we are led back into the heart of the scene and hear him speaking ; he *says*.

Thou art the Christ. A great improvement on Wycliffe's version, *Thou ert Crist*. And yet Luther's version is the same as Wycliffe's, and Piscator's the same as Luther's ; inexcusably so, on the part of both. It is as if they had allowed the Latin Vulgate to press in, dominatingly, on their memory (*Tu es Christus*). Tyndale's version was a great advance, *Thou arte very Christe* ; it was adopted by Coverdale, and in the first edition of the Geneva. In the corrected Geneva, however, the right translation was at length introduced, *Thou art the Christ.* Bengel has, correspondingly, *Thou art the Anointed (der Gesalbte).* Count Zinzendorf, Mace, and Principal Campbell have, Hebraizingly, *Thou art the Messiah.* Erasmus and Beza, in their Latin versions, have *Thou art that Christ (Tu es ille Christus,* and Erasmus Schmid improves on the expression, *Tu es Christus ille*). It was a decisive answer, and given, as even Schenkel admits, ' as out of a higher inspiration.' (*Charakterbild*, xii. 4.) The Lord Himself, as we learn from Matt. xvi. 17, traced the thought to its true Divine source. And yet it was no doubt founded on evidence which the disciple had diligently studied, and logically construed to his own inner satisfaction. It was evidence which, when impartially weighed in the balance of judicial reason, warranted the conclusion. That conclusion therefore would, we may be sure, be everything the reverse of a mere semi-mechanical reverberation of any mere assertion that had been mechanically heard from the lips of ' the Christ ' Himself. *It was not ' the Christ's ' manner to bear much testimony to Himself by His lips* (John v. 31). He left His life and His labours to speak for Him (John

Christ. 30 And he charged them that they should tell no man of him.

v. 36). Peter listened to *their* voice and was convinced. Petter explains Peter's confession thus: " Thou art that special and singular Person ordained "of God to be the Mediator between God and us, and to be the Redeemer and "Saviour of all mankind"; an admirable explanation, though its sharply cut shaping is somewhat indebted to the century, and the eminently theological ecclesiastical community, in which the commentator lived.

VER. 30. Mark omits entirely the Saviour's encomium on Peter, an encomium that budded out into specific prediction and promise of high spiritual prerogatives. If Peter himself be regarded as the chief wellspring of Mark's information, the omission is easily accounted for, as Eusebius remarks (*Demonstrat. Evang.*, lib. iii., 121, 122), on a principle honourable to the modesty of the apostle. But it would be altogether unaccountable, if it were in that encomium alone that the true basis is found for the true constitution of the Christian church. Yet it *is* in that encomium alone that Roman Catholic theologians find, or found, the doctrine of the primacy of the Roman popes. It is, they maintain, in virtue of these Roman popes being St. Peter's legitimate successors, that they are entitled to primacy. And that primacy is essential, in their estimation, to the visible hierarchy and normal existence of the church. Köstlin, from his peculiar standpoint, would say that the *Petrinism* of Mark is not so exclusive, or so strongly pronounced, as the Petrinism of Matthew. (*Ursprung*, p. 366.)

And He charged them. Peremptorily. See, on the word, chap. iii. 12.

That they should tell no man of Him. Or, *in order that they should say to no one concerning Him* (viz. *what they had said to Himself*). The reason is not, as Cartwright, under the pressure of a singular theological strain, suggests (*Harmonia*, p. 560), that men would have been deterred from putting Him to death, so that the atonement would not have been completed. Cardinal Cajetan comes nearer the reality. Men, he says, would have suspected that He was affecting the Jewish throne, and cherishing designs at variance with the rule of the Herods and the supremacy of the Cæsars. There is, it must be remembered, 'a time to keep silence,' as well as 'a time to speak' (Eccles. iii. 7); and the state of society at once in the tetrarchy of Philip, and the tetrarchy of Antipas, and throughout the rest of Palestine, was such that direct public or even private promulgation, on the part of the disciples, of our Lord's Messiah-hood would, at that particular time, have done much injury and little or no good. A favourable party, comprehending a considerable multitude of ultroneous but unindoctrinated adherents, would have sought to take Him by force and get Him crowned. (John vi. 15.) Another party, who were as yet only considering His true character, but disposed to look upon Him as exceptionally noble and mysteriously superior to all ordinary men, would have been prematurely stumbled. A third, and large, and politically influential, and adverse party were eagerly waiting to get hold of an excuse to put an instant arrest upon His proceedings. Indoctrination was needed throughout all the reaches of Jewish society, indoctrination in the grand fundamental principles of true religion.

ST. MARK VIII.

31 And he began to teach them, that the Son of man must suffer many things, and be rejected of the elders, and of the

The indoctrination of the very elite of the disciples themselves was much required. (See ver. 32.) They were seeing only patches of the Divine reality; and some of these patches they were seeing only very intermittently. The teaching of events was needed by them; more especially the teaching of the dark events which were already casting their long shadows before, and which, as they advanced, seemed to be the very 'blackness of darkness,' although to penetrative eyes the cloud was radiant on the other side, and pointing, like a pillar of fire, in the direction of the land of liberty and the kingdom of heaven.

VER. 31-33 form a little appended paragraph, closely connected with the paragraph that immediately precedes. It corresponds to Matt. xvi. 21-23. See also Luke ix. 22.

VER. 31. **And He began to teach them.** To *instruct* the disciples; for their minds, like the minds of most of their compeers in the nation, were full of fancies in reference to the Messiah.

That the Son of Man must suffer many things. Or, more literally still, *that it is necessary that the Son of Man suffer many things.* Note the present tense, *it 'is' necessary.* The substance of the Saviour's teaching is thus presented in the *direct* form of report. Hence the preliminary '*that*,' though in accordance with the Greek idiom, would almost need to be merged out of sight in our English idiom. It is, so far as the eye is concerned, somewhat equivalent to *the inverted commas* of quotation. *It is necessary :* that is, *It is, in the circumstances, inevitable.* The Saviour indeed could in a moment have lifted Himself up into a sphere in which He would have been for ever far above the possibility of human assault and personal suffering. But if He deemed it desirable to carry on the work of popular indoctrination, it was inevitable that He should meet with opposition on the part of those whose errors He exposed, and whose selfishness and selfish influence in society He resisted. And if too He had it in view, over and above, to meet one of the greatest difficulties in political economy, human or Divine, *the difficulty of granting pardon to criminals*, then there might be, and no doubt there was, a *relative necessity* of submitting, in a public and conspicuous manner, to sufferings that might have an atoning value in the Divine moral government. Both the precept and the penalty of the law,—and the penalty, like all else that is right, is, as well as the precept, unspeakably important and good,—would thus be honoured. (See Heb. ii. 10, viii. 3, ix. 12, 22, 23.) *The Son of Man :* the Saviour, while admitting the name '*the Christ*,' and rejoicing in spirit over Peter's employment of the designation, yet adheres, in His own personal phraseology, to His favourite appellation of Himself. He had voluntarily descended into the plane of humanity, and it was His delight to realize His oneness with the race. *Suffer 'many things':* it is an admirably literal translation. But if the peculiarity of idioms be taken into account, the phrase very closely corresponds to our English expression *suffer 'much.'* (See chap. ix. 26 and Rom. xvi. 6, 12.)

And be rejected by the elders, and the chief priests, and the scribes. The three

chief priests, and scribes, and be killed, and after three days
rise again. 32 And he spake that saying openly. And Peter

---

constituents of the sanhedrim. The *elders* would be chosen because of their
material and political influence; the *chief priests* because of their elevated
ecclesiastical position; the *scribes* because of their literary and rabbinical
qualifications. The word *elders* had become a term of office, its reference to
age being merged. The word *chief priests* would include *the high priest* proper,
and *the high-priests emeriti* if such there were, and the chiefs of the four-and-
twenty courses. The *scribes* of the sanhedrim would be the most eminent of
those who knew *letters*, and who would consequently be learned in the law and
the traditions.

And be killed. Or put *to a violent death*. He foresaw it all! And yet went
steadily onward to the consummation of His mediatorial career! In the midst
of His vivid anticipation of the effects of human ignorance, recklessness, rage,
and rabid bloodthirstiness, He discerned an undercurrent of grand Divine ends,
that rolled steadily onward, like wave on wave, in the direction of the weal of
the universe. Hence the next clause.

And after three days rise again. Some grand mediatorial purpose was to be
subserved by the death; but the state of death was to be only temporary, and
for an exceedingly brief period. The Saviour of men must be *alive for ever-
more*. There were indeed grand purposes which could not be realized unless He
lived. *After three days:* it was customary among the Jews, as among many
other peoples, to be somewhat indeterminate in the designation of certain
periods of time. Thus the phrase *after three days* might either mean *after the
period that is covered by three complete days*, or *after the period that is covered
by one complete day, flanked on either side by two incomplete days*. The day at
the commencement and the day at the conclusion of the whole period might,
according to circumstances, be either complete or incomplete. In the one case
the time referred to would be *after each successive day had been completed*; in
the other it would be *after the three days respectively had been more or less
touched*. This is the meaning of the phrase here, so that the expression, notwithstanding Fritzsche's protest, is equivalent to *on the third day*. Comp.
2 Chron. x. 5, 12. Compare also the two synonymous expressions in English,
this day eight days and *this day sennight* or *seven nights*. Krebs gives a large
induction of particular cases, more especially from the writings of Josephus,
in which the same latitude in the counting of time occurs. (*Observat.*, in loc.)

VER. 32. **And He spake the saying openly.** *The saying*, namely, to which He
had just given expression. He uttered it *openly*, or *plainly*, as Wycliffe and the
Geneva have it. The contrast is not with the idea of *secrecy*, but with the idea
of *mystery*. Our Saviour made the statement *explicitly* and *unambiguously*,
without any involution of parable, metaphor, or enigma (ἀπαρακαλύπτως as
Euthymius Zigabenus has it). He did not, as He had done before, speak of
being lifted up, of *building the temple in three days*, or of *being, Jonah-like,
three days and three nights in the heart of the earth* (John iii. 14, ii. 19; Matt.
xii. 40).

And Peter took Him, and began to rebuke Him. *To reprimand Him; to chyde*

ST. MARK VIII.

took him, and began to rebuke him. 33 But when he had turned about and looked on his disciples, he rebuked Peter, saying, Get thee behind me, Satan : for thou savourest not the things that be of God, but the things that be of men.

Him, as Tyndale has it ; very literally, *to rate Him*. So very partial, on the one hand, were Peter's notions of the Lord's Messiahship; and so very partial, on the other, was the normal development of his feelings in relation to his Lord. The idea of the violent death of Him who was 'the Christ,' a violent death too at the hands of the chieftains of the people, ran so thoroughly counter to all the fond conceptions he had been cherishing in reference to the success of his Master's enterprise, that for the moment his feelings of reverence were overridden. *Do not say such things ! You speak of impossibilities ! You are surely giving way to despondency ! You will dishearten us all ! Such things must not be !* "No wonder," says Richard Baxter, "if novices now think themselves wiser "than their wisest teachers." "This world," says Hofmeister, "has many "Peters, who wish to be wiser than Christ, and to prescribe to Him what it is "needful to do."

VER. 33. But He, when He had turned about. Not *to Peter*, as Meyer and Alexander strangely suppose, but *from* him, under a feeling of disapprobation.

And saw His disciples. The group of the eleven, from whom Peter had taken Him aside. Our Lord turned *toward them*, and, *when He saw them*, He spake to Peter. *He turned purposely, wishing to see them, and to make His statement to Peter in their hearing*. Wakefield freely, but admirably, renders the expression thus, *but He turned about, and, 'in the presence of His disciples,' rebuked Peter*.

Rebuked Peter, saying, Get behind Me, Satan. Though it was Peter who had spoken, the Saviour recognised the presence of a subtler intellect. He recognised his old 'Adversary' who had assaulted Him in the wilderness with the idea of worldly greatness and success (Matt. iii. 8-10). Hence His language. Peter indeed was to be blamed, and *was* blamed. But the address went intentionally farther, deeper. The word *Satan* means *adversary*, but was conventionally applied among the Jews to the great Adversary. *Get behind Me!* an expression of strong disapprobation and dislike, *Get out of My sight!* It throws light upon the *turning* of our Saviour. *In turning from Peter*, our Lord was really putting 'behind' Him the evil being who was tempting Him through Peter.

For thou mindest not the things of God, but the things of men. The Saviour, in these words, speaks home to the personality of Peter. He pays no farther heed, as it were, to the darker presence behind. Peter, under the influence of that presence, was suffering the eye of his intelligence to be eclipsed, and hence he was allowing his interests to gather clusteringly around what would be immediately agreeable to merely human feelings, instead of what would be agreeable to the mind and heart of God. *Mindest :* there is reference in the word to the *thinking* element of the *mind*, as well as to its *feeling* element ; and indeed to the *thinking* element prominently. But the Geneva version goes too far in that direction, *thou understandest*. Bengel's version is better, *thou considerest* (du bedenkest). Count Zinzendorf's is also good, *thou art concerning thyself*

ST. MARK VIII.

34 And when he had called the people *unto him* with his disciples also, he said unto them, Whosoever will come after me,

(es ist dir um zu thun). Newcome has *thou regardest*. Peter was *allowing his 'mind'* to be occupied with things human as distinguished from things Divine. *The things of God.* The reference is to the Divine idea, and the coincident Divine pleasure, in relation to the real and permanent weal of men as moral, immortal, and yet sinful beings. *An atonement was an essential element in that idea and pleasure.* And, as to the atonement again, *suffering and death were essential to its completion.* Peter was allowing his mind to get away from the impress of such thoughts, or of what, if logically pursued, would have led to them; and he was occupied with *the things of men*, or as Luther has it, *with what is human.* Man is too apt to occupy himself with what is immediately agreeable. Peter would have liked the power, pomp, wealth, and splendour of the Messiah's kingdom, in a few weeks or months.

VER. 34-38, along with ver. 1 of chap. ix., constitute a paragraph, consecutive in relation to the preceding one, and corresponding to Matt. xvi. 24-28 and Luke ix. 23-27.

VER. 34. **And He called to Him the crowd along with His disciples.** For even in that out-of-the-way locality He was identified, and followed by groups of expectant hangers on, who were eager to see and hear. At the present day nothing is easier in Syria than to gather a crowd; almost every stranger at once attracts a following. What must it have been when it was reported, in the hamlets surrounding Cæsarea Philippi, that the Great Prophet of Nazareth was in the vicinity! De Wette, however, can only see in the word *multitude* or *crowd* a wilful expansion, and therefore a real misinterpretation, on the part of Mark, of the word *all* employed by Luke, in his less determinate narrative of the occurrence (ix. 23). This *all*, says de Wette. Luke intended to be applied to *the disciples only*, inasmuch as it is said in the 18th verse that our Lord had been 'alone praying.' (*Handbuch*, in loc.) Baur accepts de Wette's idea, and thence builds an argument in relation to the interdependencies of the Gospels. *Mark*, says he, *must have had Luke's Gospel lying before him.* (*Marcuserang.*, pp. 65-67.) But it is utterly gratuitous to assume that, because our Lord was 'alone praying,' He continued 'alone' after His prayers were concluded. It is not only gratuitous, it is also a most improbable supposition. If our Lord was known to be engaged in prayer, the groups of followers would, in accordance with oriental reverence, respect His seclusion, and keep at a distance. But when they noticed that His prayers were concluded, and that He was engaged in earnest conversation with His disciples, they would naturally begin to draw nearer, although modestly refraining from pressing exceedingly near. Between Luke's *all* (not *them all*) and Mark's *crowd along with His disciples*, there is, to our view, a beautiful coincidence that bespeaks a common source of accurate information.

And said to them, Whosoever is wishful to come after Me. There was an eagerness among many of the people to 'come after Him.' The wistfulness of a considerable proportion of the northern population had been awakened. They were ruminating anxiously on Old Testament predictions, and filled with vague

let him deny himself, and take up his cross, and follow me.
35 For whosoever will save his life shall lose it; but whosoever

expectancy. They saw that the Rabbi of Nazareth was no common rabbi. He was a wonderful Being. It is not strange therefore that they pictured out to themselves all sorts of possibilities in connection with His career. *To what was He advancing? Whither was He bound? Was He on His way, or was He not, to the throne of the kingdom?* The Saviour by and by gives sufficiently explicit indications of the ultimate whitherhood of His career (ver. 38, ix. 1); but meanwhile He brings into the foreground the moral conditions of adherence to H s person and His cause.

Let him deny himself. The word is strong in the original (ἀπαρνησάσθω), *let him entirely renounce himself.* Let him be prepared to say No to many of the strongest cravings of his nature, in the direction more particularly of earthly ease, comfort, dignity, and glory.

And take up his cross. Note the *his*. It intimates that the world in general has got ready a cross for each of Christ's disciples; so determined is it in its opposition, and so remorseless in its hate. It has resolved that every Christian shall be crucified, in one way or another; if the body cannot be got hold of and transfixed, the heart may. Every true Christian must be willing to accept this treatment for Christ's sake. He must *take up his cross*, and walk with it, as it were, to the place of execution, ready for the last extremity. It is the dark side of the case; and the phase of representation, under which it is exhibited, was no doubt suggested to our Lord by the clear view He had of the termination of His own terrestrial career. (See ver. 31.) A *Christian*, says Luther, is a *Crucian*.

And follow Me. The Saviour pictures to His hearers a procession. He himself takes the lead with His cross. He is the chief Crucian. All His disciples follow; each having his own particular cross. But the direction of the procession, when one looks far enough, is toward the kingdom of heavenly glory.

VER. 35. **For whosoever would save his life.** Or, more literally, *For whosoever may will to save his life*, that is, *may wish-and will to save his life.* Whosoever may choose to avoid crucifixion, by refusing to take up his cross and follow Christ.

Shall lose it. Viz. in the sphere of the future. Very literally, *he shall destroy it.* He shall lose, in the sphere of the future, the higher life, because in the sphere of the present he refuses to part with the lower. He shall lose everlasting ease, comfort, honour, and glory, because he refuses to part, for Christ's sake, with the ease, comfort, honour, and glory which it is in the power of the world to withhold.

But whosoever shall lose his life. In the sphere of the present: *whosoever shall surrender his life to destruction.* Our English translation, though not a precisely literal rendering of the text that was lying before the translators, is in exactest harmony with the reading of the text that is given by the most modern editors, inclusive of Tischendorf, Tregelles, and Alford (ὃς δ' ἂν ἀπολέσει, not ἀπολέσῃ). The idea is, *who·oever shall, as a matter of fact, lose,* or *surrender to destruction, his life.* This reading is supported by the Sinaitic, Vatican, Ephraemi, and Cambridge manuscripts (א B C D).

shall lose his life for my sake, and the gospel's, the same shall save it. 36 For what shall it profit a man, if he shall gain the whole world, and lose his own soul? 37 Or what shall a

For My sake and the gospel's. Two sides of that one great reality, in which the motive, which constrains to the endurance of Christian martyrdom, is found. The gospel without Christ *would be nothing*. Christ without the gospel, to make Him known, *would be nothing* '*to us*.'

Shall save it. In the sphere of the future and the eternal. The best manuscripts and editors (inclusive of Griesbach and Scholz) omit the resumptive expression *the same*; *the same shall save it*. It seems to have been imported from Luke ix. 24.

The term which is translated *life* in this verse ($\psi\upsilon\chi\dot{\eta}$) is the same which is translated *soul* in the two following verses, and in many other passages. It might here too have been rendered *soul*, but not with perfect idiomatic propriety. The primary Geneva version (of 1557) gives a peculiar turn to the word, *For whosoever wyl save 'him selfe,' shal lose ' him selfe.'* But *whosoever shal lose 'him selfe' for My sake and the gospel's, the same shal save ' him selfe.'* None of the English words *soul, life, self*, exactly corresponds to the Greek term. And indeed the real comprehension of the term was left by the Greeks themselves, to a large extent, indeterminate. It originally signified *the breath*; and hence at times it was used to denote *the concrete principle of vitality*. At other times it was used to denote, more comprehensively, *the concrete principle of self consciousness or personality*. At other times still the two principles were identified; and at other times yet, as in the verse before us, a twofold form of vitality was regarded as attaching itself, potentially, to the concrete principle of self consciousness and personality. *A man,—realizing his own centre of immortal self consciousness and personality,—may, in certain critical circumstances, make choice between life terrestrial and life celestial.*

VER. 36. **For what shall it profit a man?** Or, according to the reading of the Sinaitic and Vatican manuscripts, *For what profiteth it a man?* The Saviour chooses for the present to take the standpoint of *profit* as His standpoint of measurement and remark. He speaks, says Luther, 'as an orator.' Note the *for*. It carries the mind back, through the preceding verse, to the 34th, and shows why the disciples of the Saviour should not scruple to take up their crosses. The reason is partly co-ordinate with that stated in the 35th verse, but also partly modified by it and illustrative of it.

If he should have gained. Or, as it stands in the Sinaitic and Vatican manuscripts, and in Tischendorf's text, *to gain*, or *to have gained* ($\kappa\epsilon\rho\delta\tilde{\eta}\sigma\alpha\iota$).

The whole world. With its fulness. What would it profit a man, were he to become the absolute proprietor of the whole world's soil, treasure, and population? What would this profit, if another contingency were to be concurrently realized? See next clause.

And suffer the loss of his soul. The *soul* is popularly spoken of as distinct from the man who loses it, for the reference is rather to the man's *life* than to his *being*. What would it profit a man to become the lord of the whole world, if thereby or therewith he suffer the loss of the higher life of his being,

ST. MARK VIII.

man give in exchange for his soul? 38 Whosoever therefore shall be ashamed of me and of my words in this adulterous and

the heavenly and 'everlasting life'? "How poor a price," says Richard Baxter, "is all the profit and pleasure of this life, to hire a man by sin to lose "his salvation!" "O flesh!" exclaims Luther, "how mighty art thou, that "thou canst still throw darkness over those things, even to the minds of the "holy!"

VER. 37. **Or.** Or *for*, as it is given in Tischendorf, Tregelles, Alford. The Sinaitic and Vatican manuscripts read *for*. It is *or* in Matt. xvi. 26; and there may have been a desire, on the part of some ancient transcriber, to effect a minute identity between the two evangelists. If *for* be accepted, then what follows will be regarded as an illustration, and confirmation, of the reasoning of the preceding verse.

What shall a man give? Or, according to the reading of the Sinaitic and Vatican manuscripts, and of Tischendorf and Tregelles, *what should a man give* (δοῖ).

In exchange for his soul, or *for his living self*. What should a man not give? If he had the whole world, should he not willingly give it, provided he really knew, believed, or felt, that otherwise he would be utterly lost. King Richard, in Shakespeare, says, 'My kingdom for a horse!' How many kingdoms should be willingly surrendered, if man were not utterly infatuated, for the salvation of the soul? But the reference is not exactly, as Petter assumes, to the 'irrecoverableness' of a lost soul. It is to the incomputable value of the soul, even in man's own judgment, when his judgment is unfettered. Strong doctrinal proclivity gave a twist to Luther's translation of the question, *What 'can' man give wherewith to redeem his soul?* Coverdale follows Luther. Doctrinally, it is true that man 'can' give nothing as a sufficient ransom. 'The ransom is Jesus,' as Luther remarks. But that is a direction of thought that leads away from the Saviour's present standpoint.

VER. 38. **For whosoever.** What follows is a justification, as it were, of the preceding queries. Notwithstanding the appalling nature of some of the ideas suggested by them, it was right to propose them. *Whosoever*: it matters not what his position or condition in this world may be.

Shall be ashamed of Me and My words. As many would be prone to be. The temptation to *shame* in reference to the Saviour, and the Saviour's sayings or doctrines, continues to the present day, and is pervading society to the core. even in countries called Christian. It is one of the severest temptations which young 'converts' have to encounter. The anticipation of it is one of the mightiest motives to keep men away from religion, and on the other side of Christian faith and fealty.

In this adulterous and sinful generation. A specific phase of sinfulness is put in front of the generic representation. It was outstanding and conspicuous. The men of that generation were *wantonly unfaithful to Him who was their Lord*, and who had more claims upon their faithfulness than any husband has upon the faithfulness of his wife. God had, as it were, espoused to Himself the Jewish people. (Isa. liv. 5; Jer. iii. 14.) He had conferred on them the

sinful generation; of him also shall the Son of man be ashamed, when he cometh in the glory of his Father with the holy angels. (CHAP. IX.) 1 And he said unto them, Verily I say unto you,

highest possible prerogatives and honours. And yet they had proved *adulterous*, or *advouterous* as the old translations, Wycliffe's, Tyndale's, Coverdale's, the Great Bible, the first Geneva, the Rheims, give it. (Comp. Jer. iii.; Ezek. xvi.) Norton merges the specific peculiarity of the epithet, when he freely renders it *apostate*. The free rendering of Wakefield is, in some respects, not quite so indefinite, *ungodly*. The *name of God* was, as it were, renounced by the unfaithful people. Barnes supposed that the reference was to literal adultery. Webster and Wilkinson assume that such a reference is included. Unlikely. Petter is on the wrong scent, entirely, when he explains the phrase as meaning *a bastardly brood*. Dionysius à Ryckel supposes that God may be fittingly represented as having taken to Himself in marriage all souls.

The Son of Man also shall be ashamed of him. Not in a spirit of vindictiveness or pique, but at the bidding of a high, holy, wise, and most judicial consideration and determination. The character of him who is ashamed of the Saviour is really shameful; and it is right that it should be treated as such by the Saviour.

When He shall have come in the glory of His Father, with the holy angels. To make all things right on the earth, for the ages of ages to come. He shall then judge 'the quick and the dead,' and render to every man according to his true character. (See Matt. xxv. 31-46; 2 Cor. v. 10; Rev. xx. 12, 13, xxii. 12.) In that coming, as distinguished from His first advent, He shall appear *in the glory of His Father*, accompanied and encompassed with the unmistakable insignia of the Monarch of the universe. There will then be no doubt of His dignity, and no scope for disputation concerning His authority.

CHAPTER IX. VER. 1. It was in a mood of mental somnolency that Hugo de Sancto Caro concluded the eighth chapter with the 38th verse, and carried forward into a new chapter the verse before us. This was not so much to divide Scripture into convenient lections as to rend it at random. Well might Grotius say that he 'marvelled' at the division (*miror*). The verse obviously belongs to the preceding paragraph, and is appended to it by Theophylact, by Wycliffe too and Tyndale, both of whom commence the ninth chapter with the following verse; Coverdale also does the same, and so did Luther and Piscator. It aggravates the carelessness of the existing division, that in St. Matthew the corresponding verse is correctly sundered from what follows, and attached, at the conclusion of the chapter, to what goes before (xvi. 28). In St. Luke, on the other hand, the corresponding verse occurs, such was the waywardness of the divider, in the middle of a chapter (ix. 27).

And He said to them. A favourite form of expression with Mark, when introducing some outstanding or emphatic observation. Its force here might be represented thus: *and He added*. See chap. iv. 9, 11, 13, 21, 24, 26, 30, 40.

Verily I say unto you. A deep solemnity and earnestness were resting on our Saviour's spirit when He uttered what follows; hence the *preliminary* 'verily,'

That there be some of them that stand here, which shall not taste of death, till they have seen the kingdom of God come with power.

or *prefatory* '*amen*.' The whole expression was a peculiarly solemn way of saying *I assure you*.

That. This conjunction should be omitted in our English idiom, as the report of what our Lord said is in *the direct form*. Our translators have generally left it out. Tyndale omits it here, and Luther, and Coverdale.

There be some of those standing here. Note the archaic *be* for *are*. It is Tyndale's word.

Who shall in no wise taste of death. *Of death*, or the *of* may be omitted as in Heb. ii. 9. Wycliffe omits it here. Death is regarded as a bitter poison-potion, which all have, at one time or another, to taste. It is so potent, that to taste it suffices.

Till they have seen the kingdom of God come with power. Or literally, *in power*, in the possession and manifestation of power. The kingdom of God, as developed on the earth, might appear to be a feeble little thing, as it pre-existed during the period of our Lord's humiliation; but by and by it would assert for itself a might that would defy every species of criticism or opposition, and eventually shiver into atoms, or grind into powder, every existing institution of ungodliness. Note the word *come*. It is not *coming* but *having come* (ἐληλυθυῖαν).

Many have found difficulty in understanding the Saviour's statement. "The "verse," says Alexander, "is one of the most difficult and disputed in the "whole book." And yet its difficulty arises exclusively from the partial views that have been entertained in reference to our Lord's kingdom and coming. In Matt. xvi. 28 the corresponding expression is, *There be some standing here, who shall not taste of death, till they see the Son of Man coming in His kingdom*. If *the coming of Christ in His kingdom* be regarded as applicable only to one definite event in the evolution of the ages, then the statement must indeed be the most difficult imaginable. We really could not conceive of it having been uttered in the full clear consciousness of a true perspective, stretching away out into the future. It would be a statement that would be apt to shake one's confidence in our Lord's capacity of accurate foresight, and in the reliability of the most solemn of His asseverations. We must hence suppose that while there is undoubtedly some grand culminating *coming*, which is still in the future, and which will sum up into itself all the precursive *comings* that have afforded to men provisional glimpses and foretastes of its surpassing glory, yet there have been in actual history, and may yet be, veritable instalments of the consummation. Already, in the Old Testament Scriptures, the *coming* of the Messiah is often represented as a unit, or a whole, without the formal distinction of its two great 'moments,' the *coming to suffer* and the *coming to reign*. When the prophetic telescopes of the old prophets were turned to *the coming*, the elongated interval that was to elapse between the beginning and the ending lay *out of view in their perspective*. Hence Malachi says : "Behold He shall come "saith the Lord of hosts. But who may abide the day of His coming ?" (chap. iii. 1, 2.) That day of His coming is 'the great and dreadful day of the Lord'

CHAPTER IX.

2 AND after six days Jesus taketh *with him* Peter, and

(chap. iv. 5). To the prophet's eye *the first coming* and *the final coming*, looked at in the plane of his perspective, were obviously but two sides of one entirety; and hence, although he does refer to what we call *the first coming*, the coming that was to be associated with the appearance of John the Baptist (Matt. xi. 9-14, xvii. 10-13; Mark i. 2, 3), he brings into the same cartoon of representation his reference to what we so often call *His second coming*, 'the great and dreadful day of the Lord' that is yet to come. It is on the same principle that the representations of the New Testament are to be interpreted. In the line of the successive manifestations of the majesty and glory of the exalted Messiah, the eye is generally carried forward to the overshadowing grandeur of the consummation; but at other times, as here, the view is arrested at some of the intervening illapses of the heavenly presence and power. Doubtless our Lord referred to the marvellous enlargement, consolidation, and establishment of His kingdom, which was to take place on occasion of the destruction of Jerusalem, and in which there was to be an exceedingly vivid glimpse of the greater future glory. On the occurrence of that destruction there would occur the annihilation of all the emptied and effete formalities that were connected with the Jewish temple, and that constituted the chief obstacles to the spread of the gospel among the Jews, and its chief competitors in influence among the Gentiles. The idea of Theophylact, Leo the Great, Hofmeister, Maldonato, a-Lapide, Petter, Richard Baxter, Patrizi, Ryle, and many others, that the reference of our Saviour was to His transfiguration on the mount, just about to be recorded, is exceedingly unnatural. When our Lord says, "*there are some of those "standing here who shall not taste death* till they witness the kingdom of God "come in power," He evidently refers to a date that was still remote. For the same reason, as well as for others, the reference cannot be, as Cardinal Cajetan, Calvin, and Beza supposed, to our Lord's resurrection and the consecutive events of Pentecost, etc. See *Comm.* on Matt., xvi. 28.

CHAPTER IX.

VER. 2-8 the transfiguration section. Comp. Matt. xvii. 1-8 and Luke ix. 28-36.

VER. 2. And after six days. Luke has. *about eight days* (ix. 28). There is no collision. Luke counts the fractional days at the commencement and close of the six complete days specified by Mark and Matthew. The chronological relation of the transfiguration to Peter's confession and the Saviour's consequent manifesto regarding the cross as the stepping stone to the crown seems to have engraven itself ineffaceably on the memory of the evangelical reporters. Hence the preciseness of the date in all the synoptic Gospels.

Jesus taketh with Him Peter, James, and John. The elite of the Master's

James, and John, and leadeth them up into an high mountain apart by themselves: and he was transfigured before them.

elect, the triumvirs of the apostolate. Comp. chap. v. 37, xiv. 33. They were sufficient in number to be adequate witnesses to the rest of the apostles, and to men in general. It was seemly not to take a large company. The scene into which the selected three were about to be introduced belonged to the sphere of the Saviour's privacy, rather than to the sphere of His public ministry.

And bringeth them up into a high mountain. That is, *into* some recess in some high mountain. The particular mountain referred to is not specified, and is not known. From about the time of Cyril of Jerusalem, in the fourth century, it has been popularly regarded as Tabor, a singularly beautiful 'dome-shaped mamelon,' a little to the east of Nazareth. It stands apart, and is remarkable, says Dr. Tristram, for 'its peculiar symmetry of shape.' (*The Land of Israel*, p. 125.) Tabor however could not be the scene of the Saviour's transfiguration, for the narrative impresses us with the conviction that the spot was secluded, whereas "long before and after the event of the transfiguration, the summit of "Tabor," as Dr. Robinson has shown, "was occupied by a fortified city." (*Researches*, vol. iii., p. 222.) Wilson, Porter, Stanley, and Patrizi agree with Dr. Robinson that the mountain referred to could not be Tabor. Lightfoot and Reland, even in their day, reached the same conclusion. The hallowed spot was doubtless one of the many highland solitudes in the neighbourhood of Cæsarea Philippi (chap. viii. 27). "The context of the narrative," says Dr. Porter, "shows that the Mount of Transfiguration is to be sought on the ridge "of Hermon" (*Syria*, p. 397).

Apart by themselves. Literally, *apart alone*, or as Tyndale has it, *out of the waye alone*. The word *apart* has by some, as by Norton for instance, been connected, not with the expression *and conducted them alone*, but with the expression *a high mountain*. Hence indeed one of the reasons why Tabor has been fixed on as the scene of the transfiguration. "It stands on the plain in "isolated grandeur," says Dr. Tristram (*The Land of Israel*, p. 125). "From "these and all the adjoining hills," says Dr. Wilson, "it certainly stands "apart; but it is an erroneous criticism, which finds in this circumstance any "suitableness for its being the scene of our Lord's transfiguration." (*The Lands of the Bible*, vol. ii., p. 100.)

And He was transfigured before them. Or *transformed*; literally, *metamorphos:d*. *Transformed* is Erasmus's word, and Beza's. *Transfigured* is the fine old Vulgate word. It holds its place in all the English versions which preceded King James's. Luther's translation is free, *made Himself clear* or *bright* (*verkläret sich*). Bengel's is more literal, *assumed another form*. So Felbinger's, *was changed in form*. It was a change in the externality of the person, a kind of temporary glorification, effected no doubt from within outward, rather than from without inward. It would reveal the essential glory of the spirit that 'tabernacled' within, its glory at once in that lower sphere that was human and in that higher sphere that was Divine. It would be a prefiguration of our Lord's permanent resurrection glory. And possibly, therefore, it may be legitimately regarded as an earnest of the glory that is awaiting all who have become by faith 'members of His body.'

3 And his raiment became shining, exceeding white as snow; so as no fuller on earth can white them. 4 And there appeared unto them Elias with Moses: and they were talking with Jesus. 5 And Peter answered and said to Jesus,

VER. 3. **And His garments.** Matthew and Luke draw attention to the transfigured appearance of the countenance. Mark confines his description to the effect of the personal transfiguration on the raiment.

Became resplendent. Plato applies the word (στίλβοντα) to lightning; Aristotle to the light of the fixed stars. The garments could not conceal the personal glory, but became themselves semi-translucent.

Exceeding white, like snow. When the sun is shining on it in full force. The comparison however, *like snow*, was probably imported from Matt. xxviii. 3. It is not found in the Sinaitic and Vatican manuscripts (אB), nor in C L Δ, 1, nor in the Sahidic, Coptic (cod.), Armenian, and Æthiopic versions. It is omitted by Tischendorf, Tregelles, Alford, from their texts; and Griesbach suspected its genuineness. It is not needed. The garments were *exceeding white*, or dazzlingly white, like the glow of white objects when reflecting the rays of a meridian sun.

So as no fuller on earth can wh:ten them. Or, more literally, *As no fuller on the earth can so whiten.* Tyndale's version is good, *so whyte as noo fuller can make apon the erth*, that is, so resplendently white.

VER. 4. **And there appeared to them Elias with Moses.** Or, *and there was seen by them Elias with Moses.* Elias with Moses was visible to them. It is not implied that Elijah and Moses were there, *for the purpose of making themselves visible to the disciples.* They were there for another purpose, but they were not hidden from the eyes of the disciples.

And they were talking with Jesus. They were the most illustrious representatives of 'the law and the prophets,' the greatest of the agents who had, in former times, been divinely employed for the establishment and maintenance of 'the kingdom of heaven' on earth. That kingdom is the only real refuge of humanity. It is the only efficiently aggressive institution, that is fitted to make way into the domain of the world's dominant wickedness and woes. And as Jesus was the King of the kingdom, there is no wonder that Moses and Elias wished to commune with Him, and that He wished to commune with them. Their work had prepared His way. His work was to put the copestone on their labours. Was this appearance of Moses and Elijah to the disciples *a vision?* It was (Matt. xvii. 9). That is to say, it was *something seen.* But was it a merely subjective vision? was it a thing of fancy, woven weirdly out of the woof of their own imaginations? No. It was objective to all the three, and interned within none of them. And doubtless it would become objectively visible to them in the light of Him who was for the time being so ineffably radiant with His own effulgence. Or we might put the case thus: they got a glimpse into glory, by reason of their nearness to Him who was and is, in His own most glorious person, the open Door into heaven.

VER. 5. **And Peter answered and says to Jesus.** Namely, when Moses and Elijah were just in the act of departing. (See Luke ix. 33.) The impulsive

ST. MARK IX.

Master, it is good for us to be here: and let us make three tabernacles; one for thee, and one for Moses, and one for Elias. 6 For he wist not what to say; for they

---

Peter would fain have detained and retained them on the spot. He is represented as *answering*, although no question had been proposed to him, and no remark was addressed to him. He felt rightly, however, that a revelation had been purposely made to him; and to that he was, in his own impulsive and awkward way, sincerely responsive.

Master. In the original it is *Rabbi*. It would be the common appellation which the disciples employed when speaking to their Lord. Their standpoint of appellation, as of everything else, was naturally and inevitably Jewish. The two words however, *Rabbi* and *Master* (*Magister*), correspond almost exactly in their radical signification. (See Patrizi.)

It is good for us to be here. The first ingenuous outburst of the disciple's ravishment. He was witnessing indeed only the concluding scene of the sublime spectacle; but he did not know that; and what he did witness entranced him. He had been asleep along with the other two (Luke ix. 32). Weariness had overpowered them. It was late at night. Our Saviour had been engaged in prayer. He had ascended the mountain 'to pray' (Luke ix. 28). It would seem that, as on so many other occasions, He had continued long in aspiration and supplication. He was rapt into the presence of His Father, and wrapt in communion with Him. He would gather spiritual strength and recruitment as He continued. He would draw into His recipient humanity more and more of the heavenly influences which were the efflux of the Father's presence. By and by His very body was interpenetrated, and sublimed in some celestial way or other, 'transfigured.' He conferred with Moses and Elijah; and, just as the conference concluded, the disciples awoke, and were filled with overawing wonderment and rapture. Peter gave expression to their common feelings.

And let us make three tabernacles, one for Thee, and one for Moses, and one for Elias. *Tabernacles*, that is, *tents*, or *booths*. Peter would have liked the continuance of the scene. He wished to detain the heavenly visitants; and he thus proposes to provide for their temporary accommodation. He spoke, of course, unadvisedly. 'He committed,' says Petter, 'gross errors and absurdities.' But he knew Moses and Elias nevertheless. For, most probably, in the spirit world, every one's identity will be self evident. The nature and the name will be coincident. There will be no veils possible, and none needful.

VER. 6. **For he wist not.** *Wist* or *wissed* is the preterite of a fine old verb *wiss*, still living in German (*wissen*), and meaning *to know*. It is connected with *wis-dom*, *wise*, *wit*, *wits*. In the Anglo-Saxon version the *not* is combined with the *wist*, in the same way in which *nilled* is the negative of *willed*; *he nyste*. Coverdale's version is, *he knew not*. But Wycliffe and Tyndale have *he wist not*, and hence King James's version.

What to say. A great improvement on the translation in the Geneva, the Rheims, the Great Bible, Coverdale, and Tyndale, *what he said*. The original cannot bear to be so rendered (τί λαλήσῃ, or, as Tischendorf and Tregelles read, τί ἀποκριθῇ). And yet Luther committed the same mistake, and Zinzendorf,

were sore afraid. 7 And there was a cloud that overshadowed them: and a voice came out of the cloud, saying, This is my beloved Son: hear him. 8 And suddenly, when they had looked round about, they saw no man any more, save Jesus only with themselves.

---

and even Principal Campbell and Norton. The expression means, as Beza and Bengel clearly saw, *what he should say*, or, according to the probable reading of Tischendorf and Tregelles, *what he should answer*. Wycliffe was right, *what he shulde seie*. Peter assumed that he should say something, by way of response to the revelation made to the disciples, but he was not sufficiently self collected, to determine, deliberately and judiciously, how he should express himself.

For they became sore afraid. Or *they exceedingly feared*, as the word is rendered in Heb. xii. 21, the only other passage in the New Testament in which it occurs. The meaning is, *they were exceedingly agitated*. And although a sense of bliss was profoundly pervading their hearts (see ver. 5), there was yet whirling around it a feeling of trepidation and awe. The *sore* of our Authorized version is just the Scotch *sair*, and the German *sehr, exceedingly* or *very*.

VER. 7. And there was a cloud that overshadowed them. Or, more literally, *and there came a cloud overshadowing them*. The cloud *became* (ἐγένετο). Purvey has it admirably, *and ther was maad a cloude overschadewyinge hem*. The effulgence, of which Jesus was the centre, became overcanopied, and the cloud, that overarched them all, gradually settled denser and denser down. The end of the scene was at hand.

And there came a voice out of the cloud. The voice too, as well as the cloud, *became* (ἐγένετο the right reading). The cloud, within which it formed itself, and out from which it issued, would be a cloud of glory, veiling and shading no doubt all that was aloft, but yet resplendent (Matt. xvii. 5), a fit symbol of the Divine Presence.

This is My beloved Son, hear Him. Our Lord thus "received from God the "Father," as we read in the Second Epistle of Peter (i. 17, 18), "honour and "glory, when there came such a voice to Him from the excellent glory, *This is* "*My beloved Son, in whom I am well pleased*. And this voice we ourselves "heard come out of heaven, when we were with Him in the holy mount." The voice would be finely sustaining to the heart of our Lord Himself; and, as heard by the disciples, would be eminently fitted to strengthen their faith, and predispose them to bow implicitly to the Master's instructions and declarations. (See Deut. xviii. 15.) The highest position of honour and bliss which any human being can occupy is to sit lowly at the feet of Jesus, and 'hear Him.' "Jesus," says Petter, "is the chief Doctor or Teacher of the church; and all 'Christians ought to hear and obey His teaching." True; and He is likewise the chief Light of the world, and all men everywhere ought to ' see light in His light.'

VER. 8. And suddenly, when they had looked round about, they saw no man any more, save Jesus only with themselves. Or, *they no longer saw any one but Jesus alone with themselves*. Moses and Elijah had dis-appeared: and at a certain stage of things this fact became *suddenly* or *all at once* apparent to the

10] ST. MARK IX. 239

9 And as they came down from the mountain, he charged them that they should tell no man what things they had seen, till the Son of man were risen from the dead. 10 And they kept that saying with themselves, questioning one with another what the rising from the dead should

overawed disciples. The older English translators, as well as Luther and Principal Campbell, the authors of the modern Dutch version (1868), and the English Revisers, connect the word *suddenly* with the verb *when-the y-had-looked-round-about.* Tyndale's version is, *and sodenly they loked rounde aboute them.* Principal Campbell's is, *and instantly looking about.* But King James's translators, following in the wake of Erasmus and Beza, did well in severing this connection. It is unnatural to suppose that the overawed disciples were eager to look about with suddenness. The *suddenly* is used, in an artless manner, to describe the impression made upon them *after* they had looked round about. *All-at-once* they realized, what exceedingly surprised them, that Jesus was 'alone with themselves.'

VER. 9-13 constitute a little appendix to the preceding narrative of the transfiguration. (Comp. Matt. xvii. 9-13.)

VER. 9. **And as they were going down from the mountain.** What follows transpired while they were in the act of descending.

He charged them that they should tell no one what things they saw. *Tell*, or *narrate* (διηγήσωνται). Even they themselves did not yet understand what they had seen. Still less could they, in present circumstances, make others understand.

Till the Son of Man were risen from the dead. The compound expression rendered *till* literally means, as Wakefield renders it, *save when*, or, still more literally, *except when*; *unless when the Son of Man should have risen again from the dead.*

VER. 10. **And they kept the saying.** The *saying*, namely, which is recorded in the immediately preceding verse, *the injunction.* Beza strangely understood the word as meaning, not *saying*, but *thing* (*rem* : eds. 1558, 1598), and referred it to *the fact of the transfiguration.* But the reference is evidently to the injunction ; they *kept* it, or *held it fast.* Such is the import of the verb employed (ἐκράτησαν) ; and so is it translated in Heb. iv. 14, Rev. ii. 13, 25, iii. 11. They *held fast* the injunction as a sacred thing, that was not to be tampered with.

With themselves. Our Authorized translators, along with the Syriac Peshito version, and Euthymius Zigabenus, Erasmus, Luther, Tyndale, Coverdale, Beza, Felbinger, Mill, Willes, Lachmann, Ewald, Tregelles, Ornsby, connect these words with the expression that goes before. Heumann, though entirely misunderstanding the meaning of the preceding verb, protested against such a construction as unexampled and unnatural. Dav. Scholz and Fritzsche agree with him, and hence connect the expression with the following participle. So do Hammond, Bengel, Meyer, Lange, Bisping. Rightly.

Questioning among themselves what the rising again from the dead should mean.

mean. 11 And they asked him, saying, Why say the scribes that Elias must first come? 12 And he answered and told them, Elias verily cometh first, and re-

Or more literally still, *What the rising again from the dead 'is.'* The three discussed among themselves, in a puzzled mood, what the Master could be referring to, when He spoke of His own rising from among the dead. Things had got into confusion in their minds. Surely He cannot be referring to what we have hitherto been accustomed to speak of as 'the resurrection of the dead.' That must still be in the far future. But He seems to be speaking of something that is to take place soon, and while we ourselves are living; something too in which He himself is to be implicated. We cannot understand what He means. And yet it must be of a momentous nature, for He spoke it with awful solemnity.

VER. 11. Probably the Saviour, after having charged His disciples not to divulge the scene of the transfiguration until after His resurrection, stepped on before, wrapped in His own contemplations. The disciples, falling behind, would then, in mingled awe and perplexity, ventilate among themselves the Saviour's meaning; and at the same time, no doubt, they would be, with unwavering fealty, encouraging one another to keep the secret which had been committed to their trust. But by and by their thoughts take another turn, though into a strictly adjacent field, and they make up to the Master to state their difficulty.

And they asked Him, saying, Why say the scribes that Elias must first come? There had been many debates among the people as to who Jesus was, and whether or not He might not be, notwithstanding the humility of His appearance, the Messiah promised to the fathers. The scribes were positive in maintaining the negative, for this among other reasons, that Elijah had not yet reappeared, according to Malachi's prediction (iv. 5). There seemed, at first sight, to be some force in the objection. And certainly if the resurrection of the just were to take place soon, it would be very wonderful indeed if Elijah should not make his appearance 'before the coming of the great and dreadful day of the Lord.' *Why?* Such is the general rendering of the term employed by the evangelist (ὅτι; Lachmann prints it ὅ τι;). It is a fragmentary interrogative, admirably appropriate in the mouths of questioners, labouring under a feeling of diffidence. Ewald however, and the English Revisers, regard it as being simply 'recitative,' and therefore to be left untranslated in English and German, *And they questioned Him saying, The scribes say, Elias must first come* But this interpretation is not so natural as the other. Tischendorf, instead of the single expression *the scribes*, reads *the Pharisees and the scribes*, under the insufficient authorization of the Sinaitic manuscript and the Vulgate version.

VER. 12. **And He said to them** (ὁ δὲ ἔφη αὐτοῖς) Such is the simple reading of Tischendorf, Tregelles, Alford. It is the reading of both the Sinaitic and Vatican manuscripts, and of C L Δ.

Elias indeed cometh first, and restoreth all things. According to the prediction in Mal. iv. 5, 6. He *restoreth all things*, so far as issuing a new order of the

storeth all things; and how it is written of the Son of man, that he must suffer many things, and be set at nought.

day is concerned, an order involving a return to first principles. In his preaching he puts all things to rights. He shows what should be; he shows what should not be. If his preaching were to be practised, the way would be admirably prepared for the highest prosperity and glory of the Israelites, and the ultimate regeneration of the whole of mankind. The wounds and divisions of society would be healed. 'The heart of the fathers would be turned to the children, and the heart of the children to their fathers.' The reform would spread from the family circle to all the other circles of society. Man would be heartily united to man. Webster and Wilkinson correctly note that the expression which denotes the advent of Elias is not, in the original, *coming*, but *having come* (ἐλθών). If we could, in our English idiom, have said *caming* instead of either *coming* or *having come*, the reproduction of the evangelist's phrase would have been complete. We cannot however. And our translators have admirably accommodated our English idiom to the Greek, *Elias indeed cometh first 'and' restoreth all things*. The use of the conjunction '*and*' sufficiently indicates that the 'restoration of all things' *follows after* the 'coming first.' The particle (μέν) rendered *indeed* in the Revised version or, in King James's version, *verily*, has no analogue in English. It finely bends the mind forward, in expectancy, toward some complementive fact that remains to be stated.

And (καί). This conjunction introduces the complementive fact, though the evangelist, in employing it, departs, *so far as form is concerned*, from the mode of representation which is initiated in the preceding clause. Form apart, what the conjunction introduces is something to be taken *on the other hand*, in relation to what goes immediately before.

How it is written of the Son of Man. A phrase which has, as Fritzsche expresses it, 'vehemently harassed interpreters.' He himself thinks that the reading of the existing manuscripts is in a state of hopeless confusion. Beza too was perplexed to the last degree. Daniel Heinsius, however, seems to have hit upon the true method of interpretation. He puts an interrogation point at the close of the clause, *And how stands it written concerning the Son of Man?* Lachmann, Tischendorf, Meyer, Lange, accept this interpretation. The Saviour wished the disciples to couple with the fact concerning Elijah another fact concerning the Messiah himself. It was a fact of the greatest moment, though utterly ignored by the Pharisees. The Saviour excites His disciples' attention to it, by introducing it interrogatively, *how stands it written concerning the Son of Man?* The Saviour answers His own question as follows.

That He should suffer many things and be set at nought. To lose sight of the sufferings of the Messiah, and of His rejection by the mass of the people, was to lose sight of one of the most obvious and important features of Old Testament prophecy. The word aptly rendered *set at nought* (ἐξουθενωθῇ) is exceedingly graphic and emphatic. Our Saviour was to be *treated as if He were Nothing at all*. He was not only to be ignored, He was to be ignored with the utmost possible contempt. See the predictions in Psalm xxii. and Isaiah liii. The expression '*that*' *He should suffer*, if very literally rendered, would be '*in order*

R

13 But I say unto you, That Elias is indeed come, and they have done unto him whatsoever they listed, as it is written of him.

---

that' He should suffer. Our Saviour's very presence on the earth was *in order that He might suffer.* He came *when* He came, and *as* He came, and *where* He came, in order that He might face the very difficulties, and endure the very trials, which were now to rise up around Him in these circumstances, while engaged in the prosecution of His great undertaking. Over and above His more general aim, which would not have been modified in whatsoever age and in whatsoever sphere He had appeared, *He came to enter that particular sphere and arena, and to sacrifice Himself there.*

VER. 13. **But I say unto you.** A solemn and autocratic way, becoming in our Lord, of giving utterance to an important idea or truth.

That. It is the *recitative* '*that*,' and may be omitted in translation, as has been done by Wakefield, Meyer, Ewald.

Elias is indeed come. A free translation. The particle rendered *indeed* is the common conjunction that means *and* or *also* (καί). Many translators, such as Luther, Tyndale, Coverdale, omit it altogether. And many interpreters, on the other hand, have supposed that it looks forward to the *and* in the beginning of the following clause, *and they have done unto him what they listed.* They would accordingly translate it *both,* as if the meaning were as follows : *It is the case,* '*both*' that Elias has come, '*and*' that they have done to him what they listed. So Edgar Taylor and Norton translate. The Vulgate translator, and Erasmus Schmid, and de Wette, seem to have taken the same view (*et...et*). But if such a relationship of the clauses had been the idea of the evangelist, we should have expected, as Meyer observes, another order of his words (καὶ ἐλήλυθεν Ἠλείας). It is more likely therefore that the particle tacitly glances at Another One who had come, *Elias* '*too*' *has come.* The disciples were certain that the Messiah had come. He was standing before them, and speaking to them. Jesus assures them that *Elias also had come.* In the Rheims the translation is *Elias also.* Principal Campbell's version is, *Elijah too.* Bishop Hammond puts it well, 'He is come *as well as I.*'

And they did to him what they listed. That is, *what they desired.* Compare the German *Lust.* The two English words, *list* and *lust,* were originally one, and one with the German word, and meant *desire.* The leading Jews, in dealing with the New Testament Elijah, John, did not take into account for a moment *what God desired.* They only considered what was agreeable to their own feelings. And it was agreeable to their feelings to pay little regard to his spiritual instructions while he prosecuted his ministry at large, and to use no influence to get him liberated, after Herod had laid hands upon him.

As it stands written concerning him. Literally, *upon him.* It is an idiom in English also, to speak of *writing* '*upon*' *a subject.* But where, it has been often asked, is there anything written in the Old Testament Scriptures concerning the treatment which John, as the New Testament Elijah, was to receive? Grotius ingeniously says that since the prophet speaks of John as Elijah, *he leaves it to be understood that Ahabs and Jezebels would not be wanting.*

14 And when he came to *his* disciples, he saw a great multitude about them, and the scribes questioning with them. 15 And straightway all the people, when they beheld him, were

---

There was hence, he would conclude, a virtual prediction of John's maltreatment by Herodias and Herod. Wetstein takes the same view; *it stands written concerning John*, he says, *in the history of Elijah, who typified him*. So Elsner; Meyer acquiesces; so do the authors of the new Dutch translation. Patrizi actually thinks that the pronoun *him* refers not to John at all, but *to Elias his type*. Fritzsche says that the view of Grotius and Wetstein is 'the most *tolerable*' that has been suggested. But it appears to be more 'tolerable' and natural to admit that Mark was no purist in composition, and that his mind was resting on the chief assertion, *Elias too has come*, although he had let drop interveningly the secondary statement *and they did to him what they listed*. Robert Stephens took this view of the matter, and hence, in his 1550 and 1551 editions of the New Testament, enclosed within parentheses the intervening clause. He was followed by the authors of the Rheims version, and by le Clerc in his Latin New Testament. In his French version le Clerc omits the last clause altogether. Le Cene, Mace, and Principal Campbell transpose the clause into the middle between the two preceding clauses. Campbell gives the verse thus: *But I tell you that Elijah too is come, as was predicted, and they have treated him as they pleased*. This is too great freedom; and the brackets are too artificial. But the conception that underlies both the expedients is substantially correct. It was also Bengel's conception, and du Veil's.

VER. 14–29 contain a paragraph parallel with Matt. xvii. 14–21 and Luke ix. 37–43. The narrative of Mark, however, is much fuller, and more vivid, than the accounts of the other synoptics.

VER. 14. **And when He came to the disciples, He saw a great crowd around them.** In the Sinaitic and Vatican manuscripts, and the Armenian version, the expression runs thus, *and when 'they' came to the disciples 'they' saw a great crowd around them*. It is more likely, however, that the reading of the Received Text is the original.

And the scribes questioning with them. Or rather, *and scribes disputing with them*. There is no article before the word *scribes*. As to the phrase, *disputing with them*, see chap. viii. 11 and chap. ix. 10. It is the translation of Purvey, Tyndale, Coverdale, and the Geneva.

VER. 15. **And immediately all the crowd, when they saw Him, were greatly amazed.** Why? A debated matter. Some have supposed that their amazement arose from seeing His countenance, like that of Moses, supernaturally radiant from the effects of the transfiguration. Both Euthymius Zigabenus and Theophylact, as also John Wesley, make mention of this opinion, without however deciding for it. Bengel and de Wette favour it. Whitby and Wynne adopt it. But inconsiderately; for Mark does not mention at all, in his account of the transfiguration, the radiance of our Lord's countenance; and he does mention that our Lord expressly enjoined on the three favoured disciples to keep the fact of the mountain-glory a secret. We may be sure therefore, as

greatly amazed, and running to *him* saluted him. 16 And
he asked the scribes, What question ye with them? 17

Elsner remarks, that our Lord would not carry with Him, on His own person, the visible tokens of what had transpired. We must look in another direction for 'the reason why.' The Lord's *opportune appearance* seems to have struck the people with amazement. The disciples had got into a great difficulty. They were at their 'wits' end.' They had failed in an attempt to effect a cure. Their failure had been signal and conspicuous. The scribes, ever lying in wait to detect flaws, had taken advantage of their discomfiture to ride roughshod over their humiliated feelings; and no doubt they would be improving the opportunity to throw discredit on the name of the Master himself. Very likely they would be insinuating that it was a matter of good policy for Him to be out of the way, when a case that would really have tested His power of wonder-working was to turn up. The imbroglio of insinuation, disputation, crimination, and recrimination, had just reached its climax, when lo, in the 'very nick of time' the Saviour made His appearance, walking calmly along in the direction of the scene of contest. This is the view that has been generally entertained in reference to the *great amazement* of the people. It is sufficient. Instead of *greatly amazed*, Wells translates the word *overjoyed*. Unwarrantably, however. Wakefield renders it *surprised*; also unwarrantably. *There was surprise*; but it was superlative in degree.

And running toward Him, saluted Him. They hailed His advent with the greatest respectfulness and delight.

VER. 16. **And He asked the scribes.** Or, according to the reading of the modern critical editors, *and He asked 'them*,' that is, *the people in general*. As the Saviour advanced into the thick of the hubbub of disputation, He viewed collectively the general crowd, instead of disintegrating it into *scribes* and *the rest*. The Sinaitic, Vatican, and Cambridge manuscripts (א B D), along with L Δ, 1, and the Vulgate, Coptic, Armenian, and Æthiopic versions, read '*them*.' Mill had no doubt at all that *them* must be the autographic reading. Griesbach and Fritzsche were of the same opinion. But all three of these critics differed as to the reference of the pronoun. Mill supposed that it referred to *the disciples* alone, and that the second clause of the verse should be rendered thus, *what dispute ye 'among yourselves*,' for, says Mill, *they had no doubt begun to dispute among themselves*. (*Prol.*, § 406.) Griesbach supposed that it referred to *the disciples and the scribes*, and hence he too would translate the second clause of the verse in the same manner with Mill. Fritzsche again espoused the view that had been taken by the very ancient annotator whose annotation now forms part of the *Textus Receptus*. He supposed that the reference is to *the scribes*, and that the second clause of the verse should therefore be rendered as in our Authorized version. It is far more probable however that the reference of the pronoun is, indefinitely, *to* the people in general, as distinguished from the disciples.

What question ye with them? Or rather, *What dispute ye with them?* Or the phrase might be rendered thus, '*Why*' *dispute ye with them?* that is, *Why dispute ye with My disciples?* He would be already in the midst of the disciples when He spoke, as one of their company, so that His reference to them would

18]   ST. MARK IX.   245

And one of the multitude answered and said, Master, I have brought unto thee my son, which hath a dumb spirit; 18 and wheresoever he taketh him, he teareth him:

be manifest. *Why this uproar? Why those keen and biting words, which fell upon My ears as I approached?* As to the verb rendered in our Authorized version *question*, see on chap. viii. 11 and ix. 10, 14. It is rendered *dispute* by Purvey, Tyndale, Coverdale, and in the Great Bible and the Geneva. As to the general import of the interrogation, compare a corresponding phrase in chap. viii. 17. *With them:* In some important manuscripts, inclusive not only of the Alexandrine (A), but also of the Sinaitic at first hand (א*), the expression is reflexive (πρὸς ἑαυτούς), and means *with one another*, as Mill and Griesbach understood it. The other reading however (πρὸς αὐτούς) is the best supported, and the reference is no doubt to the disciples. Lachmann, Tischendorf, Tregelles support it.

Ver. 17. **And one out of the crowd answered and said.** Or simply, according to the reading of the Sinaitic, Vatican, and Cambridge manuscripts, and 33 'the queen of the cursives,' *answered Him.*
Master. Literally, *Teacher*, that is, *Rabbi.*
I have brought my son. Or rather, *I brought my son* (ἤνεγκα). The father was not referring to an action that was just completed as he spoke, but, indefinitely, to an action that was now among things past.
To Thee. It was *to Thee* that I wished and intended to apply in his behalf, though, when I arrived, I found Thee not.
Who has a dumb spirit. That is, according to a common idiom, *who has a spirit that makes him dumb*. The poor lad was a demoniac, and the demon had deprived him of the use of the affiliated organs of speech and hearing. (See ver. 25.) There is nothing incredible in such power, if evil spirits there be at all. Even some 'men' have power to deprive, for the time being, some of their fellow men of speech, hearing, feeling, seeing; and what marvel, then, that unincarnated spirits should have a corresponding power? There are assuredly in existence, as W. G. Palgrave says, 'malignant cosmical influences, be they what they may.' (*Central and Eastern Arabia*, vol. ii., p. 273.) "The spirit world," says Delitzsch, " good as well as bad, has been in all times the background of "the events that transpire on earth." (*Bib. Psychologie*, p. 22.) As to demons and their influence, see on chap. i. 23, 32.

Ver. 18. **And wheresoever** (ὅπου ἐάν). The right translation, giving the adverb its proper *local* import. Erasmus and Coverdale take the word in its rare *temporal* import, *whensoever*; but without any good reason. It is never used *temporally* in the New Testament.
It taketh him. The expression is somewhat ambiguous in English. It might be supposed to mean, *it conducteth him.* But it really means, *it seizeth him,* that is, *taketh hold on him.* The word in the original (καταλάβῃ) is the term from which we have our pathological word *catalepsy.* No doubt the poor afflicted lad would be an *epileptic*, and during his epileptic seizures he would be *cataleptic.*
It teareth him. Such is the literal meaning of the evangelist's term (ῥήσσει).

and he foameth, and gnasheth with his teeth, and pineth away: and I spake to thy disciples that they should cast him out; and they could not. 19 He answereth him, and saith,

It is a natural description, from a primitive standpoint, of the *convulsions* to which epileptics are subjected. Something seems to be *tearing*, or *tearing at, them*. In the margin of King James's version the term is rendered *dasheth him*, the Rheims translation. Purvey's corresponds, *hurtlith hym down*. They both reproduce the Vulgate version (*allidit illum*), which corresponds with the Peshito Syriac. Euthymius Zigabenus gives the same interpretation to the term. Hesychius too gives it, in his lexicon, as one of his interpretations of the term. Fritzsche approves. With some reason; and yet the evangelist's term is more generic, and exhibits as it were a more primitive attempt to represent the worry to which the poor sufferer is subjected.

And he foameth. Principal Campbell, having rendered the preceding clause *dasheth him on the ground*, freely renders this, *where he continueth foaming*; and no doubt the evangelist intends to describe the progress of the symptoms consequent upon seizure.

And gnashes with his teeth. More literally and simply, *and gnasheth his teeth*, or *grindeth his teeth*. The word *gnash* is onomatopoetic, and is painfully expressive, as is also Luther's word *knirschet*, and the corresponding word in all the Dutch versions, *knarst*, as also the Gothic word in the version of Ulfilas, *kriustith*.

And pineth away. Literally, *and is becoming dried up*, like a *withering* thing. The word is rendered *wither away* in Matt. xiii. 6, xxi. 19, 29 ; Mark iv. 6, xi. 21. It graphically represents that wasting condition of the body, which results in a haggard appearance. Celsus mentions that while the *morbus comitialis*, or *epilepsy*, is commonly not 'perilous to life,' it nevertheless sometimes 'consumes the man.' (*De Medicina*, iii. 23.) Euthymius Zigabenus misunderstood the reference of the evangelist's expression. He supposed that it describes the *insensibility* that is the concomitant of the attacks in detail. Principal Campbell has a corresponding idea, 'where he continueth foaming, and grinding his teeth, *till his strength is exhausted*.' Heinsius and le Cene blundered remarkably over the phrase. They thought that it had reference to the demon, and denoted the termination of the attack. They would translate it, *and departeth*.

And I spoke to Thy disciples, in order that they might cast it out, and they were not able. They had actually tried, but had failed.

VER. 19. **But He answered him, and saith.** Instead of *him*, it is *them* in the oldest and most important manuscripts, such as ℵ A B D L Δ II, 1, 33. Griesbach, consequently, and also Lachmann, Tischendorf, Tregelles, have replaced *them* in the text. Mill, in his day, approved (*Prol.*, § 1493). And no doubt, as being by far the more difficult reading, it must be the autographic. Our Saviour did not direct His remarks, in the first place, to the father of the afflicted lad. He spoke *to the crowd in general*, as embracing all the different parties ; and, as He spoke, He realized that they were but representatives of a far larger crowd. His spirit spread itself out over *the population in general*. See the following words. The expression however is not, *He answered and saith to*

ST. MARK IX.

O faithless generation, how long shall I be with you? how long shall I suffer you? bring him unto me. 20 And they brought him unto him: and when he saw him, straight-

---

them; it is *He answered them and saith*. In the Received Text, and indeed in all Stephens's editions, there is a comma before the clausule *and saith*. The Saviour thus is represented *as turning Himself responsively to the crowd in general, and the population in general, and then saying what follows*. He looks, as it were, at the prevailing state of mind, as if it had been vocally expressed to Himself. It had in it a relation of challenge or defiance, which was as real as actual speech.

O faithless generation. Or rather, according to our modern idiom, *O unbelieving generation!* Such is the translation of the Vulgate, Ulfilas, Erasmus, Luther, Calvin, Beza, le Clerc, Bengel, Newcome, Principal Campbell, Sharpe, Lange, Rilliet. It is not unlikely however that the word *faithless* was used by our translators in its primary import, *destitute of faith*, that is, *unbelieving*. The original term was generally translated by them *unbelieving*, or *not believing*. See 1 Cor. vii. 12, 13, 14, 15, x. 27, xiv. 22, 23, 24; 2 Cor. vi. 14, 15; 1 Tim. v. 8; Rev. xxi. 8. Note too the contrast in John xx. 27, 'Be not *faithless*, but *believing*.' The cognate noun moreover is always translated *unbelief*. (Matt. xiii. 58; 1 Tim. i. 13; Heb. iii. 12; etc.) In the passage before us the Geneva has *faithless*; and so has Cromwell's Bible. But Tyndale and the original Geneva (of 1557) have 'O generation *without faith*,' which corresponds to Wycliffe's *out of bileve*, that is, *out of belief*, or *without belief*. The Saviour lamented the unbelief of the generation, their unbelief in relation to Himself, their unbelief in relation to His Father.

How long shall I be with you? I have come *to* you ($\pi\rho\delta s$), how long shall I require to remain in the relationship thus established, ere the end of My mission be realized? How long shall I require to be *with* you, ere you get to know Me and the Father? *How long?* literally, *until when?* At what point of time will there be a prospect of My mission being understood?

How long shall I bear with you? If the force of the verb were very literally given, the interrogation might be expressed thus, *How long shall I 'hold Myself up' in relation to you?* That is, *How long shall I tolerate you?* The Saviour speaks as from a Divine standpoint, and realizes that there are limits to Divine forbearance.

Bring him unto Me. How full and unwavering His consciousness of Divine power! The verb *bring* is in the plural ($\phi\epsilon\rho\epsilon\tau\epsilon$), so that the father, while specially referred to (Luke ix. 41), is not exclusively addressed.

VER. 20. **And they brought him to Him.** *They*, the excited people, would eagerly take part with the father.

And when he saw Him. 'It is possible,' says Bleek, to regard the subject of the seeing as the demon, and not the demoniac. It may be 'possible,' but it is extremely improbable; for (1) the last clause of the verse, running in a corresponding groove, must refer to the demoniac; and (2) the gender of the participle which is rendered *when 'he' saw* ($i\delta\acute{\omega}\nu$) is at variance with the supposition.

way the spirit tare him; and he fell on the ground, and wallowed foaming. 21 And he asked his father, How long is it ago since this came unto him? And he said, Of a child. 22 And ofttimes it hath cast him into the fire, and into the waters, to destroy him: but if thou canst do any thing,

Straightway the spirit tare him. Or, *convulsed him*, or, better still, *the spirit immediately threw him into convulsions*. Such is the appropriate rendering of Mace, Worsley, and Principal Campbell. (Compare Plutarch's expression, κραυγὰς σπαραγματώδεις, *convulsive screams*, or *paroxysms of screaming*: *Op.* vol. ii. p. 130. C.)

And he fell on the ground, and wallowed foaming. *Wallowed* or *rolled (himself)*. The word *wallowed* (connected with the Latin *volvo*) just meant *rolled*. The expression in Matt. xxvii. 60, that is rendered in our version *and he 'rolled' a great stone to the door of the sepulchre*, is rendered by Wycliffe thus, *and he 'walowid to' a grete stoon at the dore of the biriel*. See also Mark xv. 46.

VER. 21. And He asked his father, How long ago is it since this happened to him? '*This*,' that is, *this* affliction. '*Since* this,' or more literally, '*when* this'; exceedingly literally, '*as* this.' Compare the German *als*. As to the final end of the Saviour's asking, we certainly do not need to seek it in our Saviour himself. (See John vi. 6.)

And he said, From a child. That is, *from childhood*, or rather, as Richard Watson remarks, *from boyhood*. In the oldest and best supported reading of the original phrase there is a pleonasm (ἐκ παιδιόθεν), somewhat corresponding to our English pleonastic phrase *from thence*.

VER. 22. The father of the lad continues. And ofttimes it hath cast him. Tyndale has *casteth him*; literally, (*it*) *threw him*. The father thinks of particular instances.

Into (the) fire. There was no article in the text that was lying before our translators, and there is none in the best manuscripts and critical editions. It is found however in the Alexandrine manuscript; and Bengel and Fritzsche have introduced it into their texts. *Into fire*: not simply *into 'the fire' at home*; but, indeterminately, *into fire*, when he happened to be near it, and, it might be, in various places. In the original the expression is *both into fire*, the mind being thus prepared for a reference to some other dangerous element.

And into (the) waters. The article here too is wanting, even in the Alexandrine manuscript, and in Bengel. It is foisted in however by Fritzsche; wilfully. The lad had been precipitated at various times, and in various places, *into waters*, or *into water*, as Wycliffe renders it. Tyndale and Coverdale also use the singular number. There is something both singular and plural in water; the many drops or droplets run together into unity. In Hebrew the word for *water* is plural only.

In order to destroy him. The father recognised demonic malice in the seizures.

But if Thou canst do anything. The afflicted parent was not sure whether such an aggravated case was within the reach or scope of the great Healer's

have compassion on us, and help us.   23 Jesus said unto him, If

power. He did not question indeed that Jesus was a wonderful Healer. But there was, he seems to have thought, a peculiarity in his son's particular case, that made it doubtful whether even so wonderful a Healer could do anything that would be adequate to remove or even to alleviate the affliction. In short he did not understand Jesus as the Son of God and the Saviour of men, their Saviour both inwardly and outwardly.
Have compassion on us, and help us. The 'us' is touching. The father, with beautiful benevolence of love, identifies himself instinctively with his son. He felt that whatever was done to his son was done to himself.

VER. 23.   An exceedingly important verse, but to many minds beset with difficulties, both critical and doctrinal.
But Jesus said to him, If thou canst believe. This word *believe*, though apparently so indispensable, is wanting in both the Sinaitic and Vatican manuscripts (א B), and in the Parisian Ephraemi (C*); as also in L Δ and 1. It is wanting likewise in the Coptic, Armenian, and Æthiopic versions, and in k* of the Old Latin version. Griesbach thought that it was 'probably' spurious; and Tischendorf and Tregelles have actually omitted it from their texts. Neander approved of the omission (*Life of Christ*, § 187); and so do Ewald and Meyer, and the English Revisers. No doubt rightly. For although, at first sight, when the word is left out the Saviour's answer seems cut short of significance at its very commencement, yet, when we look deeper, we see that there is a fine subtle significance that is blurred out of sight by the presence of the word. In the original the neuter definite article (τό) stands before the expression, so that very literally the Saviour's reply runs thus, *The If thou canst (believe), all things are possible to him who believeth.* The presence of this article changes the whole aspect of the case; for if the word *believe* be retained, the article is a stumbling block. It puzzled the writer of Beza's old manuscript (D), who hence left it out altogether. It puzzled Beza too, so that he actually turned the sentence right round, *If thou canst believe 'this'* (viz. *that I can help thee*). Krebs again regarded it as forming no part at all of our Saviour's reply, but as standing before it, fingerpost-wise, after the manner of its use in Luke i. 62, ix. 46, xxii. 2, 4, 23, 24, 37; Acts xxii. 30; 1 Cor. iv. 6. Lösner and Kuinöl agree with Krebs. Their interpretation would be so far legitimate, if we could conceive any reason that might have led the evangelist to give a special emphasis to this reply of our Saviour, as distinguished from the many other replies that were made by Him on other occasions. Fritzsche imagined that the text must be corrupted; Lachmann (*Preface to vol.* ii., p. 7) was of the same mind, and proposed a modification of reading (πιστῶσαι), *make certain the (uncertain)* '*If thou canst.*' Burton, accepting the text and the Received reading, would remodel its import by a peculiar punctuation and accentuation, *Believe what you have expressed when you said If Thou canst* (Τό, Εἰ δύνασαι, πίστευσαι). Sir Norton Knatchbull and Grashof had the same idea regarding *believe* (that it was an imperative in the middle voice); but they took a simpler view of the remainder of the expression. The verb however in its New Testament usage never occurs in the middle voice. D. Heinsius proposed as an emendation of the text that, instead of the article

thou canst believe, all things *are* possible to him that believeth.

---

the (Τό), we should read the interrogative *What?* (Τί ;) But there would be no end to conjecture, if conjecture were to be the order of the day. All real difficulty vanishes when we accept the reading of the oldest manuscripts, and omit the word *believe*. Then the Saviour's answer fastens upon the unbelieving expression which the man had employed, ' but *if Thou canst* do anything.' Taking hold of that expression, the Saviour draws the man's attention to it, and thence starts immediately in the direction of the ability that was really indispensable. It is as if He had said, " The phrase *If Thou canst* is a phrase which " should not have been used by thee in relation to Me. It is in truth applicable " only to thyself; for *all things are possible to him who believeth.*" The Saviour refrained from *spreading out* His rebuke. He only *suggested* it, by holding up to view the man's own phrase, and then abruptly turning from it to the condition on which, in all ordinary cases, His special favours were suspended. There is therefore a kind of *break-off*, or *aposiopesis*, at the conclusion of the articulated expression, ' *If Thou canst !* All things are possible to him that believeth.' Tischendorf employs an interrogation point, ' *If Thou canst ?* ' It is as if he would interpret thus, 'Did you really say so ? ' Ewald also brings out the idea interrogatively, ' *What ? If Thou canst ?* ' The recent Dutch translators (1868) give the same interrogative rendering, only omitting the preliminary *What ?* Griesbach disliked the interrogative form, but explains, in substantial accord, as follows : " Thou saidst, *If Thou canst*. With the highest possible right do I " throw back to thee that expression ; for there is nothing that is impossible to " him who finds it possible to believe." (*Comm. Crit.*, in loc.) Wetstein had substantially the same idea, though he did not see clearly how to work it out.

All things are possible to him who believeth. The expression does not mean, in this connection, *It is possible for the believer to* ' *do* ' *all things*, but *It is possible for the believer to* ' *get* ' *all things*. Omnipotence is, in a sense, at his disposal. But the universality of things contemplated by our Lord was not, as the nature of the case makes evident, the most absolute conceivable. We must descend in thought to *the limited universality of things that would be of benefit to the believer.* We must indeed descend still farther. We must consider the benefit of the believer not absolutely, or unconditionally, but relatively to his circumstances, and thus relatively to the circumstances of the other beings with whom he is connected. With these limitations, inherent in the nature of the case, ' *all things* ' *are possible for him that believeth.* But why, it has often been asked, for only *him that believeth?* Why insist on *faith* from the afflicted father, and from others in corresponding circumstances? Why not dispense favours of health, with indiscriminative generosity, on *believing* and *unbelieving* alike ? *It was because faith in the fact of Christ's Divine power or authority, or, at all events, in the propitiousness which is involved in that fact, is, in the nature of things, absolutely necessary to the enjoyment of the highest* ' *spiritual* ' *blessings.* Being, in the nature of things, thus necessary in that high spiritual sphere, it was wise that our Lord should, by a positive enactment or determination, make it, in all ordinary cases, a prerequisite for obtaining His peculiar favours in all inferior spheres. He thus, in the material department of His work, held up the mirror to the spiritual ; and flashed light on the inner by the reflective power of

24 And straightway the father of the child cried out, and said with tears, Lord, I believe; help thou mine unbelief.

the outer. He made His visible life a parable of high invisible realities; it was the perfection of symbolism.

VER. 24. **And straightway the father of the child.** Note the expression *the child*. It is a diminutive in the original, so that we may conclude that the sufferer was *but a 'lad.'* The first Geneva and the Rheims render the word *boy*.

Cried out. He was profoundly agitated, and hence spoke in a loud and earnest way, with vehemence of intonation.

And said with tears. It would appear that the expression *with tears* has crept into the text from the margin. It is wanting in the three most important manuscripts, the Sinaitic, Alexandrine, and Vatican (א A* B), as well as C* L Δ; and in the Coptic, Armenian, and Æthiopic versions. It is left out of the text by Lachmann, Tischendorf, Tregelles, and is not needed. Meyer and Ewald approve of its omission.

Lord. This too has been carried in from the margin. It is wanting in *all* the best manuscripts, inclusive of A B C D, as well as in the Syriac versions, and the Gothic, Coptic (Schwartze's ed.), and Armenian (Zohrab's ed.). Even Griesbach and Scholz omit it.

I believe. The poor man, looking eagerly and excitedly from the standpoint of his great trial, caught a glimpse of the Divine glory that was radiating from the personality of Jesus. *Yes, I believe!* He exclaimed his faith.

Help (or *succour*) **mine unbelief.** 'A prayer,' says Martin Bucer, 'most needful (*pernecessaria*) for us all.' Yet it is a rather peculiar expression. Does it mean, *Help me against my unbelief?* So Dr. Adam Clarke explains it, 'assist me against it.' Ryle too, who says, 'What shall we do with our unbelief? We must *resist it*, and pray against it.' Doddridge gives the same explanation; and Rodolphus Dickinson introduces it into his translation, 'Fortify me against unbelief.' But this can scarcely be the exact idea. It seems to be one thing to *help unbelief*, and another to *help 'against'* it. Wesley looked at the expression from quite a different standpoint. He explained it thus, 'Although my faith be so small that it might rather be termed unbelief, yet help me.' He thus did not regard the suppliant as supplicating for increase of faith. This explanation was the alternative interpretation of Bengel. It was also Grotius's idea, who thinks that "it is scarcely credible that the man could have expected from "Jesus, and in particular suddenly, an augmentation of faith." Principal Campbell agrees with Grotius, and follows Mace in his version. Meyer too, in all his editions, adheres to the same interpretation, *Deny me not Thy help, notwithstanding my unbelief.* So Bleek, and also Webster and Wilkinson. But this view of the expression, notwithstanding the eminence of its supporters, seems far-fetched and strained. It is more likely that the man while exclaiming 'I believe!' realized, as he spoke, that his belief was but struggling, as it were, into existence. It was merely a rudimentary thing, scarce worthy of the name of belief. It was not defiant infidelity indeed: far from that. It was not deliberate and self-complaisant antagonism to faith: far from that. But

25 When Jesus saw that the people came running together, he rebuked the foul spirit, saying unto him, *Thou* dumb and deaf

still there was more of what was negative in it than of what was positive. While, when looked at on one side, it might be called *belief*, yet, when looked at on another, it was rather *unbelief*, though unbelief in the throes of transformation into belief. Hence many interpreters, such as de Lyra, Dionysius à Ryckel, Petter, Trapp, Kuinöl, Holden, Bland, Grashof, Alexander, Burger, explain the word as the man's own depreciatory expression for his *weak* or *imperfect faith*. The man was probably in the very act and agony of a vital change; and hence, at the moment that he caught a glimpse of the Divine power of Jesus to succour the disordered body, he also caught a glimpse of His equal power to succour the disordered soul. He therefore prays Him on his own behalf. But Wynne surely misunderstood the prayer when, on a principle of cool reflectiveness, he interpreted it thus: 'Remove my doubts by performing the cure, which will strengthen my wavering faith.' Yet le Clerc gives the same interpretation. Calvin seems to look upon the *faith* and *unbelief* here mentioned as the two permanent foci in the ellipse of all Christian experience, and hence he extends the application of both parts of the expression to all Christians. He says, 'As their *faith* is never perfect, it follows that they are partly *unbelieving*.' 'This,' says Richard Baxter, ' is alas the case of most Christians.' Note the 'alas,' for Alexander goes too far when he says, ' the reply itself is one of the most beautiful on record, even in the Gospels.' See next verse.

VER. 25. But (δέ). Tyndale and our translators did wrong in omitting this conjunction. It is rendered *now* by Coverdale and Luther. Wycliffe and the Rheims, following the Vulgate, render it *and*. Bengel has *aber*, that is *but*.

When Jesus saw that the crowd came running together. Or more literally, *comes running together*. The object seen is, as it were, *directly* represented. *when Jesus saw* (this to wit) *the crowd comes running together*. The verb rendered *comes running together* (ἐπισυντρέχει) is freely thus rendered, though Liddell and Scott give, in their lexicon, the same import, ' to run together to (a place).' So too Robinson in his lexicon; also Erasmus, Grotius, Beza. The verb is unknown in classical Greek; but one should suppose, on the principle of analogy, that the first preposition would denote *addition* (see Fritzsche), *But when Jesus saw the crowd running together more and more*, viz. in the direction of Himself. Bretschneider, in the first and second editions of his lexicon, explained the word as Liddell and Scott have done. In his third and last edition he combined, unwarrantably, the two forces of the preposition. Schleusner overlooked the force of the preposition altogether. And so did Wahl, in the first and second editions of his lexicon, but he explained it correctly in his third.

He rebuked the unclean spirit, saying to it, Thou dumb and deaf spirit, I charge thee. Or, as Wycliffe and the Rheims give it, *I comaund thee*. The spirit is called *dumb and deaf*, because dumbness and deafness were two of the characteristic results of its occupancy. 'The demon,' says Delitzsch, ' stood related to the dumbness and deafness as cause to the effect.' (*Bib. Psychologie*, § 16, p. 296).

29] ST. MARK IX. 253

spirit, I charge thee, come out of him, and enter no more into him. 26 And *the spirit* cried, and rent him sore, and came out of him: and he was as one dead; insomuch that many said, He is dead. 27 But Jesus took him by the hand, and lifted him up; and he arose.

28 And when he was come into the house, his disciples asked him privately, Why could not we cast him out? 29 And he

---

Come out of him, and enter no more into him. It was thus not merely deliverance from the present epileptic seizure which the Saviour granted. It was a deliverance from liability for the future to all similar attacks and the other calamities involved in ' possession.' It will be noted that it is not said that the Saviour wrought the miracle here recorded, because of His high approbation of the state of mind that was manifested by the afflicted father. Comp. Matt. viii. 10-13; Mark vii. 29. Exorbitant ideas of the excellency of that state of mind have been entertained by Alexander and others, as if it were the *beau ideal* of true spiritual self consciousness and humility. But it is another motive-cause of action that is brought into view by the evangelist. It was *when the Saviour saw the multitude gathering rapidly, in yet denser crowds*, that He cut short His interview with the agitated man and delivered his son.

VER. 26. **And after it cried, and severely convulsed him, it came out, and he became as dead, so that the more part say, He is dead.** It is Alford's rendering, and Rilliet's (*la plupart*). It is not needful however to suppose that there was much of a formally comparative estimate of the numbers of two distinct parties.

VER. 27. **But Jesus took him by the hand.** Or, according to the reading of the Sinaitic, Vatican, and Cambridge manuscripts (א B D), a reading received into the text by Lachmann, Tregelles, and Tischendorf, *But Jesus took hold of his hand.*

And raised him up. *Awaking him to consciousness.* He infused into his frame a divinely reviving and healing energy.

And he arose. Namely, to his feet, ' perfectly whole and sound ' (Petter).

VER. 28. **And after He entered into (the) house.** There is no article before the word *house* in the texts that were lying before King James's translators; and it is wanting in almost all the best manuscripts, and in all the critical editions. Still the meaning is not exactly *into a house*, the rendering of Wycliffe, Wakefield, Norton, Godwin. The idea is, *after He was housed, after He had retired from the outside crowd.* And no doubt the Saviour would be domiciled just in ' *the* ' *house* where He had been lodging for the time being. Comp. chap. ii. 1, iii. 19, vii. 17.

His disciples asked Him privately. After they had got to be with their Lord, by themselves.

Why (ὅ τι or ὅ, τι) **were we unable to cast it out?** They had made the attempt and had failed, though in other cases they had succeeded. See chap. vi. 13.

VER. 29 Jesus seizes the culminating point of what was reprehensibly

said unto them, This kind can come forth by nothing, but by prayer and fasting.

30 And they departed thence, and passed through Galilee; and he would not that any man should know it. 31 For

---

deficient in the disciples. Comp. Matt. xvii. 20, 21. **And He said to them, This kind.** Not *this kind of faith*, as le Cene strangely supposes; nor *this kind of unbelief*, as Sieffert as strangely supposes (*Ursprung*, pp. 100, 101); nor *this kind of beings* (namely the whole tribe of demons), as Fritzsche, Bleek, and Alexander suppose; but *This kind of demons, this kind of peculiarly determined and malicious demons*. For, among evil spirits, as among evil men. there are varying degrees of energy, determination, and malice. They are not all cut and clipped after one precise model.

Cannot come forth. Or *go out*, as it is rendered in Wycliffe, Coverdale, and the Rheims. It '*cannot*' *go out*, that is, it *cannot be compelled to go out*.

By anything except by prayer and fasting. Not pathologically on the part of the demoniac, as Paulus fancied, but propaedeutically on the part of the exorcist. It is not meant, however, that *faith* might be omitted (Matt. xvii. 20). Neither is it meant that faith must be merged in prayer and fasting. It is meant that faith must be in maximum degree, and that consequently those spiritual exercises which condition its highest attainable exaltation must be realized. *There must be prayer*, the uplifting of desire till it settle in the will of God. *There must be fasting*, the denying of all in the periphery of self that would hinder the uprising of the desire to God, or its absolute repose in His will. When the desire reaches the will of God, and entering into it settles itself there, it has laid hold of Omnipotence. No wonder therefore that 'all things are possible' to the faith that goes along with it. No wonder that 'mountains' are 'removable.' No wonder that the promise is illimitable, 'Ye shall ask *what ye will*, and *it shall be done unto you*.' (John xv. 7; comp. Mark xi. 23, 24.) It is into *the will of God* that the desire has risen; hence subjective caprice is excluded. And thus, if not always in the physical sphere, yet always in the moral sphere, demons the most inveterate are cast out, mountains the most frowning are swept aside, and miracles the most marvellous are achieved. It is remarkable that in the Sinaitic and Vatican manuscripts (ℵ B) the words *and fasting* are wanting, and Tischendorf has left them out. Meyer condemns them, as do our English Revisers. The authorization, however, is not sufficient. But even if it were overwhelming, *fasting* would, *in its essence*, be implied.

VER. 30-32 form a little appendix to the preceding paragraph. Comp. Matt. xvii. 22, 23; Luke ix. 43-45.

VER. 30. **And they departed thence.** From the neighbourhood of the mount of transfiguration, the district of Cæsarea Philippi. See chap. viii. 27.

And passed through Galilee. Literally, *and passed along through Galilee*. They did not tarry much at any particular place. Tyndale's translation is, *and toke their iorney thorow Galile*.

And He did not wish that any one should know. He wished to be really, and not merely technically, incognito. For the reason see next verse. The expression in the original brings *aim* into view (ἵνα τὶς γνοῖ). Our Lord had no wish

he taught his disciples, and said unto them, The Son of man is delivered into the hands of men, and they shall kill him; and after that he is killed, he shall rise the third day. 32 But they understood not that saying, and were afraid to ask him.

---

that involved within it as an aim that He should be known. In other circumstances He might wish and aim, and no doubt often did wish and aim, to be known; but not now.

VER. 31. **For He taught His disciples.** The verb is in the imperfect, *He was teaching His disciples.* And as it was on this teaching that His heart was set, He sought seclusion. In teaching His disciples He was teaching the teachers of the world.

And said to them, The Son of Man is delivered into the hands of men. *Of men,* mark. He refers to the chief priests and elders and scribes (see chap. viii. 31), but He chooses here to merge the specific representation in the generic, ' of men.' There is a gleam of antithesis in the generalization. Our Lord realized His own essential superiority to *men.* Note the present tense, *is delivered.* He has gone forward in thought into the approaching future, and is present there. He sees it all as vividly as if it were actually present. *Delivered,* viz. by His own traitorous disciple. To deliver indeed properly means to *free from*, and thus *to set at liberty*; a *deliverer* is one who gives *liberty.* But when a captor gives liberty to his captives, and hands them over to the people with whom he had been at variance, he puts them, in freeing them, *under the control of others*; hence the secondary meaning of the word *deliver, to give up to the control of another.* It was in this sense only that Jesus was *delivered* by Judas.

And they shall kill Him. Instead of welcoming Him as the Son of God, they will murder Him. The verb used (ἀποκτενοῦσιν) is of intense import, *to kill off.*

And after that He is killed, He shall rise. Literally, *He shall rise up,* that is, He shall rise up from the prostrate condition of death. In substance therefore the idea is, *He shall rise again,* and so the word is rendered by Wycliffe, Tyndale, Coverdale, the Geneva, and the Rheims, as also by the great majority of the modern translators.

The third day. In the most ancient manuscripts, and the most modern critical editions, the expression is, *after three days.* It has the same meaning as the expression in the Received Text. See chap. viii. 31. As the expression in the Received Text is the form of the phrase in Matt. xvii. 23, it seems to have commended itself to some early transcriber as the more precise or perspicuous way of putting the idea.

VER. 32. **But they understood not that saying.** It is simply *the saying* in the original. Erasmus translates the phrase freely, *what He had said.* Principal Campbell's version is also admirable, though free, *what He meant.* In accepting it we might then revert to a still more literal rendering of the verb, ' but they knew not what He meant.' To us, looking backward, the meaning of the prediction is as clear as sunlight; but when the disciples looked forward, from their standpoint of rabbinical anticipation, no utterance could appear more enigmatical.

And were afraid to ask Him. To inquire of Him, to question Him. They

33 And he came to Capernaum: and being in the house he asked them, What was it that ye disputed among yourselves by the way? 34 But they held their peace: for by the way

were 'afraid.' Mace far too freely renders it *ashamed*; Principal Campbell, influenced by Mace, uses a still more objectionable word, *shy*. It was not a case of mere *shyness*, or even *shame*. They saw clearly that some dark cloud was lowering. The Master's mind was profoundly affected. Billows of 'a sea of troubles' were dashing in upon Him. Their hearts were like to fail them for fear, and they dreaded to look with inquisitiveness into what was impending. They remembered too the strong words that had been uttered to Peter, when he ventured to remonstrate: see chap. viii. 33. Thus *they feared to make inquiry*.

VER. 33-37 form a paragraph corresponding to Matt. xviii. 1-5, and Luke ix. 46-48. It is peculiarly interesting as containing evidence of the historical impartiality of the disciples. They did not suppress from their memorabilia of the Saviour what reflected discredit on themselves, if it served to reflect their Master's excellence or glory.

VER. 33. **And He came to Capernaum.** Or, as it runs in the Sinaitic, Vatican, and Cambridge manuscripts (א B D), *and 'they' came to Kapharnaum*; the Lord, to wit, and His disciples. Mill approved of the plural reading, and it has been introduced into the text by Lachmann, Tischendorf, Tregelles. The little company, in passing southward from the region about Cæsarea Philippi, at length arrived at Capernaum, our Lord's headquarters in Galilee. See chap. i. 21.

And being in the house. Or rather, as it stands in Lord Cromwell's Bible (1539), *and when He was come into the house* (ἐν τῇ οἰκίᾳ γενόμενος). Tyndale's version is *and when He was come to housse*; but the phrase *to house*, though idiomatic in German, has not grown into an English idiom. Coverdale's translation is more idiomatic, but still not quite satisfactory, *and whan He was at home*. The expression informs us that our Lord deferred questioning His disciples until He was once more domiciled in the house where He was accustomed to reside when He was living in Capernaum.

He inquired of them, What was it that ye disputed among yourselves by the way? Or, *What were you discussing in the way*, or *on the road?* The expression *among yourselves* is omitted in the manuscripts א B C D L, and in the Vulgate and Coptic versions, and in a great majority of the Old Latin codices. It is left out by Lachmann, Tischendorf, Tregelles, Alford. Our Saviour did not make the inquiry in order to get information. (See ver. 34-36.) He made it in order to prepare their minds for certain ideas which He wished to communicate.

VER. 34. **But they held their peace.** Or, as Coverdale has it, *they held their tunges*. Mace and Campbell with exact literality render it, *They were silent*. Shame sealed their lips.

For they discussed with one another by the way. In the original, the expression *with one another* occupies a position of emphasis, by standing at the commencement of the clause, *for with one another they discussed on the road*. They had

ST. MARK IX.

they had disputed among themselves, who *should be* the greatest. 35 And he sat down, and called the twelve, and saith unto them, If any man desire to be first, *the same shall*

allowed a question, which should have been kept for ever far away from the hallowed enclosure of their fellowship, to get within their little circle.

Who (should be) the greatest. Literally, *Who (should be) greater*, viz. than the rest; who should occupy the chief position under the King, the position of prime minister as it were, in the kingdom that was about to be inaugurated. It is not likely that each of the disciples would put forward a claim to the primacy; there was a triumvirate that stood out conspicuously, and the rest of the disciples would probably be divided for the time being into cliques of partisans. We need not suppose indeed that the rivalry had been very strongly 'pronounced'; but it existed, and the discussion to which it gave rise had been unhappy.

Ver. 35. **And having seated Himself.** The Saviour was going to deal with the matter as a Teacher, solemnly.

He called the twelve. To come close to Him. See Matt. xx. 32; Luke xvi. 2, xix. 15; Acts x. 7. They had probably been engaged with their individual concerns; or they might be clustering in groups, which somewhat represented the cliques into which they had broken up.

And saith to them, If any one wishes to be first, he shall be last of all, and servant of all. This whole clause is regarded as apocryphal by Volkmar; and it is wanting in Beza's celebrated manuscript (D), now in Cambridge; it is however manifestly genuine. Instead of *he shall be* (ἔσται), the San Gallensis manuscript (Δ) and a good many others of lesser note read *let him be* (ἔστω); and many interpreters, who accept the common reading, that of the Received Text and also of the critical texts, interpret the expression after the mind of the San Gallensis transcriber. Petter, Wakefield, Worsley, Wesley, Rodolphus Dickinson, translate the phrase *let him be*. Calvin gives the same translation as an alternative rendering (*qu'il soit*). Heumann and Newcome have *he must be*; and so substantially, Luther, Meyer, Grashof, Lange, and expositors in general. They regard the entire apophthegm as coincident in import with chap. x. 43, 44, and Matt. xx. 26, 27. And so it is undoubtedly, in substrate of idea at least. It would be quite possible indeed to understand the expression as denoting the penal result of ambition. In the estimation of the Highest, he who seeks to be first shall be the last and least. But, on the whole, it is more likely that our Lord was designedly uttering, in a somewhat enigmatical way, the great principle of promotion in the kingdom of heaven: *If any one in My kingdom wishes to be first (to be*, says Cardinal Cajetan, *not to appear to be, not to be held to be, but to be*), *he shall not seek the pre-eminence in the usual way; he shall seek it in the reverse way; he shall go down, and be the last of all and the servant of all;* he shall ascend descendingly, and thus descend ascendingly. It is not necessary indeed that a man think untruths regarding himself, and his mental endowments or other talents; but it is necessary, if a man would be a Christian, that he do not make himself his own end. He must not coil himself on himself, and terminate himself in himself. He may ascend over

s

be last of all, and servant of all. 36 And he took a child, and set him in the midst of them: and when he had taken him in his arms, he said unto them, 37 Whosoever shall receive one of such children in my name, receiveth me: and whosoever

others, but not for himself. He may also descend below others; he must; but not for himself. His selfhood must not take a circuit, just to get back to itself; it must not go round about in order to reach itself by and by, enriched with the results of a wide-spreading sweep. The great sociological law of the kingdom of heaven is not this, *Use thyself for thyself*; still less is it this, *Use others for thyself*; but it is this, *Use thyself for others*.

VER. 36. **And He took a little child, and placed it in the midst of them.** Acting a parable. The action seemed to say: *Look there! In that child you have a charming picture of an unambitious spirit. I wish you not to be 'childish'; but I wish you to be 'childlike,' so far as ambition is concerned. Why should any one seek to be uppermost? or to gain an advantage over all the rest? It is surely nobler to give than to get. This child is not thinking of using us for the sake of itself. Its whole soul is beaming forth with fulness of unselfish love upon us all!*

And after taking it up in His arms. This is a graphic touch which Mark alone preserves. The Saviour felt impelled to lavish His love on the little one. He '*embraced*' it, in the literal sense of the word, *folding it within His arms.* (French *embrasser*, from *bras* the 'arm,' Lat. *brachium.*) The old corresponding Saxon word, *beclyppan*, has for long dropped out of use, though Wycliffe retained it in the passage before us, *whom whanne He hadde byclippid*. (To *clip*, now, is to bring a thing within the arms of scissors or shears.) Luther's word is fine, *herzete; He pressed the child to His heart.*

He said to them. No doubt among other remarks. See Matt. xviii. 3–5. The evangelist goes rapidly on with his narrative, only touching, as he passes, certain points and peaks of biographical events and remarks.

VER. 37. **Whosoever shall receive one of such little children.** Or, *If any one should receive one of such little children* (ὃς ἂν . . . δέξηται). *Of such little children* is the reading of Lachmann and Tregelles as well as of the Received Text. Tischendorf reads *of these little children*, under the authorization of the Sinaitic manuscript (ℵ) and C Δ, etc. It is an unimportant variation. **Shall receive:** to his house or his heart; an orphan child, for instance. But it is possible to receive to the heart when it is impossible or unnecessary to receive to the home; and what is applicable to the literal child is just as applicable to the intellectual or spiritual child. Comp. ver. 42; Luke xvii. 1, 2.

In My name. Literally, *upon My name*, that is, *on the ground of My name, influenced by regard to My name*. We should lay emphasis on this expression. The Saviour is thinking only of actions that are associated *with His name*. Kindness, *unlinked to His name*, is not at present taken by Him into account. But what if, nevertheless, it be implicitly connected? What if all that is beautiful and good in man be but some reflected rays from the beauty and goodness of the Ideal Man? The Saviour however is here speaking of *explicit* recognition; hence His use of the word *name*. His *name* indeed, apart from Himself, would be but an empty sound, sign, or symbol, something not worth

shall receive me, receiveth not me, but him that sent me.
38 And John answered him, saying, Master, we saw one
casting out devils in thy name, and he followeth not us:

knowing. But Himself, apart from His name, would be The Unknown. We cannot think of objects which are beyond our senses but by means of names.

Receiveth Me. The Saviour will take what is done to the child ' for His name's sake' as done to Himself. Comp. Matt. xxv. 40.

And whosoever receiveth (δέχηται ℵ B L) **Me, receiveth not Me, but Him who sent Me.** *Not Me* as separated from the Father. The man's action does not find its terminus in Christ; it goes farther, and terminates on the Great Father: so that the will of him who receives Christ is in harmony with the Infinite Will; his heart beats in sympathy with the Infinite Heart.

VER. 38-40 contain further particulars of the conversation that is referred to in ver. 33-37. Comp. Luke ix. 49, 50.

VER. 38. **And John answered Him, saying.** In the Sinaitic and Vatican manuscripts, as also in Δ, and the Peshito Syriac version, and the Coptic, the word *answered* is omitted. The expression simply runs thus, *John said to Him*. Tischendorf and Tregelles have introduced this reading into their texts. It is more likely, however, that the Received Text is genuine. It is the more difficult of the two readings. Jesus had not asked any question which needed to be *answered*; but when He said *Whosoever shall receive one of these little ones in My name receiveth Me*, John's mind got a gleam of light, and his conscience smote him. And hence, in response to the idea expressed by his Lord, he ' took words ' and spoke.

Master. That is *Rabbi*, literally *Teacher*.

We saw one casting out demons in Thy name, who followeth not us. *One, or a certain (individual)*. The expression, *who followeth not us*, omitted on insufficient evidence by the English Revisers, implies, *firstly*, that the individual referred to *did not follow Jesus* as one of His personal attendants and pupils (Luke ix. 49); and, *secondly*, that he *did not follow* '*the twelve*' as one occupying a subordinate position to theirs. There were individuals who *followed the twelve*, pious women for example, and, most likely, others. The individual here referred to, though probably not even of 'the seventy,' was no doubt one who had listened at some time or other to Jesus, and had faith in Him as the great Deliverer. Petter arbitrarily says, " he was faulty, in not being so forward "as he should have been in following Christ." Richard Baxter too speaks of him as 'faulty.' So does Matthew Henry: " I know of nothing that could hinder " him from following them, unless he was loath to leave all to follow them ; and "if so, that was an ill principle." But it was not to be expected that all who listened to our Saviour's words, and believed on Him, should leave their respective vocations and homes, and 'itinerate' in the company of our Lord's personal attendants. Our Lord wished, and had chosen, a limited number of 'itinerant' followers. The great majority of the rest, His inward followers, would require to adorn the doctrine of godliness in their local spheres, and in the management of their private and personal affairs. Some however would have peculiar gifts, and would hence be called to peculiar spheres of service.

and we forbad him, because he followeth not us. 39 But

The individual here referred to had one of those gifts, *he had power over evil spirits, and could exorcise them.* We know that there were such individuals in our Saviour's time, even among those who had never had any external connection with Him. See Matt. xii. 27. We know also that there were many in later times, as there had been before, who professed to be possessed of exorcistic power. Justin Martyr says, in his *Apology to the Roman Senate*: "Many of our people, the Christians, by using adjuration in the name of Jesus "Christ who was crucified under Pontius Pilate, have cured, and are still "curing, in Rome and throughout the world, multitudes of demoniacs, whose "cases had utterly baffled all other exorcists." (Chap. 6.) In his *Dialogue with Trypho the Jew* (chap. 85) he affirms that while exorcism, as practised by the Jews, failed, when the adjuration was "by kings (such as Solomon), or "saints, or prophets, or patriarchs," and often failed when the adjuration was simply "by the God of Abraham, the God of Isaac, and the God of Jacob," it was emphatically successful when administered "by the name of the Son of God, "who was born of a virgin and crucified under Pontius Pilate." Then, says he, "every demon is overcome and subdued." There would however, we may be sure, be many mountebank pretenders to exorcistic power. See Acts xix. 13, 14. And some perhaps, on the other hand, would have real power, who knew nothing outwardly of Jesus. Josephus witnessed the marvellous feats of a professed exorcist, called Eleazar, who performed in the presence of the emperor Vespasian. See *Antiq.* viii. 3 : 5. It is not incredible that, in certain peculiar idiosyncrasies and circumstances, incarnated spirits should have power to a certain extent over unincarnated spirits. It is but the reverse of the obverse fact, so often referred to in the New Testament, that unincarnated spirits have power, to a certain extent and in certain idiosyncrasies and circumstances, over spirits that are incarnated. The generic phenomenon is, *that spirit has power over spirit in many subtle ways, not yet explained by science.*

And we forbad him. We *prohibited* him. Very literally, *we hindered him*, viz. so far as blaming him, and insisting on his abandonment of the exercise of his gift, were concerned. Comp. Num. xi. 28.

Because he followeth not us. Tischendorf, under the sanction of the manuscripts ℵ B Δ, reads *because he was not following us* (ἠκολούθει), an unimportant variation. Mill rejected the clause altogether (*Prol.*, § 407), and Fritzsche cuts it off because of the 'intolerable loquacity' which it ascribes to John. It is no doubt genuine however. Note the '*us.*' Although no exegetical emphasis is lying on it, yet it is well to read it with some doctrinal intonation. It is the point at which the principle of exclusiveness crops up, that spirit of intolerance that so easily develops itself into fagot and fire. It was rife in the Jewish nation. It had been rife among other peoples. And although it was nipped in the bud by the Saviour the moment it sprang up among His disciples, yet by and by it rose again within the circle of Christendom, and grew into a upas tree that spread its branches, and distilled its blight, almost as far as the name of Christ was named. The tree still stands, alas, though many a noble hatchet has been raised to cut it down. It stands; but the hatchets have not been plied in vain. It is moribund. And here and there some of its larger boughs

ST. MARK IX.

Jesus said, Forbid him not: for there is no man which shall do a miracle in my name, that can lightly speak evil of me. 40 For he that is not against us is on our part.

have been lopped off, so that the sweet air of heaven is getting in upon hundreds of thousands of the more favoured of those who were sitting in the shadow of death. "Better a thousand times," says Ryle, "that the work of warring "against Satan should be done by other hands, than not done at all. Happy "is he who knows something of the spirit of Moses when he said, *Would God* "*that all the Lord's people were prophets*, and of Paul when he says, *If Christ* "*is preached, I rejoice, yea and will rejoice*" (Num. xi. 29; Phil. i. 18).

VER. 39. **But Jesus said, Forbid him not.** The Great Master had no sympathy with that exclusive spirit which was the germ of ecclesiastical persecution. The expression *prohibit him not* has been perplexing to some, inasmuch as the man was already prohibited. Petter says: "His meaning is, they should "not forbid him any more hereafter, nor yet any other that should attempt the "like in the same manner." We are probably to explain the injunction on the common rhetorical principle, that the scene in which the disciples encountered the exorcist was summoned up before the imagination, as if it were present. When we penetrate beneath the rhetorical form of the expression, we find in it both reproof for the past and direction for the future.

For there is no one who will do a miracle in My name. Or literally, *upon My name*, that is, *resting upon My name*. See on ver. 37. The word translated *a miracle* (δύναμις) properly means *power*. Wycliffe renders it *vertu* (virtue); Luther, *a deed (eine That)*; Bengel, *a mighty deed*. It is often, when used in the plural, rendered, in our English version, *mighty works* (Matt. vii. 22, xi. 20, 21, 23, xiii. 54, 58; 2 Cor. xii. 12). *Miracle* is Tyndale's and Coverdale's word. So too Piscator, *ein Wunder*. It is a *miracle* that is meant, but a miracle not considered as *an object of wonder*, but regarded as *a manifestation of power*.

That can lightly speak evil of Me. Literally, *and will be able quickly to speak evil of Me*. The verb translated *speak-evil-of* is the exact antithesis of the frequently recurring verb that is rendered *to bless* (εὐλογέω). Instead of *quickly* (ταχύ), or *soon*, as Wycliffe and Coverdale have it, Tyndale introduced the free translation *lightly*. The idea is, that if any man be conscious of exerting, either in an extraordinary or in an ordinary way, a great and beneficent influence through the name of Jesus, *it will take a considerable time*, to say the least of it, before his mind can become so altered that he would either speak or think depreciatingly of the 'worthy name' in which he has found a source of power and blessing. Nature, as Leibnitz and other thinkers used to say, does not advance *by leaps*. And mind too, even when in the act of transition and conversion, in either an upward or a downward direction, never takes *an entirely sudden leap*.

VER. 40. **For he that is not against us is for us.** Note the social *us*. The Saviour graciously associates His disciples with Himself. On another occasion (Matt. xii. 30) He said, *He that is not with Me is against Me*. The two apophthegms are but the obverse and reverse of one idea. *There is no neutrality*

41 For whosoever shall give you a cup of water to drink in my name, because ye belong to Christ, verily I say unto you he shall not lose his reward.

---

in relation to Christ and Christianity. He who is not with them is against them. He who is not against them is with them and for them. For, in all the spheres of things moral, there is no belt of border land between right and wrong. He who is not good is bad. He who is not bad is good. In the highest sphere, Christianity and goodness are identical. Christ is impersonated Goodness. And thus the great law of no-neutrality comes into operation. *He who is not with Christ is against Him: He who is not against Him is with Him and for Him.* When, in applied morals, we sit in judgment on ourselves, we should in ordinary circumstances apply the law obversely and stringently, *He who is not with Christ is against Him.* But when we are sitting in judgment on others, into whose hearts we cannot look directly, we should in ordinary circumstances apply the law reversely and generously, *He who is not against Christ is with Him and for Him.*

VER. 41. **For.** In the apophthegm of ver. 40 there is a substantial return to the sentiment of ver. 37; and hence this ratiocinative *for*, while strictly referring back to the immediate antecedent, implicitly refers farther back to the remoter antecedent in ver. 37. But Burton puts this latter link of connection too strongly when he says: "The 41st verse seems to be connected "*immediately* with ver. 37; our Saviour's discourse about the child having "been interrupted by the question put by John." Du Veil however took the same view; and Patrizi takes it strongly.

If any one should give to you a cup of water to drink. An inexpensive gift, but most precious and delicious, especially in such a thirsty climate as that of Palestine.

In My name. Having thought of Me and regard for Me. Note the *My*. It is recognised as genuine by Tregelles, and at length too by Tischendorf. It is in the Sinaitic manuscript. It had been given up by Griesbach, Lachmann, Scholz; by Fritzsche too, and Meyer; and also by Tischendorf in his 1849 and 1859 editions. It is no doubt genuine. And yet the Saviour was no egotist. He did not attribute, to the extent of one particle, too much importance to Himself. Neither did He intend to depreciate acts of kindness that had no explicit reference to Himself; no one was so ready as He to appraise at their true value such embodiments of love. But, instead of referring for the present to generic *acts of kindness*, He refers for a special purpose to such as were done *for His name's sake.* See on ver. 37, and comp. Matt. x. 42, where the same seed-thought was sown on another occasion.

Because ye belong to Christ. Or, as it is more simply in the Rheims, *because you are Christ's*. The word *Christ* is here used as a proper name, and yet with its significance unmerged. *They belonged to the Messiah.* The expression is epexegetical of the preceding *in My name.* But it does not suggest, specifically, *following* or *disciplehood* or *service*; the relationship indicated is generically *possession*.

Verily I say unto you, he shall on no account lose his reward. The action is

42 And whosoever shall offend one of *these* little ones that believe in me, it is better for him that a millstone were hanged about his neck, and he were cast into the sea.

---

worthy and rewardable, and shall therefore obtain reward. Not that there is anything in it, that should, or could, be erected on a high pedestal of merit. But, being right and good, God will smile on it.

VER. 42. See Matt. xviii 6, and Luke xvii. 2.

And whosoever shall offend. Or, as the idea of the original might be expressed, *And if any one should offend.* It is not possible to reproduce the original phrase to a nicety. The word *offend* too does but scant justice to the original term (σκανδαλίσῃ). It is rather, as Jonathan Edwards remarks (*Notes*, in loc.), *cause to offend*; Edgar Taylor's version. But neither is that the exact idea. The Rheims version is *scandalize*, a mere Anglicising of the original word, in despair of otherwise doing it justice. So too the French Geneva, in such editions as 1562, 1606, 1616, 1710. Calvin also, in his French version, uses the same word; and Martin, Ostervald, Rilliet. These all followed in the wake of the Latin Vulgate. But not only is *scandalize* not a translation; the term, in so far as it has become a denizen of our English language, has obtained a signification that is quite aside from the idea intended in the passage before us. Le Clerc renders the word, *make to fall*; Mace, *cause to transgress*; Norton, *cause to fall away from Me.* But Principal Campbell has hit on the proper translation, *insnare.* The Greek *scandal* was the stick of a trap, which, when struck, sprang and insnared the animal. *Men are 'insnared' when they are 'caught tripping.'* They are *caught tripping* when they go where they should not go, and touch what they should not touch. "If any one," says Calvin, "trips through our fault, or is turned aside from the right path, or retarded, "the Scripture says that we *scandalize* him."

One of these little ones who believe in Me. The Saviour has passed in thought from the literal child to the childlike; the childlike not merely in spirit, but in experience and intellect. There are little ones, intellectually, in the family of the Great Father. Tyndale uses the one word *lytelons.* Note that the Saviour says *one of these lytelons,*—even *one*, 'though,' says Petter, 'it be the least or meanest of them.'

It is better for him. Literally, and as the Rheims gives it, *it is good for him rather.* The word rendered *good* properly means *beautiful* (καλόν). It is implied that, as there is a species of ethical *beauty* in what is honourable and honest (or '*fair*'), so there is a species of semi-ethical *beauty*, or *attractiveness*, in what is profitable or advantageous. As many good things are not absolutely good, but only *good for certain other things*, so many beautiful things are not absolutely beautiful, but '*do beautifully*' *for the attainment of other things.*

That a millstone were hanged about his neck. More literally, *if a millstone is hanged about his neck.* Very literally, *if a millstone is laid about his neck.* Note the present tenses, *it 'is' better for him, if a millstone 'is' hanged about his neck.* It is primitive representation. We are taken, in imagination, into the presence of a certain dreadful scene; we see a millstone attached to a man's neck; the fastening, passing through the central perforation of the stone, is

43 And if thy hand offend thee, cut it off: it is better for thee to enter into life maimed, than having two hands to go into hell,

---

made secure; it is a sad sight. Yet, turning from another scene, we say, "This *is* better:" it is better than that the same man should act the part of a seducer, and entrap a childlike follower of Jesus. Instead of the simple expression, *a millstone*, the critical editors, Lachmann, Tischendorf, Tregelles, Alford, read *a great millstone*, literally, *a donkey millstone*, that is, such a millstone as it required a donkey to work. (See on Matt. xviii. 6.) This reading is supported by the best manuscripts, inclusive of ℵ B C D, and by the Vulgate, Peshito Syriac, Gothic (*asiluquairnus*, i.e. *a donkey quern*), Armenian, and Æthiopic versions.

And he were cast into the sea. There is no *he* in the original. Sharpe supplies *it* instead, understanding the reference to be to the millstone. Wakefield took the same view. But it is better to regard the millstone as an appendage of the man, than to think of the man as an appendage of the millstone. The sensational scene is represented as by an eye-witness. He sees the man lifted up, weighted with the enormous appendage of the millstone; he sees him cast into the sea. It is a sad temporal end to which to come. But how much sadder would it be to incur, in the world to come, the doom deserved by the seducer!

VER. 43. **And if thy hand offend thee.** Or, *And if thy hand should insnare thee* (ἐὰν σκανδαλίσῃ σε, the rendering of the Sinaitic and Vatican manuscripts). If thy hand should tingle, to its finger tips, with a longing to do what is bad; and if thou canst not repress it.

Cut it off. Wycliffe's version is, *kitt it awey*; Tyndale's and Coverdale's, *cut him off*. Use unsparingly spiritual surgery. Don't tamper with the temptation.

It is better for thee. Very literally, *it is good*. Gothic, *goth*.

To enter into life crippled. Very literally, *to enter into the life*, that is, *into the life* emphatically so called, the life of heavenly glory. (See ver. 47.) Every other state, comparatively speaking, is a state of lifelessness or death.

Than having two hands. Literally, *the two hands*, the full complement of hands, 'both hands.'

To depart into the Gehenna. That is, *the Valley of Hinnom*, the place of future punishment. It was a common Jewish representation; and a most graphic hieroglyph it was. The literal Gehenna was a valley to the south of Jerusalem, naturally 'pleasant,' as Milton describes it; but having become the scene of the worship of Molech, 'the abomination of the children of Ammon' (1 Kings xi. 7), its associations became frightful. Human sacrifices had been offered. Innocent children were made to pass through the fire to the 'grim idol.' "According to the rabbins," says Dr. Porter, "the statue of Molech was of brass, "with the body of a man and the head of an ox. The interior was hollow and "fitted up with a large furnace, by which the whole statue was easily made red "hot. The children to be sacrificed were then placed in its arms, while drums "were beaten to drown their cries." (*Syria*, p. 92.) These were horrible rites, and king Josiah, in consequence, caused the 'pleasant' place, where they had been perpetrated, to be desecrated and 'defiled.' (2 Kings xxiii. 10, 13.) The

into the fire that never shall be quenched: 44 where their worm dieth not, and the fire is not quenched. 45 And if thy foot

---

locality became a place of sepulture (Jer. vii. 32); and to this day the surrounding rocks are pierced in all directions with ancient tombs. It would appear also that it had become in later times a place of refuse, where carcases and other abominations were thrown. The consequence was that 'worms' would be there; and no doubt, occasionally also, as required, 'fires' would be kindled to consume the noisome accumulations. Altogether the uses to which the place had been put made it a graphic symbol for the refuse-place of the universe; 'black Gehenna,' says Milton, 'type of hell.' (*Par. Lost*, i. 405.) "Having," says Dr. Barclay, "been the scene of such pollution, wickedness, "and torment, it became a fit emblem of everlasting punishment." (*City of the Great King*, p. 90.)

Into the inextinguishable fire. The fires that were occasionally lit in the literal Gehenna or Tophet were necessarily only temporary; they died out for want of fuel. It was to be otherwise with the 'fire' of the other and ultimate Tophet. The 'fire' referred to is, of course, a mere symbol of the sum total of certain dreadful realities, positive and privative, for which there are no adequate representations in human language.

VER. 44. *Where their worm dieth not, and the fire is not quenched.* There is some reason for supposing that these words, which are repeated in ver. 46, have been added by a later hand out of ver. 48, where they are unquestionably genuine. It is noticeable that at the conclusion of ver. 47 the word *inextinguishable* is not found, and thus, when in ver. 48 it is said *where the fire is not quenched*, there is no approach to what might be considered an idle repetition or redundancy. There seems however to be something like such repetition or redundancy in the relation of ver. 44 to the conclusion of ver. 43. Tischendorf has cancelled the verse altogether; so has Ewald in his German version. Meyer approves of the omission, and Klostermann. The verse is wanting in the Sinaitic, Vatican, and Parisian manuscripts (א B C), as well as in L Δ; and in 1, and other cursives. It is wanting too in the Coptic version, and in Zohrab's Armenian version. It is certainly more probable that it would be deliberately added than that it would be wilfully omitted; for there was no fastidiousness in early times in reference to the doctrine of everlasting punishment. There was rather, in harmony with a peculiar development of society, that presented but a limited breadth of spiritual surface for the operation of higher and diviner motives, a tendency to give peculiar emphasis to the dreadful effects, within the sphere of sensibility, of persisted-in wickedness. Some very early transcriber therefore, having his eye upon effective ecclesiastical lection, might introduce the words on a principle of solemn liturgical refrain, and be sincerely persuaded all the time that he was doing no injury to the text, inasmuch as the words actually occur in ver. 48. See on that verse.

VER. 45. *And if thy foot insnare thee.* Feeling, as it were, restless and eager, until it get thee conveyed into some improper place. Our Saviour of course specifies *hand* and *foot* only for rhetorical purposes. It is a fine, bold, graphic way of bringing home to the imagination and the bosom the idea of

offend thee, cut it off: it is better for thee to enter halt into life, than having two feet to be cast into hell, into the fire that never shall be quenched : 46 where their worm dieth not, and the fire is not quenched. 47 And if thine eye offend thee, pluck it out : it is better for thee to enter into the kingdom of God with one eye, than having two eyes to be cast into hell fire : 48 where their worm dieth not, and the fire is not quenched.

what is near and dear to our natural feelings. He speaks in hieroglyphics. "We are to understand," says Petter, " not the parts of the body so called, but "anything which is as near and dear to us in this world." "The meaning is "not," says Richard Baxter, "that any man is in such a case, that he hath no "better way to avoid sin and hell; but if he had no better, he should choose "this. Nor doth it mean that maimed persons are maimed in heaven; but if " it were so, it were a less evil."

Cut it off. The Rheims version is *brusque, choppe it of*.

It is better for thee to enter into life lame, than having both feet to be cast into the Gehenna. The manuscripts א B C L Δ, 1, and the Syriac Peshito and Coptic versions, stop here. So does Zohrab's Armenian version ; so do Tischendorf and Tregelles. The Received Text adds the words *into the inextinguishable fire*. See on ver. 43, 44.

VER. 46. This verse is omitted by the same authorities which omit ver. 44. In addition, the latter half is omitted in the Æthiopic version.

VER. 47. **And if thine eye insnare thee.** 'Lusting,' as it were, to see in thine own possession what, of right, belongs to others ; or if it otherwise allure thee to what is forbidden, as when Eve felt that the fruit of the forbidden tree was ' a desire to the eyes' (Gen. iii. 6).

Pluck it out. Literally, *cast it out*. Tyndale has *plucke him oute* ; Coverdale, *cast him from thee*.

It is better for thee to enter into the kingdom of God. In glory, to wit. See ver. 43.

With one eye. Literally, *one-eyed* ($\mu o\nu \acute{o}\phi \theta a\lambda \mu o\nu$). Wycliffe strangely renders it *gogil-yghed*. The Attic purists would have used a different word from that employed by the evangelist ($\dot{\epsilon}\tau\epsilon\rho\acute{o}\phi\theta a\lambda \mu o\nu$). See Phrynichus, Thomas Magister, and Moeris).

Than, having two eyes, to be cast into the Gehenna. While it is said in ver. 43 ' *the* two hands,' that is, *both hands*, and in ver. 44 ' *the* two feet,' or *both feet*, the expression in this case is simply 'two eyes.' Thus there was no slavish attachment to one form or formula of representation.

VER. 48. **Where their worm dieth not, and the fire is not extinguished.** An expression borrowed from the last verse of Isaiah, and probably in current use among the Jews of our Saviour's time, as applied to the state of future retribution. There is a commingled reference to two modes of destruction, vermicular putrefaction and fire. When men's bodies are destroyed, it is generally either by the one agency or by the other. Both are here combined, for cumulative rhetorical effect. And the dread climax of the whole representation is found in the ceaselessness of the twofold operation. Theophylact explains the

49 For every one shall be salted with fire, and every sacrifice shall be salted with salt.

worm and the *fire* as metaphorical representations of the conscience and memory of the lost. The explanation is too narrow; but doubtless the representation is intended to be hieroglyphical. When Fritzsche says that no figure was intended (*dicuntur sine ullâ figurâ*), he either attributed arbitrarily to our Lord, or to the evangelist, an abject sensuousness of conception, or he failed to apprehend that sentences as really as words may be figurative. They are but words of greater length. Note the difference in the two expressions, '*their* worm' and '*the* fire.' The worm is regarded as *belonging* to the body; the fire is considered as something outside. The representations are both popular, but eminently graphic.

Ver. 49. **For every one shall be salted with fire, and every sacrifice shall be salted with salt.** Almost all expositors and critics speak of these expressions, and especially the former, as among the most difficult in the Bible. "The "passage," says Grimm, "is exceedingly difficult" (*perdifficilis locus*). "It "is," says Jansen, "exceedingly obscure" (*perobscurus*). "It is," says Wolf, "exceedingly vexed." "It is," says Heumann, "exceedingly vexing." "There "is perhaps," says Bloomfield, "no passage in the New Testament which has "so defied all efforts to assign to it any certain interpretation." "It is," says Ryle, "one of those knots which are yet untied, in the exposition of Scripture." "It has put to the rack the ingenuity of many learned men," says Grotius. "It is," says Fritzsche, "one of those passages in which, because of their extra-"ordinary obscurity, crosses seem to be fixed on which to torture expositors." "It is certainly," says Spanheim, "among the passages that are *hard to be* "*understood*" (*Dubia*, iii., p. 451). Many separate treatises have been published on it, and very many long and elaborate notes, full of ingenuity and learning, have been written to throw light upon it. We do not despair however; and we feel persuaded that the true view will not be far removed from simplicity. Beza's celebrated manuscript, now in Cambridge (D), omits the first clause of the verse, *every one shall be salted with fire*, and that clause accordingly is wanting in Whiston's *Primitive New Testament*. It is wanting too in some copies of the Old Latin version. The transcribers of these copies and of D had evidently been puzzled by the phrase. But if it had not been in Mark's autograph, we may rest assured that no annotator would ever have spontaneously introduced it. Some high manuscriptural authorities again omit the second clause of the verse, *and every sacrifice shall be salted with salt*. Both the Sinaitic and the Vatican manuscript (א B) omit it; and L Δ; and 1, and a considerable number of other cursives. It is omitted too in certain manuscripts of the Coptic version, and in Zohrab's Armenian version. David Schulz suspected its genuineness (*glossam olet*); and Tischendorf has left it out in his eighth edition of the text; unreasonably. It is the necessary stepping stone to what comes after; and yet its connection with what goes before is not so obtrusively evident as to make it astonishing that some transcribers should have looked upon it as an apocryphal addition to the original text. The repetition, moreover, of the concluding verb (ἁλισθήσεται) might in one or two cases mislead the transcriber's eye. We must retain both clauses of the verse ; we must also retain both in their integrity. The celebrated Joseph Scaliger, a man of marvellous force of intellect, was deeply interested in the passage. But he was confident that the first clause had got to be corrupted at a very early period in the dissemination of the Gospel. He was also confident that he had discovered the original reading. The connective *for*, he assumed, should be cashiered, and then the whole verse should be read thus : ' *Every burning (πᾶσα πυρία, i.e.* every offering made by fire) *shall be salted, and every sacrifice shall be salted with salt.*' He mentioned this conjectural emendation of the phraseology to Grotius. He contended for it strongly once and again in his letters still extant. (See Wolf) And in Rouiere's edition of the Greek Testament, ' *with Joseph Scaliger's Notes on some of the more difficult passages* ' (1619), the emendation is repeated. Petter accepts it; and Louis Cappel thought it ' exceedingly probable.' But Grotius did right to reject it ; as did Gataker (*Adversaria*, xliii., Op. p. 889) ; and also Spanheim (*Dubia*, iii., p. 452). Also Dr. Adam Clarke, who says : 'This, I fear, is taking the text *by storm.*' In fact Scaliger *invented* a sacrificial word for the occasion, and was fascinated by the ingenuity of his invention. The phraseology needs no tinkering. The introductory *For* is genuine, and is of itself fatal to Scaliger's conjecture. We are by no means however shut up to the conclusion of Maldonato, Jansen, Meyer, and many others, that the reference of the reason-rendering conjunction is simply to what is said at the conclusion of the preceding verse, *and the fire shall not be quenched.* There is no occasion whatever for insisting on such a short and narrow bridge of transit. It is far more probable that the reference is to the great pervading idea of ver. 43-48, *that it is indispensable for all such as would escape the retribution of inextinguishable fire to be unsparing in their treatment of the insnaring members of their own persons.* Let them not hesitate for a moment to mortify, cut off, and cauterize these rebellious members. Such is the Lord's graphic way of representing the sacrifices which His disciples would require to make for conscience sake These sacrifices, says He, must be made, *for every one shall be salted with fire. Every one*, viz. of those who are referred to in the preceding context. And these are not, as has been too often assumed, (as by Maldonato, Jansen, Lightfoot, Grotius, Elsner, Wesley, Rosenmüller, Alexander, Patrizi,) the *unbelieving* ; but, on the contrary, *the believing* So Erasmus, Luther (*Gloss*), Flacius (*Clavis*, ii. 601), Calvin, Spanheim, Gataker, Wetstein, Heumann, Richard Watson, Glöckler, Dav. Brown. The Saviour is addressing *His disciples*, and counselling them in reference to the temptations to which they were sure to be subjected in consequence of their relationship, ' in the flesh,' to the manifold corruptions of ' the present evil age.' Yield not to these temptations, says He. On the contrary, cut off unsparingly the occasions of them, as far as in you lies, and thus escape the doom of those who allow themselves to be insnared, *for every one (of My disciples) shall be salted with fire.*

What does this mean ? It means, says Theophylact, *shall be tried by fire*, a mere guess of an interpretation. And yet it is reproduced by Dionysius à Ryckel. It also found its way into some unimportant cursive manuscripts. Grotius translates the phrase, *shall be consumed with fire.* This translation is accepted by Hammond, le Clerc, Dr. Samuel Clarke, Wells, Mace, and Storr (*Opuscula*, ii. 212), on the ground that the Hebrew word that means *to be salted* also means *to be consumed*, or *to vanish away* (Isa. li. 6). But it is enough to say that the Greek word has no such meaning. And it would be hard to believe that the Hebrew usage could so dominate Greek Palestinian usage as to ascribe to the same word, in the same verse, two meanings so contrary as *consumed* and *salted*; and more especially as the best Hebrew philologers maintain that the Hebrew word is indeed not one word, but two, accidentally coincident in sound, but belonging to totally different roots. We must adhere then to the translation, *shall be salted with fire*. But what can be made of it? Lightfoot, supposing that the reference is to *the unbelieving*, explains thus : " shall be "seasoned with fire itself, so as to become unconsumable, and shall endure "for ever to be tormented, as salt preserves from corruption." Alexander Morus gives the same interpretation (*Notæ*, in loc.), and Michaelis (*Anmerkungen*, in loc.), and Patrizi too. But it certainly involves a violent and unnatural wrench of conception. For while it is conceivable that, by the application of something incombustible, a substance might be preserved from the consuming influence of fire, it is really inconceivable that any substance should be rendered 'unconsumable' by the application to it of the very element that consumes. Elsner and others, also assuming a reference to the doom of unbelievers, suppose that the imagery of the expression is borrowed from the catastrophe of Sodom and Gomorrha and the other 'cities of the plain,' *for every one shall be immersed in that abyss of fire and salt*. Eccentric ; a shift. Schöttgen, Macknight, and Baumgarten-Crusius render the expression *shall be salted 'for' the fire*. Eccentric too, though in another line of things; a subterfuge. But what then? How can there be 'salting *with* fire'? We must in the first place, distinguish 'letter' from 'spirit' in the two terms *salted* and *fire*. Our Saviour is not, in either of the terms, referring to the literal realities. It is *salting* metaphorically viewed, and *fire* metaphorically viewed, of which He speaks ; and hence the possibility of perfect congruity in the apparently incongruous idea of 'salting *with* fire.' Among the various uses of salt, two are popularly outstanding : *seasoning*, and *preserving from corruption*. In the passage before us there is no reference to *seasoning*, although Principal Campbell actually translates the word *shall be seasoned*. The reference is exclusively to *preservation from corruption*. In hot countries in particular, killed meat hastens to a tainted condition, and could not be preserved from spoiling, either by cooks or priests, for any appreciable length of time, *were it not for salting*. It is on this antiseptic property of salt that the Saviour's representation is founded. *Every one of His disciples shall be preserved from corruption by fire*. The *fire* referred to however is not *penal*, like the inextinguishable fire of Gehenna. It is intentionally *purificatory*. And yet when we take the preceding context into account, we may rest assured that its purificatory efficacy is referred to, *not merely because it is purificatory* (comp. Matt. iii. 11), but also because, in its purificatory action, *it is painful, though not penal*. It scorches, and pierces to the quick. It is such *fire* as is in certain '*fiery* trials ' willingly endured for righteousness sake (1 Pet. iv. 12). It is *fire* that 'eats the flesh' (Jas. v. 3), and is 'sent into the bones ' (Lam. i. 13). It is its cauterizing smart and energy that are felt, when a hand, or foot, or eye, is parted with for the sake of purity. What then is this *fire*? It is not simply and generically, as Heumann supposed, the purifying influence of the Holy Spirit, an influence purifying the soul as fire purifies silver. Neither is it simply, as Luther and

Calov supposed, the purifying power of the gospel. Still less is it, as others have supposed, such as Baxter, Wolf, Hofmeister, Kuinöl, the painfully purifying influence of afflictions in general, or of persecutions in particular for the gospel's sake. It is another phase of purifying influence. It is, as Cardinal Cajetan, Beza, Spanheim, and Wetstein saw, *the unsparing spirit of self sacrifice*. It is the *spirit* to which our Saviour refers in ver. 43-48, *the spirit that parts, for righteousness sake, with a hand, a foot, an eye*. But instead of representing it here once more as manifesting itself in acts of amputation or excision, He takes occasion, from the incidental reference to *the fire of Gehenna*, to depict it, in striking and vivid antithesis, as an alternative fire (*opponit ignem igni, presentem futuro*: Spanheim, p. 454), which indeed scorches the sensibility to agony, but which in the end consumes only what is bad, and leaves the soul freed from those moral combustibles on which the penal fire of Gehenna could feed. Every disciple of Christ is thus *salted with fire*. He is *preserved from corruption, and consequent everlasting destruction, by the fire of unsparing self sacrifice*.

And: Le Clerc and Beausobre-et-L'Enfant, in their respective French versions, as also Schöttgen and du Veil, translate this conjunction *even as*. Heumann and others defend the rendering. But it not only does violence to the conjunction, it throws the whole clause which it introduces into the position of a mere foil, to give emphasis to the idea of the preceding clause. There is no need for thus ' vexing ' the word. It has its ordinary signification, and introduces a statement which it is of importance for us to add to the preceding. Glöcklern traslates it *also*.

Every sacrifice shall be salted with salt: The Saviour is alluding to what is said in Lev. ii. 13, "*and every oblation of thy meat offering shalt "thou season with salt; neither shalt thou suffer the salt of the covenant "of thy God to be lacking from thy meat offering. With all thine offerings "thou shalt offer salt.*" At the commencement of this verse there is reference to such offerings as were derived from the *flora* of the earth. ' Meat offerings,' in our version, mean *vegetable* or *farinaceous offerings*. At the conclusion of the verse the reference is extended to all offerings, inclusive therefore of such as were derived from the *fauna* of the earth, animal offerings. See Ezek. xliii. 23, 24. The expression *seasoned with salt* is admirably adapted to ' meat offerings,' which did not require salting to preserve them from corrupting. But the Hebrew phrase so rendered is simply, like the Greek phrase in the passage before us, *salted with salt*. All kinds of offerings *were to be salted with salt*, just as, generally speaking, all kinds of food used by the people *were salted with salt*, in order to ensure that they should be at once wholesome and pleasant. Our Saviour, in using the word *sacrifice* (θυσία), instead of the expression *oblation of meat offering*, employed a term which naturally suggests an animal offering; and hence the *salting with salt*, in so far as He gives it emphasis, recalls the antiseptic virtue of salt, as distinguished from its seasoning influence, and thus brings into view not merely, in a generic way, what was required to make food palatable, but, in a specific way, what was needed to preserve animal food from taint and loathsomeness. Our Lord transfers to New Testament times, and exalts into spiritual and world-wide maxims, the rudimentary principles of the dispensation of shadows. And thus the *salt* of the Old Testament priest is reproduced in the *spirit* of the New Testament wor-

50 Salt *is* good: but if the salt have lost his saltness,

---

shipper, that *spirit* which is a moral antiseptic, because instinct with the influence of the Holy Spirit of God. The idea of our Saviour amounts to this: *Every true self sacrifice, presented to God, is presented in a state of (comparative) purity, sweetness, and consequent acceptableness, in virtue of the purity-imparting spirit of the sacrificer.* God's ancient dispensation as a whole, and every particular ordinance in it as an integrant part, was *a covenant of purity*, the purity in particular of reciprocal faithfulness. It was 'a covenant of salt' (Lev. ii. 13 ; Num. xviii. 19). God and man, as it were, met together in amity, as under one roof, and pledged themselves to one another in rites of a sublime hospitality. This 'covenant of salt' runs on into New Testament times ; and man's part in it is fulfilled when he remembers never to present to the Infinite Guest who condescends to enter his heart (John xiv. 23) any other sacrifice or service than what is *salted with salt.*

VER. 50. **Salt is good.** Such is the general conviction of men ; and yet there was extensively advertised a few years ago an English publication, in which it was contended that almost all the ills to which flesh is heir are attributable to the use of salt! *Good*, literally *beautiful*. Spanheim explains the word as meaning *useful*. But *good* is better, *good* for most important purposes, especially *seasoning* and *preserving*. Some have supposed that the *salt* here spoken of is to be viewed as a metaphorical impersonation, just as when it is said in Matt. v. 13, *ye are the 'salt' of the earth.* So Petter for instance, who says that the term here " signifies *the ministers of the word*, yet not simply " considered in regard to their persons, but in regard of their ministerial " calling and office." He would thus interpret the expression, '*salt is good*,' as meaning " the true and faithful ministers of the gospel, lawfully called to their " office, are necessary, profitable, and useful in the church of God, in regard of " their persons and ministry." This interpretation however is harsh, artificial, and grotesque. Our Saviour evidently uses the term in the same acceptation as in the preceding verse. What He says indeed is true of literal salt ; but it is in a higher plane of reference equally true of the metaphorical salt of *a holy spirit*, a spirit instinct with *the Spirit of God.* Such salt is emphatically *good*. It is *good as a means*; it is the best possible human means for the highest possible human ends.

But if the salt should become saltless. The Saviour speaks popularly ; and His idea would be readily caught in Palestine. Maundrell mentions that in *The Valley of Salt, which is about four hours from Aleppo*, " there is a kind of dry " crust of salt, which sounds, when the horses go upon it, like frozen snow " when it is walked upon." He adds: " along on one side of the valley, viz. " that toward Gibul, there is a small precipice about two men's lengths, oc- " casioned by the continual taking away the salt ; and in this you may see how " the veins of it lie. I broke a piece of it, of which the part that was exposed " to the rain, sun, and air, though it had the sparks and particles of salt, yet " had perfectly *lost its savour* (as in St. Matt., chap. v.). The inner part, which " was connected with the rock, retained its savour, as I found by proof." (*Journey from Aleppo to Jerusalem*, pp. 161, 162, ed. 1749.) Whatever may be

wherewith will ye season it? Have salt in yourselves, and have peace one with another.

---

the case with literal salt, the Saviour is referring to spiritual salt, which undoubtedly, in so far as it consists of a phase of character, may be metamorphosed into its negative or contradictory. Such metamorphic changes of character are possible in two directions; they may be realized upwardly, in bad beings becoming good, or downwardly, in good beings becoming bad. Hatred may be transformed into love, or love into hatred. In either case there is 'conversion' from contrary to contrary.

Wherewith will ye season it? Or, '*in what*' will ye *season it?* '*in what*' will ye steep it as it were, so as to restore its sapidity? If it should be replied, *in other salt*, then it suffices to remark that the Saviour was representing to Himself a case which did not admit of such an alternative. With Him all salt is a means to an end; it is the means of salting, but of course not of salting saltless salt; for if animal food for instance should require to be preserved from wasting, or other food to be seasoned, why take the circuitous way of first salting insipid or saltless salt, and then applying this for preserving or seasoning? No good end could be subserved by such a circuit, and hence the ridiculous process itself was never contemplated by our Lord or by any one else. Our Lord simply intimates, by a striking mode of thought, that as nothing in the natural world would be more useless than saltless salt, so nothing in the spiritual world would be more hopelessly useless than Christianity which is no longer Christian, or holiness which is no longer holy, or evangelicism that has ceased to be evangelical, or religiousness that has degenerated into irreligion. What if a man have 'a name to live' while he is 'dead'? What if a church have such a name? Could they be blessings in the world? It is impossible. It is in vain to try, by any process of galvanism, to restore life to a putrid or putrescent mass. Omnipotence alone could meet such an emergency. But in all ordinary cases, so far as spiritual life is concerned, it is a moral result which the Omnipotent One desires; and it is therefore moral means which He employs.

Have salt in yourselves. A practical inference, says Cardinal Cajetan, from 'the parable of salt.' Note the '*in*.' The true spirit of holiness or good doing is not a thing that can be put on. It is within. It may come out indeed; it must come out; but it must come out from within, seasoning at once works and words (Col. iv. 6), and rendering our sacrifices pure and acceptable (ver. 49).

And have peace 'one with another.' A corresponding expression is employed 1 Thess. v. 13, *Be at peace 'among yourselves.'* Tyndale combines, to a certain extent, the two phrases in his translation of the passage before us, *Have peace amonge youre selves one with another*. The Saviour, in thus winding up His conversation, reverts to the subject with which He had started. His disciples had disputed *who should be greatest* (ver. 34). The dispute had threatened to break up the circle into cliques of partisanship. Harmony was endangered; and if harmony were lost, their moral influence in the world would be crippled. It was needful that they should cooperate; it was needful therefore that they should 'be at peace with one another.' But there would be security for their unity only if they had salt, the spirit of purity, 'in themselves.' It is difficult

ST. MARK X.

CHAPTER X.

1 AND he arose from thence, and cometh into the coasts of Judæa by the farther side of Jordan: and the people resort

to restrain the conviction to which Bishop Hammond gives expression, that our Lord had a touch of reference, in the injunction *and be at peace with one another*, 'to that other quality of salt, as it is a sign of union.' If it be true that God and man have entered into 'a covenant of salt,' then surely His children should pledge themselves to each other in a corresponding covenant. Since they sit at one table, and are partakers of the common salt, and have it 'in' them, they should be inviolably true to one another.

CHAPTER X.

VER. 1-12 of this chapter constitute a paragraph corresponding to Matt. xix. 1-9.

VER. 1. **And He arose from thence and cometh.** A more awkward expression than there was any occasion for in translation. In the original the phrase *from thence*, or *thence*, or *from there* (ἐκεῖθεν), stands before the whole of the clause, so that its incidence reaches to *cometh; And thence, when He had risen up, He cometh*, that is, *And He rose up and came*. It is a primitive mode of representation, exemplifying a kind of 'preraphaelite' particularity of detail. We not only see the Saviour setting out on His journey, we see Him *rising up* that He might set out. The representation is analogous in principle to the expression, 'and *He opened His mouth* and taught.' (Matt. v. 2; comp. Mark vii. 24.) The point of departure was Capernaum, on the west side of the sea of Tiberias (chap. ix. 33).

Into the borders of Judæa. The evangelist leads our thoughts meanwhile not to the terminus of our Lord's journey, in the heart of Judæa, but to the boundary line at which He entered the district. It was apparently the last southward journey of our Lord, though not the first. Modern critics indeed, of the sceptical school, insist that no other journey into Judæa was known either to Mark or to the two other synoptic evangelists. But both Matthew and Luke represent our Lord as saying: "O Jerusalem, Jerusalem, *how often* would I have "gathered thy children together, . . . and ye would not" (Matt. xxiii. 37; Luke xiii. 34). It was moreover most improbable that our Saviour and His disciples would refrain from going up to the great festivals. And there is not in Mark's narrative here the slightest indication that he regarded our Lord as entering upon a novel or unprecedented career.

And beyond the Jordan. That is, *and in particular beyond the Jordan*. Not only did He come into the border lands of Judæa, He approached these border lands beyond the Jordan. Our Saviour did not visit Samaria; or, if He did (Luke xvii. 11), He crossed over thence into Peræa before He entered the border lands of Judæa.

And the people went unto Him again. In the original the reference is not to any 'people' that may have been formerly spoken of. The term employed is indeterminate, *crowds* (ὄχλοι), *And crowds again come together to Him.*

unto him again; and, as he was wont, he taught them again.

2 And the Pharisees came to him, and asked him, Is it lawful for a man to put away *his* wife? tempting him. 3 And

And again He taught them, as He was wont. It is not meant *that He taught the same people again.* The idea is that He resumed His former plan of operation, no longer shunning crowds because in quest of seclusion with His disciples; He chose, on the contrary, favourable amphitheatres of assembly along the line of His route, and taught the congregated masses as had been His wont.

VER. 2. **And.** At a certain unspecified stage in His progress.

The Pharisees. Note the article. It is in the Received Text, and it has been readmitted by Tischendorf in the eighth edition of his critical text. It is found in the Sinaitic and Ephraemi manuscripts (א C), as also in N V X; but it is omitted by Griesbach, Scholz, Lachman.., Tregelles, Alford. It is wanting in the great body of the uncial manuscripts, inclusive of the Alexandrine and Vatican (A B). It is a matter of no moment whether it be admitted or rejected. If admitted, it marks the party or sect to which the individuals referred to belonged. If it be omitted, then the evangelist leaves it indeterminate whether the individuals introduced to our notice should be regarded simply as individuals, or as representing the entire Pharisaic body.

Came to Him, and asked Him. They came forward from the rest of the people, *approached and questioned Him.*

Is it lawful for a man to put away his wife? Or more literally, *if it is lawful for a man to put away his wife*; or, as Tyndale gives it, *whether it were laufull for a man to put awaye his wyfe.* So too Coverdale and Luther. The nature of the case makes it evident that the meaning of the query is, Whether it is lawful for a man to put away his wife, *at his pleasure* as it were, or, as it is expressed in Matt. xix. 3, *for every cause.* It is altogether gratuitous in Saunier to say that the representation of Matthew is 'obviously the more correct' (*Quellen*, p. 120). It is equally gratuitous in F. C. Baur to maintain that Mark 'intentionally' made a variation from the representation of Matthew (*Marcusevangelium*, p. 81). There is no discrepancy to be accounted for, as is obvious when we look at the subject from the standpoint of common sense, and, as will be specially obvious, when we take into account that it is, as a general rule, only certain salient points of our Lord's conversations, discussions, and remarks that are recorded. We may reasonably assume that on the present occasion there would be details of colloquy of which neither the one evangelist nor the other makes mention. In the course of these details the varied recorded forms of remarks, or their equivalents, and no doubt many others from which other evangelists might have selected, would occur.

Tempting Him. The English word *tempting* has, in its modern use, a much stronger twist in the direction of what is evil than it had in our older literature and in the passage before us. And yet it was intended by our translators to have here a bend in that evil direction. Rightly so, apparently. The word originally means *trying*, or *attempting* as it were. Tyndale translates it here, *to*

ST. MARK X.

he answered and said unto them, What did Moses command you? 4 And they said, Moses suffered to write a bill of divorcement, and to put *her* away. 5 And Jesus answered and said unto them, For the hardness of your heart he wrote

---

prove Him; Principal Campbell, *to try Him.* So Wakefield, Newcome, Edgar Taylor. Rilliet has *wishing thus to put Him to the test (à l' épreuve).* Norton, following in the wake of Mace, goes much farther in the direction of the evil meaning, *with a design to insnare Him.* There had been among the Jewish rabbis great discussions on the subject of divorce, and serious dissension. The Hillelites, the followers of Hillel, maintained that divorce might be lawfully effected at the pleasure or caprice of the husband; while the Shammaites, the followers of Shammai, contended that 'putting away' was lawful only on condition of the occurrence of unchastity. (See Michaelis's *Mosaisches Recht*, § 120.) Our Lord's questioners were probably confident in their own particular notion on the subject, and imagined that they would be able to get Him to say something which they could make use of to 'corner Him up' or to diminish His influence with the people. (See *Comm.* on Matt. xix. 1-12.)

VER. 3. **But He answered and said unto them, What did Moses command you?** Or, as Tyndale has it, *What dyd Moses byd you do?* He wished them to have in view their own political statute on the subject. It had been much abused in the controversies that had been waged.

VER. 4. **And they said, Moses permitted to write a bill of divorcement and to put away.** See Deut. xxiv. 1. Instead of *a bill of divorcement* Wycliffe hað *a libel of forsakinge*, and Tyndale *a testimoniall of devorsement*. The word thus rendered *bill, libel, testimonial,* properly means *a little book* (βιβλίον), that is, *a formal writing* or *document.* *Libel,* in its original signification (*libellus*), exactly corresponds to the evangelist's term; and if *bill* be *libel* cut down, it too will be an exact rendering. Our Lord's questioners used the word *permitted,* or *suffered.* It was legitimate. And yet it brought into view only one aspect of the case, and that not the most important, when the question was considered not so much politically as morally. See next verse.

VER. 5. **And Jesus answered and said to them.** Or, as it stands more briefly in the manuscripts אBCLΔ, and the Coptic version, as also in Tregelles' and Tischendorf's texts, *And Jesus said to them.*

For your hardness of heart he wrote you this precept. It was a *precept* therefore, or *injunction*, as really as a *permission.* It was a statute that was intended to throw some restraints upon summary dismissal. Such dismissal was constituted illegal. Divorce, henceforth, could not be effected until a regular instrument or document was legally drawn up, and handed over to the unfortunate wife. "In this way," says Michaelis, "a marriage could never be dissolved "in the first heat of passion; and the husband might perhaps change his mind, " or the person employed to write the bill of divorce (probably a priest or Levite) " might perhaps be a man of principle, who would speak to the husband before " he set about the writing. This delay, affording time for reflection, could not " fail to put a stop to many divorces resolved on under the influence of passion."

you this precept. 6 But from the beginning of the creation God made them male and female. 7 For this cause shall a

(*Mosaisches Recht*, § 119: 3.) The legislation of Moses on the subject was thus benevolent in its aim. It had to deal, we may presume, with an exceedingly lax and latitudinarian use-and-wont, that would press crushingly upon the weaker sex. It did not indeed, and could not, accomplish all that is morally desirable. What legislator can? What legislation can, if it be intended to meet the actual requirements of exceedingly imperfect and perverted states of society? The political institutions of the Jews, though Divinely devised, could scarcely even initiate an approximation to an ideal state of society. That goal was contemplated indeed; but it was far off in the distance. And meanwhile the uncultured people required as much political restraint and constraint, and just as much, as was politically practicable. The marriage statute, we need not doubt, would have been far more stringent in its restraints, had it not been for the people's moral unpreparedness, *their hardness-of-heart*. They were far from being in an ideal state of heart. They were as yet, comparatively speaking, coarse in their views and insensitive in their feelings, irresponsive to highly refined principles of delicacy and purity. Hence there was no alternative between giving them imperfect political institutions, up to the level of which they could be lifted, and thence prepared for farther ascent, or giving them absolutely perfect institutions, which could not have been transferred into their practice even for a single day. Absolutely perfect political institutions would be adapted only to an absolutely perfect people, or a people who were on the eve of emerging into absolute moral perfection. The expression '*for*' (πρός) *the hardness of your heart*, does not so much mean *because of* as *in reference to, in respect to*, that is, *to meet the case of, the hardness of your heart*. Politics, while ever aspiring toward a moral ideal, must yet be proportional in the ratio of their development to the actual moral condition of the people.

Ver. 6. **But from the beginning of the creation.** Very literally, *from creation's beginning*. The word *creation* properly means *the act of creating*; but here it denotes *the object in which the act terminated, the thing created, the world*. The original word (κτίσις) has no inherent reference to *absolute creation*, or *production out of nothing*. Neither was it intended that the word *beginning* should be pressed to a nicety. Men were not in existence at the absolute beginning. The idea is substantially this: *From the time when men were first Divinely introduced upon the scene of creation.* Petter explains it, 'from the time when God did first create mankind.'

God made them male and female. It is not *God made them*, but *He made them*, in the manuscripts ℵ B C L Δ, and such is the reading of Tischendorf and Tregelles. It is no doubt the correct reading. The Saviour was simply quoting the words of Gen. i. 27, as they stand in the Septuagint; and it would have been well if our translators had suggested the fact of verbal quotation by preserving the very collocation of the original phraseology, '*male and female made He them*.' *Male and female*, that is, *a male and a female*. The reference is to two, and two only. The one was the counterpart of the other. Each was fitted to be the other's complement, both physically and morally. It is one of the

man leave his father and mother, and cleave to his wife; 8 and they twain shall be one flesh: so then they are no more twain, but one flesh. 9 What therefore God hath joined together, let not man put asunder.

---

marvels of Providence, and a striking demonstration of the continuous working of the Creator, that, notwithstanding the multitudinous perturbations of things that are the result of sin, the proportional monogamistic numbers of the sexes are still maintained, as in a balance, all the world over.

VER. 7. **For this cause.** The Saviour continues to quote, but from another part of the early record, viz. Gen. ii. 24. The *cause* or *condition of things* referred to is *the counterpart and complementive relationship of the two sexes*.

Shall a man leave his father and mother. Because in marriage a higher relationship supervenes, which dominates the antecedent filial relationship. A new domestic centre is to be established.

And cleave to his wife. These words are wanting in the Sinaitic and Vatican manuscripts (אB), and also in the Gothic version. Tischendorf has omitted them in his eighth edition, without sufficient warrant. *Cleave* is Wycliffe's word; it is Coverdale's too, and adopted in both the Geneva and the Rheims. It is an admirable translation, much better than either Purvey's *draw* or Tyndale's *bide*, '*and bide by his wife.*' It is rendered *join himself* in Acts v. 36. The original term (προσκολληθήσεται) denotes the closest possible attachment and adherence. Very literally rendered, it means, as Petter remarks, *shall be glued*.

VER. 8. **And they twain.** An archaism for *the two* (οἱ δύο). The expression does not occur in the Hebrew passage from which our Lord quotes. He freely supplies it, as embodying the manifest meaning of the original.

Shall be one flesh. Literally, *shall be into one flesh*, that is, shall be so intimately united that, in their earthly or bodily relationships, they shall constitute as it were a unit of being.

So that they are no longer two, but one flesh. What has preceded is quotation from Gen. ii. 24. This is the Saviour's own inference from the language quoted. Husband and wife, though in a sense *two*, are yet, if they fulfil the Divine ideal, *no longer two*. They are but halves of a whole, 'one flesh.' Were it not for the intervenience of sin, the most delightful union conceivable would be realized in their experience.

VER. 9. **What therefore God joined together.** Namely, in His institute of marriage. Note (1) the word *what*; it is in the singular number, *what thing* (ὅ). The Saviour's mind had gone forward, in conception, beyond the stage of duality into the stage of unity. Note (2) the phrase *joined together*, or *cuppled*, as Tyndale has it. Coverdale has *coupled together*; so the Geneva. The word strictly means *yoked together*. Husband and wife are under a common yoke; and under this yoke, 'lined with love,' they are to work together as 'true yoke-fellows.' Note (3) that it is 'God' who yokes them together in the institute of marriage. Marriage is His institute, His idea. And He acts, not directly indeed but indirectly and institutionally, when man and woman take each

10 And in the house his disciples asked him again of the same *matter*. 11 And he saith unto them, Whosoever shall put away his wife, and marry another, committeth

---

other for husband and wife. But man and woman act too. They act directly, in subordination to the Divine institution. They choose each other. If they choose thoughtlessly, recklessly, capriciously, or selfishly, what wonder that human perturbations should be introduced into the Divine institution?
Let not man put asunder. Or, as Tyndale has it, *Let no man separate.* What? Not even when there are insurmountable incompatibilities? There should be no such incompatibilities. Not one, or at least scarcely one, of the multitudinous perturbations which so often perplex the marriage relation would ever have scope for operation if the Divine will regarding a 'pre-established harmony' were duly regarded. God's *institute has never got justice done it in the world*. It is impossible to make happy in wedlock those who make no moral provision for united happiness in the interblendings of every-day life. And yet, instead of the evil of unhappiness being lessened, by the degradation of the Divine ideal over the length and breadth of society, and the consequent relaxation of the matrimonial tie, it would be but intensified into greater and more intricate perplexities. Legislative relief may, in certain circumstances, be politically necessary, *because of the hardness of men's hearts*. But it is always an evil. And when legislation has to descend, step by step, from the Divine ideal of things, and even from the highest human ideal, instead of maintaining a gradual progression of ascent towards its own normal pinnacle of development, it is a symptom of social decay. Legislation should move in another direction, and initiate and foster measures that may tend to fit the rising youth for understanding and working out the laws of physical, æsthetical, and moral correspondencies and harmony.

VER. 10. **And in the house.** Namely where they were lodging. In the very ancient manuscripts ℵ B D, as well as L Δ, the expression is not *in the house,* but *into the house.* Lachmann, Tischendorf, Tregelles, Alford have admitted this more difficult reading into their texts. Rightly, no doubt. It is an abrupt and irregular phrase; but its meaning is obvious enough. The evangelist's mind was thinking of our Lord and His disciples, *as they entered 'into' the house.*

His disciples. Or, as the Sinaitic, Vatican, and Ephraemi manuscripts have it, *the disciples.*

Questioned Him again. As the Pharisees had done before.

Concerning the same (matter). Or, as the reading is in a large proportion of the best manuscripts, *concerning this.* This demonstrative reading is accepted by all the modern critical editors.

VER. 11. **And He says to them, If any one should put away his wife.** The exception, specified in Matt. xix. 9, *except for conjugal unfaithfulness*, is of course to be understood. It had been specified in our Lord's remarks to the Pharisees outside; and it was really self evident.

And should marry another. Roman Catholic theologians contend that to marry another is unlawful, so long as the first wife, however unfaithful, remains

adultery against her. 12 And if a woman shall put away her

alive. (See Denzinger's *Enchiridion*, §§ 597, 853, 878.) They allege that the exceptive clause, *except for conjugal unfaithfulness*, as occurring in Matt. xix. 9, has reference only to the contingency of *putting away the unfaithful wife* (*videlicet, quoad thorum*), and does not extend to the second contingency of *marrying another*. The indissoluble union of Christ and the church is, as they hold, the type and archetype of the union of husband and wife, under the New Testament dispensation; and the union therefore must remain indissoluble 'till death do part them.' (Denzinger's *Enchirid.*, § 597.) Luther and Calvin however, and Protestants in general, hold that adultery is in fact, at heart and in principle, the rupture of wedlock, and that it therefore affords a legitimate ground on which the injured party may sue out a complete divorce (*non solum quoad thorum, sed etiam quoad vinculum*). They think hence that the exceptive clause in Matt. xix. 9 is not meant to be attached with lawyerlike exclusiveness to the contingency with which it happens to be formally connected, and detached from the second contingency; just as they think that, in the passage before us, the exception is not intended to be ignored, although it is not formally introduced. This is no doubt the right view of the case; and, among Roman Catholic writers, both Erasmus and Cardinal Cajetan were of the same mind; but still it should ever be borne in mind that the existence of 'sin' has introduced all but inextricable confusion into the whole subject.

He committeth adultery against her. Though the husband has put away his wife in fact, she is still his wife; he has merely put her *out of the way*. The expression *against her* is literally *upon her* (ἐπ᾽ αὐτήν), and is so rendered in the Vulgate version. Hence some expositors suppose that the reference is not to the wife who has been put away, but to the woman who has been superinduced into her place. This is the view of Theophylact and Euthymius Zigabenus (δηλαδὴ τὴν ἐπείσακτον), as also of Elsner, Ewald, Bleek, Lange. It is more likely however that the view entertained by the great majority of expositors is correct, the view that is embodied in our Authorized translation. The man commits adultery *in relation to his wife, in opposition to her rights and interests*. His adultery comes *upon her*, and is *against her*. The preposition is frequently rendered *against*; see Matt. x. 21, xii. 26, xxiv. 7, xxvi. 55, etc. Erasmus interprets the expression, *to her injury*.

VER. 12. **And if a woman.** Such is the reading of the Received Text, and also of Lachmann. Some exceedingly ancient and important manuscripts however, instead of *a woman* (γυνή), read *she* (αὐτή). Such is the reading of ℵ B C L Δ. It is also the reading of the Coptic and Æthiopic versions, and has been introduced into the texts of Tregelles, Tischendorf (eighth edition), Alford. It is no doubt the original reading. The other can be accounted for on the principle, so often acted on by transcribers, that it is innocent to amend or improve a mere matter of phraseology.

Should put away her husband. It is implied that, in our Saviour's judgment, wives and husbands have equal rights in reference to divorce, and in reference to all therefore that is implied in divorce. Josephus indeed says "that while, "according to the Jewish laws, it is lawful for a husband to dissolve his

husband, and be married to another, she committeth adultery.

13 And they brought young children to him, that he should touch them: and *his* disciples rebuked those that brought

"marriage by giving a bill of divorce to his wife, yet it is not lawful for a wife, "who voluntarily departs from her husband, to be married to another, unless "her former husband renounce her" (*Antiq.*, xv. 7: 10). No doubt Josephus expressed the common opinion of his countrymen. But this opinion was founded on Deut. xxiv. 1-4, which merely brings into view a certain duty devolving on husbands, but does not on that account deny the equivalent rights of wives. As a matter of fact, Jewish wives, in ordinary circumstances, did not enjoy equivalent rights; but that matter of fact was founded, not on Divine statute, but on a barbarous use-and-wont, which had descended from the days when right was arbitrarily merged in might. In marriage however, as Richard Baxter remarks, the wife and the husband are equally 'contractors.' Among Greeks and Romans, in the age of our Lord, the wife's right of divorce was recognised; and whenever among the Jews the wife had the power as well as the inclination, she asserted her right. (See Danz's Dissertation, *Uxor Maritum Repudians*, in Meuschen's New Test., pp. 677-701.)

And be married to another. Or, as it stands in the modern critical editions and in a great majority of the best manuscripts, *and should marry another* (γαμήσῃ). The woman is recoguised as not only *being married*, but as also actively *marrying*. Note the word *another*, that is, according to our translation *another husband*. But in reality the woman does not, according to our Saviour's supposition, marry *another husband*; she only marries *another man*, who cannot be her *husband*. In the original the awkwardness is avoided by an idiom which is literally reproduced in Scotch and German, *and if she put away her 'man' and marry another*. Purvey avoids the awkwardness by a free translation, *and if the wiif leveth hir housbonde and be weddid to another man*.

She committeth adultery. It is not said *against him*, probably because it is in the case of the weaker sex that the injury, as distinguished from the sin of wanton divorce, is most severely felt.

VER. 13-16 constitute an exquisite paragraph, corresponding to Matt. xix. 13-15, and Luke xviii. 15-17.

VER. 13. **And.** On some unspecified part of the Saviour's route southward.

They were bringing little children to Him. It would doubtless be the parents who were bringing them, fatherly fathers and motherly mothers. Their instincts assured them that He would be a lover of children, and they were convinced in their hearts that there would be some peculiar value in His benediction.

That He might touch them. They wished that He should lay His hand on their heads and bless them. They had faith that His touch would be more than mere symbolism. Must not His whole person be surcharged with 'virtue'?

And the disciples were rebuking (ἐπετίμων) **those who were bringing them.** 'The erroneous apostles,' as Richard Baxter calls them, thought that the Great Rabbi would be annoyed, and His attention diverted from matters of greater importance than anything connected with little children. Any such thing

them. 14 But when Jesus saw *it*, he was much displeased, and said unto them, Suffer the little children to come unto me, and forbid them not: for of such is the kingdom of God. 15 Verily I say unto you, Whoso-

---

would be, in their apprehension, as Petter remarks, 'a small and leight matter.' On the word translated *were rebuking*, see chap. i. 25, iv. 39. It is here equivalent to *chiding*.

VER. 14. **But when Jesus saw it.** The original expression (ἰδὼν δέ) does not imply that any time elapsed before Jesus had cognisance of what was transpiring. It only implies that what follows the *seeing* in the narrative also followed as an effect in the sequence of the narrated events. Jesus *saw what the disciples did*, and then was affected according to the peculiarity of their action, on the one hand, and the peculiarity of His own character on the other.

He was much displeased. The *much* is superfluous in translation, and is wanting in Luther, Tyndale, Coverdale, and the Geneva. The Rheims renders the expression thus, *He tooke it il.* The word may often, in its classical usage, be translated, *He was vexed.*

And said to them, Suffer the little children to come to Me. *Suffer,* that is, *permit. Take your hands off the little ones!* The expression is applicable to the case of children who were eagerly making their way, on their own feet, to the Saviour.

And. This conjunction, found in Matthew and Luke, is omitted in the texts of Tischendorf, Tregelles, Alford. It is wanting in a large number of the uncial manuscripts, inclusive of the Vatican. It is more likely to have been intentionally added than intentionally or unintentionally omitted.

Forbid them not. Or rather, *Hinder them not* (μὴ κωλύετε). That is the word which is given in the versions of Mace, Wakefield, Principal Campbell, Norton, Alford. The disciples had been putting forth their hands to keep back the little ones.

For of such. That is, *of such little children as these.* The Saviour does not mean, *of persons like little children in disposition* ; otherwise, as Richard Baxter says, " He might have taken up lambs or doves, and blessed them, and said, *Of "such is the kingdom of God.*" He refers to the little children who were there (comp. Acts xxii. 22 ; Rom. i. 32); but not to them exclusively. All little children everywhere are embraced within the compass of His reference. (See *Comm.* on Matt. xix. 14.)

Is the kingdom of God. The kingdom of heaven, in its privileges, *belongs to* little children. They are ' in ' it, and have a right through grace to its prerogatives. They will never be ' far,' or only ' not far,' from it, unless they wilfully expatriate themselves, or be subjected to banishment because of rebellion. If they die in infancy, they will but ascend from a lower to a higher province, in which they will be nearer to the throne of the King.

VER. 15. **Verily I say unto you.** That is, *I solemnly assure you.* The Saviour takes the opportunity of adding a remark that has reference to such as are not children.

ever shall not receive the kingdom of God as a little child, he shall not enter therein. 16 And he took them up in his arms, put *his* hands upon them, and blessed them.

17 And when he was gone forth into the way, there came one running, and kneeled to him, and asked him, Good Master,

---

Whosoever shall not receive the kingdom of God, as a little child, he shall in no wise enter into it. While little children do not need voluntarily to *enter into* the kingdom of God, adults do; for by sin they have become expatriated. But as it is a spiritual kingdom, *to which* men can return without any local transference of their personality, they may be said to *receive it*, as well as to *enter into it*. They allow it to enter into them, until they are absorbed within it and assimilated by it. Or we may distinguish thus: they *receive it*, so far as its principles are concerned; they *enter into it*, so far as its privileges are concerned. They must however receive it and enter into it, *in the spirit of little children*, who do not think of alleging any claim of merit, or presenting any price for their position and privileges.

VER. 16. **And** having taken them up in His arms. Infolding or clasping them. It is the same beautiful word that is used in chap. ix. 36 (ἐναγκαλισάμενος). Wycliffe has *biclippinge hem*.

He blesses them, putting His hands upon them. This is the collocation of the clauses that is adopted by Tischendorf, Tregelles, Alford. While the little ones were successively folded to His breast, He disengaged His right arm, laid His hand on the little head, and uttered His benediction. The word rendered *blesses* (κατευλόγει), as adopted into the texts of Tischendorf, Tregelles, Alford, from the ancient uncial manuscripts, occurs nowhere else in the New Testament. It is stronger than the uncompounded verb, and 'may,' says Alford, 'be rendered, *He fervently blessed them*.' The Saviour lifted up to His Father, in behalf of the little ones, the fervent desires of His heart, and thus invoked '*down*' *upon them a blessing*. See Matt. xix. 13.

VER. 17-21 constitute a paragraph parallel to Matt. xix. 16-26 and Luke xviii. 18-27.

VER. 17. **And.** At some unspecified period in His southward journey.

As He was going forth into the way. *The way, road, track,* or *route*, that led southward. Edgar Taylor translates, *as He was going forth 'along' the highway*. But the evangelist's expression denotes the action of our Lord *in going from the house where He had been 'into' the highway*.

One came running up, and, kneeling to Him, asked Him. His mind had been 'under concern' on a practical matter, and, hearing that the celebrated Galilean Rabbi was about to pass by, he had come with haste to get the benefit of His counsel.

Good Master. Literally, *Good Teacher*. He assumed that the Galilean Rabbi, with whose good deeds the whole country had been ringing, must be *good*. But perhaps, in the employment of such an epithet, there might be, as there sometimes is in our familiar English idiom, a germ of self-assumption, such self-

19] ST. MARK X. 283

what shall I do that I may inherit eternal life? 18 And
Jesus said unto him, Why callest thou me good? *there is
none good but one, that is*, God. 19 Thou knowest the commandments, Do not commit adultery, Do not kill, Do not steal,

---

assumption as is ready enough to admit in others some excellency of motives,
while no other superiority is conceded.

What shall I do that I may inherit eternal life? He was in a state of
'anxiety' in reference to everlasting things. He had faith in a retributive
future; and, desiring a state of bliss in the world to come, he wanted to know
what would be necessary to secure that state. He was persuaded apparently
that eternal life was not to be obtained *by purchase* It was to be obtained *by
Divine allotment and will, by inheritance*. But he was also persuaded, and so
far rightly, that subjective conditions required to be fulfilled, ere he would be
'meet' to enter on possession as a 'portioner' or heir. We have no reason to
think that Mark intended to report, exhaustively, the whole language employed by the interrogator, and all the aspects of conversation that ensued.
Hence the variations in Matthew's account. (Chap. xix. 16, 17. See *Comm.*
in loc.)

VER. 18. **But Jesus said to him, Why dost thou call Me good?** Our Lord saw
that the 'young man' (Matt. xix. 20) only assumed that He was good; and in
the very facility with which he made the assumption he bewrayed an inadequate
conception of the true import and importance of goodness.

There is none good but One, God. Tyndale's translation is awkward, *There is
no 'man' good but one, which is God*. Goodness, moral and spiritual, is Divine.
Absolute Goodness and God are one. God is impersonated goodness, just as
He is impersonated love. Primarily, essentially, independently, none is good
but God. When goodness is found in a creature, it is just a reflection of the
moral glory of the Creator; it is godlikeness. The young man was not taking
this lofty view of goodness; otherwise, before he called Jesus good, he would
have taken some pains to ascertain how far there was in Him a reflection, or
'express image,' of the glory of the Divine Father. The Saviour is not repel-
ling however, as some have imagined, the notion of His own *sinlessness*. He is
only criticising the loose language, and loose ideas, of His interrogator, regarding that moral condition of spirit which is the contradictory of sinfulness.

VER. 19. After uttering His mild rebuke, our Lord proceeds to answer the
young man's question, by exhibiting the moral character requisite as 'meetness' for the enjoyment of everlasting life.

**Thou knowest the commandments, Do not commit adultery, Do not kill, Do not
steal.** There is considerable diversity in the manuscripts, as regards the relative position of these commandments. Lachmann, under the authority of the
Vatican, puts *Do not commit adultery* after *Do not kill*. The Syriac Peshito
version again puts *Do not kill* after *Do not steal*. The Sinaitic manuscript,
on the other hand, omits *Do not commit adultery* altogether. The order of
the Received Text, and consequently of our Authorized version, is the best
supported.

Do not bear false witness, Defraud not, Honour thy father and mother. 20 And he answered and said unto him, Master, all these have I observed from my youth. 21 Then Jesus behold-

Do not bear false witness, Do not defraud, Honour thy father and thy mother. A good deal of debate has been raised in reference to the second of these three commandments. Beza and Lange suppose that it gathers up and generalises all the preceding commandments, being equivalent to this, *Do injury to no one.* Petter, Heupel, Fritzsche, Bloomfield, contend for something much more specific. They suppose that it is a return, under a particular phase, to 'the eighth commandment,' *Do not steal.* Hofmann again supposes that it bends forward to the next clause in the list, in which ' the fifth commandment ' is specified, *Defraud not thy father and thy mother of the honour which is their due.* (*Schriftbeweis*, ii. 2, p. 365.) Owen (*Modes of Quotation*, p. 45) and Kuinöl suppose that there is a reference to the particular injunction contained in Lev. xix. 13, *Thou shalt not defraud thy neighbour, neither rob him,* or, as the Septuagint renders it, *Thou shalt not injure* (ἀδικήσεις) *thy neighbour, nor rob.* Meyer again supposes that the reference is to Deut. xxiv. 14, *Thou shalt not oppress a hired servant that is poor and needy*, which, in the Alexandrine manuscript, is rendered thus, *Thou shalt not withhold the hire* (ἀποστερήσεις μισθὸν) *of the poor and needy.* It is far more likely however that the words are really, as Bishop Hammond expresses it, 'St. Mark's rendering of the tenth commandment'; and if so, we find in our Lord's specification of commandments the complement of duties in the entire manward circle, or second table, of the decalogue. He who covets what belongs to another *has in his heart already deprived him of it.* The verb (ἀποστερήσῃς) that is rendered *defraud* in our version and *begyle* in Coverdale, is too narrowly so rendered. It means to *deprive* of what is one's due, whether by ' hook,' ' crook,' or force, or in any other way. (See Wetstein *in loc.*) Le Clerc takes Hammond's view of the commandment, and so do Bengel, Wetstein, de Wette, Holden, Alexander, Bisping.

VER. 20. **But he answered and said unto Him.** Or, as it is more briefly in both the Sinaitic and Vatican manuscripts, *But he said to Him.*
Master. Literally, *Teacher*, that is *Rabbi.*
All these have I observed from my youth. Or more literally, *All these I observed from my youth.* He is thinking of his past life as a distinct unit of time, back on which he looks from the standpoint of the present. The word translated *observed* properly means *guarded.* The young man acted toward the commandments as *wards* committed to his keeping. So he thought at least; and to a certain extent correctly. So far as the letter of the law was concerned, that letter which was incorporated in the political constitution of the Jewish polity, and which formed the groundwork of unchallengeable position in Jewish society, the young man had kept the commandments. His outward demeanour had been irreproachable. (Comp. Phil. iii. 6.)

VER. 21. **And Jesus beholding him.** Fixing His eyes upon him, so as to read him.
Loved him. Many of the older expositors, from Victor of Antioch downward, wondered at this statement. It surprised them that our Saviour should be repre-

ing him loved him, and said unto him, One thing thou lackest: go thy way, sell whatsoever thou hast, and give

---

sented as *loving* one who was not prepared to give up all on earth for the sake of the kingdom of heaven. Hence various attempts were made to find in the expression something less inward than real love. Some supposed that the words *loved him* meant *kissed him*. (See Casaubon's note and Wolf's.) Even Lightfoot hesitates to object to this interpretation. Others have supposed that it means *spoke to him kindly*. So Casaubon, Elsner, de Dieu, Vater. Norton has a similar idea; only he blends the phrase with the following expression *and said to him*, interpreting thus, *affectionately said to him*. Others again maintain that the phrase means *pitied him*. Alexander says: " Most probably love, as in " many other places, here denotes, not moral approbation, nor affection founded " upon anything belonging to the object, but a sovereign and gratuitous com- " passion, such as leads to every act of mercy upon God's part. The sense will " then be, not that Jesus loved him on account of what he said or what he was " or what he did, but that, having purposes of mercy towards him, He proceeded " to unmask him to himself, and to show him how entirely groundless, although " probably sincere, was his claim to have habitually kept the law. The Saviour's " love is then mentioned, not as the effect of what precedes, but as the ground " or motive of what follows." It should however be borne in mind that those who love both wisely and well take cognisance invariably of lovable qualities in the objects of their love. It would not be to the glory of any being to love the utterly unimportant, insignificant, and unlovely. Beauty of moral character may indeed be wanting; but excellency of capability, or superiority of constitution, or some other beauty or worth, must be discernible, as an indispensable condition of such love as challenges the approbation of conscience and the admiration of intelligence. Love of compassion is never absolutely separated from love of appreciation. Our Saviour's love would be no exception. He would discern in the young man not a little that was really amiable, the result of the partial reception and reflection of gracious Divine influences. There was ingenuousness for instance, and moral earnestness. There was restraint of the animal passions, and an aspiration of the spirit toward the things of the world to come. There was still, indeed, ' one thing ' that was wanting, ' one thing ' that was wrong; and in that ' one thing' many things would be involved. But there were other things that were the fit objects of complacency.

And said to him, One thing thou lackest. Or, *in one thing thou comest behind, in one thing thou comest short* (Rom. iii. 23). Wycliffe's version is, *o thing failith to thee.*

Go thy way. Or simply, *Goo*, as Tyndale has it. The Saviour thus, instead of stating categorically *what was the one thing* in which the young man came *behind*, tells him how to act, if he were willing and wishful to be set right.

Sell whatsoever thou hast. This is not, as certain defenders of Roman Catholic monasticism have maintained, Patrizi for instance, *a counsel of supererogatory perfection*, in complying with which something more would be achieved than what was requisite for personal righteousness. Neither is it, as communistic theorists have contended, a rule of life for all the disciples of Christ in all ages. It was an injunction addressed to a particular individual, and intended to meet

to the poor, and thou shalt have treasure in heaven: and come, take up the cross, and follow me. 22 And he was sad at that saying, and went away grieved: for he had great possessions.

---

his particular spiritual difficulty, that he might master the particular temptation to which he was exposed, and before which he was in danger of succumbing. The same individual, if living in another age and amid other circumstances, might probably have received some modification of the injunction. The one thing aimed at was, no doubt, the deliverance of the young man's heart from some subtle species of self-indulgence that endangered his soul. He was not realizing, we may presume, that he was *but a steward* of the property of the Great Proprietor; he was in other words overlooking the moral responsibilities of wealth, the duties which it superinduces on its privileges.

And give to the poor. We need not imagine anything like indiscriminate or injudicious distribution. It is enough that the Saviour recognised that some people have too much of the world, and others too little; and that they who have too little should be the objects of an unceasing solicitude.

And thou shalt have treasure in heaven. Thou shalt have riches of glory. The righteousness of liberality, which is thus represented as rewardable with the riches of glory, is not the perfect and spotless righteousness of systematic theology. That perfect and spotless righteousness is the work of the Mediator, and the objective ground of forensic justification. But the righteousness of liberality is a single phase of that imperfect personal righteousness of the believer which is, notwithstanding its imperfection, the indispensable moral meetness for the employments and enjoyments of the heavenly state. See on ver. 27.

And come. Very literally, *and come hither.*

Take up the cross and follow Me. The words *take up the cross* are wanting in very high and ancient authorities, the Sinaitic, Vatican, Ephraemi, and Cambridge manuscripts (ℵ B C D), as also in Δ, and the Vulgate version. Tregelles and Tischendorf have thrown them out of their texts. Mill's critical instinct led him of old to condemn them (*Prol.*, § 407). It is likely, as both Mill and Tischendorf remark, that they have been marginally added from chap. viii. 34. Comp. Matt. xvi. 24 and Luke ix. 23. It was enough, we may presume, that, in the first instance at least, it should be laid on the conscience of the young man to attach himself to the Galilean Rabbi as a personal follower.

VER. 22. **But he, saddened at the saying.** The word rendered *sad* or *saddened* (στυγνάσας) is applied to the sky in Matt. xvi. 3, and is there translated, in our Authorized version, *lowring.* A gloom came over the young man's heart, and threw its shadow on his face. *Discumforted* is Tyndale's rendering; *chagriné*, Rilliet's; *ful sori*, Purvey's.

Went away sorrowing. This present participle, as distinguished from the past of the preceding clause, denotes the grief that continued after the first shock of vexation.

For he had great possessions. Wycliffe's rendering is, *Forsoth he was havynge many possesciouns.* The possessions which he was holding (ἦν ἔχων) were numerous (πολλά).

23 And Jesus looked round about, and saith unto his disciples, How hardly shall they that have riches enter into the kingdom of God! 24 And the disciples were astonished at his words. But Jesus answereth again, and saith unto them, Children, how hard is it for them that trust in riches to enter into the

---

VER. 23. **And Jesus looked round about.** Withdrawing His eyes from the young man, who had now turned away.
And saith to His disciples. After having surveyed them round and round.
How hardly shall they who have riches enter into the kingdom of God! *How hardly*, that is, *with what difficulty*. The expression *who have riches* is literally *who have 'the' riches*. The article was somewhat perplexing to Fritzsche; but he hit apparently on the true explanation. The Saviour had it in His option either to consider *riches* indefinitely, or to take into account *the definite sum-total of the riches of the world*. He chooses the latter view. The few, who divide among themselves *these riches*, are in general regarded by their fellow-men as 'the favourites of fortune.' But their position has its drawbacks as well as its advantages. While they have great facilities for getting good and doing good, they are encompassed with great temptations.

VER. 24. **And the disciples were amazed at His words.** They had been accustomed to think little of the dangers, and much of the advantages, of wealth.
But Jesus answereth again, and saith unto them. The *again* grated on the ear of Fritzsche, and he struck it out of his text. Unwarrantably, although it is wanting in the Alexandrine manuscript and a few unimportant cursives. The evangelist did not intend it to qualify the word *answereth*, but rather the remainder of the introductory expression, *But Jesus again says to them in reply*. He *replied* to what was *implied* in their amazement; and in His reply He repeated, though under a variation, the idea which He had expressed in what goes immediately before.
Children. His affection overflowed, as He realized that the objects of His solicitude were spiritually young and inexperienced. All those of them who were genuine had in them a true spiritual life, which they had derived from Himself. Comp. chap. ii. 5, v. 34; John xiii. 33, xiv. 18.
How hard is it for them that trust in riches to enter into the kingdom of God. Might we not rather have expected our Lord to have said, *How hard it is for them 'who have riches'*? And this is really what is said in the Æthiopic version. Some copies of the Old Latin version (c, ff²) have simply, *How hard it is for a rich man* (divitem). Another Old Latin co₁y (a) has alternatively, *How hard it is for those who have riches or who trust in them.* Such variations in the Old Latin copies almost suggest that the Received Text must contain an ancient marginal annotation. And then, in another Old Latin copy (k), the text runs thus, *How hard it is to enter into the kingdom of God!* And this is the reading that is actually found in a certain important Coptic manuscript (*petr.* 3). It is too the reading of the important San Gallensis manuscript (Δ). And it is likewise the reading of the two most ancient and most important manuscripts yet known the Sinaitic and the Vatican (אּ B). Tischendorf has accepted it. Rightly, no doubt. The Saviour indeed had His eye, specifically

kingdom of God! 25 It is easier for a camel to go through the eye of a needle, than for a rich man to enter into the kingdom of God. 26 And they were astonished out of measure, saying among themselves, Who then can be saved?

---

upon the rich; but for a moment He enlarges His field of vision, and makes the more generic statement, *How difficult it is to enter the kingdom of God!* What barriers are in every one's way! Hence the tenderness of His address, *Children!* It would, when one considers it, be strange that He should have said, *How difficult it is 'for those who trust in riches' to enter into the kingdom of God!* Those *who trust in riches* are very far indeed from being meet for the kingdom of heaven. They are most unmeet. Their god is gold. It is at the shrine of Mammon that they perform the rights of adoration. The hand therefore of an annotator is surely bewrayed in the reading of the Received Text. He wanted to explain wherein the danger of riches consists. His explanation is admirable. The rich *are* apt to 'trust in their riches' for their happiness. It is self evident. But for that very reason it seems almost preposterous to suppose that our Saviour would, in the solemnity of the case before us, utter the commonplace, as if it were something of very deep significance.

VER. 25. **It is easier for a camel to go through the eye of a needle, than for a rich man to enter into the kingdom of God.** A fine, bold, hieroglyphic, hyperbolical, way of speaking, that need impose upon no one who has a spark of poetry in his soul. The key to its import is hung at the girdle of common sense. Southey caught its spirit:

> "I would ride the camel,
> Yea, leap him flying, through the needle's eye,
> As easily as such a pampered soul
> Could pass the narrow gate."

'The text,' he says, 'is gospel-wisdom.' The Saviour intended to represent vividly and memorably the extraordinary difficulty of discharging the responsibilities, and overcoming the temptations, of riches. The expression *the eye of 'a' needle* is, in the original, as it was lying before our translators, *the eye of 'the' needle.* Such too is Tischendorf's reading, supported by the Vatican manuscript and other considerable authorities. A preponderance of the best authorities however, inclusive of the Sinaitic, Alexandrian, Ephraemi, and Cambridge manuscripts (א A C D), omit both the articles, *a needle's eye*; and this is Lachmann's and Tregelles' reading. The attempt to substitute *cable* for *camel*, patronized even by Calvin, and the kindred attempt to explain away the phrase *a needle's eye*, as if it must mean something far less impervious to a camel than the actual *eye of a needle*, proceed on an entire and prosaic misconception of the sacred imagery. (See *Comm.* on Matt. xix. 24.)

VER. 26. **And they were astonished exceedingly.** They were astounded; they were confounded.

Saying unto Him. Or rather *to themselves*, that is, *to one another*, but in the hearing of the Master.

Then who can be saved? A free translation, but correct. The expression, if very literally rendered, would run thus, '*And*' *who can be saved?* It has been

27 And Jesus looking upon them saith, With men *it is* impossible, but not with God: for with God all things are possible.

perplexing to many scholars, to Grotius among the rest. It is quite an intelligible idiom however, resting like many others on a faithful representation of an actual mental experience. The astounded disciples advanced, not *oppositively* as Fritzsche supposed, but *continuatively* in the direction of the train of thought that had been started by the Saviour. And as they thus advanced they were shut up to the question, *who is able to be saved?* Their minds had gone beyond the special case of the rich. They saw, as the Saviour had indicated in ver. 24, that the temptations which assail the rich are just a particular species of the temptations that assail generically all without exception. All, in all circumstances, are liable to insidious temptations to selfishness; and selfishness is the essence of unrighteousness.

Ver. 27. **Jesus, looking upon them.** The tenderness of His heart looking forth from His eyes.

Saith, With men it is impossible. *With men*, that is, *on the part of men.* It does not mean, as Fritzsche strangely supposed, *in the judgment of men.* When the Saviour says *It is impossible,* He means, *It is impossible to work out salvation,* in the sense, namely, of working out such a perfect righteousness as would be the meritorious cause of salvation. When the Saviour spoke of the difficulty of rich men in particular, and of men in general, He had reference not to the righteousness which is the 'meritorious cause' of everlasting glory, but to the righteousness which is the ' moral meetness ' of the soul for the enjoyment of such glory. The two righteousnesses are intimately inter-related, and in the case of unfallen beings are but two aspects of one identical reality; in the case of sinful beings like men, however, they are distinct realities. The righteousness which is the meritorious cause of everlasting glory was wrought out and brought in by ' Jesus Christ the righteous,' and is for ever in Him. It is forensically imputed to those who believe in Him. But the righteousness which is moral meetness for the enjoyment of everlasting glory is wrought out in the believer's heart and life, under the mighty impulse of the Holy Spirit of God; it is the righteousness of which mention is made in the sermon on the mount (Matt. v. 6, 20). The other is the righteousness of which Paul speaks when he says that *" the gospel is the power of God unto salvation to every one that believeth, for " therein is the righteousness of God (i.e.,* the work of the Saviour) *revealed from " faith to faith."* (Rom. i. 16, 17.) He who looks merely in the direction of the requisite subjective righteousness, with all its inherent imperfections, cannot but say in despair, 'Who can be saved?' And if the Saviour be speaking to one who is looking exclusively in that direction, He cannot but say ' with men salvation is impossible,' absolutely impossible.

But not with God. It is possible for God to save even the unrighteous, and to ' justify the ungodly ' (Rom. iv. 5), for it is possible for Him to provide the perfect righteousness which is the meritorious cause of salvation.

For all things are possible with God. All *things,* all ' *thinks.*' All that man can think as possible is possible with God. *All that does not involve a contradic-*

28 Then Peter began to say unto him, Lo, we have left all, and have followed thee. 29 And Jesus answered and said, Verily I say unto you, There is no man that hath left house, or brethren, or sisters, or father, or mother, or wife, or children, or lands, for my sake, and the gospel's, 30 but he shall receive

---

tion in thought is possible with God. It is impossible to think that God should cease to be God, or that infinite wisdom should become infinite folly, or that badness should be goodness, or that twice two should be three; but it is not impossible to think that a Divine Saviour should appear in human form, and magnify the law, and bring in an everlasting righteousness for men who have been unrighteous.

VER. 28–31 constitute an appendage to the preceding paragraph. Corresponding appendages are found in Matt. xix. 27–30, Luke xviii. 28–30.

VER. 28. **Peter began to say to Him.** Observe the *began*. It is one of Mark's peculiarities to note *beginnings*; he leaves the mind to go forward from them of its own accord. See chap. ii. 23, iv. 1, vi. 2.

Lo, we have left all, and have followed Thee. We have let all go. Unlike the rich young man, we have surrendered all that would be a fetter to us in attending on Thee; we have surrendered all, that we may follow Thee from place to place, and be moulded by Thee for the work which may be given us to do in connection with Thy kingdom. Peter was sincere, but too retroverting toward self; see Matt. xix. 27.

VER. 29. **Jesus said** (ἔφη ὁ Ἰησοῦς), **Verily I say to you.** That is, *I solemnly assure you.*

There is no man that hath left house, or brothers, or sisters, or mother, or father. There is difference among the manuscripts regarding the sequence of the words *father* and *mother*. Tischendorf and Tregelles reverse the order of the Received Text; they follow the Vatican manuscript. The Received Text has the support of the Sinaitic. The Received Text adds *or wife*; but this item is omitted by both the Sinaitic and Vatican manuscripts (א B), as also by D Δ, 1, 66, and the Vulgate, Coptic, and Armenian versions, and many copies of the Old Latin. Lachmann, Tischendorf, Tregelles, Alford throw it out. It is a matter of no moment whether it be formally retained or formally excluded; it is virtually included; for it is evident that the relationships specified are specified representatively.

Or children. Tyndale in both his editions has *other children*, thus interestingly presenting to view the full original form of the disjunctive conjunction *or*; compare the German *oder*.

Or lands. Literally *fields*, that is, properties or possessions. The specific for the generic.

For My sake, and for the gospel's sake. The Saviour formally distinguishes between Himself and the gospel; and yet with lofty self-consciousness He realized that He and the gospel were inseparable. Without Him the gospel would be nothing; without the gospel men would know nothing of Him.

VER. 30. **But he shall receive.** Principal Campbell and Norton translate, *who*

an hundredfold now in this time, houses, and brethren, and sisters, and mothers, and children, and lands, with persecutions; and in the world to come eternal life. 31 But many that are first shall be last; and the last first.

shall not receive. Very literally it is, *unless he should receive.* The idea is that it is in no case a fact that any one has left all for Christ's sake, *unless it be at the same time true that he shall receive* sublime compensation.

A hundredfold. A definite for an indefinite proportion. The meaning is that the compensation will be far more than double, triple, quadruple, etc. It will mount up to *a hundredfold* as it were, a truly glorious reward.

Now in this time. Even on earth the reward will be transcendent.

Houses, and brothers, and sisters, and mothers. There is no *and fathers*, the omission being apparently without any specific intention. Several manuscripts and Fritzsche read *and mother and father.*

And children, and lands. It is with beautiful delicacy that our Saviour refrains from inserting as an item *and wives*; and thus Julian's scoff, referred to by Theophylact, that the Christian has a promise of a hundred wives, had no vestige of foundation but in his own foul imagination. In the preceding verse the connective between the items is *or*, here it is *and.* There is great propriety in the exchange, for here the Saviour is giving as it were *an inventory of the Divine fulness of blessing,* so far as it is available for the most ample compensation of those who have suffered loss. And there is besides in the spiritual sphere of things a kind of mutual involution of blessed relationships; the sum total of them all belongs to every true disciple. He gets a hundredfold more bliss, even 'now in this time,' than he loses in the surrender of house, or brother, or sister, or mother, or father, or wife, or children, or fields.

With persecutions (μετὰ διωγμῶν). It is grandly added. The idea is not, *in the midst of persecutions*; still less is it, as Kuinöl imagined, *after persecutions* The preposition employed never means *after*, when connected with the genitive case. And it was in vain that Heinsius, le Clerc, and Wetstein conjectured that the evangelist had written in his autograph *after persecution* (μετὰ διωγμόν). We must occupy a loftier standpoint of observation, although Campbell and Fritzsche, as well as Heinsius, le Clerc, and Wetstein had difficulty in reaching it. The Saviour represents *persecutions* as, in some wonderful manner, belonging to the inventory of the believer's blessings on earth. There is a certain lofty sense in which it can be said, 'if ye suffer for righteousness sake *happy are ye*,' '*rejoice and be exceedingly glad.*' Comp. Matt. v. 10–13; Phil. i. 29; 1 Pet. iii. 14, iv. 12–16.

And in the world to come eternal life. Which, with its 'eternal weight of glory,' makes up for all the Christian's trials, not merely a hundred times over, but thousands of thousands of times. The phrase *in the world to come* is literally *in the age to come.* It is the age of the Messiah's undisputed reign, coincident with the age of man's perfected glory. It will be the beginning of an endless series of corresponding ages.

VER. 31. **But many that are first shall be last, and the last first.** One of our Saviour's seed thoughts. (See Matt. xix. 30, xx. 16; Luke xiii. 30.) The con-

ST. MARK X.

32 And they were in the way going up to Jerusalem; and Jesus went before them: and they were amazed; and as they followed, they were afraid. And he took again the twelve,

---

trast of what is and of what ought to be is not greater than the contrast of what is and what shall be. In the great sphere of the world at large, many are at present uppermost who shall by and by be undermost; and even in the hemisphere of Christian society many have pressed forward to the front, who shall by and by be consigned to the rear. Not a few of the noblest and wisest and best have been pushed aside into corners and hidden places by the more bustling, self asserting, and self elevating. But by and by the tables will be Divinely turned, and every one will be found, high or low, in his proper niche. In the pyramid of the glorified it will not be the highest dignitaries of the church, or the most applauded scholars, or the most splendid orators, who will be found at the apex. Perhaps not even Peter, James, or John will be 'first.'

VER. 32-34 constitute a little paragraph corresponding to Matt. xx. 17-19 and Luke xviii. 31-33.

VER. 32. **And they were in the way going up to Jerusalem.** The scene with the rich young man happened while they were going out *into the highway* (ver. 17). Now they had reached the highway, *and were in it*, with their faces set toward Jerusalem.

And Jesus was going before them. Pressing on, with high resolve, in the direction of the final scenes. He foresaw all, and yet marched on unflinchingly toward the conflict, 'for the joy that was set before Him.' (Heb. xii. 2.)

And they were amazed. Or *astounded*. It is the same verb that occurs in ver. 24. The majesty and heroism of His bearing, as He strode along in advance, wrapt in His own lofty meditations, struck them as something extraordinary. They were *confounded*. Principal Campbell very unhappily renders the expression, *a panic seized them*.

And they that followed—or better, *they that were following*—were afraid. This is no doubt the correct reading; it is that of the Sinaitic and Vatican manuscripts (אB), as also C*LΔ and 1; it is, at first sight at least, the more difficult reading. Ewald, Tregelles, Tischendorf approve of it. The evangelist distinguishes between the apostles who would be nearest to our Lord, though at a distance, and the miscellaneous crowd who had been looking on wistfully, and listening as they had opportunity, and 'following.' To them the Saviour was an impenetrable Mystery; He was entirely unique and unearthly; and as He strode along sublimely, in advance even of His chosen disciples, their reverence rose up into a weird feeling of awe, under which they began to tremble and be afraid. 'Who can tell,' they would be thinking, 'what is portended by the appearance of such a Being?'

And He took again the twelve. *The twelve*, as distinguished from those referred to in the immediately preceding clause. Jesus *took them* '*to Himself*.' Such is the import of the word. He gathered them around Him, apart from the rest of the 'following.' He took them *again*. This *again* refers to the fact that after He had advanced for a time on the highway apart and alone, *He rejoined His apostles*.

and began to tell them what things should happen unto him, 33 saying, Behold, we go up to Jerusalem; and the Son of man shall be delivered unto the chief priests, and unto the scribes; and they shall condemn him to death, and shall deliver him to the Gentiles : 34 and they shall mock him, and shall scourge him, and shall spit upon him, and shall kill him : and the third day he shall rise again.

35 And James and John, the sons of Zebedee, come unto him, saying, Master, we would that thou shouldest do for us whatsoever we shall desire. 36 And he said unto them, What

And began to tell them the things that were to happen to Him. He had done so before, but they had only the dimmest apprehension of what He meant (chap. viii. 31, ix. 31). They needed 'line upon line,' 'here a little, there a little.'

VER. 33. Here follows an abstract of what He said to them.

Behold, we are going up to Jerusalem, and the Son of Man shall be delivered to the chief priests and the scribes. An informal way of referring to the supreme Jewish council or sanhedrim. The *elders* might also have been specified (see chap. viii. 31); but they were, so to speak, the lay element, and in ecclesiastical cases would be dominated by the more ecclesiastical members.

And they shall condemn Him to death, and shall deliver Him to the Gentiles. The Romans, to be by them ignominiously executed.

VER. 34. And they shall mock Him. *They*, the Gentiles to wit.

And shall spit upon Him, and shall scourge Him, and shall kill Him; and after three days He shall rise again. Such is the reading of the best manuscripts (ℵ B C D L Δ) and of the great majority of the Old Latin codices. It is approved of by Griesbach, and received into the text by Lachmann, Tischendorf, Tregelles, Alford. See chap. viii. 31, ix. 31.

VER. 35-40 exhibit a strange freak of ambition on the part of the two disciples, James and John, who seem to have thought that a momentous crisis in our Lord's history was at hand. A corresponding paragraph occurs in Matt. xx. 20-23.

VER. 35. And. At some subsequent stage of their progress southward.

James and John, the sons of Zebedee, approach Him, saying to Him. This repetitive expression '*to him*,' though not occurring in the Received Text, is found in the manuscripts ℵ B C D L Δ, and is no doubt genuine.

Master. Or *Rabbi*. Literally, *Teacher*. See chap. ix. 5.

We would that Thou shouldest do for us whatsoever we shall ask of Thee. The pronoun *of Thee* (σέ) is found in the manuscripts ℵ A B C L Δ, and is doubtless genuine. The phrase *we would that*, if very literally rendered, would be, *We desire in order that*, that is, *We have a desire, the aim of which is that, whatever we should ask, Thou shouldest do for us*. The whole expression just means, *We have a request to prefer to Thee*.

VER. 36. And He said to them, What would ye that I should do for you? The

would ye that I should do for you? 37 They said unto him, Grant unto us that we may sit, one on thy right hand, and the other on thy left hand, in thy glory. 38 But Jesus said unto them, Ye know not what ye ask : can ye drink of the cup that I drink of? and be baptized with the baptism that I am bap-

---

reading is a little perplexed in the oldest manuscripts; but the meaning is obvious. Our Lord wished the two disciples to spread out, under the light of His observation and of their own reflection, what was lying in their hearts.

VER. 37. **And they said to Him, Grant to us, that we may sit, one at Thy right hand, and one at Thy left hand, in Thy glory.** The request was certainly more honest than modest. Apprehending that some great apocalypse was at hand, they seem to have had it in view to steal a march on Peter, their most formidable rival for the primacy. They were sure that their Lord must be a King, though at present in disguise. In imagination they saw the disguise thrown off ; and, lo, He is seated on a gorgeous throne, surrounded with all the insignia of royal state. They wish to bask in His immediate sunshine, and to be the highest of the high who should be privileged to surround His person. The expression, *at Thy right hand, and at Thy left hand*, is, in the original, *from Thy right (parts), and from Thy left*. It is an idiom, as is also the form of the phrase in our English version and in Tyndale, '*on*' Thy right hand, and '*on*' Thy left. Wycliffe's translation is picturesque, *Gyve to us that we sitten, the toon at Thy right half, and the tothir at the left, in Thi glorie*.

VER. 38. **But Jesus said to them, Ye know not what ye ask.** Ye know not what is involved in your request. The degree of exaltation in ultimate glory is not to be a matter of capricious or arbitrary determination. It must be regulated by the degree of the spirit of self-sacrifice during probation.

Are ye able to drink the cup that I drink? When the Saviour says *that I drink*, He regards *His present* as extending into *His future*. He might have said, *which I shall drink*, for although He was drinking already He had not yet reached the dregs of the draught. See Matt. xx. 22. The *cup* to which He refers was the cup with the bitter potion in it, the bitter death potion which He ultimately drained. (Comp. chap. xiv. 36 ; John xviii. 11 ; Heb. ii. 9.)

Or to be baptized with the baptism that I am baptized with? Rather a peculiar expression, and explained by Campbell, Bleek, Meyer, Grimm, as denoting *immersing*, or *immerging*, and *consequent whelming*, in calamities ; *Can ye bear to be plunged into the trials into which I am plunged, and which are about to overwhelm Me?* Or, as Petter explains, "Are ye able and fit to be dipped or "drenched in those deep waters of affliction, pains, and miseries, in which I "must shortly be drenched?" Principal Campbell's version is, *Can ye undergo an immersion, like that which I must undergo?* It is more likely however that the word *baptism* has, not its etymological, but its conventional Palestinian import (see chap. vii. 4), so that the idea of *purification* is brought into view: *Can ye endure the purifying ordeal through which I am passing, and which is just about to reach its climax in My experience?* Meyer objects that the idea of a *purifying ordeal* was not applicable to our Lord. Unreasonably. There was indeed no personal impurity in His character. He 'knew no sin ' (2 Cor. v. 21).

tized with? 39 And they said unto him, We can. And Jesus said unto them, Ye shall indeed drink of the cup that I drink of; and with the baptism that I am baptized withal shall ye be baptized: 40 but to sit on my right hand and on my left hand

As He passed through the ordeal, not the least atom of alloy was discovered. He stood the test ; He came out of the fiery trial victorious. But it *was* a fiery trial, a most searching test and ordeal. It was, in a peculiar sense, *a baptism of fire*, or, to change the figure, *a salting with fire* (chap. ix. 49). It burned into His inmost sensibility, and produced ' agony ' (Luke xxii. 44). He willingly endured it, and came out ' perfected through sufferings ' (Heb. ii. 10). He now asked James and John *if they could endure such a baptism of fire.*

Ver. 39. And they said to Him, We are able. They did not, we may be sure, think of any nice psychological distinctions between *ability* and *willingness*. They just meant that they had sufficient strength of attachment to their Lord's person and cause to nerve them for any preliminary ordeal. They would not flinch from enduring, along with Him, any amount of trial however formidable or fiery, through which it might be requisite to pass while He was on His way to His throne. They were sincere, we need not doubt, in this profession.

And Jesus said to them, The cup that I drink ye shall drink. The prospective particle rendered in King James's version *indeed* (μέν) is omitted in the Sinaitic, Vatican, and Parisian manuscripts (אּ B C), and by Tischendorf, Tregelles, Alford. If it be retained it looks forward to the antithetic *but* of the following verse. The two ambitious disciples would have to drink the same bitter potion which the Lord was drinking, so far namely as was possible for them in their circumstances. They would have to suffer as He suffered, so far as such suffering was a possibility to them. There were indeed elements of trial which were peculiar to our Lord in His peculiar position, and in virtue of His peculiar personality and character. And there would be elements of suffering on their part in which their Lord would not be able to share. No two beings in the universe are absolutely alike, or in absolutely identical condition. But, to a large extent, as Jesus was ' in this world,' so would they be.

And with the baptism, with which I am baptized, ye shall be baptized. So far as essential differences in personality and relationship admitted.

Ver. 40. But to sit at My right hand, or at My left hand, is not Mine to give. An expression that has unnecessarily perplexed many who had high ideas of the Lord's sovereignty. It was an old perplexity, and hence the Vulgate version and the Æthiopic, and many copies of the Old Latin, add the pronoun *to you*, as a conducting rod to draw aside the emphasis of the negation. Patrizi contends for it. No such conducting rod however is required. The Saviour is speaking popularly, and *from* or *to* the standpoint of His petitioners. They thought that by an arbitrary act of will the Lord might confer on them the honour which they desired. The Saviour denies to Himself the prerogative which they ascribed to Him. He denies it, that is to say, as apprehended by them. He tells them that it was not His to put forth any such arbitrary act as they had been imagining. The highest posts of honour were to be assigned on

is not mine to give; but *it shall be given to them* for whom it is prepared.

41 And when the ten heard *it*, they began to be much displeased with James and John. 42 But Jesus called them *to him*, and saith unto them, Ye know that they which are accounted to rule over the Gentiles exercise lordship over

---

a totally different principle, in which the arbitrary will of the Sovereign did not at all come into play.

But (it is for them) for whom it has been prepared. The expression is fragmentary in the original, being intended to suggest, to such as were at the right standpoint of thought, more than it plainly declared. The Father had a plan in reference to the honours of the kingdom. It was perfect and unalterable. According to it the chief places were disposed of (in purpose), and could be given to no others. The lowliest would be the loftiest. They who gave up most would get most. He who goes nearest in time to Christ the crucified shall get nearest in eternity to Christ the glorified. See ver. 41-45.

VER. 41-45 constitute an appended paragraph, which corresponds to Matt. xx. 24-28 and Luke xxii. 25-27.

VER. 41. **And when the ten heard it.** We know not how. Perhaps they had noticed the approach to the Saviour of the two disciples, along with their mother (Matt. xx. 20), and had suspected their errand, and pressed them for an explanation of the private interview.

They began to be moved with indignation at James and John. Literally, *concerning James and John*. Principal Campbell, merging the word *began*, translates the whole phrase thus, *conceived indignation*; so Norton, *they were angry*. But there is significancy in the *began*. Mark delighted to note the beginnings of things (see ver. 28), and in the case before us it is natural to suppose that our Saviour interposed before the altercation had time to rise high.

VER. 42. **And Jesus called them to Him, and says to them, Ye know that they who are accounted to rule over the Gentiles.** The expression rendered *they who are accounted to rule over*, and by Grotius *they who have the honour to rule* (οἱ δοκοῦντες ἄρχειν), literally means *they who seem to rule*. It does not signify simply *they who rule* (Matt. xx. 25), as Hombergk, Heumann, Rosenmüller, Kuinöl, Norton, Edgar Taylor, suppose; nor does it necessarily bring into doubt the fact of their rule. Strictly speaking, it neither admits nor denies the fact (Gal. ii. 6). It simply allows *an apparent reality*. Some realities are apparent, or appear, just because they are realities. In other cases, unrealities, though mere delusions, have all the appearance of realities. The persons referred to by our Lord *appeared to rule*. Casaubon, Meyer, Bisping, suppose that the expression means that their rule was *obvious, evident, admitted*; but it seems more likely that our Lord leaves the question of the reality undetermined, more especially as the word rendered *rule* brings the notion of *firsthood* or *primacy* into view. It is a legitimate question certainly whether they who seem to be the primates and princes of the Gentiles are really the first and the most princely. Wetstein supposes that the expression is intended to represent the

them; and their great ones exercise authority upon them.
43 But so shall it not be among you: but whosoever will be
great among you, shall be your minister: 44 and whosoever
of you will be the chiefest, shall be servant of all. 45 For
even the Son of man came not to be ministered unto, but

Gentile rulers as but imposing on themselves when they seemed to themselves to be lords, while they were really moral serfs or slaves. Fritzsche, without accepting any such contrast, supposes that the expression means *they who assume to themselves the position of rulers, who think that they rule.* But our Lord simply admits that the persons to whom He refers *seem,* so far as appearances go, *to be first and chief.*

Lord it over them. Lord it down on them (κατακυριεύουσιν αὐτῶν). They keep themselves exalted over the others, who are, in relation to them, *subjects, subjected, subjacent.*

And their great ones. Their *magnates.* They are great in certain respects, although some of the finest phases of greatness may be entirely wanting.

Exercise authority over them. But not so much '*up*'-*on* them as '*down*'-*on* them (κατεξουσιάζουσιν, a verb unknown in classical Greek).

VER. 43. **But it is not so** (ἐστίν) **among you.** Such is the reading of certain very important manuscripts (א B C* D L Δ), and of the Vulgate version, and many of the Old Latin codices. It is rather the *constitution,* than the *law,* of the kingdom of heaven that is expressed.

But whosoever would become great among you shall be your minister. Your *deacon* (διάκονος). Greatness in the kingdom of heaven consists in *doing* rather than in *being,* and in doing for others rather than for self. No man has a right to be his own end. While it is the case that he is an end to himself, it is not the case that he is his own chief end, or the end that lies immediately underneath the chief. There is a hierarchy of ends; and the man who seeks to make himself his own principal end is an inverted pyramid.

VER. 44. **And whosoever would be first among you.** Your foremost man as it were, your primate.

Shall be servant of all. *Of all,* mark. The width of the ministry determines the degree of the majesty.

VER. 45. **For even the Son of Man came not to be ministered unto, but to minister.** To act as a 'deacon' to men (διακονῆσαι). He came *not to be served, but to serve.* So far as He is a Mediator He sought not 'His own things,' but men's. In teaching, it was not renown as a teacher that was His aim, but men's instruction; in giving an example, it was not His own fame as an exemplar which He sought, but men's elevation; in reigning, it is not His own glory that He desires, but men's prosperity and bliss. In atoning, see next clause. There are indeed relations, more comprehensive than those of mediatorship, in which He who is 'God over all, blessed for ever,' must find His final End in Himself. In the sphere of these relations it is His pleasure *to be served,* and not *to serve.* But there is no sphere whatever in which He will ever consider it to be a greater glory to be a Receiver than a Giver.

to minister, and to give his life a ransom for many.
46 And they came to Jericho: and as he went out of Jericho

And to give His life a ransom for many. So emphatically did He come *to serve*, at whatever cost to Himself. He came to make a sacrifice of Himself *for the sake of men*. A *ransom* is *a price of deliverance* (λύτρον from λύω). Jesus came to give Himself as such. He looked upon men as captives. They had been transgressors, and therefore Divine justice had to lay hold of them. They were 'lawful captives.' They were exposed to the full desert of their transgressions, and hence were in danger of ' the wrath that is to come.' What was to become of them ? There were difficulties in the way of liberation pure and simple. Had they been liberated without any ransom, there would have been no security that they would care, for the future, to renounce ' the way of transgressors.' If all who transgress were always liberated the moment they transgress, the sanctions of law would cease to be sanctions except in name; the law would be no longer law, but mere opinion or advice. Thus a ' ransom ' was needed if there was to be salvation, needed for the sake of the transgressors, and for the sake of the law which they had transgressed. Jesus came ' to give Himself ' as such a ' ransom.' He came, that is to say, to present to the Divine justice what would afford a sufficient guarantee for the authority and honour of the law, in the event of the liberation of the guilty, and what would be fitted to have a wholesome ethical influence upon the hearts of the liberated. *For many.* The Saviour merely looks at the multitudinousness of the objects of His gracious intent. " The word *many*," says Calvin wisely, " is not put definitely " for a fixed number, but for a large number; for the Saviour contrasts Himself " with all others. And in this sense it is used in Rom. v. 15, where Paul does " not speak of any part of men, but embraces *the whole human race* " (*Harmony*, in loc.). The preposition translated *for* (ἀντί) does not mean *for the benefit of*, or *in behalf of*. It properly means *over against*, and here represents the ransom as *an equivalent* for the persons for whom it was paid. *Substitution* is implied; *equivalence* is expressed.

VER. 46-52 constitute a paragraph that corresponds to Matt. xx. 29-34, and Luke xviii. 35-43.

VER. 46. **And they come to Jericho.** Or, more strictly, and as Tyndale gives it, *Hierico*, the city of aromas, situated between the Jordan and Jerusalem. " Its palm groves and balsam gardens were given by Antony to Cleopatra. " From her Herod the Great bought them, made it one of his royal cities, and " adorned it with a new hippodrome and many stately buildings ; and here too " that monster of iniquity died." (Porter's *Syria*, p. 184.) The modern representative of the ancient city is sadly degenerated ; it is called *Riha* or *Eriha* ; and, says Dr. Porter, " a more filthy and miserable village could not be found " in all Palestine. Its few inhabitants too are not only poor, but profligate, " retaining some of the vices for which the cities of Sodom were rendered " notorious four thousand years ago." (*Ditto*, p. 185.)

And as He was going out of Jericho. The case about to be recorded seems to have begun as He entered into the city (see Luke xviii. 35), but it culminated, in all likelihood, as He departed. (See *Comm.* on Matt. xx. 30.)

ST. MARK X.

with his disciples and a great number of people, blind Bartimæus, the son of Timæus, sat by the highway side begging. 47 And when he heard that it was Jesus of Nazareth, he began to cry out, and say, Jesus, *thou* son of David, have mercy on me. 48 And many charged him that he should hold his peace: but he cried the more a great deal, *Thou* son of David, have mercy on me. 49 And Jesus stood still, and commanded him to be called. And they

---

With His disciples, and a great multitude. Literally, *and a sufficient crowd*, that is, *and a considerable crowd*, or, as Beza in his last edition (1589) explains it, *no small crowd*.

Timæus's son, Bartimæus, a blind beggar, was sitting by the way side. He had been, or he subsequently became, a somewhat noted individual; hence the preservation of his name, though it is recorded by Mark alone. His father too would appear to have been noted for some reason or other. Perhaps they both became ultimately attached to the cause of the Saviour and the fellowship of the disciples. (See ver. 52.) The word *Bartimæus* just means in Aramaic *son of Timæus*; and hence it may seem strange to some that the evangelist should say ' *Timæus's son, Bartimæus*.' There is no real redundancy however; for the patronymic was used as the son's proper name. In Syria and the adjacent lands ophthalmic affections were in ancient times, and are still in modern times, of very frequent occurrence. W. G. Palgrave, speaking of Arabia, says: "Ophthalmia is fearfully prevalent, especially among children, and goes on "unchecked, in many or most instances, to its worst results. It would be no " exaggeration to say that one adult out of every five has his eyes more or less " damaged by the consequences of this disease." (*Central and Eastern Arabia*, vol. ii., p. 34.)

VER. 47. **And when he heard that it was Jesus of Nazareth.** Literally, *that it is Jesus of Nazareth*. The thing heard is reported in the direct form, and hence the introductory *that* is what is called *recitative* by critics, *and when he heard* (this to wit) *It is Jesus of Nazareth*.

He began to cry out, and say, Jesus, Thou Son of David, have mercy on me. Or, *Son of David, Jesus, pity me*.

VER. 48. **And many rebuked him, that he should hold his peace.** Literally, *chid him in order that he might be silent*. He seemed, by his vociferative appeals, to disturb the solemnity that was brooding over that part of the caravan procession in which our Saviour was moving.

But he cried out the more, a great deal, Son of David, have mercy on me. He had faith in Jesus as not merely the Great Rabbi of Nazareth, but as also the Great Deliverer of Israel; and he was not to be thwarted in his application.

VER. 49. **And Jesus stood still.** Or, more literally and simply, *stood*. He made a halt.

And said, Call him (φωνήσατε αὐτόν). He said this to the persons who were near Him.

call the blind man, saying unto him, Be of good comfort, rise; he calleth thee. 50 And he, casting away his garment, rose, and came to Jesus. 51 And Jesus answered and said unto him, What wilt thou that I should do unto thee? The blind man said unto him, Lord, that I might receive my sight. 52 And Jesus said unto him, Go thy way; thy faith hath made thee

And they call the blind man, saying to him, Be of good cheer, rise, He calleth thee. Instead of *Be of good cheer*, it might be better to adopt the more literal rendering of Worsley, Newcome, Edgar Taylor, Norton, *Be of good courage* (θάρσει). If the expression *cheer up* were not so exceedingly colloquial, it would admirably represent the force of the original verb.

VER. 50. **And he, casting away his garment.** Namely, the loose outer robe that was wrapped around him over his tunic. Newcome has the word *mantle*; Tyndale, the Geneva, Norton, Sharpe, use the word *cloak*, the term that is employed in Matt. v. 40. The man was in haste, and wished to be disentangled from its folds.

Sprang up, and came to Jesus. Instead of the simple word *rose* (ἀναστάς), the reading of the Received Text, the Sinaitic, Vatican, and Cambridge manuscripts (א B D) among others, along with the Old Latin, Vulgate, Coptic, and Gothic versions, support a more graphic term (ἀναπηδήσας), *sprang to his feet*. Lachmann, Tischendorf, Tregelles, have received this term into the text. Griesbach reclaimed against its acceptance, and apparently with some reason, for it is difficult to suppose that if it had been the original term it would ever have been deliberately pushed out.

VER. 51. **And Jesus answered him and said, What wilt thou that I should do to thee?** This question the Saviour is said to have put by way of *answer*. It was the answer which He graciously gave to the original request of Bartimæus, *Pity me*.

And the blind man said to Him, Rabboni, that I might receive my sight. Very literally, *that I might look up*. The *up* is not to be ignored. In the midst of his blindness he would, in all likelihood, be sensitive in some degree to the light of the sun streaming down upon him from above. *Seeing* would therefore he naturally associated in his mind with *looking up*. *Rabboni* was equivalent to the term *Rabbi*, but more reverential. (See *Drusii Præterita*, in loc.) It was akin to the French *Monseigneur*, as distinguished from *Monsieur*.

VER. 52. **And Jesus said to him, Go thy way, thy faith hath made thee whole.** Not efficiently indeed, but instrumentally in a certain respect. His faith had laid hold of omnipotence; and omnipotence had made him whole. Very literally rendered, the expression is, *thy faith hath saved thee*. But our word *saved*, just as truly as our phrase *hath made whole*, is not a precise reproduction of the idea of the original verb. Here the reference, we need not doubt, is, mainly at least, to the cure that had taken place in the man's body, so that he was now *sound and well*. Comp. Matt. ix. 21; Mark v. 23, 28, vi. 56; Luke viii. 36, 50; Acts iv. 9, xiv. 9. But it is not impossible, perhaps not unlikely, that the Saviour, with His deep view of the correspondencies of things outward and

ST. MARK XI.

whole. And immediately he received his sight, and followed Jesus in the way.

CHAPTER XI.

1 AND when they came nigh to Jerusalem, unto Bethphage

inward, employed the word with a two-edged reference. What was happening in the man's body was really, we may presume (ver. 47, 48), but the outward picture or hieroglyph of what had happened in his soul.

And immediately he received his sight. He *looked up.*
And followed Him in the way. *The way*, that is *the route* that led to Jerusalem. Bartimæus joined the caravan of which Jesus was the central object. He wished to attach his fortunes to 'the Son of David'; and he became, we may suppose, a devoted and well-known disciple. (See ver. 46.)

CHAPTER XI.

JERUSALEM is now near, and the tragic end of our Saviour's terrestrial career begins to loom into view.

VER. 1-10 contain *the approach to the capital city by way of Bethany and Bethphage.* The paragraph corresponds to Matt. xxi. 1-11; Luke xix. 29-38; John xii. 12-15.

VER. 1. **And when they come nigh.** Note the tense. The reader is, as it were, carried along with the procession or caravan, and is present at the approach. (See Jelf, 395, 2.)

To Jerusalem, to Bethphage and Bethany. A cumulative expression. Jerusalem is mentioned first, though it was remotest, for it was the grand terminus. Bethphage and Bethany were suburban villages, near to one another, and lying on the direct line of road that led to Jerusalem from the east. They were on the east side of the mount of Olives, which was on the east side of the holy city. Though the exact site of Bethphage is uncertain, yet it is probable that it lay westward of Bethany, and that it was thus a stage in advance toward the city. The evangelist, consequently, is to be regarded as enumerating the three places in their reverse topographical order, putting the last first and the first last. Instead of the expression *to Bethphage and Bethany*, Lachmann and Tischendorf read *and to Bethany*, the reading of the Cambridge manuscript (D), and, very decidedly and critically, of Origen in two distinct passages, as also of the Vulgate version and of a preponderance of the Old Latin codices. But it looks like a torso of an expression, and the Received reading is overwhelmingly supported. (See in particular Griesbach's *Comm. Crit.* in loc.) All trace or almost all trace of Bethphage has disappeared, though the place is often referred to in the Talmudic writings, in a puzzling way. (Lightfoot's *Chorographical Century*, chap. xxxvii.) As to Bethany, it has lingered on to the present day; but it is, as Tristram calls it, a 'miserable village.' (*The Land of Israel*, p. 199.) 'Bethany,' says Dr. Robinson, 'is a poor village of some twenty families; its inhabitants are without thrift or industry.' (*Researches*, vol. ii.,

and Bethany, at the mount of Olives, he sendeth forth two of his disciples, 2 and saith unto them, Go your way into the village over against you: and as soon as ye be entered

---

p. 101.) And yet when the writer visited it in 1855 he found, among the children who were clustering about, a boy carrying *an inkhorn by his side*. On being asked if he could write he answered in the affirmative, and wrote with his reed on the blank leaf of our New Testament the words, in Arabic, *God is Love*. It was of his own accord that he selected the words, much to our gratification.

At the mount of Olives. *At* or *toward* (πρός). The preposition is attached, as by a longer thread of reference than the preposition in the two preceding clauses (εἰς), to the verb *come nigh*. The meaning is not that either Jerusalem itself or the suburban Bethphage and Bethany were *at* the mount of Olives; it is that the caravan procession, in approaching Jerusalem by way of Bethphage and Bethany, *moved in the direction of the mount of Olives*. It is a little geographical remark, intended for such as were not familiar with the topography of the locality. It is introduced without any phraseological jointing, simply in the aggregative way. *The mount of Olives*, or *the mountain of the olive trees*, was the natural name of the beautiful mountain that rises close to Jerusalem on the east, the home or favourite habitat of the olive tree. "The sides of the "mountain," says Dr. Robinson, "are still sprinkled with olive trees, though "not thickly, as was probably the case of old." (*Researches*, vol. i., p. 348.) "At present," says Horatio Hackett, "the mountain exhibits, on the whole, a "desolate appearance. Rocky ridges crop out here and there above the surface, "and give to the hill a broken sterile aspect. Yet the mount is not wholly "destitute of verdure even now. A few spots are planted with grain; and fruit "trees, as almonds, figs, pomegranates, olives, are scattered up and down its "sides. The olives take the lead decidedly, and thus vindicate the propriety of "the ancient name." (*Illustrations of Scripture*, p. 165.) The mountain rises about 220 feet above Mount Moriah over against it on the west, and affords a magnificent and most commanding view of Jerusalem and the surrounding country. "Surely," says Dr. Barclay, "there is not in all the world a prospect "so delightful to behold as the panorama to be enjoyed by ascending the "minaret alongside the Church of Ascension, that now crowns the elevation "nearest the city." (*City of the Great King*, p. 60.)

Ere the company had yet turned the apex of the mountain, the Saviour **sendeth two of His disciples.** He *sendeth forth* (ἀποστέλλει), that is, *He details and despatches.*

VER. 2. **And says to them.** Or, as we might now express it, *with the following instructions.*

Go into the village that is over against you. Bethphage, most likely. Comp. Matt. xx. 1, 2. Both Dr. Barclay (*City of the Great King*, p. 66) and Dr. Hanna (*The Passion Week*, p. 4) suppose that the village must have occupied a certain 'tongue-shaped promontory or spur of Olivet,' across the hollow which the road avoids, and just a few hundred paces before reaching the turning point of the mountain ridge. There are on that spot tanks and discernible foundations of buildings.

into it, ye shall find a colt tied, whereon never man sat; loose him, and bring *him*. 3 And if any man say unto you, Why do ye this? say ye that the Lord hath need of him; and

And straightway as ye enter into it, ye shall find a colt tied. It might, according to circumstances, be the foal of a horse or the foal of an ass. The circumstances and habits of the Jewish people in general, and, if more evidence were required, the special circumstances of the class of people with whom our Lord was accustomed to associate, made it certain that it was the humbler animal that was meant. It was no stigma however, or diacritical mark of poverty, to ride upon an ass. The horse was for long reserved for war purposes; and, as among the Aryans (Lenormant's *Ancient Hist. of the East*, vol. ii., p. 5), it was used for the war chariot before it was used for riding on.

Whereon no man ever yet sat. In the action which the Lord contemplated He meant to be no man's successor.

Loose it, and bring it. Mark makes no reference to the mother ass, beside which the colt would be found standing. (See Matt. xxi. 2.) It was the colt alone which was really to be used.

VER. 3. **And if any one say to you, Why do ye this? say ye, The Lord hath need of it.** The expression *the Lord* was in itself of somewhat indefinite reference, for there were then, as there are still, 'lords many.' There is no good reason for supposing that the disciples would be enjoined, or would be inclined, to point upward to heaven as they spoke, so as to indicate *that 'Jehovah' had need of the colt*. Such an assumption, on the part of persons who had no instructions to present any special credentials of a Divine commission, would not have been fitted to command the confidence and acquiescence of the owner. It is more natural to suppose that the intended reference was to our Saviour himself in His visible personality, although surrounded with no other insignia of lordship than His own native majesty and moral glory. He had arrived with His numerous 'following' two days before, the day before the sabbath which had just been ended. He had lodged in the immediate vicinity, either in Bethany or, as is more probable, on one of the northern slopes of the mountain, on which the Galilean pilgrims were accustomed, year by year, to fix their temporary booths. (Comp. Robinson's *Researches*, vol. i., 565, 566.) He was the centre of an intense curiosity and enthusiasm. His fame had travelled before Him. His appearance, though confoundingly humble so far as paraphernalia were concerned, did not, in respect of a certain indescribable grandeur of bearing, belie His fame. His works were unprecedentedly marvellous. His words were, if possible, more marvellous still. His secret demeanour was without a speck on which doubt could fasten. Those who were nearest Him, and saw most of Him when He was ungirt, admired and revered Him the most. Who could He be? What might He be? Everybody was putting such questions. His face had been set unflinchingly Jerusalem-ward. And the nearer His approach to the city of the Great King, the more abstracted His gaze, as if He were looking into a future of infinities. Was it not possible, was it not even probable, that He was the long-looked-for King of the Jews, coming to His people in disguise? Who could say what He would do when once He should

straightway he will send him hither. 4 And they went their way,

---

enter His capital and be in the midst of the temple? Such ideas as these might be, or would be, whirling about, in more or less of confusion, within many an expectant mind. Speculation would be rife. And throughout the whole village, crowded as it was with strangers who were on their way to the passover solemnities, there would be much eager inquiry and earnest discussion. Eyes would be frequently turned toward the spot where our Lord and His disciples formed the centre of the widely distributed multitude, with which the whole mountain side was alive. When messengers came forth from this centre, a kind of avenue would be made for them as they passed along from group to group; and it would be known, or telegraphed from individual to individual, that they were *the Great Rabbi's disciples*. When consequently they made their appearance in Bethphage, and when, looking perhaps in the direction of the surging central crowd whence they had emanated, they said, *the Lord hath need of it*, there would be no doubt remaining regarding the Personage referred to.

And straightway he will send it hither. The Lord foresaw, as by a miracle of knowledge, every link, however minute or complicated with human free will, in the future train of events. But, strange to say, there is a great difficulty regarding the expression. We do not refer to the fact that instead of the future verb, *he will send*, there is in an immense preponderance of the uncial manuscripts, including all the oldest (א A B C D), the present tense, *he sends*. This, though something peculiar in such a statement, is capable of sufficient explanation. The present may, as often elsewhere, be idiomatically employed to express complete certainty of future occurrence, such certainty as is warranted when the event is seen in the very act of transpiring. We refer to the fact that in the Sinaitic, Vatican, Parisian, and Cambridge manuscripts (א B C D), as well as in L Δ, the adverb *again* (πάλιν) is found in connection with the verb *sends: and immediately he sends it again hither*, that is, *and immediately he will return it hither*. The expression, in other words, is, according to these manuscripts, not to be regarded as informing the commissioned disciples that the colt, when claimed, would forthwith be sent by the owner. It is to be regarded as part of the commission which they were to discharge, embodying a promise that was to be made to such as it might concern, *that the Lord would without delay return the animal*. Origen, in two distinct passages of his *Commentary on Matthew* (iii. 722, 740), inserts this *again*, and interprets the expression as a promise of a speedy return. Dav. Schulz hesitated to reject the adverb, and Tischendorf and Tregelles have received it into their texts. We cannot think however that it is genuine. Internal congruity recoils. And it is a notable fact that no trace of the adverb is found in any of the ancient versions, the Old Latin, the Vulgate, the Peshito Syriac, the Philoxenian Syriac, the Coptic, Sahidic, Æthiopic, Gothic, Armenian. Even Origen omits it in his *Commentary on John* (iv. 181). It must, we conclude, have been inserted in the margin of some very early copy of the Gospel, as an expository note, and thence have crept into the text of the ancient manuscripts in which it is found. It was, we doubt not, an inaccurate expository note.

and found the colt tied by the door without in a place where two ways met; and they loose him. 5 And certain of them that stood there said unto them, What do ye, loosing the colt? 6 And they said unto them even as Jesus had commanded: and they let them go. 7 And they brought the colt to Jesus,

---

VER. 4. **And they departed, and found a colt.** It is simply *colt*, that is *a colt*, in the great body of the most ancient manuscripts. So too Griesbach, Scholz, Lachmann, Tregelles, Alford, and Tischendorf in his 1849 and 1859 editions. In his eighth edition, however, Tischendorf re-inserts the article under the sanction of the manuscripts ℵ C Δ. The sanction is not sufficient.

Tied by the door without. It had been led *to* (πρὸς) *the door outside*, and there tied. '*The*' door: the Received reading and the right reading, that is, *the door* of the dwelling house that belonged to the proprietor of the animal. It is as if St. Mark were reporting from the lips of an eye-witness, perhaps, as Papias expressly asserts (Eusebius' *Eccles. Hist.*, iii. 39), from the lips of Peter, who might not unlikely be one of the two disciples sent to fetch the colt. (Comp. Luke xxii. 8.) It is probable that the owner of the animal would belong to the 'well to do' class in the village, and that hence his house would have a court, which would open out to the street by a great door. It is on the basis of this supposition that we see the propriety of the expression *outside*, that is, *outside the court*, instead of *inside*, where, in oriental houses of that description, it is common to have horses or asses standing, ready for use.

In a place where two ways met. But this is rather, as Alexander remarks, a translation of the Vulgate version (*in bivio*) than of the Greek original, which strictly means *on the roundabout road* (ἐπὶ τοῦ ἀμφόδου). It is a topographical note that could only be given by an eye-witness. The likelihood is that the village would be straggled along a road that deviated from the highway, but came round to it again.

And they loose it. They engage in loosing it. He who was Lord of all had need of it.

VER. 5. **And certain of them that stood there.** Most likely domestics of the proprietor, in the first instance. The imagination is left to fill up the minuter details of the incident.

Said to them, What do ye, loosing the colt? *What do ye?* an idiom corresponding to the German *Was machet ihr?* or to the English *What are ye about? What is that you are doing?*

VER. 6. **And they said to them even as Jesus said; and they let them go.** That is, the people ceased interference with them by hand or otherwise. *They let them go.* The word is rendered *suffered* in chap. i. 34, v. 19, vii. 12, x. 14. It primarily means *sent away*. It is sometimes translated *forgave* (that is, as it were, *forth-gave* or *gave up* what was due), as in chap. ii. 5, 9, 10, iii. 28, iv. 12.

VER. 7. **And they bring the colt to Jesus.** The past is 'présented' to us, or 'presentiated,' and thus 'presénted.' *They :* we are not, in our imagination, to draw a very precise line between the disciples and the surrounding crowd.

and cast their garments on him; and he sat upon him. 8 And many spread their garments in the way: and others cut down branches off the trees, and strawed *them* in the way. 9 And they that went before, and they that followed, cried, saying,

---

And cast on it their garments. An extemporized housing, instead of the lofty oriental saddle. It was however quite seemly, as the *garments* referred to were the loose outer robes which were worn above the tunic. The word *cast* is equivocal in English, as regards tense. It was meant however to be past, *threw*. But in the modern critical editions of the text the verb is in the present, *throw*. The scene continues to be 'présented.' Such is the reading of ℵ B C D L Δ, and of the Vulgate and Coptic versions.

And He sat upon it. He mounted, that He might enter the holy city with all the significance of a triumph. He would not enter it indeed like a haughty warrior on his steed; He was the Prince of peace. Neither would He enter it in a bedazzlement of purple and pomp and pageantry; He was the Meek and Lowly One. And yet He was a Conqueror and a King; and the ideas that were incarnated in His career, and emblazoned in His final sufferings and death and resurrection, are destined to be triumphant all the world over.

VER. 8. The procession began. **And many.** Catching the enthusiasm of the moment, and rising to the greatness of the occasion.

Spread their garments. That is, *strewed their mantles* or *cloaks*, in place of tapestry or webs of cloth.

Upon the way. Literally, *into the way*. The attention is turned to the enthusiastic action of the people, in pressing in from either side, that they might succeed in bringing their garments *into* that precise line along which the mounted Monarch would pass, in the broad irregular highway.

And others branches, which they had cut from the fields (ἄλλοι δὲ στιβάδας *small leafy branches*, κόψαντες ἐκ τῶν ἀγρῶν). The expression, *having cut them out of the fields*, is pregnant. The branches were cut 'in' the fields, and then carried 'out.' Branches are natural decorations; no triumphal procession could well take place without them. At the conclusion of the Franco-German war, in the course of which Napoleon III. became a captive and was dethroned, the victorious German troops made their triumphal entry into Berlin, on 16th June, 1871, and it is written in the newspapers now lying before us (June 23, 1871), that "on each side of the way were placed gilt "pedestals, and between each pedestal hung a festoon of *laurel and fir*." "After the flags, come the Guards. They are covered with *laurel and fir*." " The altars and cannons are covered with *leaves and with branches of fir trees*."

VER. 9. **And they who marched before, and they who followed:** namely, Him who was the great Centre of attraction in the procession.

Shouted, Hosanna. The sacred Hebrew *Hurrah*, literally meaning *Oh save!* It would originally be used when captives, rebels, or submissive subjects, supplicated mercy from some conqueror or lord. But it had grown, in the course of ages, into a mere acclaim. The shouting people, in the case before us, were ntentionally catching up and repeating the acclaim of Psalm cxviii. 25.

Hosanna; Blessed *is* he that cometh in the name of the Lord: 10 blessed *be* the kingdom of our father David, that cometh in the name of the Lord: Hosanna in the highest. 11

Blessed is He. Or, *Blessed be He*, the rendering of Mace, Wakefield, Principal Campbell, Norton, Edgar Taylor. Rightly so, and in harmony with the view of Luther, Piscator, Bengel, Zinzendorf, Heumann, Fritzsche. In the English version of Psalm cxviii. 26 the expression is, *Blessed be He*. It was not so much the intention of the enthusiastic multitude to make a doctrinal affirmation as to express a devotional desire. They lifted up their hearts actually or virtually to God, and prayed: *May God bless Him!—God who 'says' and 'it is done.'*

Who cometh. *Who is coming.* It is the expression of Psalm cxviii. 26, and beautifully represents the Messiah as *on His way!* All along the ages His advent had been imminent, for He was *on His way*. Time was on tiptoe; people were looking out; the ages were ages of expectancy; for *He was on His way! He would come, and would not tarry!* But now the shout would have a greater emphasis in it than ever. Were not the eyes of the people beholding Him going along the way? going to that terminus, where it would be proper for Him to withdraw His veil, and let His glory shine forth?

In the name of the Lord. That is, *in Jehovah's name*. It is *Jehovah*, or *Jahveh*, that is the Hebrew word in Psalm cxviii. 26. The Messiah was not to come as a Principal, or as Supreme. He was *to be sent*. He was to be an 'Apostle' (Heb. iii. 1) or Commissioner, but of the highest possible dignity. He was to be *Jehovah's Lord High Lieutenant* or *Viceroy*. Hence He was to come in all the authority that could be communicated by the authorizing 'name' of the Supreme.

VER. 10. **Blessed be the kingdom that cometh, the kingdom of our father David.** Or rather, according to the reading of Griesbach, Lachmann, Scholz, Tischendorf, Tregelles, supported by the manuscripts ℵ B C D L U Δ, 1, 69, and the best ancient versions, *Blessed be the coming kingdom of our father David!* The enthusiasm of the people, having got vent for its first up-gushings in the fine old triumphal language of the 118th Psalm, extemporized for itself another channel in the common popular representation of the collective import of the prophecies. *The coming kingdom of our father David* was just, under a particular phase of expression, *the coming Messianic kingdom, the coming kingdom of God, the coming kingdom of heaven*. It was called *the kingdom of David*, because it was regarded as at once the restoration, continuation, and antitypical culmination and completion, of that system of society that was established in the reign of David. The royalty was to continue in the line of king David, who was regarded as the father not only of the Messiah in particular, but of the Jewish people in general. The triumphal processionists, getting a glimpse of the glory of the lowly but lofty One who was in the midst of them, felt persuaded that He was about to re-establish the kingdom of David. And so He was, though on a far higher plane of things than was conceived of in their imaginations.

Hosanna in the highest! That is, *Hosanna in the highest places, in the heavens.* Norton totally misunderstood the expression. He renders it, *Hosanna*

And Jesus entered into Jerusalem, and into the temple: and when he had looked round about upon all things, and now the eventide was come, he went out unto Bethany with the twelve. 12 And on the morrow, when they were come from Bethany, he was hungry: 13 and seeing a fig tree afar off having

---

'*Thou*' *in the highest heavens.* But it was no circuitous naming of Jehovah. It was a particular way of intensifying, to the utmost conceivable degree, the enthusiasm of their welcome. It corresponds, in a parallel line of things, to the appendage *for ever* connected with the *vive* or *viva* of other national acclaims. *Life* is intensified to the superlative degree in *life for ever*; and, correspondingly, the *salvation*, which is the kernel-idea of *Hosanna*, is intensified to its superlative degree in *salvation that is consummated in the highest heavens.* (See *Comm.* on Matt. xxi. 9.)

VER. 11. **And He entered into Jerusalem, into the temple.** The entrance of our Lord *into the temple* is represented, not as something in addition to the entrance into Jerusalem, but as the continuative result of entering into Jerusalem. (Comp. ver. 1.) He had *entered into Jerusalem*, because He purposed to *enter into the temple*, His Father's house.

And when He had looked round about upon all things. Not simply as one might gaze who had never been there before: an arbitrary and wanton idea; but as one who had a right to inspect the condition of the place, and who was determined to assert and exercise that right. See ver. 15–17.

It being now eventide. That is, *the hour being now late*.

He went out to Bethany with the twelve. To *Bethany*, where He had some devoted adherents (John xi. 5), with whom He might choose to spend part of the evening. The night would probably be spent quietly and secludedly in the neighbourhood, where His disciples and Himself might have their booths or tents. It was the custom of the Galileans and other strangers to camp out at the time of 'the great congregation,' when the city overflowed.

VER. 12. **And on the morrow, when they had come out from Bethany.** Or, *after they came out from Bethany*. It was then, and only then, that what follows was realized.

He hungered. Or, as we should now say, *He was hungry*. A certain proof, one should suppose, that He had not spent the night under the hospitable roof of Martha and Mary. He had most likely spent it in the open air, communing with His Father, and brooding over the condition of Jerusalem, the Jews, and mankind.

VER. 13. **And seeing a fig tree afar off.** Or, *from a distance.* "Mount "Olivet," says Dean Stanley, " besides its abundance of olives, is still sprinkled "with fig trees." (*Sinai and Palestine*, p. 422.) In the very name Beth*phage* there is probably a reference to *figs*. Modern critics in general agree with Lightfoot that the word means, not, as Origen thought, *the house of jawbones*, but *the house of green figs*.

Having leaves. A rather remarkable phenomenon at that early season of the year. If the Saviour was crucified on the 15th of the month Nisan, the day

leaves, he came, if haply he might find any thing thereon: and when he came to it, he found nothing but leaves; for

---

after the passover lamb was slain, then it is probable that He entered Jerusalem triumphantly on Sunday the 10th. It would hence be on Monday the 11th that *He saw the fig tree from a distance, having leaves*. This 11th of the lunar month Nisan would correspond to an early day in our solar month April, a time when fig trees in general would not be in leaf. But it sometimes happens that there is an exceptional precocity in a tree's foliation; there had been such precocity in the case before us.

He came, if haply. Coverdale supplies *to see* after the expression *He came*; so does the Cambridge manuscript (D). Our translators, in using the word *haply*, left the lead of Tyndale and Coverdale, followed the Rheims version (*happily*), and thus returned to the translation of Wycliffe and the Vulgate (*forte*). The word so rendered however (ἄρα) brings into view a different idea from that of *chance* on the one hand, or *good luck* on the other. It has an illative force, and means, in such an instance as the present, *that being the case*, that is, *it being the case that the tree had leaves*.

He might find anything. Literally, *He will find anything* (εὑρήσει). He came to the fig tree to see, by actual inspection, if anything eatable was to be found. But the evangelist, instead of reporting historically the aim of our Saviour, carries us back in imagination to the scene, and sets us down, chronologically, beside our Lord, at the very time when He was approaching the tree. Hence he says, *if He will find*, instead of *if He might find*.

Thereon. Or more literally, *therein*, or *in it*, within the umbrageous circumference of the tree.

And when He came to it. Or, very literally, *upon it*, that is, *close upon it*, so *close to it* as to be, as it were, *on it*.

He found nothing but leaves. Was He then disappointed? Had He 'erred' in seeking for fruit? 'If,' says Augustine, 'He really sought for it, then He erred.' (*Si vere quæsivit, erravit*: *Serm*. lxxxix. 4.) The evangelical and reverential Witsius does not use the word 'erred'; but he maintains (*haut illubenter*) that our Lord was 'truly ignorant' (*revera ignorasse*) whether there would be any fruit on the tree or not. (*Meletemata, X., De Ficu Maledicta*, § 4.) Episcopius too held the theory of *true ignorance* (*Responsio ad Quæstiones*, § 9); and Calvin himself alleges that there is 'nothing absurd' in the idea. Wolf too adopts it, and puts it strongly thus: 'He abdicated for the time the use of His omniscience.' Our Lord was acting, says Witsius, not as *God*, not even as *Mediator*, but simply as *a man*, who 'grew *in wisdom*,' and therefore *in knowledge*. But certainly it was not simply as *a man* that He acted when He forthwith 'answered and said, No man eat fruit of thee hereafter for ever'; and it seems to be sharp discrimination to find in that judicial sentence the superhuman element, while the merely human element is recognised in the investigation that immediately preceded it. Augustine says that He only *feigned to seek for fruit* (*finxit*). His phrase is tantamount to that of Euthymius Zigabenus, *He simulated* (ὑπεκρίνατο). But he no sooner gives expression to the idea than he finds that he has to confront the objection that '*feigning*' or '*fiction*' *is, to all appearance, as inconsistent as 'erring' with perfection*. Hence he discrimi-

the time of figs was not *yet.* 14 And Jesus answered

nates between legitimate or 'laudable,' and illegitimate or 'criminal,' *fiction,* and elaborately contends that the fiction in the case before us was laudable, because it was *figuratively significant.* (*Serm.* lxxxix., §§ 1-6.) He means that it was *a kind of figure of speech.* It was a *figure of action.* It was, as Cardinal Cajetan represents it, *a parable in act.* If there were any necessity for employing at all, in reference to such action, the word *fiction,* then it was not a fiction in morals, but a kind of literary fiction, a symbolic or hieroglyphic representation of spiritual realities. Augustine was undoubtedly right in the substrate of his idea. Our Lord took occasion from the relation of His own physical hunger to a certain pleasant and nutritious fruit, to illustrate to His disciples some great spiritual verities, into the reaches of which it was of the utmost moment for them to get glimpses. See next clause and next verse. See also *Comm.* on Matt. xxi. 19.

For it was not the season of figs. This statement has occasioned to expositors and critics, needlessly, an immensity of perplexity, issuing in a perfect forest of tangled controversial and conjectural literature. Schöttgen gave up in despair the attempt to explain it. He honestly said : " I cannot interpret it, or account " for it; and I prefer to avow my ignorance, than to make myself ridiculous by "the proposal of ineptitudes" (*nugas effutiendo: Horæ Hebraicæ,* i., p. 171). De Wette says, 'I find it absolutely unintelligible' (*ich finde ihn schlechthin unbegreiflich: Handbuch,* in loc.). Toup too despaired, and, measuring objective possibility by his own subjective inability, denounced the expression as an ignorant gloss that had been, by some unhappy accident, foisted into the text. (*Emend. in Suidam,* p. ii., p. 219.) Wassenbergh ultimately acquiesced in this decision. (*De Glossis Nov. Test.,* in loc.) Scholten also, but looking at the whole subject from a very different standpoint, speaks of the expression as 'a senseless glossema.' (*Het Oudste Evangelie,* p. 225.) Friedrich C. Baur does not impugn its genuineness, but he regards it as evidence of Mark's mental poverty (*Armuth*), and liability to misconception (*Missgriff*), whenever he let go the leading-strings of Matthew! (*Marcusevang.,* p. 90.) Michelsen also regards the expression as senseless, but supposes, not only that it was absent from the text of the Proto-Markus, but also that, as it stood originally in the text of the Deutero-Markus, it was precisely the reverse of what it now is. He supposes that it stood thus, *for it was fig season* (ἦν γὰρ ὁ καῖρος σύκων). It came to be transmuted into its present form, as he imagines, when 'some one or other,' with a little more sense than the evangelist, noticed that passover time was 'not' the time of figs! (*Het Evang. van Markus,* pp. 22, 30.) It is a curious fact, when looked at in connection with this conjecture of Michelsen, that the 'not' is wanting in the Anglo-Saxon version. The translator apparently had not been able to account for it, and therefore quietly left it out. Rolof suggested, in his dissertation on the subject (*De Ficus Imprecatione*), whether we might not read the expression interrogatively, *for was it not the season of figs?* Woolston proposed the same translation (*Miracles,* iv., p. 28). And Heinsius, having the same idea substantially as Rolof, suggested that we should alter the 'breathing' of the negative particle (οὗ for οὐ), and by that means annihilate the negation. He would translate thus, *for where He was it was the season of* *figs.* (*Exercitationes*, in loc.) It is an ingenious suggestion, and was approved of, at least to a qualified extent, by the illustrious Gataker (*Marc. Antonin.*, ix. 10). It was adopted too by Sir Norton Knatchbull; and le Cene introduced it into his French translation of the Bible. And yet it is too ingenious by far, besides being geographically untenable. Passover time was 'not' the time of figs on Mount Olivet. Rilliet is totally mistaken when he says that 'figs are ripe in Palestine about the middle of the month of March'; they *never* are so, he antedates the earliest fig season by at least a full quarter of a year. And yet the same mistake was unwittingly committed by Lambert Bos and Wolle, when they proposed to render the phrase *for it was no (longer) the time of figs*, that is, *for the time of figs was past.* The 'early figs' or 'boccôre,' the earliest, the 'precursors,' were in June; the 'summer figs' were in August; the 'winter figs' survived the leaves. What then are we to make of the evangelist's saying? Wakefield, working on the same basis of conception as Heinsius, only leaving the text unaltered, advocates a transposition of reference, and, in his version, makes an actual transposition of clauses. He renders the verse thus: "*And, seeing a fig tree at a distance with leaves on, He went, if He might chance to find some fruit upon it; for the season of gathering figs was not yet come: but when He got up to it, He found nothing but leaves.*" He supposes apparently that the evangelist is accounting for the reasonableness of searching the tree for figs, *inasmuch as they could not, at that season, have been all gathered off.* If the season of gathering figs had been past, it might have been unreasonable to have expected to find any. It would at all events have been unreasonable to have inferred, from the fact that none were found, that the tree was barren. Such is the representation of the case that Wetstein gives, whose view is coincident with that of Wakefield. Iken also contends for the same interpretation, in his dissertation on the subject (*De Ficu ad imprecationem Serv. Exarescente*). Archbishop Newcome likewise took the same view, and hence, in his *Revision of the Authorized Translation*, inserted in a parenthesis the words '*but, when He came to it, He found nothing but leaves.*' The Unitarian 'Improved Version' adopted this parenthesis; while Principal Campbell and Edgar Taylor transposed the clauses after the manner of Wakefield; so too, in substance, Bland, Holden, Lange. It is an ingenious shift of exegesis; but a real *shift* nevertheless, and quite unnatural, more particularly if the phrase *fig season* denote, as it evidently does, not specifically *the time of gathering figs*, but generically *the time when figs are ripe and ready for gathering*. (See Deyling's *Dissertation* on the phrase, iii., § 29.)

What then? Has conjecture exhausted itself? Far from that. Bishop Hammond supposes that the expression means 'the year being unseasonable for that fruit.' Le Clerc, in his French Testament, took the same view, *for that season had not been favourable for figs.* So too Goesgen in his *Dissertation* on the subject (§ 44); and Hombergk, and Bornemann (*De Glossematis*, p. xlix.). Most unnaturally however on both philological and exegetical grounds. Had the *fault*, so to speak, been in the season, the *blame* could not attach to the tree. Elsner saw this, and hence tried (*invitâ Minervâ*) another shift. He supposed that the meaning must simply be, *for there was no crop of figs on that tree!* Alberti's shift, though not so utterly vapid as to the 'letter,' is still more objectionable as to the 'spirit,' *for the figs were not yet ripe on that tree.* They would however, he adds, be so by and by! (*Observationes*, in loc.)

Triller's shift is unobjectionable in 'spirit,' but most objectionable as a matter of philology; he thinks that the word *season* has no reference to time, but to the locality where the tree was, or, better still, to the constitution of the tree itself, *for there was no aptitude for figs in the tree*. (See his long note in Bernard's edition of *Thomas Magister*, pp. 489-491.) Hoogeveen's shift of punctuation is still more objectionable, both as a matter of philology, and as a matter of natural history. He renders the passage thus, *He found nothing except leaves; nothing at all (οὐ γάρ). It was the time of figs.* (*De Particulis*, pp. 920-1.)

But what then are we to do with the vexed expression? We are manifestly just to take it as it stands, and to interpret it, without 'vexation,' according to its plain and obvious sense. Our Saviour found nothing but leaves on the tree, *because it was not the season for figs*. The remark is a good reason for the fact *that He did not find figs to eat*. And it was of importance for the evangelist to make it, inasmuch as there is nothing in the preceding context to indicate to the reader, and more particularly to the Gentile reader, the particular time of the year when Jesus was visiting Jerusalem. But why then did our Lord punish, as it were, the tree, for not having figs, when it was not the season of figs? See next verse. And why did He 'come' to it, to see 'if, in accordance with the promise of its leaves, He might find anything thereon,' when He must have known, as well at least as the evangelist, that it was not the time of figs? This leads us at once to the heart of the whole matter, and out of the reach of the whole difficulty. *Our Saviour was not expecting to find figs, in order to satisfy His bodily hunger*. His mind was bent on higher things. "He came "to the tree," says Zuingli, "not for the sake of eating, but for the sake of per- "forming an adumbrative action (*sed aliquid præfigurandi causa*)." It was true 'He was hungry.' *His hunger too was the occasion that gave shape to His adumbrative action, when He went to the leafy tree to see if there was fruit on it*. But in every step that He took toward the tree, and in every act that He performed after He reached it, as in all the details of His engagements before and after, in those memorable Jerusalem days, He was actuated by a far profounder 'hunger' than that of the body. If this be ignored, the whole action of our Lord in the case before us, and the whole peculiarity and mystery of His life and death, become an inexplicable enigma.

Grotius caught sight of the reality of the case, but overdid its exposition. He interprets the expression thus, '*He hungered*: namely, after the salvation of the Jewish people represented by the fig tree.' It is a true idea, and takes into account ninety-nine proportional parts of the whole reality of the transaction, while too many expositors have stuck on the remaining hundredth, and paltered with it. But it merges nevertheless out of view, unnecessarily and violently, the physical 'occasioning cause' of the whole parabolic action. Even Theophylact, galled as he was by the difficulties which beset his superficial view, had insight sufficient to say 'but Jesus hungered for their salvation.' And Cardinal Cajetan, with his keener eye, saw deeper, and with his masterly hand touched the case thus: "Jesus knew that it was not the time of figs; but He *came*, com- "posing a figure by the act of coming (*componens figuram actu veniendi*)." This hits the nail on the head, and rivets the correspondence of the outer and the inner. In this act of 'coming' the Lord was engaged in composing and enunciating part of His parable. In the act of searching, after He had come,

15] ST. MARK XI. 313

and said unto it, No man eat fruit of thee hereafter for ever. And his disciples heard *it*.

15 And they come to Jerusalem: and Jesus went into the

He was composing and enunciating another part. And then in the sentence which He passed, after careful judicial examination, He composed and enunciated another part still. The adumbration, after the manner of Ezekiel and other Old Testament prophets, is complete. In the oral parable of *the barren fig tree*, as preserved in Luke xiii. 6–9, there is something analogous. The proprietor of the vineyard '*came seeking fruit*.' It is on a corresponding principle of graphic anthropomorphic representation, that we read in Genesis that, when the cry of Sodom and Gomorrah was great and their sin was very grievous, the Lord said, "*I will go down now and see whether they have done altogether according to the cry of it, which is come unto Me; and if not I will know*." (Gen. xviii. 21.)

VER. 14. **And He answered.** Note the word *answered*. Petter says it is 'an Hebraism'; but that explains nothing. The tree, as Bengel remarks, is regarded as having *refused to give fruit*. The people, whom the Saviour had in view as He spoke, had covered themselves indeed with the leaves of religious profession; they had been too forward in that respect. But, as regards 'the fruit of righteousness,' they were not merely wilfully backward; they were wilfully barren. Not only was there no fruit fit for eating, there was no promise of such fruit. There were no young figs or 'grossi.' (See Altmann's *Observationes*, ii., p. 445.)

And said to it, No man eat fruit of thee. That is, *It is My pleasure that no one should eat fruit of thee*. Our Lord was thinking of the Jews as 'a peculiar people,' formed into a peculiar Messianic community, enjoying peculiar privileges, and lying under the obligation of a peculiar vocation. All this peculiarity was to 'cease and determine.' The world was no longer to be dependent on Jews, as Jews, for spiritual nourishment and enjoyment.

Henceforward. Or *hereafter*, or more literally, *any longer*. More literally still, according to the double negative in Greek, *no longer* (μηκέτι). It is implied that the tree had been probably fruit-bearing in former times. The Jewish people *had been* useful in the world.

For ever. An excellent translation, though there is no reference to *eternity* as we now understand that word. Tyndale's version is also excellent, though not quite literal either, *whill the worlde stondith*. The phrase cannot be made intelligible by a very literal rendering, *to the age*.

"I hope," says the scoffing Woolston (iii. 8), "He asked leave beforehand "of the proprietor." But there is not the shadow of evidence that the tree was private property; and He who came seeking was the Great Proprietor.

And His disciples heard it. They were listening, in an attitude of attention, to what their Master said.

VER. 15. **And they come to Jerusalem: and He entered into the temple, and began to cast out.** That is, to *drive out*, as the word is rendered in Luther's translation, and in Bengel's, and Zinzendorf's.

temple, and began to cast out them that sold and bought
in the temple, and overthrew the tables of the moneychangers,
and the seats of them that sold doves; 16 and would not suffer
that any man should carry *any* vessel through the temple.

Them that sold and them that bought in the temple. Namely, lambs for the
passover supper, and oxen for specific sacrifices. A market for these animals
was allowed, by the priests, in some of the ample spaces belonging to the court
of the Gentiles. So thoroughly had the spirit of trade invaded the sphere of the
spirit of devotion. It would have been well indeed to have had accommodation
for the beasts in the vicinity of the temple; but to take them inside, and to
sell and buy and haggle there, was a climax of indecorum and irreverence.

And overthrew the tables. A fine exemplification of the primary import of
the word *overthrew*. We should now say *overturned*, only in *overthrew* there
is the additional idea of violence implied. Wycliffe's translation is *turnyde
upsodoun*.

Of the money-changers. Or, as the Rheims has it, *of the bankers*, the money-
traders who, for a certain *agio* or premium, were ready to give Jewish money in
exchange for the coins of the countries from which the worshippers had come.
The business of such traders was in itself most important. But it was shameful to erect their stalls in the very courts where devotional worship was to be
performed.

And the seats of them that sold the doves. Or *pigeons*, for the accommodation
of such as required to offer that kind of sacrifice, and of poor mothers and
others, who could not afford costlier offerings. See Lev. v. 7, xii. 6-8, xiv. 22,
xv. 14, 29; Num. vi. 10.

Matthew, in *his* picture of our Lord's procedure at Jerusalem, gives the detail
of the temple purgation under the head of the first day's proceedings. (Chap.
xxi. 12.) We need not be surprised at this. There was neither in his case,
nor in that of Mark, any scientific attempt to exhibit in their *Memorials* a precise chronology. But it is possible that the purgation may have extended over
more days than one, for it is scarcely to be supposed that the traders would be
so overawed as to make no attempt to re-establish their position. They would
imagine no doubt that they had rights. They would have a licence, it may be
presumed, obtained from the sacerdotal authorities, and most probably by
purchase.

VER. 16. **And He would not suffer.** An admirable idiomatic translation. It
is literally, *and He did not suffer* or *permit*.

That any one should carry a vessel through the temple. Principal Campbell
has *vessels* instead of *vessel*. Norton gives it freely *any article*; Mace, *any
baggage*. The word, though strictly meaning a *vessel*, was used by synecdoche
to denote all kinds of *utensils*. Our Lord would not allow that a mere convenience should be made of the temple as a thoroughfare of traffic. There
would be no temptation indeed to use any other portion of it for this purpose,
than the immense court of the Gentiles. It was so immense that tedious
circuits would be avoided, in going from place to place, by passing through it.
And then, *being only the court of the Gentiles*, it was not regarded by the super-

17 And he taught, saying unto them, Is it not written, My house shall be called of all nations the house of prayer? but ye have made it a den of thieves. 18 And the scribes and chief priests heard *it*, and sought how they might destroy him : for they feared him, because all the people was astonished at his

---

cilious Jews as entitled to that respect which they acknowledged to be due to the other parts of the enclosure. But our Lord set His foot on all such disdainful distinctions, and the profane practices to which they led.

VER. 17. **And He taught, and said to them** (καὶ ἔλεγεν αὐτοῖς). Our Lord gave reasons for His conduct, reasons that were intended and fitted to instruct the people.

Is it not written? Or as Luther gives it, *Stands it not written?*

My house shall be called a house of prayer for all the nations; but ye have made it a den of robbers. See John x. 1, 8, in which *robbers* are expressly distinguished from *thieves* (κλέπται). Our Saviour intimates that a system of unblushing robbery, or fleecing, was carried on by the traders who transacted business in the court of the Gentiles. Exorbitant profits were extorted from the people who needed to purchase sacrifices or to obtain exchange of moneys. Coverdale however goes too far when, in imitation of Luther, he renders the phrase, *a denne of murthurers*. The word *den*, or rather *cave*, is evidence that our Lord was referring to *robbers* as distinguished from *thieves*. (See Trench's *Synonyms, sub voce*.) He thinks of *a cave in the mountains* as the rendezvous and retreat of highwaymen. What a transformation for the temple ! Instead of *a den*, Mace has *a harbour*.

VER. 18. **And the chief priests and the scribes.** The leading men of the sanhedrim.

Heard it. The reference is not simply or principally to what our Saviour had just said to the traders, but also to what He had done in driving them out.

And sought. This verb is in the imperfect tense (ἐζήτουν), and, as distinguished from the aorist of the preceding verb, it embodies an idea of incompleteness, *and began to seek*.

How they might destroy Him (ἀπολέσωσιν not ἀπολέσουσιν). It was a foregone conclusion that He must be destroyed ; *but how to effect His destruction*, that was the question. In the use of the word *destroy*, as distinguished from *kill* or *put to death*, there is a reference to our Lord as a Power, or living Energy in society.

For they feared Him. The verb is in the imperfect tense, *they stood in fear of Him*. Their fear was the reason why, instead of laying hands on Him at once, they planned and plotted, or *sought*, 'how they might get rid of Him.'

Because all the people. Or more literally, *For the whole crowd*, namely, that was collected within the precincts of the temple.

Were astonished at His teaching (διδαχῇ). The word is not so much objective, *the thing taught*, as subjective, *the teaching*. See chap. i. 22, 27, iv. 2. It was the strange imperial power of the great Speaker that amazed them. He

doctrine. 19 And when even was come, he went out of the city. 20 And in the morning, as they passed by, they saw the fig tree dried up from the roots. 21 And Peter calling to remembrance saith unto him, Master, behold the fig tree which thou cursedst is withered away. 22 And Jesus answering saith

---

spoke home to their hearts and consciences, and swayed them, they knew not why or how.

VER. 19. **And whenever even was come** (every day as evening set in). Literally, *And whenever it became late.* The gates of the city would be shut then, as now, at sunset.

He went forth out of the city. To some spot or other on His favourite mount of Olives, where there would be multitudes of pilgrims from Galilee and other places. See ver. 11.

VER. 20-24 constitute a paragraph corresponding to Matt. xxi. 20-22. The chronology in Mark seems to be more explicit, and the narration less *conglomerate*, than in Matthew.

VER. 20. **And as they were passing by in the morning.** Namely, on their return to the city. Note the *they*. The Saviour is for the moment shaded off behind His disciples.

They saw the fig tree withered from the roots. Luther's version, adopted by Coverdale, is free, *to the root.* So Mace, *to the very roots.* But the pole of the evangelist's representation is better, for no doubt the blight would operate from within outward, and thus from below upward.

VER. 21. **And Peter, calling to remembrance.** Or simply, *recollecting.* The original participle however is passive. He was, on occasion of seeing the tree, *reminded*, viz. of the whole transaction of the previous day.

Saith to Him, Rabbi. "The ordinary title of honour," says Petter, "which "the disciples used to give unto our Saviour."

Behold. The word is used absolutely, *Look!* or *Lo!*

The fig tree, which Thou cursedst, is withered away. Or better, and more literally, *has become withered* (ἐξήρανται). The *away* is superfluous, and inapposite too, inasmuch as the tree was too solid to have disappeared on withering, as might have been the case with a mere flower. The *away* is omitted in the Rheims, and is wanting in Wycliffe; it was introduced by Tyndale. *Which Thou cursedst:* it is Peter's word, but not inappropriate, though possibly he might not at the time have a fully developed view of the Lord's action. The Lord *cursed*, not passionately, but judicially, and 'in a figure.'

VER. 22. **And Jesus, answering, saith to them.** He addresses not Peter only, but the whole circle, for they were all no doubt correspondingly affected and interested.

Have faith in God. Very literally, *Have faith of God.* The genitive however represents the object, not the subject, of the faith, and hence the translation given in our Authorized version is correct. The same construction occurs in

unto them, Have faith in God. 23 For verily I say unto you, That whosoever shall say unto this mountain, Be thou removed, and be thou cast into the sea; and shall not doubt in his heart, but shall believe that those things which he saith shall come to

Gal. ii. 16, 20, where we read of 'the faith *of Jesus Christ*,' and 'the faith *of the Son of God*,' rather obscure expressions in English idiom. We can readily speak of 'the love *of God*,' meaning, according to circumstances, either the love *of which He is the subject*, or the love *of which He is the object*. But the phrase *the faith of God*, or *the faith of Christ*, has not got fixed, in its objective signification, into an easy-going idiom. Hence, Dr. Adam Clarke so entirely misunderstood the import that he supposed the words *of God* to be a kind of oriental or Hebraistic adjective, equivalent to *great*, 'Have strong faith.' When the Saviour says, *Have faith in God*, He means, *Have faith in the illimitable resources of God*.

VER. 23. **Verily I say unto you.** A favourite formula, with our Saviour, of solemn assurance.

Whosoever should say to this mountain. Viz. this mount of Olives on which we are standing. *Whosoever should say*, or *If any one should say*.

Be thou taken up. Or *Be thou raised up*, viz. from thy foundations. The verb is frequently rendered *to take up*, as in Mark ii. 9, 11, 12, vi. 29, 43, viii. 8, 19, 20, 34. It is rendered *to lift up* in Luke xvii. 13; John xi. 41; Acts iv. 24; Rev. x. 5.

And thrown into the sea. A fine vivid idea, representing, in a bold hieroglyphic manner, a great result. The Saviour did not mean that it would ever be desirable that the mount of Olives should be literally torn from its socket and hurled into the ocean. If however it were desirable, it would take place. But He meant that there would be occasion, within the moral area of human experience, for changes as great intrinsically, and every way as remarkable and difficult, as the transference of mountains. 'By the mountain,' says Zuingli, 'He understands whatsoever things are arduous.'

And should not doubt in his heart. That is, *in his mind*. No amount of mere words, or vehement utterance of words, or loud profession, will be of any avail. The thing signified by pious words or pious profession must be present in the interior of the being. And that interior must not be distracted by an internecine contention of confidence and no-confidence, trust and distrust, in reference to the action of God. Utter moral impotence would be the result of such intestine distraction. There is really no room for legitimate doubt in reference to the desires which are the offspring of faith; and it is to *such desires only* that the Saviour refers. *All such desires are invariably fulfilled.* They cannot but be fulfilled; for they really root themselves in the desires of God Himself.

But should believe that what he says. It is likely that the autographic expression was singular (ὅ instead of ἅ), *the thing which he says*. This is the reading of the Sinaitic and Vatican manuscripts, as also of 'the queen of the cursives' (33), and of Tischendorf, Tregelles, Alford.

Cometh to pass (γίνεται). The present tense is employed to bring out the

pass; he shall have whatsoever he saith. 24 Therefore I say unto you, What things soever ye desire, when ye pray, believe that ye receive *them*, and ye shall have *them*. 25 And when ye stand praying, forgive, if ye have ought against any:

---

idea of absolute certainty. It is as if it had been said, *comes, as a matter of course, to pass*.

He shall have it. Or, *It shall be to him*.

VER. 24. Therefore. That is, since it is the case that *faith in God* efficaciously unites the believer to the omnipotence of the Almighty.

I say to you, All things whatsoever ye pray and ask for, believe that ye have received them. Viz. in the purpose of God. In the Cambridge manuscript, or *codex Bezæ* (D), the verb is in the future, *Believe that ye shall receive* (λήμψεσθαι). In the Alexandrine manuscript (A), on the other hand, and in many others, both uncial and cursive, the verb is in the present, *ye receive* (λαμβάνετε), the reading of the Received Text, and therefore reproduced in King James's version. But in the Sinaitic and Vatican manuscripts (אB), as also in C L Δ, the verb is in the past, *ye received* (ἐλάβετε). And this is the reading that has been received into the texts of Lachmann, Tischendorf, Tregelles, Alford. Rightly: for it is a reading which would never have suggested itself as an emendation. It puts the Saviour's idea in the strongest possible form. His disciples were to be as assured as they would be *if they had received*. "It shall "come to pass that *before they call, I will answer*; and while they are yet "speaking, I will hear" (Isa. lxv. 24).

And ye shall have them. Literally, *And they shall be to you*. God knows beforehand the prayers that are about to ascend, and sends on His answers in anticipation. A great promise; and available not to apostles merely, but to all believers. Comp. Matt. vii. 7–11; 1 John iii. 22, v. 14, 15; Jas. i. 4, 5, v. 15. *Every desire of the human heart, which is the progeny of faith in God or faith in Christ, will be fulfilled.* (Ps. cxlv. 19.) It is in absolute coincidence with the desire of God's own heart. Should there be, interwarped or mingled with it, any atom of desire that is not in coincidence with the Divine will, then the true believer, in the heart of his heart, desires that that desire should not be fulfilled. When his real prayer is stripped of all its unessential accessories, it is found that the presentation of that particular item is an excrescence, and forms no part at all of the essence of his petition.

VER. 25. An essential condition of prevailing prayer, for any object whatsoever, is specified. And whensoever ye stand praying. The common attitude assumed in prayer is here incidentally specified, *standing*.

Forgive if ye have aught against any one. *Aught*. See on chap. vii. 12. Wycliffe has *ony thing*; Tyndale, *eny thinge*; Coverdale, *ought*. *Forgive*: absolutely and unconditionally? Yes, so far as private feeling is concerned, and as far as the well-being of society will permit. As there are limits however to the Divine forgiveness itself, so there are corresponding limits to legitimate human forgiveness. Parents must sometimes punish; not to gratify ignoble passion, but for the welfare of their children (Prov. xiii. 24), and for the maintenance of wholesome parental authority. Magistrates must sometimes

ST. MARK XI.

that your Father also which is in heaven may forgive you your trespasses. 26 But if ye do not forgive, neither will your Father which is in heaven forgive your trespasses. 27 And they come again to Jerusalem : and as he was walking in the temple, there come to him the chief priests, and the

---

punish ; not to gratify a spirit of personal revenge, but to guard the interests of the community. Private persons must sometimes prosecute and sue ; not from a narrow spirit of malevolence, but from a spirit of broad benevolence. In all cases a forgiving spirit may be cherished, and will by Christ's disciples be felt and fostered.

That. Or, *In order that.* The word brings into view one of the aims which it will be legitimate for Christ's disciples to have in view when forgiving.

Your Father also who is in heaven may forgive you your trespasses. Note the *also,* i.e. *on His part, as you on yours.* In some circumstances the action of God is conditioned on the action of men ; for, as Creator, Father, and Governor, He is not the Absolute One, but Relative. Comp. Ps. xviii. 25, 26 ; Jas. iv. 8. It is legitimate for Christ's disciples to have in view their own forgiveness ; but it would be altogether illegitimate and selfish to be either solely or supremely under the influence of that motive.

Ver. 26. This verse, **But if ye do not forgive, neither will your Father, who is in heaven, forgive your trespasses,** is omitted altogether from the texts of Tischendorf and Tregelles ; and it is condemned as ' adulterate ' by Fritzsche. These critics regard it as ' freely ' borrowed from Matt. vi. 15. It is noticeable that it is wanting in both the Sinaitic and the Vatican manuscript (א B), as well as in L S Δ, as also in some important manuscripts of the Coptic, Armenian, and Æthiopic versions. It is wanting too in Erasmus's editions of the text, and in his Latin translation. In the *Annotations* of his first edition he says that it is not in the Greek manuscripts. In the *Annotations* to the second and subsequent editions he says that it is wanting in most Greek manuscripts, but present in some, and that therefore, and because the words are found in ancient authorities, *he has added them.* They *are not added however.* Luther too omitted them in all his editions of his translation ; and the omission continued for long after his death. It is a matter of no exegetical moment whether they be admitted or omitted. But the external evidence in favour of their admission is, if numerically considered, very preponderant ; while, as regards the internal evidence, there is nothing to allege against their retention that might not with equal propriety be urged against the counterpart statement in ver. 25, which is of unquestionable genuineness. If the verse be genuine, it shows us that the Saviour readily diverged, in His discoursing, from the miracle of the blighting to the still more practical, and in some respects more difficult, subject of personal forgiveness.

Ver. 27-33, a paragraph corresponding to Matt. xxi. 23-27 and Luke xx. 1-8.

Ver. 27. **And they come again to Jerusalem.** *To,* or *into.*

And as He is walking about in the temple, there come to Him the chief priests, and the scribes, and the elders. Representatives of the sanhedrim. There had

scribes, and the elders, 28 and say unto him, By what authority doest thou these things? and who gave thee this authority to do these things? 29 And Jesus answered and said unto them, I will also ask of you one question, and answer me, and I will tell you by what authority I do these things. 30 The baptism of John, was *it* from heaven, or of men?

---

probably been an extemporized meeting of the council, or of its principal members, to consider what should be done. See ver. 18.

VER. 28. **And they said to Him, By what authority.** Literally, *in what authority*. Authority has a sphere *within which* it is operative. The *what* denotes *quality* (ποίᾳ). The inquisitors wished to know the *quality* or *kind* of the authority under which our Lord acted.

Doest Thou these things? The reference is doubtless to the authoritative cleansing of the court of the Gentiles. See ver. 15-17.

And who gave Thee this authority to do these things? Literally, *in order that Thou mayest do these things* (ἵνα). Instead of the conjunctive *and*, the Sinaitic and Vatican manuscripts have the disjunctive *or* (ἤ), which represents the second question as but another phase of the first. Tischendorf has accepted this *or*, and so have the English Revisionists. But it is probable that it is a transcriber's emendation, simplifying the relationship of the two queries. It is a matter of option to run the queries into unity, or to keep them apart as representing two distinguishable, though affiliated, elements of the case. The kind or quality of authority may be discriminated from its source. It might, for instance, be merely that of a rabbinical reformer, or that of a Divinely commissioned Messiah.

VER. 29. **And Jesus said to them, I will also ask you.** Or, more literally, and as the Rheims has it, *I also will ask you*, i.e. *I, on My part*. The *also* however, along with the pronoun (κἀγώ), is omitted in the Vatican manuscript and a few other authorities; and it is hence left out by Tischendorf and Tregelles. On insufficient grounds.

One question. A free but excellent translation. It is *one word* in the original (ἕνα λόγον); and such is the Rheims translation, and Wycliffe's, 'o word.' Coverdale has 'a word'; Tyndale, 'a certayne thinge.'

And answer Me, and I will tell you by what authority I do these things. It is again '*in*' *what authority* in the original. See ver. 28. The Saviour, though eminently 'meek and lowly,' yet stood erect, in the presence of His inquisitors, on a pedestal of dignity.

VER. 30. The question was as follows: **The baptism of John, was it from heaven, or from men?** Was it a truly Divine or a merely human ordinance? Did it bear the impress of the Divine will, or merely of a human assumption? It was a crucial question to the priests, scribes, and elders, and was eminently fitted to determine whether they were qualified, in their present mood, to understand the ground or reason and reasonableness of our Lord's procedure. See next verse. The 'baptism' of John is specified representatively, in consequence of its conspicuousness in his ministry. But the idea, as Zuingli cor-

answer me. 31 And they reasoned with themselves, saying, If we shall say, From heaven; he will say, Why then did ye not believe him? 32 But if we shall say, Of men; they feared the people: for all *men* counted John, that he was a prophet

---

rectly remarks, is, *The mission of John, was it Divine, or merely self assumed and human?*

Answer Me. He would give them leisure for deliberation; but He insisted on a determinate answer. As He spoke, they would feel the presence of an indescribable authority and majesty.

VER. 31. **And they reasoned with themselves.** That is, *among themselves*, turning to one another. Tyndale's version is, *they thought in themselves*, but the preposition employed (πρὸs) naturally suggests the idea of conference.

Saying, If we shall say, From heaven; He will say, Why then did ye not believe him? It is noteworthy that in reasoning with one another it was not their aim to get such an answer to our Lord's query as would embody the truth, or even their own conviction in reference to the truth. They simply, on a plane of low expediency, considered what would serve their purpose as inquisitors. They therefore came to the conclusion that it would be inexpedient to say that John's baptism was from heaven. They dreaded that, if they should make such an answer, they would expose themselves to the retort that they had paid no heed to his message, either as it regarded themselves or as it regarded the Messiah. John had not been welcomed by them as a herald of Divine news. He had been to them, on the contrary, as a thorn in their side.

VER. 32. **But should we say.** The *if* of King James's version is wanting in almost all the great manuscriptural authorities, and is hence omitted not only by Lachmann, Tischendorf, Tregelles, Alford, but also by Bengel, Matthæi, Knapp, Scholz. It was disapproved of by Mill (§ 1344), and suspected by Griesbach; and it was omitted from the Complutensian edition, and the two ' O mirificam ' editions of Robert Stephens. The sense of the clause is not affected by the omission.

From men. The evangelist leaves us to supply what, in the estimation of the inquisitors, would be the result of such an answer. The inquisitors themselves deemed it prudent to be silent. Hence they would, by shrug of shoulder, or by finger on mouth, or by some other movement, indicate *aposiopesis*. In some editions a point of interrogation is put after the alternative, *But should we say, Of men?* This point is given by Robert Stephens in his second ' O mirificam ' edition, that of 1549, and it has been adopted, not only by Bengel, but also by Lachmann and Tischendorf. It is approved of too by Meyer. It is just another and earlier form of representing the hypothetical or deliberative nature of the expression. But it is not needed in English, Greek, or German.

They feared the people. We are left to extract from this historical expression the idea which was in their minds, but which they would not like to bring out to one another in explicit words, *we fear the people* (Matt. xxi. 26).

For all verily held John to be a prophet. It is a rather rugged expression, but it represents a real ruggedness in the original, *held John indeed that he was a*

indeed. 33 And they answered and said unto Jesus, We cannot tell. And Jesus answering saith unto them, Neither do I tell you by what authority I do these things.

CHAPTER XII.

1 AND he began to speak unto them by parables. A *certain* man planted a vineyard, and set an hedge about *it*,

---

prophet, that is, *held John to be indeed a prophet*, a man inspired by God to make known Divine ideas. (See chap. vii. 6.)

VER. 33. **And they answered Jesus, and say, We know not.** Or, as Wycliffe has it, *we witen nevere*. It was an unconscientious answer, their real idea being, if they had only possessed sufficient moral manliness to have uttered it, *We think it inexpedient to say*.

And Jesus saith to them, Neither tell I you by what authority I do these things. Our Lord acted on a principle at once of equity and of dignity. Since they dealt unconscientiously in reference to John's testimony, He was justified in retributively withholding from them, in present circumstances, His own testimony. It became too His superior position; for He was above them, even as John was, only to a much higher degree. If they had been conscientiously seeking or wishing to ascertain His true position and authority, they had His works to enlighten them; and He would have rejoiced to have added such words as might have been of still further service.

CHAPTER XII.

THERE is no winding up of a distinct department of narrative at the conclusion of the preceding chapter. The break into a new chapter is topical only, as a matter of convenience in lection and reference.

VER. 1-12 constitute a paragraph which is parallel to Matt. xxi. 33-46 and Luke xx. 9-19.

VER. 1. **And He began to speak to them in parables.** *To them*, that is to the inquisitorial representatives of the sanhedrim, who had asked Him to produce His credentials for interfering in the affairs of the temple. See Matt. xxi. 28. There would however be an immense concourse of people clustering about, who would in part overawe the deputies of the council, and constitute at the same time the great body of our Lord's auditors. See Luke xx. 9. *In parables :* Or, as it is in Tyndale's version, *in similitudes*. Such too is the import of Luther's translation of the word (*Gleichnisse*). See, on the radical import of the term, chap. iii. 23.

A man planted a vineyard. Our Lord draws, as was His wont, His illustration from common life and familiar objects. Palestine was emphatically a vine-growing country, and fitted, in consequence of its peculiar configuration and climate, for rearing the very finest grapes.

And set a hedge about it. Or, *And surrounded it with a fence*; it might be

ST. MARK XII.

and digged *a place for* the winefat, and built a tower, and let

a wall (Prov. xxxiv. 31); it might be *a quickset hedge* (Prov. xv. 19); or it might be a combination of both (Isa. v. 5). "In addition," says Horatio B. Hackett, "to a stone wall, or as a substitute for it, the Eastern vineyards have "often a hedge of thorns around them. A common plant for this purpose is "the prickly pear, a species of cactus, which grows several feet high, and as "thick as a man's body, armed with sharp thorns, and thus forming an almost "impervious defence." (*Illustrations*, p. 109.) This cactus hedge is much used about Joppa for instance; but still it is of itself no sufficient defence against jackals, and some other wild animals, which abound in Palestine, and infest the vineyards about the vintage season.

And digged a pit for the winepress. Or, more simply and correctly, *digged a wine-vat*. The *wine-fat* or *wine-vat* was not *digged* in the sense of being delved out of the soil, and hence Wycliffe's translation *and dalf a lake* is not appropriate. But it was *digged* in the sense of being *scooped* out of the rock. See Isa. v. 2 (margin). Tyndale's translation is peculiar, *and ordeyned a wynepresse*, that is, *and set in order a wine-press*. Multitudes of the wine-vats referred to are still to be found in the vicinity of Palestine; and from them we learn that, a sloping rock being selected, a trough was hollowed out, two or three feet perhaps in depth, and four or five, or more or less according to circumstances, in length and breadth. This was the *winepress* proper. Then immediately below in the same slope, another trough, or lake (*lacus*), as the Romans called it, of smaller dimensions, was cut out, with an aperture or apertures communicating with the compartment above. Into this the juice of the grapes ran when they were trodden in the press. Thence it would be taken out and put into large bottles or skins. The word that is used in the passage before us (ὑπολήνιον), though freely used to designate the whole complex excavation, properly denotes this lower trough or lake. (See Bruinier *De Verbis compositis*, p. 170.) The word used by Matthew (xxi. 33, ληνός) brings prominently into view the upper compartment, the *press* or *torcular*. Comp. Rev. xiv. 19, 20; xix. 15. The translation of the Geneva of 1557 is exceedingly periphrastic, *and digged a pit to receave the lycour of the wynepresse*.

And built a tower. That is, a watchtower, which however would also serve as a residence during the vintage season. "Watchtowers," says Horatio B. Hackett, "are confined chiefly to vineyards and orchards. . . . They caught my "attention first as I was approaching Bethlehem from the south-east. They "appeared in almost every field within sight from that direction. They were "circular in shape, fifteen or twenty feet high, and, being built of stones, looked "at a distance like a little forest of obelisks. I was perplexed for some time "to decide what they were. My travelling companions were equally at fault. "Suddenly, in a lucky moment, the words crossed my mind, *a certain man* "*planted a vineyard, and set an hedge about it, and built a tower, and let it out* "*to husbandmen, and went into a far country* (Mark xii. 1). This recollection "cleared up the mystery. There before my eyes stood the towers, of which I "had so often read and thought. . . . Those which I examined had a small "door near the ground, and a level space on the top, where a man could sit and "command a view of the plantation. I afterwards saw a great many of these

it out to husbandmen, and went into a far country. 2 And at the season he sent to the husbandmen a servant, that he might receive from the husbandmen of the fruit of the vineyard. 3 And they caught *him*, and beat him, and sent *him* away empty.

"structures near Hebron, where the vine still flourishes in its ancient home." (*Illustrations*, p. 108.) Dr. W. M. Thomson had experience of the watchfulness of the watchmen on these towers. Passing on a certain occasion through the vineyards of Lebanon, " I was," says he, " suddenly startled by a long loud note " of warning, swelling up the steep cliffs of the mountains, and responded to " by others before and behind, ringing together in concert, and waking the " echoes that sleep in the wadies and among the rugged rocks. Then one of the " watchmen, leaving his lofty station, descended to meet me with hands laden " with the best clusters for my acceptance, and this too without money and " without price. Courteously accompanying me to the end of the vineyards, he " then dismissed me with a graceful bow, and the prayer of *peace* on his lips. " If however one attempts to take without permission, these watchmen are " required to resist even until death, and in the execution of their office they " are extremely bold and resolute." (*The Land and the Book*, p. 599.)

And let it out to husbandmen. Literally, *and gave it out*, viz. in his own interest (such is the force of *the middle voice*). A company of practical vine-dressers became the lessees of the vineyard. The word rendered *husbandmen* (γεωργοῖς) properly means *earthworkers*, *tillers*, or as Wycliffe has it, *tilieris*. The English word *husbandman* had originally a higher meaning, denoting *a man who was the centre and band of a household establishment*.

And went into another country. The translation in King James's version is, *and went into a far country*; but there is nothing in the original (καὶ ἀπεδήμησεν) to vindicate the insertion of the word *far*, at least in its modern acceptation. The idea simply is, *and went from his own people*, that is, *and went abroad*. The translation of Tyndale, Coverdale, the Geneva, and the Rheims is, *and went into a straunge countre*. He went *forth* or *furth* from his native land, a common enough practice in our Lord's days, when travelling was general, and Rome was a great centre of attraction for the wealthy in all surrounding lands. For the application of the parable see on ver. 9.

VER. 2. **And at the season.** The vintage time.

He sent to the husbandmen a servant. Instead of *the husbandmen* Tyndale has it, freely, *the tennauntes*.

That he might receive from the husbandmen of the fruits of the vineyard. A partitive expression. The rent was to be paid in kind, the servant or commissioner being no doubt instructed by his lord to commute the fruits received into money, by means of some of the traders in the adjoining city.

VER. 3. **And they took him.** They caught hold of him.

And beat him. Or, as the Rheims has it, *bette him*. Tyndale and Coverdale have *bet*. They cudgelled him. Literally, *they flayed him*.

And sent him away empty. They dismissed him with nothing in his hands.

ST. MARK XII.

4 And again he sent unto them another servant; and at him they cast stones, and wounded *him* in the head, and sent *him* away shamefully handled. 5 And again he sent another; and him they killed: and many others, beating some, and killing some.

Ver. 4. **And again he sent to them another servant.** Perhaps of a higher position, or of a more commanding nature.

It is then added in King James's version, *and at him they cast stones*. But this clause is wanting in the Sinaitic, Vatican, and Cambridge manuscripts (ℵ B D), as well as in L Δ, 1, and 33 'queen of the cursives.' It is wanting too in the Italic, Vulgate, Coptic, Sahidic, and Armenian versions. Griesbach suspected it (*Comm. Crit.*); Mill condemned it (*Prol.*, p. xliii.). Lachmann, Tischendorf, Tregelles omit it. Rightly, most likely. It would be introduced at first into the margin to explain what follows, or as an import from Matt. xxi. 35. Omitting the word translated *they cast stones*, the clause runs thus, **and him they wounded in the head.** The word employed occurs nowhere else in the form in which it is found in the Sinaitic and Vatican manuscripts and L (ἐκεφαλίωσαν). They '*headed*' *him*, that is, apparently, they '*broke his head*,' as Tyndale and Coverdale have it. *They inflicted severe and dangerous wounds upon his head.* The word is in the other manuscripts spelled differently (ἐκεφαλαίωσαν), and is a common enough term, but never occurring in the sense which, if it be the true reading, it must bear in the passage before us. It everywhere else means *to reduce to a head or heads, to sum up.* Wakefield ingeniously supposes that here the meaning is, *they dealt with him summarily*; but such a use of the verb, with a person for the object of its action, is unexampled and unlikely. It is probable that the evangelist's word had been a term that was common, in the acceptation accorded to it, in certain circles of provincial society, though it had never got the sanction of any classical writer. (See Lobeck's *Phrynichus*, p. 95.)

And shamefully handled (καὶ ἠτίμασαν). Or *dishonoured*, or as Tyndale has it, *all to revyled*, that is, *altogether reviled* It is the generic summing up of all that the imagination naturally suggests when we think of what must have been done to the man, in the affray in which his head was seriously wounded.

Ver. 5. **And he sent another.** His forbearance was something remarkable. **And him they killed.** Him they killed *outright*.

And many others, beating some, and killing some. An incomplete expression, but easily understood. There should not be, as is common in the modern editions of King James's version, a mere comma after the preceding clause, *and him they killed*, and then a semicolon after the expression *and many others*; thus detaching to a distance the subsequent clauses. The result of this punctuation is, that the mind is led to carry forward the word *killed* to the expression *and many others*. That however is not the idea of the original. The clause *and him they killed* is self-contained and complete, with its pronoun preceding its verb, as in the two foregoing clauses. But when it is added *and many others*, the mind of the writer or speaker, instead of looking backward in the direction of the verb of the preceding clause, looks forward, in quest as it were of some more comprehensive verb that would embrace in its import not only actual murder, but also such other violent and shameful treatment as might stop short

6 Having yet therefore one son, his well-beloved, he sent him also last unto them, saying, They will reverence my son.

---

of murder. Instead however of laying hold of such a verb, the mind assumes it, and then proceeds to trace out derivatively the two courses of conduct pursued, *cudgelling some, and killing others outright*. The punctuation of Blayney's " *Standard Edition* " of the English Bible, published in 1769, is wrong, having the now current comma after *killed*, and the semicolon after *others* ; but in the *editio princeps* of 1611, as also in the second issue of that year, and in the four succeeding folio editions of 1613, 1617, 1634, and 1640, as in almost all the other editions, larger or smaller, for many years, the punctuation is correct: a colon after *killed*, and only a comma after *others*. Tyndale's punctuation is the same, and so is that of the Rheims ; so was that of Beza, in all his editions, as also of Bengel in all his, Greek and German. It was the punctuation too of Robert Stephens in his last edition, that of 1551. It is reproduced in the Elzevir, and in Mill.

VER 6. **Having yet therefore one son, his well beloved.** A very touching statement, especially in the original, although there is some difficulty in determining the autographic form of some of the minute details of phraseology. The *therefore* for instance, which is found in the Received Text, is omitted by Tischendorf, Tregelles, Alford. It is omitted in ℵ B L Δ, 1, 33, and in the Coptic, Armenian, and Æthiopic versions. But tinkeringly, no doubt. It seems to embarrass the connection ; and certainly it would never have been inventively thrust in if it had been originally wanting. It is easy to account for its omission, but difficult to conjecture a reason for its intrusion. And yet in such a style as Mark's it is interestingly significant. It recalls attention to the fact that all the messengers hitherto sent had failed to have effect upon the lessees. The lord of the vineyard *therefore* thought of a superior kind of messenger. *He had therefore yet one.* Instead of *having* ($\mathit{\xi\chi\omega\nu}$), Tischendorf, Tregelles, Alford read *he had* ($\mathit{\epsilon\tilde{\iota}\chi\epsilon\nu}$) on the authority of ℵ B C² L Δ, 33. It is the reading too of the Philoxenian Syriac, and is supported by the Peshito Syriac. We are disposed to look upon it as genuine. Its inartificiality is obvious ; it does not naturally coalesce with *therefore*. The participial reading smooths the expression, and would not, one should imagine, have ever been altered had it been original. But the artless evangelist, though evidently meaning what is expressed by the participial reading, sets down his thoughts, with less nicety of interdependency, in a semi-detached way, *he had therefore yet one*, *a beloved son* ; he had *one* individual more, whom he could send with some prospect of success, *a beloved son*. Wycliffe renders the adjective *most dereworth* ; the Geneva, *dere beloved* ; the Rheims, *most deere* ; Tyndale, *whom he loved tenderly.*

He sent him last to them, saying, They will reverence my son. Very literally, *they will turn-themselves-in-upon-themselves* ($\mathit{\dot{\epsilon}\nu\tau\rho\alpha\pi\dot{\eta}\sigma\text{o}\nu\tau\alpha\iota}$) *in relation to my son*. When erring or unworthy people thus turn-themselves-in-upon-themselves, they naturally feel *ashamed* of themselves (see 1 Cor. iv. 14 ; 2 Thess. iii. 14 ; Tit. ii. 8), and are hence humiliated and *reverent*.

7 But these husbandmen said among themselves, This is the heir; come, let us kill him, and the inheritance shall be our's. 8 And they took him, and killed *him*, and cast *him* out of the vineyard. 9 What shall therefore the lord of the vineyard do? He will come and destroy the husbandmen, and will give the vineyard unto others. 10 And

---

VER. 7. **But those husbandmen.** Very literally, *But they, the husbandmen*, or as Wycliffe has it, *the tenauntis*, i.e. *the tenants*.

Said among themselves. Or, more literally, *to themselves*, that is, *to one another*.

This is the heir; come, let us kill him, and the inheritance shall be ours. An idea as infatuated as it was ferocious and unjust. Why should they presume that their lord would be tolerant for ever?

VER. 8. **And they took him, and killed him, and cast him forth out of the vineyard.** We may suppose, either that the idea is that *they killed him, and then cast his body outside of the vineyard*, or that the evangelist, after stating the lamentable issue of the struggle, *they killed him*, returns, on the principle exemplified in such an expression as '*far and near*,' to the specification of one of the preliminaries of the tragedy, *they dragged him in the struggle outside the vineyard, and there despatched him*. It is probable that this latter view is his idea. Comp. Matt. xxi. 39; Luke xx. 15. But it is by no means necessary or warrantable to make, with Mace, Heumann, and Principal Campbell, a transposition of clauses in translation. It is as unwarrantable to employ, with Norton, the word *body* in the last clause.

"Who did this?" asks Richard Baxter, looking to the application of the parable; and he answers, "The only national church on earth." "No wonder," he adds, "that no innocency or worth can preserve the Lord's ministers from "their rage, and from being cast out of the vineyard."

VER. 9. **What, therefore, will the Lord of the vineyard do?** The question was addressed to the audience, and we may conceive, if we choose, of our Lord pausing for a reply. Comp. Matt. xxi. 40, 41.

We could not learn from Mark or Luke whether any of the auditors of our Lord answered His question. But if any did, our Lord took up the answer and iterated it, as from Himself, thus making it His own. It is this, His own answer, which is here recorded, **He will come and destroy the husbandmen.** Putting them, as they deserve, to a violent death.

And will give the vineyard to others. To farm it for him. More worthy lessees would be obtained.

The application of the parable is obvious. God was the Lord of the vineyard. The vineyard was an enclosed portion of the human race, the chosen and peculiar people. They were enclosed within fences, that were requisite to protect them from the evil influences rampant in the world at large. There should have been valuable results from such advantages, and from the labours of the appointed workers and overseers. There should have been results acceptable to God. Such results however were not forthcoming. The priests and

have ye not read this scripture? The stone which the
builders rejected is become the head of the corner: 11 This

---

other leaders of the people were shamefully unfaithful to their obligations.
But the Lord was gracious, and sent prophet after prophet to remonstrate with
them, and to induce them to repent of the error of their ways, and to act in
conformity with the covenant to which they had given their assent. But they
would not; and only 'shamefully entreated' the noble men who had been sent
to them as commissioners. By and by, after the greatest patience and long
suffering, God sent 'His only begotten Son,' Jesus Himself, the speaker of the
parable, to put all things to rights. As He spoke to the priests, and scribes,
and elders, He was engaged in His work. But He foresaw that they would
persist in their mad and wicked opposition, and finish it by imbruing their
hands in His blood. The result would be that their peculiar privileges would
be taken from them, and handed over to others. There *is* consequently a
change in the theocracy. There is still indeed an enclosure; but it is no longer
given to mere formalists of priests, and paltry pedants of scribes, and sordid or
worldly minded elders, to have office and power. The theocracy is spiritual,
and all its officers and administrators are spiritual. The fence that surrounds
it is spiritual; and, in the fence, there is a spiritual door of entrance for all who
are spiritual.

VER. 10. **Have ye not read even this scripture?** Very literally, *And did ye
not read this scripture?* that is, in substance, *And did ye never, at any point of
time past, read this scripture?* Note the continuative expression, '*And* did you
not' (οὐδέ). Only one query is formally uttered; but two are implied. It is as
if the Saviour had said, '*Do you not* understand the application of My parable?'
'*and*' *did you never* read this scripture? The two things coalesce. *This
scripture:* viz. Psalm cxviii. 22. The term *scripture* is, in its own nature,
indefinite in its applicability, and may be used with propriety in reference either
to a single written statement or to a sum of such statements. It is used here
with reference to a single written statement, a small component part of that
which is emphatically '*the*' *Scripture*, in Luke iv. 21, John xix. 37, Acts i. 16.
The stone which the builders rejected. *The stone;* literally, *a stone. Rejected. Refused* is Coverdale's rendering, and Tyndale's; and is the word that
is employed in the Authorized version of the Psalms. *Dispisid* is Wycliffe's
rendering. The term means *disapproved*, and suggests that the stone was subjected to scrutiny, and then condemned and rejected. The reference is probably
to some incident that had occurred in the building or rebuilding of the temple.
Some stone had been disapproved of for the foundation. It was too insignificant! But ere the building was finished, that very stone was elevated into a
most conspicuous position. The incident is turned to account by the psalmist,
and by our Lord. It is regarded as adumbrating the treatment accorded to the
Messiah by those who, in the preliminary dispensation, had to do with the
erection of the temple of humanity, the great spiritual worship-house of the
Most High.

The same was made the head of the corner. Or, more literally, *this became
head of a corner*. More literally still, *this became into a corner's head*. The

was the Lord's doing, and it is marvellous in our eyes.
12 And they sought to lay hold on him, but feared the
people: for they knew that he had spoken the parable
against them: and they left him, and went their way.

---

reference is not, as is generally supposed, to a chief corner stone *in the foundation* (Eph. ii. 20; 1 Pet. ii. 6), but to a corner stone *in the cornice*. Jesus, in the temple of humanity, is both; but He cannot be represented in the twofold relation, within the limits of one and the same hieroglyphic picture. He is at the head moreover of *every* corner, as well as *at every corner's base*. He is at once the foundation all round and round, and the crown all round and round, of the entire erection. But the architectural figure will not stretch to body forth the vast reality. (See *Comm.* on Matt. xxi. 42.)

VER. 11. The quotation continues. **This was from the Lord.** More literally, *this came to pass from the Lord.* The reference of the *this* has been disputed. The word is feminine in the original (αὕτη), as if it referred to the *head* of the corner, a word that is also feminine (κεφαλή). But it is more probable that, being taken from the Septuagint, it is a mere verbatim translation of the Hebrew pronoun (זאת), which, although really meaning *this thing* (that is, here, *this occurrence*) is idiomatically of feminine gender. (See *Comm.* on Matt. xxi. 42.) The occurrence referred to, the elevation of the despised stone to the cornice at an angle, or rather, the elevation of the Person adumbrated by the stone, was traceable to the overruling agency of the Lord. His heart and His hand were in the matter.

And it is marvellous in our eyes. The occurrence is a fitting object of human wonder. And such 'wonder' is not merely 'the daughter of human ignorance.' It is the sister of admiration, and may be allied to the very highest possibility of knowledge.

VER. 12. **And they sought to lay hold on Him.** *They*, the priests, scribes, and elders. They were anxious to get our Lord arrested, so that they might, in some way or other, get rid of Him. *They sought.* They desired, and consulted, and schemed.

And they feared the multitude. That is, *the crowd that was there and then surrounding our Saviour.*

For. This introduces a reason for what is stated, not in the immediately preceding clause, but in that which goes before it, and which was of overshadowing significance.

They perceived that He spake the parable against them. Or, more literally, *in reference to them.* Their *amour propre* was thus wounded. Meyer unnaturally interprets the *they* as designating the crowd, in order to avoid the hyperbaton, or vaulting, of the reference in the reason-rendering particle. He has hence to assume a leaping back of the reference in the *they* of the following clause.

And they left Him, and departed. They could not at that time make anything more of the case.

13 And they send unto him certain of the Pharisees and of the Herodians, to catch him in *his* words. 14 And when they were come, they say unto him, Master, we know that thou art true, and carest for no man : for thou re-

---

VER. 13-17 constitute a paragraph corresponding to Matt. xxii. 16-22 and Luke xx. 20-26.

VER. 13. **And they send to Him.** *They*, the baffled priests, scribes, and elders. Meyer fancies a contradictory account in Matthew, because the Pharisees are there specified (xxii. 15). But what more likely than that the scheme should originate with a certain class? and indeed in an individual mind? They send **certain of the Pharisees.** Picked men no doubt, able, unscrupulous, and subtle.

And of the Herodians. Politicians, who had lost faith in everything supernatural and Divine in Judaism and the Jewish Scriptures. The radiance from above that rested on the superincumbent darkness was, to them, mere moonshine. The aspirations of the ancient 'fakeers' of the nation, and thence of the masses of the people, after a glorious royalty and theocracy, were, in their estimation, reasonably and sufficiently realized in the Herodian dynasty. See on chap. iii. 6.

That they might catch Him in talk. Or, as it is in Wycliffe, *in word*. But more literally yet, *by word*. The term *word* however is far from doing justice to the Greek original (λόγῳ). We have no precise English equivalent. It is rendered *His talk* in Matt. xxii. 15. The aim of the 'hunters' was to get hold of our Lord *by means of something that He might say*. They resolved to construct, out of their discordances, a snare for getting Him to say something that might be available against Him, either with the Jewish people on the one hand, or with the Roman authorities on the other. The verb rendered *they might catch* (ἀγρεύσωσιν) is a 'hunting' word. They wanted to throw a lasso round Him, or otherwise entrap Him. We shall see how, in what follows.

VER. 14. The scheme has been agreed upon, and the 'hunters' stealthily approach their game. **And when they were come, they say to Him, Master.** Or *Teacher*. No doubt, the word actually employed would be the Jewish one, *Rabbi*. They would use the title obsequiously, as if they were animated by feelings of the profoundest deference.

We know that Thou art true. *True*, that is, ingenuous, honest, transparent. There is no veneering in Thy teaching. The word *true* in Greek is beautiful and suggestive, ἀληθής, *unconcealed, real*. It is probable that the 'hunters' had at bottom a kind of actual faith in the honesty of our Lord. The very consciousness of their own duplicity and unreality might suggest, on the principle of contraries, the turn which they gave to their compliment.

And carest n t for any one. False in a certain sense, for our Lord cared for every one. But *it was true* in the sense intended by the 'hunters.' Our Lord would not trim to please any one ; He would not shrink from declaring 'the *present* truth,' however much offence it might give to the high and mighty on the one hand, or to the many headed and many handed multitude on the other.

14] ST. MARK XII. 331

gardest not the person of men, but teachest the way of God in

For Thou regardest not the person of men. A strange kind of expression, full of phraseological fossils. The word *person* originally meant *a mask, through which a play-actor made sounds* (per-sona). It then denoted *a certain character played*; and thence *a self regulating actor, a self conscious agent*. In the expression before us it has an intermediate meaning, *the outward appearance*; and such is the translation of the word in Myles Coverdale's version (1535), and in Lord Cromwell's Bible (1539). The Geneva and the Rheims have *person*. Tyndale has, still more freely, *degree*. But the Greek word (πρόσωπον) neither corresponds to *degree* nor *person*, nor exactly to *outward appearance*. It simply means *face* or *countenance*, so that the 'hunters' say, *for Thou lookest not into the countenance of man*. What did they mean? Viewing the expression from a purely Greek standpoint, one might suppose that it meant *for Thou regardest not mere appearance, or profession. Thou lookest behind to the real character.* That however is not the idea. The expression has within it the fossil of a popular Hebrew idiom. The phrase *to lift up the face of any one* (נָשָׂא פָנִים) meant, in Hebrew, *to be gracious to him, to show him favour*. When suppliants came before a king, in those olden times when the idioms of the Semitic tongue were being formed, they prostrated themselves on the ground. If the monarch was disposed to be gracious, *he lifted up their countenances*, that is, *he allowed them to look him in the face and to present their case before him*. He thus too himself looked upon their faces, and beheld them graciously. If he was resolved however not to be favourable, he refused to let them look up. In Hebrew idiom *he turned away their countenances*, and caused them *to return back whence they came*. See 1 Kings ii. 16, 17, 20 ; 2 Chron. vi. 42. It was bountiful in a sovereign to lift up the countenance of a suppliant. But if the sovereign was acting at the time as a judge between contending parties who had carried their appeal to his bar, then, to have prejudged the case by lifting up the face of one of the litigants, while the other's countenance was turned away, would have been criminal partiality. Hence the evil of *respect of persons* in a judge, or the lifting up of the face of one of the contending parties at the bar. (Ps. lxxxii. 2 ; Prov. xviii. 5 ; Mal. ii. 9.) But the principle of impartiality extends its application beyond the professional acts of professional judges. All men are more or less judicial, and they should be impartial when they judge. More particularly should they guard against bias in the presence of the rich and the great. Public teachers very particularly, or preachers and rabbis, should be constantly on their guard against favouritism for persons who owe their elevation in society to causes that have no connection with moral superiority. Hence the adroitness of the address of the 'hunters' who came to our Lord, *for Thou lookest not into the face of men*. It is as if they had said, *Thou art far removed from a spirit of partiality and favouritism. There is no fear of Thee having regard to the great, however great, when Thou givest Thy judgment regarding any act or course of action.*

But of a truth teachest the way of God. Not *the way in which God Himself goes*, but *the way which He has laid out for men to go in*. *Of a truth :* Literally *upon truth*, that is, says Euthymius, *truly*. And such is the translation of Tyndale, Coverdale, and the Geneva. The 'hunters' tried to flatter our Lord

truth : Is it lawful to give tribute to Cæsar, or not? 15 Shall

by saying that His teaching was based *upon truth*. All up to this point was 'flattering,' and flattering, and clearing of the way. Now comes the lasso: **Is it lawful to give tribute to Cæsar, or not?** That is, *Is it lawful, or is it not, to pay taxes to the Roman emperor?* It is often supposed that the reference of the querists was to the capitation-tax imposed on the Jewish people by the Romans. So Schleusner, Bretschneider, Wahl, Robinson, Schirlitz, Grimm, among the lexicographers. So too Hesychius in his lexicon (*sub voce κίνσος*), and the writer of the *Codex Bezæ*, who, in place of the generic Latin term *census*, used by the evangelist, substitutes the specific Greek term for poll-tax (ἐπικεφάλαιον). But the question addressed to our Lord derived its significance not from the particular form of any of the taxes imposed by the victorious Romans. It drew deeper, *Had any Gentile a right to tax the chosen people of God? Should any Jew recognise such a right?* The Pharisees in general had high ideas of the prerogatives of the chosen people. When they paid their taxes to the Romans, it was under a silent protest; and they would have been glad to witness the inception and consummation of any movement that would have lifted the foreign yoke off the neck of the people. The Herodians again, though politicians rather than religionists, were of patriotic principles, and wished to see at the head of the nation a Herod, into whose exchequer, in place of that of the Roman emperor, all taxes, dues, or customs should be paid. In their heart they were opposed, like the Pharisees, to the payment of taxes to Cæsar. They knew that Jesus would be well aware of their distinguishing principles. The Pharisees too were sure that He would be aware of their distinctive views. And hence they unitedly hoped that He would not fear to speak out in their presence, if He really was opposed in His heart to the Roman rule. And if He should thus speak out, they had resolved apparently to denounce Him to the Roman governor as disaffected, like Judas of Galilee (Josephus, *Ant.*, xviii. 1 : 6 ; *Wars*, ii. 8 : 1), to the Roman emperor, and politically dangerous to the Roman supremacy. But if, instead of saying *Nay*, He should chance to say *Yea*, they were resolved in that case not to be baulked of their prey, but to denounce Him to the people as basely acting in collusion with their oppressors. It was a cunningly constructed lasso.

Ver. 15. **Shall we give, or shall we not give?** The break in King James's version, between this verse and the former, comes awkwardly in at this place, and no doubt in consequence of some casual oversight or mistake. Robert Stephens in his 1551 edition, the edition in which the verse-divisions were introduced, appropriately postponed the break till after the clause, *Shall we give, or shall we not give?* Beza too. The Elzevirs too. Mill too. And in fact all the critical editions of the Greek text; and the uncritical too. The same postponement occurs in the German, Dutch, and French versions ; and also in the English editions of Wells, Mace, Worsley, Wakefield, Young, Godwin. The awkward break occurs however in the Geneva, and had thence been inadvertently imported into our Authorized version. A more literal translation of the clause would be, *Should we give, or should we not give?* In the former clause, at the

17] ST. MARK XII. 333

we give, or shall we not give ? But he, knowing their hypocrisy, said unto them, Why tempt ye me? bring me a penny, that I may see *it*. 16 And they brought *it*. And he saith unto them, Whose *is* this image and superscription ? And they said unto him, Cæsar's. 17 And Jesus answering said unto them, Render to Cæsar the things that are Cæsar's, and to God the things that are God's. And they marvelled at him.

---

conclusion of the preceding verse, the question concerns a general principle; in this there is reference to the application of the principle to the acting of the people.

But He, knowing their hypocrisy. Or, as Tischendorf gives it, on the authority of the Sinaitic and Cambridge manuscripts, *But He, seeing their hypocrisy* (ἰδών instead of εἰδώς). Their masks could not conceal from His eye. He saw at a glance that they were playing a part on a stage of unreality, for the iniquitous purpose of entrapping Him. They were not wishing advice from Him how to act, neither were they wishing His help to solve for them a perplexing problem. They were simply laying a snare, or constructing a lasso.

Said to them, Why tempt ye Me? Why play recklessly with your consciences in *trying Me*, and *trying to wile Me* to My injury? To *tempt* is to *try*; see on chap. x. 2.

Bring Me a penny. Literally, *a denarius*, the standard silver coin of the Romans, of somewhat less value, so far as amount of silver is concerned, than a shilling sterling.

That I may see it. He wished to intermix the element of ocular demonstration with the remarks which He was about to make.

VER. 16. **And they brought it.** The picture of the scene is so vividly drawn by the evangelist, that we seem to see with our eyes the successive occurrences. The coin is handed to our Lord; He examines it.

And He says to them, Whose is this image and superscription ? As if He had said: *The coin, I perceive, has the likeness of some royal personage stamped upon it; and it bears an inscription or legend. Whose is the likeness ? Whose name is mentioned in the legend ?* The word translated *superscription* does not denote that the name was written *above* the head; it has only reference to the fact that it was written *upon* the coin. Wycliffe renders it *the in-wrytinge*. If he had said *the on-writing*, the translation would have been perfect.

And they said to Him, Cæsar's. *Cæsar* was properly the surname of the Julian family, and in particular of the great Julius; but, being assumed by Octavianus Augustus, became thence for a considerable time attached to his successors in the imperial throne. Purvey and Coverdale render the word *Emperor*. To this day *Kaiser* is the word used in Germany for *Emperor*.

VER. 17. **And Jesus said to them, Render to Cæsar the things that are Cæsar's, and to God the things that are God's. And they marvelled greatly at Him.** They *marvelled*. It is the imperfect tense, *they stood marvelling*. No wonder. Instead of finding Him eager to plunge headlong, as they had expected, into the determination of an exciting political question, and thus into the pit which

18 Then come unto him the Sadducees, which say there is no

they had digged for Him, they saw Him vaulting at a bound to an eminence on the other side of their snare, whence He preaches to them a lesson which could not fail to command the homage of their consciences. He assumes, what could not be denied, that they had relations to Cæsar as well as to God. The currency of Cæsar's coin among them was evidence of the fact. It was hence the case that they had obligations, of some kind or other, to discharge toward him. *See*, said He, *that you conscientiously discharge these. See that you be not merely recipients of benefits. In whatsoever sphere you get, in that same sphere you have to give.* All men have duties to discharge to the civil rulers or magistrates under whose authority they enjoy protection and other blessings. They owe something, they owe much, to society around them, and hence to its representative men. But there is a wider sphere still, that comprehends and dominates all the spheres of social organization. There is the sphere of the Divine and the infinite. Men are placed there; and there they 'live and move and have their being.' There and thence they enjoy all the blessings which make 'being' desirable or delightful. Hence they have duties to perform toward God. Even in relation to Him, infinite though He be, they should not be receivers only; they should be givers too. They should 'render to Him the things that are His,' that is, they should *give away, and from themselves* (ἀπόδοτε), to Him, the things which of right belong to Him. It is their duty, and their privilege too. For even in relation to God ' it is more blessed to give than to receive.' And when He actually gets the things which constitute the fitting tribute of the homage, service, and love, which are His due, then a principle is got hold of which adjusts into its proper proportion the amount of tribute, material or moral, that is due to men. The Saviour thus, instead of leaping into the thicket of a petty political question of the day, ascended a peak of ethical thought, and legislated for all peoples and persons, in all places and times.

VER. 18-27 constitute a paragraph that corresponds to Matt. xxii. 23-33 and Luke xx. 27-38.

VER. 18. **And there come to Him Sadducees.** That is, *certain Sadducees*. The interest in the Great Rabbi got more and more contagious. Within the courts of the temple there would be numerous representatives of all the classes of Jewish society. Some would be walking up and down, wrapped in their meditations, or conversing together; others would be standing in clusters, engaged in keen debate. But Jesus gradually became *the* centre of attraction. Some around Him might be in the secret of the sanhedrim's plot; others would be ingenuously charmed by the wonderful matter, and equally wonderful manner, of His teaching; while others still, big with theological or philosophical self-conceit, would be eager to try their hand in shutting Him up dialectically within one or other of their favourite commonplaces. Among this last class apparently was the knot of Sadducees who now approached, and threw out upon Him their grappling hooks of argumentation.

Who say that there is no resurrection. It is a compound pronoun that is rendered *who*, or *which* (οἵτινες), it represents the Sadducees specified as

resurrection; and they asked him, saying, 19 Master, Moses wrote unto us, If a man's brother die, and leave *his* wife *behind him*, and leave no children, that his brother should take his wife,

---

belonging to a certain class. *They were of that class of people who say that there is no resurrection.* Note the negative form of their tenet. All their distinctive tenets were negative. (See Reuss's article in Herzog's *Encyklop.*) And not only did they object to the doctrine of the resurrection, they objected to the kindred and more comprehensive doctrine of immortality. They seized indeed on the idea of resurrection simply as vantage ground, on which to dispute the idea of immortality. "They deny," says Josephus, "the immortality of the "soul, and the punishments and rewards of hades" (*Wars*, ii. 8: 14). They had thus no basis in their thoughts for the highest and most ennobling of aspirations.

And they asked Him, saying. As follows in ver. 19-23.

VER. 19. **Master.** Literally *Teacher*, or *Rabbi*.

Moses wrote to us. Viz. in Deut. xxv. 5. There follows a conjunction in the original, standing before the quotation (*that* or ὅτι). But it is, as critics say, *recitative*, and therefore not to be translated in English; it simply points demonstratively forward.

If a man's brother die, and leave a wife behind him, and leave no children. It is *no child* in the Vatican manuscript and a few other authorities; and Tischendorf has received that reading into his text. But wrongly. The reading bewrays an annotator's hand, who took into account, lawyer like, that the want of *a single child* exposed the widowed woman to the contingency about to be specified. The word *leave* occurs twice in our translation; but two distinct verbs are used in the original. The first (καταλίπῃ) means properly *to leave down*, at one's feet as it were, and then *to leave behind*; the second (ἀφῇ) means primarily *to send forth*, and thence *to throw up*, *to relinquish*, *to leave*. Wakefield's translation of the whole clause is, *and leave a wife without children*.

That. Literally, *in order that* (ἵνα). It is at this point that the emphasis of what Moses wrote comes in. What precedes is but preamble. The gist and aim of his writing was *in order that* the domestic result hereafter specified might be realized.

His brother should take his wife. Viz. in marriage. Instead of *his wife*, Tischendorf, Tregelles, Alford read *the wife*, under the sanction of ℵ B C L Δ, 1, and the Coptic version. Right. A species of 'communal' relationship is subindicated. The statute must be regarded as relative to some exceedingly offensive matrimonial condition which had prevailed, probably *polyandry*. It is the obverse of the more common *polygamy*, and had, in certain conditions of social degradation, cropt up into use and wont. "Polyandry," says Sir John Lubbock, "is far less common than polygamy, though more frequent than is "generally supposed" (*Origin of Civilization*, p. 115). Sometimes one band of brothers, kenneling in one homestead, would be the common husbands of one wife. "Among the Todas of the Neilgherry hills," says Sir John, "when a "man marries a girl, she becomes the wife of all his brothers as they success- "ively reach manhood, and they also become the husbands of all her sisters

and raise up seed unto his brother. 20 Now there were seven brethren : and the first took a wife, and dying left no seed. 21 And the second took her, and died, neither left he any seed : and the third likewise. 22 And the seven had her, and left no seed : last of all the woman died also. 23 In the

---

"as they become old enough to marry. In this case the firstborn child is "fathered upon the eldest brother, the next born on the second, and so on "throughout the series" (*Origin of Civilization*, p. 74). Sir John says again : "Polyandry is no doubt very widely distributed over India, Thibet, and Ceylon. "In the latter island the joint husbands are always brothers" (*Ditto*, p. 117). When such a custom has unhappily got ingrained in the habits of a degraded people, it is not possible to induce them to leap, at a bound, to a lofty pinnacle of marital purity. The ascent, in general at least, must be gradual ; and hence the utmost that can be achieved by progressive legislators is to take one step upward at a time. It was thus that Moses had to deal with the Hebrews, who had been for so long a period trampled down, in Egypt, into the mire of a degraded servile condition. Hence the statute referred to by the Sadducees. It was no doubt intended to limit the rights of brothers to succession, in place of contemporaneity, and thus to promote as much as might be the development of the idea of monogamy. It would be intended too to protect the interests of widowed females, by giving them, when inheritances were involved, a claim upon those who would obtain their deceased husband's effects. A corresponding custom still prevails, or till recently prevailed, among the Kalmucks. "If a "husband die, his widow becomes the property of his brother, provided the "brother chooses to accept of her." (Clarke's *Travels in Russia, Tartary, and Turkey*, vol. i., p. 315.)

And raise up issue to his brother. Perhaps that the line of inheritance might, as far as possible, run on according to the ideal of the first marriage.

VER. 20. **There were seven brothers.** We may either suppose, with Theophylact, that the Sadducees feigned, for argument's sake, the case which they state ; or, with Petter, that they had got hold of some extraordinary fact which had actually occurred once upon a time, and which, when got hold of by them, became their favourite armoury of argument while debating on their peculiar views. This latter view is probably the more correct.

And the first. The eldest of the brotherhood.

Took a wife, and, dying, left no issue.

VER. 21. **And the second took her, and died;** leaving no issue behind him ; **and the third likewise.** The Sadducees make their argument graphic by spreading out the case. We may imagine that there had been some idiosyncrasy in the physical constitution of the brothers, that developed into fatal results in early manhood.

VER. 22. **And the seven left no issue.** Such is the simple reading of the manuscripts ℵ B C L Δ, and 33. Tischendorf, Tregelles, Alford have received it into the text ; and Meyer approves of it. Rightly.

Last of all the woman also died. *Also*, for sooner or later every one must fall.

resurrection therefore, when they shall rise, whose wife shall she be of them? for the seven had her to wife. 24 And Jesus answering said unto them, Do ye not therefore err, because ye know not the scriptures, neither the power of God? 25 For when they shall rise from the dead, they neither marry, nor are given in marriage; but are as the angels which are in heaven. 26 And as touching the dead, that they rise,—

VER. 23. In the resurrection whose wife shall she be of them? Literally, *of which of them shall she be wife?*
For the seven had her to wife. That is, *to be wife,* or, *had her as wife.* There is nothing however in the original corresponding to *as* or *to.* Wycliffe gives it literally, *hadden hir wyf.* The seven *had her successively a wife.* Wakefield and Norton translate freely, *for all the seven married her*; so Principal Campbell, *for she hath been wife to them all.*

VER. 24. Jesus said to them, Is it not for this cause that ye err? *Err.* or *wander,* viz. from the right view of the subject. We have our word *planet,* or *wandering star,* from the term that is employed (πλανᾶσθε). The expression *for-this-cause,* or *on-account-of-this* (διὰ τοῦτο), looks forward, as Erasmus remarks, to the twofold clause that immediately follows. The interrogative form of the address challenges the assent of the unbiased reason. The ground on which the challenge is supported is found in ver. 25–27.
That ye know not the Scriptures, nor the power of God. Ye do err by not knowing the Scriptures on the one hand, nor the power of God on the other.

VER. 25. For when they shall rise from the dead. *They,* that is, men in general, for by this time the thought has travelled forward from the specific standpoint to the generic. *From the dead :* literally *from among the dead,* or *out of the dead.* But the expression had got to be idiomatically equivalent to *from the state of death.*
They neither marry, nor are given in marriage. A specific phase of conventional marriage customs in relation to females is brought into view. Not only *are they married,* they are *given in marriage.* Comp. 1 Cor. vii. 38.
But are as angels in heaven. In the resurrection state there will not be a repetition, pure and simple, of present conditions; there will be advance of inward and outward development. Love will continue; but in the case of the holy it will be sublimed. 'The power of God' is adequate, not only to the re-formative, but also to the trans-formative changes that may be requisite; and His wisdom will see to it that they be in harmony with the perfectibility of individual personality and the general procession of the ages. Even on earth there are loftier loves than those that are merely marital.

VER. 26. But as touching the dead. The Saviour turns from the consideration of the plastic 'power of God' to the doctrine of the Old Testament Scriptures.
That they are raised. This is the position that was gainsaid by the Sadducees, and affirmed by their theological opponents. It is expressed, with a kind of technical precision, in the form of a thesis.

z

have ye not read in the book of Moses, how in the bush God spake unto him, saying, I *am* the God of Abraham, and the God of Isaac, and the God of Jacob? 27 He is not the God of the

Have ye not read? It is the aorist tense. As if it were said, *Did ye never read?* In the Book of Moses. The Pentateuch. (Exod. iii. 2-6.)
What follows in our Revised version and in the original is not the adverb *how*, but the expression *in the bush*, or more literally, *on the bush* (ἐπὶ τοῦ βάτου). The *how* comes immediately after, and should, by King James's translators, have been kept in that, its proper place. Erasmus however, and Tyndale, Coverdale, Calvin, Beza transposed the adverb, putting it, in their various versions, before the expression *in the bush*. None of these critics saw that the expression had a titular and topical reference to a certain portion of the Pentateuch. Such however is undoubtedly the case, *in the passage or paragraph on the Bush*. Comp. Rom. xi. 2. It was customary for the Hebrews to refer in this manner to outstanding portions of their Scriptures. See Jablonsky. The Greeks and Romans had a corresponding custom. Bloomfield says that Beza explained the expression in this, the natural way; but the fact is emphatically otherwise. In every one of his editions Beza gives and defends the transpositive interpretation; and his influence, we doubt not, weighed with King James's translators. Almost all modern critics however oppose his view; and Luther and Wycliffe, in their respective versions, give the natural and correct translation. Wycliffe's is as follows: *have ye not read in the book of Moyses on the bousche, how God seide to him.*

How God spake to him, saying, I am the God of Abraham, and the God of Isaac, and the God of Jacob. Such is the statement on which the Saviour erects His argument. See next verse.

VER. 27. **He is not the God of the dead but of the living.** This is the best-supported reading. See Tischendorf's eighth edition. The Saviour considers (1) that the declaration of God to Moses demonstrates that Abraham, Isaac, and Jacob are alive; and He assumes (2) that if Abraham, Isaac, and Jacob are really alive, there will be a resurrection. He does not argue the validity of His assumption; for He knew that the real difficulty of the Sadducees did not concern the specific doctrine of the resurrection, over and above the generic doctrine of immortality. It centred in the generic doctrine, "for the Sadducees "say that there is no resurrection, *neither angel nor spirit*" (Acts xxiii. 8). Josephus merges out of view altogether their difficulty in reference to the resurrection, when he says, "They take away the belief of the immortal dura- "tion of the soul, and the punishments and rewards in hades" (*Wars*, ii. 8: 14). Their objection to the idea of resurrection was, in short, just their outward and pictorial way of objecting to the idea of immortality. It was the external robe of a more inward idea. Prove to them immortality, and they would no longer contend against resurrection; for the idea of resurrection was to them, and, when looked at from the highest standpoint, it is to all, simply the complement of the idea of immortality. It resolves itself into this, *If men are to live for ever, they will live in their entire selves*. Everlasting life will not be realized in a fragmentary existence, as in an arch of being springing for ever but half way over. The Saviour agreed with the Sadducees in this conception;

ST. MARK XII.

dead, but the God of the living: ye therefore do greatly err.

and hence, assuming it, He contented Himself with demonstrating *that Abraham, Isaac, and Jacob are alive.* The only question that remains therefore is this. *Is the demonstration valid?* It must be; though many a critic, looking only at the surface of the phraseology, has failed to lay his finger on the vital nerve of the argument. The argument, it is manifest, is not caught when the word *am* is laid hold of, *am* as distinguished from the præterite *was*: 'I am the God of Abraham, and the God of Isaac, and the God of Jacob.' There is no *am* in Mark's Greek, and none in the Hebrew of Moses. The argument therefore dips deeper. What is it? God sustained a relation of gracious peculiarity to Abraham, Isaac, and Jacob. He was 'their God.' He opened out, that is to say, in a peculiar manner, in His relation to these patriarchs, the fulness of the resources of His 'Godhead.' Why? Was it because of a feeling of capricious favouritism? Was it to make the specified patriarchs wealthier than all others? Or healthier? Or more cultured? Or more sensuously happy? Or more powerful? No. In these respects they did not excel all others; in several of these respects they were inferior to some others. Consider Abraham himself, the chief of the three. He 'went out, not knowing whither he went,' and 'sojourned in the land of promise, as in a strange country, dwelling in tabernacles' (Heb. xi. 8, 9). So far was it from being the case that he was, in all terrestrial respects, superior to all others. What then? In what way was the fulness of the Godhead lavished on the Hebrew patriarchs? *In a way that had reference to a life to come.* " These all died in faith, not having received the promises. "but having seen them afar off, and were persuaded of them, and embraced "them, and confessed that they were strangers and pilgrims on the earth. For " *they that say such things declare plainly that they seek a country.* . . . God " is not ashamed *to be called THEIR GOD, for He prepared for them a city* " (Heb. xi. 13, 14, 16). If it was not with reference to the life to come, that God became 'the God of Abraham, and the God of Isaac, and the God of Jacob,' then there was nothing peculiar in God's relation to the Hebrew patriarchs. And if all peculiarity of relationship be denied, then all the peculiar Jewish institutions, founded on these relations, were illusory, and 'the book of Moses' was a fable. This however the Sadducees, as self-conscious Jews, were not prepared to admit; and hence the Saviour's demonstration, based on the Scriptures which they and He held in common, was unanswerable and irrefragable. It amounted to this: *If there was at all a patriarchal dispensation, embracing a Messianic or redemptive scheme, and thus involving a divinely commissioned Messiah or redeemer, who was to be in due time incarnated, then there must be a life to come. But there was such a dispensation, if it be the case that God became 'the God of Abraham, and the God of Isaac, and the God of Jacob,' in any distinctive sense whatever.* And then moreover, as Abraham, Isaac, and Jacob took personal advantage of the Messianic covenant into which God entered with them, they 'live.' They have 'life,' 'everlasting life,' in the intense acceptation of the term. They not only exist consciously. Their self-conscious existence is normal, and harmonious with itself. It is ideal life. It is bliss. 'The righteous by faith *shall live*' (Hab. ii. 4; Rom. i. 16, 17.)

Ye do greatly err. The Sadducees entirely misunderstood the mystery and

28 And one of the scribes came, and having heard them reasoning together, and perceiving that he had answered them well, asked him, Which is the first commandment of all? 29 And Jesus answered him, The first of all the commandments *is*, Hear, O Israel; The Lord our God is one Lord: 30 and

---

meaning at once of their own Jewish Scriptures, and of the various ordinances which entered as elements into the peculiarity of the national constitution of their people.

VER. 28-34 constitute a paragraph which corresponds to Matt. xxii. 35-40.

VER. 28. **And one of the scribes came, and heard them reasoning together, and knowing [or rather *perceiving* (ἰδών)] that He had answered them well, asked Him.** It is rather a complicated string of clauses in the original, resolving itself into two clusters: the first, *and one of the scribes came, who heard them reasoning together*; the second, *perceiving that He answered them well, he asked Him*. There should be a pause, in reading, between the two clusters. *One of the scribes*: of nobler nature than the most of the rest, or of more unsophisticated character. *Came*: that is, approached. He stepped forward from the multitude, and respectfully addressed our Lord. *Who heard them reasoning together*: he had listened to the discussion between our Lord and the Sadducees. *Perceiving that He answered them well*. Very literally, *beautifully*. *Admirably*, as it were. Rodolphus Dickinson uses freely the word *ably*. Petter explains thus, 'truly and soundly, as also wisely.'

Asked Him, **What commandment is the first of all?** The *what* denotes quality (ποία). *Of what nature, of what kind, is the first commandment of all?* What is its essence? The expression is one of several possible ways of putting substantially the same question. There is a peculiarity in the gender of the original word *all* (πάντων instead of πασῶν). The logical neutrality of the idea of the things referred to immerges out of sight, for a moment, the rhetorical femininity of the vocable employed. *The first*: 'the principal,' says Wesley, 'and most necessary to be observed.'

VER. 29. **Jesus answered, The first is.** There are great variations in the manuscripts as regards the form of this clause; but they are of no exegetical moment. They seem all to be expansions of the reading, *The first is*.

Hear, O Israel, the Lord our God the Lord is one. See Deut. vi. 4, 5. This is the preamble to the commandment, and is, as Wesley says, 'the foundation of the first commandment, yea of all the commandments.' All the Infinities must be modes of one Absolute Infinity; and that one Absolute Infinity must be the Being of God. If however, instead of the word *God*, we substitute the word *gods*, we annihilate the idea of Godhead; for we have then, in our conception, but parts and parcels of infinity. We have in fact descended from the infinite to the finite.

VER. 30. **And thou shalt love.** 'Love,' says Richard Baxter, 'is the final act of the soul.' It is the soul's essence seeking, in some 'otherhood,' its

thou shalt love the Lord thy God with all thy heart, and with all thy soul, and with all thy mind, and with all thy

---

final end. In its consummation it is the soul's self embracing its perfect 'otherhood.'

The Lord. In Hebrew, *Jehovah*, or *Jahveh*. He is the Perfect 'Otherhood' of the soul.

Thy God. The term *Jehovah* is absolute, but the term *God* is relative. We cannot say, *my* or *thy Jehovah*; but we can say, *my God, thy God, our God*. God is relative to us as the perfect Object of our adoration, obedience, confidence, and love. The fulness of His Godhead is the inexhaustible source out of which we get all that is truly desirable.

With all thy heart. Literally, *out of thy whole heart*. The representation in Matthew (xxii. 37) is different, but harmonious. Our love to God is to drain, not one district only of the heart, or several, but the entire length and breadth of the domain. The word *heart* has not here its modern psychological import of the special seat of the affections. It has its more primitive import of *the interior of our nature*, the centre or core of our complex being, as distinguished from the physical periphery. See chap. ii. 6, 8; iii. 5; iv. 15; vi. 52; vii. 6, 19, 21; viii. 17; xi. 23. (See also Oehler's article on *Herz* in Herzog's *Real-Encyklop.*)

And with all thy soul. Literally, *and out of thy whole soul*. The word *soul*, like the word *heart*, does not denote any particular power, energy, or capacity of the inner nature, but the inner nature itself, under the phase of *the self-conscious life-essence*. The heart *is* the self-conscious life-essence; or, under another phase, it is the sphere in which the life-essence is self-conscious. There is an idea of locality in the word *heart*. The soul is at home in the heart. Hence we do not, in general, speak of *the immortality of the heart*; but we speak of *the immortality of the soul*. Herodotus, in his day, used the same expression: he says that 'the Egyptians were the first who maintained that the soul of man (ἀνθρώπου ψυχή) is immortal' (ii. 123).

And with all thy mind. Or, *and out of thy whole mind*. The word here rendered *mind* (διάνοια) naturally denotes some act of the discriminative intelligence. But, as in Plato's *De Legibus*, (xi. 2,) it is freely and indefinitely employed to designate the mind itself, as the subject of the acts of intellectual discrimination. Plato, in the passage referred to, uses the word to denote that entire hemisphere of our being which is over against the body (σῶμα). The *mind* thus *is* the *heart* and the *soul*; but it is the *heart* and *soul* in that particular phase that brings intelligence into view. 'It is the *mind* that makes the *man*.' There is an etymological connection between the two English words. In Sanscrit the verb *man* means to *think*; and thus '*man*' is impersonated '*mind*.' Man is the being on earth who can see *meanings* in things. And it is hence his duty to draw out of this faculty a constant succession of materials, with which to feed his love to God. It is worthy of observation that the expression, *out of thy whole mind*, has nothing corresponding to it in Deut. vi. 5. There is no antagonism however between the two representations. The superadded clause, as Calvin remarks, 'does not alter the sense.' It is merely

strength. This *is* the first commandment. 31 And the second *is* like, *namely* this, Thou shalt love thy neighbour as thyself. There is none other commandment greater than these. 32 And the scribe said unto him, Well, Master, thou hast said the truth: for there is one God; and there

---

the explicit specification of a part of what *is* latently comprehended in the words *heart* and *soul*.

And with thy whole strength. For man has *strength*, or *ability*, the gift of God. Our responsibility is measured by it. Our whole inner being is *force* or *energy*, just as it is *heart, soul, mind.* There is quadruplicity, as well as triplicity, in our nature. There are indeed manifold multiplicities.

Such is the 'first' of the commandments, in the order of importance. Obedience to it would turn our earth into a paradise. The striving toward it, consciously or unconsciously, is the secret of all the civilization that has hitherto been realized.

VER. 31. **The second is this.** A clause that exists under a great variety of forms in the manuscripts, indicating apparently that it had been modified by transcribers out of some brief original phrase. It would seem to have been modified into harmony with the phraseology of Matt. xxii. 39. Tischendorf and Alford read simply and compendiously thus, *The second, this*, the Vatican reading, and found also in L Δ, and in the Sahidic and Coptic versions. The Sinaitic reading corresponds, *The second is this*. Meyer approves of Tischendorf's judgment.

Thou shalt love thy neighbour as thyself. *Thy neighbour.* Thy neighbours. It is just the circumference of the duty whose centre is represented in the preceding commandment. Whosoever really loves God supremely is emancipated from selfishness; and whenever this emancipation takes place, the unselfish spirit goes out with its love to all kindred spirits around. In imperfect man indeed sometimes the Godward tendency overweighs too much the manward; and sometimes, on the other hand, it is the philanthropic tendency that is 'loaded.' But the two tendencies are not in antagonism. They are complementive, the one of the other; and when either is clear and pure, it involves the other. Let a man love the Father unselfishly, and not merely as an Almighty Servant, and assuredly, when freely and fully developed, he will love, also unselfishly, the Father's family. Let a man, on the other hand, love the Divine family unselfishly, and he too, when freely and fully developed, will assuredly rise in his affection to the Divine Father.

There is none other commandment greater than these. All other commandments are binding, just in proportion as they partake of the essence of these.

VER. 32. **And the scribe said to Him, Of a truth, Master, Thou hast well said that He is one.** Or rather, *And the scribe said to Him, Excellently! Master. Thou hast said truly that He is one.* Excellently! (καλῶς): the phrase is not to be connected, as by Luther, Bengel, Coverdale, Principal Campbell, Norton, Webster and Wilkinson, with the following verb *Thou hast said*. It is in itself, as the Syriac Peshito translator saw, a condensed sentence, self contained, and assuming the form of an exclamation, *Well! Right! Just so! Admirably!*

ST. MARK XII.

is none other but he: 33 and to love him with all the heart, and with all the understanding, and with all the soul, and with all the strength, and to love *his* neighbour as himself, is more than all whole burnt offerings and sacrifices.

Literally, *Beautifully!* corresponding to the German *Schön*, which is Ewald's word. The recent Dutch translators have seized the correct idea, setting the term by itself, and rendering it *Juist*. So too Zinzendorf. *Master:* or, as Wycliffe has it, *Maister*. Literally *Teacher*, that is *Rabbi*, as it is in the Peshito Syriac. *Thou hast said truly that He is one:* The word *God* is wanting in a great preponderance of the best manuscripts, as well as in the Syriac Peshito, Gothic, and Æthiopic versions. It is omitted from the text by Bengel, Griesbach, Matthæi, Fritzsche, Scholz, Lachmann, Tischendorf, Tregelles, Alford. It must be spurious, so that the subject of the preposition has to be mentally supplied. The scribe's mind was full of the idea of *God*, so that it seemed to him to be enough that he should speak *of Him*, without expressly *naming Him*.

And there is none other but He. With this clause the scribe *insensibly* moves off from the attitude of a mere reporter of what our Saviour had 'truly said,' and begins to express independently his own ideas. *There is not another 'God.'* Such is the idea. The great monotheistic truth had taken a strong hold of his mind.

VER. 33. **And to love Him with all the heart, and with all the understanding.** *Understanding* ($\sigma\nu\nu\epsilon\sigma\epsilon\omega s$): a different word from that employed in ver. 30, but having a corresponding import. It properly means *an act of understanding*, but is here freely and indefinitely used to denote the mind as characterized by such acts. So Grimm. The word is finely significant, etymologically considered. It denotes that act by which the mind *sends out its thought to get into company with an object*. When subject and object are joined, an act of understanding is accomplished. The English word *understanding* goes still farther in its significance. It represents that act in which the 'thought' not only associates itself with the 'thing,' but goes to its bottom and gets under it, *stands-under* it.

And with all the strength. It is likely that the scribe confined himself to this triplicity of representation, corresponding to the Hebrew original in Deut. vi. 5, and may thus have used the word *understanding* as substantially equivalent to *soul*.

And to love his neighbour as himself. Literally, and as Wycliffe gives it, *and to love the neighebore as him silf*, that is, *and to love one's neighbour as one's self*.

Is much more ($\pi\epsilon\rho\iota\sigma\sigma\acute{o}\tau\epsilon\rho\sigma\nu$). The idea of quantity is carried into the idea of quality. All that is really meant however by the quantification is the idea of *superiority*.

Than all whole-burnt-offerings and sacrifices. More literally, *than all the whole-burnt-offerings and the sacrifices*, that is, *than all the holocausts* (in particular), *and the sacrifices* (in general), *that are offered upon the altar, in accordance with the prescriptions of the ritual law.* The scribe's mind had got a glimpse of the significance of things, and thus of the supremacy of the moral over the ceremonial.

34 And when Jesus saw that he answered discreetly, he said unto him, Thou art not far from the kingdom of God. And no man after that durst ask him *any question*.

35 And Jesus answered and said, while he taught in the temple, How say the scribes that Christ is the son of David? 36 For David himself said by the Holy Ghost, The Lord said to

---

VER. 34. **And when Jesus saw that he answered discreetly.** The original form of the expression is exceedingly inartificial, *And Jesus, when He saw him, that he answered discreetly.* The inartificiality proved a stumbling-block to some of the early transcribers; and hence the *him* is omitted in the Sinaitic and Cambridge manuscripts, as also in L Δ. Unnecessarily. *Discreetly : sensibly, intelligently*; Wycliffe has *wysely*. *Answered :* No question had been asked; but the scribe's remark was responsive to our Saviour's statement, it was an echo of the truth

He said to him, Thou art not far from the kingdom of God. The *kingdom of God* is, for the moment, pictorially represented as *localized*, like the ordinary kingdoms of the world. The scribe, walking in the way of conscientious inquiry, and thus making religious pilgrimage, had nearly reached its borderland. He was bordering on the great reality of true religion, *subjection of spirit to the sovereign will of God.* The kingdom of God is the community of those who bow to the sceptre of God. In the plane of earth it is realized in an incipient stage. In the plane of heaven it is perfected.

And no man after that. No one thenceforward.

Durst ask Him any question. Viz. in a captious or argumentative way. Every man in the immense surrounding crowd felt that there was such a reach of insight in the Lord that it was in vain to dispute with Him.

VER 35-37 form a little appended paragraph, corresponding to Matt. xxii. 41-45 and Luke xx. 41-44.

VER. 35. **And Jesus answered and said.** Though no question was proposed to Him, yet there were many ideas in the minds of His opponents and of the people in general, which seemed to challenge remark.

As He taught in the temple. While He continued His teaching in the area of the temple.

How say the scribes? *How?* on what principle of consistency is it that they make the representation?

That the Christ is David's son? When the scribes spoke to the people of the promised Messiah, they were accustomed to represent Him as *David's son.* It was a true representation. (See Matt. i. 1 ; Luke iii. 31 ; Rom. i. 3 ; Rev. xxii. 16.) And it was true that He was to mount David's long vacated throne, and to render it more illustrous than ever. (See Acts ii. 30.) But nevertheless, as apprehended by the scribes, it was only a half-truth.

VER. 36. **David himself said in the Holy Spirit.** The Holy Spirit is represented as *comprehending* the royal psalmist, and thus interpenetrating his being.

The Lord said to my Lord. A quotation from a psalm (cx.) which cannot be

my Lord, Sit thou on my right hand, till I make thine enemies thy footstool. 37 David therefore himself calleth him Lord ;

explained, except on the principle that it is *Messianic* on the one hand and *inspired* on the other. (See Reinke's *Messianische Psalmen*, ii., p. 151, ff.) Even Strauss is unable to deny that ' the majority of ancient Jewish interpreters apply the psalm to the Messiah.' (*Leben Jesu*, ii. 6, 79.) *The Lord said:* In Hebrew, *Jehovah said.* To my Lord: that is, to my Suzerain or Sovereign. When King David thus spoke, he had been anticipatively rapt into the far future, where he saw scenes, and heard words, which would no doubt occupy him long in ' searching what and what manner of time,' and what and what manner of event, ' the Spirit of Christ, which was in him, did signify' (1 Pet. i. 11). He was gazing, though most likely he knew it not, on a scene that was consequent on the death, burial, and resurrection of his illustrious Descendant. The scene is laid in heaven; and its chronology, when sacred history holds up its torch that we may see, is coincident with the triumphal ascension of our Lord. While David gazed on the Royal Personage whom Jehovah welcomed to His side, he forgot his own little royalty, and spoke as the humblest seer that ever lived might have spoken, ' Jehovah said to *my* Lord.'

Sit. There is no *thou* in the Greek or Hebrew, for there is no emphasis intended to distinguish the person addressed from other persons. The emphasis has reference to the place of honour to which the person is invited. There is more dignity in the omission than in the insertion of the pronoun.

On My right hand. That is, *On the place at My right hand.* It is better however to merge the *on* altogether, and substitute some other preposition, *Sit at My right hand.* *At* is nearer the import of the Hebrew than *on*; and the expression in Greek is '*from*' *My right hand*, which separates the space to be occupied *from* the person of the speaker. *My right hand :* There is no word for *hand* in either the Greek or the Hebrew. The phrase in Greek is plural, *My right (parts).* Wycliffe has it, *My right half.* The place at the right side of a monarch was the place of highest honour, under himself. In vision David saw the Monarch of the universe pointing *to the place at His right side;* and he heard Him welcoming to that place, as to a second throne, a glorious personage who had just entered. This personage David calls ' my Lord.'

Till I make thine enemies the footstool of thy feet. Note the ' I.' Jehovah is Himself to act. His hand is to be supreme in all the arrangements that are to be conditioned on the accomplished work of the Messiah. Note the expression ' thine enemies.' It touches a sad reality. Christ *has enemies*, the enemies of Christianity, of Christliness, of God, of man. Note the vividly pictorial and artlessly redundant expression ' the footstool of thy feet.' It is borrowed from the customs of a remote antiquity, when men were fierce and rude, and required extremely striking symbols of ideas for their instruction. In such a state of society the necessity of submission to rightful authority, and thus to right and righteousness, would be emphatically taught by compelling some of the ringleaders of anarchy and wrong to act as ' footstools' to the representatives of legitimate order and law.

Ver. 37. David himself calleth Him Lord, and whence is He his son? The

and whence is he *then* his son ? And the common people heard him gladly.

38 And he said unto them in his doctrine, Beware of the

whence is logical. *How comes it to pass that He is his son?* The Saviour would not put the question merely to corner up, and puzzle, or humiliate. He had no love for dialectic feats on the 'diamond cut diamond' principle. His life was too earnest for that. His spirit would be moved with emotion, when He saw how persistently the most learned men of the nation, the accredited interpreters of the sacred writings, skimmed the surface of things, and refused to turn for a moment in the direction of anything different from the most superficial conceits. Hence His question. With their view of the Messiah, as a mere monarch somewhat like David, and in the line of David, it was not wonderful that the scribes did not find anything in Jesus to elicit the echoes of their hopes. They found much that was inconsistent with their fondly cherished anticipations. It was enough for them. They concluded offhand that it was absurd to suppose that He could be the Being to whom the fathers had pointed. They were not in quest of the Divine. They were off the scent entirely, and hence off the track that would have led them to the recognition in our Lord of the fulfilment of the promises made to the fathers. No view of the Messiah could be a true view, that did not take into account that there would be such a complement of elements, in His glorious personality, as would constitute Him at once *David's son* and *David's Lord*.

And the common people. Not quite a correct translation. There is no antithesis intended to the higher classes of society (as might be supposed to be the case in Plutarch, *Opera*, i., p. 34, F). The expression is literally *the numerous crowd* (ὁ πολὺς ὄχλος), and does not mean, as Webster and Wilkinson interpret it, *the greater part of the crowd*, but *the great crowd*. Young and Alford render it, *the great multitude*. Wakefield, *the multitude, which was great*. Comp. Acts xxvi. 24. The expression, without the article, occurs repeatedly in Mark, *a great crowd*. See chap. iv. 1, v. 21, 24, vi. 34, ix. 14. xiv. 43. Here the greatness of the crowd is historically assumed, and it is pictorially referred to in one of those graphic touches, so frequent in Mark, which bewray the hand or tongue of an eye witness.

Heard Him glad y. Literally *sweetly*, that is, *with keen relish, with delight*. The masterliness of the reasoning would tell. The power of the speaking would tell. The transparent elevation and earnestness of the character would tell. And, overarching all, there would be a certain indescribable grandeur of spirit, which would make them feel exalted, as toward God and heaven, in the very act of hearing.

VER. 38–40 constitute a condensed paragraph, parallel to Luke xx. 46, 47. It exhibits in a few touches the sum and substance of what is detailed at length in the 23rd chapter of Matthew.

VER. 38. **And in His teaching He said, Beware of the scribes.** Be *on your guard* in reference to them. Literally, *Look from* them ; look for a way of escape from the onset of their influence. Comp. chap. viii. 15. The *scribes* were the learned class in Jewish society. But they seem to have, in general,

scribes, which love to go in long clothing, and *love* salutations in the marketplaces, 39 and the chief seats in the synagogues, and the uppermost rooms at feasts : 40 which devour widows'

used their knowledge of letters for purposes that were far from being noble. They were puffed up with conceit, and turned their intellectual advantages into an instrument for feeding an insatiable appetite of selfishness. See on chap. i. 22.

Who desire to walk in long robes. The word translated *desire* (θελόντων) is frequently translated *will*, and generally denotes either *wish*, or *wish-and-will*. The scribes *wished and willed* to walk in long robes. It was *their pleasure* thus to walk. They *took pleasure* in the display. Brameld omits the translation of the word altogether. Alford renders it *desire*; Newcome, *like*; Mace, *affect*; and so too Wakefield, Principal Campbell, Rodolphus Dickinson, Edgar Taylor, Young. *To walk: to walk about*, to promenade, showing themselves off in the chief places of concourse. *In long robes:* literally, *in stoles*, long robes reaching to the ankles, such as ladies of rank were accustomed to wear, and kings, and nobles, and certain priests, and other high personages.

And (to have) salutations. Deferential greetings. It gratified them to be called *Rabbi*, and to see the people bowing before them in obeisance. The verb that governs the expression *to walk in long robes* has to be carried on to govern the word *salutations*.

In the market places. The places of popular resort, where the people promenaded, and where consequently stalls were erected for the sale of fruits, confections, articles of ornamentation, etc. Our British market places do not quite correspond.

VER. 39. **And chief seats.** *Prominent seats.* Literally, *first seats*, or *front seats.* Wycliffe has it, *the firste chaires.*

In the synagogues. They carried their vanity even into the places of worship.

And chief places at feasts. Literally, *in the suppers*, the fashionable entertainments to which they were invited. Wycliffe's translation is, *the firste sittinge places.* The original expression means, *first reclining places.*

VER. 40. **They who devour widows' houses.** King James's translators had regarded this clause as a continuative addition to the preceding clauses. So too Luther, Beza, Erasmus Schmid, Sebastian Schmidt, le Clerc, Heumann, Alford, and English translators in general. There is however a change in the construction. The nominative is used in place of the genitive. This change *might* be accounted for on a principle of unconscious transition; but it is better to suppose a pause at the conclusion of the 39th verse. Then our Saviour resumes, and makes a self-contained sentence of this 40th verse, *They who devour widows' houses, and for a pretence make long prayers, these shall receive greater damnation.* There is more spirit in this method of construction. And though the reference to the scribes, or to some prominent individuals among them, is merged in a more generic statement, yet the undercurrent of allusion is evident. This self-contained construction is approved of by Grotius, Felbinger, Bengel, Zinzendorf, Lachmann, Tischendorf, Tregelles, Meyer, Bisping, Lange. *They who devour widows' houses* · it is a vivid hieroglyph. What

houses, and for a pretence make long prayers: these shall receive greater damnation.

41 And Jesus sat over against the treasury, and beheld

an extraordinary 'swallow' the devourers must have had! The very idea of it apparently either shocked Principal Campbell, or failed to effect an entrance into his conception, and hence he renders the phrase *the families of widows*, a most unhappy emendation. It was not their families that the scribes coveted, but *the literal houses*. Having, as the lettered class, to do almost all the writing that required to be done, they would be universally employed in making wills and conveyances of property. In some notorious cases, perhaps in many, they had been abusing their influence with widows.

And for a pretence make long prayers. *And in pretence pray long.* They did not really pray. They did not open up their hearts to God, and thence lift up their desires. They merely pretended to pray. And, that they might succeed the more effectually in the imposition, they continued long at the 'exercise.' The base hypocrites! It was to impose on the widows, or to minister in other ways to selfish aims, that the prayers were lengthened out.

These. This resumptive word indicates a peculiar edge of feeling on the Saviour's spirit.

Shall receive greater condemnation. It is *judgment* (κρίμα) in the original. And so the Rheims. Wycliffe's word is *doom*, or *dom* as he spells it. It means properly *judicial sentence*, and then, as here, *the award objectively specified in the sentence*. It is assumed that the judicial sentence would be condemnatory. *Greater*: The word is rendered *more abundant* in 1 Cor. xii. 23. Principal Campbell renders the whole phrase, freely, *the severest punishment*.

VER. 41-44 constitute a paragraph which has no parallel in Matthew. There is however a corresponding paragraph in Luke xxi. 1-4.

VER. 41. **And He sat down over against the treasury.** In that great central quadrangle or court of the temple, that was accessible to the Jewish women. It lay in front of the sanctuary, 'forming,' says Thrupp, 'a kind of ante-court to the rest of the inner temple' (*Jerusalem*, p. 329). It was environed, on the three remaining sides, by the vast spaces of the court of the Gentiles. In a certain portion of this spacious quadrangle was *the treasury* (comp. John viii. 20 and Josephus, *Ant.* xix. 6: 1), where, as we are informed in the Talmud, there were thirteen receptacles for receiving certain religious dues and the people's free-will offerings for the benefit of the temple. These receptacles were called *shopheroth*, or *trumpets*, because they were trumpet shaped, swelling out beneath, and tapering upward into a narrow mouth or opening, into which the contributions were put. (Buxtorf's *Lexicon Talmud.*, p. 2506.) Each receptacle had a label upon it which specified the particular object, or charity, to which it was reserved. (Lightfoot's *Prospect of the Temple*, chap. xix.) It was over against the place where those treasury receptacles were arranged that our Saviour sat, in the covered piazza, or colonnade, toward the right hand on going toward the sanctuary. (See Vogué's *Temple*, plate xv.)

And beheld. *And He was beholding.* He was deliberately observing, as one who had a right to take note of the moral acts of the people.

how the people cast money into the treasury: and many that were rich cast in much. 42 And there came a certain poor widow, and she threw in two mites, which make a farthing.

How the multitude. Or, *the crowd-of-people* (ὁ ὄχλος). Note the *how*. It is more primitive and expressive than such a semi-demonstrative phrase as *how that*. The Saviour noticed not merely the fact or acts of contribution, but also the wonderfully diversified modes in which the acts exhibited themselves. Mode is inseparable from act, and, when outward, reveals the inward essence of the act. We may suppose that our Saviour *looked in*, through the diversified modes that struck His outward eye, *to the diversified characters of the contributors*, as they passed in succession before Him. If so, it would be with far more interest and innerliness than was ever manifested by Lavater, and with an intuition that was unerring. " On Sundays, after the sermon," says the poet Goethe, " it was Lavater's duty, as an ecclesiastic, to hold the short-handled, " velvet alms-bag before each one who went out, and to bless as he received the " pious gift. Now, on a certain Sunday he proposed to himself, without look- " ing at the several persons as they dropped in their offerings, to observe only " their hands, and by them silently to judge of the forms of their donors. Not " only the shape of the finger, but its peculiar action in dropping the gift, was " attentively noted by him, and he had much to communicate to me on the " conclusions he had formed." (*Autobiography*, vol. ii., b. xix., p. 137.) As the idiosyncrasy and form of the whole body were revealed to Lavater's eye by the form and action of the fingers, so the idiosyncrasy and moral condition of every soul were unveiled to our Saviour's gaze, as He noticed ' *how* ' the offerings were cast in.

Cast money into the treasury. The word *cast* is ambiguous in English, so far as tense is concerned. But the verb in the original is in the present, *are casting*. The evangelist, as so often on other occasions, goes back in thought to the scene, and looks at the acts of contribution. The crowd-of-people are casting in *money* ; literally, *copper* (χαλκόν), and so no doubt the word should have been translated. Comp. Matt. x. 9. The great bulk of the people, then as now, would contribute the lowest metal coinage. But it should be borne in mind by modern contributors that the relative value of *copper* was much greater then than now. What Trapp so cynically says will surely not be always true, ' Something men will do, but as little as they can.'

And many that were rich were casting in much. An expression that may mislead, for the word *much* is a free translation. It is literally *many (pieces)*. Perhaps some might be giving silver or gold. But it is likely that the great majority of even the rich would be contenting themselves with giving *a considerable quantity of the current copper coins*, ' a handful of halfpence ' as it were, according to the suggestion of Dr. Adam Clarke. *Many pieces:* even at the present day a European, when travelling in Palestine, is amazed at the multitude of little pieces which he receives in exchange for silver or gold.

VER. 42. **And there came a poor widow.** Or literally, *one poor widow*, or as Wycliffe gives it, *o pore widowe*. The evangelist singles her out.

And she threw in two mites, which make a farthing. An admirable translation,

43 And he called *unto him* his disciples, and saith unto them, Verily I say unto you, That this poor widow hath cast more in, than all they which have cast into the treasury: 44 for all *they* did cast in of their abundance; but she of her want did cast in all that she had, *even* all her living.

---

when the words *mites* and *farthing* are considered etymologically. *Farthing* is just a corrupt way of saying *fourthing* or *fourthling*, Anglo-Saxon *feorthling*; and thus it denotes *the fourth part* of some standard coin or sum. And this is the precise idea of the term employed by the evangelist (κοδράντης = *quadrans*). In English a *farthing* is the fourth part of a 'penny.' In Latin a *quadrans* or *quadrant* was the fourth part of an 'as.' But the coinage of the Hebrews, under the Romans, was so exceedingly mixed that it may be difficult to determine what proportion of a Greek *drachm*, or Latin *denarius*, was represented by their *quadrant*. (See Beza, de Dieu, and Fischer.) The word *mite* has come to us apparently as a contraction of the word *minute* (Latin, *minutum*). As a *minute* of time is just a *minute* portion of time, so a *minute* or *mite* of money is just *a minute coin*. Wycliffe has here *tweie mynutis*, that is, *two minutes*. The Greek word (λεπτά) denotes *thin* (*pieces*).

Ver. 43. **And He called to Him His disciples, and said to them.** It is *said*, instead of *saith*, in a great majority of the best manuscripts.

Verily, I say to you, This poor widow cast in more. Not *hath cast in more*, but *cast in more*, according to the aoristic reading of Lachmann and Tregelles. It is supported by A B D L Δ, 33, and substantially by the Sinaitic also.

Than all they who are casting into the treasury. Such is undoubtedly the correct reading. It is supported by ℵ A B D L X Γ Δ Π, and accepted into the text by all the modern critical editors. The Saviour does not wait till the stream of contributors has flowed past. While it is still flowing, He makes an unerring comparison, and utters His commendation of the poor 'lorn' woman. She *gave* more than all the rest *are giving*. Note the word *more*, proportionally to wit, to her means, and thus *more* in the estimation of God, who measures quantity by quality.

Ver. 44. **For they all did cast in.** We might have expected that it would have been said, *For they all are casting in*. And such no doubt was in substance the meaning of our Lord, only He chooses to vary His standpoint of observation, and to specify those alone of the continuous stream of contributors who had already thrown in their offerings.

Out of their superfluity. So Tyndale and Coverdale translate: their *surplusage* as it were. He, whose eye could see, had taken note (John xxi. 17).

But she of her want. Or *her penury*, that condition in which *she came behind her neighbours*. She had no superfluity.

Did cast in all that she had, even all her living. Her whole *means of living*, every particle of money that she had in the world. He, who 'knew all things,' knew; and His simple notification of the fact, and true appraisement of the quantity involved in the quality of the offering, have touched the hearts of generations of admirers. The collective voice of all the ages of the Christian era has been this: '*O woman, great was thy munificence! Great was thy faith.*'

CHAPTER XIII.

1 AND as he went out of the temple, one of his disciples saith unto him, Master, see what manner of stones and what buildings *are here!* 2 And Jesus answering said unto him, Seest thou these great buildings? There shall not be left

---

CHAPTER XIII.

THIS chapter of 'eschatology' corresponds to Matt. xxiv. and Luke xxi. 5–36. The end of our Saviour's terrestrial career was at hand. He knew it well. Its imminency led Him to improve to the utmost the limited opportunities which were still available for enlightening, forewarning, and thus fore-arming, the minds of His disciples. In this chapter He sheds light upon certain 'coming events' of great significance and moment. They were partly in the more remote, and partly in the nearer, future. All men have prophetic longings, and look instinctively more or less forward. But if a man's soul be lofty he looks far forward.

VER. 1. **And as He went forth out of the temple.** *Went,* or rather *was going.* What follows occurred while He was in the act of going out of the temple.

One of His disciples says to Him, Master. Literally, *Teacher.* The actual word employed would no doubt be the Hebrew title, *Rabbi.* See chap. ix. 5, xi. 21, xiv. 45.

Behold, what manner of stones and what manner of buildings! Or, *See! what stones! and what buildings!* The great size of the blocks, and the massiveness and magnificence of the erections, the colonnades or porticos, gateways, and other structures that were grouped around the inner sanctuary, riveted the disciple's attention and evoked his admiration. No wonder. The temple of Jerusalem was one of the wonders of the world. Whosoever had not seen it, said the old rabbis, had not seen the perfection of architectural beauty. (See Wetstein, vol. i., p. 493.) Josephus, in his *Antiquities,* xv. 11 : 3, speaks of the stones of a certain part of the edifice as being 'each, in length twenty-five cubits, in height eight, in breadth about twelve.' In his *Wars* (v. 5 : 6) he speaks of 'some of the stones as forty-five cubits in length, five in height, and six in breadth.' Stones these, of a magnitude almost baffling to the imagination of those who have not travelled in the East. They have their analogues only in some of our greatest, but unchiselled, ' megaliths.'

VER. 2. **And Jesus said to him, Seest thou these great buildings?** Mace, Worsley, Principal Campbell, and Godwin give the words affirmatively, *Thou seest these great buildings.* There is probably a touch of both the modes of representation, or a hovering between the two, *Thou seest, dost thou ? these great buildings.* The verb translated *seest* (βλέπεις) means *beholdest,* and here suggests an idea akin to *contemplatest.* Norton's rendering is too strong however, *are you gazing on ?*

There shall not be left here one stone upon another. Literally, *stone upon stone:* or, as with our English indefinite article, we might express it *a stone upon a stone.* That is Wycliffe's version, *a stoon upon a stoon.*

one stone upon another, that shall not be thrown down.
3 And as he sat upon the mount of Olives over against the
temple, Peter and James and John and Andrew asked him

Which shall not be thrown down. Very literally, *which shall not be loosened down*. A progressive process is depicted. Demolition proceeds, and is nearly completed. Still here and there *a stone is left upon a stone*; but the demolition advances till it is consummated. *Every stone that had been left lying on a stone is detached and thrown down.* It is not the Jewish temple that is to be eternal. 'The words have emphasis,' says Zuingli. They have: and they have been fulfilled to the letter, so far as the area of the temple platform is concerned. The substructures of the surrounding walls, some of which still stand, would not be referred to. The disciple was not pointing to them or looking at them. 'It is a figurative speech,' says Petter. It is enough to take it as such. And then the figure is a fine instance of natural hyperbole, bold, and grandly graphic. None but a paltering mind could be stumbled at it, or have difficulty in interpreting it. Comp. chap. x. 25. (As to the aorist subjunctive with the double negative, see Clyde's *Greek Syntax*, pp. 93, 115.)

VER. 3. The conversation would probably cease for a little; but the company solemnly proceeded, and by and by Mount Olivet was reached. The ascent began, in silent meditation we may suppose. The Saviour is in advance. At some convenient spot He pauses, and, turning His face toward the beloved but faithless city, He seats Himself. **And as He sat.** Or, *And as He was sitting*, *while He was sitting*.

On the mount of Olives. Very literally, *to the mount of the olives*. The motion of the person *to* the mount, ere rest was obtained *on* it, is primitively suggested.

Over against the temple. Thus looking westward, as the façade of the temple faced the east. The temple, with its surrounding perspectives, as seen from the mount of Olives, must have been one of the grandest terrestrial sights on which the eye of man could rest.

Peter and James and John and Andrew. It is noteworthy that the sons of Zebedee come, in the enumeration, between Peter and his brother Andrew. Spiritual relationship overrides the physical. It is noteworthy also that James takes, as usual, precedence of John, no doubt because he was the older of the two. It was only gradually that John's intrinsic pre-eminence asserted itself, though to the Saviour himself he seemed to get nearer than his brother.

Asked Him privately. The excluding reference of the expression is not likely to have relation to the other disciples (see Matt. xxiv. 3; Luke xxi. 7), but to the people in general who might be hovering about outside their little circle. No doubt there would be many, attracted by the presence of our Lord, who would feel loath to lose sight of Him; they would be straggled around and behind, individually and in groups, waiting on, respectfully or wistfully, in the hope of getting access to listen. The Saviour however wished to be alone with His disciples for a season. His wish would be understood, and strangers would retire or keep at a distance.

privately, 4 Tell us, when shall these things be? and what *shall be* the sign when all these things shall be fulfilled? 5 And Jesus, answering them, began to say, Take heed lest any *man* deceive you. 6 For many shall come in my name,

---

VER. 4. Tell us, when shall these things be? The *things*, namely, that were involved in the total demolition of the Jewish temple. The ideas of the disciples would no doubt be confused. Their notions in reference to the futurities of the kingdom of heaven would be immature; they would be very imperfectly apprehending the relation of Judaism to Christianity, and of the Jews to the rest of mankind, and of Jesus to peoples in general; and consequently the relation of the Jewish temple, the Jewish worship, and Jerusalem, to the dispensation of the fulness of the times. Even still, on some of these points, much confusion of idea prevails among 'the students of prophecy'; lines of discrimination are sometimes too rigidly drawn, and at other times they are lost sight of altogether. And no wonder therefore that the apostles, whose minds had been steeped for long in crude rabbinic conceptions, but who had been beginning to see rays of light struggling in through their darkness, were unable to work out for themselves a consistent scheme of the future, in its relation to their Lord and His kingdom.

And what shall be the sign, when these things are all about to be accomplished? The same *class of things* are referred to, but their radius gets elongated; their range expands; and hence, as the disciples think of them, they now say, *all these things.* They wonder when *all these things* '*shall be accomplished*' (μέλλῃ συντελεῖσθαι), *finished* (Rom. ix. 28), *brought to a conclusion.* They do not so much reflect on the commencement and progress as on the consummation of the dread events. With that consummation they would be connecting, in their ideas, the overturning of all human institutions, the winding up of all the probationary affairs of the world, the great judgment, and thus the glorious epiphany of their Lord to act as Judge of the whole earth, and to inaugurate, with befitting pomp and all the visible insignia of universal royalty, the dispensation of the new heavens and the new earth. They were eager to know what would be the *sign* or *signal* of this great œcumenic crisis. Their ideas would be indistinct, and very particularly in a chronological point of view; but, as faithful servants of their Lord, they wished to be on their watchtowers, looking out for the fulfilment of their Messianic hopes.

VER. 5. **And Jesus began to say to them.** Viz. what follows. The evangelist, as often elsewhere, fixes his attention on the *beginnings* of addresses or statements. Comp. chap. i. 45; iv. 1; v. 17, 20; vi. 2, 34; viii. 11, 31, 32; x. 28, 41; xii. 1.

Take heed that no man lead you astray. Be on the outlook, not merely heavenward but earthward. Depend upon it there will be danger of seduction unless you are wary.

VER. 6. **Many shall come in My name.** Literally, *on My name,* founding on it; they shall assume the name that belongs to Me alone, '*the Messiah,*' '*the Christ.*' On that assumption they will erect an imposing edifice of claims which, crazy with its own intrinsic unreality, will fall disastrously on all who

saying, I am *Christ;* and shall deceive many. 7 And when ye shall hear of wars and rumours of wars, be ye not troubled: for *such things* must needs be; but the end *shall* not

rally round it. There would no doubt be many of these pretenders in the period that elapsed before the destruction of the temple of Jerusalem, just as there have been many since. They have in general indeed been too insignificant to leave their mark in history; but their pretences would be none the less perilous to the little circles of the simple-hearted who might be within the reach of their influence. Even at the present day there is a sprinkling of strange individuals, dotting society here and there all over the world, who claim to be either Christ come back again, or the Holy Spirit, or some kindred Incarnation. Some of these go at large, and address their fellow men, or write books and manifestoes, and wield other kinds of influence.

Saying I am He. There is no word *Christ* in the original, though it is freely supplied in the Coptic, Sahidic, Armenian, Anglo-Saxon versions, and by Erasmus, Luther, Tyndale, Beza. The expression is exceedingly expressive without it, when, as should be the case, the emphasis is laid not on the ' *am* ' as in the name of God ' *I AM* ' (Exod. iii. 14), but on the ' *I.*' The egotism of the respective pretenders is graphically exhibited.

And shall lead many astray. More especially among the ignorant and ingenuous. When such persons cannot be seduced by gross baits of sensualism, they can sometimes be caught in the snares of a wild and lurid enthusiasm.

VER. 7. **And when ye shall hear of wars, and rumours of wars.** *Ye :* the Saviour, as He speaks, is not thinking merely of the twelve individuals, as individuals, who were around Him. They were *His disciples*; He was thinking of them *as such*; and in thinking of them *as such*, His field of vision widened. He thought of *His disciples in general.* There were indeed ' *rumours of wars* ' rife enough before the destruction of Jerusalem. The whole Roman empire was uneasy. A far firmer hand than that of the animalized Vitellius, who lived to eat, was needed on the imperial throne. The firmest that could be got was not firm enough. Hence the *rumours of wars,* which agitated the empire. And besides these there were to some small extent actual ' *wars,*' which certain students of prophecy have succeeded in hunting up in the byeways of history. But minute and microscopic research is not needed. There have been, since the destruction of Jerusalem, actual ' *wars* ' innumerable, and ' *rumours of wars* ' innumerable. All these were embraced within the scope of the Saviour's vision. He was looking to another ' end.'

Be not troubled. *Be not alarmed.* Literally, *Do not cry out* (μὴ θροεῖσθε). Wycliffe, *Drede ye not.* The word occurs only here and in Matt. xxiv. 6, and in 2 Thess. ii. 2. Do not conclude from such occurrences that the pangs of the world's dissolution are imminent.

These things must needs come to pass. Or, more simply, *they must needs be.* Or still more simply, *they must be. It is necessary that they be.* The adverb *needs* (Anglo-Saxon *neades,* i.e. *of need* or *of necessity*) only intensifies the idea which is already expressed in the *must.* The idea however has no reference to any absolute necessity, or fatality, overriding and enslaving the wills of men.

ST. MARK XIII.

be yet. 8 For nation shall rise against nation, and kingdom against kingdom; and there shall be earthquakes in divers places,

It does not refer to what Archbishop Bramhall calls 'antecedent and extrinsical necessity.' Such necessity, as he remarks, "destroys liberty, and dishonours "the nature of man. It makes second causes and outward objects to be the "rackets, and men to be but the tennis balls, of destiny. . . . Excuse me," he adds, " if I hate this doctrine with a perfect hatred. . . . It were better to be "an atheist, to believe no God ; or to be a Manichee, to believe two gods, a god "of good and a god of evil ; or, with the heathens, to believe thirty thousand "gods; than thus to charge the true God to be the proper Cause, and the true " Author, of all the sins and evils which are in the world." (*Defence of True Liberty*, pp. 60, 61.) The necessity referred to is relative to the antecedent elections, or choices of the human will; but, within that sphere, it is real, inevitable, irresistible. If men persist in choosing to be selfish, grasping, haughty, then a Higher Hand comes into operation, and whirlwinds must be reaped. What multitudes of these have already swept across the area of human society! What multitudes more will yet require to do their appointed work as 'besoms of destruction'!

But the end is not yet. There is no verb in the original, *but not yet the end*, the great end, the end of the age, 'the present evil age,' the age that is to run on till all things be made new and glorious. It may be that, in the disciples' ideas, this 'end' and the end of the temple would be synchronous. Most likely. The whole subject would be lying in confusion before their view. And the Saviour would see that it would have but ministered to further confusion, had He attempted, by the introduction of niceties of chronology, to rectify into precision their scheme of the futurities. He acted with consummate wisdom. He confined Himself to leading lines of processional evolution, now taking up one and now another. Instead of scattering attention on matters of minute detail, He contented Himself, as was His wont, with summations of particulars, and the enunciation of great general principles. It was ever His leading aim to throw practical seed thoughts into the minds of His disciples and auditors in general.

VER. 8. **For nation shall rise against nation.** Literally, *upon nation*. One nation shall rise in its anger to come *down upon* another. A kind of gigantic collective personality is ascribed to nations. There will be wars of nationalities.

And kingdom against kingdom. Whether they be, as in some cases, the subdivisions of a single nationality, or, as in others, greater communities, or empires, embracing within one political sphere various distinct nationalities. Kingdoms will rise up to put down kingdoms; and terrific in their clash will be the collisions.

There shall be earthquakes in divers places. For not yet is the earth, which 'the meek shall inherit' (Matt. v. 5; Rom. iv. 13, 14), a fit residence for the glorious community. Neither will it be, so long as there is scope for the incidence of such fearful phenomena as earthquakes. In 'the new earth, wherein dwelleth righteousness' (2 Pet. iii. 13), there will no longer be anything 'to hurt.'

and there shall be famines and troubles. These *are* the beginnings of sorrows.

9 But take heed to yourselves: for they shall deliver you

There shall be famines. Terrible scourges, when they occur. And, notwithstanding all the resources and appliances of modern commercial inter-relationships, they still do occur. When they happen among a people who are supplied with only a scanty circulation of the precious metals, the effects are necessarily of the most melancholy description. Witness the state of Persia and India of late. If mankind were once a self-realizing brotherhood, famines would be impossible. The scarcity of one region would be readily supplemented out of the abundance of others.

It is added in the Received Text, and troubles. That is, *disturbances*, or *social perplexities and tumults*, such as are the natural result of widespread 'want.' Men who are pinched with hunger are apt, unless of noble character, to become desperate and reckless. In ℵ B D L, however, and the Vulgate, Coptic, and Æthiopic versions, the phrase *and troubles* is wanting. Mill approves of the omission (*Prol.*, § 408), and Griesbach (*Comm. Crit.*). The phrase is left out of the text by Lachmann, Tischendorf, Tregelles. But on insufficient grounds. The omission truncates, as Fritzsche justly observes, the evangelist's phraseology; and the wilful addition of the expression cannot be accounted for, except on some violent hypothesis. Mill supposed that it had been originally a political explanation of the word *earthquakes*. Unnatural. Griesbach thought that if the expression had been genuine it would have come in before, not after the *earthquakes* and *famines*. He did not notice the natural connection that subsists between the want of the necessaries of life and political perplexity. Origen expressly notes (*Op.*, iii., p. 855) that 'Mark adds *and troubles*' (Marcus eadem, addit autem *et turbelas*).

These are the beginning of travail. Literally, *of parturition pangs*. There is hope in the word. The *regeneration* of the world will be the ultimate result. But the anguish that precedes will be inexpressible. The Saviour has but touched on the *beginning* of that anguish. Its consummation would have been utterly unintelligible to the apostles. It is, we doubt not, all but utterly unintelligible even yet. The greater the complexity of society, the more intricate the interdependency of the various classes, the vaster the accumulation of the results of civilization, the higher the refinement of thought and feeling, so much the more tremendous will be the unutterable woes that must be experienced when the crisis of universal revolution takes place. In all Beza's editions, with the exception of the first in 1556, the clause *these are the beginning of sorrows* is transferred to the commencement of ver. 9. Unhappily. But the Elzevirs followed his example; and hence continental editions in general, inclusive of Bengel's, Lachmann's, Scholz's, and Tischendorf's, exhibit the same awkward arrangement. So too Mill and his followers, and even Alford. But not Calvin, Castellio, Erasmus Schmid, Zinzendorf, Tregelles.

VER. 9. But take ye heed to yourselves. *But look ye to yourselves.* The Saviour, after having swept with His eye a vast circumference of society, stretching away downward through time, returns to the disciples that were

9] ST. MARK XIII. 357

up to councils; and in the synagogues ye shall be beaten: and ye shall be brought before rulers and kings for my sake, for a testimony against them.

around Him, and addresses them, partly as individuals, and partly as the representatives of such others as might eventually be associated with them. He gives them allowance to be careful of life and limb. He does more, He enjoins them.

For. Their utmost care would be needed, *for* they would be exposed to very ruthless persecution. The *for* however is wanting in the Vatican manuscript (B), and in L, as also in the Coptic, Armenian, and Æthiopic versions. Tischendorf has omitted it. But on insufficient grounds.

They shall deliver you up. *They*, the reference is indefinite, corresponding to *on* in French, and *Mann* in German. *You shall be delivered up.*

To councils, and in synagogues shall ye be beaten. It should rather be, *to councils and to synagogues* (καὶ εἰς συναγωγάς); *ye shall be beaten.* This is the most natural interpretation. It is given by Erasmus, Luther, Tyndale, Cardinal Cajetan, Coverdale, Calvin, Castellio, Beza, the Geneva, le Clerc; and also by Heumann, Lachmann, Meyer, Tregelles. And though it is opposed by many, inclusive of Bengel, Bleek, Rilliet, Alford, Klostermann, the opposition rests on insufficient grounds. The word *councils* or *sanhedrims* denotes such civil, or ecclesiastico-civil, courts or 'consistories of justice' (Petter), as had power to deal with individuals who might be regarded as disturbers of the peace, or dangerous to society. *Synagogues* were assemblies for worship, but possessing, within certain limits, jurisdiction, jurisdiction that could take effect not merely on spiritual relationships, but also on the outer person. In the word *councils* or *sanhedrims* the reference is conventionally to the persons met in conclave, as distinguished from the literal or topical conclave itself, the meeting-place. The term however is sometimes used topically. See Acts iv. 15. Comp. Herodotus, viii. 79, and Xenophon *Hist. Gr.*, ii. 4:23. In the word *synagogues* again the reference is conventionally rather to the places of assembly than to the persons assembled. But the term nevertheless originally referred to *the persons assembled*, and is so used here in consequence of its connection with *sanhedrims*. It is similarly used in Acts ix. 2 and xiii. 43, as also in Luke xii. 11. *Ye shall be beaten:* literally, *skinned*, that is *scourged*. The statement stands on its own pedestal. But it may be assumed that, in many cases at least, the torturing infliction would be made in the presence of the council, or within the walls of the synagogue. See Matt. x. 17; Acts xxii. 24. "There were two ways of "scourging; one with thongs or whips, the other with rods or twigs. The "punishment was inflicted on the offender lying on the ground (Exod xxi. 20; "Lev. xix. 20; Deut. xxii. 18; Prov. x. 13, xiii. 24, xx. 30, xxiii. 13, 14; Ps. "lxxxix. 32; 1 Kings xi. 12). In later times the offender was tied by his arms "to a pillar, and his back laid bare to the *virgæ* or rods of the lictor." (Bastow's *Bible Dictionary*, p. 654.)

And before governors and kings shall ye stand for My sake. The preposition translated *before* literally means *upon* (ἐπί). i.e. *up on*, and thus, in such a case as this, means *in the elevated presence of*. See Matt. xxviii. 14. *Governors:* such as Roman *proconsuls, proprætors, procurators,* or other *presidents* or *pre-*

10 And the gospel must first be published among all nations.

11 But when they shall lead *you*, and deliver you up, take no thought beforehand what ye shall speak, neither do ye pre-

---

fects. *Kings:* such as Agrippa for instance, and many other monarchs in many parts of the world. *For My sake: on account of Me, because of your loyalty to Me.*

For a testimony to them. Not, as Petter and others would have it, *for a testimony against them.* The forcible arrestment of Christ's disciples, and their consequent trial at the bar of the highest terrestrial authorities, would be divinely permitted and overruled for this, as for other ends, to give them an opportunity of bearing testimony to the high and influential classes of society, in reference to the truth, purity, power, and glory of the gospel.

VER. 10. **And the gospel must first be preached to all the nations.** *First*, before the 'end' come, the 'end' spoken of in ver. 7, the end of the age that is to precede the new and glorious epoch. *Preached:* published, heralded. The word is generally rendered in our Authorized version *preached*, sometimes *proclaimed* (Luke xii. 3; Rev. v. 2). The office of the minister of Christ is heraldic in its nature; it is his duty to make public proclamation of the good news of salvation. *To all the nations:* the gospel has a world-wide destiny, and until that destiny be fulfilled the 'end' will not be. Köstlin thinks that this 10th verse is ineptly introduced into its present position between ver. 9 and 11, causing an unnatural rupture in the practical instructions contained in these verses. (*Ursprung und Komposition*, p. 352.) But a deeper and juster view of the Saviour's aim would have shown that it was of the utmost practical moment that the Lord's apostles, and His other disciples, should bear in mind that, however severe the persecutions to which they might be individually exposed, the great crisis would not be imminent till the gospel should have fairly fulfilled its world-wide mission.

VER. 11. **And when they lead you to judgment.** Or rather, *whenever they may be leading you* (ὅταν ἄγωσιν), viz. in fetters, or, at all events, as persons under arrest. The Saviour transports His disciples, in imagination, to the road along which they might be forcibly conducted to appear before the civil authorities.

And deliver you up. Or, as Bengel and Principal Campbell render it, *to deliver you up.* It is, literally, *delivering up.* The act of *delivering up* is represented as beginning with the act of compulsory *leading.*

Be not anxious beforehand what ye shall speak. Whatsoever the etymology of the word rendered *anx ous* (see G. Curtius's *Grundzüge*, p. 308), its companion phrase in Luke x. 41 throws light upon the idea intended, 'thou art *anxious* and *troubled* about many things.' The disciples were not to be *troubled* beforehand; they were not to be *careful* beforehand, in the disquieting sense which is sometimes attached to the word *carefulness.* (See *Comm.* on Matt. vi. 25.) The *beforehand* was not intended to limit the period of exemption, and to open a door to legitimate anxiety, after the preliminary stage of things had been passed. It simply brings into natural prominence the time when anxiety is apt

meditate: but whatsoever shall be given you in that hour,
that speak ye: for it is not ye that speak, but the Holy
Ghost.

12 Now the brother shall betray the brother to death, and the

to be intensest on the one hand, and is sure on the other to be of the least
possible avail.

It is added in King James's version, *Neither do ye premeditate*. But this clause
is omitted in the manuscripts ℵ B D L, 1, 33, 69, and in the Vulgate, Sahidic,
Coptic, and Æthiopic versions, and in a large proportion of the Old Latin
codices. Tregelles and Tischendorf leave it out. It is not unlikely that the
expression was originally a marginal explanation of the preceding clause. Our
English translators, in using the compound word '*p*remeditate,' reproduced
exactly the form of the original word as it is given by Origen (προμελετᾶτε: *Opera*,
vol. i., 295), but not its form as it occurs in the Received Text. It is simply
meditate, study, con over. The Geneva of 1557 renders it *prepare*; Tyndale,
ymagion, i.e. *imagine*. There is, of course, if the clause be genuine, no absolute prohibition of *premeditation*, but only, as Petter remarks, of such ' as is
joined with distracting care.' The idea is, *you need not distress yourselves by
anxiously considering beforehand how you ought to speak before such high and
august personages. Be calm, collected, inartificial, and a higher wisdom than
your own will guide your thoughts and mould your words*.

But whatsoever may be given you in that hour, that speak ye, for it is not
ye that speak, but the Holy Spirit. Many, besides the apostles, have had experience of this high assistance, and have been themselves amazed at the
aptness of the ideas and words that were flashed, as occasion required, into
their minds. Some fanatics however have arbitrarily stretched the Saviour's
instructions, to the length of covering the idea that it is wrong for preachers,
even in their ordinary preaching, to make previous preparation. But the
Saviour is not at all referring to the ordinary ministrations of preachers, or to
the expositions of expounders of the 'lively oracles.' He is referring to the
contingency of compulsory appearance at the bar of governors and kings. And
the design of His instructions is to prevent unmanning disquietude or distress.
It is not eloquence, or fine rhetoric, that is needed, when an innocent man is
called upon to answer for his conduct in a court of justice. It is candour, calm
self-possession, and confidence in a Higher Presence and Power as the Shield
of the upright. In that spirit, the reflex of the brooding Spirit of truth, let a
man stand before his judges, and he is far more likely to say the right thing
and to say it well, than if he were, with ever so much disquietude, to 'ymagion'
or con over beforehand what he ought to say.

VER. 12. **And brother shall deliver up brother to death, and the father his
child.** As there is nothing that excites such love as the gospel, when intelligently received, so there is nothing that occasions such hate as this same
gospel, when passionately rejected. In that reception or rejection the heart of
the heart is concerned. Woodman, the Sussex martyr in Queen Mary's days,
" was," says Petter, " betrayed and taken by means of his own father and
" brother and other friends; whereupon he professed that this very text of
" Scripture was verified in him, and he did comfort himself with it."

father the son; and children shall rise up against *their* parents, and shall cause them to be put to death. 13 And ye shall be hated of all *men* for my name's sake; but he that shall endure unto the end, the same shall be saved.

14 But when ye shall see the abomination of desolation,

And children shall rise up against parents. Literally, *upon parents*. The children shall rise up *to come down 'upon' them*.

And cause them to be put to death. Even although the murder be committed through the moral machinery of information, and consequent judicial examination and technical condemnation, it is still true that the unnatural children themselves are the murderers. Coverdale's translation imitates Luther's, *and shall help them to death*.

VER. 13. **And ye shall be hated of all men for My name's sake.** The real significance of the 'name' will not be considered by the masses. The real mission and aims at once of the servants and of the Master will not be so much as looked at. The public in general will take its cue from the representations of its natural leaders, and hence will hate zealously and remorselessly all who bear the brand of the blessed name. 'The vulgar of all sorts,' as Richard Baxter expresses it, 'will be seduced to take you for the plagues of the world.' The expression *all men* is used of course popularly, by a fine graphic kind of hyperbole. *Expect not that the people will pour forth in torrents to welcome you as preachers of the glad tidings. They who extend to you a cordial welcome will be so few, compared with those who neglect or reject your message, that I can scarcely see them at all as I pass My telescope of prevision across the millions of society.*

But he that endureth to the end, he shall be saved. With that everlasting salvation which, when consummated, merges in everlasting glorification. 'The end' referred to is not specifically *the end of the age*, but the end of each individual's probationary career. Instead of *endureth*, Principal Campbell and Norton have *persevereth*; Purvey, *lastith*. But our English translation is admirable, for there is more than *lasting* or *persevering* implied. There is *lasting* or *persevering* '*under trials*.'

VER. 14. **But whenever ye see.** *Ye*, My disciples. The Saviour recognised in His apostles the representatives of all the disciples who might be living at the time of the destruction of Jerusalem; and therefore, in speaking to the former, He realized that He was speaking to all their representees.

The abomination of desolation, spoken of by Daniel the prophet. A much better translation than Wycliffe's, *the abhomynacioun of discomfort*. It would be better still however, and more literally, *the abomination of 'the' desolation*, that is, *the abomination connected with the particular devastation that was predicted by Daniel, and that was imminent over Jerusalem and the whole of the Jewish territory*. It is the *devastation* that is referred to in Dan. ix. 27, though the form of the phrase is slightly modified from the Septuagintal plural, and thus conformed, so far as the singular number of the word is concerned, to the analogous Septuagintal expressions in Dan. xi. 31 and xii. 11.

spoken of by Daniel the prophet, standing where it ought
not, (let him that readeth understand,) then let them that

Comp. also 1 Macc. i. 54. The *devastation* to which Daniel and our Lord referred is manifestly that desolating devastation of the Holy City and the Holy Land that was effected by the Roman army Comp. Luke xxi. 20. In the Hebrew of Dan. ix. 27 there is brought into view the personal agency that was to be at work in this devastation, *the abominations of the devastator*, that is, of the collective devastator, the Roman army. Such variations in the phraseology are the natural result of unfettered thought; they can occasion no difficulty to any method of interpretation that is free from artificiality and narrowness. Hence too we have, in the Hebrew of Dan. ix. 27, the plural word *abominations* instead of the singular *abomination*, as given in the Septuagint and by the evangelist. Both are equally veracious representations. There was to be *a collection of abominations*, and thus there was unity as well as plurality. The reference is undoubtedly, according to the conventionalism of the Old Testament usage, and as was discerned by Victor of Antioch, to the abominations, or collective abomination, of *the idolatrous standards of the Romans*. See *Comm.* on Matt. xxiv. 15.

Standing where it ought not. That is, in the temple. Comp. Matt. xxiv. 15. It is a very remarkable fact that Josephus expressly records that the victorious Romans " brought their ensigns into the temple, and placed them over against " the eastern gate; *and there they offered sacrifices to them*, and with the loudest "acclamations proclaimed Titus emperor" (*Wars*, vi. 6: 1). Such intrusion of the military standards into the holy place, followed by the deliberate act of causing them to *stand* there, was a wanton desecration, which no exigency of battle, siege, or storming could justify. The abomination *stood where it ought not*. Petter, looking at the expression from the peculiar standpoint of his theology, says, ' in respect of God's decree, *it ought to stand there!* ' It is an unnecessary and unhappy ' antinomy.' It suffices for all legitimate theological ends, to regard the sphere of God's decree as coincident with the sphere of His voluntary activity.

Let him that readeth understand (νοείτω). Let him *exercise his intelligence* (his νόος). Let him *think*. The translation of the word in 2 Tim. ii. 7 will suit admirably, *let him consider*. Coverdale's version is forcible and ' sun-clear,' though free, *let him marck it well*. We are to regard this parenthetical counsel as uttered by our Lord himself, in reference to Daniel's prophecy, not as an interjected *nota bene* of the evangelist. Such a *nota bene* on the part of the evangelist, though approved of by Principal Campbell and others, would be an unprecedented intrusion of the narrator's own personality; and it would carry with it something of immodesty, as a kind of presumptuous selection of one from among the other utterances of our Lord, as worthy on the part of a biographer of very peculiar emphasis, and, on the part of his readers, of very special consideration. Our Lord's counsel is reported by Matthew also (xxiv. 15); and it is analogous, as Wolf remarks, to the oft repeated ' he that hath ears to hear, let him hear '; only as there is a reference to a written prophecy, the counsel points to the duty, not of the *hearer* but of the *reader*. It is not unlikely that it is the echo of the counsel of the angel Gabriel to Daniel himself,

ST. MARK XIII.

be in Judæa flee to the mountains: 15 and let him that
is on the housetop not go down into the house, neither enter
therein, to take any thing out of his house: 16 and let him

'therefore understand the matter and consider the vision' (Dan. ix. 23). See
Comm. on Matt. xxiv. 15.

Then let them that are in Judæa flee to the mountains. It will be in vain for
them to persist in the expectation that there will be a Divine interposition, at
the last moment, to destroy the Romans and to restore the Jewish state. It is
the will of God that the Jewish state should 'cease and determine.' It is His
pleasure to permit the Romans to play out their part in the procession of the
dispensations. Let the disciples then, who may have been wistfully hovering
around the doomed city, betake themselves, without any further delay, to the
securest fastnesses, that they may be spared for ulterior duties.

VER. 15. **And let him that is on the housetop.** The *dome* (δῶμα). The word
originally meant *house*, but in the New Testament usage it invariably means
housetop, or *roof*; and indeed, in primitive times and hot climates, the house
would be, in a great measure, a roof or cover. Such would be, and such still
are, the *booth* and *tent* : '*On*' *the housetop*. For it is a common thing for the
Oriental to be ' on ' his housetop. It is flat, with frequently a little cupola in
the centre. It is a fit place for repose in the cool of the evening, as also for
meditation or for observation.

Not go down (it is added in the Received Text) **into the house**. The addition
is wanting in the Sinaitic and Vatican manuscripts, and L ; the Syriac Peshito
version too, and the Sahidic and Coptic. Tischendorf omits it. The omission,
when taken in connection with the next clause, seems to promote the concinnity
of the composition ; but for that very reason it is to be suspected as a literary
pruning. The Saviour intimates that the greatest haste would be requisite, if
there was to be a chance of escape from captivity or death. They who, hoping
against hope, had lingered on till the storming of the city and the burning of
the temple, had lingered too long. Every moment thenceforward was precious.
The Roman cavalry would be instantly flying hither and thither, scouring the
country in quest of plunder and captives ; and if any one therefore was ' on the
housetop' when news arrived that the temple was carried, let him flee at once.
Let him, if that would give him a start even of a few moments, just step
across the parapet of his own housetop, and run along the line of roofs till he
get out to the country, and thence by the shortest road to the fastnesses in the
hills.

Nor enter in to take anything out of his house. The phrase *nor enter* seems
superfluous after the preceding clause. But it may be accounted for, either on
the common principle of repetitiousness, or more probably on the assumption
of an interior beyond an interior in the house. It is common, in oriental houses
of a respectable size, for the stairs that lead from the roof to terminate *in the
court*; he therefore who descends such a staircase is landed *in the court*, and has
thus 'come down *into the house.*' But when in the court he may either rush
out by the front gate, or enter *into one or more of the chambers* which open from
the court. The Saviour glances, both generically and specifically, at both

19] ST. MARK XIII. 363

that is in the field not turn back again for to take up his
garment. 17 But woe to them that are with child, and to
them that give suck in those days! 18 And pray ye that
your flight be not in the winter. 19 For *in* those days shall
be affliction, such as was not from the beginning of the

---

interiors, but specifies, in the second place, that which is inner, because in the
order of nature one must go *into the court* before one can *enter into the other
parts of the house.* To take any thing out of *his house :* though the things might
be precious, time would be much more precious still.

VER. 16. **And let him that is in the field.** Viz. working. It is literally *into
the field.* In primitive representations, processes as well as results would be
indicated even in the simplest matters ; and when, for brevity's sake, the one
or the other of the two elements was omitted, sometimes an arrest took place,
phraseologically, at the stage of process, though it was assumed of course that
thought would go forward to the stage of result.

Not return back to take his cloke. His outer robe, which would only have
encumbered him while working in his field, but which would be of the greatest
advantage to him when resting by night out in the open air, away from the
comforts of home ; the time gained however by fleeing without it would be of
far greater advantage still.

VER. 17. **But woe to them that are with child, and to them that give suck, in
those days.** Or, as Godwin renders it, *But alas for the women who are with child,
and for them who suckle, in those days.* The Saviour's heart was more tender
than a woman's, and bled when He thought of the anguish that would, in many
cases, be inevitable in the hasty flight. How dreadful is defeat in an embittered war ! How dreadful too is victory, in its pursuit of the defeated !

VER. 18. **And pray ye that it be not in winter.** That is, *pray that all this
that I have been speaking of do not take place amid the severities of wintry
weather.* These would greatly aggravate the sufferings of the sufferers. The
word for *winter* may mean *a storm* or *stormy weather.* See Matt. xvi. 3, and
Acts xxvii. 20. Wakefield renders it here *rainy weather.* The whole expression,
that it be not in winter, exhibits in the original not so much the subject matter
of the prayer as the end that was to be contemplated in praying. *Pray, in order
that it be not in winter (ἵνα).* The idea of the act of prayer is accordingly
modified. Were the subject matter of the prayer coming up into prominence,
the idea of the act would be narrowed into that of petition ; but when prominence is given to the final cause of the act, then the idea of prayer is widened
into that of general address or appeal to Him who ruleth over all, and can and
will overrule whatever may be brought to pass by His creatures.

VER. 19. **For.** Such prayer will be much needed, as a means of obtaining
some little mitigation of the inevitable woes.

The following expression is very striking, *For* **those days shall be tribulation.**
Instead of the tribulation being represented as *occurring in the time,* the days
are, so to speak, transubstantiated into the affliction.

Such as there hath not been the like from the beginning of the creation which

creation which God created unto this time, neither shall be.
20 And except that the Lord had shortened those days, no

God created until now, and never shall be. One might explain this language on the principle of that graphic hyperbolism that pervades, to so large an extent, the speech of all peoples. It is quite common, in many languages at least, if not in all, to say of any very extraordinary affliction, it is *the greatest possible*. Superlatives are often employed, when there is really no definite intention of asserting a perfectly absolute prominence. It is at the same time however worthy of consideration, whether there was not, in this catastrophe of the Jews, a minglement of elements, physical, intellectual, moral, and spiritual, which was so unique as to render the anguish that was consequent on the overthrow of Jerusalem unprecedented, and incapable of future recurrence. Many peoples have been vanquished. Often have surviving populations been 'peeled,' and scattered or led captive. Often have capital cities been stormed and sacked. But the case of the Jews was peculiar. They were convinced that they were the favourites of heaven; they regarded their capital as 'the city of the Great King,' and the predestined mistress of the world. Their temple was to them the one house of God; it could not be dispensed with in the world. Hence they expected, up to the last moment, that 'the Lord's arm' must needs be made conspicuously 'bare' in the extremity of their necessity, to smite the beleaguering hosts, like the hosts of Sennacherib of yore, and thus to rescue the beloved place and the beloved people! When one mingles the elements of such thoughts and feelings, and their effects, with the effects of the utter social disorganization that prevailed, and consequently with the unutterable physical woes that preceded and succeeded the capture of the temple, it is easy to see that the tribulation endured may have had an edge of agony, which never was before in the history of any people, and which will never be again. See *Comm.* on Matt. xxiv. 21. The word *creation* is used objectively, as equivalent to *the created world*.

VER. 20. **And except the Lord had shortened the days.** The Saviour does not particularly refer to Himself when He says *the Lord* ; He refers to Him who is the absolute One, *Jehovah* or *Jahveh*. *Shortened*, or *curtailed*. It is not said *should curtail*. The reader is transported forward to the time when the tribulation referred to had passed its culminating point. He looks back from his standpoint upon the anguish, as it was at its intensest ; and he is told that the reason why it is already past is, *Jehovah had curtailed the days of its duration*. *The days :* the days referred to were really curtailed in number, beyond what might have been anticipated. A concurrence of contingencies contributed to this result. Titus, the commander, was personally disposed to clemency and moderation. He loved a Jewess too, Bernice, the sister of Agrippa. He esteemed Josephus moreover, the Jewish historian; and he was in haste besides to get to Rome that he might share in the triumphal entry of his father Vespasian, and enjoy the splendid festivities of such a jubilant occasion. All these things and others might be Divinely overruled, and no doubt were, to curtail the days of Judæa's anguish.

No flesh would have been saved. *No flesh*, that is *none*, viz. of the Jews.

flesh should be saved : but for the elect's sake, whom he hath chosen, he hath shortened the days.

21 And then if any man shall say to you, Lo, here *is* Christ ; or, lo, *he is* there ; believe *him* not : 22 for false Christs and

---

There would have been an almost total extermination of the race. So exasperated were the Romans, and so fitted were they by their victories to carry this exasperation into fatal effect. The idiomatic phrase 'no *flesh*' was a Hebraism, remarkably corresponding to our English 'nobody.'

But for the elect's sake, whom He chose, He shortened the days. The motive that moved the will of 'the Lord' is revealed. He had a special regard to *the elect 'in Christ'* (Eph. i. 4), whom He elected ; and hence, that they might not be extirpated, He overrulingly curtailed the days of tribulation. *He*, and no other, *elected* them. He *selected* them, that is to say, for the enjoyment of peculiar blessings and the performance of peculiar duties. They were hence objects, so to speak, of a peculiar solicitude or care, that affected the Divine heart, moved the Divine will, and guided the Divine hand. This solicitude however, or special Divine care, was not the result of any arbitrary predilection. *The elect in Christ,* or in other words, *the true Christians,* were, for all the great moral ends which were contemplated by the Divine Grace, the flower of the population ; and, so far as human agency was concerned, they were the hope of the world.

Ver. 21. **And then.** *Then* and thenceforward indefinitely. No definite chronological measurements are made by our Lord, beyond the period of the great Jewish crisis. The varying elongations, in time, of the succeeding futurities do not come within the scope of the prophetic perspective.

If any one shall say to you, Lo here is the Christ ! Lo there ! believe it not. When *the Christ* does appear again, it will be in no obscure way. Human testimonies or telegrams will be altogether unnecessary. No one will need to be dependent on another for information concerning the fact. 'Every eye shall see Him.'

Ver. 22. There is need for such a warning. **For there shall arise false Christs.** There have been many of them. David George, for instance, who ultimately settled at Basle, where he died in 1556. He claimed, according to the account of Dr. Henry More, *to be the true Christ, the dear Son of God, born not of the flesh, but of the Spirit. He was to restore the house of Israel and re-erect the tabernacle of God, not by afflictions and death, as the other Messiah, but by that sweetness, love, and grace that were given him of the Father. He had the power of the remission of sins, and had come to administer the last judgment.* He averred that " *the Holy Scriptures, the sayings and testimonies of the prophets, of* " *Christ, and of His apostles, do all point, if rightly understood in their true* " *mystery, to the glorious coming of David George, who is greater than the former* " *Christ, as being born of the Spirit and not of the flesh.*" (*Enthusiasmus Triumphatus,* § 34.) This David George, says Dr. More, was a man 'of notable natural parts, of comely person, and a graceful presence.' And he had many adherents, who believed in him. In our own day there are persons, out of asylums, who put forth corresponding claims. There is lying before the writer

false prophets shall rise, and shall shew signs and wonders, to

a "Tract on the Second Advent fulfilled," in which it is said that "the enrolling "of the saints commenced on the anniversary of the last day of the Feast "of Tabernacles of the year 1868, that is, on the 9th October, 1868. The "following," it is added, "is the declaration to be made and signed: *I believe* "*Jesus of Nazareth to be the Messiah at His first coming and the antitypical* "*Paschal Lamb who died for sin in allegory. and I believe John Cochran of* "*Glasgow to be that Messiah at his second coming and the antitypical High Priest* "*who has taken away sin in reality.*" Of all such persons it has, in consequence of their obscurity, to be said *Lo here! Lo there!* "Believe not," says our Saviour.

And false prophets. They have been legion in number. Lodowick Muggleton, for instance, who on the title page of his *True Interpretation of the whole Book of the Revelation of St. John* (1746), describes himself as "one of the two last "commissionated witnesses and prophets of the only high, immortal, glorious "God, Christ Jesus." Madame Antoinette Bourignon, before him, was a far nobler being, yet she dec'ared to Christian de Cort: "I am sent from God to "bring light to the world, and to bear witness to the truth. He has sent me to "tell that the last times are come; that the world is judged, and the sentence "is irrevocable; that the plagues are begun, and will not cease till all evil be "rooted out ; and that Jesus Christ will come shortly to the earth to finish this, "and then He will continue to reign with 'men of goodwill,' who shall enjoy "eternal peace. I am sent with a commission to declare all these things to "men, to the end that peradventure some of them may be converted and repent, "that they may reign with Jesus Christ in His glory. . . . I am certainly "sent from God to declare the truth of everything." (*The Light of the World*, part iii., pp. 45, 46, ed. 1696.)

And shall show signs and wonders. Literally *and shall 'give.'* viz. as evidence. It is a somewhat peculiar and semi-awkward word; but, notwithstanding its peculiarity, it is strange that Tischendorf should actually reject it from the text, and on the mere authority of the Cambridge manuscript (D), a few cursives, and some free quotations or allusions of Origen, substitute, in its place, *do* or *perform* (ποιήσουσιν). It seems hard to suppose that any fastidious or critical transcriber would ever have turned *perform* into *give*, if he found *perform* in the codex from which he was copying. But it is easy to conceive that occasionally a transcriber, of little depth or perspicacity of judgment, might be tempted to substitute the easy going *perform* for the more rugged *give*. imagining all the time that, instead of doing any harm to the sacred text, he was merely, without modifying the idea, smoothing and improving a comparatively unimportant expression. It is noteworthy moreover that many modern translators, who had no other word in the texts that were lying before them than *give*, have taken nevertheless the liberty of freely rendering it *do*. So Luther, Piscator, Zinzendorf, Heumann (all of whom have *thun*); Worsley renders it *work*; Principal Campbell, *perform*. It is *give* which is the reading of ℵ A B C L, and indeed of all the rest of the uncials, except D. It is supported too by all the ancient versions. *Signs and wonders :* 'Lying wonders' (2 Thess. ii. 9) no doubt, wonders that serve a purpose of imposition, partly it may be on the wonder

seduce, if *it were* possible, even the elect. 23 But take ye heed: behold, I have foretold you all things.

---

workers themselves, and partly on those whom they wish to attach to themselves. There are wonderful idiosyncrasies among men, that give scope for the performance of such wonders. In some natures, as in Valentine Greatrakes and Gassner (see Howitt's *History of the Supernatural*), singular therapeutic energies instinctively well up and flow over; in others there is a singular power of something like ' second sight ' or ' clairvoyance,' turning fitfully its penetrative eye, now upon objects distant in space, and now upon objects distant in time, though in a way far removed from infallibility. This clairvoyant eye often takes cognisance of only frivolous realities, and seems blind to things of moment. Still its peculiarity is fitted, (when once a willing and shallow fanaticism tries its hand at understanding it,) to be a ' lying wonder.' There are other remarkable endowments and instincts, which crop up at times in exceptional idiosyncrasies, and may give occasion either to self-delusion, or to deliberate artifice, or to a minglement of the two perversities.

That they may lead astray. Or *seduce*. Intention is expressed, even though it should be the product of self-delusion. At the base of the self-delusion there must be unconscientiousness, if insanity be absent; and if so, the whole outcome becomes morally tainted. There is something that is resolvable into *an intention to seduce*, or *to proselytize to one's self*. Instead of *lead astray*, Tyndale and the Geneva have *deceive*; Wakefield, *draw away*; Campbell, *impose on*. Literally, *cause to wander off*.

If possible, the elect. An expression crowded in. It is not meant to represent subjectively a detail in the intention of the pretenders; it rather depicts objectively the subtlety of the imposition. There is such a plausibility of evidence, that, *if it were possible, even the elect would be seduced*. *The elect:* the truly Christian, who are Divinely segregated, not only from the world at large, but also from all such as are but superficially or nominally Christian. See on ver. 20. These true Christians, the Saviour intimates, it is not possible to seduce. As a body, that is to say, or in their entirety. They ' cannot err damnably, says Tyndale the Reformer; ' nor any long time; nor all of them.' (*Prologue to Exposition of Sermon on the Mount*.) The last idea should get prominence. Individuals have often no doubt been sadly imposed upon, and led far astray in their notions, and in those actions that are the natural outworkings of notions. But in the midst of the spiritual freedom that is the spiritual birthright of all truly spiritual persons, there is no fear of universal delusion. A seed to do God service will never fail. The holy bush that burns will never be consumed, whatever may become of withered branches and some sickly sprays.

VER. 23. **But take ye heed.** There is an emphasis on the *ye*. *But look ' ye.'* The Saviour no doubt addresses the disciples who were seated around Him, hanging on His lips. But the caution would be meant to be handed down from generation to generation.

Behold, I have foretold you all. The Saviour had omitted nothing that was needed to set them, and to preserve them, on their guard. It may have been unwelcome to their Jewish prejudices and fervid anticipations to be told of such

24 But in those days, after that tribulation, the sun shall be darkened, and the moon shall not give her light, **25** and the stars

difficulties, intricacies, dangers, and trials; no doubt it would be. But the Lord did not on that account leave them unwarned. He sought to send them forward into the future forearmed.

VER. 24. **But.** It is as if He had said, *Now to turn for a little to another view*. **In those days.** In those future days, forward to which the Saviour's eye was looking.

After that tribulation. Of which He had been speaking in ver. 14–20; that is, after the tribulation connected with the destruction of Jerusalem and the dissolution of the Jewish state and dispensation. The Saviour does not enter farther into chronological measurements and adjustments. Possibly, as He looked beyond the scene which presented to His view 'the abomination of desolation' in the 'temple,' and the connected catastrophes and woes, the whole perspective may have had no precise chronological subdivisions, indicated by means of milestones of time, and marking off the exact stages of succession. But the things toward which He looked, and of which He now begins to speak, belonged, as Calvin saw, and still more clearly Luther, Zuingli, Wesley, not to the end of the Jewish state and dispensation, but to *the end of the present age*, or as it is often, though less properly, represented, *the end of the world*. So too Petter. (See, among many other dissertations, Schott's *Commentarius Exegetico-dogmaticus*, pp. 73–124.)

The sun shall be darke ed, and the moon shall not give her light. Eclipses are described. Bengel, in his German translation, has *and the moon shall not give 'his' light*, inasmuch as the moon is masculine in German, and the sun feminine. So Emser, Piscator, Felbinger, Zinzendorf, Stolz, Meyer, in their respective German versions. Luther deftly throws a veil over the genders: *the sun and moon shall lose 'their' light*. Their *light*, their *lustre*, their *shine* as Luther has it. The language is not intended to be pressed into the service of scientific representation; otherwise there would not have been a coincidence of solar and lunar eclipses. The representation is a method of sublime hieroglyphic imagery, meaning that a great and portentous change will, at some future time, take place in the world at large, in relation to the rest of the universe. Of this great ultimate crisis and change there have been, in times past, and there will no doubt yet be in times to come, many partial or local rehearsals. Compare the language of Isa. xiii. 9–19, xxiv. 19–23; Ezek. xxxii. 7.

VER. 25. **And the stars of heaven shall fall.** Or, as the reading runs in Lachmann, Tischendorf, Tregelles, as in the manuscripts ℵ A B C U II*, and in the Syriac Peshito, Coptic, Sahidic, and Æthiopic versions, *and the stars shall be falling out of the heaven*. This grand rhetoric is by no means, in its basis, purely imaginative, any more than the expressions in the preceding verse. It is founded on those extraordinary and awfully magnificent meteoric phenomena, which occur in full force periodically every thirty-three years, in the month of November. Our earth at that time passes through the nucleus of a belt of meteors, and the result is an unintermitting shower, for hours, of 'falling stars.'

27] ST. MARK XIII. 369

of heaven shall fall, and the powers that are in heaven shall be shaken. 26 And then shall they see the Son of man coming in the clouds with great power and glory. 27 And then shall he send his angels, and shall gather together his elect

---

This spectacle, so splendid on the one hand, and so appalling on the other to such as are ignorant of astronomy, occurred last on the night between the 13th and the 14th days of November, 1866.

And the powers that are in the heavens shall be shaken. Wahl supposes that these *powers* are the *stars*. So Bretschneider and Grimm. Robinson, that they are 'the sun, moon, and stars.' But either the wider or the narrower of these suppositions introduces unnatural tautology into the phraseology. Cardinal Cajetan supposes that the reference is to *the active powers of those heavenly bodies which exert an astrological influence on things terrestrial*; while Petter prosaically imagines that the phrase denotes 'the natural force, strength, or virtue which is' intrinsic 'in the whole body and frame of the starry heavens.' It is more likely that the reference is to invisible or personal *powers* or *hosts*, as distinguished from hosts visible and impersonal. We may think of the high and holy hosts that surround the throne of the Eternal. (See 1 Kings xxii. 19; Ps. ciii. 21, cxlviii. 2.) Or we may think of the lower hosts which are subject to 'the prince of the power of the air' (Eph. ii. 2), and which, under certain fixed limitations, have malign influences under their control. It is more likely that there is a reference here to these latter; for the great cosmical changes spoken of seem to be introductory to that dissolution of the 'heavens' as they at present are and the 'earth,' which is to precede the emergence of 'the new heavens and new earth, wherein dwelleth righteousness.' See 2 Pet. iii. 10-13.

VER. 26. **And then.** Ere the end, but yet toward ' the beginning of the end.'
Shall they see the Son of Man coming in the clouds. Or, more literally, *in clouds*, i.e. *amid clouds*. It might also have been said *on clouds*. See Matt. xxiv. 30. Comp. Ps. civ. 3, and Isa. xix. 1. The clouds, which will be rolling over the troubled sky, and which are the fitting symbols at once of the impending crisis and of the impenetrable mystery that surrounds the throne of Him who rules over it, will be, as it were, the sublime drapery of His presence, illumined ' with the brightness of His coming' (2 Thess. ii. 8). *Shall they see Him: They*, men in general, men universally. ' Every eye shall see Him.' (Rev. i. 7.)
With much power and glory. With that pomp of appearance and attendance that is fitted to make known to all, at once His inherent *power* and His essential *glory*.

VER. 27. **And then shall He send forth His angels.** The *His* is undoubtedly genuine, though it is wanting in the Vatican and Cambridge manuscripts, and has been left out by Tischendorf and Tregelles. The angels belong to our Lord as His 'ministering spirits' (Heb. i. 14).
And shall gather together His elect. Tischendorf and Tregelles omit *His* in this clause too; but on quite insufficient grounds. It is found in א A B C, and indeed in all the uncials except D L. The elect on earth belong to Christ, as

B B

from the four winds, from the uttermost part of the earth to the uttermost part of heaven.

28 Now learn a parable of the fig tree; When her branch truly as the angels in heaven. The proprietorship is assumed by Him as a matter of course; so thoroughly imperial and Divine was our Lord's self consciousness, even in the depth of His humiliation. *Gather together:* To meet Himself, and to be with Himself, so as to be preserved in safety and exalted to glory. All the details however of the physical and moral machinery, by means of which the ultimate glory is to be reached, are shaded off; and hence nothing is here said of the resurrection, or of physical transformation, or of the general judgment. See 1 Thess. iv. 14–17.

From the four winds. Literally, *out of the four winds*, for the word *winds* is used in its secondary acceptation, to denote the *quarters* of the earth's surface, from which the winds blow, east, west, south, and north. The earth, to every spectator, is optically a circle. If the circle be subdivided into four equal segments, these segments are the *quarters*, on which the various points of the compass may be calculated. The Hebrews, in distinguishing the quarters, supposed themselves to be looking to the rising of the sun. The east was in *front*; the west *behind*; the south was *the right hand*; the north, *the left.* (Compare *the Hebrew words.*)

From the uttermost part of the earth to the uttermost part of heaven. Or, more literally, *from earth's extremity to heaven's extremity.* Bleek supposes that there is a reference, in the one phrase, to the saints that shall be alive on the earth, and in the other to those who shall have fallen asleep in Jesus, and whose souls shall be in heavenly places. But in that case we should have expected the expression to have run thus, *from earth's extremity, and 'from' heaven's extremity,* that is, *from earth's extremity all over 'its' plane, and from heaven's extremity all over 'its' plane.* It is far more probable that the expression is only a variety of phrase for *from horizon to horizon.* Comp. Matt. xxiv. 31. "The extremities," says Petter, "of the heavens and of the earth are sup-"posed to be the same, and are put for one and the same." Optically the earth and heavens meet at the horizon, so that the idea is, *from one extremity of the world (take the horizon at what point you please) to the other.* Tyndale's translation actually is, *from one ende of the worlde to the other;* and this, though free, is certainly much to be preferred to Principal Campbell's, *from the extremities of heaven and earth.*

VER. 28. The filament of thought that floated into the far future is let go with what precedes. The Saviour returns to the consideration of what was more immediately to transpire.

But (δέ) from the fig tree learn 'the' parable. That is, *from the fig tree, as for instance in its present state, learn 'the' indirect instruction, which it is so admirably fitted to suggest, and which is so appropriate to the case in hand.* It is probable that a fig tree was close by. Perhaps the little company were sitting under its shade, as they looked west toward Jerusalem.

Whenever her branch. The word properly means *a young branch* or *spray*, which may be easily *broken off* (κλάδος). Note the *her.* The pronoun *its* was

is yet tender, and putteth forth leaves, ye know that summer is near: 29 so ye in like manner, when ye shall see these things come to pass, know that it is nigh, *even* at the doors.

only coming into use at the time when our translation of 1611 was made, and was not adopted by our translators. (See *Comm.* on Matt. v. 13.) Hence either *his* or *her* had to do duty in its place. It is *her* in the Greek, for the word *fig-tree* is feminine; but it is *his* in German and therefore in Luther, for the word *tree*, in German, is masculine. Tyndale too has *his*, and King James's translators preserved the *his* in Matt. xxiv. 32.

Has already become tender. *Tender*, under the reviving influences of spring, when the 'hibernacles' or winter-quarters of the leaves become flushed with the living juices, out of which the new growths are to be elaborated.

And putteth forth its leaves. Or rather, *and the leaves have sprouted forth.* The verb is in the passive, so that the expression *the leaves* forms the *subject* of the proposition. (Read, not ἐκφύῃ with Beza, the Elzevirs, and Tischendorf, but ἐκφυῇ with Erasmus, Bengel, Matthæi, Fritzsche, Lachmann, Tregelles. It was the reading too of Schott ultimately, and of the first, third, and fourth editions of Robert Stephens.)

Ye know that the summer is nigh. Its outriders have arrived.

Ver. 29. **So also ye.** There is emphasis on the *ye* (ὑμεῖς). The same parties indeed were both spoken of, and spoken to, in the preceding verse; for it is *they* who are referred to, as knowing the signs of coming summer. Yet, in the approach of summer and in the signs which herald it, they had no special interest. They were hence referred to in a merely representative way; and our Lord meant that the signs of coming summer are known *of men in general*. But the coming of the great national crisis, which our Lord had in view in His illustration, was a matter that had bearings of very special importance for the disciples.

When ye see these things coming to pass. *These things:* not the last things spoken of in ver. 24-27, but the things that had formed the bulk and burden of His prophetic utterances, and that were referred to by the disciples when, in ver. 4, they asked 'when shall *these things* be?' The reference is to the precursors of the destruction of the temple and city of Jerusalem. See *Comm.* on Matt. xxiv. 33.

Know that it is nigh, at the door. Literally, *on (the) doors.* Note the plural. *Folding doors* are referred to, as so frequently in Homer. The outer doors of oriental houses at the present day are generally folding, if the houses have courts. But, idiomatically, *at the door* is identical with *at the doors*; and it is more consonant with our British ideas, for folding doors are exceptional in Britain, and even when they are used they are still *the door*. The Saviour does not specify, by name, *what it is that would be at the door*. It is *that which constituted the burden of His thoughts, and the burden of the thoughts of His disciples, that which occasioned the whole of the long prophetic discourse contained in this chapter*, viz. the destruction of the city and temple of Jerusalem. See ver. 2. This, the subject of the proposition, did not need to be formally stated, being perfectly well understood.

30 Verily I say unto you, that this generation shall not pass, till all these things be done.
31 Heaven and earth shall pass away : but my words shall not pass away.

Ver. 30. Verily I say to you. Christ's solemn way of saying, *I do assure you.*

This generation shall not have passed away till all these things have taken place. The *things*, namely, which were to be the precursors of the national crisis, and which were to terminate in that crisis. The crisis therefore is itself included. The destruction of Jerusalem did happen, in harmony with our Saviour's prediction, within the limits of the existing generation. It happened in the year 70 of the Christian era, between thirty and forty years after the prophecy was uttered. Many expositors, missing their way through the discourse as a whole, and thus unable to disintegrate the references to *the end of the age* from the references to *the end of the Jewish temple and temple service*, have been driven to their wits' end to account for the statement of this verse. Hence attempts have been made to interpret *this generation* as having reference to quality of characteristics, rather than to time and contemporaneity. Some suppose that the expression means *this race of Jews.* Among others, Bishop Ryle takes this view. He says: "I take this opportunity of expressing my "decided opinion that *this generation* can only mean *this nation* or *people*, the "Jewish nation." (*Thoughts on Mark*, p. 290.) Others suppose that it means *this race of men*, ' the totality of men.' So Klostermann, in recent times. We would not object, with Alexander, to the principle of these interpretations on the ground that the word *generation* (γενεά) always means, and must always mean, *a contemporary race.* The ineptitude that would be characteristic of the prediction, on either of the two hypotheses, is a far weightier objection. M. Roustaing's interpretation is still more objectionable, though given spiritualistically, as he alleges, by the evangelists themselves assisted by Moses ! He supposes that the meaning is, *this generation when re-incarnated (in the latter days*). See *Les Quatre Évangiles expliqués par les Évangélistes*, tome ii., pp. 639-645. The expression *this generation* was a familiar one with our Saviour, and in all other cases was used by Him to denote *the sum total (in some given sphere) of the persons then living.* Comp. Matt. xi. 16, xii. 41, 42, 45, xxiii. 36 ; Mark viii. 12, 38 ; Luke vii. 31, xi. 30, 31, 32, 50, 51, xvii. 25. The statement before us is definitely fixed down and explained by the equivalent and unequivocal expression in Matt. xvi. 28, *Verily I say unto you, There be some standing here, which shall not taste of death, till they see the Son of Man coming in His kingdom.* Richard Baxter correctly reproduces the idea, ' Some now alive shall live to see it.' See *Comm.* on Matt. xvi. 28 and xxiv. 34.

Ver. 31. The heaven and the earth shall pass away. Notwithstanding their apparent stability. They are ever changing, and passing on to farther change. They are never for two successive millenniums, or for two successive moments, in exactly the same state. Witness the revelations of geology and of astronomy. Consider the prodigious dissipation of heat or ' energy ' into space. Suns burn out. Solar systems must collapse. (See Kant's *Naturgeschichte*, c. vii.) Our

32 But of that day and *that* hour knoweth no man, no, not the angels which are in heaven, neither the Son, but the Father.

Saviour assumes it. Those who are on the summits of science see it, and can demonstrate it. (See the papers of Sir William Thomson and Dr. Croll on *Geological Time.*) "The earth," says Sir William Thomson, "is filled with "evidences that it has not been going on for ever in the present state, and that "there is a progress of events toward a state infinitely different from the pre- "sent" (§ 20.) The sun, he elsewhere says, is most probably "simply an in- "candescent mass cooling." (*Geological Dynamics*, § 40.)
But My words shall not pass away. *My words* concerning the fate of Jerusalem, as concerning other things. They partake of the immortality of truth. How towering the self consciousness of our Lord! And yet He was no sciolist on the one hand, and no braggart on the other. Was He then deluded? It cannot be: *His prediction was literally fulfilled.*

VER. 32. **But of that day.** Literally, *but concerning that day.* There is a strong emphasis on the *that*, the intended effect of which is that the thought takes a vault to a time far beyond the things referred to in the preceding verse : *that day of days; that great day, the culmination of all the days of this preliminary age.* Comp. 2 Tim. i. 12, 18, iv. 8.

And that hour. The *that* is not repeated here in the original. There is simply the article, *and* '*the*' *hour.* But in the uncial manuscripts A B C E G H K L M U V W X Γ Δ II, as in the Vulgate and Philoxenian Syriac versions, it is not '*and*' but '*or*' *the hour*, a variation from the representation in Matt. xxiv. 36. The *or* is accepted by Griesbach, Fritzsche, Lachmann, Tischendorf, Tregelles. The idea suggested is, that whether the great crisis-time be looked at in its nearer or in its remoter proximity to the actual chronological point of occurrence, the relation to it of finite foreknowledge is the same.

Knoweth no man. Literally, and better, *knoweth no one.* See the exceptive clause at the conclusion of the verse.

Not the angels who are in heaven. The negative represented by the English *not* has a continuative import imbedded in it (οὐδέ); and the idea in such a case as the one before us may be thus expressed, *not even the angels.*

Neither the Son. It is more than *neither*, '*nor yet*' *the Son* (οὐδέ again : see Clyde's *Greek Syntax*, § 56, c.).

But the Father. Very literally, *if not the Father*, that is *unless the Father*, *except the Father* (εἰ μή). The expression is to be connected with the clause *no one knoweth, no one except the Father.* The Father's absolute omniscience, and His consequent absolute prescience, is assumed by the Saviour, even although the object of the prescience is chronologically conditioned on millions of intervening free acts on the part of millions of free agents. When absolute prescience however is denied by the Son on the part of Himself, He is of course referring to Himself *as Son, begotten on a certain day* (Ps. ii. 7; Acts xiii. 33) *in the virgin's womb* (Luke i. 35). He is, in other words, referring to Himself as He was self-realized in His finite nature, to be for ever distinguished from that infinite essence in which He made the worlds (John i. 3), sustains them (Col. i. 17), sees the end from the beginning (John vi. 64), and 'knows all things'

33 Take ye heed, watch and pray: for ye know not when the time is. 34 *For the Son of man is* as a man taking a far journey, who left his house, and gave authority to his servants, and to every man his work, and commanded the

(John xxi. 17). The expression perplexed Ambrose; he suspected that it had been interpolated by the hand of a heretic. (*De Fide*, lib. v. 16) It perplexed Dr. Adam Clarke too, who was likewise disposed to suspect its genuineness. But it is certain that it is no interpolation. And there is really no embarrassing difficulty. It is only when we proceed on a 'monophysist' hypothesis, and assume that our Saviour's Divinity was His only mind, and the soul of His humanity, that overwhelming difficulty is encountered. Some ardent 'students of prophecy' have supposed that it is merely the 'hour' and 'day' of the second coming of our Lord that are inscrutable, not the year, month, or week of the occurrence! And hence the numerous predictions of the dawning 'year' of the millennium, which have shot, time after time, across the literary heavens like meteors. They have, one and all, been fictitious. And to persist in similar experiments of calculation is but to persist in a waste of ingenuity.

VER. 33. Other exercises than those of calculative ingenuity become us. **Take ye heed, watch and pray.** That is, *See that ye watch and pray. See*, or *Look to it* (βλέπετε). Wakeful watchfulness and prayerfulness constitute the proper attitude of the souls of men, all down through the ages to the great day.

For ye know not when (πότε = ὁπότε) **the time is.** *The right point of time* (ὁ καιρός) *for the glorious epiphany.* It is well therefore to be always 'looking for,' and 'longing for,' or 'hasting to,' the coming of the day of God (2 Pet. iii. 12), for, so far as the individual interests of individual souls are concerned, it is certain that a great change will soon and perhaps suddenly occur; and it matters little, so far as these same individual interests are concerned, whether Christ comes to us or we go to Christ.

VER. 34, 35. There is a fine comparison in these verses. But it is only partially wrought out. Yet, though partial, it is not so decidedly a torso as it seems to be in King James's version, as also in the Geneva, and in Beza's version, from which our translators borrowed the supplementary clause at the commencement of ver. 34.

VER. 34. **As a man who is gone abroad.** Or, as Tyndale gives it, *as a man which is gone in to a straunge countrey.* The man is thought of, not as *going*, but as *gone*.

Having left his house. The mind reverts to what he did before he went abroad; and, in thus reverting, it heaps together in a peculiar order a series of successive acts. One of these is, *he left his house.* But before this took place, certain other acts were performed. See next clause.

And given to his servants authority. Very literally *the authority*, namely, that was requisite to regulate their demeanour in his absence.

And to each one his work. The *and* is wanting in א B C* D L, and is left out by Lachmann, Tischendorf, Tregelles.

ST. MARK XIII.

porter to watch. 35 Watch ye therefore: for ye know not when the master of the house cometh, at even, or at midnight, or at the cockcrowing, or in the morning:

Also commanded the porter to watch. The conjunction in this clause was perplexing to Beza. He regarded it as standing in the way. He therefore 'expunged' it. Arbitrarily however. Bengel understood it correctly, and hence renders it *also*. So Meyer, '*also*' *enjoined the porter that he should be watchful*, or, *in order that he should be watchful*. The other acts of the gentleman abroad are regarded for the moment as subordinate to this. What then? See next verse. But there should not be a full point at the conclusion of this. The application of the comparison is contained in what follows.

VER. 35. **Be watchful therefore.** The *therefore* crowds into itself the whole force of the comparison contained in the preceding verse. It is as if it were said: *As the person abroad, whom I am depicting on the tablet of My imagination, gave strict injunctions to the gatekeeper to be perpetually on the outlook for his return, so say I to you, Be ye watchful*. The word for *watchful* in this and the preceding verse is a term of the later Greek, and denotes a *waked-up* condition. The proper name *Gregory* is derived from it. The word employed in the 33rd verse is different, and denotes *sleeplessness*.

For ye know not when the Master of the house cometh. The figure in the comparison of the preceding verse is kept up. The Saviour, instead of saying *he who corresponds to the master of the house in the comparison*, just speaks of Himself as *the Master of the house*, for He is indeed a Master, and has a household and a house. '*Ye*' *know not:* the disciples of all ages are addressed through their representatives, the apostles. It is in vain therefore for any one to fix the precise date of the millennium.

At even. In the manuscripts א B C L Δ the disjunctive particle is found before this expression, and has been received into the text by Tischendorf, Tregelles, Alford; *or, either*, and here *whether*. It is probably authentic. The word rendered *even* properly means *late evening*. It began at sunset and lasted for three hours, or till the middle point between sunset and midnight. Originally the Hebrews seem to have divided the night into three watches. (See Jud. vii. 19, where we read of *the middle watch*; and compare Buxtorf's *Lexicon Talmudicum*, p. 2454, and Lightfoot's *Works*, vol. iv., p. 198.) But in the time of our Lord the Roman division into four watches had superseded the older Hebrew style.

Or at midnight. The second watch extended from nine till twelve o'clock. The various watches were named from their terminations, rather than from their beginnings.

Or at the cock-crowing. More literally, and better, without the article, *at cock-crowing*. So Wycliffe and Purvey, *(at) cockis crowynge*. The Roman word was *gallicinium*. In some of the Jewish towns, at the present day, the emulative cock-crowings in the stillness of the night, about midway between midnight and sunrise, is something quite startling to a stranger.

Or at morning. The watch that concluded with the sunrise. It is dimly assumed that the master of the house will come *during night*. It is night, as it

36 lest coming suddenly he find you sleeping. 37 And what I say unto you I say unto all, Watch.

CHAPTER XIV.

1 AFTER two days was *the feast of* the passover, and of un-

---

were, so long as he is away. (See Cardinal Cajetan.) Theophylact however dispels the charm of the parabolic scene, when he supposes the evening time to be representative of old age, midnight of middle life, cock-crowing of manhood, and morning of the time of childhood.

VER. 36. **Lest coming suddenly He should find you sleeping.** Though it is night-time with the church and the world, till the dayspring of Christ's universal epiphany, yet it is not time for sleeping. There is no time Divinely allotted, or humanly required, for spiritual slumber and sleep. A-Lapide mentions that when Theophylact the commentator was dying, he said, *Blessed are you, Father Arsenus, for you always kept this hour in view.* (See *Evangel.*, p. 451, ed. 1735.)

VER. 37. **And what I say to you, I say to all, Watch.** The Saviour realized that He was not speaking to His apostles alone. He was speaking, through them, to the people of every generation and age. How vast the comprehension of His aim! How godlike the self consciousness of His own commanding position in the very centre of universal humanity!

CHAPTER XIV.

THE last week of our Saviour's life on earth is drawing rapidly to a close. Two days more, and the last day will be reached, the day of the consummation, the day when the typical passover feast was to be enjoyed, and when the antitypical passover Lamb was to be sacrificed. (See Matt. xxvi. 2.) Ver. 1, 2 correspond in brief to Matt. xxvi. 1-5. So Luke xxii. 1, 2.

VER. 1. **But after two days.** It is probable that the triumphal entry into the city had been on Sunday, the 10th of the month Nisan, the day after the Jewish sabbath. It would therefore be on Monday, the 11th, that the fig tree was blighted and the temple purified. Tuesday, the 12th, had been a peculiarly busy day, at once in the temple and on the mount. The prophecies of the preceding chapter had been delivered during the latter part of it. Wednesday and Thursday, the 'two days' specified by the evangelist, had yet to intervene, and then came ' *Good* Friday,' the 15th of the month. (See Hanna's *Passion Week*.)

Was (the feast of) the passover and of unleavened bread. Literally, *was the passover and the unleavened.* A two-sided way of designating the chief of all the Jewish festivals. It was really but one and the same festival, a week of festal days. But the elements of the prolonged festivity connected themselves, respectively, with the eating of the paschal lamb on the first of the seven festal days, and with the using of unleavened bread during the whole succession of holidays. Hence the twofold designation in Mark's phraseology. Luke combines the elements into unity, *the feast of the unleavened, which is called the*

ST. MARK XIV.

leavened bread: and the chief priests and the scribes sought how they might take him by craft, and put *him* to death.

passover (xxii. 1). Josephus, in his *Antiquities* (xiv. 2: 1), speaks correspondingly of 'the festival of the unleavened, which we call phaska,' or passover. Phaska, *paska*, or *pascha*, is the Aramaic form of the Hebrew word *pesach*. In his *Jewish War* (ii. 1: 3) the historian expresses himself thus: 'the festival of the unleavened, it is called phascha by the Jews.' The word *passover* is a fine English translation of the Hebrew term. It properly denotes *the act of God in 'passing over'* the houses of the Hebrews on that night in which He passed through the land of Egypt and smote the firstborn. (See Exod. xii. 12, 13.) But, as that gracious act was joyfully remembered by the people on the annual recurrence of the day on which it occurred, the day itself, and the whole connected week, and sometimes the specific supper, and sometimes also the paschal lamb itself, receive respectively the designation. The day, the supper, the lamb, were not literally the 'pass-over'; they were the memorials of it. It is on the same principle that the bread and wine of the Lord's supper are not literally, even when 'blessed,' the body and blood of the Saviour, though so called in free sacramental phraseology. They are the memorials of the sacred realities. (See Harrison's *Answer to Dr. Pusey's Challenge*, chap. iv.) Instead of the fine word *passover*, Tyndale and Coverdale, after Luther, give the heathen word *Easter*, and Wycliffe the Hebrew word *pask*. *The unleavened:* That is, *the unleavened (bread)*, or, more literally still, *the unleavened (things or cakes,* λάγανα). The phrase is in two ways cut short, for not only is the word *cakes* left out, the word *festival* is also omitted: *the festival of the unleavened cakes*. Those cakes indeed would in themselves be unadapted for sensuous festivity; they would not be so agreeable to the taste as leavened bread. They were 'bread of affliction' (Deut. xvi. 3). But still they constituted an important element in the spiritual festivity of the occasion, for they were memorials, to the Hebrews, of the trying circumstances of their forefathers when they could not afford time for the tedious process of leavening, but "baked unleavened cakes "of the dough which they brought forth out of Egypt: for it was not leavened, "because they were thrust out of Egypt, and could not tarry, neither had they "prepared for themselves any victual" (Exod. xii. 39). Rather unhappy, consequently, is the translation of Luther, Tyndale, Coverdale, and Amandus Polanus, *swete bread*. Emser, in this, as in a few other cases, improved on Luther's version, 'the days of the unleavened cakes' (*der ungesaurten Brot*). So Piscator, Zinzendorf, Bengel, Grynäus. And yet, as the German word for *leaven* is '*sour*-dough,' there is a semi-justification for Luther's translation.

And the chief priests and the scribes. The leading men in the state, and thus the leading members of the great council of state, or sanhedrim.

Sought. Or rather, *were seeking, were engaged in seeking*. It is the imperfect tense. The excitement occasioned by our Lord's appearances in the temple on the Sunday, Monday, and Tuesday, had put spurs into their malice. They were, before Wednesday, Thursday, and 'Good Friday,' busily engaged in concocting how they could get finally quit of such an impracticable Rabbi. *Seeking:* Desire, eagerness, effort, are implied.

How they might lay hold of Him by stratagem, and put Him to death. They

2 But they said, Not on the feast *day*, lest there be an uproar of the people.

3 And being in Bethany in the house of Simon the leper,

---

were afraid to seize Him publicly, as He was the favourite of a large proportion of the unsophisticated people. *By stratagem:* in the exercise of some kind of treachery (ἐν δόλῳ), such as has so often been resorted to in the case of the followers of the Lord. Of Tyndale for instance, the noble English martyr and Bible translator, who was basely entrapped in Antwerp by Philips, who pretended to be his friend, and who acted his miscreant part ' not without the help and procurement of some bishops of this realm.' (See Demaus's *William Tyndale,* p. 424.) Wycliffe's translation is, *with gile* (guile); Coverdale's, *with disceate* (deceit). The same word is translated *subtilty* in Matt. xxvi. 4.

VER. 2. **But they said.** It is *For they said* in the manuscripts ℵ B C* D L, as also in the Coptic version and the margin of the Philoxenian Syriac, and in a very large proportion of the Old Latin codices. The *for* has been received into the text by Lachmann, Tischendorf, Tregelles, Alford: with reason, as being by far the most difficult reading; whereas *but* is the reading of Matt. xxvi. 5. Tregelles says that the Syriac Peshito has no conjunction at all ('ἔλεγον *tantum*'). But it has *and.* The *for* adduces the reason why they were just *seeking,* not acting. *They said:* The verb is in the imperfect. *They kept saying.*

Not during the festival. The supplement *day* in King James's version is unhappy, for the *festivity* extended over seven days. It is however an old supplement. It is in the Vulgate, and hence in Wycliffe; in Erasmus too, and Tyndale, Coverdale, Castellio, and the Geneva. But not in Luther, Beza, Piscator, Sebastian Schmidt, or Erasmus Schmid.

Lest there be. Or, *Lest there should be.* Very literally, and according to Greek idiom, *Lest there shall be.*

A riot of the people. Or *tumult* (the Rheims and Geneva word), or *uproar* (Coverdale's word, and suggested to him by Luther's *Aufruhr*).

VER. 3-9 constitute a paragraph corresponding to Matt. xxvi. 6-13 and John xii. 1-8. It introduces another thread of things which got interwarped with what is recorded in the two preceding verses. It is probable that the narrative in Luke vii. 36-50 refers to a different, though somewhat kindred, occurrence. Events in common life frequently repeat themselves, *with variations.*

VER. 3. **And while He was in Bethany.** The precise chronological relationship is left indeterminate. In reality however, as we learn from John's subsequent narrative, the evangelist steps backward a few days, to take up the thread that henceforward got intertwined with the action of the chief priests and scribes. See John xii. 1, 2.

In the house of Simon the leper. Simon or Simeon was a common name among the Jews, and hence recourse was had to various expedients to differentiate any particular individual who required to be specified. The Simon in the case before us had been a leper, and may have been cured by our Lord. If he was presiding at his own table, his leprosy must have been removed, though the designation of his former unfortunate state stuck to him.

as he sat at meat, there came a woman having an alabaster

As He sat at meat. More literally, *as He was reclining (at table).* There is reference to the recumbent posture, which, in imitation of the Greeks and Romans, had been adopted for banquets by the Jews. (See Hi. Mercurialis, *De Accubitus Origine.*)

There came a woman. Her name is suppressed both by Mark and by Matthew. But we learn from John that it was Mary, the sister of Martha and Lazarus (xii. 2, 3). There may have been motives of prudence, or of delicacy, leading the earlier evangelists to veil the personality of the ' woman.'

Having an alabaster box of ointment. Such is King James's version. But there is no word for *box* in the original; and there is no reason to suppose that the vessel in which the perfume was contained would be of the nature or shape of a box. Doubtless *alabaster boxes* would be in use among ladies to hold their jewels, cosmetics, perfumes, and toilet etceteras; but it would most probably be in some kind of minute bottles that the volatile scents themselves would be kept. Hammond uses the word *cruse*, and his rendering has been accepted by the Revisers. (Compare Petronius's phrase *nardi ampulla.*) The expression in the original is simply *having an alabaster of ointment.* Pliny expressly says that *perfumes are best preserved in alabasters.* The vessel, because made of alabaster, was called *an alabaster*, just as, with ourselves, a particular garment, because made of waterproof stuff, is called *a waterproof*; and a small glass vessel, for drinking out of, is called generically *a glass*. Herodotus (iii. 20) uses the identical expression employed by the evangelist. He says that the Ichthyophagi were sent by Cambyses to the Ethiopians " bearing, as gifts, a " purple cloak, a golden necklace, bracelets, *an alabaster of perfume*, and a cask " of palm wine." *Perfume:* Or *balsam* as it were, or *otto* or *âtar.*

Of spikenard. If the *of* be retained, then the word *spikenard* will be regarded as literally in the 'whence-case,' and as denoting the plant from which the essential scent was obtained. If the *of* be dispensed with, and a comma substituted in its place, then the word *nard* will be in simple apposition with *ointment*, as denoting, not the plant from which it was obtained, but the specific kind of perfume. We are disposed to take this latter view. So Robert Stephens, Henry Stephens, Beza, Mill, Wetstein, Schöttgen, Griesbach, Vater. *Spikenard:* Certainly a wrong translation, though not involving error of any serious consequence, even in a botanical point of view. The original expression is just, as Jeremy Taylor reproduces it (*Works*, iii., p. 272, ed. 1839) without any attempt at translation, *nard pistic* (νάρδου πιστικῆς). So too Erasmus. What this word *pistic* means is the question in dispute, and has much exercised the ingenuity and stimulated the research of critics. The Latins, from the earliest period, were puzzled by the word. A considerable number of the codices of the Old Latin version just reproduce the Greek term, as Erasmus and Jeremy Taylor do (*nardi pistici*). But as this was quite unintelligible to Latin ears, the expression was, by a slight modification (*nardi spicati*), changed in other copies into *bearded nard*, or *spiked nard*, that is *spikenard.* This modified term was retained in the Vulgate. Hence Wycliffe's version, *spicanard*; and the Rheims, *spike-narde*; and the Geneva, and our English version. It is defended as the probable original form of the word by Castellio, Grotius,

Hammond, Wetstein. Unreasonably. Augustine supposed that the evangelist's word must have reference to some place, unknown to him, ' whence the precious ointment was obtained,' and he conjectured that this topographical reference was specified by the evangelist, because the name recalled, in a mystic or ' sacramental ' way, the idea of *pistis* or *faith*. (*Tract. in Johannem*, xii. 3) John Hartung of Friburg crowned the conjecture of Augustine by supposing that the term had suffered elision in the hands of transcribers, who were ignorant of oriental geography, and that, as it came from the pen of the evangelist, it was *Opistic*, the reference being to *Opis*, a place in the vicinity of Babylon. Scultet was charmed with this fancy of Hartung's, and declared that it entirely superseded all the disputations of theologians, botanists, and grammarians, on the term. (*Observationes in Matt. et Marc.*, c. lxxx.) Petter too inclined to it. But there is no trace of *Opistic* in either manuscripts or versions; and, though there were, the adjective would have had a different conformation if the reference had been to Opis. Joseph Scaliger, always fertile in ingenuities, had, as Nansius, the teacher of Gerard Jo. Vossius, reports, another conjecture, emendative of the word. (Vossii, *Harm. Ev.*, I., iii., § 9.) He supposed that it should be *ptistic*, and that the entire expression meant *perfume of 'pounded' nard*. But this too is a mere and impracticable guess. A considerable number of eminent critics have supposed that the word must be derived from πίω = πίνω, *to drink*, or, as Fritzsche contends, from πιπίσκω, *to give to drink*, and that its meaning is either *potable*, strictly so speaking, or, more generically, *liquid*. This supposition has been approved of by the lexicographers Henry Stephens, Pasor, Fischer, Schleusner, Passow, Liddell and Scott; and likewise by Casaubon in his Notes, and by Beza, Maldonato, Felbinger, Erasmus Schmid, Sebastian Schmidt, and others. Fritzsche, in particular, contends strongly for it, and adduces good evidence to show that nard was really 'potable,' and sometimes drunk. The word *pistic* however never occurs in Greek writers with the meaning contended for; not even in Eusebius, *Dem. Evan.*, ix. 439. And although it did occur with such a signification, it would seem strange that the nard's potability should be specified here, as the perfume was not mixed by Mary with the Saviour's wine, but poured upon His person. What then? Is there any other more likely interpretation of the term? There is. The word occurs in both Xenophon (*Cyrop.*, I., vi. 10) and Plato (*Opera*,vol. iv., 21, *Bipont.*) with the signification *persuasive*, or *producing persuasion*. In later writers, such as Plutarch, Artemidorus, and Cedrenus, the idea of *persuasion* passed over to that of *faith* or *trust*, and the word is used as meaning *producing faith* or *trust*. Artemidorus for instance, in the second book of his *Oneirocritica* (ch. 33), speaks of ' a wife, who is rich, *trusty* (πιστικήν), and a keeper at home, and obedient to her husband,' *trusty, trustworthy*, or, as viewed from a slightly varied standpoint, *faithful*. Things however may be trustworthy as well as persons; and no doubt the *nard* referred to by the evangelist was a *pistic* thing, in the sense of being *trustworthy*, that is, *genuine, pure, unadulterated*. Heumann supposes that this might be a *plebeian* use of the word *pistic*. But le Clerc seems nearer the mark when he suggests that it would probably be the term that was used *in the trade* to denote the genuine article. Such too was Winer's opinion (*Grammar*, p. 110). And we know from Pliny's *Natural History* (xii. 26) that there was, as might have been expected, an ' adulterated ' article in circulation, which he calls *pseudonard*. Theophylact gives this mean-

box of ointment of spikenard very precious; and she brake the box, and poured it on his head. 4 And there were

ing of *unadulterated* as an alternative explanation of the term: he says, "under-"stand by *pistic nard* either a kind of nard so called, *or the genuine nard, faith-*"*fully prepared* (τὴν ἄδολον νάρδον καὶ μετὰ πίστεως κατασκευασθεῖσαν)." The interpretation is approved of by Faber, Luther, Tyndale, Coverdale, Kypke Bengel, Michaelis, Heumann, de Wette, Bleek, Ewald, Meyer, Lange, Volkmar. It is also approved of by the lexicographers Parkhurst, Bretschneider, Wahl, Robinson, Schirlitz, Grimm. Otto too and Eckard, in their respective *Dissertations* on the expression, support it. And it is supported likewise by the Syriac Peshito version, in which the phrase is rendered freely by an expression which means *the principal* or *best nard*. (See Reusch.)

Nard: A word which, though in common use among the Greeks, was not of Greek origin. It was used too by the Hebrews (Cant. i. 12, iv. 13, 14), but was not a native of their language either, or of any of the Semitic tongues. It had no doubt come from the farther East; but from what part is still uncertain. Sir William Jones mentions, on the authority of Dr. Anderson of Madras, that 'in the Tamul dictionary most words beginning with *nár* have some relation to fragrance.' But, adds Sir William, "I have not met with "any such root in Sanscrit; and in Persian, which has a manifest affinity "with it, *nár* means a *pome-granate* and *nárgíl* a *cocoanut*, neither of which "have any remarkable fragrance." (*The Spikenard of the Ancients*: Works, vol. v., p. 27.) Sir William says that "it seems clear that the Greeks "used the foreign word *nard*, generically, for odoriferous plants of differ-"ent natural orders" (p. 37). He was led however, in consequence of our Authorized translation of the term, to concentrate his researches upon *spikenard*, which certainly may have been the *genuine nard* which Mary lavished on her Lord, although the evangelist does not say that it was. Sir William Jones concludes thus: "My own inquiries having convinced me that "the Indian spikenard of Dioscorides is the *Sumbulu'l Hind*, and that the "*Sumbulu'l Hind* is the *Jatámánsí* of Amarsinh, I am persuaded that the true "nard is a species of *Valerian*, produced in the most remote and hilly parts of "India, such as Nepál, Morang, and Butan, near which Ptolemy fixes its native "soil" (p. 44). As to the construction of the adjective *very-precious*, or rather *very-expensive, very costly*, we may either leave it appositively by the side of the expression *genuine nard*, or transpositively connect it thus, *very-costly genuine nard*. This latter we prefer.

And she brake the alabaster. Probably in the way of striking off the narrow neck, or such part of it as had been tightly and hermetically plugged and sealed to prevent evaporation and unlawful abstraction. She would bring it sharply in contact with some hard substance at hand (συντρίψασα). To suppose, with Hammond and Alford, that the vessel was entirely *shattered*, or 'crushed in the hand,' is to introduce incongruities of imagination. Fritzsche specifies them naively thus, "probable injury to the hand of Mary, possible injury to the "Saviour's head, and plashing of the nard on the floor."

And poured over His head. As an 'oil of gladness.' Very literally, the clause would run thus, *poured down Him, down the head*. In Greek idiom, as well as

some that had indignation within themselves, and said, Why was this waste of the ointment made? 5 For it might have been sold for more than three hundred pence,

in English, we can speak either of *pouring down a person*, or of *pouring down upon a person*. In the reading of אׁ B C L Δ, 1, received by Lachmann, Tischendorf, Tregelles, Alford, the detached preposition is omitted, *poured down His head*. It seems a more elegant phrase; but for that very reason we should scarcely expect that it would, if genuine, have been disturbed and transformed into the more repetitious and inartificial expression of the Received Text.

VER. 4. **But there were some that had indignation.** A peculiar and very expressive word in the original (ἀγανακτοῦντες). They felt as if *full of aches*. *Some:* a veil is drawn over the personalities. But we learn from Matt. xxvi. 8 that it was the 'disciples' themselves whose equanimity had been disturbed. The more shame to them. And from John xii. 4 we learn that the centre and the source of the 'cantankerous' disturbance was Judas Iscariot. 'Just like him.'
Within themselves. More literally, *to* or *toward themselves*, that is, *to* or *toward the individuals of their own circle*, to or *toward one another*. The expression implies that, instead of bottling up '*within themselves*,' and burying, the aching fretting grudging feelings of which they were conscious, they *turned to one another*, and gave expression to them.
And said. These words are not found in the manuscripts אׁ B C* L, and may not improbably have been absent from the evangelist's autograph. They can be mentally supplied with ease. Had they occurred indeed before the clause *to one another*, their omission from the manuscripts specified might have been accounted for on the principle of similar endings of short lines (*homoioteleuton*. See the Sinaitic MS.); but as they are found after '*to one another*,' their accidental omission is not so easily accounted for, while their deliberate insertion on the part of **some** transcriber, who wished to smooth the phraseology, need occasion no surprise.
Why was this waste of the ointment made? Or, *to what end has this destruction of the perfume been made?* They speak of the perfume as having been *destroyed*, not thinking, in their censorious zeal, that if it should ever be used at all it must be evaporated. *To what end?* They were blind meanwhile to the very end which the All-wise Creator intended in the creation of such sweet perfumes. Why should they not be enjoyed? If enjoyed by others, why not by our Lord? Why should not Mary have the joy of ministering to the joy of her Saviour? Could 'the oil of gladness' be more worthily employed?

VER. 5. **For it.** Or rather, as it is in the best manuscripts and ancient versions, *for this ointment*. All the modern editors, inclusive of Griesbach and Scholz, have accepted the reading.
Might have been sold. Or *could have been sold*. Very literally, *was able to be sold*.
For more than three hundred pence. Literally, *for above three hundred denarii*. The *denarius*, or *silver penny*, was the standard silver coin of the Romans, larger than a sixpence and smaller than a shilling. Three hundred denarii would be about £10 sterling, a very large sum in those days.

and have been given to the poor. And they murmured against her. 6 And Jesus said, Let her alone; why trouble ye her? she hath wrought a good work on me. 7 For ye have the poor with you always, and whensoever ye will ye may do them good: but me ye have not always. 8 She hath done what she could: she is come aforehand to anoint my

And given to the poor. True; and it was also true that the individual who might be supposed to buy it could, instead of buying it, give his money to the poor. Must he not buy it then? Must no one buy it? And must the poor cease to cull the plant, and prepare the perfume, that it may be sold to the rich? Must there be nothing used in life but the barest and most absolute necessaries? Must all fine arts and elegancies be abolished? It is evident that the grumblers were taking extremely narrow views of what is good for human society in general, and for the poor in particular.

And they murmured against her. It is a most expressive word in the original (ἐνεβριμοῦντο), and suggests something stronger than *murmuring*. There was a kind of *rumble-grumble muttering* bursting out. The word recalls the hoarse dissonant sounds emitted by fretted beasts.

VER. 6. **But Jesus said, Let her alone; why trouble ye her?** Or, as the Rheims admirably renders it, *Why do ye molest her?* Our Lord's spirit rose up against their rasping censoriousness.

She hath wrought a good work on Me. Literally, *she wrought.* Namely, in the act that is past. *A good work:* very literally, *a beautiful work.* There was beautiful propriety in it. **On Me;** literally, *in Me:* such is the reading of all the uncial manuscripts without exception, and hence of all the modern editors. The reading in the Received Text must have been simply borrowed from Matt. xxvi. 10. The expression *in Me* represents the Saviour's person as the sphere in which the beautiful work was performed.

VER. 7. **For ye have the poor with you always, and whensoever ye will ye may do them good.** Literally, *ye are able to do good to them.* You will have plenty of opportunities for your charities.

But Me ye have not always. The Saviour was looking steadfastly to the crisis that was imminent, and wished to direct, in an indefinite way, the minds of His disciples and other auditors to the same 'coming event.' Any trifle of expenditure therefore that might be lavished on Him, during the few remaining hours of His career, would abstract but little indeed from the sum total of the resources that might be available for the poor.

VER. 8. **She hath done what she could.** Literally, *she did what she had,* that is, *she did what she had to do, what she had it in her power to do.* A noble eulogium; the noblest possible. We are not responsible for not doing what we have it not in our power to do; but to do up to the measure of our power, that is Christian perfection.

She anticipated to anoint. That is, *she anticipatively anointed,* or *embalmed* as it were, though not in the Egyptian way. See John xix. 40. The custom of embalming rested on a principle of hope for the future, and indicated emphatic-

body to the burying. 9 Verily I say unto you, Wheresoever this gospel shall be preached throughout the whole world, *this also that she hath done shall be spoken of for a memorial of her.*

---

ally that endearment did not cease with life. (See the fine dissertation of Faselt *De Unctura Christi Sepulchrali.*)

My body. The Saviour's thoughts have gone forward beyond His decease. He is thinking of His lifeless body.

To the burying. Or *for the entombment* (εἰς τὸν ἐνταφιασμόν), ' the ' *entombment that is to take place.* The Saviour knew that He was to die according to the Scriptures, *and to be buried*, and to rise again the third day according to the Scriptures. In *His* mind therefore the action of the loving woman was connected with His death and consequent burial. And in *her* mind too when, under the folds of her explicit faith, gratitude, and devotedness, we reach the substrate of what was implicit. We come to a point where her anointing connected itself, in a spirit at once of holy hope and true devotedness, with all that was essential for human salvation. It connected itself therefore with ' the entombment.'

VER. 9. **And verily I say to you.** That is, *I solemnly assure you.*

Wheresoever this gospel shall be preached. *This gospel, of which we have been speaking at this table this evening, and which has to do with My death, burial, and resurrection.* It is noteworthy however that in the Sinaitic, Vatican, and Cambridge manuscripts (אׁ B D), as also in L and 69, the expression is simply *the gospel.* And this is the reading given by Tischendorf, Tregelles, Alford. With reason apparently, the 'Received' reading being borrowed from Matt. xxvi. 13, where it is genuine.

Throughout the whole world. Literally, *into the whole world.* The phraseology is abrupt and condensed. The idea is. *wheresoever the gospel shall be proclaimed by My heralds, as they go ' into ' the whole world.* See chap. xvi. 15; and compare, for the mode of expression, chap. xiii. 16. Principal Campbell's translation is free, but not remarkably elegant, *in whatsoever corner of the world the gospel shall be preached.*

That also which this (woman) has done shall be spoken of. Other doings indeed shall be prominent, the doings of Another. But the deed of this woman shall not be overlooked. It shall be *rehearsed*, as Tyndale has it; or *told*, as it is in Wycliffe, Coverdale, and the Rheims; or *mentioned*, as Mace and Principal Campbell give it.

For a memorial of her. That is, to preserve the memory of her among men. Comp. Acts x. 4. The word used (μνημόσυνον) is connected with *Mnemosyne*, the mother of the Muses, and so called because, before the invention of writing, a capacious and tenacious *memory* was a prime prerequisite in every effort of literary genius.

VER. 10 and 11 form a little paragraph concerning Judas, the betrayer, corresponding to Matt. xxvi. 14–16 and Luke xxii. 3–6.

VER. 10. **And.** This conjunction indicates that what follows is a thread of things that should be taken up in connection with what goes before. There

ST. MARK XIV.

10 And Judas Iscariot, one of the twelve, went unto the chief priests, to betray him unto them. 11 And when they heard it, they were glad, and promised to give him money. And he sought how he might conveniently betray him. 12 And the first day of unleavened bread, when they killed

---

was even a closer connection than is apparent on the surface of Mark's narrative. Comp. John xii. 3-7.

Judas Iscariot. See chap. iii. 19. The great drawbacks to every good cause on earth are: (1) the imperfections of the good workers; and (2) the ultroneous presence and poisonous influence of workers who are not good.

He that was one of the twelve. This expression would possibly get attached to the traitor's name in society at large. When man told to man the sensational news regarding the arrest and execution of the great Galilean Rabbi, who, with His twelve humble disciples, was 'turning' the Jewish world 'upside down,' it would be said that He was sold and betrayed to the chief priests by *Judas Iscariot, 'one of the twelve.'* Why did our Lord, it may be asked, admit him into the number? The man, we imagine, would be honest when admitted. And though he might not be noble, yet our Lord had to accept, not the best that were conceivable, but the best that were available.

Went to the chief priests. *Went off* privately from Bethany, that very night apparently on which he had been checked by our Lord for his petty and illiberal grumbling in reference to the perfume.

In order that he might deliver Him over to them. His temper was 'up.' And, as his Master was now habitually speaking of imminent and ignominious death, he perhaps began to think that it was not prudent to be attached to a 'losing concern.' Should he not therefore get out of it without delay, and if possible with something in his pocket?

VER. 11. **And they, when they heard it, were glad, and promised to give him money.** Probably a large sum. The thirty pieces of silver, spoken of in Matt. xxvi. 15 as then and there paid to him (see *Comm.* in loc.), were probably only a sum in hand to whet his cupidity, and spur him on to go through with his treason.

And he sought. From that time *he set about seeking* ($\dot{\epsilon}\zeta\dot{\eta}\tau\epsilon\iota$), he applied his mind to mature a plan.

How he might conveniently deliver Him up. The word rendered *conveniently* means *opportunely* ($\epsilon\dot{\upsilon}\kappa\alpha\iota\rho\omega s$). He began to plot how he might improve the first good opportunity that occurred, to deliver up his Lord.

VER. 12-16. The evangelist leaves the traitor to work out his dark plot, and here take up another thread of events, our Lord's personal preparation for celebrating the paschal supper. See, as corresponding paragraphs, Matt. xxvi. 17-19, and especially Luke xxii. 7-13.

VER. 12. **And on the first day of the Unleavened.** That is, *of the unleavened cakes*, or, in the singular, *of the unleavened bread*. The day referred to, the 14th of the month Abib or Nisan (Exod. xii. 6), was only in a loose and popular sense *the first day* of the festival. It was strictly *the preparation day*, when all

the passover, his disciples said unto him, Where wilt thou that we go and prepare that thou mayest eat the passover ? 13 And he sendeth forth two of his disciples, and saith unto them, Go ye into the city, and there shall meet you a man bearing a pitcher

arrangements had to be completed for the commencement of the festivities, immediately after sunset. As however these arrangements were, so to speak, the inception of the festivities, the day was sometimes, as here, spoken of as the first day of the festival. Hence in Josephus's *Antiquities*, ii. 15 : 1, we read, 'we keep a feast for *eight days*, which is called the feast of the unleavened,' while in the same *Antiquities*, iii. 10 : 5, he says, 'the feast of the unleavened falls on the fifteenth day of the month, and continues *seven days*.' In the one case the historian freely attached the preparation day to the sacred days, and thus made *eight days*. In the other he spoke strictly of the sacred days, and hence numbered them *seven*. If our Lord's decease be reckoned as having happened in the 29th year of the Christian era as now calculated, then the day referred to here, the 14th of the month Nisan, would fall on the 16th of March, A.D. 29. (See Patrizi, *De Evangeliis*, lib. ii., p. 423.)

When they sacrificed the passover. For it was needful that the paschal lamb, which was to be eaten on the 15th, immediately after the setting of the sun on the 14th, should be killed on the 14th, ' between the two evenings,' that is after the ninth hour of the solar day, but before the conclusion of the twelfth, or between three and six o'clock in the afternoon. See Exod. xii. 6 ; Lev. xxiii. 5, 6 ; Num. xxviii. 16, 17, xxxiii. 3. *When they sacrificed :* the verb is in the imperfect tense, and here means *when they were wont to sacrifice*. *To sacrifice :* that is, to kill in a sacred way, or *sacrificially*. Hence the appropriate translation of the word in 1 Cor. v. 7, ' Christ our Passover is *sacrificed* for us.' In the passage before us too it is rendered *sacrificed* in the Geneva, and the Rheims, and by Calvin too in his French version, and Wakefield and Principal Campbell. The Vulgate has *immolated* ; Luther, *offered*. The lambs were killed in the temple, either by the owners or by the Levites (2 Chron. xxx. 17). The blood would be received by the Levites, and then handed to the priests to be sprinkled (2 Chron. xxxv. 11). *The passover :* that is, *the lamb which was the memorial of the historic passover*. The thing commemorating gets the name of the thing commemorated.

His disciples say to Him, Where wilt Thou that we go, and prepare, in order that Thou mayest eat the passover ? Note the reverential feeling that dominated the disciples. They did not say, *in order that ' we ' may eat the passover*. They hid themselves behind their Lord.

VER. 13. And He sendeth off two of His disciples. They were Peter and John. See Luke xxii. 8.

And saith to them, Go into the city, and there shall meet you a man bearing a pitcher of water. Showing, by that servile act, that the day was not strictly *a holy day*. There is a kind of emphasis on the word *man*. It was women in general who carried home, poised on their heads, the earthenware pitchers, pots, or 'cans' of water, which needed to be replenished for domestic use. There might be many of these veiled females wending their respective ways

14] ST. MARK XIV. 387

of water : follow him. 14 And wheresoever he shall go in, say ye to the goodman of the house, The Master saith, Where is the guestchamber, where I shall eat the passover with my dis-

through the streets, at the time that the two disciples would be entering the city ; a considerable supply of water would be requisite for the holidays. But the disciples were to look out for *a man* thus engaged, no doubt *a serving-man* in some ' hostelry ' or ' hospice.'
Follow him. Our Lord's instructions rested on His infallible prevision.

VER. 14. **And wheresoever he shall enter in.** Into whatsoever house he shall enter, enter ye too, and then act as I tell you.
Say to the goodman of the house. Literally, *to the master of the house*, or, as Wycliffe has it, *to the lord of the hous*. The expression *goodman*, as used by Tyndale and preserved in our English version, is a relic of an olden time, when the heads of a household establishment expressed to one another, in their habitual intercourse, their mutual esteem. In some parts of the country the custom still lingers, and husbands and wives address each other as *goodman, goodwife*. The goodness was sometimes regarded as transferred to the house. Over the door of some of the houses of the ancient Egyptians the inscription was occasionally put, ' the good house.' (Wilkinson's *Ancient Egypt*, vol. i., p. 6.)
The Master saith. Literally, *the Teacher*, that is, *the Rabbi*. We may reasonably suppose that *the goodman of the house* would know the Saviour, and would have such a knowledge of the disciples too that the expression *the Rabbi* would be enough to determine for him who was meant.
Where is My guestchamber, where I may eat the passover with My disciples? '*My*' *guestchamber*, or *apartment, for which I made arrangements with thee.* The word (κατάλυμα) freely translated *guestchamber* by Tyndale, and condemned altogether by Thomas Magister (under καταγώγιον), properly means, when spoken by a Jew or other Oriental, a *khan* or *caravanserai* where travellers *untied* their travelling ' traps ' or equipages, and got rest for their beasts of burden and themselves. It is translated *inn* in Luke ii. 7. " Caravanserais are " generally built of the most solid and durable materials ; have commonly only " one storey above the ground floor, the lower of which is arched, and serves for "warehouses to store goods, and for stables, while the upper is appropriated to "lodgings. A fountain is commonly in the centre of the open quadrangle, and " itinerant cookshops are found nigh at hand to supply the wants of travellers· " The lodging chambers are often little better than cells, where the visitor "finds nothing else than bare walls, dust, and sometimes scorpions. The "traveller must bring with him his bed, and not unfrequently his cooking " utensils and provender." (*Rays from the East*, p. 39.) The establishment in Jerusalem, to which the disciples were directed, would be conducted on more accommodating principles, especially at passover time, when there would be much demand for accommodation. See next verse. The word used by the evangelist was applicable, it would appear, either to the entire establishment or to a particular apartment within it, which would be indeed but a miniature of the whole. Each was *a resting place* or *lodging place.* The Rheims translates

ciples? 15 And he will shew you a large upper room furnished *and* prepared : there make ready for us. 16 And his disciples went forth, and came into the city, and found as he had said unto them : and they made ready the passover.

---

it *refectorie*, the Geneva *lodging*, and Wycliffe, picturesquely and alternatively, *fulfilling* or *eating place*, a place where people might *eat* till *filled full*.

VER. 15. **And he himself will show you a large upper room.** Literally *a large upper place*, or *a place raised above the ground* (ἀνάγαιον = ἀνώγαιον). It might be a whole floor, or it might be a single chamber in a floor. Here it was the latter. It needed to be relatively large however, as it was to accommodate not merely two or three, but thirteen.

Furnished. Literally *strown*, or as Wycliffe has it, *strewid*, namely *with couches round a table*. The couches were *strewed* or '*strawed*,' ready for convivial use. The rooms in caravanserais were generally unfurnished. But this was prepared for the passover feast. Luther, Tyndale, and Coverdale misunderstood the word; they rendered it *paved* (Luther, *gepflastert*) ; the Geneva too was off the scent, *trimmed*.

Ready. Already swept and clean, and in order for the feast. Even at the present day the very humblest Jewish family generally has, at the passover time, "the walls of the house whitewashed, the floor scrubbed, the furniture "cleaned, and all things made to put on a new appearance." (Mills' *British Jews*, p. 195.)

There make ready for us. It is *And there* in ℵ B C D L, and in the Vulgate, Coptic, Gothic, and Æthiopic versions.

VER. 16. **And the disciples went forth.** Literally, *went out*, namely from the place where the Lord and the rest of them were remaining.

And came into the city, and found as He said to them, and made ready the passover. That is, they got the paschal lamb, took it to the temple to be there sacrificed, so that its blood might be sprinkled by the priests. Then taking it to the caravanserai, they engaged themselves in getting it cooked, and in providing all the etceteras of the feast, such as the unleavened cakes, bitter herbs, wine, and the water that was required for baptismal purification. At the present day, in Britain, the Jews are still punctiliously particular in making preparation on the same day for the feast. They provide for themselves unleavened cakes, made under the supervision of the chief rabbi, and all the other etceteras specified. But instead of the literal paschal lamb they have only, on a representative principle, a bone having a small bit of meat adhering, which is roasted brown on the coals. Along with this they have, in the same dish, as supplementary to the bone, an egg roasted hard in hot ashes. This is intended to signify that the lamb was to be roasted whole. (Mills' *British Jews*, p. 196.) The company all 'lay hold of the dish,' and the evening is turned into the principal festivity of the year.

VER. 17-21 correspond to Matt. xxvi. 20-25, and Luke xxii. 14, 21-23. The shadows are thickening around our Lord.

VER. 17. **And in the evening.** Or, *and when evening came*; very literally,

17 And in the evening he cometh with the twelve. 18 And as they sat and did eat, Jesus said, Verily I say unto you, One of you which eateth with me shall betray me. 19 And they began to be sorrowful, and to say unto him one by one, *Is it I?* and another *said, Is* it I? 20 And he answered and

---

when evening became. The reference is to the *later evening* of the Jews, the evening that set in with the setting of the sun.

He cometh with the twelve. After the two deputed brethren had finished their preparations, and were ready to leave the lamb roasting in its earthenware or excavated oven, they would doubtless return to their Master, and the whole company would thereafter walk together to Jerusalem. The city and the entire neighbourhood would be tremulously astir as the sun went down.

VER. 18. A space of time intervenes, and many little incidents occurred, but a veil is drawn over them. The evangelist touches only on some salient points, which were relevant to his practical purpose.

And while they were reclining (*at the table*), **and eating, Jesus said, Verily I say to you.** That is, *I do solemnly assure you.*

One of you, who eateth with Me, shall deliver Me up. His heart was full. It was a feast of holy gratitude and gladness which they were celebrating and enjoying, a feast too of mutual love. And yet a traitor's heart was present, and a traitor's hand was partaking. The existence of such treason was a burden on the Saviour's spirit, and a bar to free fellowship.

VER. 19. **And they began to be sorrowful.** The true-hearted disciples had, no doubt, been disposed before to be joyful on the joyful occasion. But a dark cloud now flung its shadow o'er their spirits.

And to say to Him, one by one, Is it I? The question is of such a nature ($\mu\eta\tau\iota$ $\epsilon\gamma\omega$;) that the expectation of a negative reply is carried in its breast, *Surely it is not I?*

And another *said,* **Is it I?** The supplementary *said* should be omitted. It interferes with the construction, *they began to say, first one and then another, Is it I? and another, Is it I?* The evangelist's expression is not punctiliously trimmed. He first goes over the whole company summarily, '*one by one*'; and then, as if he had merely commenced the enumeration and said '*one*,' he proceeds to specify '*another*.' Schulz says correctly that the clause, '*and another, Is it I?*' is not needed after the expression '*one by one, Is it I?*' And so have the writers of some of the earliest manuscripts thought; for the clause is wanting in א B C L P Δ, as also in the Vulgate, Syriac Peshito, Coptic, Armenian, and Æthiopic versions, and in the text of the Philoxenian Syriac. It is condemned also as spurious by Erasmus, Beza, Grotius, Mill, Fritzsche. Tregelles omits it from his text; and so does Tischendorf in his eighth edition. Volkmar too rejects it. And yet *it must no doubt be genuine*; for, while there was strong temptation, on the ground of concinnity of composition, to reject it, there would be none to insert it. It bears the mark of a true Markism. It is found in the Alexandrine and Cambridge manuscripts (A D), as also of W^b X Γ Π, and other eight uncials. It is found too in the majority of the Old Latin codices, as also in the margin of the Philoxenian Syriac. And Origen, in collating Matthew's

said unto them, *It is* one of the twelve, that dippeth with me in the dish. 21 The Son of man indeed goeth, as it is written of him : but woe to that man by whom the Son of man is betrayed ! good were it for that man if he had never been born.

---

representation and Mark's, expressly gives it (*Opera,* iv., p. 436). Griesbach approved of it in his *Critical Commentary.* Lachmann retained it. So did Alford. And Meyer and Lange acquiesce.

VER. 20. **And He answered and said to them.** The word *answered,* though undoubtedly genuine in Matt. xxvi. 23, is omitted here in the oldest manuscripts and versions, and hence is left out by the modern editors.

One of the twelve, that dippeth with Me in the dish. There is emotional abruptness in the appositive expressions. A shower of questions *Is it I?* had fallen around our Lord. He paused deliberately, and then said, *One of the twelve,* (*one*) *who dippeth with Me in the dish.* It is as if He had said : *He belongs to My own little band; and he partakes of My hospitality, as if he were animated with the kindliest feelings !* *Dippeth:* There would be frequent dippings. But perhaps there was a simultaneous dipping at the time that our Lord uttered the words before us. Besides the roasted lamb, there would probably be other viands ' sodden ' (2 Chron. xxxv. 13), and swimming. There would at all events be some liquid preparations into which the hands would be dipped either with or without bread. Such dipping, in lieu of forks on the one hand and of spoons on the other, is still a common custom in the East. *In the dish :* literally, *into.* The conveyance of the hand *into* the vessel is depicted. The nature of the vessel or tureen is not now determinable. Wycliffe, Tyndale, Coverdale have *platter.* It is the Rheims that supplied our translators with the word *dish.*

VER. 21. **The Son of Man goeth.** *Departs, withdraws from this terrestrial scene of things.* The reference is of course to death. In the Sinaitic and Vatican manuscripts (א B), as also in L, and in the Sahidic and Coptic versions, there is, at the commencement of this clause, the conjunction *because* (ὅτι). It has been received into the text by Tischendorf and Alford, and is probably genuine. In the Vulgate, most of the Old Latin codices, as also in the Peshito Syriac, and the Philoxenian Syriac, there is instead the conjunction *and*, supplanting apparently the more difficult *because.* Comp. Luke xxii. 22. The Saviour is not strictly giving a reason for the base act of treason to which He has referred ; but He is giving a reason for the Divine permission of such an act. It would have been easy to have prevented, by a miracle, the flagrant deed. But such prevention was not thought of; for a victim's death, as an offering for the sins of the world, was really contemplated by the Divine Mind.

As it is written of Him. Literally, *as it has been written concerning Him.* For instance, in the 22nd Psalm, and the 53rd chapter of Isaiah, and in the whole sacrificial symbolism of the Old Testament economy.

But woe to that man by whom the Son of Man is delivered up. There is a sound of *wailing* in the *woe.* Compare the use of the word in the only other case in which it occurs in Mark, chap. xiii. 17, as also Rev. xviii. 10, 16, 19. Reprobation and increpation are indeed implied ; but lamentation is expressed.

Good were it for that man if he had never been born. More literally, *Good*

22 And as they did eat, Jesus took bread, and blessed, and

---

would it be for him, if that man were not born. As for the potential import of the substantive verb *would it be*, see Clyde's *Syntax*, § 43. The apophthegm is rather remarkable when microscopically examined, for, strictly speaking, nothing would be *good* to a man who never existed. But our Saviour's meaning is not microscopic but obvious and most solemn: *A man's existence is turned into a curse to him, when he inverts the grand moral purpose contemplated in its Divine origination.* But was not Judas's treason indispensable, and also the murderous action of the Jews and Gentiles? God forbid! Dr. Beard says: "Whatever "God may have appointed, Judas committed a great crime; and the Jews were "murderers in the most unmitigated sense of the term. I present an illustra- "tion: A man is condemned to death; a regular infliction of the punishment "would not be murder; but when the day of execution arrives, an impatient "and vindictive mob turns aside the course of law and takes the work into its "own hands. Death is the result; but was the agency of the mob necessary to "the end? Did it make any part of the original appointment? . . . I can- "not make the admission that sin is necessary to any good, great or small. ". . . God did appoint the Saviour to sufferings and death for sin. But I "insist that God did not appoint the particular agencies which employed them- "selves in the transaction, nor the manner in which those agencies acted." (*Lectures on Theology*, vol. iii., pp. 38, 23.)

VER. 22–25 contain an account of the institution of the New Testament passover feast, the Lord's Supper. Comp. Matt. xxvi. 26–29; Luke xxii. 17–20; 1 Cor. xi. 23–26.

VER. 22. **And while they were eating.** Namely, at another period of the protracted festal supper, and no doubt after Judas had gone out. See John xiii. 21–30. Lightfoot however, in his racy '*Battle with a Wasp's Nest*,' contends that the traitor 'received the sacrament.' So many others.

Jesus took bread. 'To invite them,' says Calvin, ' to partake of a new supper.' The bread of course would be such as was lying on the table, *unleavened bread*. But it would be finical to insist, at the present day, on the necessity of using the same kind of bread. It is not now so much *the bread of affliction* that we need to eat as *the bread of true nourishment, the bread of life. The best bread in itself is the best bread for us to use.*

And when He had blessed. He uttered a *benediction* (εὐλογήσας), a *eulogy* (εὐλογία) as it were. The eulogy would rise up in the form of a *thanksgiving*. (See next verse, and also Luke xxii. 19 and 1 Cor. xi. 24.) He would give thanks for the bread, and for what it signified. So outstanding was the act of *thanksgiving* that the entire ordinance came, in course of time, to be frequently called *the Eucharist*, that is, *the thanksgiving*. This name was common even in Justin Martyr's time, in the second century. (*Apol.*, i., § 66.)

He brake. The unleavened bread consisted of *cakes*, something like *water biscuits*; and hence it was naturally subdivided, not by *cutting*, but by *break- ing*. The *breaking* was symbolical of *the ' breaking ' of His own body by the act of crucifixion*. See 1 Cor. xi. 24.

brake *it*, and gave to them, and said, Take, eat: this is my body. 23 And he took the cup, and when he had given

And gave to them, and said, Take ye. Namely, with the hand, and then eat. In some ecclesiastical communities the bread is put by the officiating minister into the mouth of the communicant, as if it were too holy to be handled by the laity. The reason for such a mode of acting is superstitious. But if the superstition be veiled, then the practice suggests an infantile condition of the communicant, although it is only the ' carnal,' and not the ' spiritual,' who continue to be ' babes in Christ ' (1 Cor. iii. 1).

Eat. This word was not in the autograph of the evangelist, but must have been added, by some harmonist, out of Matt. xxvi. 26 and 1 Cor. xi. 24. It is wanting in all the chief old manuscripts, such as ℵ A B C D K L M P U II, and in all the chief old versions, the Vulgate, the two Syriacs, the Coptic, Sahidic, Armenian, Æthiopic. It is omitted by all the modern editors. The word however is manifestly implied. In making a narrative, or in giving instructions, it is not needful to state everything expressly.

This is My body. *This*, that is, This ' *thing* ' which I give you (τοῦτο). that is, *This bread.* When He says *This* ' *is* ' *My body*, it cannot be that He meant, *This is My real body in a transubstantiated condition.* He was ' at home ' in His real body at the moment He was speaking. His hand, a part of His real body, was handling the ' sacramental ' bread, and was therefore distinct from it His tongue with which He was speaking, and His eyes through which He was looking, were certainly no parts of the bread which He handled and handed, but were at some considerable and mensurable distance from it. It cannot be, therefore, that the body which gave the bread was gathered up into the bread, so as to displace and annihilate the substantive reality of the bread, while it continued nevertheless, even when *given*, to be the organism *giving*. There was neither trans*form*ation, nor trans*substant*iation. What was there then? Symbolisation, or sacramental representation. Patrizi says indeed, as spokesman for the whole Roman Catholic church, " By the words, *This is My body*, Christ " converted the bread into His body." (*Comm. in Marcum*, in loc.) But Augustine, on the other hand, says : " How is the bread His body? and the cup, or " that which the cup contains, how is it His blood ? *These are therefore called* "*sacraments, because in them one thing is seen, while another thing is under-* "*stood.*" (*Sermo* cclxxii.) " *Signs*," he says again, " when they pertain to "Divine things, are called *sacraments.*" (*Epist.* cxxxviii. 1, 7.) Sacraments then are signs, not miracles of reciprocal annihilation and creation. " *Sacra-* " *ments,*" he says in another place, " would not be *sacraments*, if they had not " a certain similitude to the things of which they are sacraments. But from " this similitude *they also very frequently receive the names of the things them-* " *selves.*" (*Epist.* xcviii. 9.) Hence the ' sacramental bread ' receives the name of *the Lord's body.*

VER. 23. **And He took a cup.** It is simply *a cup* in ℵ B C D L X Δ, 1. So in Matthew. The modern critical editors omit the article. It is not unlikely, nevertheless, that there was only one cup on the table. Comp. Luke xxii. 20 and 1 Cor. xi. 25.

And having given thanks. For the cup, as formerly for the bread. The feast

24] ST. MARK XIV. 393

thanks, he gave *it* to them: and they all drank of it. 24 And he said unto them, This is my blood of the new testament,

---

itself was protracted into a second course, and hence the appropriate repetition of the thanks-offering.

He gave (it) to them, and they all drank of it. Very literally, *out of it*. The evangelist hastens, anticipatively, along the historic line of action. But doubtless before the completion of the communicating act, and probably indeed before any one of the disciples partook of the cup, the words of institution, or rather the words of explanation, as contained in the next verse, would be spoken.

VER. 24. **And He said to them, This.** That is, *This thing*, or, as it is expressly supplemented for us in Luke xxii. 20 and 1 Cor. xi. 25, *This cup*. And yet the reference is obviously and admittedly to the wine in the cup. The freedom of the expression should be a lesson to those who insist on excluding every vestige of freedom from the phraseology of the 22nd verse.

Is My blood. Augustine used to explain the copula by referring to the expression in 1 Cor. x. 4, 'that Rock *was* Christ.' Or we might refer to Matt. xiii. 38, 'The field *is* the world: the good seed *are* the children of the kingdom; but the tares *are* the children of the wicked one.' The red wine employed at the passover was an appropriate symbol of the Saviour's blood, and especially in this respect, that when added mystically to the mystic bread it made a mystic feast. There was reason indeed for mourning too. For, while the *bread* pointed forward to nourishment and strength that were to be, the *breaking* of it pointed backward to manglement and woe. The poured out wine too not only pointed forward to festivity and joy, it also pointed backward to a sacrifice, by blood shedding, of an inestimably precious life. So strangely near to each other, and interconnected, are sorrow and joy. In death there is the fount of life; in the anguish of the heart there is the wellspring of bliss and joy. It is the paradox of saving grace.

Of the new covenant. The word is thirteen times translated *testament* in King James's version of the New Testament, and twenty times *covenant*. Its Hebrew equivalent properly means *covenant*; but its classical import is *latter will* or *testament*. Neither of the translations does full justice to the unique transaction referred to. Indeed no human word could. And to have used a Divine word would simply have been to speak an unintelligibility. The reference is to that *disposition of things*, in virtue of which mercy, and the possibility of true and everlasting bliss, are extended to the sinful human race. It was a glorious device, culminating in the atoning sacrifice of 'the Lamb of God.' It was *a covenant*, inasmuch as there is inherent in it an element of conditional reciprocity. God, on His part, does something; He does much. But the blessing involved in what He does is suspended, so far as men's enjoyment of it is concerned, on acquiescence on their part, or cordial acceptance, or faith. It is also of the nature of a *testamentary deed*. For there is involved in it a *disposal of the effects or goods* which constitute *the property of God*; in virtue of which disposal it is that men who acquiesce or believe become His 'heirs.' The deed is a real testament, for it is duly and solemnly

which is shed for many. 25 Verily I say unto you, I will drink no more of the fruit of the vine, until that day that I drink it new in the kingdom of God.

attested and testified. And it is also really *a last will*, for it is a final expression of the will and wish of God. There was need too, in contemplation of certain sublime moral and political ends to be subserved, for an interposing death (Heb. ix. 16, 17), although there was no need for the final departure of God from the midst of His own property. His presence in the midst of it, and His enjoyment of His goods, do not interfere with the presence and enjoyment of His 'heirs,' but only crown their privileges and happiness. The Divine plan of mercy has thus in it the essentials of both a *covenant* and a *testament*. But still *covenant* is the more prominent idea. And as the covenanting parties must, in so peculiar a case, approach each other through the solemnity of a sacrifice, the Saviour says 'This is My *blood* of the new covenant.' There is some reason for regarding the word *new* as imported from Luke xxii. 20 and 1 Cor. xi. 25. It is wanting in the uncial manuscripts ℵ B C D L, and in the Coptic and Sahidic (Ming.) versions, and it is left out by Tischendorf, Tregelles, Alford. Griesbach and Meyer approve. The reference indeed is undoubtedly to *the* '*new*' covenant, which was in truth just the one grand scheme of mercy. The 'old' one, the Jewish, was but adumbrative, the shadow, cast before, of the coming reality.

Which is shed. Or, *which is being shed*. Our Saviour might have used a future expression, for the real blood shedding was still future. He might also have used a past expression, for the actual blood shedding was the logical antecedent of the commemorative ordinance. But He chooses to use a present expression, for to His mind the little space of time that was yet to elapse before His decease was as it were no time at all.

For many. How many is not indicated. But they must be so many as to constitute a *multitude*. We know from other passages that the *multitude* consisted of *the whole of mankind*. See 1 Tim. ii. 6; 2 Cor. v. 14; Heb. ii. 9; 1 John ii. 2. "By the word *many*," says Calvin, "He means not a part of the "world only, but the whole human race, for He contrasts *many* with *one*, as if "He had said that He would not be the Redeemer of one man only, but would "die to deliver *many* from the condemnation of the curse." The preposition *for* before *many* (ὑπέρ) means properly *over*, that is, *in behalf of*. It is indeed just the Greek form of our English word *over*.

VER. 25. **Verily I say to you.** I solemnly assure you.

I shall drink no more. The negative is triple in the original, and thus very strong; *I shall not drink, no more, never.*

Of the fruit of the vine. The word *fruit* means literally *progeny*, and is here applied to the wine, which is the elaborated product of the vine. Note that, according to our Saviour Himself, the liquid contained in the cup was not literal blood, but *the fruit of the vine*.

Until that day when I drink it new—as drink it I assuredly shall—**in the kingdom of God.** Namely, when, at the second coming of our Lord, the heavenly kingdom shall be established in all its intrinsic glory. The wine then used will

ST. MARK XIV.

26 And when they had sung an hymn, they went out
into the mount of Olives. 27 And Jesus saith unto them,
All ye shall be offended because of me this night: for it

be *new*, not in the sense of being *newly pressed from the grapes*, for 'the old is
better' (Luke v. 39), but in the sense of being one of the 'all things' that are
to be made 'new.' See 2 Pet. iii. 13; Rev. xxi. 5. The word rendered *new*
(καινός) is quite a different word from that which is employed when *new wine*
or *must*, as distinguished from that which is *old*, or ripe by means of age, is
referred to (νέος).

VER. 26–31 take us through another of the scenes that were preliminary to
he crisis. A corresponding paragraph is found in Matt. xxvi. 30–35. Comp.
Luke xxii. 39 and John xvi. 32.

VER. 26. **And when they had sung a hymn.** Wycliffe has *the ympne*, that is,
the hymn. So Luther, Principal Campbell, Alford. But it is neither *a hymn*
nor *the hymn* in the original. The phrase is participial, *having hymned*; and,
if the custom that prevailed in our Lord's time corresponded with the custom
represented by the subsequent rabbinical writers and practised to the present
day, more psalms than one would be chanted at the conclusion of the feast.
The 'Hallel,' a very simple oratorio of the *Hallel*ujah description, was chanted
during the paschal feast. It consisted of Psalms cxiii., cxiv., cxv., cxvi., cxvii.,
cxviii., which group of hymns "they cut in two parts," says Lightfoot; "a
"part of it they repeated in the very middle of the banquet, and they reserved
"a part to the end. . . . The hymn which Christ now sang with His disciples,
"after meat, was the latter part," which, according to the school of Shammai,
extends over Psalms cxiv.—cxviii., while according to the school of Hillel it
extended only over Psalms cxv.—cxviii. (*Lightfoot's Works*, xi., pp. 435, 436.)
The British Jews, before partaking of the fourth and last cup, 'the cup of blessing,' repeat, says Mills, Psalms cxv., cxvi., cxvii., cxviii., and cxxxvi. (*British
Jews*, p. 201.) Tyndale and Coverdale take all the poetry out of the evangelist's
expression by rendering it, *when they had sayd grace.*

They went out to the mount of Olives. So Tyndale, Wakefield, Campbell,
Edgar Taylor, Godwin. They *went out*, viz. from the place where they were in
the city, and from the city. The scene, whence the exit took place, consisted
of concentric spaces. *The mount of Olives:* Where our Lord, as well as many
of the other sojourners, was accustomed to spend His nights. See chap. xi.
11, 12, 19.

VER. 27. **And Jesus saith to them, Ye all shall be offended because of Me this
night.** But the expression *because of Me this night* has been imported from
Matthew's narrative. It is wanting in the best manuscripts, and is left out by
Tischendorf, Tregelles, Alford. It was condemned as spurious by both Mill and
Griesbach, as also by Fritzsche. Mark's narrative is briefer than Matthew's,
but quite harmonious. *Ye all shall be offended;* literally, *ye all shall be scan-
dalized.* Such is the Rheims version. Edgar Taylor's is, *ye will all offend*;
Worsley, *ye will all be made to offend*; Mace, *you will all be staggered*; Norton,
very paraphrastically, *There is none of you whose faith will not be shaken*;
Principal Campbell, with remarkable faithfulness to the idea, *I shall prove a*

is written, I will smite the shepherd, and the sheep shall be scattered. 28 But after that I am risen, I will go before you into Galilee. 29 But Peter said unto him, Although all shall

tumbling-block to you all. Wakefield and Rodolphus Dickinson, too freely, *ye will all forsake Me.* The idea is, *You will all be unwittingly caught and insnared (so that you will be staggered in your faith, and scandalized in your feelings).* See chap. iv. 17, vi. 3, ix. 42, 43, 45, 47. They would, under the malign influence of insnaring circumstances, lose confidence in the Lord as the long hoped for Messiah.

For. An event, necessary for the weal of universal man, but not yet fully understood by the disciples, was imminent. In its very approach it would shake their faith.

It stands written. Viz. in Zech. xiii. 7, in the midst of a remarkable oracle, which still needs, for its satisfactory interpretation, a considerably increased amount of scrutiny.

I will smite the Shepherd. In the original Hebrew the same idea is more poetically put, *Sword! awake against My Shepherd, even against the Man, My Fellow* (*My neighbour*), *saith Jehovah of hosts; smite the Shepherd!* It is thus the Divine sword that is to awake and smite. " Many hands were raised to wound Him, | None would interpose to save ; | *But the awful stroke that found Him | Was the stroke that Justice gave.*" (Kelly.) The passage, says Henry Cowles, "remarkably recognises the Divine agency in the atoning death of the "Lamb of God." (*The Minor Prophets*, p. 366.) " The great doctrine here "set forth," says Dr. Moore, " is, that the death of Christ was a judicial act, in "which He endured the penalty of the law, whose penal power was symbolised "by this sword of Divine wrath." (*Prophets of the Restoration*, p. 293.) Man acted coincidently, it is true, and most wilfully and wickedly, at some points in the scene; indeed, his agency, in some respects, as so often in other cases, outran the Divine order of things. But still the Divine agency went on, in uninterrupted dignity, with the dread solemnities of its own high and holy work, and completed the sacrifice. (See Stroud's *Physical Cause of Christ's Death.*)

And the sheep shall be scattered abroad. The sudden withdrawal of the Shepherd's presence will loosen for a season the bond that bound the sheep together. They will be scattered hither and thither in dismay.

VER. 28. **But after I am raised up.** Namely, from the condition into which I shall be smitten by the awakened sword. The disciples however would have no proper conception of what their Lord meant. Comp. chap. ix. 10. Their thoughts, though vibrating with solemnity and pathos, yet ran in lines that led far away from the reality that was actually imminent.

I shall go before you into Galilee. Namely, like a shepherd who goes before his sheep, that they may follow him. Though the sheep were for the moment to be scattered, yet they would continue, and especially the lambs of the flock, to be Divinely cared for. ' I will turn My hand,' saith the Lord, ' on the little ones' (Zech. xiii. 7), to rescue and protect them. This would be realized when the Shepherd reappeared on the scene.

VER. 29. **But Peter said to Him, Although all shall be offended.** Or *scandalized,*

ST. MARK XIV.

be offended, yet *will* not I. 30 And Jesus saith unto him, Verily I say unto thee, That this day, *even* in this night, before the cock crow twice, thou shalt deny me thrice. 31 But

---

or *staggered and stumbled*. The expression rendered *although* is more emphatic than our translation would suggest. It is literally *even if* (καὶ εἰ). Such is the reading, not of the Received Text only, but also of the great majority of the uncial manuscripts. In ℵ B C G L, 1, 69, however, the expression is reversed, *if even* (εἰ καί). This last reading has been accepted by Tregelles, Tischendorf in his eighth edition, and Alford. The variation is of trifling significance; but we feel disposed to adhere to the Received reading as the less likely to have been tinkeringly modified.

Yet (will) not I. The *will*, even in English, can be very well dispensed with, as in Wycliffe and the Rheims. Literally the expression is, *but not I*. The whole remark of Peter was compressed. It might be unfolded thus: 'Others may be staggered and stumbled, *but not I*. Even if they all shall falter, *I will not*.' 'Just like Peter,' a child of manly impulse, but far too impetuous and self-reliant. "This was indeed," says Petter, "his principal and most danger- "ous error and fault at this time, that he presumed too much upon himself."

Ver. 30. **And Jesus saith to him, Verily I say to thee that thou to-day, this very night.** Note the limitation of the time. The day had begun. It began with the night; and already was the night far advanced. Not only, however, some time or other during the day, but before even the first or nocturnal half of it should be concluded, the event about to be predicted would take place. So short was to be the distance between Peter's presumption and his fall.

Before the cock crow twice, thou wilt deny Me thrice. The time is still further limited. Long before the dawn of the morning the denial would take place. In the other evangelists the word *twice* does not occur. It is said in Matt. (xxvi. 34), *Before the cock crow, thou shalt deny Me thrice*. The expressions in Luke xxii. 34 and John xiii. 38 correspond. But as the expression *before the cock crow* seems to mean *before the cock crow once*, there has been perplexity among some of the reverent students of the word, while there has been no little cock-crowing, not once only or twice, on the part of those who will not admit that there is anything Divine in the Gospel. Evanson, for example, says: "This relation is absolutely irreconcileable with what is given in the Gospel "according to Matthew." (*Dissonance*, p. 265.) Scholten contends that the word *twice* must have been a gloss introduced into the text of the Proto-Mark. (*Het Oudste Evang.*, p 229.) So Michelsen. (*Het Evang. van Markus*, p. 170.) But there is really no difficulty, if the subject be looked at, not microscopically and crotchetously, but in a broad and genial spirit. "The difference," says Alexander, "is the same as that between saying, *before the bell rings*, and *before* "*the second bell rings* (for church or dinner); the reference in both expressions "being to the last and most important signal, to which the first is only pre- "liminary." Or we may conceive the matter thus: No doubt there would be more said in the conversation than is recorded, much more. It is, as in most other cases, but snatches of the interview that are narrated. And in the different narratives different aspects of the one sum total are presented to view. Mark, very likely instructed by Peter himself, presents one particular item of what

he spake the more vehemently, If I should die with thee, I will not deny thee in any wise. Likewise also said they all.

32 And they came to a place which was named Gethsemane:

---

was said, which was merged by the other evangelists in their more generic representations. Hence his '*twice*' and '*thrice*,' the echoes no doubt of the actual utterances of our Lord. Our Lord may have said, at one part of the interview, *Ah Peter, thou dost not know thyself; this very night thou shalt deny Me thrice.* Intervening remarks may then have occurred, and our Saviour may have said again, *Yes, this very night. even before the cock crow, thou shalt deny Me.* At another stage of the conversation our Lord would say. *Before the cock crow twice, thou shalt deny Me thrice.* The respective records of the fulfilment of the Lord's prediction admit of easy explication and adjustment, when looked at in the light of this variety of detail. And although these records may not be constructed with lawyer-like scrupulosity of phrase and iterative particularity, yet they are really admirable reflexes of the actual occurrences, and admirably adapted, when accepted in the spirit in which they were given, to secure all the grand purposes intended. *Deny :* The verb is compound and very strong (ἀπαρνήσῃ), *thou shalt utterly deny.*

VER. 31. **But he.** That is, *Peter.* The name indeed is added in many of the manuscripts, and also in the Armenian, Æthiopic, and Philoxenian Syriac versions; intrudingly however.

Spake. A happy version, by accident or instinct, on the part of Tyndale, of the right reading (ἐλάλει), but not of the reading that was before him (ἔλεγε). He may have been influenced by the Vulgate (*loquebatur*). The verb is in the imperfect, *he persisted in speaking.* There was repetitiousness, though the evangelist did not deem it needful to preserve the minute details.

Exceeding vehemently, If I must die with Thee, I will not deny Thee. A compressed way of saying, *If it should be necessary for one to die with Thee, to avoid denying Thee, I shall die, but I shall not deny Thee.* No doubt Peter was honest in his repeated asseverations. His whole soul would be revolting from the idea of renouncing and denying his Lord; but, like so many others, he did not know, till he was put to the test, how weak he was.

And in like manner also said they all. That is, *And all the rest also expressed themselves in like manner.* Of nothing were they more convinced, than that they would stand true to their Lord, happen what might either to Him or to them.

VER. 32–42. The Lord's agony and the disciples' sleep. Comp. the corresponding paragraphs in Matt. xxvi. 36–46, and Luke xxii. 40–46.

VER. 32. **And they come.** We are taken back, and look on.

To a place which was named Gethsemane. The word means *oil-press.* And, no doubt, originally there would be, in the spot, an olive-oil press. The real locality cannot now be precisely determined; neither is it necessary. There is an enclosed spot, lying at the base of the western slope of the mount of Olives, which is called Gethsemane (*El-Jesmániye*). It is kept by the Latin Christians, and contains eight extremely aged olive trees. "If," says Dr. Wilson, "the

ST. MARK XIV.

and he saith to his disciples, Sit ye here, while I shall pray. 33 And he taketh with him Peter and James and John, and began to be sore amazed, and to be very heavy; 34 and saith unto them, My soul is exceeding sorrowful unto death : tarry ye here, and

'Gethsemane of the Bible be not here, and we can see no reason for disturbing "the tradition regarding it, it cannot certainly be far distant, as must be "apparent from the incidental notices of the evangelists." (*Lands of the Bible*, vol. i., p. 481.)

And He saith to His disciples, Sit here, until I shall pray. Until My prayer shall be past (ἕως προσεύξωμαι). The great crisis was at hand; and it was casting its dark shadow before on the spirit of our Lord. He felt that He must get into comparative retirement, in order that He might, without distraction, grapple with the appalling difficulties of the trial, and open up His heart, in the time of extremity, to His Father.

VER. 33. **And He taketh with Him Peter and James and John.** The elite of his elect, who had been witnesses of the counterpart scene, the transfiguration (chap. ix. 2). They were admitted by their own brethren to be a representative triumvirate, and *primi inter pares*. For, even among those who are good and true, some are better fitted than others for posts of eminence, and for intimacy of intercourse.

And began to be dismayed. *Stunned*, as it were. That is the radical idea of the word. (See G. Curtius, *Grundzüge*, p. 206.) He was *astonied*. Probably never before, within the limitations of His finite experience, had the sphere of our Lord's vision, in reference to sins, and their desert and effects, been so vast. Probably never before had the corresponding sphere of His emotions, in relation to these sins, been so profoundly agitated and heaved. This state of things now 'began.' And, as it 'began,' it caused an *amazement*, that culminated in consternation. Wycliffe translates the verb *to drede* (to dread) ; Coverdale, *to waxe fearefull*.

And greatly distressed. Comp. Phil. ii. 26. Tyndale's version is borrowed from Luke, *to be in an agony*.

VER. 34. **And He saith to them.** Namely after the terrible experience had 'begun' to roll in on His spirit.

My soul is exceeding sorrowful. The idea is, *My soul is sorrowful all round and round* (περίλυπος). It was a kind of moral midnight within the periphery of His soul. At no point in the circumference was there a single gleam of light.

Unto death. Not a mere rhetorical addition. The weight of woe was literally crushing out the Saviour's life. In bearing it He was making more literal sacrifice of Himself than ever had been made on literal altar. The sacrifice would have been complete, then and there, had it not been that it appeared to Him and to His Father that certain momentous purposes of publicity, in reference to the conclusion of the tragedy, would be better subserved by shifting the scene.

Remain here and watch. He had wished His chosen three to be near Him in His woe; and yet, as it advanced, He felt that He must retire even from them, and be alone with Himself and His Father. 'Of the people' none could be

watch. 35 And he went forward a little, and fell on
the ground, and prayed that, if it were possible, the hour
might pass from him. 36 And he said, Abba, Father, all
things *are* possible unto thee; take away this cup from me:

'with Him' in the agony, none on the altar. Still He wished that His chosen
ones should not be at a great distance, and hence He said, *Remain here*. He
desired to be the object of their active sympathy, and hence He said, *and watch*.

VER. 35. **And He went forward a little**. Still farther from the spot where the
eight disciples had been asked to halt (ver. 32).
And fell on the ground. Gradually. The verb is in the imperfect. He would
kneel first of all (Luke xxii. 41).
And prayed. He continued in prayer. The verb is in the imperfect. He
kept addressing His heavenly Father. His aim in thus addressing His Father
is brought out in the next clause.
That. *In order that* (ἵνα).
If it were possible. Very literally, *if it is possible*. We are taken back to
the very time when the Saviour's prayers were uttered, and to the spot whence
they were uttered, and we hear the very words which He used. *Possible:* the
reference is not so much *to absolute* as to *relative possibility*, possibility in consistency with the great objects contemplated in the mission of the Saviour.
The hour might pass from Him. *The hour* that was imminent, and that
embraced within its compass His betrayal, His arrestment, and the desertion of
His disciples. He did not pray that the hour of the atoning sacrifice might pass
by. It was the incidental woes, inflicted so superfluously and wantonly by men,
and to no small extent by His own chosen disciples, it was these apparently,
these more particularly at least, to which the cry of His spirit referred.

VER 36. **And He said, Abba Father.** The filial element in His spirit rose up
and overshadowed all the other elements of relationship. Mark alone records
the 'bilingual' appellation, Aramaic and Greek. No doubt it would be genuine;
and most likely it would be current in certain 'bilingual' home circles, more
especially at moments of earnest address on the part of children. At such
moments there is often a tendency to emphatic redundancy or repetitiousness of
expression. Comp. Rom. viii. 15, and Gal. iv. 6. As employed by our Lord,
the dual form of the appellation is delightfully fitted to suggest that, in His
great work, He personated in His single self not Jews only, but Gentiles also.
All things are possible to Thee. Literally true. *A thing* is *a think*; and all
things thinkable are possible to almightiness. To imagine that there are actual
limits to God's power is merely to bewilder oneself in *unthinkabilities*. In the
preceding verse the reference is to conditional possibility: hence the '*if*.' In
this the reference is to absolute possibility: hence the '*all*.'
Remove this cup from Me. The Rheims translation is, *transferre this chalice
from Me*. Not that our Saviour rued His enterprise, or desired to 'back out of
it.' Infinitely far from that. The cup, which He felt it so dreadful to drink,
had in it ingredients which were never mingled by the hand of His Father, such
as the treachery of Judas, the desertion of His disciples, denial on the part of

nevertheless not what I will, but what thou wilt. 37 And he cometh, and findeth them sleeping, and saith unto Peter, Simon, sleepest thou? couldest not thou watch one hour? 38 Watch ye and pray, lest ye enter into temptation. The

---

Peter, the trial in the sanhedrim, the trial before Pilate, the scourging, the mockery of the soldiery, the crucifixion, etc., etc. All these incidental and unessential ingredients were put into the cup by men, wilfully and wantonly. Hence the petition, *Remove from Me this cup*, this cup as it is. Without these superadded ingredients the potion would have been unquestionably bitter enough; and it need not be doubted that, in consideration of that bitterness, the exquisite sensibility of our Lord would be conscious of a feeling of shrinking and instinctive recoil. But still He had come for the very purpose of 'tasting death for every man,' and was no doubt willing and wishful to die.

But not what I will, but what Thou wilt. *But the question is not, What will I? but What wilt Thou?* The reference in the word *will*, in so far as it is applied by the Saviour to Himself, is to that which Petter calls the *sensitive will*, and the schoolmen *voluntas sensualitatis*. The more literal translation however of the verb is *wish* rather than *will*. The question with the Saviour was not, *What do I wish?* but *What does My Father wish?* There was infinite submissiveness to the wish and will of His Father. If the Father deemed it best that the cup, just as it was, should be drained, the Son was absolutely acquiescent. It is easy to conceive of the greatest possible diversity in the circumstantial incidents of the atoning sacrifice. The Saviour would have wished them to have been different from what they were. Who would not? But on almost everything that is done in this world, or that has to be endured, the foul fingers of sin are laid.

VER. 37. **And He cometh.** To His disciples, viz. at some intermission in the agony of His spirit, when He had got strength through prayer. See Luke xxii. 43.

And findeth them sleeping. So far were they from profoundly realizing the solemnities that were imminent.

And saith to Peter. Peter is no doubt singled out, partly because he was the leader of the three, and partly because he had singled himself out but a little before. See ver. 29, 31.

Simon, sleepest thou? Although thou sawest that I was in such distress, and although I expressly desired thee to keep awake and watch?

Couldst thou not watch one hour? Hadst thou not strength for that? Surely thou wilt not say so. Why then not use thy strength to watch, when I desired it, that I might have the consolation of thy sympathy? Note the expression *one hour*. It seems to indicate that our Saviour had suffered an entire hour of agony. How long that period! when we remember that every moment would be stretched to its utmost.

VER. 38. **Watch ye.** The three disciples, we may suppose, had waked up when Peter was addressed. What our Lord said to one, He meant for all; and here He expressly addresses all.

And pray, that ye may not enter into temptation. They were in danger of

spirit truly *is* ready, but the flesh *is* weak. 39 And again he
went away, and prayed, and spake the same words. 40 And
when he returned, he found them asleep again, (for their eyes
were heavy,) neither wist they what to answer him. 41 And
he cometh the third time, and saith unto them, Sleep on now,

---

losing confidence in Him as the Messiah. There was therefore much need for
faithful watching and earnest praying.

The spirit indeed is willing, but the flesh is weak. The Saviour's gracious
apology for the languor of His disciples. Even while He spoke to them, they
had but imperfectly waked up. He saw them struggling with the oppressive
languor, but ineffectually. And yet, true, as well as gracious, though His
apology was, *the spirit was nevertheless to be somewhat blamed.* If it had been
sympathetic to the quick, it would have roused the *flesh.* Some have supposed
that the words, *the spirit is willing, but the flesh is weak,* are the Saviour's
explanation of His own distress. Unnatural. The supposition proceeds on the
false assumption that the Saviour's horror *was a weakness,* and that it would
have been more magnanimous and glorious to have had no experience of shrinking from the ingredients of the dreadful cup.

VER. 39. **And again He went away.** His agony returned on Him. Perhaps
the very lethargy of His disciples might call up before His view the whole
appalling succession of incidental and unessential woes that were about to
overtake Him.

And prayed, saying the same words. More literally, as the Rheims has it,
saying the selfsame word. The term *word* is used collectively, as when we speak
of *the word of God.*

VER. 40. **And when He returned, He found them asleep again, for their eyes
were heavy.** Were, so to speak, '*weighted*' (βεβαρημένοι), or, according to the
better reading (καταβαρυνομένοι), *weighed down.* The *for* introduces, not a
reason for, but an illustration of, their sleepiness. It would appear that they
had not deliberately surrendered themselves to sleep. They did not lie down, for
instance. They sat, and, to a certain extent, sought to keep themselves awake.
But ever and anon, and prevailingly, their eyelids closed.

And they wist not what to answer Him. They knew not what they could
say to Him in reply. They had no excuse which they could honestly plead.
Wist, or *wissed* as it were, that is *knew,* is now obsolete, but is connected with
an interesting group of words, *wise, wisdom, wizard,* and the German *wissen* 'to
know.' On another line it is connected with the Anglo-Saxon *witan,* the Dutch
weten, and the Gothic *vitan,* ' to know,' around which we have another group of
words, *wit, wits, witty, witless, witch, outwit, to-wit.*

VER. 41. **And He cometh the third time.** After a third retirement for a
solitary endurance of His overwhelming agony.

And saith to them, Sleep on now. A rather unhappy translation, almost
suggesting irritation and irony on the part of our Lord. Petter actually thinks
that our Lord spoke 'in a taunting manner.' But the verb rendered *sleep on,* a
translation got from Coverdale, is simply *sleep,* the translation of Tyndale, the

ST. MARK XIV.

and take *your* rest: it is enough, the hour is come; behold,

Geneva, and the Rheims; and the expression rendered *now* means literally *the remainder* (τὸ λοιπόν), that is, *the remainder of the time that is available*. Tyndale and the Geneva render it *henceforth*. *Sleep the remaining interval!* It was in compassion that our Lord thus spoke. His own struggle was meanwhile past. He did not feel the same need of the intense active sympathy of His disciples which, in the crisis of His agony, He had so fervently desired. He saw too that they were still overpowered with drowsiness, notwithstanding the persevering efforts they were making to wake up. He hence spoke to them soothingly; and, as Cardinal Cajetan expresses it, 'indulgently,' that they might get the refreshment they so much required, *Sleep for the interval that remains. I can now calmly wait and watch alone.*

And take your rest. Or, as the Rheims has it, *and take rest*. *Rest yourselves*, that is, *refresh yourselves*. The word is so rendered in 1 Cor. xvi. 18; 2 Cor. vii. 13; Philem. 7, 20.

It is enough (ἀπέχει). An expression that has given almost infinite trouble to critics. It fairly puzzled the Syriac translator. He renders it, *the end is at hand*. Our English translation is just a reproduction of the Vulgate version (*sufficit*), which must, one should suppose, have been dashed off in a fit of despair. But howsoever dashed off, or otherwise introduced, there it stands; and Luther, in his version, simply accepted it, without any attempt at an independent judgment; as did Erasmus also, and Tyndale, and Coverdale. Henry Stephens, the lexicographer, was much perplexed with the word, and in particular with its Vulgate translation; but at length he found a solitary passage, in one of the apocryphal *Odes of Anacreon* (xxviii. 33), in which the term would seem to bear no other interpretation. It afforded him great relief. Beza too found in the same ode a corresponding relief, and speaks indeed of the passage 'occurring to him,' in the midst of his doubts, as if it had been he, and not Henry Stephens, who had first alighted on it. He makes no reference at all to Stephens. The translation of the Vulgate, thus fortified out of Anacreon, was thenceforward regarded as confirmed. It was accepted by Castellio, the Geneva, Piscator, Erasmus Schmid, Sebastian Schmidt. It is found in all the Dutch versions, the earlier, the later, the latest. So too in Diodati, Zinzendorf, Rilliet; and in many other versions. Accepting the translation (and Wetstein hunted up another passage from Cyril on Hag. ii. 9), the great body of expositors have interpreted the expression as a repetition ' in earnest' of the ironical expression that precedes, as if our Lord were now saying plainly, *ye have had enough of sleep*. See Diodati, Petter, and Schleusner. But Wolf supposes that the Saviour refers to His own sufferings, *I have suffered enough for the present, and it only remains that I endure the sufferings that are to come!* Neither phase of thought seems satisfactory. Grotius felt this, and imagined that the phrase must have an idiomatic import, corresponding to the technical expression employed in the Roman amphitheatre, when a gladiator was wounded, '*Habet*,' *He has it, he has got it, he has got the fatal wound.* The Saviour, according to Grotius, as it were says, *It is all over with Me now. The time is past for any benefit to Me from your sympathy.* An unlikely interpretation, both on philological and on moral grounds, but accepted nevertheless by

the Son of man is betrayed into the hands of sinners.

Principal Campbell, who renders the phrase *All is over*. Bengel's translation corresponds to a degree (*es ist aus*), only he gives it a turn in the direction of the disciples, not of the Saviour, *It is over*, viz. *with your rest*. So Felbinger. Kypke's interpretation is, *The time is up*. Heumann again, and Wahl, and Godwin, would render the phrase, *It is past*, or *It is away*, that is, *My agony is past*. Le Clerc, *The thing is past, My resolution to go on is taken*. There are other modifications of idea suggested by other expositors. But the great objection to all such interpretations is that the verb does not mean, *to be away*, *to be past*, or *to be up*, or *to be over*, or *to be all over*. It means, when used intransitively, *to have off*, *to hold off*, *to be distant*. Such is its meaning in all the other passages of the New Testament in which it occurs with its intransitive signification. So Matt. xv. 8 and Mark vii. 6, 'their heart *is far* from Me,' '*is distant* from Me.' So Luke vii. 6, 'when He *was* now not far from the house,' that is, 'when He *was* now not far *distant* from the house.' So Luke xv. 20, 'when he *was* yet a great way *off*,' that is, 'when he *was* yet a long way *distant*.' And Luke xxiv. 13, 'A village called Emmaus, which *was* from Jerusalem about threescore furlongs,' that is, 'which *was distant* from Jerusalem.' We see no reason for departing, in the passage before us, from this, the word's accredited and ordinary signification. But the question arises, to what, or to whom, does the Saviour refer, when He says 'is distant'? He refers, as we apprehend, not to a thing, but to a person, of whom He was thinking much, as is evident at once from the last clause of this verse, and from the next verse. But, though thinking much of him, He did not feel inclined expressly to name him. The reference we take to be to Judas, *He is distant, He is at a distance*. The expression is thus not the unmasking of a previous sarcasm. It is the gracious utterance, partly to His own mind, and partly to the minds of His lethargic disciples, of a reason for indulging them in a few minutes more of rest. We shall lose much of the true significance of the whole scene, and of the grandeur of the Saviour's demeanour, if we imagine that there was anything like hot haste and semi-irritation on the part of our Lord. There is not the slightest need for supposing that all the words, recorded by the evangelist, were spoken in rapid succession. It was, we believe, far otherwise. After our Saviour had got relief from the overwhelming pressure of His agony, and had graciously approached His disciples, and sympathised with them in their feelings of oppression, He would most probably seat Himself beside them, and say soothingly, *Sleep for the remainder of the little time that we still have, and refresh yourselves*. Then He would add, as a reason for this indulgence, the word before us, a word which did not demand, on the part of the disciples, any mental determination regarding the subject of the proposition. It was enough that they knew that, whether a person or a thing were referred to, *distance* was affirmed. They might indeed have waked up, and inquired, ' — *is distant?*' *what is? who is?* But this was not necessary, if they understood that the reason for making a final effort to shake off their drowsiness was yet *at a distance*. After the Lord had said (*He*) *is at a distance*, we may suppose that He paused, and, turning His eyes in the direction of Jerusalem, wrapped Himself up in His own meditations. At length, when the moving lights of

42 Rise up, let us go; lo, he that betrayeth me is at hand. 43 And immediately, while he yet spake, cometh Judas, one of the twelve, and with him a great multitude with swords and staves, from the chief priests and the scribes and the elders.

---

the band around Judas became visible, the Lord broke silence, and spoke as follows.

The hour has come. *The hour*, the crisis time, the beginning of the end.

Lo, the Son of Man is delivered up. *Is in the act of being delivered up*, viz. by Judas. The verb is in the present tense. The event was now so imminent that the Saviour speaks of it as transpiring.

Into the hands of sinners. Literally, *of the sinners*. The word is used, as often elsewhere, in its emphatic acceptation, and hence Godwin's translation does justice to its spirit, *of the wicked*. Such was the character of the white-washed men who bore sway in the sanhedrim, and of the others who would co-operate with them in their eagerness to get rid of all who might disturb them in their hypocritical repose.

VER. 42. **Rise up.** *Rouse yourselves up.* There was no longer time for repose.

Let us be going. *Let us voluntarily lead ourselves on* (ἄγωμεν), viz. that we may confront the traitor and his band. How sublimely does the heroism of our Lord reveal itself!

Lo, he who delivereth Me up is at hand. Instead of naming Judas, the Lord described him, and, in the description, verified His own former predictions regarding Himself.

VER. 43–50. The delivering up of our Lord by the traitor Judas. For corresponding paragraphs, see Matt. xxvi. 47–56, Luke xxii. 47–53, and John xviii. 1–12.

VER. 43. **And immediately, while He yet spake.** Or, more literally, *while He is yet speaking*, viz. to the effect of what is recorded in the two preceding verses.

Cometh Judas. The Alexandrine and Cambridge manuscripts (A D), as well as a few more uncials, add *Iscariot*. So do the Italic and Vulgate versions, as likewise both the Syriac Peshito and the Syriac Philoxenian. The great majority of the uncial manuscripts however omit the addition, as do the Sahidic, Coptic, and Gothic versions; and it is more likely that, in this case, the transcribers would add than it is that they would subtract.

One of the twelve. It was such an astonishing thing that 'one of the twelve' should be the chief agent in the arrestment of our Lord, that the phrase got linked, in the people's speech, to his name. Comp. ver. 10.

And with him a great crowd. The word *great* has been probably added from Matt. xxvi. 47. It is wanting in both the Sinaitic and Vatican manuscripts, and in the Sahidic, Coptic, Gothic, Philoxenian Syriac, and Armenian versions, as well as in several of the Old Latin codices.

With swords and staves. Or *sticks, cudgels, 'shilelahs.'* The *crowd* was to a large extent a *mob*.

From the chief priests, and the scribes, and the elders. The highest authorities

44 And he that betrayed him had given them a token, saying Whomsoever I shall kiss, that same is he; take him, and lead *him* away safely. 45 And as soon as he was come, he goeth straightway to him, and saith, Master, master; and kissed him. 46 And they laid their hands on him, and took him.
47 And one of them that stood by drew a sword, and

in the state were represented by the crowd. There had been a council held, and authority communicated.

VER. 44. **And he that betrayed Him.** It is a participial expression, which we cannot well reproduce. It means *the deliverer up, he who was being engaged in delivering Him up.*

Had given them a token. The word for *token* is compound (σύσσημον), and literally means *a token between parties*, a mutually agreed-on token, sign, or signal, 'a concerted signal' (Bloomfield).

Saying, Whomsoever I shall kiss, He it is. To what a depth of callousness the infatuated man had sunk!

Take Him. *Seize Him, arrest Him.*

And lead Him away safely. Wycliffe, Tyndale, Coverdale, have *warily*; and Wycliffe has an alternative word *queyntely* (or *quaintly*), that is, *knowingly, skilfully.* The word means *securely* (*so that there may be no chance of His escape*). Mace's translation of the whole clause is, *seize Him, and don't let Him escape.* It was, on the part of Judas, a detestable superfluity of instruction.

VER. 45. **And having come, he immediately came up to Him.** Without hesitation or falter. The tide of feeling was still strong, though the moment of ebbing was at hand.

And saith, Master, Master. Or, as it is in the original, *Rabbi, Rabbi*. But in the ℵ B C* D L M Δ, and in a large proportion of the Old Latin codices, as well as in the Coptic and Æthiopic versions, the word is single. *Rabbi* was evidently the designation by which our Lord was usually and familiarly addressed by His disciples. See chap. ix. 5, xi. 21.

And kissed Him. Viz. in an emphatic manner (κατεφίλησεν). The word is stronger than the uncompounded term used in the preceding verse.

VER. 46. **And they laid their hands on Him.** Or, more literally, *they clapped their hands on Him* (ἐπέβαλαν).

And took Him. That is, *and held Him fast.* Wycliffe has, *and heelden Him.*

VER. 47. **But one of them that stood by.** Literally, *but one certain (individual) of those who stood by.* His name is withheld by all the evangelists but John (xviii. 10). No doubt wisely. Feelings of revenge might have been awakened. Blood-thirst was strong in the East. But by the time that John wrote the actors and sufferers had alike passed from the scene.

Drew a sword. Or *his sword.* More literally, *having drawn 'the' sword.* What sword? It is as if the reader were expected to know that he had a sword. And indeed the circle of the disciples knew it well, and, no doubt, in their familiar narrations of the occurrence, they would naturally use the definite

smote a servant of the high priest, and cut off his ear. 48 And Jesus answered and said unto them, Are ye come out, as against a thief, with swords and *with* staves to take me? 49 I was daily with you in the temple teaching, and ye took me not: but the scriptures must be fulfilled.

---

article. There were two swords among them (Luke xxii. 38). The Saviour allowed it, for a parabolic purpose (Luke xxii. 36-38). It was needful for His disciples to bear in mind that, in the warfare which awaited them, they would have enough to do to guard their lives. And when all was done that could be done by them, their lives, so far as earth was concerned, would by no means be secure. Peter was one of the two disciples who had provided themselves with swords. It was customary of old in Syria, as it is still, for peaceful inhabitants to wear weapons of defence. As there is no proper system of police, every man has to be his own policeman.

And smote a servant of the high priest. *Smote* or *struck*. *A servant*: it is *the servant* in the original. The high priest seems to have sent one particular confidential servant, who might exercise a careful surveillance over Judas and the rest of the company.

And cut off his ear. The stroke, aimed at the head, had been parried, but took partial effect.

VER. 48-50. The fact recorded in the preceding verse stands apart by itself. So does the fact recorded in ver. 48, 49. So does the fact recorded in ver. 50. The evangelist adds, artlessly and aggregatively, detail to detail.

VER. 48. **And Jesus answered and said to them.** His words were *responsive* to their acts, for their acts were as significant as words.

Are ye come out as against a thief? Or, more literally, *As against a robber are ye come out?* More literally still, *As against a robber came ye out?* viz. from the city. **With swords and cudge's to apprehend Me.** Swords and cudgels would not have been required against a mere thief. But robbers or brigands were men of arms, who were prepared to defend themselves to the last, and, in the ultimate extremity, to sell their lives at as dear a cost as possible. The word is always mistranslated *thief* in King James's version of the three synoptic Gospels; but it is correctly translated *robber* in John's Gospel (x. 1, 8; xviii. 40), and in 2 Cor. xi. 26. Luther did the word more justice than our English translators, but yet not full justice. He rendered it *murderer*. Bengel in his German version put it right, *Räuber*, i.e. *Robber*.

VER. 49. **I was daily with you in the temple teaching.** Or, as Rotherham gives it in the original collocation, *day by day was I with you in the temple, teaching.*

And ye took Me not. *And ye did not arrest Me.* Our Lord knew that He was not addressing the high authorities, though there were representatives of their number who had come out in the crowd (Luke xxii. 52). But He desired to make asseveration of His innocence, and to declare that such nocturnal stratagems were inconsistent with the dignity of justice.

But the Scriptures must be fulfilled. The language is abruptly broken off in

50 And they all forsook him, and fled.
51 And there followed him a certain young man, having a

the original, *But that the Scriptures might be fulfilled—*. We must mentally add *this takes place*. It was Divinely permitted to take place, because the same Mind which foresaw what it was that Judas and the high priest, and their co-conspirators, would voluntarily do, resolved to permit it, inasmuch as their act, however wicked and infatuated, would not frustrate the final end contemplated in the mission of our Lord, His sacrificial death as 'the Lamb of God bearing the sin of the world.'

VER. 50. **And forsaking Him, they all fled.** The disciples namely. The evangelist's own mind had turned from our Lord's enemies to His friends. But, not being practised in ' the wisdom of words,' he omits to mark the transition of reference. The disciples *forsook* or *left* their Lord, being, as their Master had predicted, stumbled or staggered in their faith. See ver. 27. They had never taken up the idea that it would be consistent with the ends contemplated in the mission of the Messiah, that He should be ignominiously arrested.

VER. 51, 52, contain another connected incident, standing by itself in the evangelist's narrative.

VER. 51. **And a certain young man.** Very literally, *and one certain young man*. But the present indefinite article ' a ' or ' an ' is just the original numeral *one* or *one*. There have been many speculations and conjectures regarding this young man. Who was he? It is impossible to say with absolute certainty. Epiphanius (*Adv. Hæres.*, lxxviii. 13) assumes that it was James the Just, the brother of our Lord, who was reported, in early times, to have confined himself ascetically to a single ' cloth ' or garment. A whimsical reason for an unlikely conjecture. Others, inclusive in modern times of Ingraham (*Prince of the House of David*, Letter 29), have supposed that it was the apostle John; also a most unlikely conjecture, resting on no basis of probability whatever. Theophylact supposes it probable that the person referred to was a youth belonging to the house where our Lord ate the passover · also a baseless conjecture. Cardinal Cajetan thinks that he may have been the son of the Gethsemane gardener. Grotius and Petter content themselves with the more generic conjecture that he would probably be a youth who lived in some contiguous villa. If conjecture at all be allowed, we should, along with Bisping and Klostermann, give the preference to the opinion of those who imagine that the evangelist refers, veilingly, to himself. The incident is in itself so exceedingly trifling, as compared with other incidents omitted from the narrative, that it seems difficult to account for its introduction unless on the principle that the narrator had a deep personal interest in its occurrence, and delighted, though in an unobtrusive and modest manner, to link himself on, in what may have been to him the turning point of his spiritual history, to the great event that was transpiring. We would agree, with Bisping, that it is most likely that the incident occurred, not in Gethsemane or on the way to Jerusalem, but in the streets of the city. The evangelist has been setting down, one by one, a number of events only loosely connected; and this is one of them.

53]   ST. MARK XIV.   409

linen cloth cast about *his* naked *body*; and the young men
laid hold on him: 52 and he left the linen cloth, and fled
from them naked.

53 And they led Jesus away to the high priest: and with
him were assembled all the chief priests and the elders and the

Followed Him. The verb is in the imperfect tense, *was following Him.* In the manuscripts ℵ B C L however it is compound (συνηκολούθει), *was following with the rest who were there.* Note that it was not the crowd which he followed: *it was Jesus.* His interest was in Jesus. Possibly as the crowd were passing along the streets, they would be excited, perhaps uproarious. The young man had been in bed; but, hearing the noise, he had started up, and rushed out undressed. He found it was Jesus, the Great Teacher, to whom we may suppose he had been listening with rapture in the temple,—it was Jesus who was being led off under arrest. He followed on for a little, and then perhaps began impulsively to interfere with the conductors, or to remonstrate. It is noteworthy that Mark and his mother lived at Jerusalem (Acts xii. 12).

Having a linen cloth cast about (his) **naked** (body). He had, on starting up, wrapped himself hurriedly in a loose robe or coverlet of fine linen, under which most probably he had been lying. The linen referred to was that peculiar texture, brought originally (not from Sidon, as Chifflet supposes (*De Linteis*, p. 23), but) from Sind or India, which was used for inwrapping the bodies of the dead. See Matt. xxvii. 59; Mark xv. 46; Luke xxiii. 53.

And the young men laid hold on him. Or, more literally, *lay hold on him,* or *seize him.* He was regarded as in sympathy with their Prisoner. He was therefore obnoxious to the virulent partisans in the crowd. Instead of *and the young men lay hold on him,* the reading in the manuscripts ℵ B C* D L Δ, and in the Vulgate, Syriac Peshito, and Coptic versions, is simply *and they lay hold on him.* Griesbach suspected the genuineness of the Received reading. Mill had previously condemned it. (*Prol.,* § 409.) And it is omitted from the text by Lachmann, Fritzsche, Tischendorf, Tregelles, and by the Revisers of 1881. No doubt correctly.

Ver. 52. **But he left.** In their hands.

The linen cloth, and fled from them naked. It would be a memorable event to the young man himself.

Ver. 53. See, for parallels, Matt. xxvi. 57; Luke xxii. 54; John xviii. 13, 14.

And they led off Jesus to the high priest. Viz. Caiaphas. Indeed the name is added in several of the ancient manuscripts and versions. Intrusively however. The detour to the house of Annas is merged out of view. See John xviii. 13.

And with him were assembled all the chief priests and the elders and the scribes The prominent members of the sanhedrim. The expression *with him,* or as Fritzsche interprets *to him,* was suspected by Mill (§ 409), and is omitted by Tischendorf on the authority of ℵ D L Δ and 69, as also of the Italic, Vulgate, and Æthiopic versions, etc. The phrase is more likely however to have been wilfully dropped than to have been wilfully added. It should no doubt be rendered as in our Authorized version. See Luke xxiii. 55; Acts ix. 39, x. 23, 45,

scribes. 54 And Peter followed him afar off, even into the palace of the high priest: and he sat with the servants, and warmed himself at the fire.

55 And the chief priests and all the council sought for witness against Jesus to put him to death; and found none. 56 For many bare false witness against him, but their witness

---

xi. 12, xv. 38; and also John xi. 33. And the reference is not, as Meyer supposes, to our Lord, but to the high priest.

VER. 54. Comp. Matt. xxvi. 58; Luke xxii. 54, 55; John xviii. 15–18.

And Peter followed Him afar off. Or, as Mace, Campbell, Norton give it, *at a distance*; or, according to the Greek idiom, *from a distance*.

Even into. The original phrase is repetitious, *until within into* (ἕως ἔσω εἰς).

The palace of the high priest. Or rather *the court* (viz. of the high priest's palace), the interior *hall* or *quadrangle*, around which the chambers of the residence were constructed.

And he was sitting along with the servants. The reader's mind is thrown anticipatively forward to something special that occurred *while he was sitting*. There would be quite a crowd of servants and hangers on, and, in particular, the sweepings of the band which had gone to Gethsemane. Peter would expect to get jostled into the heart of the crowd unobserved.

And warming himself at the fire. Literally, *toward the fire*; more literally still, *toward the light*. The preposition brings into view *that he turned himself toward the fire*, in order to get warmed. The word *light*, again, brings into view the *blazing* of the fire, by which his countenance would be illuminated and thus by and by identified. The word is everywhere else translated *light*.

VER. 55–64 constitute a paragraph corresponding to Matt. xxvi. 59–66. The narratives in Luke and John are much more fragmentary.

VER. 55. **But the chief priests and the whole council.** Or, *the whole sanhedrim*. It was an informal meeting of the sanhedrim, and the members present seemed to be animated with the same deeply prejudiced spirit that was dominating the high priest.

Sought-for. The verb is in the imperfect, *were engaged in seeking-for*.

Testimony against Jesus. It was right in them to require testimony. But it was iniquitous for them to go hunting for it *against* the Prisoner. Such prejudication and partisanship were a virtual abdication of their function as judges.

To put Him to death. This laid the copestone on their iniquity. They not only prejudged the case, they were eager to inflict the highest penalty possible. Their eagerness resolved itself into the spirit of murder.

And found none. Literally, *and did not find*; more literally still, *and were not finding* it. This was what *went on* in the court for a time.

VER. 56. **For many bare false witness against Him.** Literally, *were bearing false witness*. There was a succession of cases.

But. Strictly *and* (καί). The clause introduced forms part of the succession of things.

agreed not together. 57 And there arose certain, and bare false witness against him, saying, 58 We heard him say, I will destroy this temple that is made with hands, and within three days I will build another made without hands. 59 But neither so did their witness agree together. 60 And the high priest stood up in the midst, and asked Jesus, saying, Answerest thou nothing ? what *is it which* these witness against thee ?

Their witness agreed not t gether. Literally, *the testimonies were not equal.* They did not tally, or match, the one with the other. Hence there was a difficulty in getting the sentence desired, for two accordant witnesses, at the least, were indispensable. See Deut. xvii. 6.

VER. 57. **And some arose and bore false witness against Him, saying.** This case was worthy of specification. They *bore* false witness. They persisted in it for a time. The verb is in the imperfect.

VER. 58. **We heard Him saying, I will destroy this temple that is made with hands, and within three days I will build another made without hands.** Of course the Saviour never made any such statement. See John ii. 19. He made a mystic reference indeed to His own death and resurrection. But He never intimated that He would destroy any temple whatsoever. Neither did He distinguish, at that time, between a temple made with human hands, and another made without such hands. The expression *within three days* should rather be *in three days*, for the phrase does not intimate that the period required would be *less than three days*. It is literally, *through three days*. Our Saviour, *in passing through three days*, would accomplish the work of which He spoke.

VER. 59. **But neither so.** Literally, *and not even so*, that is, *and not even to that extent*, nor even to the extent of the allegation, as given summarily in the preceding verse.

Was their testimony equal. The witnesses had so much in common that they were sure that the Lord had said something or other about the 'destruction of the temple,' and something or other about 'raising it again in three days.' But they differed in the details of their testimony, which was consequently so vitiated that a conviction could not be obtained. It would appear that either the witnesses were, as Meyer supposes, examined separately, or else that they got positive in contradicting one another.

VER. 60. **And the high priest rose up in the midst.** More literally, *into the midst*. He would seem to have stepped forward nearer the Prisoner.

And interrogated Jesus, saying, Answerest Thou nothing? What do these testify against Thee? Instead of this double interrogation, Luther gives it thus: *Answerest Thou nothing to that which these testify against Thee?* So the Vulgate before him, and Baumgarten-Crusius, Lachmann, Tischendorf, Bleek. But the two interrogatories are more in harmony, at once with the nature of the phraseology, and with the exasperated spirit of the interrogator. He had been baffled, and was chagrined. Laying aside everything like judicial impartiality and calmness, he chides our Lord for His dignified silence amid the Babel of

ST. MARK XIV.

61 But he held his peace, and answered nothing. Again the high priest asked him, and said unto him, Art thou the Christ, the Son of the Blessed? 62 And Jesus said, I am: and ye shall see the Son of man sitting on the right hand of power, and coming in the clouds of heaven. 63 Then

---

accusation, *Answerest Thou nothing?* He would have liked that our Lord had lost command of His reticence, and had returned railing for railing. When he added, *What do these testify against Thee?* the meaning is, *Though the testimonies of these witnesses do not quite agree in details, yet there was evidently something extraordinary said by Thee on the occasion referred to. What was it?* It was a most improper question. The construction of a double interrogation has been accepted, not only by our Authorized translators, but likewise by Erasmus, Tyndale, Castellio, Beza, Bengel, Meyer.

VER. 61. **But He was silent, and answered nothing.** He could not descend, even for a moment, from the pinnacle of true dignity on which He stood. It was no part of His duty, as a defendant, to unravel the contradictions of His unprincipled accusers.

Again the high priest interrogated Him, and says to Him, Art Thou the Christ, the Son of the Blessed? This was a legitimate question to put. It was quite right to call upon our Lord to declare who and what He was. It is right that every man in society should be prepared to tell who and what he is. No man can have a legitimate claim to the privileges of society who cannot give account of himself. The expressions employed by the high priest were taken from the second Psalm, which was then considered to be Messianic, and which can never be rationally interpreted on any other hypothesis. See ver. 2, 7. *The Blessed:* An indefinite appellative way of referring to God, who is emphatically *the Blessed One.* The word is not here, as in 1 Tim. i. 11 and vi. 15, equivalent to *happy* (μακάριος). It represents the Lord as the appropriate object of *eulogy* or *praise* (εὐλογητός).

VER. 62. **And Jesus said, I am.** It was the fitting time and place to declare, in terms the most unequivocal and unmistakable, that He was the Divine Messiah.

And ye shall see (sooner or later) **the Son of Man.** While our Lord was in the very act of avowing that He was *the Son of God* He delights to think and speak of Himself as the *Son of man.* He realized His identification with the human family.

Sitting at the right hand of power. Very literally, *of the power*, i.e. *of the supreme power.* He represents Himself as seated at the right hand of the absolute and irresistible Sovereign of the universe. As *Son of man* indeed He was essentially subordinate to the Father, so as to have His appropriate place in a secondary position. But as *Son of God* He was fit to sit on the throne with His Father. Compare the first verse of that remarkable Messianic psalm, the 110th.

And coming in the clouds of heaven. Literally, *with the clouds of the heaven*, that is, encompassed with them. *Coming:* namely, to judge the world, and thus to judge the judges who were now judging Him. When Jesus shall thus

the high priest rent his clothes, and saith, What need we any
further witnesses? 64 Ye have heard the blasphemy : what

come, He will not be alone. He will indeed be the active agent in conducting
the judgment, for 'the Father judgeth no man, but hath committed all judgment to the Son' (John v. 22). But the Father, 'the Ancient of days,' will be
present (Dan. vii. 9), a 'very present' Assessor on the one throne of judgment,
and rejoicing that His mind can be infallibly manifested through Him who is '*a*
Word,' and '*the* Word,' and '*His* Word.' How august the self consciousness of
our Lord, to realize all this, at the very moment when He was standing like a
felon at the high priest's bar !

VER. 63. **But the high priest rent his clothes.** No doubt in some normal
and formal manner. In a primitive state of society indeed, when inward feeling
is, with but little restraint, immediately mirrored in outward action, the tearing
of one's robes violently might often occur ; and when it did occur, it would be
expressively indicative of a perfect tumult of passion. See Gen. xxxvii. 29 ;
Jud. xi. 35 ; Job i. 20 ; Isa. xxxvi. 22, xxxvii. 1. But in a more disciplined
condition, when art has been interwoven with nature and restrains it at almost
every point of the warp, the tearing of the robes, when there is a wish to convey
the impression that something dreadful has occurred, must be regarded as
an entirely artificial symbolism. In the case before us the high priest would
probably be careful to regulate the rending, both topically and longitudinally,
according to the rules of the most approved rabbinical etiquette. See *Comm.*
on Matt. xxvi. 65. *Clothes :* Or, literally, *tunics*. It is the word, but in the
plural, which is almost always rendered *coat* in the Authorized version, as
distinguished from the loose outer robe or *cloke*. It had only the remotest
analogy however to a European *dress coat*. The poor contented themselves
with wearing one tunic. The rich in general wore two, the inner one plain
and of fine linen, the outer ornamental and of stronger stuff. See Braunius *De
Vestitu Sacerdotum Hebræorum*, p. 554. The high priest, when rending his
tunics, would have on his unofficial robes. See Braunius, p. 842.

And saith, What farther need have we of witnesses? Very literally, *Why still
have we need of witnesses ?* That is, *Why should any one suppose that we still
require witnesses in this case, ere we could be warranted to come to a judgment ?*
See next verse.

VER. 64. **Ye have heard.** Literally, *ye heard*, viz. within the last few
moments.

The blasphemy. The defamation of God, of which this man was guilty. The
high priest, in his self sufficiency, did not distinguish between *a claim* and *a
false claim*. If our Lord's claim to be *the Christ, the Son of the Blessed*, had
been false, it would have been a blasphemy. But no evidence had been brought
to show that it was false. And the high priest was travelling far beyond his
judicial function when he merely assumed that it was. If there was any foundation for the existence and maintenance of the office of the high priesthood
among the Jews, or for the existence and maintenance of the other peculiarities
of Judaism, some One, at some time or other, must appear as *the Christ, the
Son of the Blessed*. Why might not our Lord be that One?

think ye? And they all condemned him to be guilty of death. 65 And some began to spit on him, and to cover his face, and to buffet him, and to say unto him, Prophesy: and the servants did strike him with the palms of their hands.

What think ye? Literally, *what appears to you?* That is, *what appears to you to be the desert of this blasphemer?*

And they all condemned Him to be guilty of death. The meaning is not, *that they condemned Him to die.* They had not such power (John xviii. 31). But they passed sentence on Him as one who, in their judgment, was *worthy of death*, one who had brought Himself *within the grip of the penalty of death*, as one consequently who should be delivered over to the Roman governor to be dealt with according to their finding. See chap. iii. 29. The word *guilty* has a far-off connection with *gilding* and *gold*, and has thus embedded in it a reference to that which is *precious*. *Guilt* was in some respects *a price*. It often merged in *a price*. It could be replaced or cancelled by *a price*. A person offending *had a price to pay*. The *price* was a penalty. A *guilty* man is one who is *liable to 'pay' a penalty*. The expression *guilty of death* means *liable to pay the penalty of death*. The word rendered *guilty* is translated *in danger of*, in Matt. v. 21, 22. It literally means *in the grip of*. Tyndale renders it, here, *worthy of*.

VER. 65. Compare for parallel statements Matt. xxvi. 67, 68, and Luke xxii. 63–65. The wild beast element was stirred in the breasts of some of the baser beings around our Lord.

And some began to spit on Him. Alas, alas! But 'this,' says Richard Baxter, 'the Son of God endured for our sins.'

And to cover His face, and to buffet Him, and say unto Him, Prophesy. That is, *Tell us by inspiration who the individual was who struck Thee.* The word *buffet* means *to cuff*. *to strike with the fists.* Tyndale's translation is, *and to bete Him with fistes*; Wycliffe's, *and smyte Him with boffatis* (i.e. *buffets*).

And the servants did strike Him with the palms of their hands. A free translation of a tinkered text. The word rendered *the palms of their hands* means *slaps*, or *blows* (ῥαπίσμασιν). The verb rendered *did strike* (ἔβαλλον) is a transcriber's substitute for a different verb altogether, which means *received* (ἔλαβον). This latter is the reading of ℵ A B C I K L N S V Γ Δ Π; and so, in substance, of D G. 1, 69. It must be genuine. The meaning is, *the officers received Him with blows*, that is, they *received Him into custody* till the regular meeting of the sanhedrim, which could not be held sooner than in the morning: but the moment He was committed to them they *received Him with blows*. Alas, alas! And yet no wonder. They but imitated their superiors. 'Like master, like man,' says Petter.

VER. 66–72. The episode of Peter's lamentable fall and speedy penitence. Compare, for corresponding paragraphs, Matt. xxvi. 69–75; Luke xxii. 54–62; John xviii. 15–18, and 25–27.

VER. 66. **And.** The narrative goes back a little. The main current of events was followed to the point recorded in the preceding verse. The evangelist returns thence to take up the following incidents.

66 And as Peter was beneath in the palace, there cometh one of the maids of the high priest: 67 and when she saw Peter warming himself, she looked upon him, and said, And thou also wast with Jesus of Nazareth. 68 But he denied, saying, I know not, neither understand I what thou sayest. And he went out into the porch; and the cock crew. 69 And a

---

While Peter was beneath in the palace. Or rather, *down in the court*, that court that was open above, and round the sides of which the chambers of the mansion were built. *Down;* it is not implied that the apartment in which our Saviour was tried was an upstair floor or storey. It is only implied that the reception hall, that entered off the quadrangular court, was raised a little above its level. There would perhaps be only a curtain intervening, which would be opened and closed as servants or others entered or retired. See Luke xxii. 61.

There cometh one of the maids of the high priest. Excited by what was transpiring in the reception hall, and eager to get talking about it to the people.

VER. 67. **And seeing Peter warming himself, she looked on him.** She was led to fix her eyes on him. Something in his appearance stirred her recollections.

And says, And thou wast with Jesus of Nazareth. Literally, *and thou wast with the Nazarene, Jesus.* See, in particular, the modern critical editions.

VER. 68. **But.** Now was Peter's time for acting a hero's part, *but.*

He denied, saying, I know not. A broken statement. He meant, *I do not know Him.* See Luke xxii. 57. But in his agitation he only got the length of *I do not know*, and then he takes up another line of self defence.

Neither do I understand what thou sayest. In the original of the correct text the language is singularly indicative either of Galilean rudeness of speech, or of agitation, or of both combined (σὺ τί λέγεις).

And he went out into the porch. With all his assumed hardihood, he trembled in his skin, and felt that the sooner he got more into the shade the better. So he left the vicinity of the blazing fire, and returned into *the vestibule,* or the arched entrance passage which extended from the great outside gate to the quadrangle of the court.

And the cock crew. Or rather, *and 'a' cock crowed.* It was distinctly audible; and though it did not succeed in touching the deepest spring in Peter's heart, yet no doubt it would excite some tremulous emotion : *What! is the prediction to be literally fulfilled after all? And yet this prisoner, being a prisoner, cannot surely be the Messiah for whom we hoped, and in whom I misplaced so fondly and devotedly my confidence.*

VER. 69. **And a maid.** It is *the maid* in the original, no doubt the same maid, although there is no reason whatever why we should not suppose that she had some companion or companions, who would take a part in the conversation. Hence we read in Matthew of *another maid.* Luke refers to *others* who were *males.*

maid saw him again, and began to say to them that stood by, This is *one* of them. 70 And he denied it again. And a little after, they that stood by said again to Peter, Surely thou art *one* of them : for thou art a Galilæan, and thy speech agreeth *thereto*. 71 But he began to curse and to swear, *saying*, I know not this man of whom ye speak. 72 And the second time the cock crew. And Peter called to mind the word that Jesus said unto him, Before the cock crow twice, thou shalt

Seeing him again, began to say. Tischendorf reads, under the authority of ℵ C L Δ, *seeing him, began again to say*. But there can be little doubt that the same reason which led our translators to say *a maid* led the transcribers on whose authority the reading of ℵ C L Δ rests to shift the position of the *again*. Under the pressure of the same supposed difficulty the *again* was sometimes altogether dropped out, as in the Vatican manuscript, and in the Coptic, Sahidic, and Æthiopic versions.

To them that stood by, This is (one) of them. She was confident, notwithstanding his strong denial, that she had seen him with the Nazarene, probably in the temple area. And she would be able also to see self consciousness and self condemnation in his face.

Ver. 70. **But he again denied.** Poor fellow ! He was in the hands of the Philistines and of his conscience.

And after a little, again they who stood by said to Peter, Surely thou art of them. Instead of *again*, Wycliffe has, throughout the whole of this paragraph, the fine old word *eftsoone*, i.e. *soon after*. *Surely :* this word is now too hesitative. It is *truly* in the original, that is *certainly*, or *without doubt*. Wycliffe, *verily*.

For thou art a Galilean. There is an untranslatable *and* in the original before these words ; but it is very significant. It suggests, on the one hand, that there were other things that proved that Peter belonged to the circle of the Nazarene; but asserts on the other that this was an additional proof. His accent bewrayed him to be a Galilean, and, if a Galilean, what was he doing skulking about in the high priest's house if he was not one of the 'set'?

And thy speech agreeth thereto. This clause is omitted by Lachmann, Tischendorf, Tregelles. It is wanting in the manuscripts ℵ B C D L, 1, and was wanting in the copies before Eusebius and Augustine, as also in the Sahidic and Coptic versions. It was most likely imported from Matt. xxvi. 73.

Ver. 71. **But he began to curse.** " As if he should say, the curse of God " alight upon me if I know Him " (Petter).

And to swear, I know not this man of whom ye speak. Ah Peter, alas!

Ver. 72. **And.** The word *immediately* is added in ℵ B D G L, 69, and in the Old Latin, Vulgate, Syriac Peshito, Armenian, and Æthiopic versions. No doubt it is genuine. It is received by Griesbach, Lachmann, Fritzsche, Tischendorf, Tregelles.

The second time a cock crowed. And Peter called to mind the word that Jesus said unto him. More literally, *and Peter was reminded of the saying, how that Jesus said to him*.

deny me thrice. And when he thought thereon, he wept.

B-fore the cock crow twice, thou shalt deny Me thrice. And when he thought thereon, he wept. King James's translators have happily hit upon the true import of the last clause (καὶ ἐπιβαλὼν ἔκλαιεν). The Geneva version pointed in the same direction, but not by any means so felicitously as King James's translators, *And waying* (i.e. weighing) *that with himselfe, he wept*. The word rendered *when he thought thereon* has been puzzling to interpreters from the earliest times. ' There are not many words in Scripture,' says Bland, ' which have undergone more interpretations than this.' The Vulgate version renders the whole phrase thus, *and he began to weep*. So the Old Latin before it, and the Peshito Syriac, Philoxenian Syriac, Sahidic, Armenian, and Gothic versions. So too Erasmus, Luther, Tyndale, Coverdale, and many others. The Cambridge manuscript (D) actually cancels the original phrase, and substitutes, no doubt out of a marginal gloss, the common word for *began* (ἤρξατο κλαίειν). Faber Stapulensis, having the same view of the import of the phrase, gave, as far as possible, a fine idiomatic turn to his translation, *broke forth into weeping* (prorupit in fletum). He was followed by Vatable and Cajetan. It is however, in all its phases, a violent, and indeed, when the participial form of the word is taken into account, impossible rendering. Theophylact takes an entirely different view of the import of the word. He explains it thus, *having shrouded his head*. The word etymologically means *having thrown upon*. Theophylact supposes that Peter *buried his head in the folds of his cloak*, and then wept. The great French scholar Salmasius, the antagonist of Milton, was of the same opinion, and quite positive indeed that this is the only legitimate interpretation. (See his *Epistola ad Colvium*, pp. 656–7.) Many subsequent critics and expositors, inclusive of Bos, Wolf, Suicer, Elsner, Krebs, Heumann, Mace' Fritzsche, coincided in his judgment. In the absence however of any word to suggest the idea of *robe* or *cloak*, the interpretation is violent, and the expression so interpreted would be unexampled. Grotius, followed by le Clerc, thought that the phrase was a kind of Hebraism, *and adding he wept*, that is *and in addition he wept*, or, *and he wept also*. The guilty apostle *not only recollected* his Lord's prediction, *he added weeping to his recollection*. But this is, almost as much as Theophylact's, a violent and unlikely interpretation. Bleek however, misunderstanding it, thought that Grotius and le Clerc wished to interpret the expression thus, *he wept still more*; and this misconception of their meaning he adopts as the true interpretation of the evangelist's phrase, though he admits that there is nothing in what goes before to lead us to suppose that Peter had formerly wept. He thinks it likely however that Mark tacitly assumed *that the apostle had wept at the first crowing of the cock*. Most unlikely. Beza interprets the expression thus: *And when he had rushed forth* (from the high priest's house) *he wept*. The force of the participial word however he admits to be such that the meaning is not so much, *he rushed forth 'from'* (the high priest's house), as *he threw himself ' upon '* (the place that was beyond). Henry Stephens endorsed this interpretation, and it is adopted by Piscator, Erasmus Schmid, Felbinger, Raphel, Schleusner, Bretschneider, Wahl, Vater. It is however, notwithstanding such great names, utterly unworthy of being accepted, except in despair. Bishop Hammond and Palairet would interpret thus, *and when he cast* (his eyes on Christ) *he wept*. It is manifestly a suggestion of despair, and clearly inadmissible, unless despair should rise to its maximum. It is Luke alone who mentions the fact that Jesus was visible to Peter (xxii. 61). What then? Must we despair? By no means. Our English translators have given to the word a thoroughly legitimate and idiomatic rendering. The idea is, *when he threw (his thought) upon* (the prediction which he recollected) *he wept*. As a matter of fact, the word was often employed 'absolutely' by the later Greek writers, with this peculiar idiomatic reference. See a long list of passages in Wetstein (and compare the secondary meaning of the noun ἐπιβολή). Casaubon finally settled in this interpretation. Wetstein powerfully supported it. And it has been approved of by Petter, Kypke, Principal Campbell, Glöckler, de Wette, Bland, Bloomfield, Alexander, Meyer, Bisping, Grimm, Godwin, Volkmar. *He wept:* the verb is in the imperfect tense, and suggests more than a mere outburst of tears. His tears kept flowing.

CHAPTER XV.

THE tragical story hastens to its consummation. There is no pause, on the writer's part, for emphasising, or moralising, or philosophising, or even theologising. There is the most perfect simplicity and artlessness of narration.

The events narrated happened in the course of a single day, 'dark and dreary.' It was the very day before the Jewish sabbath, Friday, which hence became the most historical of all Fridays, the first 'Good Friday.' All that our Lord did, while enduring the pangs that were thrust into Him, and the woes that were heaped upon Him, was pre-eminently '*good*' *in Him*, and pre-eminently '*good*' *for man*.

VER. 1-5 constitute a condensed paragraph, corresponding in its brief outlines to the fuller details in Matt. xxvii. 1, 2, 11-14; Luke xxiii. 1-16; and John xviii. 28-38.

VER. 1. **And straightway.** Or *immediately*, one of Mark's favourite words. It is not to be interconnected with the following expression, as if the meaning were, *as soon as it was morning*. The idea rather is, that no delay was required in the way of waiting for the morning. The morning was just about to break as the preliminary meeting in the high priest's house drew to a close.

In the morning. Literally, according to the text that was before our translators, *on the morning*, that is, *on the occurrence of the morning*. The preposition and the article are both wanting however in the texts of Lachmann, Tischendorf (eighth edition), Tregelles. But it seems less likely that they would be added by a critical transcriber than that they would be subtracted.

The chief priests held a consultation with the elders and scribes and the whole council. One would be apt to infer from this translation that it was the evangelist's intention to represent the chief priests as initiating the consultation

ST. MARK XV.

and bound Jesus, and carried *him* away, and delivered *him* to Pilate. 2 And Pilate asked him, Art thou the King of the Jews? And he answering said unto him, Thou sayest *it*.

with the whole council. But that is not quite the idea, though no doubt the chief priests would, as a matter of fact, be prominent. The expression is complicated, but may be represented thus: *the-chief-priests-with-the-elders-and-the-scribes, even the whole sanhedrim, held a consultation.* The evangelist first specifies the component elements in the membership of the sanhedrim, and then adds in an artless manner the sum total composed. *Held a consultation:* Very literally, *made counsel*, that is, *took counsel together.* Three uncial manuscripts, ℵ C L, read *prepared counsel*; and Tischendorf has received this word into the text of his eighth edition. But it is likely to have been a graphical error.

And bound Jesus. They caused Him to be manacled, that He might be impeded in any attempt to escape. It is probable that, for form's sake, they would try Him afresh, though hurriedly, and making use of the finding of the extemporized meeting in the high priest's residence.

And carried Him away. *Bore Him off* from the sanhedrim house. It is an idiomatic expression, denoting forcible transference of the person. Origen has *led off*, instead of *carried off*; and so too do the manuscripts C D G N and 1 read; tinkeringly however. Comp. Matt. xxvii. 2.

And delivered Him to Pilate. That he might adjudge Him to death. See John xviii. 31. After Archelaus, son and successor of Herod the Great, had been banished by the Roman emperor to Gaul, Judæa was added to the province of Syria, and governed by deputies called procurators. Of these Pontius Pilate was the fifth.

VER. 2. **And Pilate asked Him.** Or, *put the following question to Him*, no doubt among other interrogatories. Though by no means remarkable for uprightness, he had too much of the Roman spirit of justice in him to pass summary sentence, on the simple representation of the sanhedrim.

Art Thou the King of the Jews? Or, assumingly, and with a dash of mingled nonchalance and sarcasm, *Thou art the King of the Jews? Thou art, I believe, the King of the Jews?* The sanhedrim had obviously informed the procurator that the Prisoner, who was delivered up to him, was aiming at the Jewish crown, and that therefore the case submitted to his lordship's administrative decision was one of treason, a capital crime.

And He, answering, said unto him. Or, as it is in the manuscripts ℵ B C D, *says to him.* We listen as He speaks, as if we had been 'present.'

Thou sayest. Theophylact supposes that our Lord returned to Pilate an intentionally ambiguous answer, that might be understood as meaning, either *Thou sayest truly what I am*, or *I do not say that, but thou*. The expression however was a strong, though strange, idiomatic affirmation, precisely equivalent to *I am*. Comp. Matt. xxvi. 64 with Mark xiv. 62. Norton renders it, *I am*; Mace, *yes*; Zinzendorf and Godwin, *as thou sayest*; Newcome and Edgar Taylor, *thou sayest truly*; Principal Campbell, *thou sayest right*. The rationale of the idiom is that *when the interrogative form is withdrawn from the class of*

3 And the chief priests accused him of many things: but he answered nothing. 4 And Pilate asked him again, saying, Answerest thou nothing? behold how many things they witness against thee. 5 But Jesus yet answered nothing; so that Pilate marvelled.

---

interrogations referred to, the saying that remains is the reality. One sees, readily and clearly, the perfect pertinency of the idiom, when the interrogative form of the utterance is found exclusively in the peculiarity of the intonation, and not in any peculiarity in the collocation of the vocables, as for example in the case before us, *Thou art the King of the Jews?*

VER. 3. **And the chief priests accused Him of many things.** Or, *accused Him much.* The reference is rather to a multiplicity of allegations than to a multiplicity of misdemeanours. They made 'a great ado,' and used repetitiously a multitude of words, in making and enforcing their charge. The word rendered *many things* (πολλά) is often used idiomatically as equivalent to *much.* It is so rendered in Mark i. 45, v. 10; John xiv. 30; Rom. xvi. 12; Rev. v. 4. Luther's version corresponds, *accused Him 'hard,'* or *'sore,'* as Coverdale renders it. Zinzendorf uses the German word corresponding etymologically to *sore,* viz. *sehr,* that is, 'very (much).'

But He answered nothing. This clause seems to have been imported from Matt. xxvii. 12. It is wanting in all the best manuscripts and versions, and is omitted by all the modern editors, inclusive of Griesbach and Scholz. By Bengel too.

VER. 4. **And Pilate asked Him again.** Or rather, *And Pilate again interrogated Him.* The question put by the procurator was different from that which he previously asked.

Answerest Thou nothing? Or, *Art Thou not answering anything?* He was surprised at His calm dignified reticence amid the Babel of accusation.

Behold, how many things they witness against Thee. Or, as it is in ℵ B C D, 1, and in the Italic and Vulgate versions, as also in the texts of Lachmann, Tischendorf, Tregelles, *Behold, how many things they accuse Thee of!* Tischendorf thinks that the reading of the Received Text has been borrowed from Matt. xxvii. 13. Not improbably. *How many things:* the expression is the reflex of the plural phrase employed in ver. 3, and should be interpreted in the light of the import of that phrase. Luther maintains his consistency, *See how hard they accuse Thee!* Meyer's version is, *See how much they testify against Thee!* So Godwin.

VER. 5. **And Jesus still answered nothing.** Namely, to the accusations made against Him by the chief priests. Although invited, as it were, by the procurator to speak out in self-defence, He maintained a perfect and dignified silence.

So that Pilate marvelled. It was an unwonted spectacle at his bar. He would be accustomed to stormy scenes of fierce and fiery recrimination.

VER. 6-15 may be compared, as a paragraph, with Matt. xxvii. 15-26, Luke

6 Now at *that* feast he released unto them one prisoner, whomsoever they desired. 7 And there was *one* named Barabbas, *which lay* bound with them that had made insurrection with him, who had committed murder in the insurrection. 8 And

---

xxiii. 17–25, and with John xviii. 39, 40, etc. The procurator cannot in his conscience acquiesce in the decision of the sanhedrim, but he weakly yields.

VER. 6. **But at feast time.** It is a very idiomatic phrase in the original, denoting a course of time extending down from feast to feast in annual recurrence: *But feast by feast,* that is, *But at every recurring passover.*

He released. The verb is in the imperfect tense, *he was accustomed to release.*

To them. The reference has expanded, in the evangelist's mind, from the authorities of the nation to the people in general.

One prisoner, whomsoever they desired. Or, *whom in particular they asked* (ὅνπερ ᾐτοῦντο). But the three oldest manuscripts, the Sinaitic (ℵ), the Alexandrine (A), and the Vatican (B) have a slightly different reading (ὃν παρῃτοῦντο), *whom they begged,* or *whom they petitioned for.* The compound word is translated *intreated* in Heb. xii. 19. Tischendorf has received it into his eighth edition of the text; with probability. It may seem strange that it should be regarded as a favour to a people to get the release of a prisoner. But sometimes noble men have been imprisoned for noble deeds; and often, when a people has been subjected to a foreign yoke, the patriotic and heroic have had to suffer with felons in their cells.

VER. 7. **And there was one named Barabbas.** There was *the so-called Barabbas.* The spirit of the representation would not be greatly exaggerated if we rendered the expression thus, *there was the notorious Barabbas.* This freebooter would seem to have been of respectable parentage, though he had gravitated into the profession of a brigand. The word *Barabbas* means *Son-of-father,* that is, *Son-of-Father (so and so).* He had been the son apparently of some *rabbi,* who was highly esteemed, and called *father* in his circle.

Who lay bound with them that had made insurrection with him. That is, *with h's fellow rioters.* In some of the best manuscripts however, such as ℵ B C D K, 1, 69, the word for *fellow* is omitted, *with the rioters.* This reading has been approved of by Schulz, and received into the text by Lachmann, Tischendorf, Tregelles. It is supported by the Syriac and Vulgate versions, and is, in all likelihood, the autographic. If it be accepted, then there is no explicit statement in the text to the effect that Barabbas was one of the rioters; yet it is implied. He would no doubt be their ringleader.

Who had committed murder in the insurrection. *In the riot.* Note the article, *in 'the' riot which issued in the imprisonment of Barabbas and the other rioters.* It is a compound and indefinite relative (οἵτινες) which is translated *who.* The idea is, that the rioters had not only been guilty of rioting, they were *such as* had committed murder in the riot. The riot had been got up in antagonism to the authorities, and hence was a kind of *insurrection* on a small scale.

VER. 8. **And the multitude, crying aloud** (ἀναβοήσας). Such is the reading of the great majority of the existing manuscripts. But in the Sinaitic, Vatican,

the multitude crying aloud began to desire *him to do* as he had ever done unto them.

9 But Pilate answered them, saying, Will ye that I release unto you the King of the Jews? 10 For he knew that the

---

and Cambridge manuscripts (א B D) there is a very different reading (ἀναβάς), meaning *going up*. This reading was approved of by David Schulz, and has been received into the text by Lachmann, Tischendorf, Tregelles, Alford. Griesbach hesitated whether to accept or reject it. (*Com. Crit.*, in loc.) It is supported by the Vulgate version and the Italic; and also by the Coptic, Sahidic, and Gothic. The Æthiopic version combines the two readings, *going up and crying out*. It is more likely, on the whole, that the evangelist's word would be expanded to convey the idea of *crying out*, an idea in harmony with the usual characteristics of a crowd or mob, than that it would be contracted or cut down to bring out the idea of *going up*, which at first sight seems to be an almost meaningless, if not incongruous, item of information in the narrative. But as Mark was a resident in Jerusalem (Acts xii. 12), and knew the topography of the city to perfection, nothing after all was more natural than that he should, in his own artless style of composition, use the expression. The procurator's residence would either be in Herod's palace, occupying a conspicuously elevated position on Mount Zion, or in the castle of Antonia at the northwest angle of the temple area, also a conspicuously elevated site, down from which, and up to which, the *Via Dolorosa* leads. The people *needed to go up* to the procurator.

Began to desire (him to do) as he had ever done unto them. The word *ever* is wanting in the manuscripts א B Δ, and in the Syriac Peshito, Sahidic, and Coptic versions. Tischendorf omits it. And we can easily suppose that it was a marginal expletive. The verb itself brings out a frequentative idea, *as he was accustomed to do to them*. Comp. ver. 6. *The crowd began to ask (that he should do) as he was wont to do to them*. The preliminaries of this appeal on the part of the populace are not stated by Mark; but see Matt. xxvii. 16-18.

VER. 9. **But Pilate answered them, saying, Will ye that I release?** Is it your pleasure that I should release?

Unto you. It was the populace he wished to gratify. And most likely he would not have regretted, but rather rejoiced, if the choice of the populace had been at variance with the wishes of the high priest's party.

The King of the Jews. There might be a minglement of feelings prompting the procurator to use this expression. Very possibly there would be something of only half concealed sarcasm and contempt. But very likely too he might know that only a few days ago the Prisoner had entered the city in a kind of triumphal manner, as if He were some royal personage; and that He was received as such by the populace. Knowing this, in part perhaps by the accusations of the chief priests, and in part perhaps by previous report or distant personal observation, he might wish to show the people that, as a faithful and loyal Roman, he was not in the least jealous of Jesus as a rival to the emperor. He really had no sympathy with the representations of the sanhedrim. He did not believe that any political complication was intended by the Prisoner, or

chief priests had delivered him for envy. 11 But the chief priests moved the people, that he should rather release Barabbas unto them. 12 And Pilate answered and said again unto them, What will ye then that I shall do *unto him* whom

---

that there was any danger of insubordination and insurrection. If therefore they would take it as a compliment that one, whom only a few days before they had hailed as *the king of the Jews*, should be set at liberty, he intimated that he would be glad to gratify them.

VER. 10. **For he knew that the chief priests had delivered Him for envy.** *Or, on account of envy.* Wakefield renders the word too generically, *hatred.* Mace and Norton, also too generically, *malice.* It was *envy* that was the deepest feeling in their spirits. They saw that Jesus was getting a hold of the hearts and consciences of the people, in a way and to a degree that was quite beyond their reach. They hence concluded that if He was not arrested in His career, He would gradually make Himself the living centre of such an extended spiritual interest that they would be left outside, high and dry! They could not bear the prospect. The expression *on account of envy* stands emphatically, in the original, in the front of the sentence, *for he knew that on account of envy the chief priests had delivered Him up.* It is well to say *delivered Him up*, rather than simply *delivered Him*, as *delivered*, when used absolutely, is apt to suggest the idea of *deliverance* in the sense of *liberation.* The chief priests however had nothing further from their intent than liberation. They handed our Lord over to Pilate, that He might receive from the hands of the Roman a severer handling than could be given to Him in their own hands. See on chap. ix. 31.

VER. 11. **But the chief priests.** Wycliffe here gives the strange translation, *the bischopis*, i.e. *the bishops.*

Moved the people. *Moved* is scarcely strong enough (ἀνέσεισαν). They '*stireden' the cumpenye of peple,* as Wycliffe has it. They *urged* or *instigated* them. Mace and Principal Campbell have *incited. The people :* that is, the people there assembled, *the crowd.*

That. Literally, *in order that.* What follows brings out the aim they had in view.

He might rather release Barabbas to them. Any one rather than Jesus. They would represent to the people that Jesus was so insidiously dangerous to their interests and principles that the greatest scoundrel or freebooter in the country would do less harm than He.

VER. 12. The fickle crowd yielded to the priestly pressure. **And Pilate answered, and said again to them.** In ℵ B C, and 33 'the queen of the cursives,' the *again* comes in connection with the word *answered ; But Pilate again answered, and said to them.* This connection is favoured by the Vulgate, Sahidic, Philoxenian Syriac, Æthiopic, and Gothic versions, and by Augustine in his *Consensus.* The position is of little exegetical moment. Pilate did not 'give in' without making another attempt to rescue the innocent Being at his bar.

What then is it your pleasure that I should do to Him whom ye call the King of the Jews? He artfully threw the responsibility of the royal designation upon

ye call the King of the Jews? 13 And they cried out again, Crucify him. 14 Then Pilate said unto them, Why, what evil hath he done? And they cried out the more exceedingly, Crucify him.

15 And *so* Pilate, willing to content the people, released Barabbas unto them, and delivered Jesus, when he had scourged *him*, to be crucified.

---

the people, instead of saying *Him who calls Himself the King of the Jews*. He understood that the meek Being, whose life was at stake, and who would no doubt have a majesty in His bearing far transcending the dignity of the high priest, was popular with the common people. He knew that they supposed that He had some intimate relation to their inextinguishable national yearnings. He held on therefore to the hope that they would not wish Him to be given up to an ignominious execution.

VER. 13. **And they cried out again.** That is, when they did once more tumultuously express their pleasure. They had already shouted out, *Release to us Barabbas!*

Crucify Him! "The cry of the infatuated rabble really means, Deal with "Him as you would have dealt with Barabbas" (Alexander). It was the voice and concentrated essence of the wild-beast spirit. The chief priests and their associates had breathed it into the people. It is saddening to think how frequently this spirit obtains the ascendant in human affairs. Not only is righteousness outvoted, goodness is overridden roughshod; and, most likely, not until men find out, from bitter experience, that they cannot get up to the heights of prosperity by going down to the depths of wickedness, will they be persuaded to try the Divine way of equity and love.

VER. 14. **But Pilate said to them, Why, what evil hath He done?** A peculiar idiomatic phrase in Greek. Literally, *For what did He evil?* The *for* points to the suppressed expression of surprise, (*You surprise me*,) *for what did He evil?* The procurator was seeking to introduce an element of reason into the excited populace.

But they cried out the more exceedingly, Crucify Him. They were past the stage of reasoning. They were thirsting for blood, and would listen to nothing that seemed to come between them and their thirst. The phrase *the more exceedingly* ($περισσοτέρως$) is positive, instead of comparative, in a very large proportion of the uncial manuscripts, ℵ A B C D G H K M Δ II. *They shouted exceedingly* ($περισσῶς$). It was as if showers of shouting fell on the procurator's ears.

VER. 15. **And Pilate, willing to content the people.** Very literally, *to do 'the sufficient' to the people*, or, as Wycliffe has it, *to do ynow* (i.e. *enough*) *to the people*, that is, *to 'satisfy' the people*, to do to the crowd what would be *sufficient to please them*. Pilate was *deliberately desirous* ($βουλόμενος$) of doing this.

Released Barabbas to them. Or, according to the collocation of the original, *released to them Barabbas.*

And delivered up Jesus, when he had scourged Him. Viz. by the hands of the lictors. (See Stockbauer's *Kunstgeschichte des Kreuzes*, p. 40.) This *scourging*

16 And the soldiers led him away into the hall, called
Prætorium; and they called together the whole band. 17

with rods, or with what Horace calls the 'horrible flagellum' (*Sat.* i. 3, 119),
was deemed a fitting prelude to crucifixion. (See Lipsius *De Cruce*, ii. 2, 3.)
The aim was to make crime as odious as possible, by prefixing pain to pain, and
infamy to infamy. The prospect of such anguish and ignominy would be fitted
to act as a deterrent on the minds of the servile and the selfish. But when
justice missed its aim, and punishment fell on the innocent, the pure, and the
noble, then the effects on delicate and high strung sensibility must have been
terrible in the extreme. They must have been superlatively so in the case of
Jesus.

To be crucified. Literally, *In order that He might be crucified.* The high
priests and their coadjutors gained their end, and yet lost it. They wished to
stamp ignominy on the impracticable Galilean Reformer, and to stamp out His
reforming influence, as if it were a pest and a disgrace. But His cross has
become an actual ornament to beauty, personal and impersonal, wherever
civilization has been triumphant. It is the symbol, almost everywhere among
the progressive races, of the pathway to the crown. And His reforming influence is silently reforming society all the world over. 'The Stone which the
builders disallowed, the same is made the Head of the corner.'

VER. 16-20. A paragraph that opens up to view immeasurable descents of
human degradation, and, on the part of our Lord, immeasurable ascents of
noble self sacrifice. It corresponds to Matt. xxvii. 27-31. See also John
xix. 2, 3.

VER 16. **And the soldiers.** Into whose hands our Lord was committed for
execution.

Led Him away into the court. More literally still, *led Him off inside the court,*
the open court or quadrangle of the procurator's mansion house. Pilate had
met the sanhedrim and the people outside, on the paved esplanade in front of
his residence. See John xviii. 28, xix. 13.

Called Prætorium. It was not the court, *as distinguished from the buildings
that were massed around it,* which was called Prætorium. The whole pile, inclusive of the court, was the *Prætorium,* or *Governor's residence.* But as the
evangelist had, in what precedes, been narrating occurrences which took place
outside, he now speaks of the soldiers as entering what was at once a part and
the whole of the pile, at once the court in particular and the Prætorium in
general. He might have said, *inside the court of the Prætorium.* But he chooses
to say *inside the court*; and then he artlessly adds a clause which determines
the particular building referred to, *which is (the) Prætorium.* The word *prætorium*
originally meant the tent or residence of the *prætor* or *leader*; but after *leaders*
became subdivided into various orders, and only some continued to be called
prætors, the name for the residence still retained its generic hold. And hence
Pilate, though no *prætor,* resided in a *prætorium.*

And they call together the whole band. Or *cohort,* which was doing military
duty in the city. The rough brutal fellows, accustomed to gladiatorial shows,
and other savageries, wanted to get some sport out of their Hebrew prisoner.

And they clothed him with purple, and platted a crown of thorns, and put it about his *head,* 18 and began to salute him, Hail, King of the Jews! 19 And they smote him on the head with a reed, and did spit upon him, and bowing *their* knees worshipped him. 20 And when they had mocked him, they

---

VER. 17. **And they clothe Him with purple.** *They invest Him with* '*a purple*,' that is, *with* '*a purple robe.*' It had been apparently some cast off robe of Herod Antipas. See Luke xxiii. 11.

And having plaited a crown of thorns, they put it about His head. And thus, says Hiller mystically, 'the curse that began in thorns (Gen. iii. 18) ended in thorns' (*Hierophyticon,* i., p. 473). The hardened legionaries however thought it splendid drollery. "The thorns," says Malan, "were most likely twigs of the "commonest thorn bush in Palestine, growing everywhere on waste ground, "and ready at hand. The branches are long, slender, and very thorny, though "the thorns are far apart; so that it was well suited to the purpose of the "Roman soldiers." (*Notes on John,* p. 127.)

VER. 18. **And they began to salute Him, Hail, King of the Jews.** "*Hail,* an "ancient form of saluting such as we honour or respect, which signifies as "much as *All health to you!*" (Petter.) "Our ancestors," says Verstegan, "used it instead of *Ave,* as a word of most well-wishing." (*Restitution,* p. 247.) The salutation would be the more incisively derisive, that the word rendered *Hail!* literally means *Rejoice!* "Alas, mad sinners," says Richard Baxter, "little know you whom you scorn."

VER. 19. **And they smote Him on the head.** Very literally, *and they smote His head.* Not gently, we fear. They smote Him too again and again. The verb is in the imperfect tense, and hence Rotherham renders it, *they were striking Him.*

With a reed. The particular reed, most probably, which they had attempted to stick into His hand as a sceptre. See Matt. xxvii 29.

And did spit on Him. Repeatedly, alas. The verb, like the preceding one, is in the imperfect tense.

And bowing their knees. Literally, *and placing the knees,* namely, in position. Not unlikely, the posture would be a studied imitation of the most obsequious oriental mode.

Worshipped Him. Did humble obeisance to Him. The whole body would be bent forward, prostratingly and adoringly. The Rheims version is, *adored.* The word *worshipped,* given both by Wycliffe and Tyndale, was formerly employed in a more generic acceptation than what is now common. The expression in Matt. xix. 19 for instance, '*honour* thy father and thy mother,' was rendered by Wycliffe '*worshipe* thi fadir and thi modir.' Hence, too, certain survivals of complimentary address or designation, '*your worship,*' '*worshipful,*' as applied to certain 'honourable' magistrates or corporate bodies.

VER. 20. **And when they had mocked Him.** That is, after the mocking was finished. The word rendered *mocked* turns, in its significance, on the idea of the sports of children (ἐνέπαιξαν).

ST. MARK XV.

took off the purple from him, and put his own clothes on him, and led him out to crucify him.

21 And they compel one Simon a Cyrenian, who passed by, coming out of the country, the father of Alexander and Rufus, to bear his cross.

They took off the purple from Him, and put His own clothes on Him. Some texts conclude a paragraph here, and hence commence a new paragraph with the following clause. It is better however to make no break. And although it is advantageous, for purposes of arrangement and harmony, to set ver. 16-20, and then ver. 21-26, respectively, apart as distinct groups or paragraphs, yet there is no real division in the evangelist's composition. He hastens on continuously.

And led Him out that they might crucify Him. A portion of their number would be told off to see the execution completed.

VER. 21-26 constitute a group or paragraph corresponding to Matt. xxvii. 31-37 and Luke xxiii. 26-31. Comp. also John xix. 17-24.

VER. 21. **And they compel.** Or *impress*. The original word is of Persian origin, and derived its conventional acceptation from the Persian postal system.

One Simon a Cyrenian, who passed by. Or, *a certain individual, passing by, Simon of Cyrene*. There were many Simons, or Simeons, among the early Christians. But this one was distinguished from all the rest as *Simon of Cyrene*, a great and flourishing city of that North African district which somewhat corresponds to the modern Tripoli. It lay between the territory of Alexandria on the east and that of Carthage on the west, and was called Cyrenaica, or Pentapolitana. Cyrene was several miles inland from the Mediterranean Sea, and in virtue of a charter of Ptolemy I. had become a favourite resort of Jews. It is now a heap of ruins, and called *Cairoan* or *Ghrenna*. (See Bastow's *Bible Dictionary*, p. 202.)

Coming from the country. He was not only *passing by*, he was *on his way 'in from the country*,' and would be totally ignorant of the immense commotion that had been heaving, that morning, the great heart of Jerusalem.

The father of Alexander and Rufus. They are mentioned by name as being well known among the early Christians. They were probably devoted and conspicuous disciples. Paul sends, in his Epistle to the Romans (xvi. 13), a salutation to ' Rufus, chosen in the Lord,' and to ' his mother,' concerning whom he adds most touchingly, ' and mine.' Possibly this Rufus might be he who is specified by the evangelist. Possibly the whole family may have been converted to Christianity in consequence of the impressment of the father on the streets of Jerusalem. Coming in contact with the Saviour, he might recognise, even in the depth of His humiliation, the unmistakable gleams of His Messiahship, and become inspired with faith and fealty.

To bear His cross. Or, *in order that he might take up His cross*, and carry it when taken up. Our Saviour had been so exhausted in body by His want of rest, and His agony in Gethsemane, and the abuse to which He was subjected in the respective courts in which He had been tried and mocked, that He was unable to drag after Him the cross which had been laid on His shoulder. (See Gruner's *Commentatio de J. Christi morte vera*, pp. 34-37.) It was customary

22 And they bring him unto the place Golgotha, which is, being interpreted, The place of a skull.
23 And they gave him to drink wine mingled with myrrh: but he received *it* not.

---

for the great coarse scoundrels who were condemned to crucifixion to be compelled to carry their crosses to the place of execution. (See Salmasius, *De Cruce*, p. 435.) In general they would be quite able to undergo that humiliating preliminary. But Jesus was of a different mould, outwardly and inwardly, and was therefore stumbling and falling under His oppressive burden. Thus it was necessary to impress some one to assist. The soldiers would disdain to lend a helping hand. So would the mob. And hence Simon was eagerly pounced upon, as he was coming in from the country, and perhaps expressing surprise, in a remonstrating manner, that a Being, so evidently different from the criminal class, should be led off toward Golgotha. He was nothing loath to comply with the impressment. He went to the fallen Sufferer, and '*lifted up*' the cross. Then placing himself behind the meek mute Burden-Bearer (Luke xxiii. 26), he cheerfully took over on himself the greater portion of the burden, and so got linked for ever to the Lord.

VER. 22. **And they bring Him to the place Golgotha.** Literally, *upon the Golgotha place*. The preposition *upon* thus denotes, not the direction taken, but the position, or super-position, ultimately attained. *Golgotha* represents, in Greek letters, the Chaldaic *Gulgaltha*, or Syriac *Gugaltho*, which is a modification of the Hebrew word *Gulgoleth, a skull*.

Which is, being interpreted, The place of a skull. Or better still, and more literally, *skull-place*; and 'skull-place' is just 'Calvary-place.' When we drop the word 'place,' as Luke does (xxiii. 33), then the Aramaic 'Golgotha' is identical with the Latin 'Calvary,' or the English 'Skull.' It had no doubt, wherever situated, been a little knoll, or *monticule* of a place, a kind of '*head*-land,' somewhat like a rounded skull. It was thus *Mount Calvary* in a certain dwarfish application of the word *mount*. Its true topography however is only matter of conjecture. The current ecclesiastical tradition, that it is embraced within the compass of the present *Church of the Holy Sepulchre*, is imaginary, and evidently apocryphal. For the site of that church is now, and must apparently have been in the Saviour's days, within the circuit of the walls of the city, and not 'outside the gate' (Heb. xiii. 12). The word *interpreted*, in all the places in which it occurs in the New Testament, has reference to that simplest phase of the interpretation of a foreign word, *translation*. Rilliet's version of the clause is, *which signifies, when translated, place of the skull*.

VER. 23. **And they gave Him to drink.** The expression *to drink* is wanting in the Sinaitic (א), Vatican (B), and Parisian (C*) manuscripts, as also in L Δ, and in the Coptic and Armenian versions. It is omitted from the text by Tischendorf, Tregelles, Alford, and was condemned by David Schulz. It is certainly more likely that it would be added than that it would be subtracted.

Wine mingled with myrrh. Literally, *myrrhed wine*, that is, drugged wine, to produce heartening it might be (see Bartholinus, *de vino myrrhato*, in his *De Cruce*, p. 136), or to induce comparative anæsthesis or insensibility. Myrrh is

24]   ST. MARK XV.   429

24 And when they had crucified him, they parted his garments, casting lots upon them, what every man should take.

---

a strong stimulant. The administration of drugged wine to criminals about to suffer was a merciful custom, which relieved to a small degree the excessive ferocity so characteristic of the executions of those olden times. (See Buxtorf's *Lexicon Talmudicum*, p. 2131, and Wetstein, *in loc.*)

But He received it not. Or, as the reading is in the Sinaitic and Vatican manuscripts, and 'the queen of the cursives' (33), *who however received it not* (ὅς instead of ὅ). Our Lord did not wish to use any artificial means to mitigate, or otherwise modify, His sense of the sufferings connected with the culmination of His work. The value of these sufferings centred in the free activity that, first of all, chose their endurance, in consideration of the sublime moral ends to be subserved, and then self-sacrificingly held out, under their undiminished superincumbence, till all was finished.

VER. 24. **And when they had crucified Him.** That is, *affixed Him to the cross.* This was generally done, it would appear, after the cross was erected. (See Lipsius, *De Cruce*, ii. 7, and Salmasius, *De Cruce*, pp. 333, 447 ff., ed. 1646.) Sometimes however it was done before the act of elevation. (See Lipsius, as above, and Gallonius, *De Cruciatibus*, p. 8.) The evangelist, by means of his participial expression, draws a veil over the act of crucifixion, and hastens on with his narrative. In the Vatican manuscript however the reading is, *And they crucify Him*; and Tischendorf and Tregelles have received it into their texts. Unadvisedly: for it would be difficult to conceive of any translator wilfully substituting the participial for the indicative expression, as there is an entire absence of literary art in here making use of a participial bridge. There is no attempt, by any kind of emphatic representation, to produce a sensational effect on the one hand, or to throw out the least particle of doctrinal hint on the other.

They parted His garments. *They parted*, that is, *they distributed among themselves* (διαμερίζονται). It was a customary perquisite to the officiating executioners.

Casting lots upon them. More literally, *casting a lot upon them.* The word for *lot* is sometimes used for *the thing allotted*, and is, with reference to *the church*, translated *heritage* in King James's version of 1 Pet. v. 3, from which passage it is that the words *clergy*, *clerk*, and *clerical* have come into use.

What every man should take. A strange expression in the original, the interblending, in an untranslatable way, of two distinct questions (τίς τί ἄρῃ). The one might be resolved thus: *Who* (τίς) *should receive this, and who that?* The other might be represented thus: *What* (τί) *should each one receive?* The two questions were simultaneously answered by casting lots. But were lots cast in reference to all the garments, or in reference to the seamless tunic only? (See John xix. 23, 24.) We may either suppose that the evangelist *masses* his expression in an artlessly free and easy manner; or we may suppose that after the garments were sorted into two divisions, (1) the precious tunic by itself, and (2) the other parts of the dress by themselves, there would be an arrangement of those other parts into four portions, as nearly equal in value as possible.

25 And it was the third hour, and they crucified him.

Each soldier of the quaternion might then get his portion by *lot*. And, after that, the seamless tunic, instead of being shared among them, would, by consent of all, be disposed of in particular by another casting of the lot.

VER. 25. **And it was the third hour; and they crucified Him.** An artless and Semitic way of saying, *And it was the third hour when they crucified Him.* There has been much discussion among expositors in reference to the horological expression *the third hour* in its relation to John's notation of the time when Pilate made a last attempt to move the Jews by saying, ' Behold your King! ' It was, says he, 'about *the sixth hour*' (John xix. 14). Augustine discusses the matter at great length in his *Harmony of the Evangelists* (lib. iii., cap. xiii.). But the solution which he proposes is far too ingenious. He supposes that Mark refers, not to the crucifixion as it was effected *by the hands of the Roman soldiers*, which would be about noon, or the *sixth hour* of the day, but to the crucifixion as it was *effected by the tongues of the Jews*, when first they began to cry out *Crucify Him!* This, the real crucifixion according to Augustine, *the crucifixion proper, so far as their guilt was concerned*, took place about three hours earlier than the final decision of the procurator. " Produce," says Augustine, "a better reconciliation of the two representations, and I shall " most readily acquiesce; for it is not my opinion that I love, but the truth of " the Gospel." It would certainly be impossible to produce a more ingenious conciliation. The Pseudo-Jerome, in his *Breviary* on Psalm lxxvii., supposes that the word *three* in the existing copies of Mark's Gospel is an error of the transcribers for *six*. He supposes still further. that the error might be occasioned by the employment, in the earliest manuscripts, of numeral signs (Γ and the 'digamma' F) instead of numeral words. The Æthiopic version, it is worthy of note, reads *sixth hour*. And the same reading occurs in the margin of the Philoxenian Syriac. In *The Acts of Pilate* the crucifixion is represented as taking place ' in the sixth hour of the day.' (Tischendorf's *Evan. Apocrypha*, B., chap. x., p. 284.) Cardinal Cajetan agrees with the Pseudo-Jerome, and thinks that *third* is a transcriber's error for *sixth*. But Patrizi, while having no doubt that one or other of the representations is a transcriber's error, supposes that the fault occurs, not in Mark's Gospel, but in John's. (*De Evangeliis*, vol. i., pp. 434-5.) If transcriber's fault there be, it is likely that Patrizi is right in attaching it to the text of John. (So Griesbach.) Mark's representation seems to harmonize at once with Matthew's (xxvii. 45), and with Luke's (xxiii. 44), and with the general requirements of the case. Comp. Mark xv. 33. We must either apparently accept this alteration, or suppose, with Dr. Ward, that John's principle of horological computation was entirely different from Mark's. (*Dissertations*, p. 127.) The full discussion of the subject belongs to the *Exposition of John's Gospel*. (See Zeltner *De Horologio Johannis*.)

VER. 26. **And the superscription.** Or *inscription*, as almost all the modern translators render it. The word has no reference to the position of the placard as affixed above the head. The *super* has reference to the relation of the letters of the inscription to the whitened board, *on* which they were written. The

26 And the superscription of his accusation was written over, THE KING OF THE JEWS.

27 And with him they crucify two thieves; the one on

word means *on-writing*, though it is always rendered *superscription* in King James's English version. (See Matt. xxii. 20; Mark xii. 16; Luke xx. 24, xxiii. 38.) Doubtless however the ticket would, as a matter of fact, be attached to that part of the perpendicular beam that surmounted the arms of the cross.

Of His accusation. Literally, *of His cause*, that is, *of the cause of His condemnation to death*, or simply, according to the expression in Acts xiii. 28 and Luke xxiii. 22, *of the cause of His death*. The inscription announced the crime which had been laid to the charge of our Lord, and which the Roman governor had, against his inclination and his judgment, been, as it were, constrained to endorse as a sufficient *cause* of condemnation. It was a *demeritorious cause*.

Was written over. That is, *ran as follows*. Had the expression been very literally rendered, the whole statement would have stood thus, *And the superscription of the cause was superscribed*, or, *and the inscription of the cause was inscribed*; namely, as follows. It is an artless mode of speech, somewhat corresponding to the use of cognates in such a phrase as Matt. ii. 10, *they rejoiced a great joy.*

The King of the Jews. That was the crime of which our Saviour had been guilty! The procurator would intend that the inscription should have a sting in it for the chief priests and elders and scribes. He had been frustrated and galled; and he took his revenge by flashing the idea before the public mind, that it was a crime, in the estimation at least of the chief priests and scribes and elders, to seek to have a Jewish king. In the different Gospels there are minutiæ of variation in the representation of the contents of the inscription. These might, in part, arise from minute diversities of expression in the different languages employed. But evidently it was not the aim of the evangelical biographers to give the identical words, nothing more, nothing less, nothing else. It was only the substance of the meaning to which they had regard, and in which they felt interested.

VER. 27-32 correspond to Matt. xxvii. 38-44, and Luke xxiii. 32-43. Compare the cursory remark in John xix. 18.

VER. 27. **And with Him they crucify.** Note the present tense. We, as it were, see the deed in process. (*They*) *crucify:* there is no nominative to the verb in the original. The agents are veiled. The whole expression is equivalent to the impersonal one, *and with Him are crucified*. No doubt however, the executioners would be the quaternion of soldiers who had been detailed for the crucifixion of our Lord.

Two thieves. Or rather, *robbers*. See chap. xiv. 48. Possibly they were the accomplices of Barabbas; and if so, the procurator might intentionally seek to show his displeasure, by precipitating their execution. He would thus let the people see in what light he regarded the man whom it had been their pleasure to honour. The names of the robbers are given in *The Acts of Pilate* as Gestas and Dysmas! In the Old Latin manuscript 'c' they are given as Zoathan and Chammatha!

his right hand, and the other on his left. 28 And the scripture was fulfilled, which saith, And he was numbered with the transgressors.

The one on His right hand, and the other on His left. Or, more literally, without the articles, *one on His right side, and one on His left*. The expression is idiomatic in the original, and would not bear unidiomatic rendering, *from His right parts and His left*. The position of our Lord between the two malefactors would not be fortuitous. He was treated as the most criminal of the three. Perhaps it was at the express desire of the procurator, that the idea might stand out, in the boldest relief, before the public mind, *that for any one but Cæsar to claim to be the king of the Jews was the greatest of crimes*.

VER. 28. This entire verse is omitted by Tischendorf and Alford, and bracketed by Tregelles. It is wanting in the most ancient manuscripts at present known, the Sinaitic (א), the Alexandrine (A), the Vatican (B), the Parisian (C), the Cambridge (D), as also in X, and in the Sahidic version. But then it is present in all the most ancient versions, the Old Latin or Italic (with one exception, *k*,) the Vulgate, the Peshito Syriac, the Philoxenian Syriac, the Coptic, the Gothic, the Armenian, the Æthiopic. It must therefore have been in the manuscripts from which these versions were made; and these manuscripts, or at all events the great majority of them, must have been older than the oldest now extant and known. The clause is also found in the excellent uncial manuscripts P S, as well as in the remainder of the uncials. It is found too in the best of the cursives, 1, 33, 69. It seems to be recognised by Origen. (See *Opera*, vol. i., p. 420, and note the plural word 'Gospels.') Tischendorf thinks that it was probably omitted by Eusebius. But in this he seems to be mistaken. (Comp. the 'Canon' 8 in Luke xxii. 37.) It is far more difficult to account for an arbitrary insertion of the verse, more particularly when we take into account Mark's limited reference to Old Testament predictions, than it is to admit the supposition of an accidental omission of the whole statement in some very early copy. The first word, as Griesbach reminds us, of both the preceding and succeeding verse, is *and*; and this is also the first word of the 28th verse. Thus the eye of an early transcriber may have been inadvertently misled. It is difficult to suppose an intentional suppression of the verse, Comp. Luke xxii. 37.

And the scripture was fulfilled which saith. Namely in Isa. liii. 12. It is a very striking statement, to which the Saviour had Himself drawn attention in the passage of Luke referred to. His reference to it is one among many evidences of the Messianic nature of the oracle.

And He was numbered. Or *reckoned*, as the same word is rendered in Luke xxii. 37. It is too Tyndale's version in the passage before us, and is certainly to be preferred to Wycliffe's *gesside* (i.e. *guessed*) and the Rheims *reputed*. Campbell has *ranked*. The word has, no doubt, in its primary import a reference to *counting*, or *laying thing to thing*. But there is a fine connection between *counting* and *accounting*. There is *reckoning* in both cases.

With the transgressors. Or more literally without the article, *with transgressors*. But *transgressors* is too feeble a version. The word means *lawless*

ST. MARK XV.

29 And they that passed by railed on him, wagging their heads, and saying, Ah, thou that destroyest the temple, and buildest *it* in three days, 30 save thyself, and come down from the cross. 31 Likewise also the chief priests mocking said among themselves with the scribes, He saved others; himself he

---

(*ones*), *those who set the laws at defiance.* Coverdale's version is *with well doers*; the Anglo-Saxon, *mid unrihtwisum* (with the unrighteous); Wycliffe, Tyndale, and the Rheims, *with the wicked.*

VER. 29. **And they who passed by.** The passers by. Calvary would seem to have been by the side of one of the thoroughfares into the city. There would be a continual flux and reflux of passers by.

Railed on Him. Or, *reviled Him.* Literally, *blasphemed Him.*

Wagging their heads. Derisively and insultingly. Comp. 2 Kings xix. 21; Job xvi. 4; Ps. xxii. 7, cix. 25; Lam. ii. 15.

And saying, Ha! An admirable and simple translation (οὐά = '*vah*,' not *oval*, as in Mill and D and E). But, admirable and simple as it is, it seems to have been reached with difficulty by our British translators. Wycliffe has *fie*; Coverdale, *fie upon The* (for Luther had *fie to Thee*); Tyndale, *Awretche*; the Geneva, *Hey*; the Rheims, *Vah.* The exclamation expresses here the bitterest irony and scorn.

Thou who destroyest the temple, and buildest it in three days. Principal Campbell has a fine word for *destroyest, demolishest.*

VER. 30. **Save Thyself, and come down from the cross.** Or, according to the reading of Lachmann, Tischendorf, Tregelles, supported by ℵ B D L Δ, and the Vulgate and Coptic versions, *Save Thyself by descending from the cross.* But this reading seems less inartificial than the other, which is probably therefore the autographic. The substantive meaning of both expressions is identical.

VER. 31. **Likewise.** That is, *in like ways*, or *in like manner*. It was not the common people alone and the casual passers by who rudely and unfeelingly insulted.

Also the chief priests. Forgetting the dignity that befitted their position and office.

Mocking among themselves. Or, literally, *to one another.* But what they said *to* each other they said *at* the surrounding people. They had come out of the city for the very purpose, apparently, of gloating over their Victim.

With the scribes. Who, notwithstanding the emollient tendencies of literature, were, in this matter, of one heart and mind with the chief priests.

Said, He saved others: Himself He cannot save. *Is not His real impotence as regards others, notwithstanding all that has been said by Him or for Him, mirrored in His manifest impotence as regards Himself?* Yet, in uttering their taunt, they unconsciously stumbled on expressions which involved the highest truths. The crucified One *did save others*. It was not merely a profession; it was a historical fact. And for the very reason that He was engaged in still further equipping or qualifying Himself for saving others, *He could not*, in consistency with His high and holy mediatorial aim, save Himself. He must needs *sacrifice Himself.* (See Luke xxiv. 26; Heb. ii. 10, 14.)

cannot save. 32 Let Christ the King of Israel descend now from the cross, that we may see and believe. And they that were crucified with him reviled him.

33 And when the sixth hour was come, there was darkness over the whole land until the ninth hour.

VER. 32. **Let the Christ, the King of Israel, descend now from the cross.** Ewald connects the nominative expression *the Christ* with the preceding clause, *The Christ cannot save Himself*. Lachmann took in the following designation also, *The Christ, the King of Israel, cannot save Himself.* No doubt, however, Robert Stephens did right in drawing the line where he did, by beginning here a new verse and thus a new sentence. Jesus had confessed before the high priest that He was *the Christ* (chap. xiv. 62), and before Pilate that He was *the King of Israel* (chap. xv. 2). His revilers try to work with the twofold confession as if it were a lever of overwhelming refutation, *let Him show, by coming down, the legitimacy of His claims!*

That we may see and believe. They knew not that what they scoffingly urged would have left the atoning decease unaccomplished. They knew not moreover the sophistical disingenuousness of their own spirits; for had the Saviour complied with their challenge, they would have been ready at once to attribute the prodigy to 'black art' and 'Beelzebul.'

And they who had been crucified with Him. His fellow-sufferers!

Reviled Him. *Reproached Him* for not delivering both Himself and them. They had both apparently joined in flinging their barbed insults at our Saviour. But one of the two seems to have speedily discovered the irrationality and wanton wickedness of the assault. (See Luke xxiii. 39–43.) Perhaps he was convicted by the very meekness and the unruffled self control and self abnegation that were manifested in the manner in which our Lord endured their insults.

VER. 33–39 constitute a paragraph corresponding, as Eusebius long ago noted, to Matt. xxvii. 45–54, and Luke xxiii. 44–47.

VER. 33. **And when the sixth hour was come.** The sixth hour from the dawn. It was thus near mid-day.

There was darkness. It *became* (ἐγένετο) dark. And this although the sun was in the meridian of his strength.

Over the whole land. A much better translation than that given in Luke xxiii. 44 by King James's translators to the same phrase, *over all the earth*; though the word rendered *land* in Mark, and *earth* in Luke, does not find its precise geographical or chorographical synonym in either of the translations.

Until the ninth hour. The darkness seems to have lasted from two to three hours. It was not occasioned by an eclipse, for the full moon cannot intervene between the earth and the sun. It was no doubt supernaturally contrived or overruled, as a fringe of the entire supernatural drapery of the great supernatural event which was transpiring within the supernatural Sufferer on the cross. Not that any universal laws were contravened or suspended. But a new force came in, which limited the scope and modified the direction of the other forces that were ordinarily at work. Or when we go to the ultimates of thought, and to the

34 And at the ninth hour Jesus cried with a loud voice, saying, Eloi, Eloi, lama sabachthani? which is, being interpreted, My God, my God, why hast thou forsaken me? 35 And some of them that stood by, when they

corresponding ultimates of objective reality, we may represent the case thus: a peculiar volition took place in the Divine Mind, which modified the action, in that particular scene, of the omnipotent Divine Hand. It was meet that there should be around our Lord a penumbra of darkness. It at once reflected the mediatorial eclipse that was going on within, and cast a fitting shade over the guilty population in the immediate vicinity of the scene.

VER. 34. And at the ninth hour. Just about the time of the evening sacrifice. The great antitypical sacrifice was about to culminate.

Jesus cried with a loud voice. Very literally, *a great voice*, the generic for the specific. The pang of the protracted sacrificial act elicited the cry.

Saying, Eloi, Eloi. An Aramaic way of saying *Eli, Eli* (Matt. xxvii. 46), and not unlikely the precise form in which the words were enunciated by our Lord. (See the Syriac version.) We must not think with Patrizi of a repetition of the exclamation, first in the one form and then in the other. It is probable that Matthew purposely quoted the original Hebrew of the psalm. It was not, however, we may be assured, a matter of interest to the evangelists to record the particular dialectic pronunciation given to the words uttered by our Lord. The only matter of real interest in their estimation was the fact that He appropriated and uttered the initial words of the 22nd Psalm.

Lama Sabachthani. The manuscripts B D and 1 read *lama*; the Vulgate *lamma*; ℵ C L Δ, *lema*, and this reading has been received into the text of his eighth edition by Tischendorf. The Alexandrine manuscript and many others read *lima*, Tischendorf's former reading. Many others read *leima*. It is not unlikely that the autographic form might be *lema*.

Which is. That is, *which means, which is in meaning*.

Being interpreted. Or, *when translated*, for the *interpretation* referred to is simply what we now call *translation*.

My God, My God. The repetition denotes intensity and urgency of feeling. Wave, as it were, surges upon wave. The *My* indicates clinging and trust. The use of the word *God*, instead of *Father*, shows that it was in the human element of our Lord's complex personality that the darkness and agony had been experienced. To the human soul the Father was *God, the object of adoration*.

Why hast Thou forsaken Me? Or, *Why forsookest Thou Me?* The Saviour was looking back to an experience, out of which He was now emerging. He had been *forsaken* or *left* by the Father; not, of course, physically or metaphysically, but politically or governmentally. In the sphere of the Divine moral government He was, as the world's Representative and Substitute, 'left' alone with the world's sin, 'bearing' it. See *Comm.* on Matt. xxvii. 46.

VER. 35. And some of them who stood by. For, notwithstanding the incubus of preternatural darkness, a proportion of the common people still hovered around, wishful to see the end. The very fact indeed of the darkness may have

heard *it*, said, Behold, he calleth Elias. 36 And one ran and filled a spunge full of vinegar, and put *it* on a reed, and gave him to drink, saying, Let alone; let us see whether Elias will come to take him down.

37 And Jesus cried with a loud voice, and gave up the ghost.

38 And the veil of the temple was rent in twain from the top to the bottom.

---

determined them to remain, if they belonged, as is likely, to the more superstitious class of the population.

When they heard it, said, Behold, He calleth Elias. Or, Elijah. The exclamation took them by surprise ; and, not catching the precise words, nor following to the end the sentence which was uttered, their excited and untutored imaginations, fixing on the first shrill cries, leaped suddenly to the conclusion that Elijah was called for. The sounds were sufficiently akin ; and even the least religious of the people would probably know that some peculiar relationship of Elijah to the Messiah was predicted in the Scriptures (Mal. iv. 5). In their weird state of mind, it would scarcely have taken them by surprise, if Elijah had suddenly alighted at the cross in his robe of rough hair.

Ver. 36. **And one ran and having filled a sponge full of vinegar, put it on a reed.** Or, more literally, *round a reed*. The reed was, at its extremity, surrounded with it.

And gave Him to drink. Holding the sponge persistently to our Saviour's mouth. The verb is in the imperfect tense. The man may have seen that the Saviour was apparently near His end, but may have hoped that, by the help of the refreshment, life might be protracted a little, so that Elijah, if he were coming, might have time to make his appearance.

Saying, Let alone. An idiomatic expression, *Let go ! Stop !*

Let us see whether Elias will come to take Him down. More literally, *Let us see if Elias is coming to take Him down*. And the man would look wistfully into the air as he spoke.

Ver. 37. **And Jesus cried with a loud voice, and gave up the ghost.** Or, more literally, *But Jesus, having emitted a loud voice, expired.* He exclaimed, *Father, into Thy hands I commend My spirit.* (Luke xxiii. 46.) The expression *gave up the ghost* is an archaism. The word *ghost*, the analogue of the German *Geist*, just means *spirit.* It is now however narrowed in its reference to actual or supposed apparitions of the disembodied human spirit. The biblical and theological phrase, *the Holy Ghost*, just means *the Holy Spirit.*

Ver. 38. **And the veil of the temple.** The curtain that separated the innermost recess from the anterior apartment of the sanctuary. It would be strong in its texture, as well as precious in its tissues.

Was rent in twain. Literally, *into twain*, or, in more modern phrase, *into two*, that is, *into two parts.*

From top to bottom. The rent was throughout. It was no doubt supernatural, indicating, by a sublime ' figure of fact,' as by a sublime ' figure of

39 And when the centurion, which stood over against him, saw that he so cried out, and gave up the ghost, he said, Truly this man was the Son of God.

40 There were also women looking on afar off: among whom was Mary Magdalene, and Mary the mother of James the

---

speech.' that in virtue of the decease, which had been accomplished, the way into the heavenly holy of holies was now Divinely opened up. See Heb. ix. 7, 8.

VER. 39. **And.** Here follows another interesting and significant fact.

When the centurion. The Roman officer who had charge of the quaternion of soldiers, who had been told off to see the execution consummated.

Who stood over against Him. *Who stood near, opposite Him, or facing Him.*

Saw that He so cried out, and expired. In the Sinaitic and Vatican manuscripts, and hence in Tischendorf's eighth edition of the text, the reference to the 'cry' is omitted. The expression runs simply thus, *Saw that He so expired.* It is not likely however that any transcriber would arbitrarily introduce the reference to the 'cry' as an object that was 'seen' by the centurion. It is more likely that some fastidious critic thought the expression awkward, and therefore curtailed the autographic statement. There is no need however for such fastidiousness in relation to artless composition. The meaning is obvious: *the centurion perceived* or *observed the various complex phenomena of the decease.* He joined fact to fact, and connected them with the manifest peculiarity, dignity, and meekness of the wonderful Sufferer.

He said, Truly this Man was the Son of God. Too strong a translation. There is no definite article in the original before the word *Son.* Perceiving this, some critics have contended that the rendering should be *a son of a god, a hero.* They have maintained moreover that such a translation is most in accordance with what might be expected from the lips of a man who was a Roman and a heathen. But yet there is nothing corresponding to the indefinite article *a* in the original. The literal rendering of the expression excludes both articles, and is perfect, *Truly this man was God's Son.* It is left entirely indeterminate whether the centurion thought of other *sons of God,* or not. Note however the *was.* It was the centurion's notion that all was now over with our Lord.

VER. 40, 41 constitute a little Ammonian section, corresponding, as Eusebius noted, to Matt. xxvii. 55, 56, and Luke xxiii. 49.

VER. 40. **There were also women.** More literally, *And there were also women,* besides the other persons who have been referred to in the preceding verses.

Looking on afar off. Or, *Looking on from a distance.* Their attachment to the Saviour chained them to the spot; their modesty kept them in its outskirts.

Among whom were both Mary Magdalene. Or, *Mary the Magdalene,* that is, *Mary of Magdala.* She was one of the most devoted of the Lord's disciples, and had experienced in her own person the marvellous effect of His mediatorial power and beneficence. (See chap. xvi. 9, and Luke viii. 2.) There seems to be no good reason for identifying her with Mary of Bethany, the sister of Martha ; or for supposing that either she, or Mary of Bethany, was 'the woman who was a sinner' (Luke vii. 37).

And Mary the mother of James the less. Or rather, *of James the little.* (See

less and of Joses, and Salome; 41 (who also, when he was in Galilee, followed him, and ministered unto him;) and many other women which came up with him unto Jerusalem.

---

chap. iii. 18.) He had been, it would appear, diminutive in stature, as were doubtless the ancestors of the considerable English families of *Littles* and *Smalls*.

And of Joses. A common name among the Jews. See chap. vi. 3. The Joses here mentioned must have been well known in the original circle of disciples, seeing he is here particularized, along with his brother James-the-little, to differentiate the second Mary referred to. Wieseler would read *Joseph* instead of *Joses*, and understands the reference to be to *Joseph of Arimathea*. Unlikely.

And Salome. The wife of Zebedee, and the mother of James and John, the 'duumvirate' who stood next among the apostles to Peter, the 'primate.' Was she the sister of the mother of our Lord? See John xix. 25.

VER. 41. **Who also.** The *also* is omitted in the Sinaitic (א) and Vatican (B) manuscripts, and 'the queen of the cursives' (33), apparently in consequence of 'homœoteleuton' (αι και). See the manuscripts A C L Δ, which omit the *who* and insert the *also*.

When He was in Galilee. Or better, *While He was in Galilee*, for the *was* is in the imperfect tense, and its idea of continuance is reflected in the *while*.

Followed Him. *Were in the habit of following Him* (ἠκολούθουν), namely, from place to place, as He went about doing good by word and work. Why? Partly no doubt because, unlike other rabbis, He delighted to admit females to the full participation of the rights of pupils. Partly because of the wonderful spiritual attraction which He exerted. Partly perhaps for another reason; see next clause.

And ministered unto Him. They were *in the habit of ministering to Him* (διηκόνουν). They knew that, notwithstanding the mysterious glories of His higher being, into which it baffled them to see far, He had, at those humbler points of His personality in which He touched the conditions of ordinary mortals, numerous little wants to which they were capable of ministering, and by their attention to which they could leave Him disembarrassed for His higher engagements.

The first moiety of the verse attaches itself parenthetically to the last moiety of the preceding verse. The ladies specified were, so to speak, the regular attendants of our Lord. But many others, who could not get into the innermost circle, or whose circumstances did not permit their frequent absence from home, had yet been blessed by our Lord, and felt irresistibly attracted toward Him. Hence they too lingered on in view of the cross **And many other women who came up with Him to Jerusalem.** To be present at the passover, and to enjoy whatever manifestations of His royal nature and office it might please the great Master to make.

VER. 42–47 form a paragraph which, as was noted by Eusebius, has its correspondencies in all the other evangelists. See Matt. xxvii. 57–61; Luke xxiii. 50, 51; and John xix. 38–42.

42 And now when the even was come, because it was the preparation, that is, the day before the sabbath, 43 Joseph of Arimathæa, an honourable counsellor, which also waited for the kingdom of God, came, and went in boldly unto Pilate, and craved the body of Jesus. 44 And Pilate marvelled if

---

Ver. 42. **And now when the even was come.** The first of 'the two evenings,' or the space of time that extended from mid-afternoon to sunset.

Because it was the preparation. Literally, *since it was preparation*, that is, *since the day, whose evening had set in, was preparation day*. The idea of the particular preparation referred to was in itself so definite that the evangelist did not even need to say '*the* preparation.' The *since* looks, reason-renderingly, forward to the action of Joseph, about to be narrated.

That is, the day before the sabbath. Literally, *which is fore-sabbath*, that is *which preparation* is *fore-sabbath*, or *sabbath eve*. Compare the German *Sonnabend*. The reference therefore is generically to preparation for the sabbath as sabbath, not specifically to preparation for the paschal sabbath, as paschal sabbath. (See John xviii. 28, xix. 31 and 42.) Every sabbath needed 'preparation,' both outward and inward, if it was to be hallowed as a season of rest from the toils of other days.

Ver. 43. **Joseph of Arimathea.** Literally, *Joseph, he from Arimathea.* So designated to distinguish him from other Josephs. The site of Arimathea is still undetermined. Many, inclusive of Grimm, suppose it probable that it was the Ramah, or Ramathaim-Zophim, of Mount Ephraim, where Samuel was born. But where that *Ramah*, or *Ramathaim*, or *Double-Height*, was, is 'one of the puzzles of biblical geography.' "It is," says Dean Stanley, "without "exception, the most complicated and disputed problem of sacred topography." (*Sinai and Palestine*, p. 224.) See Whitney's *Bible Geography*, p. 313.

An honourable counsellor. *Honourable*, viz. in a social position, as belonging to the higher classes of society. He was, as it were, a 'gentleman' or a 'noble.' The same term is applied to ladies in Acts xiii. 50, xvii. 12. Joseph was a *councillor*, or *senator, i.e.* a member of the sanhedrim.

Who also waited for the kingdom of God. Or more literally, *Who also himself was waiting for the kingdom of God.* He had been a student of prophecy and of the signs of the times, and had come to the conclusion that the crisis of the ages was at hand. Notwithstanding his high position in society, and the consequent influences that were blowing in upon him in the direction of spiritual indifference, *he also himself*, as well as the humbler and avowed disciples of Jesus, looked for the speedy establishment of the Messianic kingdom.

Came Upon the scene.

And went in boldly unto Pilate. He dared all the consequences that might be involved in the act (τολμήσας).

And craved the body of Jesus. But not in a *craven* spirit. The verb just means *asked*, and so it is generally rendered in the numerous passages in which it occurs. It is so rendered here in the Geneva and the Rheims. It is nowhere else translated *crave*. In the corresponding passages of Matt. xxvii. 58 and Luke xxiii. 52 it is translated *begged*. Tyndale has *begged* here too; Wycliffe and Coverdale have *axide* or *axed* (that is, *asked*).

he were already dead: and calling *unto him* the centurion, he asked him whether he had been any while dead. 45 And when he knew *it* of the centurion, he gave the body to Joseph. 46 And he bought fine linen, and took him down, and wrapped him in the linen, and laid him in a sepulchre which was hewn out of a rock, and rolled a stone unto the door of the sepulchre.

47 And Mary Magdalene and Mary *the mother* of Joses beheld where he was laid.

VER. 44. **But Pilate wondered if He were already dead.** It is the perfect tense that is employed, *if He were already in a dead state*. As crucified persons generally belonged to a strong coarse class of people, it was no uncommon thing for them to linger on in life for more than a day. Pilate had seen with his eyes that Jesus did not belong to that class; but still he would feel surprised if He should be already deceased.

And calling to him the centurion. Who had charge of the execution. See ver. 39.

He asked him whether He had been any while dead. The verb here, unlike the preceding one, is in the aorist, *if He died*, and the adverb literally means *formerly*, or *some time ago* (εἰ πάλαι ἀπέθανεν). It is rendered *long ago* in Matt. xi. 21, and *a great while ago* in Luke x. 13, and *of old* in Jude 4. The Vatican and Cambridge manuscripts read *now* (ἤδη) instead of *some time ago*. And Lachmann and Tregelles have introduced this reading into their texts. Wrongly. Not only is the strong adverb of the Received Text overwhelmingly supported by the manuscripts, it harmonises, admirably though artlessly, with the tense of the verb employed. Pilate does not ask *if Jesus died just now*, but *if He died some time ago*, so that there might be no doubt that He was *now in a dead state*.

VER. 45. **And when he knew it of the centurion.** As soon as he got knowledge of the fact from the centurion.

He gave the body to Joseph. He *gifted* it (ἐδωρήσατο). *The body*: Literally, *the corpse* (πτῶμα).

VER. 46. **And having bought fine linen.** Such as was used for swathing the bodies of the dead. See Herodotus, ii. 86.

He took Him down, and wrapped Him in the linen. *Wrapped* or *rolled.*

And laid Him. More literally, *deposited Him.*

In a sepulchre which was hewn out of a rock. *Sepulchre*, or *monument*. The Greek word (μνῆμα or μνημεῖον) means *monument*, for sepulchres that were hewn out of rocks, or rendered otherwise conspicuous, were intended to maintain the *memory* of the departed.

And rolled a stone to the door of the sepulchre. It would no doubt be a stone that was artificially fitted to the aperture. *To*: literally, *upon*. *The door*: that is, *the entrance*. The word does not denote the mechanical contrivance by which passages may be closed. It denotes the passage itself, which was the *thoroughfare* through which there was entrance and exit.

VER. 47. **And Mary the Magdalene and Mary the mother of Joses beheld where He was laid.** They *were beholding.*

ST. MARK XVI.

CHAPTER XVI.

1 AND when the sabbath was past, Mary Magdalene, and Mary the *mother* of James, and Salome, had bought sweet

CHAPTER XVI.

A veil is drawn over the anguish of the following day. It was 'the day of rest.' But it would be emphatically, to the disciples, a day of restlessness. It was the day of the expiry of the old dispensation. With the dawn of the first day of the new week, there came the dawn of a new era for the whole world of mankind. Our eyes are turned, by the evangelist, to the first streaks of the dayspring.

VER. 1-8. Comp. Matt xxviii. 1-10, Luke xxiv. 1-10, John xx. 1-18.

VER. 1. **And when the sabbath was past.** Or, *was passed through* (διαγενομένου). Wakefield totally misunderstood the phrase. He translated it, *on the sabbath between*.

Mary the Magdalene, and Mary the mother of James. She is called *the mother of Joses* in the preceding verse, and *the mother of James the little and of Joses* in chap. xv. 40. So artlessly does the evangelist compose, now touching on one differentiating relationship, and now on another.

And Salome. See chap. xv. 40.

Had bought. It is not a pluperfect in the original, but an aorist, *bought*. So Wycliffe, Tyndale, Coverdale, the Geneva, and the Rheims; Luther too and Calvin. The pluperfect translation was a device of Tremellius, Beza, Grotius, and such other translators and expositors as Piscator, Petter, Erasmus Schmid, Wolff, Wells, Whitby, Schaff, to produce an artificial harmony with Luke xxiii. 56, " and they returned, *and prepared spices and ointments*, and rested the sab-" bath day, according to the commandment." There is however no contradiction or disharmony between the two narratives. And there is no occasion for resorting, with Greswell and Bloomfield, to the subtle expedient of supposing a reference to two distinct bands of women, a Salome band and a Johanna band. Neither is there any occasion for supposing, with Doddridge, that the evangelist's statement is founded on a resolution of the women to purchase ' a *larger* quantity of aromatic drugs.' There is simply artlessness of representation, especially on the part of Mark. He had not in his mind the least intent to represent the purchase of the spices as chronologically subsequent to the sabbath day. Neither on the other hand did he mean to intimate that it was chronologically anterior. He is not constructing at all a chronicle of chronological details. He was intent on only one great chronological event, the resurrection of our Lord, according to His own explicit predictions, on the third day after His decease. Hence the preliminary obtrusion of the expression, *when the sabbath was past*. But after having made that statement, he seems, so to speak, to pause and stand on tiptoe to get the earliest possible glimpse of the great event. And it is while thus in an attitude of expectancy that he makes the statement regarding the women's purchase of the spices, without any intention of determining the date of the transaction.

spices, that they might come and anoint him. 2 And very early in the morning the first *day* of the week, they came unto

Sweet spices. Or simply *spices*, as the same word is rendered in Luke xxiii. 56, xxiv. 1; John xix. 40. It is also so rendered here by Coverdale, and in the Rheims. Wycliffe has simply *oynementis*, and Tyndale *odures*. But Purvey, in his revision of Wycliffe, has *sweete smellynge oynementis*; and in Lord Cromwell's Bible of 1539 Tyndale's simple *odures* is expanded into *sweete odoures*. The word in the original is *aromas* (ἀρώματα), a term which, according to Max Müller, primarily denoted *field-fruits* in general, and then came to be restricted to really *aromatic herbs*, on a principle corresponding to what is exemplified in the word *spices*, which originally meant unrestrictedly *espèces* or *species*. (*Lectures on Language*, vol. i., p. 293, sixth ed.)

That they might come. The evangelist had the journey of the women in view, and hence this clause that might otherwise have seemed superfluous.

And anoint Him. Namely with the liquid aromas. Instead of *anoint*, Bishop Hammond suggests *embalm*; and his word is accepted by Dr. Samuel Clarke, Whitby, Mace, Principal Campbell, Dr. Adam Clarke, and others. It is, for several reasons, an excellent word; but it must not be supposed that there was a precise analogy, or closely running parallel, between the Jewish and the Egyptian process. On this matter Harmer was quite mistaken. (*Observations*, vol. iii., 75.) The Jews did not disembowel, or use measures to prevent corruption. (See John xi. 39.) They merely showed their love and esteem by 'anointing to the burying.' (Mark xiv. 8.) They neutralized, for a limited season, some of the unpleasantnesses of death, and indicated the persistence of affection. They thus too subindicated the existence of a certain lively hope. The women, in the instance before us, wished to supplement the attentions of Joseph of Arimathea (chap. xv. 46). Perhaps they were ignorant of what Nicodemus had done (John xix. 39). Or perhaps they simply desired to add their contribution to his.

VER. 2. **And very early in the morning.** Or simply, *and very early*. The clause *in the morning* is superfluous, and is omitted in ver. 9; as also in John xx. 1. Wycliffe omits it here, *ful eerli*.

The first day of the week. Or '*on*' *the first day of the week*. It is a strange idiomatic expression in the original, *on the one of the sabbaths*. It has occasioned perplexity to translators. Luther renders it puzzlingly, *on one of sabbaths*. Coverdale, still more puzzlingly, *upon a daye of the sabbathes*. The Rheims, *the first of the sabboths*; Lord Cromwell's Bible (1539), *the first daye of the sabbath*. Wycliffe is far superior in his version, *in oon of woke dayes* (i.e. *in one of the week days*, i.e. *in No. one of the week days*). Tyndale apprehended the idiom precisely, *the nexte daye after the saboth day*. The Greeks sometimes pluralized the word *sabbath*, in consequence of the Aramaic way of pronouncing the term, *sabbatha*. And the Hebrews sometimes counted the days of their week *from the sabbath*, or *toward the sabbath*. Or rather they, as it were, absorbed their week in the sabbath, so that Sunday was *one of the sabbath*. (See **Arias Montanus**'s *note, in loc.*)

They came to the sepulchre. Very literally, *they come upon the sepulchre*.

ST. MARK XVI.

the sepulchre at the rising of the sun. 3 And they said among themselves, Who shall roll us away the stone from the door of the sepulchre? 4 And when they looked, they saw that the stone was rolled away: for it was very great. 5 And

---

The preposition denotes proximity. The evangelist is in haste, as it were, to see them 'on' the spot.

At the rising of the sun. Not quite a correct rendering. The expression rather means, *after the sun had risen* (ἀνατείλαντος τοῦ ἡλίου). It was correctly rendered by Wycliffe, Purvey, Tyndale, and in the Rheims. King James's English translators, along with the authors of the Geneva, were misled by Beza, who praised the reading (ἀνατέλλοντος) of his 'very ancient manuscript,' the Cambridge (D), though he did not introduce it into the text or into his version. All the other uncial manuscripts are against the reading. It was obviously a tinkering to bring Mark's phraseology into closer harmony, as was supposed, with Matt. xxviii. 1, Luke xxiv. 1, and John xx. 1. The tinkering, however, is entirely unnecessary. There is no collision of representations, although scope is left, amid their variations, for the reproductive faculty to adjust into unity, as best it can, diversities of details. (See an exceedingly ingenious attempt in this direction by E. Greswell in his 43rd *Dissertation on the Principles and Arrangement of an Harmony of the Gospels*.)

VER. 3. **And they were saying to each other.** Namely, as they were approaching the spot.

Who shall roll away for us the stone out of the door of the sepulchre? The magnitude of the stone, and the way perhaps in which it had been fixed in, occasioned them concern, though they might be hoping to procure assistance from such casual labourers as would be stirring out to their work. It is noteworthy that they make no reference to the Roman soldiers. The likelihood is that they knew nothing at all of their appointment. The military guard was an afterthought with the priests and Pharisees, and had been obtained, not on the preparation day, but on the sabbath. See Matt. xxvii. 62–66.

VER. 4. **And having looked up.** The *up* is found in the renderings of the word in chap. vi. 41, vii. 34, viii. 24. The sepulchre had been, as was common with such tombs, on the face of a sloping eminence of rock.

They see that the stone has been rolled away. In the Sinaitic and Vatican manuscripts, and in the texts of Tischendorf and Tregelles, the verb is ἀνακεκύλισται, *has been rolled back*. It is likely to be the autographic reading, and modified to that of Matthew and Luke by the early harmonists.

For it was very great. A clause that comes as artlessly in at the end here, ætiologically, as the first clause of the first verse comes in chronologically. A less inartificial writer would have put the clause at the conclusion of the third verse; whither indeed the writer of the Cambridge manuscript (D) has actually transferred it. So too Eusebius, in his quotation of the passage in his *Demonstratio*, x. 493. Wassenbergh thinks that the clause must have been anciently torn off from its natural position (*De Trajectionibus N. T.*, p. 34), a most unlikely occurrence. Yet Dr. Adam Clarke took the same view; and Mace,

entering into the sepulchre, they saw a young man sitting on the right side, clothed in a long white garment; and they were affrighted. 6 And he saith unto them, Be not affrighted: Ye seek Jesus of Nazareth, which was crucified: he is risen; he is

---

Wakefield, Principal Campbell, Rodolphus Dickinson, actually make the transposition in their respective versions; while Wolle throws the preceding part of the verse into a parenthesis (*De Parenthesi Sacra*, p. 38.) He was preceded in this device by Hammond and Petter, and has been followed by Worsley, Newcome, and Edgar Taylor. There is no need for such surgical manipulation. Neither need we, with Meyer and Alford, imagine that the great size of the stone is particularized as a reason why they could not escape taking notice of the fact that it was rolled aside. It is enough, as Bleek judiciously decides, that the evangelist's phraseology is artless.

VER. 5. **And entering into the sepulchre.** Or rather, *and when they entered into the sepulchre.* It is not implied that they entered immediately, or hasted as it were. The clause is not so much successive to what goes before, as preliminary to what comes after. It would be with trembling, and awe, and hesitation, that they would enter; and perhaps too after Mary of Magdala had sped off to inform the apostles. See Matt. xxviii. 5, and John xx. 1, 2.

They saw a young man. Or simply, *a youth.* Wycliffe has *a yong oon* (a young one); and Purvey, *a yonglyng.* This last is Luther's precise word (*Jüngling*). It is assumed that the bloom and beauty of youth are never effaced from angelic natures.

Sitting on the right side. As they entered, apparently. He might be sitting on one of the ledges or platforms, which are common in the oriental sepulchres, and which are convenient for the accommodation of the body during the process of anointing.

Clothed in a long white garment. *Arrayed in a white robe.* The idea of *long* is only implied. *Stole* is the word used. Wycliffe's version is *hilid* (= *heeled*, i.e. *covered*) *with a whit stoole.*

And they were affrighted ($\dot{\epsilon}\xi\epsilon\theta\alpha\mu\beta\dot{\eta}\theta\eta\sigma\alpha\nu$). The idea of *amazement* is more prominent than that of *fright*. See the only other passages, with the exception of next verse, in which the word occurs in the New Testament, Mark ix. 15, xiv. 33. *They would be frightened.* But they were in particular amazed to see the empty tomb. They could not yet realize the possibility of the resurrection. This idea of *amazement* has something to do with the conciliation of the different evangelical narratives. Each evangelist depicted the resurrection scene from his own peculiar standpoint; and, out of the multitudinous details of visits and revisits, crossing and recrossings, groupings and regroupings, he selected what sufficed to fill up his particular cartoon of representation.

VER. 6. **But he saith to them, Be not affrighted.** *Be not amazed.* Nothing else has happened than what you should have expected.

Ye seek. That is, *Ye are seeking I am aware.*

Jesus of Nazareth who has been crucified: He is risen: He is not here. You should not be looking for Him here. You should not have expected, after what He Himself said, to find Him here.

not here: behold the place where they laid him. 7 But go your way, tell his disciples and Peter that he goeth before you into Galilee: there shall ye see him, as he said unto you. 8 And they went out quickly, and fled from the sepulchre; for they trembled and were amazed: neither said they any thing to any *man;* for they were afraid.

Lo the place where they laid Him. The cerements were there, but the body was gone. Whither? Had it been stolen and hidden? Who would have been the thieves? Friends or foes? Not friends; for how could their faith be made heroic, for their crusade against the world's unbelief, by a theft and a carcase? Not foes; for it was their interest to prevent the disappearance of the body, that there might be ocular demonstration of the falsity of the predicted resurrection. The fact of the actual resurrection of our Lord is a rock-of-ages that never can be moved. See *Comm.* on Matt. xxviii.

VER. 7. **But.** Now that you see that your Lord is not here, but risen.

Go; tell His disciples and Peter. Peter in particular, because he in particular had denied his discipleship, and thus put himself as it were outside the circle.

That. This demonstrative conjunction is here used *recitatively*, and thus introduces, in the direct form instead of the indirect, what was to be said to the disciples and Peter. It is idiomatic in English to omit it altogether.

He goeth before you into Galilee: there shall ye see Him, as He said to you. See chap. xiv. 28. The appearance of our risen Lord in Galilee, where He was best known, and where He had the greatest number of followers who were intimately acquainted with His person, and therefore best qualified to judge of its identity, was the most important of all the appearances. It was *the great public appearance*, and is no doubt that which is referred to by Paul, when he says, *After that, He was seen of above five hundred brethren at once; of whom the greater part remain unto this present, but some are fallen asleep.* (1 Cor. xv. 6.)

VER. 8 **And they went out quickly, and fled from the sepulchre.** That they might fly, if possible, as upon the wings of the wind, to fulfil the behest committed to them. The word *quickly* however, though in the Erasmian or Received text, must have been a marginal annotation. It is wanting in almost all the good manuscripts, and in all the ancient versions.

For they trembled and were amazed. Literally, *for trembling and ecstasy had hold of them.* The word *ecstasy* is the evangelist's own word. It is rendered *trance* in Acts x. 10, xi. 5, xxii. 17. They were in the highest state of mental exaltation, as if their spirits could not be contained in their bodies. The *trembling* that accompanied this condition of ecstasy was not properly *fright*, but *agitation*.

And they said nothing to any one. Namely, by the way. So Cardinal Cajetan and Grotius. It is entirely gratuitous to suppose, with Meyer, followed by Alford, that the meaning is that they left their message unfulfilled. Such a conception of the case is intrinsically most improbable.

For they were afraid. Why? Certainly not, as Petter supposes, "from the "apprehension of some hurt or danger which might befall them by or upon the "apparition of the angel to them." Neither is it natural to think of any farseeing solicitude lest the news should get wind, and reach the ears of the members of the sanhedrim, so as to arouse to persecution. Dr. Edward Wells comes nearer nature; "*For*," says he, "*they were afraid to stay, and not to hasten all they could to the apostles.*" They were in a tumult of commotion, and could not pause by the way to speak to any.

VER. 9-20 have become a battle field of textual criticism.

They are wanting altogether in the two most ancient manuscripts yet discovered, the Sinaitic (א) in St. Petersburg, and the Vatican (B) in Rome: rather a remarkable fact.

Eusebius, the illustrious Bishop of Cæsarea, who died A.D. 340, and who was one of the most learned and inquisitive of the Greek fathers, says that the paragraph was wanting 'in almost all the existent copies of the Gospel,' 'the accurate ones at all events' (σχεδὸν ἐν ἅπασι τοῖς ἀντιγράφοις . . . τὰ γοῦν ἀκριβῆ τῶν ἀντιγράφων, κ. τ. λ.). He adds, less sweepingly, that it was found 'rarely; in some copies, but not in all.' (*Opera*, A. Migne's edition, vol. iv., p. 938.) These assertions, more especially when taken in connection with the evidence of the Sinaitic and Vatican manuscripts, are certainly startling.

Then Jerome, who died A.D. 420, and who was the most learned and critical of the Latin Fathers, echoes the substance of the assertions of Eusebius, but just as if he were making his own original observations. This he does in a long letter addressed to Hedibia, a pious lady residing in Gaul. He says that the paragraph in question is found 'in few Gospels, and is wanting in 'almost all the Greek copies' (*in raris fertur Evangeliis, omnibus Græciæ libris pene hoc capitulum in fine non habentibus*: Epist. cxx., c. 3). This language, like the first sweeping remarks of Eusebius, is almost sensationally strong.

But still farther, Victor of Antioch, who flourished, as is generally supposed, about the time of Jerome, and who compiled, chiefly from the writings of the preceding Greek Fathers, a *Commentary on the Gospel according to Mark*, still extant, re-echoes, though in a somewhat mitigated form, the strong assertion of Eusebius. He says that 'in most copies the passage, *Now when Jesus was risen early*, etc., is not found in the present Gospel.' (*Comm.*, as contained in Cramer's *Catena*, vol i., p. 447.)

Then there is an old Greek *Homily on the Resurrection*, which has gone a-begging for an author among the Greek fathers, in which the substance of Eusebius's sweeping remarks is strongly re-re-echoed. The passage runs thus: "In the more accurate copies, the Gospel according to Mark has its end at '*for* "*they were afraid.*' But in some copies this also is added, '*Now when He was* "*risen early the first day of the week, He appeared first to Mary Magdalene, out* "*of whom He had cast seven devils.*'" This Homily has been ascribed by some to Gregory of Nyssa, and is printed among his works. It is often referred to as his. But by Montfaucon and Cramer it is ascribed to Severus of Antioch, and printed by them as his; while Combefisius and Gallandius ascribe it to Hesychius of Jerusalem, and print it as his. Hesychius flourished in the sixth century, and it is most probable, it seems, that he is the real author of the discourse. (See Burgon's *Last Twelve Verses of Mark*, chap. v.)

Euthymius Zigabenus, who flourished in the twelfth century, does not deal in such energetic phraseology as some of his predecessors. But he says, in his annotation on the eighth verse: " Some of the expositors affirm that the Gospel " according to Mark terminates here, and that what follows was afterwards " added. It is necessary however," he adds, " to interpret it, as it is not incon- " sistent with the truth." This is mild enough, but let us see the continuity of the tradition.

In modern times few will be prepared to admit that the Gospel could have been intentionally terminated at the eighth verse (ἐφοβοῦντο γάρ). " That " ought," says Griesbach, " to seem incredible to all" (Com. Crit., p. 199). " It would be," says Michaelis, "a wonderful conclusion of a book." (Einleitung, p. 1060, fourth edition.)

Michaelis was greatly perplexed about the paragraph. It looked to him like a patch. And yet he could not shake himself entirely loose from the conviction that Mark was its author. He hence, with that inventiveness of genius for which he was distinguished, struck out the following vivid conjecture on the subject: What if Mark may have issued two editions of his Gospel, one in Rome, and another in Alexandria? What if the Roman edition was originally incomplete, while the Alexandrine was completed? Might not the evangelist, in composing the Roman one, have got just to the close of the eighth verse of the 16th chapter, at the very point of time when Peter, at whose dictation he was writing, was crucified or imprisoned? Why not? And why may not that event have put an abrupt arrest on the evangelist's composition? Why may we not account in this manner for the 'wonderful conclusion'? And why may we not further suppose that, when the evangelist subsequently published in Alexandria his second edition, he added, as best he could, out of his own penury, what was needed to complete the narrative? (Einleitung, pp. 1059, 1060, fourth edition.)

Henry Augustus Schott of Wittemberg, and subsequently of Jena, the distinguished translator and editor of the New Testament, had a conjecture somewhat akin. He had been disposed for a time, no doubt under the influence of Griesbach's judgment, to surrender the authenticity of the paragraph. But he swung back into the current belief, in virtue of excogitating a conjecture which accounted as he supposed for all the phenomena, and thus cleared away his difficulties. He supposed that ere Mark had finished his Gospel, it had got into the hands of some one, 'perhaps a friend or companion, to whom he had privately communicated it,' and this individual (the more shame to him!) surreptitiously published it. Hence the copies that were deficient in the paragraph. By and by however, Mark, when he had leisure, gave the finishing touch to his work, and published it in its present completed form. Hence the manuscripts that had or have the paragraph. But as meanwhile the thread of composition had been snapped, and a considerable time had elapsed ere the work was resumed, the addition was not very homogeneously composed or attached. (Authentia Marci, xvi., 9-20. 1813.) How long Schott continued satisfied with this conjecture we do not know. But he seems ultimately to have swung back again to the opinion which he held while he was working hand in hand with Griesbach. See his note in the fourth edition of his New Testament (1839).

Griesbach, as we have been indicating, was against the authenticity of the paragraph, and had his own conjecture on the subject. It was by no means so vivid as that of Michaelis; and it was more sober than that of Schott. Yet it is striking enough; and it has had immeasurably greater influence, than either or both of the others, upon the subsequent course of biblical criticism. He supposed that the evangelist's conclusion of his Gospel had by some accident perished, most probably from the original autograph, and that the present paragraph had been substituted in its place 'by somebody' (*a non nemine*), perhaps the editor of the collected Gospels, in the second century. (*Comm. Crit.*, pp. 197, 202.) This conjecture of the great critic, backed as it is by a skilfully adjusted array of the evidence, diplomatic and patristic, that was at his disposal, was acquiesced in by Schulthess. And the combined reasonings of Schulthess and Griesbach convinced David Schulz, Griesbach's critical successor, that the paragraph, as we have it, is ' spurious.' (*Nov. Test.*, 1827.)

Tischendorf, so justly illustrious as a textual critic, acquiesces in the decision of Schulz. "That these verses," he says, "were not written by Mark is proved " by sufficient arguments." Many details in the phraseology, as he thinks, are at variance with Mark's style (*a Marci ratione abhorrent*).

Tregelles, with all his reverence of spirit, is of the same opinion. (See his *New Test.* and his *Printed Text*, pp. 246–261.) He says, unhesitatingly, "the " *book of Mark himself* extends no farther than chap. xvi. 8," but he holds that "the remaining twelve verses, by whomsoever written, have a full claim to be " received as an authentic part of the second Gospel." (*Printed Text*, p. 258.) Dean Alford, ever faithful to his honest convictions, comes to a corresponding conclusion. "The legitimate inference is," he says, "that *the passage was placed* " *as a completion of the Gospel soon after the apostolic period*, the Gospel itself " having been, for some reason unknown to us, left incomplete. The most " probable supposition," he continues, "is, that *the last leaf of the original* " *Gospel was torn away*." (Greek Text, vol. i., p. 431, fifth ed.)

Andrews Norton, in his *Translation of the Gospels*, shows the strength of his convictions, by leaving off, in his text, with the 8th verse.

Archbishop Thomson, with the whole tide of his sympathies flowing in the direction of what is Christian, feels constrained to say, " it is probable that this " section is from a different hand, and was annexed to the Gospel soon after " the time of the apostles." (*Gospel of Mark* in Smith's *Bib. Dict.*) Bishop Lightfoot too, full of a corresponding spirit, says: " If I might venture a " conjecture, I would say that both John viii. 1–11 and Mark xvi. 9–20 were " due to that knot of early disciples who gathered about St. John in Asia Minor, " and must have preserved more than one true tradition of the Lord's life and " of the earliest days of the church." (*Fresh Revision of the E. N. T.*, p. 28.) These cautious and reverent statements contrast favourably with Fritzsche's opinionativeness. "Nothing in my opinion," says he " is so certain (*tam* " *certum est*), as that this section is due to another author than Mark " (*Comm.*, p. 752). But Meyer is almost, if not altogether, as unhesitating. He says: " The whole section of ver. 9–20 is inauthentic, not composed by Mark." Ewald prints the section in smaller type, and says that " without doubt it was " the conclusion of some other Gospel, now lost, and was appended to Mark's by " the last redacteur." (*Drei Erst. Evan.*, p. 366.) Hitzig thinks that the author of the section was Luke. (*Johannes Marcus*, p. 187 ff.) Henneberg, though not capable of adjudications that stand out so boldly in relief, was of opinion

9 Now when *Jesus* was risen early the first *day* of the

that the evidence, external and internal, decidedly "preponderates against the "defenders of the authenticity of the section." (*Die Geschichte des Begräbnisses*, etc., p. 167.) Klostermann too surrenders, still more decisively, to the same opinion. (*Marcusevangelium*, p. 298 ff.) And, before him, Bertholdt, Rosenmüller, Credner, Neudecker. After him Volkmar, who thinks that the inauthenticity of the section is proved by tradition, fact, and phraseology. (*Marcus und die Synopsis*, p. 606.) Baumgarten-Crusius surrenders ver. 9-18, but clings tenaciously to ver. 19 and 20 as Mark's own conclusion. (*Comm.*, vol. i., part 2, p. 211.) Michelsen, again, only surrenders ver. 9-14, and decides that "ver. 15-20 are the authentic conclusion of the Gospel." He thinks that the whole paragraph, 9-20, had probably been, by some accident or other, nearly illegible in the autograph copy, and that hence it was left out altogether by some transcribers, while others contrived to make out ver. 15-20, and then supplied ver. 9-14 out of Luke and John, as best they could. (*Het Evangelie van Markus*. p. 29.) But Reville will have no half measures. He is positive that the "independence of the whole section, relatively to the rest of the "Gospel, is one of the unassailable results of modern criticism." (*Études Critiques*, p. 330.) Scholten too speaks as if the matter were now conclusively settled against the evangelist. (*Het Oudste Evang.*, p. 323.) And the last section of one of the latest and ablest books on the Gospel, Weiss's *Marcusevangelium und seine synoptischen Parallelen*, 1872, is entitled "The inauthentic conclusion" (*Der unächte Schluss*).

All this looks, for the moment, serious. And yet when we separate mere opinions, vivid conjectures, and strong asseverations, from real evidence, we find extremely little to put into the scale against, and a very great deal to put into the counter scale in favour of, the authenticity of the paragraph.

As, however, it is from the peculiarity of the composition of the paragraph, that the external evidence against its authenticity has derived most of its weight, we shall, first of all, consider the passage critically and exegetically, that we may have before us the materials for giving a candid judgment regarding the *internal evidence*. Then, at the conclusion of our exposition, we shall briefly sift the *external evidence*, on which the oppugners of the authenticity insist, and lay it in the balance, along with the counter external evidence in favour of the integrity of the Gospel. (See *Note at end of ver. 20.*)

VER. 9. **But (δέ).** The particle is *connective* and *continuative*, and slightly *oppositive* too. The evangelist does not follow out the line that runs through the preceding verses. He takes up a new line, and goes on with it. Why? No one can now tell. Every writer is subject to multitudes of interruptions, and to various influences, objective and subjective, which give occasion to broken representations and other peculiarities in composition. Inartificial writers, in particular, who have no theory about the unities of composition, and no literary aim or literary ideal in view, are peculiarly liable to abrupt breaks, turnings, overlappings, and other inequalities or inconcinnities of style. It is doing them infinite injustice, to apply to their artless deliverances the rules of a nicely adjusted and fully developed scheme of composition.

When He. The absence of the noun is evidence that it was no 'other hand' that was engaged artificially in constructing a patch. Had there been deliberate intention to prepare some appropriate supplement to the evangelist's Memoirs, there would have been, we have a right to assume, care and art enough, to insert, at the commencement of the supplement, the name of the person referred to. It was different with the evangelist. His mind was without art. And he had been already intent, throughout the whole preceding context, in thinking of the risen Saviour. Hence he had, in his own artless way, already jotted down one group of events connected with the occurrence of the resurrection. (See ver. 1-8.) And now, on another plane of representation, for he had only the rudiments of what might be called *a literary style*, he exhibits another group. It is still however '*Jesus*' who is uppermost in his thoughts; and hence the artless omission of the name. If we should suppose, with Ewald and Meyer, that it is a *fragment of another Gospel* that is here artificially stuck on, then the editor who deliberately made the addition might be reasonably expected to connect it by supplying the word *Jesus*. If there was so much art as to seek for a patch, we might expect that there would be so much more as to make the patch naturally adhesive.

Was risen early the first day of the week. Put a comma after *risen*, says Theophylact, and so connect the expression *early the first day of the week* with what follows, *He appeared to Mary the Magdalene*. Euthymius gives the same advice (μετὰ τὸ εἰπεῖν ἀναστὰς, ὑπόστιξον). Eusebius himself suggested it to his correspondent Marinus. (*Opera*, A. Migne's ed., vol. iv., p. 940.) Jerome repeats the suggestion in his letter to Hedibia, as if it were his own original device. And it is re-repeated in Victor of Antioch's Commentary, and in that *Homily on the Resurrection* which has gone a-begging for its author. Grotius, in modern times, deemed the same punctuation a matter of considerable moment. So did Mill (*Prol.*, §§ 812-815). Bengel also was in favour of it; and Wakefield. *But for no good reason.* Eusebius and his followers supposed that, provided the whole paragraph were not rejected as apocryphal, the comma would be indispensable to secure the harmony of Matthew and Mark. The question which Marinus submitted to the learned father, and which elicited the reply that ver. 12-20 are not found 'in the best codices,' was this, *How is it that the Saviour appears, according to Matthew, to have risen 'late on sabbath,' but, according to Mark, 'early on the first day of the week'?* If, says Eusebius, you hesitate to discard the paragraph as apocryphal, then put a comma after the words *when He was risen*, and there will be no longer any contradiction. But, in truth, there was no contradiction at any rate. Matthew, in the passage referred to (xxviii. 1), is not speaking at all of the time of our Lord's resurrection. And though he were, still it could not be that our Lord would voluntarily rise on the Jewish sabbath; for it was *on the third day* that He was to re-rear the temple of His body. (John ii. 19; Matt. xii. 40, xxvii. 63.) It must therefore have been *early on Sunday morning*, 'the first day of the week,' that He arose. And Eusebius, instead of writing at random, either about the existent codices of Mark on the one hand, or about commas on the other, should have applied his powerful intellect to the correct observation of what Matthew was actually speaking about, and then to the correct interpretation of the phrase *the end of the sabbath*, or *late on the sabbath*. (See *Comm.* on Matt. xxviii. 1.) The great body of expositors have done right in *not* putting a comma after the word *risen*, and in regarding the chronometrical notation that

ST. MARK XVI.

week, he appeared first to Mary Magdalene, out of whom

follows as determining the time, not of our Lord's appearance to Mary, but of His resurrection. This is, says Cardinal Cajetan, the natural construction (*suavis constructio*) of the words. So le Fèvre, Luther, Beza, Castellio, Suicer (i. 311), Wolff, Rosenmüller, de Wette, Fritzsche, Ewald, Bisping, Lange, Volkmar, Weiss, etc. *Early*: namely, *in the day*, so that the word is equivalent to *in the morning*; and thus is it rendered in chap. i. 35, xi. 20, xiii. 35, xv. 1. Some of the oppugners of the authenticity of the paragraph think that, if it had been Mark himself who was writing, he would have resumptively said *very early*, using the phrase that he employed in ver. 2. But why should any writer, or why should Mark in particular, be tied down to repetition? And was there not besides a peculiar reason for the *very early* of ver. 2, which is not applicable to ver. 9? Is it not probable that the evangelist's mind was thinking of the time of the departure of the women from their lodgings? Comp. Matt. xxviii. 1, and John xx. 1. *The first day of the week*: literally, *the first (day) of sabbath*. See ver. 2. The oppugners of the authenticity of the paragraph urge that if it had been the real Mark who was writing, he would not have said '*first of sabbath*' ($\pi\rho\omega\tau\eta$), but '*one of sabbath*' ($\mu\iota\hat{q}$), as in ver. 2. But how can any be sure that he would not? '*First*' is more natural intrinsically than '*one*,' which is quite a Hebrew idiom. It is the idiom indeed that is used in Matt. xxviii. 1, Luke xxiv. 1, John xx. 1, 19, and in Acts xx. 7, and 1 Cor. xvi. 2. As the favourite Jewish idiom, it would seem to have got into use-and-wont in connection with the story of the resurrection. But still the phrase *one (day) of sabbath*, or *one (day) of the week*, as meaning *the first day after sabbath*, or *the first day toward sabbath*, is, in itself, a strange expression, not readily intelligible. It is not remarkable therefore that the evangelist, who had an eye to the benefit of Gentiles in the composition of his Gospel (chap. i. 5 ; vii. 2, 3), should have turned the peculiar Hebrew idiom into partial harmony with Greek and Roman usage. It is also sometimes urged that it is unaccountable that the word for *sabbath* or *week* should be plural ($\sigma\alpha\beta\beta\acute{\alpha}\tau\omega\nu$) in ver. 2, and singular ($\sigma\alpha\beta\beta\acute{\alpha}\tau\text{ov}$) in ver. 9. But it is enough to reply that the two forms of the word were in almost equal currency among those who had occasion to Grecise the Hebrew or Aramaic term. And it is matter of fact that Mark, having occasion to use the word only twelve times in all, actually employs it in the plural form just six times (i. 21 ; ii. 23, 24 ; iii. 2, 4 ; xvi. 2), and hence just six times also in the singular form (ii. 27 twice ; ii. 28 ; vi. 2 ; xvi. 1, 9). In both forms it has, in all the passages, a *singular* meaning.

He appeared. Even to this word Schulthess, Volkmar, and Weiss object, because in the only other passage in which the verb occurs in Mark (xiv. 64) it has a subjective instead of an objective import. Must then a writer confine himself to only one possible application of a term? If a term is ambidextrous, must he, in his peculiar use of it, cut off one of its arms?

First to Mary the Magdalene. But, says Volkmar, *three women are mentioned in ver.* 1 *and* 2. True. But the evangelist, as we have seen, is not pursuing continuously the line of things which starts with ver. 1 and 2. He has done with that line, and has taken up a new thread. Artlessly indeed and inartistic-

he had cast seven devils. 10 *And* she went and told

ally, but still not unnaturally. He was not intending to write a scientific History. He was not even attempting to compose a complete Biography. He is merely giving *very brief Memoirs*, and these simply in a way of aggregation, adding jotting to jotting.

As regards the fact of our Lord's first appearance, it accords with John's narrative that He showed Himself, first, not to any group of women with Mary the Magdalene among them, but to Mary by herself (xx. 13-18). To reconcile this representation with Matthew's (xxviii. 9), we must suppose, what is perfectly natural, that there was a variety of runnings to and fro. We may conceive the case in some such way as the following, without however imagining that it embodies the absolute historic truth. When the group of women saw the open tomb and the angels, Mary may instantly, in a kind of ecstatic bewilderment, have turned on her heels to run and carry word of the fact to the apostles. By and by the other women would follow. Ere long Peter and John would come running, and then return. Mary for a little season was alone, near the sepulchre, and Jesus revealed Himself to her. By and by the other women rejoined her, and Jesus appeared to them all, as they were on their way to the apostles. There would be in all their bosoms not only interest, strung to the highest pitch, but ecstasy, and trepidation, and an impossibility of resting anywhere longer than a few moments at a time. (See Greswell's *Forty-third Dissertation.*)

Out of whom **He had cast seven demons.** Almost all the advocates of the apocryphal theory of the paragraph look upon this interjected clause as incontestable evidence that Mark could not be the writer. For why, ask they, should he reserve for this place such an interesting incident? Why not introduce it at the first mention of Mary the Magdalene, as Luke has done (viii. 2)? Its introduction here is 'inept,' says Fritzsche. But surely it is enough to reply that, as a matter of fact, the incident is here introduced by some one or other. And if some one here introduced it, why might not Mark? If we shall suppose, according to the theory of Ewald, that the paragraph was the conclusion of some other Gospel, now lost, then the author of that Gospel had introduced into the concluding paragraph of his work the statement regarding Mary; and we have no right to suppose that he had made no previous reference to her. Why might not Mark do the same? If we shall, on the other hand, suppose, according to the theory entertained by the majority of the oppugners of the authenticity, that the paragraph was expressly compiled for the conclusion of Mark, then the compiler, though knowing that Mary had been referred to in what goes before, adds here deliberately the statement objected to. But if the compiler could act thus, why might not Mark? The statement is by no means unnatural. Mary of Magdala had, in a pre-eminent degree, experienced the gracious interposition of the Saviour. She had got rid of 'seven demons.' She had been formerly, it seems, sadly afflicted in several distinct respects, why not in 'seven'? She had been overbalanced in mind. She had been kept on edge in her bodily condition, as regards those more delicate elements which have mysteriously intimate connection with the mind. But having been wonderfully healed, she clung devotedly to her Saviour. She 'loved much.' And

10] ST. MARK XVI. 453

not in vain. She was pre-eminently favoured on the resurrection morning. But objectors take minute exception, still farther, to the mode of the expression, *out of whom He had cast*. Literally, according to the Received Text, it is '*from*' (ἀπό) *whom He had cast out*; and Mark, it is alleged, always uses with the verb *cast-out* (ἐκβάλλω) another preposition (ἐκ), or what corresponds to that other (ἔξω). True, so far. In *the two other passages* in which Mark has occasion to connect the verb with a preposition meaning *out, outside*, or *from*, he uses the two prepositions referred to. In chap. vii. 26 we read, "*that He would cast out the demon 'out of' her daughter.*" In chap. xii. 8 we read, "*and cast him out 'outside' the vineyard.*" And here, according to the Received Text, we read, "'*from' whom He had cast out seven demons.*" What then? Must a writer who has once, or perhaps even twice, used a particular phase of a phrase, go on using that phase for ever, without variation, even although the variation be legitimate and in harmony with general usage? Or, when a writer gives, for the first time, a slightly diversified turn to a phrase which he has already employed in another phase, must the authenticity of his composition be, for that reason, subjected to suspicion? It is true however that Luke has the very preposition, here objected to, in his statement regarding Mary the Magdalene (viii. 2), "'*from*' (ἀφ') *whom went out seven demons*"; and hence, it is argued, it is likely that the statement has been culled from Luke. 'It is certain,' says Fritzsche. That does not follow however, even although the Received Text be accepted as indisputable; for it is quite conceivable that the coincidence might have been the result of *a certain set form of phrase* having got into common use among the early disciples when speaking of Mary's case. But there is in reality no minute coincidence of phraseology, that might be supposed to indicate the derivation of the expression before us from Luke. The reading of Lachmann (παρ' ἦς) is accepted by Tregelles, and is no doubt the genuine autographic reading. It is the reading of the manuscripts C* D L, and 33 'the queen of the cursives,' and is a reading which we may be sure would never be arbitrarily substituted by any transcriber for the Received; whereas, in consequence of the historical coincidence of the two statements in the two Gospels, transcribers were under the greatest temptation to alter the more peculiar word of Mark into the more familiar one of Luke. The evidence thus increases that we are dealing with an entirely original writer, such as we may suppose Mark to have been; and there is no reason at all for feeling the slightest scruple on account of his peculiar preposition. It is in fact interestingly significant; for not only were the demons turned *outside*, as it were, they were driven away *from beside* their victim. Such is the import of the evangelist's word.

VER. 10. **She** (ἐκείνη). Fritzsche, Meyer, and Volkmar maintain that the demonstrative pronoun here employed is never used by the real Mark without some distinct emphasis, and that here no emphasis is intended. But there is emphasis; *She, as distinguished from all the rest of the women, she* was the first herald of the resurrection.

She went (πορευθεῖσα). Here too the objectors press in with their objections. It is a word, say Fritzsche, Meyer, Volkmar, and Weiss, which Mark has never used in the whole of his Gospel hitherto, and yet it occurs three times (see ver. 12 and 15) in this paragraph. Is it not, they would conclude, suspicious? Must not the paragraph writer be a pseudo-Mark? Why should we think

them that had been with him, as they mourned and wept.
11 And they, when they had heard that he was alive, and had
been seen of her, believed not.

---

so? Take a corresponding case: there are two words translated *repent* in the New Testament, one μεταμέλομαι, the other μετανοέω. But the apostle Paul uses the former only twice, namely in 2 Cor. vii. 8, and the latter only once, namely in 1 Cor. xii. 21. Must we therefore suspect the respective sections in which the words occur as having been written by another hand?

And told. Or *reported*, or *carried-the-tidings*.

To them who had been with Him. Even to this expression some of the objectors take exception. It is, says Meyer, a phrase 'foreign to the Gospels.' But it really is not, so far at least as its essence is concerned. Even to Mark it is not foreign, for we read in chap. iii. 14 'Jesus ordained twelve that *they should be with Him.*' We read again in chap. v. 18 that he who had been delivered from the legion ' prayed Jesus that *he might be with Him.*' The second of these passages makes it evident that the phrase is not, as Weiss will have it, 'the prerogative of the twelve.' It is elastic in its applicability, and is most appropriately employed in the case before us, seeing that the tidings would be of transcendent interest not only to the eleven (see ver. 14), but also to a considerable number of others who had been the followers of our Lord in Galilee. Hence we read in Luke (xxiv. 9) that the women who returned from the sepulchre 'told all these things unto the eleven, *and to all the rest.*' And when the two brethren returned to Jerusalem from Emmaus, ' they found the eleven gathered together, *and them that were with them*' (Luke xxiv. 33).

As they mourned and wept. Schulthess objects to these words too, as containing superfluous information, and as consequently a proof that the writer was not the true Mark. But even Fritzsche here interposes, and says that this is carrying objection too far (*argutatus est*). Volkmar however thinks that the phrase has been borrowed from Luke vi. 25, 'Woe unto you that laugh now, *for ye shall mourn and weep,*' as if the combination of terms was so peculiar that Luke must have originated it! There is really nothing to wonder at in the expression, and nothing to wonder at in the fact that those who had been the followers of Jesus were found by Mary ' mourning and weeping.'

VER. 11. **And they** (κἀκεῖνοι). This too is objected to by Fritzsche, Meyer, and Volkmar, on the ground that no emphasis is intended. Volkmar says that Mark, unlike Luke, never uses the pronoun except to express 'emphasis or opposition.' But here opposition is expressed, which is a kind of emphasis; *and they, on their part,* as opposed to their informant on her part. The real spirit and meaning of the composition is missed when this antithesis is unnoticed or ignored.

When they heard that He was alive, and had been seen by her, believed not. Or, more literally, *when they heard (that) He is living and was seen by her, believed not.* The construction is thoroughly characteristic of Mark's artless manner. The *that* (ὅτι) is recitative, and what follows is in the direct form of report. Meyer however, and Volkmar, and Weiss, take exception to the verb *was seen* (ἐθεάθη). It occurs again in ver. 14. But it never occurs, it seems, in the preceding part of the Gospel, and is therefore to be suspected as a word that

12] ST. MARK XVI. 455

12 After that he appeared in another form unto two

Mark would not use. On the same principle we might suspect Romans xv. 24, because the same verb occurs there, *whereas it is never found in any other part of the apostle's writings.* Then Schulthess objects that the word does not simply mean *was seen.* True: but some one here uses it in the sense which it actually bears; and why not Mark? It suggests beautifully that Mary had not only got a casual glimpse of the risen Saviour; she had deliberately *looked on Him,* and *contemplated* Him. The expression *believed not* (ἠπίστησαν) is also noted by Weiss and others as 'strange to Mark.' Why? Because, though it occurs again in ver. 16, it does not occur in the preceding part of the Gospel. But what of that? Should it have occurred? Or does mere non-occurrence, within a limited range, make a word 'strange' or 'foreign' to a writer? Besides, the cognate noun *unbelief* (ἀπιστία) does occur twice in Mark, namely in chaps. vi. 6, ix. 24. And the verb occurs only twice in all Paul's epistles (Rom. iii. 3; 2 Tim. ii. 13): and what then? *Believed not:* The news seemed to be 'too good to be true.' They forgot their Lord's explicit predictions. They would be supposing that Mary's nervous nature had made her the victim, for the time being, of some hallucination or optical illusion.

VER. 12. **And after that.** Or, very literally, *And after these things* (μετὰ δὲ ταῦτα). Even this expression, simple as it is, renews the suspicions of those who suspect the authenticity of the paragraph. It is, says Meyer, 'foreign to Mark.' Why so, we ask? Is it simply because he never happens to use it in the rest of his Gospel? That surely is nothing 'strange.' He never uses the word *law* (νόμος): are we therefore to suppose that that word too was 'foreign' to him? He uses the word *reward* (μισθός) only once (in chap. ix. 41). Shall we therefore suspect the passage on the ground that the word, being nowhere else employed by the evangelist, should be regarded as 'foreign' to his vocabulary? Volkmar couples with the expression before us an expression that occurs in ver. 19, '*after having spoken*' (μετὰ τὸ λαλῆσαι), and says of the two that 'they never occur in Mark.' True; but what then? Though the particular phrase, '*after* having spoken, never occurs in the preceding part of the gospel, yet the phrase '*after*' *the delivering up of John* (i. 14) occurs, and so does the phrase '*after*' *My rising again* (xiv. 28). Must these two phrases be suspected too, because the evangelist nowhere else uses them?

He appeared. Or *He was manifested,* as the same word is translated in 1 John i. 2; iii. 5, 8; iv. 9 (ἐφανερώθη). Or it might be rendered, with Luther, *He manifested Himself.* Volkmar however takes exception to this word too. He says that it is 'never used *of persons* by Mark.' Never! And yet the truth of the matter is that in all the preceding part of the Gospel the word occurs only once (iv. 22); and, as it so happens, it is there used of *things.* 'Nothing is hid, *which shall not be manifested.*' Are not such objections hypercriticism?

In another form. That is, *in a different form* (ἐν ἑτέρᾳ μορφῇ). There was not merely a numerical otherhood; it was differentiated in form. Grotius supposed that the reference is to *a different dress.* Vossius too; and Heumann also, and Wakefield, Kuinöl, Rodolphus Dickinson. Wakefield and Dickinson expressly render the expression *in another dress*; and Heumann, though not thus rendering it in his version, reminds us that the Roman soldiers had got

of them, as they walked, and went into the country.
13 And they went and told *it* unto the residue: neither
believed they them.

---

hold of our Lord's proper dress! He hence starts and debates the question,
How did our Lord obtain this different suit? He did not see, apparently, that
at least twenty other questions would require to be started and settled, before
the one which he proposes could be intelligently debated. It would serve no
purpose but that of frivolity to discuss the reciprocal limits of the subjective
and the objective in the manner of the manifestation, and also the various
ingredients of things that might enter into the determination of the ' form.'
The evangelist leaves the matter indefinite; and so should we.

Unto two of them. That is, to two of our Lord's followers; not necessarily
apostles. Comp. Luke xxiv. 13, 18.

As they walked. That is, *as they were taking a walk.* So Count Zinzendorf,
in the peculiar idiom of the Germans, *da spazieren gingen.*

Going into the country. Very literally, *going into country*, just as we say
reversely, *going into town.* It is a mode of expression exceedingly characteristic
of St. Mark. Comp. chaps. i. 45, ii. 1, iii. 1, xv. 21. We learn from Luke that
the brethren were taking a walk to Emmaus, a place that has not yet had its
site identified by modern geographers. ' All is mere conjecture,' says Whitney.
(*Bible Geog.*, sub voce.)

VER. 13. The twelfth verse is but a stepping-stone to this. And they
(κἀκεῖνοι). There is intentional emphasis on the pronoun, *They too, as well as
Mary.*

Went off and reported the tidings to the rest. Of the Lord's followers, whether
apostles or not. Comp. Luke xxiv. 33.

Neither believed they them. And yet it is said in Luke xxiv. 33, 34, that when
they got into the midst of ' the eleven and them that were with them,' they were
met with the exclamation, ' the Lord is risen indeed, and hath appeared to
Simon.' This apparent contrariety demolishes at a stroke the theory of
Hitzig, who supposes that Luke is the author of Mark xvi. 9-20. It also
completely overturns the theory of those who imagine that the section, though
not composed by Luke, was, by the hand of some other one, culled out of Luke.
But there is no real contradiction nevertheless, whatever may be said to the
contrary by Schultbess, Fritzsche, Meyer, Alford, Weiss. The disciples of our
Lord were in the midst of the inconsistencies of a tumultuating state of mind.
All their hopes had been suddenly dashed. They had been utterly disappointed.
And yet they could not bring themselves to believe that their late beloved Lord
had been an impostor. *Had He not been uniformly and perfectly pure? Had
He not been almost infinitely unselfish and noble? It could not be that He was
a deceiver.* And yet the unchallengeable fact stared them in the face, that,
instead of throwing off His disguise and assuming His royal prerogatives, as
they had anticipated, He had been seized, tried, condemned, and crucified like
a slave! What could they make of the case? Mary the Magdalene and other
women had told them that the sepulchre was found by them open, and
illumined by the presence of angels. Peter and John had run to it, and found

14 Afterward he appeared unto the eleven as they sat

the report of the women true, in its main element at least. Then Mary had told them that the Lord actually appeared to her. She was a lady. She was truthful. They could not for a moment doubt her sincerity. But surely her imagination must have imposed on her! By and by, however, the Lord appeared to Peter also, and he reported the fact to his brethren. His testimony had weight; and they received it with raptures. (Luke xxiv. 34.) And yet after a little, and because of the very preciousness of their new-born hope, they began to be inquisitive and critical in reference to its foundation. What if Peter himself had been overmastered by his imagination? What if, under the influence of his sanguine nature, and with that haste which has been all along his besetting failing, he had mistaken a mere subjective vision for an objective fact? Then perhaps the assembled brethren would question Peter, and cross-question him, going into the varied details of the appearance, until, it may be, Peter's own faith began to waver. When once in the full flow of this doubting mood, they would be ready enough to set aside the testimony of the two comparatively humble brethren who had returned from the country. They would say: *No doubt the brethren are honest. But surely it cannot be true that He who actually, on the cross, gave up the ghost, and was then buried, is now literally alive again! How could such a thing be? Must not the brethren, and Peter himself, as well as Mary, be the dupes of their fond imaginations?* Such would naturally be the state of the disciples' minds for a considerable length of time, the tide of thought and feeling surging and resurging in contrary directions. And hence the facile conciliation of Mark's statement with Luke's. There is certainly, as Heumann remarks, no contradiction. And yet the appearance of it is so obtrusive, when the narratives are looked at from certain narrow-pointed pinnacles of observation and interpretation, that it was wrong in Alexander to pass over the whole matter *sub silentio*, as if there were nothing that required a single word of explanation. Augustine's theory of conciliation is good so far. He supposes that the disciples were not all of one mind. Some were convinced; some were unconvinced. Luke, as he imagines, refers to the one party; Mark to the other. (*Consensus*, iii. 25.) It is too artificial. Theophylact's theory is that the two brethren from the country reported the news not to the eleven, but to certain others. So, though more generically, Euthymius. Also too artificial. Masius's theory is that the two brethren mentioned by Mark were a different pair from those mentioned by Luke. Painfully strained and artificial. Lightfoot has a bright but illusory glimpse; and yet he took along with it elements of reality. He thinks that Peter was one of 'the two,' and that when he and Cleopas showed their faces in the meeting in Jerusalem, a flash of hope flew over the assembled brethren, so that they exclaimed 'conjecturally,' *The Lord is risen indeed, and hath appeared to Simon!* 'And yet when he and Cleopas open the whole matter, they do not yet believe even them.' Calvin is judicious, 'they fell into their former doubts.' So is Bengel: 'they believed; but immediately suspicion, and unbelief itself, recurred.'

VER. 14. **Afterwards** (ὕστερον). The Vulgate renders it, *last of all*. So Luther, and many others, as Whedon. But the word just means, very indefi-

at meat, and upbraided them with their unbelief and hardness of heart, because they believed not them which had seen him after he was risen.

15 And he said unto them, Go ye into all the world, and preach the gospel to every creature. 16 He that believeth

---

nitely, *subsequently*. As to the precise time, see John xx. 19. The word occurs often in Matthew, but nowhere else in Mark. Shall we therefore suspect it? It is not easy to do so consistently, as it occurs only once also in John (xiii. 36), and once also in the epistles (Heb. xii. 11). But should we on that account suspect the passages in which it occurs?

He appeared unto the eleven as they sat at meat. Literally, *as they were reclining* (at table). See chap. ii. 15, xiv. 3. The word here used, though different from that employed in ii. 15 and xiv. 3, also occurs, with the same reference, in chap. xiv. 18; and hence the objectors to the authenticity of the paragraph do not get scope for founding an objection on its occurrence here.

And upbraided them with their unbelief. Or more literally and pleasantly, *and upbraided their unbelief*, as if the reproof terminated on the act. Instead of *upbraided*, Wycliffe has *reprovyde* (i.e. *reproved*); the Rheims, *exprobrated*. Instead of *unbelief*, Mace, Campbell, Dickinson have, unhappily, *incredulity*. Wakefield's version is much better, *want of faith*.

And hardness of heart. The word is used comparatively, and has reference rather to the impenetrability of their understanding than to the unimpressibility of their feelings. (Comp. chap. vi. 52, and see Luke xxiv. 25.) But it was an impenetrability, nevertheless, which was traceable to moral causes; it merged in their culpable *want of faith*. See next clause.

Because they did not believe them who had beheld Him after He had been raised up. Their minds had been full of erroneous preconceptions regarding the Messiah's career, notwithstanding His own explicit predictions, and the numerous prophecies of the Old Testament Scriptures. (Comp. Luke xxiv. 26, 27.)

Ver. 15. **And He said to them.** On some subsequent occasion. Comp. Matt. xxviii. 16–20. The evangelist, not intending to write a regular history, strides on in his Memoirs to a conclusion, compressing and welding, as he proceeds, a multitude of chronological and other details.

Go ye. Or more accurately without the pronoun, *go*. The Saviour realized that the few disciples whom He addressed were but the representatives of an innumerable multitude of associates and successors.

Into all the world. The word *all* is in its emphatic form ($\ddot{a}\pi a\nu\tau a$). *Go into the whole world:* see that no part be omitted.

And preach the gospel. The Saviour meant *the good news about Himself*. Comp. chap. i. 1. It was no self-conceit in Him to think that the news concerning His connection with our race, and the work He achieved, the sufferings He endured, and the glory into which He has been exalted, is 'the good news' for universal man. His self consciousness radiated outward and upward into infinity.

To every creature. Literally, *to the whole creation*, that is, *to all mankind*. Men, as being the masterpieces of creation, are, for the moment, brought so

and is baptized shall be saved; but he that believeth not

close to the mental eye as to shut out from view all other creatures. No wonder. Man '*is*' the copestone of terrestrial creation. All else on earth, all even that is palæontological, points up to him, and is culminated in him. Lightfoot and Hammond supposed that the expression referred to *the Gentiles*. But that is an unwarrantable contraction of its import.

VER. 16. **He that believeth.** Namely, the gospel spoken of. *Believeth*, that is, *receives it as true*. It is involved in the peculiar nature of the thing believed, that it is trusted in, whenever it is believed.

And is baptized. Namely with the Christian baptism, which we must assume to have been explained to the disciples, and which mirrored to the outward sense the baptizing influence of the Holy Spirit of God. (See *Comm.* on Matt. iii. 6; xxviii. 19.) The words given by Mark, in the verses before us, must not be regarded as containing 'a full report' of all that was said by our Lord. Comp. Matt. xxviii. 18-20; Luke xxiv. 46-49. The respective reports of the different evangelists are no doubt exceedingly condensed, and confined indeed to some prominent outlines. Mark, in giving his outlines, exhibits his wonted artlessness of style, and hence the position of this clause, *and is baptized*. He did not mean to put it on an equality with the preceding clause, as if they were like paired horses in a chariot, or to intimate that *baptism* is as essential to salvation as *believing*. See next clause. But as, in the ministrations of the apostles, baptism was to be administered to the believing, as a sublime symbol of the cleansing which they needed, and which God was seeking to impart, it is here formally but inartificially introduced under the shadow of the great essential condition of salvation. In its spiritual essence, indeed, baptism is as essential to salvation as believing. It is, if possible, more so; for it is God who baptizes, or Christ; whereas it is man who believes. But, in its outward form, baptism cannot be essential. What Christ said of His words is as true of His works, inclusive of the ordinances of His church, 'it is the spirit that quickeneth, the flesh profiteth nothing.' (John vi. 63.) The evangelist's inartificial method of collocation may be illustrated by his representation in chap. i. 2, 3, where, after saying *as it is written in* ' *the prophet*,' he introduces a preliminary prediction of another prophet. The preliminary prediction is thrown in by the way, and the reader is left to his good sense to make the proper adjustment. It is on a similarly inartificial principle that Paul himself says, in Rom. x. 9, " *If thou shalt confess with thy mouth the Lord Jesus*, and " shalt believe in thine heart that God hath raised Him from the dead, thou " shalt be saved. For with the heart man believeth unto righteousness, *and* " *with the mouth confession is made unto salvation.*" The apostle cannot mean that oral confession is as much a condition of salvation as inward believing; for salvation is complete when inward believing is completed. (Rom. iv. 5.) But as the inward moulds the outward, and confession in one way or another is sure to follow ' believing in the heart,' the apostle did not scruple, in his free and artless style, to introduce it side by side with faith.

Shall be saved. Namely, from his sins. (See Matt. i. 21.) His sins are regarded as imperilling his weal. He is in imminent danger because of them,

shall be damned. 17 And these signs shall follow them that believe; In my name shall they cast out devils;

in danger of 'perishing' (John iii. 15, 16) or of suffering 'death' in all its deadliness (John viii. 24). When he is ' saved' he is, theologically speaking, ' pardoned' and ' justified.' Sanctification follows. Glorification is the grand result.

But he that believeth not. He who wilfully turns away from the gospel, and thus refuses to let his mind be interpenetrated, and morally moulded, by that absolute truth which embodies the only true ideal of human life.

Shall be condemned. The same word ($\kappa\alpha\tau\alpha\kappa\rho\iota\nu\omega$) occurs in other eighteen passages of the New Testament, and in seventeen out of the eighteen instances it is translated *condemn*. (See Matt. xii. 41, 42, xx. 18, xxvii. 3; Mark x. 33, xiv. 64; Luke xi. 31, 32; John viii. 10, 11; Rom. ii. 1, viii. 3, 34, etc.) And such is its real meaning. It is strictly a judicial term, and determines, by itself, nothing at all regarding the nature, degree, or extent of the penalty to be endured. It is right that this condemnation should be, if there be wilful refusal to leave off sinning, and to accept the only Divine, and therefore the only possible, means of getting deliverance from the effects of sinning. If there be a Divine moral government at all, there must be amenability to the Moral Governor. And yet preachers of the gospel should take care not to saddle. even in imagination, the forthgoing of the Great Moral Governor's judgments with any little, narrow, artificial conceits, which they may have casually picked up in their childhood, and carried with them in their inward ' chamber of imagery ' ever since.

VER. 17. But these signs. *These*, such as are about to be enumerated. 'Signs' do not exist for themselves. Neither are they things that are ultimately aimed at by means of other things. They aim at other things. And it is in these things beyond themselves that the reason of their being is realized. All signs exist to be remarked. But the degrees of their remarkability may be infinitely diversified. To many the most remarkable are the unwonted and the miraculous.

Shall follow them that believe. *Shall follow accompanyingly* ($\pi\alpha\rho\alpha\kappa\omicron\lambda\omicron\upsilon\theta\eta\sigma\epsilon\iota$). They shall thus follow not those merely who preach, but them who believe, and all who believe. We are not to suppose however that every individual believer was to make use of, or to have experience of, every possible sign. " There are " diversities of administrations, but the same Lord : and there are diversities of " operations; but it is the same God who worketh all in all." See 1 Cor. xii. 5-30. Neither are we to suppose that there is in this and the next verse an exhaustive specification of the signs. There are many others, inclusive particularly of ' love' (1 Cor. xiii.) and its thousand and one gracious effluences, which have permanently consolidated themselves into beautiful lives and benevolent institutions. In the passage before us however prominence is given to the signs which were peculiarly adapted to commend and authenticate the gospel at the outset of its career.

In My name shall they cast out demons. Some of the disciples would be exorcists.

18] ST. MARK XVI. 461

they shall speak with new tongues; 18 they shall take up
serpents; and if they drink any deadly thing, it shall not hurt
them; they shall lay hands on the sick, and they shall recover.

They shall speak with new tongues. New to them, such as were spoken in ecstasy at Pentecost (Acts ii. 4–11), or uttered mystically in the church at Corinth (1 Cor. xii. 10, xiv. 2–40). Some of the disciples would have that gift. (See 1 Cor. xii. 30, xiv. 18.)

VER. 18. They shall take up serpents. With impunity, if they should be compelled, by their persecutors, to pass through such an ordeal, or if, like St. Paul in Malta (Acts xxviii. 3–5), they should be accidentally attacked. Some would have such a gift, without any mixture of legerdemain.

And if they should drink any deadly thing, it shall in no wise hurt them (οὐ μὴ βλάψῃ, the right reading). *No, it shall not hurt them.* (See Clyde's *Syntax*, § 41 a.) The cup of poison was another ordeal, too often devised by persecutors. But, when drained by those who had received the particular gift referred to, it would be innocuous.

They shall lay hands on the sick, and they shall recover. The objectors to the authenticity of Mark xvi. 9–20 cannot take exception to the word rendered *sick* (ἀρρώστους, *infirm*). It occurs only five times throughout the New Testament; and in three out of the five instances it is found in Mark. See chap. vi. 5, 13. The last clause is rendered by Lange, *And they (themselves) shall find themselves well.* But such a result would be nothing wonderful at all, no 'gift,' no 'sign.' The reference evidently is to the sick, *they shall have (themselves) well.* Some, but not all, of the Saviour's disciples would possess this *gift of healing.* (1 Cor. xii. 9, 28, 30.)

The enumeration of signs might have gone on to a much greater length. But it was unnecessary. Striking specimens had been particularized, *as specimens*; and we must mentally supply *et cetera*. The sum total could not be easily ascertained or enumerated. All the true fruits of faith are its true signs or signals. They authenticate, by Divine signature, the divinely transforming energy, and hence the Divine reality and glory, of faith's great Object. They have been continuously reproduced from the times of the apostles down to the present day, but under phases that correspond to the progression of the ages, and the development of living Christianity in living humanity. The fact that this living Christianity is the most plastic moral power in the world is itself the sign of signs. Modern European civilization, in all its finer and more moral elements, is a sign. The elevation of woman is a sign. The abolition of slavery and serfdom is a sign. Hospitals, orphanages, convalescent homes, almshouses, infirmaries, are signs. Moral chastity in art is a sign. The spirit of fraternity, working its way, fitfully but diffusively, into all classes and castes of society, is a sign. The increase of the humanity of man is a sign. The effort to connect nation with nation by ties of reciprocal beneficence is a sign. The loving labours, among the lapsed and the betrayed, of a white-robed army of Christian ladies, is a sign. The persistent advances, in politics, of right against might is a sign. In a higher plane of life's experiences, accommodated to a higher stage of development, and to an

462   ST MARK XVI.   [19

19 So then after the Lord had spoken unto them, he was received up into heaven, and sat on the right hand of God.
20 And they went forth, and preached everywhere, the

immensely widened sphere of operations, the early signs repeat themselves. The most villanous demons of society are still cast out in Christ's name. Converts speak in new tongues, and more musically and expressively than if they were employing the most felicitous idioms of foreign languages. And yet, in the matter of foreign languages, nothing in the world is so polyglott as Christianity and the Bible. Medical missions replace the ancient gift of healing, and are more extensively effectual. By and by Christianity will dry up all the fountains of disease. And meanwhile, in place of immunity here or there from the fangs of literal serpents, and the deadliness of hellebore draughts, there are hundreds of thousands of the youthful and inexperienced, who, by the power of Christianity in their hearts, are kept in security amid customs into which the old serpent has breathed his spirit of decoy, and thereby taught his dupes to allure with the poisoned chalice of indulgence.

VER. 19. **So then after the Lord had spoken unto them, He was received up into heaven.** *The Lord therefore (on His part), after having spoken to them, was taken up into the heaven.* Lachmann and Tregelles read *the Lord 'Jesus.'* But the word *Jesus*, though occurring in important manuscripts and in a majority of the ancient versions, is not sufficiently supported, and was more likely to be added than to be subtracted. The force of the little particle $\mu\acute{\epsilon}\nu$ may, in some measure, be represented by the phrase *on His part*. It looks forward to the counterpart particle $\delta\acute{\epsilon}$ in the next verse, *and they (on their part)*. When it is said *after having spoken to them*, there is no minute chronometry intended. Least of all does the evangelist mean, as Strauss would insinuate (*Leben Jesu f. d. d. Volk*, p. 614), that there was an immediate and direct ascent from the supper room which is referred to in ver. 14. The evangelist has by this time left the supper room far in the background of his thoughts, and was, as in so many other instances, massing his representation, leaving the details of chronometry unparticularized. When it is said that *the Lord was taken up into the heaven*, we must not ask for a scientific conception of '*the heaven.*' 'Eye hath not seen'; neither hath it entered into the heart of man to conceive except in childlike symbol and hieroglyph.

And sat down at the right hand of God. It sounds like the language of spiritual insight and inspiration. Our Lord took His seat in the place of highest honour in the universe. The Father welcomed Him. 'The Lord said unto my Lord, Sit Thou at My right hand' (Ps. cx. 1). It is beautiful and sublime symbolism. The actual altitudes of the reality signified may be far beyond our present power of apprehension.

VER. 20. **And they** (on their part) **went forth.** Namely, from their centre of operations, Jerusalem.

And preached everywhere. According as doors were opened for their entrance. The evangelist, in this single expression, comprises and compresses the work and outgrowth of years.

Lord working with *them*, and confirming the word with signˊ following. Amen.

The Lord working with them. That is, *the Lord Jesus*, who had promised to be ' with ' His disciples to the end of the world (Matt. xxviii. 20). He *worked with them.* There was a harmonious 'synergism,' the Lord doing what man could not do, and leaving men to do what He had fitted and commissioned them to perform. In particular, the inspiration of the whole movement was from the Lord, and hence the outburst of signs that followed, and that are still evolved in ever fresh variety.

And confirming the word. *The word preached*, the gospel, which is, like its Lord, ' the same yesterday, to-day, and for ever,' and yet ever varying in application, and infinitely full of varying applicability.

With signs following. More literally, *through the accompanying signs*. But still more literally, *through the closely following signs* (ἐπακολουθούντων). The interval between faith and its wonderful Divine effects is inappreciable. They follow close upon its heels, and hold out signals as they pass, which show that faith has gone on before and is speeding away on its errand of mercy.

Amen. This colophon has no doubt been added by transcribers. Robert Stephens inserts it, and hence Mill. It is found in the manuscripts C E F K L, etc., and the supplemental D. But it is wanting in A, 1, 33, as also in the Clementine Vulgate, the Cureton Syriac, the Peshito Syriac, the Philoxenian Syriac, and the Armenian version. It is not in the Elzevir ; and it is omitted by Bengel, Wetstein, Griesbach, Lachmann, Scholz, Tischendorf, Tregelles.

To return to the subject of the authenticity of the whole section comprised in ver. 9-20. (See pp. 446-449.)

I. As to *internal evidence*, there is, it should be on all hands conceded, a marked peculiarity in the style. There is, more particularly, a peculiarity in the way in which the connection of the section with the preceding context is effected. It is exceedingly inartificial. In the presence of these peculiarities, it is not to be wondered at that queries should be started.

But, *in the first place*, the entire artlessness of Mark, in the matter of literary composition, diminishes the first feeling of wonderment which arises on the consideration of the peculiarities referred to.

Then, *in the second place*, it seems to be quite inconceivable that the evangelist should have concluded his Gospel with ver. 8. Such a conclusion, more especially when we bear in mind that the last word in the original is a mere conjunction, would make the narrative go off like a knotless thread.

In the third place, it is unlikely that Mark's own conclusion of his Gospel should have been either, on the one hand, hopelessly illegible (see p. 449), or, on the other, entirely lost (see pp. 447, 448). Either of these suppositions is an extreme of conjecture that should never be entertained, except as the very last resort into which one may flee, previous to utter despair.

All this being the case, it is probable, to say the least of it, that ver. 9-20 must have been Mark's own conclusion of his Gospel.

II. As regards *external evidence*, it is certainly remarkable that the two oldest manuscripts extant, the Sinaitic and the Vatican, should be without the paragraph. But then these are actually *the only Greek manuscripts* yet discovered in which the section is wanting. It is present in A C D E F G H K L M S U V X Γ Δ Π, 1, 33, 69, etc., etc. And the agreement of the Sinaitic and Vatican in the omission is not perhaps of such significance, if it be the case, as Tischendorf supposes (*Nov. Test. Vaticanum*, xxi.), that the principal writer of the Sinaitic (viz. D) was also the penman of the Vatican. He transcribed indeed from different copies, when writing the two manuscripts; that is proved by the decided diversities in the readings of the manuscripts. But if he wrote the Sinaitic first, from a copy which was without the concluding section of Mark, then we may suppose that, if he found the section in the copy that was before him when engaged in writing the Vatican, he might hesitate, in consequence of its absence from the other codex, whether or not he should engross it. But at length he decided, it would appear, on the strength of his own judgment or by the direction of some superior, under whom he was working, to omit the paragraph. This is not a mere conjecture *growing up out of nothing*, like Michelsen's notion regarding the illegibility of the section, or Griesbach's surmise of the accidental loss of the leaf containing it from the evangelist's autograph. There is a peculiar fact in reference to the Vatican manuscript, which affords a basis of probability for the supposition. After the colophon ' ACCORDING TO MARK,' at the close of ver. 8, " the remaining greater portion of the column," says Dean Alford, " and the whole of the next to the end of the page are left " vacant. There is no other instance of this in the whole New Testament por- " tion of the manuscript, the next book in every other instance beginning on " the next column." (*Greek Test.*, vol. i., p. 430.) Tregelles mentions the same fact, and we ourselves witnessed it, when we were permitted in 1855 to inspect the manuscript. We may hence legitimately infer that in the copy that was before the writer *the section was present*, although, for some subjective reason or other, he omitted it from his transcript. *We thus account for the vacant column.* And the concurrence therefore of the two manuscripts in the omission of the section is not of such significance as, at the first blush of the subject, it might appear to be.

There are however, it is right to admit, some little items of diplomatic evidence that may be put side by side with the omission of the paragraph in the Sinaitic and Vatican manuscripts. The Old Latin or Italic manuscript 'k,' called the 'codex Bobbiensis,' omits the paragraph. So do certain ancient manuscripts of the Armenian version, in the Venetian library. So do two manuscripts of the Æthiopic version; as also an Arabic manuscript version in the Vatican library, described by Scholz in his *Reise*. These are however mere diplomatic jots or tittles. They are evidence indeed that the section was sometimes omitted; but they weigh for little, when we come to strike a balance for the decisive critical result.

But is there no other adverse diplomatic evidence to be dealt with? Let us see.

Griesbach, Scholz, Tischendorf, Tregelles (*Pr. Text*, p. 254), unite in asserting that the paragraph is marked by an asterisk in the two manuscripts '137,' '138,' and it is inferred that the apposition of this asterisk was equivalent to some brand of suspicion.

But it turns out to be the case that in neither of the codices specified is there an asterisk. In the former (*fol.* 150 *b*) there is a cross, which was intended to refer to a note on the following leaf (*fol.* 151 *b*), to the effect *that Mark xvi. 9-20 is undoubtedly authentic.* In the latter there is neither asterisk nor cross, but there is *the same note attesting the genuineness of the paragraph!* These witnesses have therefore, says Burgon, who has the merit of the discovery, 'been by accident put into the wrong box.' (*Last Twelve Verses of Mark*, pp. 117, 118.)

There are about thirty other cursive manuscripts, twenty-five of which are specified by Griesbach, which have, as is alleged, some note or scholion attached to the paragraph. The note is sometimes, as Griesbach admits, to the effect that the paragraph *is found* 'in many copies,' 'in very many copies,' 'in the accurate copies,' and in particular 'in the Palestinian Gospel'; while in other cases he says, though inaccurately, it is to the effect that the paragraph *is absent* 'from some copies,' 'from very many,' 'from the more accurate,' 'from almost all of the Greek copies.' This statement of Griesbach is not only in some respects inaccurate; it does, even in the respect in which it is accurate, less than scanty justice to the scholia referred to, as it leaves the respective proportions of testimony for and against the paragraph in utter uncertainty. And hence the general effect of his remark, and of the accompanying array of manuscripts, has, as a matter of fact, been such that succeeding textual critics have been led to assume that the evidence of all his five-and-twenty witnesses is, more or less, *against the authenticity of the paragraph.* Thus Tregelles says: " A similar note, or a scholion stating the absence of the following verses from " *many,* from *most,* or from the *most correct* copies (often from Victor or Severus), " is found in twenty-five other cursive codices." (*Printed Text*, p. 254.) But this is a mistake. *It is not the case that there is such a note or scholion in the twenty-five codices referred to. And Griesbach does not say that there is.* (See his *Nov. Test.*, in loc.)

Tischendorf however has fallen into the same mistake with Tregelles. He says, even in his eighth edition (p. 404): " The scholia of very many codices " attest that the Gospel of Mark terminated with ver. 8, in the more ancient, " and, as many add, in the more accurate copies." There are, he adds, about thirty of these. And then he calls on us to take note of three specimens of their number (*tres videamus*). These three will therefore, we may presume, be picked witnesses, containing the most obvious confirmation of the accuracy of his allegation.

Let us look then at the scholia contained in them.

The first, '22,' runs thus: " In some of the copies the evangelist closes here; " but in many the text goes on as follows, *But when Jesus was risen early, etc.*" Note the word 'some' as opposed to 'many.' This is not an attestation to the effect that the paragraph is wanting *in the 'more ancient' and 'more accurate' copies!*

The next witness is '1,' in which the scholion runs as follows: " In some of " the copies the evangelist concludes here, and up to this point Eusebius " canonized; but in many the text proceeds as follows, *But when Jesus, etc.*" Note here too the word 'some' and 'many.' This likewise is no attestation to the effect that the paragraph is wanting in the 'more ancient' and the 'more accurate' copies.

Tischendorf's third witness is '20,' in which the scholion runs as follows: "From this to the end is not found in some of the copies; *but in the ancient "copies the whole is found uncurtailed"* (πάντα ἀπαράλειπτα κεῖται). And is this evidence that, according to the scholia of the codices referred to, 'the Gospel of Mark ends with the 8th verse *in the more ancient and the more accurate copies*"? The witness, in express terms, contradicts the allegation.

Not one of the three witnesses adduced by the illustrious critic confirms his assertion; the last of the three expressly contradicts it. To such an extent did the spell of Griesbach's array throw a 'glamour' over the eyes of one of the most perspicacious of his critical successors.

But not only is this the case. In not one of Griesbach's twenty-five codices, or any others that have since been added to them, is there any note or scholion to the effect that *in the more ancient or accurate copies is the Gospel of Mark terminated at the 8th verse*, or to the effect that *what follows the 8th verse is inauthentic*. Dr. Davidson, evidently relying on Tischendorf's authority (the seventh edition), says that "scholia belonging to the manuscripts 1, 15, 20, 22, "206, 209, 300, and others, say that the more ancient and accurate copies "terminated the Gospel with the 8th verse." (*Introduction*, vol. ii., p. 112, ed. 1868.) *But this is, most emphatically, not the case.* We have seen the testimony of '1,' '20,' and '22,' as adduced by Tischendorf in his eighth edition. As to '300,' its scholion is identical with that of '20,' and is the precise opposite of what is alleged. As to '206' and '209,' the scholion is simply the following: "In some of the copies the evangelist here concludes, and up to this "point Eusebius canonized; but in others the text continues as follows, *But "when Jesus, etc.*" Nothing here about 'the more ancient and accurate copies.' As to '15,' its scholion is identical with that of '22,' one of Tischendorf's three, on which we have already remarked. All the witnesses, one after another, break down.

Scholz puts great reliance on '23,' '34,' '39,' and '41,' as having a note from Severus of Antioch, to the following effect: "In the more accurate copies the "Gospel according to Mark terminates with the words, *for they were afraid*; "but in some copies it is added, '*but when Jesus was risen*,' *etc.*" But in '23,' '34,' and '39' there is no such scholion; and in '41' there is a scholion to the opposite effect, *that the accurate copies contain the contents of the last twelve verses*. In '34' and '29' there are large extracts, *at the conclusion of 'Matthew's Gospel*,' from the Homily on the Resurrection, which has gone a-begging for its author, and in which Eusebius's remarks are re-re-echoed. (See Burgon's masterly sifting of all this class of evidence, in the 8th chapter of his *Last Twelve Verses of Mark*.)

When Griesbach said that the scholia of the codices, to which he referred, testified that the paragraph was wanting '*in some*,' '*in most*,' *in* '*almost all the Greek copies*,' *and in* '*the more accurate copies*,' he spoke under mental confusion, and had, as we presume, unconsciously mingled in his mind the strong, strange assertions of Eusebius, Jerome, and the author of the begging Homily, with the more sober statements of the codices.

The whole diplomatic evidence, with the exception of that of the Sinaitic and Vatican manuscripts, is breaking down. Only one other manuscript remains to be noticed, the uncial L, a codex in Paris of the eighth or ninth century:

Tischendorf ascribes it to the eighth. At the close of ver. 8 there occurs, in a sort of framework of dashes, the following notice: " In some instances there is added as follows." Then we read: "*But all the things enjoined they announced 'without delay to those who were around Peter. And afterward Jesus Himself, "from the east unto the west, sent forth through them the holy and incorruptible "message of eternal salvation.*" Then there is another framed remark: " But " there is also the following continuation after the words *for they were afraid.*" Then follows the text as we have it The manuscript is evidence that in some cases the concluding paragraph was not recognised as authentic. That is all.

To turn now to *the patristic evidence*. It runs up to Eusebius, as we have seen (p. 446), and resolves itself, to a large extent, into his admission " *that one*, "*puzzled to reconcile the representations of Matthew and Mark regarding the* " *time of our Lord's resurrection, might say* (εἴποι ἄν) *that the paragraph in Mark* " *is not in all the copies ; and that the accurate copies finish with the words, 'for* "' *they were afraid* ' : *there the end is put in almost all the copies of Mark's* " *Gospel.*" (*Opera*, vol. iv., p. 937.)

Jerome in his Letter to Hedibia simply gives a free translation of Eusebius s admission ; and indeed the query of Hedibia addressed to Jerome is simply a translation of the query of Marinus addressed to Eusebius.

The begging Homily, sometimes ascribed to Gregory of Nyssa, sometimes to Severus of Antioch, and sometimes to Hesychius of Jerusalem, just re-echoes the salient admission, and implicated assertions, of Eusebius.

Victor of Antioch goes no farther, so far as *that passage* is concerned in which he says that " *in most copies the paragraph,* ' *Now when Jesus was risen early,*' " *etc., is not found in the present Gospel.*" (Cramer, *Cat.*, i., p. 447.)

As to Euthymius, he merely says that *some expositors affirm that the Gospel terminates with the words 'for they were afraid.*'

Such is the substance of the adverse patristic testimony. *Omnia ex uno fonte promanarunt :* Matthæi, vol. ii., p. 270. But there has been, in many cases, a strange tendency to exaggerate its amount and strength.

To begin with Euthymius, the last name in our list, Dean Alford represents him as, along with Severus, Victor, Gregory of Nyssa (or Hesychius of Jerusalem), and Jerome, ' saying that the paragraph is wanting in the *greater number*, or in the *more accurate* ' copies. But this is altogether contrary to fact. Euthymius says nothing of the kind. Neither does he, as Volkmar alleges, ' condemn ' the paragraph ' as spurious.' (*Marcusevangelium*, p. 607.) He only says that ' *some* expositors ' affirm that the Gospel terminates with the words ' for they were afraid.'

Dean Alford, it will have been still further noticed, represents Severus *and* Gregory of Nyssa (or Hesychius of Jerusalem) as uniting with Euthymius, etc., in testifying that the paragraph is ' wanting in the greater number or in the more accurate copies.' A corresponding representation is made by Volkmar, Davidson, and Tregelles too. Tregelles says : " This testimony (of Severus) " *may* be but a repetition of that already cited from Gregory of Nyssa ; but if " so, it is, at least, an *approving* quotation." (*Printed Text*, p. 249.) But it is nothing of the kind. Severus is not quoting, approvingly, from Gregory of

Nyssa. The Homily in which the passage occurs is by some authorities ascribed to Gregory, by others to Severus, by others still to Hesychius. And its testimony therefore, such as it is, is the testimony of but one father, not of two, or three. Of late the Homily has been generally ascribed to Hesychius. (See Tischendorf, p. 405.)

Again, the testimony, such as it is, of both Hesychius and Victor of Antioch (in the passage referred to), *is not an independent judgment*. Neither is it *an independent statement of facts regarding the codices of Mark's Gospel*. It is *the mere echo of a hearsay*, or the confiding and unreflective repetition of the admission and implications of Eusebius. It is a mere uncritical *take-on-trust*. It counts therefore for absolutely nothing as evidence.

Precisely of the same value is the testimony of Jerome, in his letter to Hedibia. It is mere unreflective repetition in Latin of the Greek of Eusebius ; and there is real evidence to show that it must have been dashed off inconsiderately, when 'good Homer was nodding.' It certainly does not soberly represent the result of Jerome's own investigation or observation ; for he expressly contradicts, in a subsequent writing, his own sweeping asseveration. In the letter to Hedibia, which was written about the year A.D. 406, he says that her difficulty about the conciliation of Matthew and Mark, in their respective accounts of our Lord's resurrection, might be met thus : *We may reject the testimony of Mark, which is contained in few Gospels, almost all the Greek copies being deficient in the last paragraph*. (Epist. cxx., c. 3.) But in his *Dialogue against the Pelagians*, which was written about the year A.D. 415, he says expressly : "In some copies, and *especially in the Greek codices* (et maxime in Græcis "codicibus), it is written at the end of the Gospel according to Mark, *when* "*afterward the eleven were reclining at table, Jesus appeared to them, and re-* "*proved their unbelief and hardness of heart, because they listened not to those* "*who had seen Him rising (resurgentem).*" See lib. ii., § 15. The two representations are not in harmony. (*Unde hæc tanta inconstantia et levitas, sancte Hieronyme?* Matthæi, *Animadversio in Marc. xvi.* 9-20.) And, as in the former he is actually only echoing Eusebius, we may look upon the latter as representing his own observation, so far as he applied his mind independently to the subject. Jerome's testimony against the paragraph is thus doubly nullified, so far as real independent evidence is concerned.

The testimony too of Eusebius is of avail merely to the extent of affording evidence *that in some copies of the Gospel the concluding section was wanting*. What he says about 'the accurate copies' must be set down to his rhetoric, shaping itself capriciously on the spur of the moment, and putting into the mouth of a puzzled person *what, in the way of a special plea, might be said.* So must his remark about 'almost all the copies.' For not only is there evidence, as we shall soon see, outside the testimony of Eusebius, to invalidate his representation ; there is evidence, *inside his own remarks*, that he was speaking rashly and rhetorically, and neither as a critic nor as a judge. For after saying that it might be alleged that 'in *almost all the copies* of Mark's Gospel the end is put at the words *for they were afraid*,' he adds that it might be said that 'what follows is superfluous, and is *rarely* met with in the codices, *in some, but not in all*.' Why this last modification of the case ? Why, after saying that the paragraph is *rarely* (σπανίως) met with, does he add 'in *some* copies, *but not in all*'? It is evident that he felt that he had in his first expressions overstated the case. But instead of going back, and obliterating what he had written, as he would have done had he been acting judicially, he contents himself with appending a modifying remark. And yet, be it noted, *this is his ultimate representation of the case*, so that we may take it as his real evidence, so far as he felt bound, in consistency with his special plea, to give it. *The paragraph was not found in ' all copies.'* That is all.

That we are doing no injustice to Eusebius in this matter is evinced by the following facts in counter-evidence.

(1) The paragraph *is* found in all the existing manuscripts of the Old Latin version, *or the Itala*, with the exception of 'k,' a late copy. It is also found in all the codices of the Vulgate, Jerome's revision of the Old Latin. It is found likewise in all the Syriac versions, the Cureton (fragmentarily), the Peshito, the Philoxenian, and, as Adler expressly notes, in the Jerusalem Lectionary (*Versiones Syr.*, p. 177). It is found also in the Coptic version, and the Gothic (fragmentarily), and in the printed Armenian and Æthiopic versions. *In short, it is found in all the ancient versions.* And as these, in their sum total at least, represent manuscripts widely dispersed over the world, and *very much older than any now existing, much older too than the times of Eusebius*, we must come to the conclusion that he spoke rashly, and from only a limited range of observation and collation.

(2) Again, in all the existing Greek and Syriac lectionaries, or evangeliaries and synaxaries, so far as yet examined, the paragraph is found, forming part of the public lections, lessons, or readings of Scripture, that have been in use, throughout the churches of Christendom, from time immemorial, and certainly from a time anterior to Eusebius. (See Matthæi's *Animadversio ad Marcum xvi.* 9-20, in vol. ii. of his New Testament, first edition, and his note in his second edition, vol. i., p. 748; and thence Griesbach's admission, *Nov. Test.*, vol. i., p. 291. See also Burgon's *Last Twelve Verses of Mark*, chap. x.)

(3) Victor of Antioch, while in the body of his collections echoing emphatically the admission of Eusebius in reference to the paragraph, yet in the last words of his Commentary, (as has been noted by Matthæi, Tischendorf, Tregelles, Bishop Wordsworth, etc.,) leaves on record the result of his deliberate investigation. He says: " But although the words, *But when He was risen early*, with " what follows, are not found in very many copies of the present Gospel, seeing " some have deemed them inauthentic, yet we, *having found them in very many " copies, have added, out of accurate transcripts, and according to the verity of " the Palestinian Gospel* (καὶ κατὰ τὸ Παλαιστιναῖον Εὐαγγέλιον, ὡς ἔχει ἡ ἀλήθεια " Μάρκου), *the appended account of the resurrection of our Lord, following upon " the words 'for they were afraid'* : that is, we have added from the words, *But " when He was risen early*, to the words *through the accompanying signs.*" (Cramer's *Catena*, vol. i., p. 447.) Thus Victor's name, by his own express desire, falls to be struck from the list of the supposed oppugners of the section. And the evidence on which his name is struck off is evidence that directly invalidates the rash assertions of Eusebius. There was some important copy of the Gospel of Mark, that either had its resting place in Palestine, or was in some other way intimately associated with the Holy Land; and in this important codex, as well as in ' many other accurate copies,' examined either at first or at second hand, Victor found the disputed section.

(4) Then Irenæus, Bishop of Lyons, in the latter half of the second century, and thus long anterior to Eusebius, quotes the 19th verse of the chapter, and quotes it expressly as Mark's. (*Hæres.*, iii. 10 : 6.) It will be admitted that the manuscript from which he transcribed must have been *a very ancient copy.* Hippolytus too, Bishop of Portus near Rome, at the end of the second and the beginning of the third century, quotes the 17th and 18th verses in his fragment *Concerning the Gifts of Grace.* The copy or copies from which he quoted must have been *exceedingly old.* Moreover, James of Nisibis, or Aphraates the Persian sage, in the early part of the fourth century, and Ambrose later on in the same century, and then Augustine in the fifth, and Chrysostom between, all these quote explicitly from the passage, and of course quote from texts that were at least as old as themselves. A quotation from the paragraph moreover seems to be made in the *Acts of Pilate*, which Tischendorf ascribes to the third century. (See pp. 243, 356.) And it is not unlikely that Justin Martyr in his *First Apology* (c. 45) quotes from the last verse, when he says of the apostles that when '*they went forth from Jerusalem, and preached everywhere,*' their mission was the fulfilment of the ancient prediction, ' He shall send forth the rod of thy strength out of Jerusalem.'

How many very ancient manuscripts must be represented in all these quotations ! It is impossible that Eusebius's statements can be correct, though he himself seems to have had, for some reason or other, a prejudice against the section.

Possibly the accidental omission of the paragraph from some valuable copy, in consequence perhaps of being at the end of the codex, or in consequence of some other casualty now unknown, may be the only and extremely narrow foundation on which the whole fabric of doubt and opposition has been reared. It is a fabric that must, as biblical criticism advances, crumble into dust. It was not very far that John Adam Osiander saw into the subject, when in 1753 he penned his *Vindication of the Genuineness of the Last Twelve Verses of Mark xvi.* (Tübingen); but he divined correctly when he concluded that ' the paragraph must necessarily be retained in the evangelical text.' The wave of doubt, that swelled and boldly advanced for a season, must, like many similar waves, collapse and recede.

INDEX

TO THE

EXPOSITION OF ST. MARK'S GOSPEL

'A' or 'an,' *i.e.*, anc, one, 408.
'Abba, Father,' 400.
Abiathar, 60.
Ability, man's, 342.
'Abomination of desolation,' 360.
Abundance or surplusage, 350.
Acts of Pilate, 430, 470.
Adulterous generation, 231.
Affinity of spirits, 90.
'Αγανακτοῦντες, 382.
'Age (this),' 99 ; to the age, *i.e.*, to eternity, 88.
Agrippina, 156.
Alabaster, 379.
'Αλαλή, 134.
A-Lapide, 376, etc.
Alberti, 311.
Alexander, Dr. Joseph Addison, 233, 252, 285, 457, etc.
'Αληθής, 330.
Alford, Dean, 195, 464, 467, etc.
'All,' used in a free and easy sense, 7, 28 ; 'all things,' 37.
'All-to,' that is, *altogether*, 325.
Almeh, or dancing girl, 154.
Alphæus, 77.
Alternatives, moral, 67.
Altmann, 315.
Amazement, 244, 390, 448.
Ambrose, 374.
Amen or verily, 87.
Andrew, meaning of the word, 18, 77.
Andrew's (St.) cross, 77.
Anger in Christ, what? 67.
An-hungred, 60.
'Ανώγαιον, 388.
Anointing, official, 2 ; medicinal, 148.
'Anon,' 156.
'Αντί, 298.
Antonia, castle of, 422.
Aorist and imperfect, 207, 350, etc. ;
aorist and perfect, 245, etc. ;
aorist participle, 215, 241, etc.
'Απέχει, 403.
'Αφίημι, 305.
Aphraates, 470.
Apostles, twelve, 74 ; sent out in pairs, 144, 386 ; got authority over unclean spirits, 145 ; the word only once used in Mark, 159 ; their reverence for Christ, 386.
Apparition, 169.
Aretas, 115.
Arias Montanus, 179.
Arimathea, 439.
Aristotle, 236, etc.
Arnot, 109.
Aromas, 442.
Artemidorus, 380.
Article (the), its use in Greek and in English, 10, 66, 72, 73, 101, 120, 167, 189, 207, 248, 253, 256, etc.
Aryans, 303.
'As it stands written,' 184, etc.
Ass, used for riding on, 303, 306.
Atonement, 225, 228.
'Aught,' 187.
Augustine, 88, 208, 309, 380, 392, 430, 457, etc.
Authorized version, editions of, 326; primary edition of, 206 ; errata in, 152, 183, 338, etc.
Automatousness of nature, 106 ; of the mind, 106.

Banias, 221.
Baptism, meaning and mode of, 5, 6, 7, 9, 12. 180, 182, 459; of John, 320 ; of purifying fire, 294 ; spittle used by Roman Catholics in connection with it, 202.
Barabbas, 421.

Barclay, Dr., 265, 302.
Bartholomew, 77.
Bartimæus, 299.
Bartolinus, 428.
Βασανίζομαι, 167.
Baskets, 165, 208.
Bastow, 357, 427.
Battle with a Wasp's Nest, 381.
Bauer, Bruno, 119, 121, etc.
Baumgarten-Crusius, 449.
Baur, F. C., 69, 135, 141, 160, 209, etc.
Baxter, Richard, 46, 122, 185, etc.
Bazaars, 179.
Beard, Dr., 391.
Beasts (wild) in Palestine, 14.
Beclyppan. 258.
Beds in Palestine, 41, 183.
Beelzebub, Beelzebul, 83.
'Believing' and 'believing in,' 17.
Belly (the), 190.
Bengel, 80, 159, etc., etc. ; his great critical canon, 132.
Bethany, 301.
Bethphage, 301.
Bethsaida or Bethsaidan, 160, 166, 216.
Beza, 218, etc., etc.
Bible (English), editions of, 326, etc.
Bigotry, 68.
Bisping, 408, etc.
Bland, Dr., 417, etc.
Blasphemy, what ? 42, 87, 88, 193.
Blayney's Bible, 326.
Blazoning, 181.
Bleek, 247, etc.
'Bless,' 164, 208 ; 'the blessed,' 412.
Blindness cured, 217.
Bloomfield, 406 ; mistake of, 338.
— overleaping difficulties, 57.
Boanerges, 75.
Boat or ship, 92, 111, 166, 170.
Boccore, 311.
Bolten, 168, etc.
Bornemann, 311.
Bos, Lambert, 311.
'Bottles,' what ? 55.
Bourignon, Madame, 366.
Bragge, Francis, 119, 124.
Brameld, 347, etc.
Bramhall, Archbishop, 355.
Brass or copper, 145.
Braunius, 413.
Brethren of our Lord, 78, 141.
Bretschneider, 252, etc.
Bridechamber, sons of the, 52.
Bruinier, 323.
Bucer, Martin, 251.
Buchanan, George, 152.
'Buffet,' 414.
Burgon, 465, 466, 469.
'Burial' (a), 158.
Burton, 249, 262, etc.

'Bush (the),' in the Bible, 338.
Buttig, 161.
'By and by,' 156.

Cactus hedges. 323.
Cæsarea Philippi, 127, etc.
Cajetan, Cardinal, 143, 153, etc.
Calling, what ? 50, 51.
Calvary, 248.
Calvin, 143, 184, 185, etc., etc.
Cambyses, 379.
Campbell, Principal, 65, 204, etc., etc.
Camp-meetings, 206.
'Can,' used of moral ability, 53, 84, 143.
Canaanites, 197.
Candles, 101.
'Cannot,' *i.e*, cannot be compelled, 254.
Capernaum, its site, 20, etc.
Caravanserai, 387.
Care, anxious, 358 ; cares of this world, 99.
'Carpenter,' what ? 140.
Carson, Dr., 183.
Cartwright, 202.
Carus, 172.
Casaubon, 179, 418, etc.
Catalepsy, 245.
Causes, 198, 431.
Celsus, 148, 246.
Cene, le, 246, 254, 311, etc.
Censoriousness, 59.
Ceremonial and moral, 343.
Chains, 117.
Χαλκός, 349.
'Charged' or *rated*, 72.
'Charger' and 'cargo,' 156.
Chaucer, 155.
Chersa or Kersa, 116.
Chifflet, 409.
Children, natural and figurative, 258, 263 ; children and Christ, 280 ; children and the kingdom of God, 281 ; Christ's disciples so called by Christ, 287.
Chiliarchs, 154.
Chorazin, 166.
Christs, false, 365.
Christians, 'crucians,' 229.
Chronology in the Gospels, 314.
Ciacconius, 155.
Cicero, 155.
Clairvoyance, 367.
Clarke, Dr. Adam, 157, 164, 201, 349, 374, 443, etc.
Clarke, Dr. E. D., 134, 155, 336.
Clarke, Dr. Samuel, 198, etc.
'Cleave,' or *be glued*, 277.
Cleophas, 78.
Clerc, le, 311, 404, etc., etc.

'Clerk,' 'clergy,' 428.
· Clip,' what? 258.
Cloak, 54, 128.
Clyde, Dr., 352, 373, etc., etc.
Coat-of-arms, 181.
Coats or tunics, 146.
Cochran (John) of Glasgow, 366.
Cock crowing, 167, 375, 397 ; cock crowing and Peter, 415, 417.
Coffins and coffers, 165.
Comings of Christ, 233.
'Common,' i.e. *defiled*, 175, etc.
Concupiscences, 100.
Confession, what? 7.
Conversion, 96.
Convulsions, 248.
Copper, 145, 349 ; 'a copper,' 182.
Corban, 186.
Cornfields in the East, 57.
Couches, 183.
Court of a house, 415.
Covenant or testament, 393 ; covenant, old and new, 393.
Coverdale, 388, etc.
Covetousness, 192.
Cowles, 396.
Cowper, 214.
'Crave' and 'craven,' 439.
Croll, Dr., 373.
Cromwell's (Lord) Bible, 256.
Cross (the), 425 ; a cross for each of Christ's disciples, 229 ; the St. Andrew's cross, 77.
'Crucians,' 229.
Crumbs, 198.
Cups, 182 ; cups containing a bitter death potion, 294, 295 ; Christ's cup, 401.
Curiosity signs, 210, 211.
Curse, 316 ; curse of Corban, 187.
Curtius, Georg, 358, 399.
Cyrene, 427.

Dalmanutha, 208.
'Damnation,' what? 88, 348, 461.
Damosel and damsel, 136.
Dancing, 154.
Danz, 280.
'Daughter,' as used by Christ, 131.
Davidson, Dr., 466.
'Day,' among the Jews, 397.
Deaconship of Christ and Christians, 297.
Deaf and dumb, 200.
Death, tasting of, 233 ; a lofty view of, 135.
Decapolis, 115, 125, etc.
Deceit or deceipt, 192.
Deceitfulness of riches, 99.
Decorum, deficiency in, 139.

Defilement, 190 ; defiled hands, ceremonially, 175.
'Defoulen,' 194.
Defraud, 284.
Degrees of ultimate exaltation, 294.
D'Eichthal, 169.
De Lira, see *Lira*.
Delitzsch, 245, 252.
'Deliver,' meaning of the word. 255, 423.
'Demon,' meaning of the word in classical Greek, 28 ; demons, demonism, and demoniacs, 22, 23, 74, etc. ; prince of the demons, 83.
Denarius, 350, 382.
'Denkspruch,' 189.
Denzinger, 279.
Dervishes, 8.
'Destroy,' meaning of the word, 24.
De Veil, see *Veil*.
Devil, 13, 28 ; see *Satan*.
De Wette, see *Wette*.
Deyling, 311.
Διά, meanings and meaning, 64.
Διαλογίζομαι, 43, 191.
Dickinson, Rodolphus, 143, 202, etc.
Didymus, 77.
Digamma, 430.
Dionysius-à-Ryckel, 232, etc.
Dipping in a dish, 390.
Disease, *i.e.* dis-ease, 28, 132 ; habitats of diseases, 31.
'Dispute,' 209, etc.
Dixon, Hepworth, 158.
'Doctrine,' meaning of the word, 21, etc.
Doddridge, Dr., 441, etc.
Dogs in Palestine, 197, 198.
'Doors,' 371, 440.
Drawbacks to every good cause, 385.
Dresigius, 57.
Drusius, 300.
Δύναμις, 261.
Dutch translators, the recent, 250, 343.

Ἔα, 23.
'Ear,' 'hear,' 202 ; ears to hear, 94, 189, etc.
Earthquakes, 355.
Easter, 377.
Eckard, 381.
Ecstasy, 171.
Edwards, Jonathan, 263.
'Eftsoon,' 416.
'Eight days' and six days, 234.
Elephantiasis, 31.
Elsner, 269, etc.
Elzevirs, the, 80, 218, etc.
Embalming, 383, 442.
'Embrace,' what? 258.
Ἐμβριμάομαι, 33, etc.

Emser, 377.
'End (the),' 355 ; ends, a hierarchy of them, 297.
English Bible, editions of, 326 ; English versions of the New Testament, 332.
"Εννυχα, 29.
'Εντρέπομαι, 326.
Ephphatha, 203.
Epilepsy, 25.
Epiphanius, 3, etc.
Episcopius, 309.
'Επισυντρέχει, 252.
'Επιτιμαω, 25, etc.
Erasmus, 115, etc., etc.
Eschatology, 351.
Eucharist, what? 391.
Eusebius, 3, 77, 127, 380, 446, 467, 468, etc.
Euthymius Zigabenus, 226, 309, etc.
Evanson, 397.
'Everlasting sin,' 89.
Evil, moral and penal, 194.
Ewald, 80, 104, etc.
Exorcism, see *Demons*.
'Εξουσία, 44.
Explicit and implicit in faith, 384.
Eye, good or evil, 193.

Faber Stapulensis, 187, etc.
Faith saves, how? 300; faith has always two objects, 17 ; why it is a pre-requisite, 250 ; faith of miracles, 318 ; faith and prayer, 318 ; faith in relation to prayer and fasting, 254 ; the desires that spring from faith always fulfilled, 250.
Faithless, *i.e.* unbelieving, 247.
Fakeers, 330.
'Fall up,' 207.
*Familia*rising, 166.
'Far' and 'forth,' 324.
Farmer, Hugh, 119.
Farthing, 350.
'Feared a great fear,' 114.
Fenians, the Jewish. 79.
Festivities on birthdays, 154.
'Fetters,' 117.
Feuchtersleben, 117.
Fever in Palestine, 27.
Fig tree, 370.
Figure of fact, 436.
Fire, penal and purificatory, 269, 270.
Fishers of men, 19.
Fishing nets in the East, 18.
Flatten and fla'ter, 332.
Fly-lord, Filth-lord, 83.
'Foolishness,' 193.
Footstool (a living), 345.
Formalism, 68.

Fossils in words, 331.
Franks, 196.
Free-will, 188, 194, 401.
Fritzsche, 147, 163, etc., etc.
Φρονέω, 227.
Fulfilled, or filled-full, 16, 165, 197, 208, 388.
'Fuller,' meaning of the word, 54.

Gadarenes, 115.
Galilee proper, 160 ; its populousness, 30, 31 ; sea of, 17.
Gallonius, 429.
Gassner, 367.
Gataker, 268, 311.
Gaulonitis, 160.
Gehenna, 264, 265.
Geiger, 55, 56.
Gelbricht, 14.
Genethlia, 154.
Geneva version, 71, etc., etc.
Genitive of the author, 16 ; of the material, 54 ; of the object and of the subject, 2.
Gennesaret, or Gennesar, plain of, 94 ; lake of, 17, etc., etc.
George, David, 365
Ghost, 436.
Gi'pin, W., 202.
Girdles, 8 ; and purses, 145.
'Gnash,' 246.
Gobetis, 117.
God, absolute and relative, 319, 341 ; His infinity the sum of all infinities, 340 ; His omnipotence, 289 ; should get as well as give, 334 ; God and matter, 170 ; God and sin, 355 ; God and oaths, 45 ; the perfect Otherhood of the soul, 341 ; God and goodness, 283.
Goesgen, 311.
Goethe, 349.
Golgotha, 428.
Good, Dr. Mason, 113.
Good for an end, 263, 271.
'Good Friday,' 376, 418.
Goodman and goodwife, 387.
Gospel of the Infancy, 141.
Greatrakes, Valentine, 367.
Greek = Gentile, 196; Greek spoken by Christ, 54, 77.
Gregory, meaning of the name, 375 ; Gregory of Nyssa, 446.
Greswell, 441, 443, 452.
Griesbach, 3, 88, 147, etc., etc.
'Grossi,' 313.
Grote, 28.
Grotius, 220, 232, etc., etc.
Gruner, 427.
Guilt, what? 414 ; guilty, what? 89 ; guilty of death, 414.

INDEX. 475

Ha! 433.
Hackett, Horatio, 302, 323, etc.
Hail! 426.
Hallel, 395.
Hammond, Bishop, 273, 284, etc.
Hanna, Dr., 302.
'Haply,' 309.
Hardheartedness or hearthardenedness, 68, 172, 215.
Harmer, 442.
Harrison, 377.
Hartung of Friburg, 380.
Hearing and understanding, 96.
Heart, its biblical meaning, 41, 172, etc.
Hedges in Palestine, 323.
Hedibia, 447, 448.
Heel, heal, *to cover*, 39, 444.
Hegendorphinus, 31, 33.
Heinsius, Daniel, 249, 310, etc.
Henneberg, 448.
Henniker, 155.
Henry, Matthew, 22, 29, etc.
Herods (the), 115, 149, 213; Herod the Great, 149; Herod Antipas, 148, 158.
Herodians, 69. 213, 330.
Herodotus, 121.
Hesychius, 446, 467.
Heumann, 194, 220, etc.
Hexapla, Bagster's, 206.
Hibernacles, 371.
Hilgenfeld, 121, 125, etc.
Hillel, 395; Hillelites, 275, 395.
Hiller, 426.
Hinnom, valley of, 264, 265.
Hippolytus, 470.
Hitzig, 448.
Hofmann, 284.
Hofmeister, 142, 227, etc.
Holtzmann, 123, 141, 199, 205, etc.
Hombergk, 311.
Homoioteleuton, 382.
Hoogeveen, 312.
Horace, 425.
Hosanna, 306; in the heavens, 307.
House = household, 85; the word used without the article, 37; houses in Palestine, 39; housetops, 362.
Howitt, William, 367.
Hugo de Sancto Caro, 66, etc.
Hundredfold, 291.
Hurrah, the Hebrew, 306.
Hurricane on the lake of Gennesaret, 112.
Husbandman, what? 324.
Hyperbole, 288, 352, 360, 364.
Hypocrites, 181.

Idumea, 70.

Iken. 311.
'Immediately' in Mark, 20, etc., etc.
Immortality involved in morality. 87; immortality and resurrection, 335, 338.
Imperfect tense, 207, 315, 377, 421, etc.
Implicit and explicit in faith, 384.
Impressment, 427.
'In,' 116, 320, etc.
Infinities (the), 340.
Ingraham, 408.
Inspiration, 345.
Interrogation, partial, 351.
'Into' for 'in,' 363.
Ira per zelum, 67.
Irenæus, 470.
Irony, 185.
Is-cariot, 79.
'Its,' 370.

Jacob's *Precious Metals*, 162.
Jairus, 127.
'James and John.' 19, 75.
James, son of Alphæus, 77.
James 'the little,' 437.
Jericho, 398.
Jerome, 77, 446, etc.; the Pseudo-Jerome, 430.
Jerusalem, its elevation, 82.
Jones, Sir William, 381.
Joseph, the husband of Mary, 141.
Josephus, 30, 31, 148, 154, 160, 172, etc., etc.
Joses or Joseph, 141, 438.
Julian, 291.
Julias, 160.
Judas or Jude, 78, 141.
Judas Iscariot, 79; why chosen to be an apostle? 79, 385.
Justin Martyr, 140, etc., etc.
Juvenal, 165.

Καί, 242.
Kaiser, 333.
Καλός and καλῶς, 184, 197, 263.
Κατάλυμα, 387.
Kelly, 396.
Κεφαλαιόω, 325.
Kerioth, 79.
Kersa, 115, 116.
Khan, 387.
K'hāwah in Arabian houses, 49, 50.
King or tetrarch, 149.
'Kitchen,' 163.
Kitto, Dr., 39.
Klostermann, 133, 166, etc.
Knatchbull, Sir Norton, 248.
'Knavery,' 192.
'Knewing,' 215.
Knirschet, 246.

Κοπάζω, 170.
Koppe, 168.
Köstlin, 141, 224, 358, etc.
Κωφός, 200.
Κράβαττος, 41.
Κράσπεδον, 174.
Krebs, 81, etc.
Kriustith, 246.
Krüger, Sprachlehre, 199, 203, etc.
Kuinöl, 143, 148, etc., etc.
Kypke, 404.

Lachmann, 249, 434, etc., etc., etc.
Lactantius, 193.
Lamps, 101; lamp-stands, 102.
Lange, 133, 168, etc., etc.
Lardner, 154, 157.
Latchet, 9.
Lavater, 168, 349.
Leaven, 377; of Herod, 213; of the Pharisees, 213.
Lebbæus, 78.
Le Cene, see *Cene*.
Le Clerc, see *Clerc*.
Lectionaries, 469.
Leek-beds, 163.
Legion, 119, 120.
Leibnitz, 261.
Lenormant, 303.
'Leorning-man,' 21.
Leprosy, 31.
Λησταί, *robbers*, 315, 407.
Levi and Matthew, 46, 47.
Lexicographers, Greek, 380, 381.
Life or soul, 231; life lost and saved, 230.
Lightfoot, Bishop, 448.
Lightfoot, Dr., 48, 128, 148, 167, etc., etc.
Linen, 409, 440.
Lipsius, 425, 428.
Lira, De, 153.
'List' and 'lust.' 242.
Lobeck, 127, 325.
Locusts, used as food, 8.
Λόγος, what? 38.
'Look-from,' 213.
Looking and seeing, 95.
Lots, 429.
Love, what? 340, 341; the final act of being, 340; unselfish, 341, 342; in heaven, 337; Christ's to the rich young man, what? 285.
Lowliest (the), the loftiest, 296, 297.
Lubbock, Sir John, 335.
Lusts, what? 99, 242.
Luther, 76, 78, 81, 129, etc., etc.
'Lytelons,' 263.

Mace, W., 256, 327, etc., etc.
Macedonian era, 154.

Macgregor of the *Rob Roy* boat, 92, 112, 122, 166, etc.
Mackenzie, Sir George, 42.
Malan, Cæsar, 102.
Malan, S. C., 426.
Maldonato, 202, etc.
Male and female, 276.
Malevolence and benevolence, 68.
Man, what kind of being? 341; not his own End, 297; the copestone of terrestrial creation, 459; 'man,' *i.e. husband*, 279.
'Manufacture,' 181.
Many = all, 298, 394.
Market-places, 173, 181.
'*Markism*, a,' 389.
Mary of Magdala, 437, 451, 452.
Mary, mother of James and Joses, 78.
Masius, 457.
'Master' = Teacher, 113, 237, etc. = Rabbi, 237, etc.
Matibalg, 145.
Matthæi, 147, 205, 467, etc..
Maundrell, 8, 271.
Maunds, 208.
Mead, Dr., 31.
Measure for measure, 103, 104.
Megaliths, 351.
Megistanes, 154.
Mehring, 192.
Μέν, 241.
Mercurialis, 379.
Μετανοεῖτε, 6, 16, 17, 454.
Metaphors in acts, 202.
Metonymy, 7.
Meuschen's *Nov. Testament. Illust.*, 280.
Meyer, 59, 130, 194, etc., etc.
Michaelis, 61, 122, etc.
Michelsen, 45, 51, etc.
Mill, Dr. John, 195, etc.
Mill, W. H., 78.
Mills' *British Jews*, 388.
Milton, 265.
Mind, what? 341; mind and matter, 170.
Miracle, what? 261; Christ's miracles, 211.
Mishna, 186.
'Mite,' what? 349.
Mœris, 266.
Μογιλάλος, 200.
Molech, 264.
Money, 145, 162.
Money-changers, 314.
Monogamy, 335.
Monseigneur and Monsieur, 300.
More, Dr. Henry, 365.
Morning, 29.
Morus, Alexander, 269.
Mountain (the), 73.

Muchness, 99.
Muggleton, Lodowick, 366.
Müller, Max, 442.
Mustard seed, 110.
Myrrh, 428.

Names and thought, 258.
Nansius, 380.
Napoleon III., 306.
Nard, 381.
Nazareth, 11, 138.
Necessity, antecedent, 355; relative, 225.
Needle's eye, 288.
'Needs,' the adverb, 358.
Negative, a triple, 394.
Nets for fishing in the East, 18.
Neutrality (no), in relation to Christ, 261.
New wine, 55, 395.
Newcome, Archbishop, 311, etc.
'Nill,' 237.
'Niss,' 237.
'No flesh' = *nobody*, 365.
Norton, 168, etc.

'O Mirificam' editions of the New Testament, 140, 321.
Oath, the obligation of, 157; profane oaths and God, 45; truncated forms of oaths, 212; oath of Corban, 186, 187.
Oehler, 341.
'Of God,' i.e. *in God*, 317.
'Offend,' old use of the word, 98, 141.
Old-Latin version, 143.
Olives, Mount of, 302, 335
Omnipotence, what? 289.
'Openly,' i.e. *unambiguously*, 226.
Ophthalmic diseases in the East, 299.
Opis, 380.
Opistic, 380.
'Ordained,' 323.
Oriental prostration, 127.
Origen, 195, etc.
Osiander, 470.
'Other,' i.e. *or*, 290.
Otherhood, the soul's, 341.
Ὅτι, recitative, 36, etc.; interrogative 240.
Otto, 381.
Οὐά, 433.
Οὐδέ, 328, 373, etc.
'Ought' or 'aught,' 187.
'Over,' 394.
'Overthrew,' i.e. *overturned*, 314.
Owen, Dr. Henry, 284.

Pain often penal, 71.
Palairet, 417.
Palgrave, W. Gifford, 245, 299.

Πάμπολυς, 205.
Paneas, 221.
Parable, what? 84; parabolic action, 202, 312.
Pardon, difficulty of granting, 225
Particularism, 198.
Paska, 377.
Patch, 54.
Patrizi or Patritius, 115, 243, 386, 392, 430, etc.
Paulus, 148, 168, etc.
Pausanias, 121.
Penal evil a moral good, 194.
Penny or denarius, 162.
Peræa, 70.
Peripateticism, life a, 183.
Persecution, the heritage of Christians, 98; ecclesiastical persecution, 260.
Perseverance, 360.
Persius, 154.
Person, what? 331.
Peter, meaning of the name, 74; a leading spirit, 30; his impetuosity and self-reliance, 397, 407; rebuking and rebuked, 227; his successors, 224.
Petrinism, 224.
Petronius, 379.
Petter, 122, 128, etc., etc., etc.
Philip, brother of Herod Antipas, 115.
Philip, the tetrarch, 160, 221.
Phrenzy, 117.
Phrynichus, 167, 266.
Pilate, 419.
Pistic, 379.
Plagues or scourges, 71, 129.
'Planet,' what? 337.
Plato, 23, 341, 380.
Platter, 156.
Πλεονεξία, 192.
Pliny, 126, 379.
Plutarch, 346.
Politics must be proportional to a people's development, 276.
Πολλά, *much*, 35, 120.
Polyandry and polygamy, 336.
Polysyllogism, 65.
Popularity, its drawbacks, 204.
Porter, Dr., 116, etc.
Possession by demons, 22, 28.
Possibility, absolute and relative, 400.
Prætorium, 425.
Preaching, what is it? 6, 358.
Premeditation, 359.
Preparation-day, 439.
Preraphaelite style, 273.
Présent and presént, 305; present tense, 317, 318; presentiation, 38.
Procurators of Judæa, 419.
Prodigies, 211.

'Prophet,' what? 142, 184, 322; prophets, dervishes, 8; fakeers, 330.
Proposition, loaves of, 63.
Προσεύχομαι, 167.
Prostration, oriental, 127, 131, 196.
Πυγμῇ, 177.
Punctuation, wrong, 326, etc.
Punishment, everlasting, 267.
Purple, a, 426.
Purse, 162.
Purvey, 122, etc.

Quadrans, 350.
'Quaintly,' what? 406.
Quarantania, Mons, 13.

Rabbi, 113, etc.
Rabboni, 300.
Ransom, Christ a, 298.
'Rated,' 72.
'Receipt of custom,' or customs office, 46.
Recitative, ὅτι, see ὅτι.
Reclining at table in Palestine, etc., 47.
Reinke, 345.
Reland, 126, 160, 235, etc.
Renan, 158.
Rending of clothes, 413.
Repentance, what? 6, 16, 147, 454.
Respect of persons, what? 331.
Restoration of all things by Elias, 241.
Resurrection and immortality, 335, 338.
Reville, 449.
Rewardableness, 198, 263.
Richard, King, 231.
Riches, 287, 288, 289; what? 99; 'richesse,' 21; deceitfulness of, 99.
Righteousness, as meritorious cause of salvation, 289; as moral meetness for heaven, 288, 289.
Rilliet, 311, etc.
Rob Roy (the), 92, 112.
Robbers, as distinguished from thieves, 315, 407, 431.
Robinson, Dr., 166, 235, etc.
Rolof, 310.
Roofs of Palestinian houses, 39, 40.
'Rooms' at supper, 347.
Roost, 110.
Rotherham, 407, etc.
Rouiere's *New Testament*, 268.
Roustaing, 372.
Ryle, 110, 261, etc.

Sabbata, sabbaths, sabbath, 20, 442; Pharisaic views of, 59; made for man, 64; Christ the Lord of the sabbath, 64, 65; 'one of the sabbaths,' 442; 'first of sabbath,' 451.
Sacrament, what? 392; sacrament of extreme unction, 148.
Saddle, the oriental, 306.
Sadducees, 334.
'Sailing' of vessels, 181.
Salmasius, 154, 417.
Salome, 155.
Salt, covenant of, 271; salting, its uses, 267; salt without savour, 271; salted with fire, 265.
Salvation, difficulty of, 287.
Salvianus, 193.
Sandals and shoes, 146, 147.
Sanderson, Dr., 157.
Sanhedrim, 319, 357.
Satan, 13, 97; strong, 87; immortal, 87; Satan and Peter, 227; Beelzebul, 83.
'Satisfy,' what? 424.
Saunier, 61, 274.
Saved, what? 459; or healed, 129, 131, 300.
Scaliger, 268, 380.
Scandal, what? 263.
Scandalize, what? 98.
Schenkel, 114.
Schleusner, 143, 252.
Schmid, Erasmus, 57, 164.
Scholten, 59, 170.
Scholz, 466, etc., etc.
Schott, 368, 447.
Schöttgen, 81, 310, etc.
Schulthess, 448, etc.
Schulz, David, 267, 448, etc.
Scourging, 357, 424.
Scrip, 146.
Scripture, 328.
Scultet, 380.
Sea or lake, 17; sea of Galilee, 17.
Self, 194.
Self denial, 146, 229.
Selfishness, 184, 289.
'Sell whatever thou hast,' 285.
Semler, 120.
Seneca, 157, 158.
Serapis, 119.
Serving at table, 207.
Sexes (the), 277.
Shame in reference to Christ and His words, 231.
Shammaites, 275, 395.
Shaw, Dr., 39.
Shewbread, 63.
Ship or boat, 92.
Shod, 147.
Shopheroth, 348.
Sidon, 194, 199, 200.
Sieffert, 254.
Signs, what? 211, 460; wrought by

Christ, 210, 211; from heaven, 210.
Simon or Simeon, meaning of the name, 18, 74, 75
Simon of Cyrene, 427.
Sin, wonderful, 143; pardonable, 87; has an element of blasphemy in it, 88; 'everlasting,' 88, 89.
'Sinners,' emphatic use of the term, 48.
Sinaitic manuscript, 178, 485.
Σκύλλω, 132.
'Smith,' what? 140.
Son of God, Jesus was the, 2.
Sonnabend, 439.
Sons of the bridechamber, 52.
Sons of thunder, 75, 76.
Sore, sair, sehr, 170, 238, 420.
Soul, what? 341; soul or life, 230; its value, 231.
Sour-dough, 213, 377.
Southey, 288.
Spanheim, 268.
Spectacular miracles, 210.
Spectre (a), 169.
Spices, 442.
Spikenard, 381.
Spinsters, 181.
Spirit, the Holy, 10, 107; dove-like, 12; the Spirit and Christ, 11; the Spirit and man, 107; the sin against, 88, 89.
Spittle or saliva, 217; in baptism, 202
Spontaneity of the mind, 107; of nature, 106.
Sprinkling a mode of baptism, 181.
Staff or staves for Christ's apostles, 146.
Stanley, Dean, 111, 308, 439.
Stars falling, 368.
Stephens, Henry, 177, 380, 403, 407, etc.
Stephens, Robert, 49, 70, 158, etc.
Stockbauer, 424.
Stoles, 347, 445.
Stony or rocky, 93.
Storm on the sea of Tiberias, 112.
'Straitly,' 72.
Strauss, David, 104, 118, 119, 120, 131, 153, 345, etc.
Strength, man's, 342.
Stroud, 396.
'Strown,' 388.
Substitution or equivalence, 298.
'Suddenly,' or *all at once*, 238.
Sue = follow, 46.
Suetonius, 154, 157, 219.
'Suffered,' 128.
Sufficient, 424; *i.e.* considerable, 299.
Suicer, 193.

Sun, an incandescent mass cooling, 373.
Σύνεσις, 343.
Συνίημι, I understand, 171.
Superscription, what? 333.
Symbolism of Christ's life, 251.
Synagogues, 21, 126.
Syrophœnician, 196.
Swearing, see *Oaths*.
Swieten, V., 117.
Swine, 121.
Swords allowed by Christ for a symbolical purpose, 406.

Tabernacles or booths, 237.
Tabor, 235.
Tacitus, 154, 157, 219.
Talitha cumi, 136.
Take, i.e. *seize*, 245.
Tambour, 155.
Tasting of death, 233.
Taylor, Jeremy, 169, 379.
Temple, its grandeur and great stones, 351; seen from Mount Olivet, 352; cattle and sheep sold in it, 314; its court of the Gentiles, 315; the court of the women, 348; the Roman standards set up in it, 361.
'Tempt' and temptation, 210, 274, 333.
Testament or covenant, 393.
Tetrarch, 149.
Thaddeus, 78.
'That day,' 373.
Θέλω, 347.
Theophylact, 177, etc., etc.
'They' used indefinitely, 357.
'Thieves' or robbers, 315, 407, 431.
'Thing' = think, 289.
Thirty pieces of silver, the, 385.
Thomas, 77.
Thomas Magister, 266, 312, 387.
Thomson, Archbishop, 448.
Thomson, Dr. W. M., 134, 324, etc.
Thomson, Sir William, 373.
Thorns, 426.
'Thou sayest it,' 419.
'Thought,' intensive meaning of the word, 358.
'Three days,' 226, 255.
Thronging, 127, 130.
Thrupp, 348.
Θυγάτριον, 196.
Thunder, sons of, 75.
Tiberias, sea of, 17.
Tiberius, 221.
Tischendorf, 31, 44, 94, 104, etc., etc.
Titus, 364.
'To,' denoting direction, 38.
Tombs in Palestine, 116.

Tongues (new), 461, 462.
Tophet, 265.
Touch of faith, 129.
Toup, 310.
Tournefort, 134.
Transfiguration, 235 ff.
Translations of the N. T., 223.
Transposition of clauses, 311, 327.
Trapp, 41, 198, 349.
Treasury in the temple, 348.
Tregelles, 378, 448, 465, etc., etc., etc.
Tribulation, what? 98.
Tribute to Cæsar, 332.
Triller, 312.
Tristram, 17, 31, 113, 221, 235, 236.
Triumphal procession, 306.
Triumvirate (the apostolical), 75, 134.
'True,' what? 330.
Tunics, 146, 413, 429.
Tyndale, 283, 290, etc., etc., etc.
Tyre and Sidon, 70, 194, 200.
Twain, 277.
Twelve apostles, why twelve? 74.
Two by two, 144.

Ululation, 134.
Unbelief, 460; marvellous, 143; *i.e.* imperfect faith, 252.
Unclean persons, 147.
Unclean spirits, 145.
Uncleanness, ceremonial, 180, 181, 191.
Unction, extreme, 148.
Understanding, what? 343.
Universality *secundum quid*, 250.
Unleavened bread, 377, 385.
Unpardonable sin, 88.
Unvernunft, 194.
Unwashed hands, 176.
Ὑπέρ, *over*, 394.
Uproar, 378.

Vat or fat, 323.
Vatican manuscript, 446, 464.
Veil, du, 163, 262.
'Verily' or amen, 87, etc.
Verses of the N.T., 79, 356; see *Robert Stephens*.
Verstegan, 426.
Vespasian, 219, 364.
Vessels or goods, 86; or utensils, 314.
Via Dolorosa, 422.
Viaticum, 146.
Victor of Antioch, 284, 446, 450, 467, 469.
Viger, 57.
'Village' and 'town,' 217.
Villagers, 192.
Villain, 181, 192.
Villany, 192.
Vines in Palestine, 322.

Vineyard, the Jews a. 327.
Virtue or power, 130, 149.
Vision, a, 236.
Vitellius, 354.
Vitringa, 21, 126.
Vogüé, 348.
Volkmar, 73, 115, etc.
Voluntas sensualitatis, 401.
Vossius, 380.

Wahhabeeism, 59.
Wailing women, 134.
Wakefield, 33, 177, etc.
Wallet, 145.
Wallow, i.e. *roll*, 248.
Ward, Dr., 430.
Wassenbergh, 310.
Watch-towers, 323.
Watches of the night, Jewish and Roman, 167, 375.
Watchful, 375.
'Water' and 'waters,' 248.
'Wright,' 140.
Webster and Wilkinson, 128, 152, 346, etc.
Weiss, 449, 454.
Well-beloved, 326.
Wells, Dr. Edward, 446.
Wesley, 164, 340, etc.
Wetstein, 145, 164, 310, etc.
Wette, de, 69, 310, etc.
'What to me and to thee?' 118.
'What to us and to thee?' 23.
Whately, Miss, 179.
Whiston, 267.
Whitney, 449, 456.
Wickedness or knavery, 192.
Wilke, 205, 216.
Wilkinson, 387.
Will and wish, 401; see *Free will*
Willes, 215.
Willibald, 166.
Wilson, Dr. John, 235, 399.
Wilson, Thomas, 99.
Winds, the four, 370.
Wine, eastern, 55, 56; myrrhed, 428; wine-fat, 322.
Winer, 380, etc.
Wisdom, intellectually considered, 139, wisdom, wise, wissed, wist, etc., 402.
Wit, witan, etc., 402.
Withered hand, 66.
Witsius, 309.
'Woe!' what? 390.
Wolf, J. C., 309, 361.
Wolff the traveller, 8.
Wolle, 81, 311, 444.
Woman and Christianity, 165; the women who followed Jesus, 437; wailing women, 134.

Wonder, not always the daughter of ignorance, 143, 329.
Wonders, lying, 367.
Wood, J. G., 197.
Woodman the martyr, 359.
Woolston, 40, 41, 122, 310.
'Word,' used collectively, 402; the word, that is, the Gospel, 38.
Wordsworth, Bishop, 168, etc.
Work, the blessing of, 140, 141.
World or age. 99.
'Worship,' what ? 426.
'Written (it stands),' 184.

Wycliffe, 69, 130, 149, etc.
Wynne, 252.

Xenophon, 40, 380.

Ymagion, 359.
Yonglyng, 444.

Zealots (the), 79.
Zelotes, 79.
Zeltner, 430.
Zeugma, 173, 203.
Zuingli, 312, 352.

END OF THE INDEX.

www.ingramcontent.com/pod-product-compliance
Lightning Source LLC
Chambersburg PA
CBHW071430300426
44114CB00013B/1383